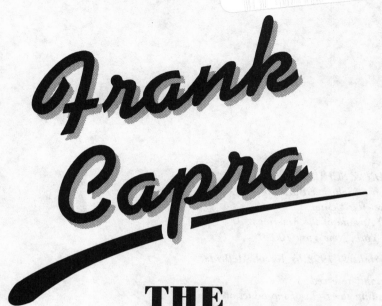

THE CATASTROPHE OF SUCCESS

by Joseph McBride

Simon & Schuster

New York London Toronto Sydney Tokyo Singapore

SIMON & SCHUSTER
Simon & Schuster Building
Rockefeller Center
1230 Avenue of the Americas
New York, New York 10020

Copyright © 1992 by Joseph McBride

SIMON & SCHUSTER and colophon are registered trademarks
of Simon & Schuster Inc.

Designed by Liney Li
Manufactured in the United States of America

10   9   8   7   6   5   4   3   2

Library of Congress Cataloging-in-Publication Data
McBride, Joseph.
    Frank Capra : the catastrophe of success / by Joseph McBride.
        p.   cm.
    Includes bibliographical references and index.
    1. Capra, Frank, 1897–   .   2. Motion picture producers and
directors—United States—Biography.   I. Title.
PN1998.3.C36M344   1992
791.43'0233'092—dc20
    [B]   92-1311   CIP

ISBN 0-671-73494-6

Grateful acknowledgment is given to the following for permission to quote from published or unpublished material: The ASC Press, for excerpts from *The Light on Her Face* by Joseph B. Walker, ASC, and Juanita Walker (ASC Press, 1984); Edward Bernds, for quotations from his diaries (1935–39); Kevin Brownlow,

(continued on page 768)

Also by Joseph McBride

Filmmakers on Filmmaking, vols. I & II (EDITOR)

Hawks on Hawks

High and Inside: The Complete Guide to Baseball Slang

Orson Welles: Actor and Director

Kirk Douglas

John Ford (WITH MICHAEL WILMINGTON)

Focus on Howard Hawks (EDITOR)

Orson Welles

Persistence of Vision (EDITOR)

To Ruth O'Hara

Contents

1. "I felt nothing"

*S*ix thousand people, virtually all the inhabitants of the Sicilian village of Bisacquino, met the old man on the highway half a mile from town. He had not seen his birthplace in almost seventy-four years, and he was stunned by the sincerity and fervor of this homecoming welcome. He remembered almost nothing of Bisacquino—running barefoot through the dusty town square; a ride on his father's mule through a mountain stream, waiting while the animal bowed its head to drink; a starkly contrasted image of black peasant hats against glaring white walls on a hot August afternoon; little more. Sicily had become a foreign country to him during these long years abroad, a lifetime that had turned him, in his own mind, into an unhyphenated American.

As Frank Capra looked out the window of his black Lincoln limousine on April 29, 1977, not one of the faces which greeted him was familiar: not the weathered faces of the old men wearing peasant caps with their best Sunday black suits; nor the hawk-eyed faces of the old women in their perpetual mourning cloth; nor the worshipful faces of his younger relatives, who knew him only from newspapers and television. But a few of the old ones still remembered "Cicco" Capra, the boy who disappeared from Bisacquino with no good-byes to his playmates one day in May 1903, and passed his sixth birthday in steerage with his family on the stormy ocean voyage to America. These old-timers, with their antiquated Sicilian dialect, still pronounced the family name as "Crahpa."

And now, because of the fame he had won in the New World as the filmmaker who "brought the meaning of the American Dream alive for generations of moviegoers past and present," these people who were strangers to Frank Capra were pulling him from the car with voracious hands and pushing him into the line of march along the narrow and winding cobblestone streets of their village. Capra's peasant origins were plain to read from his short, hardy frame, his olive skin, and his earthy features, once described by Graham Greene as "bushy eyebrows, big nose and the kind of battered face which looks barnacled with life, encrusted with ready sympathies." But he also looked jarringly out of place that afternoon in his gaudy Palm Springs attire of lemon yellow slacks and turtleneck, loud brown-and-white checked sport coat with a blue handkerchief protruding from his pocket, and a bejeweled gold medallion of Sicily (a gift from his relatives) dangling from a chain around his neck.

Escorting him on his royal progress through Bisacquino were two white-helmeted motorcycle policemen; a squad of *carabinieri*; the mayor, wearing a sash with the green, white, and red of the Italian flag; the ubiquitous village priest; the American consul general to Sicily and officials of the United States Information Service (USIS); a flying wedge of journalists and *paparazzi*; and a documentary film crew from RAI, the Italian national television network, making a special called *Mister Capra torna a casa* (*Mr. Capra Goes Home*). The municipal band, in its quaint red-and-black uniforms, followed behind the dignitaries, tubas oompahing and trumpets bleating the plaintively festive folk tunes the old man could remember his father playing on his guitar long ago in America.

It was like a scene from one of his own movies: it was Longfellow Deeds being serenaded with "For He's a Jolly Good Fellow" while leaving home at the Mandrake Falls train station, John Doe being brought back from retreat and suicide by his idealistic followers, George Bailey emerging from the snowy night of despair into a bright, warm houseful of friends at the end of *It's a Wonderful Life*. In America now they even had an adjective for this kind of scene: "Capraesque" (though there were still those who preferred to call it "Capracorn").

For Frank Capra himself, this homecoming, which should have been his moment of sweetest triumph, instead was an ordeal of the purest agony. He trudged along as if in a trance, grim-faced, ashen, unsteady on his feet. The band music was deafening. The din from the laughing, shouting, applauding crowd on the streets and balconies and rooftops was even louder, and he could barely force a smile as he waved back at them. Because of a confusion over the parade route, the crowds became unruly and swarmed through police barriers, surrounding Capra and making the American officials shout, "Don't get too close to him! Let him breathe!" The exhaust fumes from the escort motorcycles were playing havoc with Capra's skittish stomach, his surest barometer of inner crisis. And on this day of glory, Frank Capra was humbled by a ferocious attack of diarrhea.

"Oh, Jesus, it nearly killed me," he recalled in 1984, finally able to laugh at the memory. "I didn't know what the hell to do. They were going so slow, pointing out this and that, and I was just so scared I couldn't hold back. I never suffered so much."

Capra's much-publicized pilgrimage to Bisacquino was just one part of an elaborately orchestrated Italian tour on behalf of the U.S. government, an event described by Vittorio Albano of the Palermo newspaper *L'Ora* as a "grotesquely programed. . . . propagandistic parade disguised as a cultural enterprise." After returning to the United States from the Italian trip, Capra was asked what he had felt on his visit to Bisacquino.

"I felt nothing," he said. "Who the hell cares where you were born? That town meant nothing to me. You know that colored guy, that *Roots* thing? He's full of shit. I hate the word 'roots.' People are so proud of their roots it's sickening."

His homecoming left a sour taste in the mouths of many local observers, for it was obvious that Capra was, in the words of Torino's *La Stampa*, "an American in Sicily, not a Sicilian who is coming home."

In his native land, Capra time and again found himself called upon to justify his role as an official apologist for the American way of life, a position which uncomfortably exposed the deepest ambivalences in his character. To students at the national film school who disrupted his appearance there, to a journalist who called his films "a flight from reality, idyllic daydreams without engagement," he presented himself as an apolitical crusader for "the freedom of man and the right of the individual to fight against any kind of oppression," while at the same time he reveled in his symbolic status as the champion of American ideals, the pugnacious and indefatigable flag-waver. He was sure that the students who challenged him were Communists: "You can always tell 'em—they're mean and they hang together. It had been hammered into their heads that America was a lousy place. And they tried to make me a no-good moneysucker, you know—they invited me so they could give me a hard time. It took about two seconds for me to find out what was going on." So he waved the flag at them all the more vigorously and contemptuously: "I'm usually annoying because I start laughing."

Even before he arrived in Sicily, there were rumblings of discontent. Students in Bisacquino objected to the insultingly brief time the USIS had allotted to Capra's stay in their town (three hours; as it happened, he spent four hours there). And Capra's two oldest nephews in Bisacquino, seventy-five-year-old Giuseppe and seventy-three-year-old Salvatore (Toto) Troncale, claimed that they were not particularly excited over his visit. "Zio Cicco" had visited Italy several times before, but he had never bothered to visit Sicily. His relatives occasionally received largess from their illustrious uncle—CARE packages after World War II and Christmas presents every year—but since the death in 1961 of Ignazia Troncale, Capra's sister who married a peasant farmer and remained in Bisacquino, the family had not received "even a postcard" from Zio Cicco. They learned about his planned visit only from the newspaper, and Giuseppe sent his son to the American consulate for more information: "I want to know at least what he wants for dinner." After being told that his Uncle Frank would be too busy to make more than a brief visit, Giuseppe said, "I was disappointed, because he hasn't been here for seventy years. When my other uncles visited, they stayed longer than three hours."

Capra's youngest nephew, Antonino (Nené) Troncale, a fifty-three-year-old elementary school teacher, insisted on holding a lavish family celebration in his country house, Villa Rita. When USIS officials visited the house and said it might not be possible to hold the dinner there because the dining room was not big enough, Antonino tore out a wall to accommodate the dignitaries and the forty-two members of his family.

Capra acknowledged a certain feeling of guilt for having remained so distant from his family, telling a journalist in Palermo, "I felt I couldn't not know my relatives. It wouldn't have been right. That's why I came."

Capra's birthplace at 18A Via Santo Cono faces on the church of his patron saint San Francesco di Paola, where he was baptized and confirmed and in whose shadow he used to play. It was there in 1977 that he encountered a woman seven years his senior, Lucia Giasi, who remembered playing with him when he was a child. Even in those days, she recalled, "Cicco" Capra had an air about him, something brazen and pugnacious. When he pestered her, she insulted him by shouting back:

Cicchideddu   (*Little Frankie*
Supra á butte   *sitting on the wine barrel*
mangia, beve   *eats and drinks*
e se ne futte.   *and doesn't give a damn.*)

"Sorry, I don't remember," Capra said as Lucia embraced him, but she kept smiling, because she didn't understand English. He said later, "The TV guys got some old dame dressed in black, with no teeth—the oldest hag you could ever see—and they stopped someplace and she comes running and puts her arms around me. She says, 'Don't you remember me? We played so much.' Jesus Christ, I had a hell of a time shaking her off. They thought it up; the TV guys gave her a dollar and said, 'Go and tell him how you loved him.' "

Addressing the crowd from the City Hall balcony, he said through an interpreter, "I cannot believe that after so many years I'm here in these streets where I used to run up and down when I was a kid. I think I had fun here, but I don't remember very much. I remember more about the ship that took me to America. I have worked hard for seventy-four years [in America], and I have had some success. But I believe that the greater success is yours, for being so close to the earth and to God. I wish I could embrace every one of you."

His visit to his birthplace was anticlimactic: "When I went back, I thought, 'I'm not going to be able to recognize the house at all.' I didn't have a picture of it in my mind. And I worried about it as we walked toward the town. I said to myself, 'I can't tell one house from another.' They pointed it out to me, where it was, but there was some kind of a store there."

His birthplace, indeed, had changed. Capra's parents, Salvatore and Rosaria, owned a plain two-story corner house made of stone and mortar, sometimes renting half to another family. The ground floor served as a stable and a hayloft, and the second floor was the Capras' family quarters. When the rest of the family left Bisacquino, Ignazia and her husband, Vincenzo Troncale, took over the house, selling it a few years later on her parents' behalf to their next-door neighbor Bernardo Salvaggio. Bernardo and his shoemaker son, Giuseppe, the current owner, added a third story and modernized the house by changing the ground floor to a garage, which Capra mistook for a "store."

The dinner with his relatives was scheduled for seven o'clock, but at five-thirty, resting before his appearance at City Hall, Capra sent for Antonino Troncale and told him he would have to skip the dinner because of his "intestinal disturbances."

Troncale was distraught. He told his uncle about all the preparations he had made and of the long trips some of the family had made to be there. He also told Capra bluntly that "his and our prestige would have been questioned if he did not spend a few hours with us."

With that, Capra agreed, providing that he would not have to eat anything. "It was thought by some that he pretended to be ill because of the confusion created at the beginning of the visit," Troncale recalled. "We

Troncales did not believe it. It is true that he wasn't feeling good, but if I hadn't insisted he would have left, making us look ridiculous in front of the whole world. What we did for him had nothing to do with the fact that he is a famous director; it is because he is our mother's brother. Had he been less famous and less rich, we would have done the same, with even greater sincerity.

"Granted that he felt Americanized, that his hometown meant nothing to him; I believe, however, that the desire to see the place where he opened his eyes for the first time, to see the places where he took his first steps and played his first games—even if he doesn't remember which games—the desire to meet and embrace one's relatives, to take an interest in how they live and what they do, this desire cannot die in human beings. . . . Especially in a man whose films have always glorified human virtues: he who doesn't know these virtues cannot portray them."

Though Capra would admit his lack of family feeling to anyone who asked him, only his relatives knew that he harbored a black Sicilian vendetta toward the Troncales over an incident that had occurred just after World War II.

The war had drained the spirit and the resources of the island's already beleaguered inhabitants, and in 1946, Antonino, then twenty-two, wrote to his Zio Cicco in Hollywood, imploring him to bring him to America. Capra swore out an affidavit for the U.S. Immigration and Naturalization Service on Nené's behalf, guaranteeing him a job with his Liberty Films, and sent him $800 for his passage. But the Italian government refused Nené's request for an emigration permit. Nené, however, did not return the $800. His later explanation was that Capra's sister Josephine had written to him from Los Angeles, saying he could keep the money in order to continue his studies. But Capra was infuriated.

Desperate to find a way around the legal roadblock, Nené kept writing to his relatives in America, but Capra advised them to ignore his pleas. To an American nephew, Capra later said of the Troncales, "They took me. I'll never help that tribe again."

At Villa Rita the Troncales had prepared a feast with "a long table and food for four weeks," as Capra put it. Nené had enlisted the help of Biagio Rizzi, the owner of the town's only restaurant, to mediate family disagreements over the antipasto and the main course. They finally settled on a *bistecca* dinner preceded by Sicilian rosé wine and bubbling white spumante.

"How wonderful to be back with you," said Capra, lifting a glass for the newspaper photographers. Toto Troncale announced, "It's good that people remember their ancestry. We shouldn't forget our past." Another relative, caught up in the emotion of the moment, told Capra, "Uncle, you have to stay here in Bisacquino. You have been in America too long." "Yes, yes," mumbled Capra.

In fact, while they were introducing themselves, Capra was wondering desperately how he could escape from his relatives.

"They'll never forgive me," he said in retrospect. "I went to a guy who was trying to make a speech, and said, 'Look, I've got to go. Please. I know they won't understand it, but I've got to leave very, very fast.' And I left. I leapt right out the door and I got to the TV guys, I hopped into the car, and I said, 'Jesus Christ, ride like hell and get me in the country.'"

Not all of them understanding what was happening, Capra's relatives and the rest of the townsfolk who had gathered outside Villa Rita stared after the car as it disappeared down the highway.

"They got me right outside of town," Capra went on, "and I jumped out and I pulled my pants down and I just let go."

When he had finished, the TV crew suggested that Capra go back to Nené's house to finish the celebration, but he said, "I don't want to go back—I can't tell them what happened."

"Maybe I *could* have told them," he later admitted, "but I was afraid it would happen again. And I was so ashamed. They had all this wonderful table, and they don't know why I ran away. They probably thought I thought I was too good for them. It was a hell of an insult."

He had spent just one hour with his relatives.

"If he would have needed restroom facilities, my house was well equipped," Nené Troncale sarcastically observed when told of his uncle's excuse for running away.

"When he left us, we stayed together and continued to eat, though rather bitterly. We were expecting more of a show of affection from him. He is not the only one of us who succeeded. My father had nothing when he got married. Today we do have something, we are somebody in our small world, and we would have liked to have shown him. We are proud of what we have achieved, and we would have liked him to be equally proud of us. More than eating together, what we wanted most was his company, to be able to be near him, to speak to him, to ask about our relatives, to speak about ourselves and to allow him to get to know us. He was our mother's brother, our uncle. Were we asking too much?

"Perhaps his visit was more political than sentimental. But if America, fame, and wealth make a man so selfish, I am happy that I stayed in Italy, and even more, in Sicily, in Bisacquino."

* * *

Capra's ethnic heritage links him with a long history of strife and oppression on an island whose strategic Mediterranean location has caused it to be conquered and reconquered for centuries. Sicily's rulers have included the Greeks, the Romans, the Ostrogoths, the Saracens, the French, the Germans, and the Spanish, as well as the Allied armies in World War II. Because of the island's complicated history, its ethnic mixture is as richly varied as any on earth. The Sicilian's blood not only includes traces of much of Europe but also Arabic and African strains.

The name "Capra," like the names of many peasant families in Sicily, is emblematic of their closeness to the land: it means "she-goat." The English word "capricious" derives from it, evoking the animal's skittish temperament. The name neatly expresses two aspects of Frank Capra's personality: emotionalism and obstinacy.

On the Capra coat of arms is displayed a leaping goat with a two-headed eagle poised between its horns. But any nobility that may have been in Frank Capra's family tree was centuries removed. For generations before his birth his family were peasant farmers, struggling to extract a living from the ground. Frank Capra did not even remember the names of his grandparents, who never left the old country, and he said of his mother's family, "I didn't really give a damn what their name was."

His paternal grandfather, Benedetto, cultivated citrus orchards and other lands owned by the mayor of Bisacquino. Due to the repressive land system that paralyzed the Sicilian peasantry in the nineteenth century and made it impossible for them to receive a fair reward for their incentive, Benedetto never was able to buy his own land. The breakup of feudalism in 1812 had made little impact on the land system in Sicily, still leaving the vast majority of land in the hands of a few large owners; most were absentee landlords whose fields were cultivated by tenant farmers such as Benedetto Capra.

"In Sicily there were no small ranches," Frank's older brother Antonino remembered. "Those ranches ran from the mountains to the sea."

The most enduring evil of the system was the effect it had on the land itself: greedy landlords and desperate small farmers heavily deforested much of the land during the nineteenth century, causing landslides and erosion and leaving much of the once-rich Sicilian soil *stanca* (played out) and abandoned by the late 1800s. The lack of foliage on the land intensified the impact of the frequent droughts which plagued the island by lessening the ability of the soil to retain rainwater. The end results were seas of dead brown grass and the stifling, demoralizing prevalence of dusty siroccos, a condition much like the Dust Bowl of Oklahoma in the 1930s;

Frank Capra said *The Grapes of Wrath* made him think of his birthplace.

Worn out from his years of toil, Benedetto Capra eventually fell ill and had to live on the charity of the mayor in a poorhouse run by the Sisters of the Poor. He died of pneumonia in 1897, the year Francesco Capra was born, leaving five sons and two daughters, none any more prosperous than he had been.

Frank Capra's father, Salvatore, born in 1852, was the oldest of the seven children of Benedetto Capra and Luigia Maienza. Like his father before him, he cultivated citrus trees. "My father was a magician as a horticulturist," Frank Capra recalled; in California, Salvatore had "oranges and lemons and grapefruit all growing on the same tree, and red and white roses on one bush." The two lemon trees he planted in the yard of the family home in Los Angeles are still flourishing today. But unlike his industrious father, Salvatore was also a dreamer, with the poetic soul of a troubadour. He preferred strumming his guitar and mandolin, singing romantic ballads and operatic arias, and telling stories to working in the fields. In the pragmatic world of Sicily, where children were sent to work as soon as they could reach the fruit on the bushes, Salvatore was considered a ne'er-do-well.

But he was a charming ne'er-do-well: tall (5'7") for his time and place, and sinewy, with a dourly handsome face, a dashing black mustache, and unusually fair skin. In 1877, when he was twenty-five, he won the heart of a buxom seventeen-year-old girl named Rosaria Nicolosi. He serenaded her on his guitar and in time persuaded her to marry him. Rosaria had another suitor, however, a man more prosperous than Salvatore Capra, and her father would not have Salvatore for a son-in-law.

Like his father and grandfather, Antonino Nicolosi was a shoemaker. His beautifully crafted shoes, which he made with his son Giuseppe, were prized in Bisacquino. Rosaria's father also had the reputation of being a psychic and a folk healer: people would come from miles around to be touched with his *mani sante* (sacred hands), and he would never take their money. But despite the objections of their obstinate daughter, Antonino and his wife, Luigia Caronna (from a farming family herself), were not about to let Rosaria marry an idler who could not provide for her in the manner to which she was accustomed. Besides the remnants of the nobility, there were two social classes in nineteenth-century Sicily—the shopkeepers and small landowners, and the peasants—and they were rigidly stratified. The earthy Capra clan was beneath the Nicolosis socially, and, furthermore, Rosaria had been educated by the nuns of the parish school. Unlike the Capras and three quarters of the rest of the population above the age of six, she could read and write. Marriage to a Capra was out of the question.

The irate Salvatore Capra challenged his rival to a "rustic duel" with knives. But before the fateful hour dawned, an elderly nobleman, Don Nené Pancamo, saw them on his early-morning walk, marching grimly through the countryside. As Nené Troncale related, "He stopped the two young men and, after reprimanding them harshly, he first advised and then insisted that all three of them go to the woman in question and have her choose her favorite. He added that the unfavored one must, within the year, marry another woman and forget everything of the past. This they did. But my grandmother, after learning the reason they were calling upon her, disdainfully refused both of them, and, being unfavored, they married within the year as promised."

Salvatore Capra married Ignazia Catanese on February 22, 1878. But the fates seemed to be driving him back to Rosaria Nicolosi, for within six months his bride was dead from a goiter. This time he convinced Rosaria to defy her parents. When she married him, on August 8, 1879, they disowned her.

From the first, the marriage of Salvatore Capra (called Turiddu, the Italian equivalent of "Sammy") and Rosaria (called Sara, or, more familiarly, Saridda) was fraught with dissension. Her father's grim prediction seemed accurate, for, push him as she would, Saridda never was able to make much of her husband. "Turiddu was good fellow," their Sicilian-American neighbor Maria Lanza Oddo recalled. "Sang all the time. Play with kids all the time. But he no like work. I don't like to speak ill of the dead, but his wife had to work, work, work. Poor lady. He liked fool around, he liked talk to people. Lot of men are like that."

"My mother thought he was a pretty lazy guy," said Frank Capra. "She gave it to him all the time—constant bickering. He *was* lazy. He'd work more on a flower than he would on a tree. He was an artist in his own right. He liked music, playing a guitar; he dealt with the finer things of life. He had that liking for the beautiful and for the things he didn't quite understand. Life was something more than a hoe to him. It wasn't to my mother.

"My mother had a hard head and an ability to survive under any circumstances. She was much more practical than my father. My mother was really *earth*. Anything that didn't have to do with the earth didn't exist. There's where you make your living, and there's where God meant you to live and die working—the good earth. So she didn't understand anything else. Didn't want to."

By the time they left for America in 1903, when he was fifty-one and she was forty-three and they had seven living children, Turiddu had advanced no further in life than to be a straw boss in charge of seasonal tree-pruning crews on a large ranch. "He wasn't doing nothing, going around with a gun on his shoulder taking care of the place," his son Benedetto remembered. When he was hired for a long stretch of time, the family would come and live with him. He had a small piece of leased land, about two acres, called a *lòco* (literally, a place), which he worked for himself in the midst of other carefully terraced plots on a hillside just outside of town. On it he cultivated olive trees and a grape arbor, when he was not working elsewhere.

Benedetto and his younger brother Antonino were apprenticed to landowners in other towns, all of their wages going to Salvatore. Saridda, unlike most Sicilian wives of that era, also worked, using a spinning wheel to weave quilts at home with her daughters Luigia, Ignazia, and Giuseppa, for one of Turiddu's brothers to take to market twice a year in Palermo.

The family subsisted; they were not poor; they had enough to eat; they were able to buy their own small house. But the work was constant, unrelenting, and never brought in enough to get ahead.

The infant mortality rate in Sicily was appallingly high, the highest in Italy, and Saridda lost several children at birth or in infancy (Frank Capra said she lost seven, others said five). Frank was the sixth surviving child, and the children born immediately before and after him both died.

Francesco Capra was born on May 18, 1897. The birth was a difficult one, and he was weak and badly dehydrated, and not expected to live. The story handed down in the family was that Antonino Nicolosi, Saridda's father, came to see her and was appalled that the baby was being left to die while people were caring for the mother. He is said to have told her, drawing on his psychic insight, "You take care of that child. He's going to be known all over the world."

But Francesco Capra had bleak expectations.

"My father was a farmer, and he remained a farmer," Capra said many years later. "There wasn't a chance of him doing anything else. You were tied to what you were doing. You *never* moved. If you were earning a living, you stayed. The principal reason was that there was no schooling. Without schooling you have no idea how you were limited—you were limited to your language, you just took your thoughts from your father and your mother— you didn't know what was across the hill."

Even though Saridda had had some schooling, she didn't see much value in it. Her opposition to schooling was fierce and resentful: What good had it brought her? And how could learning to read and write put bread in her children's mouths?

Turiddu, while living in Bisacquino, simply did not care about educating his children. Just as he did not need to read music in order to sing and play the guitar, he needed no schooling in order to raise plants. There *was* schooling in Bisacquino—the parish school, where nuns taught boys and girls through the sixth grade—and there was a high school in Palermo, but even if the Capras had had the inclination to send their children to class, they could not have spared them for it. A child started adult work in Bisacquino at the age when today's children enter grammar school. "None of us went to school," said Frank's brother Antonino, "because when you were five or six years old you were up there on the hill herding cattle. When you were five or six years old, you were a man."

Since Francesco was just on the verge of Sicilian "manhood" when the family was uprooted, he missed being sent into the fields as a virtual slave to big landowners as his older brothers Benedetto and Antonino were; that surely would have been his fate if the family had stayed. And with three older sisters, two of them married and living nearby (Luigia had married a farmer, Giovanni Vitrano, after losing Vincenzo Troncale to her younger sister Ignazia), Cicco had no lack of care, even if he had to make plenty of noise to get noticed.

While his mother was inside cooking and weaving in the semidarkness of the flickering kerosene lamp, the lively, peripatetic little boy spent much of his time out-of-doors with his father, soaking in Turiddu's love for the soil, his delight in romantic music, his penchant for fanciful storytelling, and his dreamy peasant mysticism. In time he also would inherit his mother's practicality and her skill at handling money, but not until after his cold plunge into American life. Here in Sicily for a few brief years he was able to enjoy being a boy, riding mules and romping with his family namesake, the goat that supplied all of their milk and cheese.

The family's social life revolved around the parties his father held on Saturday nights in the grape arbor, with a long marble table filled with food and drink under the canopy of vines. The singing and dancing would go on for hours, with Turiddu and his four brothers, Giuseppe, Vincenzo, Onofrio, and Arcangelo, supplying the music. The five melodious Capras were the entire choir of the Church of San Francesco for twenty consecutive years, until, one by one, they began leaving for America.

In those days before radio, movies, or television, the illiterate Papa Turiddu's stories also provided entertainment for his family and friends. Most of the tales were humorous, and some were Bible tales or variations on old folk legends, like the one about the Sicilian Robin Hood figure from whom Saridda's side of the family claimed to be descended. Many of his stories also had supernatural overtones. Turiddu, like his fellow peasants, had a wide superstitious streak.

One of his favorites was about a peasant who was constantly bragging about his courage. His friends, tired of hearing the blowhard shooting off his mouth, dared him to spend the night in a graveyard. To prove that he had actually been there, the peasant agreed to drive a stake into the ground before leaving. But it was so dark when he did so that he inadvertently pounded the stake into the tail of his long overcoat trailing on the ground. When the peasant walked away he felt the coat tugging, and, thinking a ghost had hold of him, he dropped dead of a heart attack.

At night people would gather around with guitars and jugs of red wine to hear Turiddu tell his outlandish tales, which he would embellish as long as he could maintain interest—often tantalizing his audience with a cliff-hanger ending "to be continued."

The great hemorrhage of the Italian population to America began in the late nineteenth century.

Declining prices for food products in the increasingly competitive world market exacerbated the already tight squeeze on the nation's leading industry. The impoverished tenant farmers and *contadini* (day laborers) were squeezed the hardest, and with the failure of land reforms, they lost faith in their government and despaired of their future in their native land. In the thirty years between 1882 and 1911, nearly four million people left Italy permanently—the pace intensifying at the turn of the century, with about a quarter million a year leaving in the early 1900s.

In the first few years of the twentieth century, the only other national group which fled to the United States in such numbers as the Italians were the Russians, most of whom were Jews escaping pogroms and forced conscription in the czarist war against Japan. A staggering total of 2,104,309 Italians emigrated to the United States in the decade between 1900 and 1910, though many of them did not stay. Prior to the 1890s, more had gone to South America than had gone to the United States, but the trend changed dramatically as the States began a period of prodigious industrial expansion, with an appetite for cheap labor in great numbers. Most of the emigrants stayed in the eastern United States—about a fourth going no farther than New York City—and there were sizable Italian colonies in Louisiana and Alabama, which did heavy trade with Italian ships. But with the growth of railroad traffic to the West, some of the more adventurous began journeying to distant, still thinly populated California.

"Some notion of fitness to prosper in the future articulately or inarticulately precedes the desire to emigrate," economist Robert F. Foerster wrote in his 1919 book, *The Italian Emigration of Our Times*. Foerster saw in the emigrants "the power of the risk-taking motive, which is usually coupled with an egoistic expectation of selection of oneself for fortune's favors. . . . [A] certain superiority to circumstance appears, a ripeness and robust self-assurance."

The first of the Capra clan to leave Sicily were Frank Capra's uncles Vincenzo and Onofrio, Turiddu's young brothers, toward the end of the nineteenth century.

For a year the family did not know where they were, until Vincenzo sent for his wife and daughter to join him in New Orleans. Life was hard in Louisiana—Vincenzo and Onofrio worked in the sugarcane fields cutting cane with black people and other Italians—but it was better than life in Sicily.

Benedetto Capra, Papa Turiddu's oldest son, by that time was herding sheep for a wealthy landowner in another village. He longed to escape—from his miserable, low-paying job, which amounted to servitude, and from a land that promised nothing better for his future.

"I was fourteen years old when I started having this idea, and I didn't have but two cents in my pocket," Benedetto remembered in a 1965 interview with his nephew Joe Finochio. "When I started working I was seven years old. I was working for board the first year, just cleaning the chickens and doing little jobs like that. The second year I was getting board and a pair of shoes. Then I got to work for money—I think I was getting twenty *lire* a year. But that twenty *lire* wasn't coming into my pocket. My father used to go collect everything what I was getting.

"I didn't know what to do, but this fellow, one of his brothers-in-law, came back from America. He had been in America twelve years and he came back with $3,000. He had a face like a bulldog, but because he came with $3,000 he married the best-looking girl in the town. I was thinking, 'My gosh, why I can't-a do the same thing?' "

While he was thinking about it, Benedetto had a fight with another boy on the ranch and hit him with a rock. He ran away to see his parents. The journey home was traumatic—thunderstorms and wolves menacing him as he made his way through the hills—but he expected a happy, tearful reunion. Instead he was met with cold silence. That decided it. He would leave for America.

The year was 1900, and Benedetto was fifteen and barely five feet tall when he talked his parents into taking out a mortgage on their home to loan him the money for his passage. But when he saw the ocean for the first time at Palermo, he almost changed his mind: "I didn't know was-a so much water. I thought it was gonna be a big-a river."

He went by steerage, in the steamship *Sempione*, which sailed on September 2. His final destination was New Orleans, to join his uncles. When he arrived in the United States on September 22, 1900, he had four dollars in his pocket.

Vincenzo (called "Vince" in America) and Onofrio (familiarly known as "Nunzio") took him cutting sugarcane at a dollar a day. Out of that, the thrifty Ben repaid his parents for his passage. At the end of the season, Vince and Nunzio made plans to migrate to new employment. But Ben had contracted malaria, a common disease back in Sicily as well as in the swamps of Louisiana. His uncles didn't think he would survive, so they abandoned Ben to die in the shack where they had been staying.

A heavyset black woman the men called "Aunt Josie" would come to clean their shack, and when she found the half-dead Italian boy, she took him into her house with the ten children she was raising without a husband. She brought Ben back to life.

He left her to find work on the docks of New Orleans. But he soon lost the job, fired because he was too small for heavy lifting: "So I went walking along the river. I was very discourage. Before I left Italy, my grandfather [Antonino Nicolosi] he didn't want me to come, but he says, 'If you want to go, you take this little saint'—it was a little statue of a saint—'and in case you have-a trouble, put it in your hands and say a prayer.' So I did.

"I started looking in the river, and sure enough I could see him [his grandfather] in the water saying those words to me. I made a little prayer, and the sun shine onto my back. I turn around and I see the sun was-a nice.

"I went to sleep on a bench. Two Italian people was passin' by, and one had an awfully heavy voice. When I heard him talking in Italian in my sleep, I just jump out of the seat and I rush to him and I told him what I had been through. His name was Angelo Romano. He was very kind to me. He said, 'Don't worry, you come with us. We go to Hawaii. They have a company that wants some people there to cut sugarcane.' "

On the Hawaiian island of Maui, Ben had the company of two dozen Italians in the cane fields, but the work was rough and they were fed only rice and beans. The Italians began leaving, and Ben decided to go with two of them. "I had $150 hidden in my sock that I had saved, because over there if somebody knew that you had money, they'd hit you over the head."

They found an Australian steamer that was headed for San Francisco.

Huddling on the dock, they waited until the ship was about to be loaded with produce. Then they crept into the dark hold and hid there as the cargo was dumped in with them.

So Ben Capra, the first of the family to settle in California, arrived stowing away in a load of fruit and vegetables. "I tried to get a job in San Francisco, but nobody had any jobs for me—'too small' again. Everybody was telling me I had to go to school. They told me men gotta be educated to get a job here. But I told them I didn't have no school money."

Ben made a fateful decision. He would not stay in Northern California like most Italian immigrants—he would try his luck in the south, in a fertile area he had heard described as "a second Italy." He would go find his fortune in a place he called "Los Angelo."

He worked his way south swinging a pick and shovel from sunup to sundown with the Mexican and Italian laborers on a Southern Pacific crew digging a railway tunnel. He and a friend quit the crew and walked the last twenty miles to the San Fernando Valley, eating oranges they stole from an orchard along the way.

On his first day in Los Angeles, Ben found work as a section hand on a Pacific Electric crew laying a streetcar track to Monrovia. He settled in a mixed ethnic neighborhood just east of downtown, and in time he took a job with the Los Angeles Railway as a handyman, cleaning and repairing the yellow and green streetcars that ran within the city. He worked from six in the morning until six in the evening, seven days a week, for seventeen cents an hour. After work he studied English in night school. He lived in a tiny room—he had only a bed, a coal-oil stove, and a box he used for a dining table—for which he paid two dollars a month.

"I was famil' sick," he remembered. "I wanted my famil' awful bad.

"When I came to Los Angelo and I was working on the track for the Southern Pacific, one day we was eating lunch underneath a tree near a college. And I seen a lot of boys with their arms full of books. But I never seen no children. Finally I asked one of the fellas, 'Where's all the children? There's too many teachers and no children.' 'Oh,' he says, 'there isn't children. They go to college. Someone gonna be a doctor. Somebody gonna be a lawyer. Here in this country they go to school till they learn something.'

"That put in my head that if my famil' would come here, and my brothers would come here, Tony and Frank, my brothers they would go to school here and learn something. I had it in my head, and I couldn't rest. So in about a week I went to find some Italian fellow and asked if he could write for me to send for the folks from Italy."

* * *

Frank Capra's description of the arrival of Ben's letter in Bisacquino is the vivid opening of his 1971 autobiography, *The Name Above the Title*. More than two years had elapsed since Ben had left home (not five, as Frank stated), and though his family prayed for his return, they assumed he was dead. Ben dictated his letter to an Italian immigrant who lived in his neighborhood, a tailor named Morris Orsatti, whose son Ernie went on to fame as a major-league baseball player. Antonino Capra, seven years Frank's senior, remembered the gist of it:

"I'm sorry I couldn't write you before, but you know I can't write. I had to wait until I found somebody who would write for me. I'm doing well here. This is a second Italy. We've got oranges, lemons . . . we've got everything. So, for God's sake, Daddy, come over here from Bisacquino."

Frank Capra remembered the letter being read to his family by the parish priest, and he claimed that it was then he came to the bitter realization that his family was illiterate and that he would have to become educated to rise above their station in life.

A good story, except that his mother was educated enough to read and write Italian, even if his father was illiterate. Frank Capra undoubtedly took literary license here to construct a powerful metaphor for the opening of his book. He did not realize, or chose to forget, that his education was the idea of his brother Ben, who had a vision of his two younger brothers coming to America to "learn something."

Frank always exaggerated his differences from the rest of the family to paint himself as unique in his determination to transcend his peasant origins. "Their problem was that they didn't have the guts to do what I was doing," he said of his brothers and sisters. "I would have been a success in any place." The metaphor of rebirth pervades Capra's mythic version of his life story, just as it pervades his film work. He was unique in his family in the degree to which he ultimately rose beyond his origins, but Ben's dogged efforts on his and the others' behalf show that Frank was not unique among the Capras in having the desire, the determination, and the ability to succeed in America.

Ben kept sending letters until they made up their minds. His mother begged him to come home, but Ben refused. They would have to "come over here" instead. They would have to join him in America.

Saridda, deeply dissatisfied with her economic situation in Sicily and having no confidence in her husband's ability to do anything about it, had the pragmatist's awareness that a change could hardly leave them much worse off than they were. Turiddu, eight years her senior and constitutionally lazy, attached to his native land by deeper emotional roots, felt the pull of inertia much more strongly; he would have been happier to stay put.

There was one more factor to be considered: the mother's desire to be reunited with her oldest and favorite son. When Ben held out that carrot, he knew what he was doing.

"**A**fter about three months I got an answer," Ben remembered. "It said, 'We could come if you send us a pass [a boat ticket to bring them to America], but we haven't got-a the money.' So I managed to save every nickel I had.

"I was very skimping eating. At that time with five cents you could get a cup coffee and two doughnuts; that was my breakfast. For lunch I had a piece of salami and a part of French bread. I used to go to the bakery in the even' and get the bread stale—I got two loaves for five cents. For dinner I just fry a few eggs and a little slice bread. And so I finally save enough money, and I send-a for all of 'em."

The family with whom Ben was living thought so much of their young boarder that they loaned him the other $300 of the $500 he needed to bring his family to America. The Capras sold all the family belongings, including the animals, to help pay for the trip. They left only the house, with Ignazia. She would have come with them, but "when they went to Palermo and seen all that water," Ben recalled, her husband, Vincenzo Troncale, "was a-scared and come back." He and Ignazia never left Sicily. The second oldest daughter, Luigia, also stayed behind, but she and her husband, Giovanni Vitrano, would follow the others to Los Angeles in about three years.

Early in May 1903, Salvatore Capra loaded his wife and children into a horse-drawn two-wheeled cart, or *baròccio*, and, with hardly a backward glance, they set off on the road to Palermo. Six of them made the ocean journey: Salvatore and Rosaria; their thirteen-year-old daughter, Giuseppa; twelve-year-old son, Antonino; five-year-old son, Francesco; and three-year-old daughter, Antonia.

When Francesco first saw the Mediterranean Sea at Palermo, he "had never seen anything so big—I kept trying to stand up to see what was on the other side." There they boarded a French steamship of the Fabre line, the SS *Germania*. The ship had thirteen first-cabin passengers, including eight Americans. The Capras traveled in the steerage hold below deck with the rest of the ship's 1,414 passengers, of whom 83 were children six years or younger.

Most of the passengers' final destinations were cities in the eastern United States, where the large Italian populations were concentrated. Some were headed for the Midwest and the South, but of all the passengers only the Capras were going as far as California.

The *Germania* first sailed from Palermo to Naples, where it was given official certification for the journey by the U.S. consulate.

And then, on May 10, 1903, the ship left for America.

2. "I hated America"

*T*he immensity of the ocean, the boy would later say, "drove everything else out of my head."

The ocean crossing was a rebirth for Francesco Capra. America would write his story afresh. It was the first and most radical of the character transformations he would undergo in his lifetime, and, he admitted, "It scared the hell out of me."

His memory of the ship crossing always remained extraordinarily vivid, so much so that he would speak of it often in the present tense, as if for the rest of his life he was, in some profound sense, always on that ship, always in the process of becoming an American.

From Naples on May 10 the *Germania* traveled on a northwesterly route along the coasts of Italy and France to pick up more passengers. By the time the big black steamship crossed through the Strait of Gibraltar into the open Atlantic, it was jammed with as many people as it could hold.

For Capra and his family, the experience was hellish: "You're all together—you have no privacy. You have a cot. Very few people have trunks or anything that takes up space. They have just what they can carry in their hands or in a bag. Nobody takes their clothes off. There's no ventilation, and it stinks like hell. They're all miserable. It's the most degrading place you could ever be.

"The people who owned the boat made a lot of money on this. They just pile a lot of people in there, the boat keeps getting filled, and we get nothing. Oh, it was awful, *awful*. It seemed to be always storming, raining like hell and very windy, with these big long rolling Atlantic waves. Everybody was sick, vomiting. God, they were sick. And the poor kids were always crying. My father was the worst one of the bunch. He was vomiting all the time. I don't know if he was more delicate than my mother, but he was more aware of blood and people's sickness.

"*She* couldn't be. There were people to feed down there. She got our meals by walking up an iron ladder with a tray. Then she came back with this tray down the iron ladder hoping she can make it. Those stairs were straight up. There were six of us, and my mother was the only one of our family who would go up in a storm.

"I was two days in the hospital on the boat. I remember I could see out of a porthole, I could see the water down below. I didn't know where the hell we were going. All it was was pain and trouble. As far as I was concerned, if we'd stayed where we were I would have been much happier."

The journey took thirteen days. Eight days out, May 18, was Francesco Capra's sixth birthday. It was at four o'clock in the afternoon on Saturday, May 23, 1903, that the *Germania* arrived in New York harbor and steamed slowly toward the J. W. Elwell & Company dock with its cargo, described in *The New York Times* as "mdse. and passengers."

In the stifling steerage hold, Francesco Capra was wretched with fatigue. His father picked him up and carried him up the ladder into what he remembered as "that sea of people kneeling on deck."

For Saridda, below deck with the others, there was no exultation in their arrival. There still was one more night to spend on the boat, and she was patiently organizing the family to leave for the next leg of the trip. But as reluctant as Salvatore Capra had been to make the journey, with his emotional, imaginative nature he now had fallen under the spell of America's promise of freedom and opportunity.

Frank Capra remembered looking up from the deck and seeing "a statue of a great lady, taller than a church steeple, holding a torch above the land we were about to enter."

His father exclaimed, "Cicco, look! Look at that! That's the greatest light since the star of Bethlehem! That's the light of freedom! Remember that. *Freedom.*"

But when Cicco left the boat, all he could think about were the fleas gnawing at his dirty skin under his rancid clothing.

Late in life, alluding to the words inscribed on the base of the Statue of Liberty about America welcoming "Your huddled masses yearning to breathe free, / The wretched refuse of your teeming shore," Capra would make a revealing slip of the tongue, referring to immigrants entering America on "your wretched shore." A wretched shore, indeed, was where he felt himself to be on Sunday morning, May 24, 1903, when his feet made their first contact with American soil on Ellis Island.

The *Germania* began discharging its passengers at 9:40 A.M. Capra and his family entered the dank, cavernous waiting room, with a huge American flag looming on the wall above them, and endured the seemingly endless red tape that still separated them from the United States. They had to pass health tests; their papers had to be inspected and stamped again and again. Ellis Island, Capra recalled, was "a lot of noise and a lot of chairs and we sat on the chairs and waited for two days."

Late in the day on Monday they were taken by ferry to the mainland, and Papa Turiddu, with some difficulty, managed to find someone who could give them directions to the train station. They slept overnight there, and the next morning they boarded the train for California.

"The boat was bad, certainly," Capra said, "but after a certain amount of time you got used to it. For the kids, the train was the worst. It took eight days. The seats were wooden seats, some had covering, but mostly they were wooden, and that's where you were seated night and day. They locked the cars so you couldn't move around, and you slept there. It's simply criminal to have to keep your same clothes on for three weeks. Jesus! Kids think their parents are crazy: 'Where are they going?'

"*That's* where we cried, my sisters and brother and I, from sheer panic."

Capra would remember nothing of the vast new country he was passing through. "Goddammit, I was six years old and I saw trees!" he snapped when asked what he saw through the train windows. "Kids don't know the difference between one country and another. I was crying all the time anyhow and my ass was full of shit and I hated America then to beat hell."

The first time the train stopped and the doors were unlocked so the passengers could buy food, Papa Turiddu jumped out and found a small grocery near the station. He bought a loaf of bread, handing the grocer a twenty-dollar bill. The grocer gave him fifteen dollars in return. Turiddu knew he was being cheated, but because he could not speak English, he could not make the grocer give him the correct amount. The train was about to leave the station; Turiddu, in his helpless fury, barely made it back aboard with the loaf of bread that had cost him five dollars.

The incident impressed itself strongly on the minds of his panicky children. It taught them not only that their father hardly was able to take care of them in America (throwing their dependence even more strongly on their mother, whose stalwart behavior had been their only lifeline on the boat); Papa Turiddu's loaf of bread also taught them the even more bitter and powerful lesson that in America the immigrant was the prey of anyone who could take advantage of his ignorance and gullibility. To survive in America would require constant vigilance and suspicion.

All the way across the country they lived on bananas and bread. They did not know how to ask for anything else.

When the Capras stepped off the train at the Southern Pacific station in downtown Los Angeles on June 3, 1903, Frank Capra's father kissed the ground.

Capra remembered his mother doing the same, but she did not. While her husband was being emotional she was busy looking for her son Benedetto, who was waiting for them with a horse and wagon.

Ben Capra embraced his parents, but when Ben reached down to greet his little brother, Frank Capra pushed him away: "I hated the son of a bitch and all this trouble he'd caused."

No more physically imposing than when they had last seen him, Ben still stood barely five feet tall, but he was the man of the family now, a proud and toughened man of eighteen who had sweated and starved to bring his family to America. He drove them in the wagon to an old adobe mission called Nuestra Señora la Reina de Los Angeles. The "Plaza Mission" was the city's first church, and as such it was a fitting place for Ben Capra and his family to offer prayers of thanksgiving on this historic day in their lives.

From the mission Ben drove them up North Broadway and over the bridge spanning the dry bank of the Los Angeles River to a three-bedroom house he had rented for them at fourteen dollars a month on Castelar Street (today called Hill Street), two miles from the heart of the downtown business district.

On that early summer day in 1903 Los Angeles was, like Frank Capra, undergoing a rebirth. From a sleepy village of only 6,000 in 1876, Los Angeles was transforming itself into a metropolis. The census counted 102,479 citizens in 1900, and within ten years the population would more than triple. The railroads and other civic boosters, with their energetic promotion of Southern California's Mediterranean splendor ("The Italy of America"), were starting to fill the open spaces at the end of the line, in a new land which already seemed to function by its own rules. Multicolored railroad posters flooded the nation proclaiming California the "Cornucopia of the World—Room for Millions of Immigrants. . . . Land for a Million Farmers—A Climate for Health & Wealth—without Cyclones or Blizzards."

Just before the turn of the century, the streets of Los Angeles were laid out and paved, sidewalks were built, and an outfall sewer was constructed. Then, addressing its single greatest need, the city began to build an aqueduct to bring water from Owens Valley, and, in 1903 alone, Los Angeles drilled and tunneled for enough new water to irrigate the entire state of Rhode Island. With water came electricity: Los Angeles was the first city in the country to be lit entirely with electric lights, and the early years of the twentieth century also saw a rapid growth of the cheap, clean, and efficient interurban area transit system, the Pacific Electric. The center of population in California, previously concentrated in the north, had begun its decisive southward shift, to the area California writer Julia M. Sloane called "the land of the second chance, of dreams come true, of freshness and opportunity."

But despite the booming growth, Los Angeles when Frank Capra first saw it still had the look of a big small town. The day after the Capras arrived, the *Los Angeles Times* ran an illustrated feature on the deplorable conditions of the local streets, complaining, "Los Angeles is the only city that can boast . . . a street surfaced with boulders large enough to wreck a railroad train." Washes, ruts, and gullies were as common in the roads as burr clover and foxtail. Despite having nearly three hundred miles of improved streets, Los Angeles County had many which still were just dirt roads—including Sunset Boulevard.

The mayor hoped his constituents would be willing to invest the kind of money for improvements that a group of real estate promoters had just sunk into a newly developed housing tract west of the Cahuenga Pass, in a hitherto obscure stretch of lemon groves and vegetable fields known as Hollywood (population 700). But it would be several more years before the name of the new subdivision would become synonymous with the motion picture industry. The first motion picture theater in Los Angeles, Thomas L. Tally's Electric Theater at South Main and Third streets, had been open for only a year when the Capras arrived, and for the ten-cent admission price it still was showing travelogues, glimpses of London, Egypt, and India, not the machinery of illusion with which Hollywood eventually would seduce the rest of the world.

Frank Capra's family were not typical settlers in the early 1900s. The haven of "people of moderate means who came west to retire, to take it easy rather than to have a good time," Los Angeles was then, in Carey McWilliams's words, "the most priggish community in America. . . . A glacial dullness engulfed the region. Every consideration was subordinated to the paramount concern of attracting churchgoing Middle Westerners." The lower class—which now included the Capras—had been imported deliberately into Southern California, lured by cheap housing, the low cost of living, and the easy climate, in order to provide a malleable nonunionized labor force for the area's rapid and profitable development.

When Ben Capra drove his family in the wagon along crowded, hilly Castelar Street, he was taking them into the heart of the city's immigrant enclave, the East Side. Frank Capra in his autobiography described his Los Angeles childhood environment as a "ghetto," but that description is misleading. The neighborhoods where he lived were not restricted to Italians; they were a hodgepodge of every ethnic group in Los Angeles at that time: Russian Jews, Armenians, Greeks, Germans, Irish, Orientals, Mexicans, Italians, blacks. Nor could the East Side of Los Angeles in Capra's day be characterized as having had the hopeless poverty and squalor that the word ghetto generally implies. If the contrast between life in the East Side and the gentility of the WASP establishment quickly impressed itself upon the child, the East Side was still a much less harsh place to live in 1903 than were the tenements of the industrial Northeast, where most Italian immigrants lived. Those were true ghettos lacking the comparative spaciousness, cleanliness, warmth, and plentiful food a foreigner could find in Los Angeles.

But Frank Capra knew nothing of the ghettos of the East. His experience was intensely subjective—he *felt* himself to be living in a ghetto, and even if he never understood what the word really meant, the feeling was all that mattered to him. It became the motive and rationale for his success, the propellant that drove him. And in the end it became a trap that he could not escape, because the ghetto Frank Capra inhabited was one he carried around within himself.

The two-story wooden frame house Ben found for his family at 746 Castelar Street was in the midst of one of the city's busiest neighborhoods, just down the street from the French Hospital and the rat-infested city dump (today the neighborhood is Chinatown). Peddlers with horse-drawn fruit and vegetable wagons passed constantly along the broad, gravel-paved roadway hawking goods from outlying farms and downtown markets. For the children there was the ice-cream man with his horse shaking the tinkling bell that made them all come running. And on the corner was the grocery store run by two Greek brothers where many of the families bought their meat; a family of five could have an adequate dinner of beef for fifty cents, chicken for thirty-five, lamb chops for a quarter.

The Capras lived in the middle of a long block, next door to another Italian immigrant family, the Leones, and a couple of doors from a black widow and her five children, the Washingtons.

"We got by because of the ingenuity of our mothers," said Roscoe (Rocky) Washington, who grew up to be the first black lieutenant in the Los Angeles Police Department. "Frank's mother and my mother got closer together because they had the same problems. I wasn't race-conscious; I got along with everybody. All my little girlfriends were white girls, and my brother Julius had a crush on Frank's sister Annie. We called Annie his girlfriend, and it was really true. As I remember, there was a kind of mutual admiration society among the people who lived there. A couple of times a guy would say to me, 'Aw, nigger, shut up,' and I'd say, 'Aw, dago, kiss my ass.' Nowadays you get your throat cut if you say that. But we weren't treated any differently."

Both on Castelar Street and later in nearby Lincoln Heights, where the two families eventually moved, Frank Capra hitched rides on the horse-drawn barrel wagon Julius Washington drove for the East Side Brewery, and he palled around with Edgar Washington (called "Blue" because he was "so black he was blue"), who went on to be a movie comedian. But the member of the family Frank most admired was its warm-hearted and enterprising matriarch, Susan, who took in laundry and sewing as well as working as a janitor and running a nursery at the nearby 19th Avenue Elementary School. She further endeared herself to her neighbors by bringing food to newcomers and to sick people.

"She was superior to everything around her," said Capra. "She was a wonderful lady with a great booming laugh. I always equated blacks with kindness. Among the kids we didn't quite understand the differences. You leave kids alone, blacks and whites, there's no problem—[until] later on."

But Capra's parents, who had never seen blacks or Orientals before coming to Los Angeles, "did acquire, and I say acquire, because they didn't have it to begin with, the supposed dislike for Chinese, for Japanese, for 'niggers.' " It was only as Capra grew up and experienced discrimination himself while attempting to climb the social ladder that he lost his early sense of kinship toward blacks. "Blacks have hate in their heart," he insisted in 1984. The only blacks he approved of in his old age were those who had assimilated, "such as baseball players." The roles blacks were given in Capra films rarely were anything but demeaning and stereotypical; he was little better or worse than most other directors of his time in that regard, but modern audiences find those portrayals strangely at odds with Capra's professed egalitarianism. When prodded to justify his racial attitudes, Capra would express resentment toward blacks for supposedly expecting compensatory special treatment rather than lifting themselves up by their own bootstraps as he believed he had done.

In his boyhood, Capra's prejudice was directed not at "niggers" or "cholos" (Mexicans), but at the ethnic group he recalled as the most despised in the Los Angeles of those days, the "Japs," a catchword children used loosely for all Orientals.

For a "devilish kick," as Rocky Washington called it, Frank and the older Washington boys used to lie in wait behind the pepper tree in front of the Capras' house on Lincoln Heights' Albion Street for an Oriental man to come by with a horse-drawn wagon full of watermelons. The man often would be asleep as he drove in from the outlying farms; if he wasn't, the boys would leave him alone, so they wouldn't get a buggy whip cracked across their faces. But if he was sleeping, they would run behind the wagon and quietly toss the melons off one by one into the grass, so that when the man woke up and reached the market, he would find his wagon empty.

Asked how he would explain the evolution of Capra's racial prejudices and his continued affection for the Washington family, Rocky said, "Even real bigots usually have *one* group they like—they say, 'If all black people were like the Washingtons, Jesus, it would be a perfect world.' I can't remember anything negative about the Capras, but I can understand his parents' feelings, for whenever there was menial, backbreaking work to be done, the poor Italians, Negroes, and Mexicans had to do it. Frank kinda hitched his wagon to a star. He had visions, he was aspiring to go up, and he didn't want to stay down here with the masses. I can't fault him for that, because it turned out to his advantage, and we in the neighborhood didn't have too much to encourage us. It was dog-eat-dog."

Though he managed to escape the neighborhood, Capra could never escape a feeling of exclusion from mainstream American society, and in later years he came to view those who had not escaped, black and Italian alike, with an unconcealed contempt.

"I lived most of my early life in a ghetto," he said in 1978. "I don't mean a black ghetto; I mean a Sicilian ghetto. But they're all alike. All ghettos are alike. And all the people in them are alike. They constantly complain. About government, about jobs, about other ghettos, about this and that. But don't feel too sorry for people in ghettos. They want to live there more than you'd think. There's comfort in the ghetto. All the Sicilians where I lived would chitter-chatter in the same language, eat the same food, share the same traditions, the same church, the same values. When I was a teenager, I decided I wanted to see other things."

Saridda Capra, taking the primary responsibility for keeping her family fed and clothed, looked at her fellow "ghetto" dwellers through different eyes.

Her first job was picking strawberries for a Chinese farmer at seventy-five cents a day. After a while she found work closer to home, sitting in front of a conveyor belt pasting labels on cans of olives and bottles of olive oil at C. P. Grogan's Olive Oil Factory two miles away on Albion Street. Before she left home by 7:45 each morning she would roll the dough for bread and leave the makings of a pot of oxtail and vegetable soup for the children's lunch and a pot of spaghetti for dinner, but she could not come home to cook the lunch and she had no time to bake the bread after she finished work at four in the afternoon. So she would rely on Jennie Leone next door to start the food cooking and watch it for her during the day. People in a "ghetto" would do that for you, without complaining. And despite the hardness of her life, Saridda herself never complained. As Frank Capra recalled many years later, "I never saw my mother cry."

Salvatore Capra made halfhearted attempts at earning a living, but he felt adrift in California, cut off from the simple comforts of the old way of life, from his singing and storytelling cronies, and from the fields and trees he loved. "I didn't come here to work with a pick and shovel," he would say.

Even if his natural laziness had not interfered, Turiddu simply was too old to begin again, too old to learn the language and change his stubborn habits. A granddaughter, Josephine Campisi, who lived with the Capras off and on for several years during her childhood, said of him, "He was never happy here. He was disappointed when he came here—he didn't know what to expect—and he couldn't adjust."

Salvatore changed his name to "Sal" and then to "Sam" Capra—though his family and his Italian friends still called him Turiddu—and Ben found him a job with the Southern Pacific, on a track gang composed largely of blacks and Mexicans. It was a brief and disastrous experience. His son Antonino remembered how he lost the job: "Some nigger tripped him, knocked him down, and when he got up he hit this nigger with a shovel, sort of split his head. So he come runnin' home. That night the policemens came. They wanted to know if Salvatore Capra live here. I said, 'Yeah, he lives here.' I asked the cop what happened and he said, 'Well, if the nigger dies, we'll have to come back. If he lives, we'll forget it.' "

From time to time after that, Turiddu went to work in a brickyard, or in a glass factory, or picking fruit. For a while he had a little shoeshine stand downtown on Main Street. Being a bootblack was considered perhaps the single most demeaning job for an immigrant male in those days, and it was particularly humiliating for the proud Turiddu because almost all the other bootblacks were teenagers, either Italians or blacks. Capra said his father was "very touchy if anybody made fun of him."

"He really got discourage," Ben said. "He give up. He wanted me to make a pass [a ticket] for him to go back to Italy. But I didn't have the money. I said, 'Just wait till I get a little money. Then if you wanna go back, O.K., I pass you.' Then Papa Turiddu began to like it here. He found one of his friends he used to know over in Italy. And he could-a play a little bit and could-a sing a little bit. Boy, they went to town. Every Sunday they had the music and the dancin' out in the yard of a different Italian famil'. One had the accordion and the other had the guitar. Everyone was putting in two bits each to buy a keg of beer."

Though his grandchildren said that Turiddu was often mean to his own family as well as improvident, the neighborhood children fondly called him "Uncle Sam" and Frank remembered him as being popular with his neighbors, always ready to help if they were being bothered by the police or needed help arranging a loan.

Ben took a less sentimental view of his father. The reason Papa Turiddu had so many friends, Ben said, was that he associated with "kind of a bad gang across the street, they was all gangsters, Mafia, something like that. He was-a making some wine and these guys were going there to get drunk on his wine."

Papa Turiddu complained to his friends about Ben's unwillingness to send him back to Italy. The gang told Turiddu that since Ben had signed a paper promising to support his family in America, he had to pay his father a wage of a dollar a day whether the old man worked or not. They told Turiddu to find the "contract" and threaten to take his son to court if he wouldn't pay up. They offered to assist him in talking it over with his son.

"They was pumping in his head against me all the time," sighed the selfless Ben. "Well, I was trying to do my best, working all day, every hour I could. All I wanted was to make money for the famil'. When I get paid I was giving them pretty near all the pay, I was paying all the groceries, all the bills and everything. Well, when Mama Saridda heard them talking, she went in a little trunk and got the contract and burned it. Papa Turiddu was a tough talker, but that ended that."

Saridda usually got her way around the house, but, as her grandson Sam Capra recalled, "You always thought they were ready to kill each other. She and my grandfather would go at it tooth and nail, and she always held her own. They were always shouting. She didn't take too much sass from anybody." Their granddaughter Josie Campisi said, "They're all crazy, the Capras. They're all wired up, and they've all got tempers. My grandparents used to fight because he wanted my grandmother to bring money home. She was a tough old bird, and he gave her hell all the time."

A shift of power from the man to the woman was typical in immigrant families, and in the case of the Capras the matriarchy had begun back home in Sicily. But the process was intensified in America, and it had far-reaching effects on Frank Capra.

The fact that Saridda worked outside the home was in itself a radical difference from Sicilian mores, which kept women inside and seldom even allowed them to make money from work done at home. The pattern weakened in America, through necessity, and despite her quarrels with Turiddu, she thrived on her role as breadwinner through nineteen years at Grogan's Olive Oil Factory. Campisi observed that once her grandmother came to America she quickly shed the black garb traditional to peasant women in Sicily. Aside from her broken English, "You'd never know she came from the old country. She was very Americanized, very modernized. She was a proud lady, an independent lady."

Frank Capra grew up with what he recognized as a "mother complex." He usually sentimentalized his relationship with his mother: "I had a very strong mother—a very nice mother," he said in a 1972 interview. "I had a great respect for her ability to make do under the worst kind of circumstance and not panic. Women have always been pillars of strength to me. Always. I'm not a feminist, but I'm a real lover of women." His mother's strength of character, which impressed everyone who knew her, was reflected in the portrayals of women in his movies: "It's probably a carryover from my mother—all the women in my stories are strong. They are stronger than men. Men start crying more quickly. Jean Arthur was not about to play a harmonica. Women are more pragmatic; they think in terms of everyone's welfare. They think in terms of tomorrow and in terms of continuation. Men commit suicide. My mother was very strong in her ideas, strong in her work. She'd work night and day. She'd find jobs where nobody else could. Every month she sent five dollars to her daughter and four or five other people back in Sicily. She was a remarkable woman. She believed in being able to take care of people."

But Capra's sentimentality masked other feelings about his mother: "She was a terror. Between her and my brother [Tony] I took many a punch and slap in the face." He said his home on Albion Street "was not for me a house of joy, it was nothing but a house of pain," and he wrote that his mother reminded him of a "witch." He sentimentalized her to blunt the pain and to appease her in memory as he had tried to do in life.

"She didn't like me at all," he said, "but I *loved* her."

Josie Campisi agreed that Saridda had no great fondness for Frank, but she explained, "I don't think she really liked *any* of her kids. She was a hard woman. Maybe she couldn't express herself. She was not one for hugs and affection, but she was always there when you needed her."

One issue on which Saridda did not prevail was Frank's education. Frank claimed in his book that he was determined to get an education from his very first day in America, that the whole thing was his idea. But the idea had been planted by Ben, and Papa Turiddu also took some initiative, recognizing the special aptitudes of his youngest son and understanding, like Ben, how his own illiteracy limited his chances in America. Turiddu thought the boy should take advantage of the school right across the street. Saridda thought that if he was going to eat their food, he should work like anyone else.

They finally compromised: if Frank would go to school *and* bring in money, Saridda would drop her objections. His older brother Antonino, by now called Tony, had started peddling newspapers in the downtown business district the very day after he arrived in America. He came home the first night with eleven cents in his pocket. Before long Frank was sent out with him; Frank would peddle papers for ten years. Industriousness quickly became a habit with him: "I was always after jobs. I never was without money. I made money all the time. I don't think I missed anything in life; I think I gained. I was much smarter than any other guy. I had to be smarter. You become pretty sharp because you're constantly working against somebody else."

"When I really became aware of Frank as being a different individual from the others in the neighborhood," Rocky Washington said, "was when I realized that he was scholarly, that he wanted an education. He was a student right from the start, and he didn't compete in the playground like my brothers and others did. He was too small, anyway, but he wasn't a sissy; he wasn't tough, he just wasn't interested. He was a pretty sharp cat. Compared to the average kid in the neighborhood he was a mental giant. And you know how kids are, they would call him a 'bookworm.' That was an insult. I wouldn't say Frank was aloof, but while we were goofing off he was studying."

Frank Capra's formal education began on September 14, 1903, at the Castelar Street Elementary School, in the first-grade class of Emma C. Wisler. By then the family had moved a block and a half to 846 College Street, on the same block as the school. The earliest existing photograph of Capra was taken in the schoolyard, probably that September, although he dated it July 4. Papa Turiddu, wearing his Sicilian garb of dark working clothes, is showing off little Frank to the principal, Mrs. Isabel A. Vignolo. Frank is wearing a sailor suit his father bought him for the occasion of the boy's being chosen by Mrs. Vignolo to lead the pledge of allegiance to the flag, in English, before the other students. The patriotic ritual was not held just on July 4, but every morning in the schoolyard, part of the school's means of assimilating the mostly immigrant children to their new country. Being chosen to lead the pledge of allegiance was an honor Frank Capra never forgot.

A disgruntled bystander in the Castelar Street photograph is Frank's older brother Tony. Tony is watching with hands in pockets and an indifferent slouch. The two brothers never had an easy relationship. Tony habitually beat up on his younger brother, until Frank as a teenager passed him in height (Tony as an adult was the shortest of the male Capras, at 4'11", even shorter than Ben). Tony resented Frank because of the advantages Frank was given as a child, and, according to Josie Campisi, he "felt inferior" to Frank.

Because he had never been to school in Sicily, the twelve-year-old Tony was put into first grade with Frank, who was six years younger. Tony felt ridiculous and stupid to be in class with children so much younger and smaller than he was, and he was furious when some of them laughed at his broken English. He had to repeat the first semester, while Frank passed him, but he managed to catch up with Frank again for the second and third grades at the 19th Avenue Elementary School. In May 1906, Tony took out his rage on their third-grade teacher, Anna Fitzhugh, a cross-eyed woman with glasses. He socked her in the face, knocking her glasses off, and was sent briefly to a reform school, the last schooling he ever would receive. When he came home, his parents sent him to work in a brickyard.

Frank Capra's first years of schooling hardly were auspicious. Because of the preponderance of immigrant children, and the mixture of home languages and ethnic backgrounds, the Castelar Street Elementary School had to take a lowest-common-denominator approach, laboriously drilling the students in pronouncing and understanding basic English. Frank assimilated English quickly—within six months he had forgotten much of his Italian—and he was often bored in class.

"God, I could have jumped a class a day there," he recalled. "They were pretty low, pretty hard to teach."

He learned much more selling papers. For a while he and Tony delivered papers on a route, but mostly they sold them on the streets. Gangs of newsboys would gather in the alleys behind the downtown newspaper plants to purchase stacks of papers for two cents a copy, making a penny on each one they sold. And they had to sell all they bought, or they would be stuck with the leftovers. Frank was lucky if he made thirty-five cents a day. "Sometime he want-a get a cup of coffee and doughnuts," Ben remembered, "and he was a-eatin' some of it."

It was a job that taught diligent, aggressive salesmanship and the ability to use one's fists. The best corners, in front of the banks and the big office buildings, had to be fought for: "If you could lick the guy in front of you," Capra said, "you took his corner." As a newsboy gained in age, size, and experience, he moved closer and closer to the heart of the downtown financial center, at Fifth and Spring streets. Capra never quite made it to that corner in eleven years, but he came within "about four jumps" of it.

Though Tony bullied his little brother at home, he watched out for Frank on the streets. "We lived in a tough neighborhood," Tony recalled, "and Frank and I had to learn to be resourceful. When we were selling newspapers, I had to take a licking to support him. They all wanted to cut him out, and I had to whip the bigger boys that he couldn't handle. I was tougher than they were."

Before long they came up with a clever stratagem. "Many a night he never got to sell all his papers," Tony explained, "so we staged a fake fight. Some people would come up and stop the fight. He'd pretend to cry, and he'd say, 'My older brother beat me up because I didn't get rid of all my papers.' Right then and there he got rid of 'em all." It was Frank Capra's earliest success in manipulating public sentiment.

He avidly read the papers he sold, quickly absorbing large amounts of brisk, colloquial American prose. He acquired an awareness of world events and a familiarity with American popular culture, and he grew excited by the realization that, as Ben insisted, reading and education were the key to worldly success.

Life as a newsboy also taught Capra some more painful lessons. "I got a pretty good corner selling papers at the Jonathan Club on Los Angeles Street. They were rich people there, very rich. Those people would come out with their big long cigars and get into their big long limousines, with their black chauffeurs opening the doors. I sold them papers. And I would put them together in my mind with the little old ladies I'd see going to church in the morning. They all had to take Communion and they all had to confess. I'd say, what the hell do these women have to confess? What could they have done? What the hell is all this shit about this confession? Well, you know, I never confessed anything at all. And these rich guys, I'd say, 'Christ, these guys are not going to church. They're rich and the people that are going to church are poor.' So I put together *poor* with *church*. Nobody with any money went to church, so it had no appeal to me whatever."

And, he later recalled, the streets gave him a brutal sexual education: because he was so small when he was a newsboy, he was an easy mark for rape by older, bigger males when Tony wasn't around to protect him. That was how he accounted for his homophobic remarks in *The Name Above the Title*.

But he felt that "the selling of newspapers, and being on the street, made me much smarter than the average kid my age—street-smart. That's where I learned what it was all about. I knew more about people and money and women and what happened in the world. I knew because I saw it in the street. You see, I never played. I never was a boy. I was a man."

In October 1904, sixteen months after coming to Los Angeles, the Capras bought their first house, at 240 South Avenue 18, across the river in Lincoln Heights, two miles from where they were living. Frank, who was in second grade, transferred to the 19th Avenue Elementary School (now the Albion Street School) at the corner of Albion, half a block from his home.

This was a better neighborhood of modest, well-kept bungalows and mostly paved streets, a step up both in comfort and social status. Many of the people in the neighborhood owned their own homes, and people in this neighborhood didn't all give off an aura of having just stepped off the boat. Though the neighborhood was about one fourth Italian, including several families from Bisacquino, it still was predominantly Irish when the Capras moved there. The Washingtons, who followed later, were the only blacks.

The neighborhood would be Frank Capra's home for more than a decade. When he remembered his youth, his most vivid memories would center on Lincoln Heights, where he grew from a ragged seven-year-old newsboy to a college graduate. In his autobiography Capra created the impression that the "ghetto" he called "Little Sicily" was a joyless place of grinding poverty.

Others had quite different memories of the place.

"Uncle Frank overdid it," said Ben's son, Sam Capra. "That stuff he writes in his book about living in poverty and being from an Italian ghetto, that's a bunch of bull. We lived there. It was a pretty good place of Los Angeles when we lived there. And it was not strictly Italian; that just was not true."

Tony's widow, Marguerite Capra, said, "When we got Frank's book

Tony had me read it to him. I never did finish reading it because Tony wouldn't let me—he'd blow his top. Tony got kind of hurt about that part about them being so poor; he said it wasn't so, they never did without."

And Capra's neighbor Maria Lanza Oddo, who also had lived near him in Bisacquino, recalled, "It was nice neighborhood. Everybody knew everybody. Was poor people, oh, sure, but everything was cheap at that time. That time was so good, never come again. Everybody was getting along good. Everything was together."

Census records and the testimony of those who lived there demonstrate that the nickname Little Sicily fit the neighborhood more accurately after World War I than it did when Frank Capra was in his early youth. The neighborhood only gradually assumed the dominantly Italian character it had by the 1920s, when it became so notorious for bootlegging and Mafia activity that Avenue 19 came to be known as "Shotgun Alley."

The Capras' house had a long front yard dominated by a towering cypress tree, with a stately two-story wood frame house set far back from the street. There was a wide, elevated front porch, shady and quiet. The yard was big enough to support another house, with ample room left over. That appealed to Turiddu, whose life in the cramped hills of Sicily had taught him never to waste living space. They rented out the second floor to help pay the mortgage. One of their boarders was an unemployed carpenter, who came to Turiddu and offered to build a one-room addition in back if he could live there for nothing. Later they put up a big three-bedroom house on the front part of the lot. Ben lived in the front house after his marriage in 1908 to an eighteen-year-old Italian immigrant named Mary Gioia, and Papa Turiddu and his family moved around the corner to 1775 Albion Street, where they had three houses on one lot.

There Frank's family was able to use the big duplex in front and a tiny house in back as rental properties (Turiddu's brother Giuseppe [Joe] and his wife, Concetta, lived in back for years), while Turiddu, Saridda, Tony, Frank, and Annie squeezed into the angular two-story middle house facing dusty Avenue 17.

That wood frame house had low ceilings, a small porch, and a white picket fence. There was a good-sized rose garden on the property, which Turiddu promptly tore up and replaced with vegetables, a pepper tree, two lemon trees, and two avocado trees. The houses were situated in a cul-de-sac adjacent to the clamorous Western Pipe and Steel Company, an ice-cream factory, and a playground with a handball court smack up against the back wall of Turiddu's garden. And Grogan's was directly across the street, which at least was convenient for Saridda.

The houses on Albion Street still stand today, virtually unchanged. Like the rest of the neighborhood, time and modernization have passed them by, leaving them rundown but still functional. Even Papa Turiddu's lemon trees remain, strong-limbed and abundant.

Ben's side yard on Avenue 18 has been paved over with a driveway, but otherwise it takes little effort to imagine the joyous parties the Capras used to throw there on Sunday afternoons for all the transplanted *bisacquinesi*. Saridda supplied her homemade wine, and they hauled a keg of beer from the East Side Brewery up the street. People brought their guitars, mandolins, and accordions, taking turns playing the nonstop waltzes and polkas. No woman danced more spiritedly than Saridda. Sometimes Frank would play the guitar or an old banjo that Papa Turiddu gave him. The air was filled with raucous gaiety as men played *bocci* and tried to outdo each other in contests of impromptu badinage.

But Turiddu grew increasingly restless in Lincoln Heights. He was not a natural city dweller, and planting a few trees in his garden was not enough to satisfy his need to work with the soil. What had Ben told him? "This is a second Italy"? But the orchards Ben was talking about were out in the foothills of the citrus belt, which stretched from Pasadena to San Bernardino. Somehow he had to get there.

One of the most significant acts an immigrant can take to assume a new American identity is to change his name. Not content with having his first name changed from Francesco to the brashly American "Frank" (he rejected the more formal equivalent, Francis, because he thought it sounded like a girl's name), Capra made another change not long after he moved to Lincoln Heights. Though no middle name was recorded for him in the Bisacquino register of births, his family gave him the middle name of Rosario, the masculine equivalent of his mother's first name, and while still in grammar school he Anglicized it to "Russell." Frank Russell Capra became his legal name when he became a naturalized American citizen in 1920, and he used "Frank R. Capra" as his screen credit until 1933.

When asked why he chose his new tripartite name, which he felt evoked those of such eminent WASP Americans as Franklin Delano Roosevelt and William Randolph Hearst, Capra said simply, "It didn't smell of the ghetto."

As his self-conscious Americanism took shape, Frank Capra began to experience a larger and larger schism between himself and his family.

None of this Frank Russell Capra nonsense for them: his father still called him "Cicco," his mother called him "Franco" or "Francuzzo," and to her dying day his sister Luigia called her brother "Franga." But Frank and his family literally did not even speak the same language anymore. His parents spoke Italian around the house and broken English only when necessary outside. His siblings spoke mostly Italian too, although Annie, who followed his example by going to school, also acquired fluent English. Frank said his parents communicated with him mainly through "kicks in the ass."

"His vision of life was different from those poor people's," said Josie Campisi. "He visualized things way ahead."

The force of his inward struggles was directed against his parents, who represented what he did not want to become. In his mind, they were ignorant and superstitious peasants, hopelessly bound to habits that kept them under the thumb of the rich and powerful. In later years he admitted that as a boy he became ashamed of his parents. Asked when he had gotten over that feeling, he said, "I haven't yet. I loved my parents, but I knew what was wrong with them, and I knew what our differences were. We were growing farther and farther apart, my family and I, my brothers and sisters. And it was one simple thing: education."

It was a drama being enacted in many immigrant homes of that era. As Robert Foerster put it, "The ability to read and write, what is more to read and write in English, gives to the child a powerful instrument for adaptation which his parents lack. And his growth toward American ways rouses in him some of that contempt for his origin which has so often brought sadness to his parents."

Frank took another step upward on September 16, 1907, when he left 19th Avenue Elementary School, which went only through the fourth grade, to enter the Griffin Avenue Elementary School. It was a mile-and-a-half walk from his home, but that was part of its advantage: it was located in an area "with mostly Irish people, a better-class family than we were," said Rocky Washington, who also went there. "There weren't so many foreigners—people who spoke foreign languages in their houses," recalled Capra's classmate Evelyn Weldon. At Griffin he developed a crush on Phyllis Wilson, the prettiest girl in the class, whose parents had a grocery store. He worked up the courage to walk her to school, but the boys and girls were kept apart in the schoolyard by a cement barrier between their play areas.

Few children from Frank's neighborhood in Lincoln Heights would have been expected to continue their education beyond the eighth grade—

most could not afford it—but Griffin gave a high school preparatory education. It was at Griffin that Capra found the teacher whose belief in his potential made it possible for him to move beyond the limitations of his upbringing.

Jean McDaniel was a large, stern, but kindly Irish spinster who wore high-laced boots and addressed her class from a perch atop a tall stool. She taught Capra in the first semester of fifth grade, from September 1907 through February 1908. Capra remembered her as "motherly," and with her love of learning and her warmth toward the ten-year-old boy she began to open his intellectual horizons and fill the emptiness in him left by his own mother's indifference.

Years later Miss McDaniel recalled "a little Italian boy sitting in the second desk in the second row of seats from the windows studying his spelling lesson over the shoulder of the boy who sat in front of him, because he had no book. He never missed a word and he seemed to anticipate the word I was going to pronounce before it left my lips.

"One day I said to him, 'Frank, where is your spelling book?' He replied, 'I have none, Miss McDaniel.' 'Then how do you get your lesson?' I asked. He raised himself up in his seat as far as he could and stretched his neck to show me that he studied from the book of the boy who sat in front of him. When he finished my grade his parents thought that he would have to quit school and help to support the family. He was such a bright little fellow and was so dependable that we interested ourselves in his behalf and succeeded in getting the Parent-Teachers Association to pay his parents what he could earn and let him go on to school."

Capra remembered his fifth and sixth grades as "my toughest days," because of his mother's opposition to his schooling: "*Time* was my enemy. I was always running. All we had time to do was to work and run to work. I studied while I was in class. I was a quick learner because I had to be; I never took a book home." But it was no accident that he flourished in the two subjects Miss McDaniel liked best. His fascination with American history, which would have such a profound effect on his work in motion pictures, was kindled when he began picking up books in her classroom and reading about the American Revolution: "I thought America was a great story. They fought for liberty—I didn't know what the hell liberty meant. I thought that was better than reading a novel."*

---

*He read his first novel when he was twelve years old, and a lady on his Sunday paper route gave him a copy of The Three Musketeers: "I read that book two thousand times. I took it to bed with me. It was the only book I had for a long, long time."

Before that discovery, Capra, as he wrote in his autobiography, still "hated America." Now he was beginning to realize that those feelings of anger could be directed into ambition. "Lift yourself up by your boot-straps," Miss McDaniel would tell him, a favorite expression of hers that Rocky Washington felt "made Frank kind of sensitive to his ethnic back-ground, make him aware that people looked down on him." He had experienced a rude shock in second grade when he learned that the framers of the Constitution had decided that an American who was foreign-born could never become President of the United States. But he could see now that despite the barriers of money and birth, he did have opportunities he never would have had in Sicily. Many years later, his feelings about America still were charged with a small boy's wonderment and gratitude.

"Although I came here as a baby, I feel I was born here," Capra said in a 1941 radio broadcast for a U.S. Department of Justice series, *I'm an American!*, in which naturalized citizens talked about their adopted country. ". . . I love America, not because once I was a ragged newsboy on the streets of Los Angeles at the age of six—but because it is possible in America for a six-year-old newsboy to grow and dream, and to make his dreams materialize into realities."

While studying with Miss McDaniel, Frank also discovered that he had an aptitude for mathematics. Following his progress as he drew closer to graduation, she urged him to continue his studies. "She'd get me alone outside while the kids were playing ball or some damn thing, and she'd put her arm around me and talk to me. She'd say, 'You've got to keep going. You're not going to stop here, are you? Go on to high school. Go on to high school.'

"She kept after me. But it didn't register [at first]. I couldn't see that far."

3. "A terrible wop"

*T*he idea Miss McDaniel planted in Frank Capra's brain became an obsession. He still had no idea what he would become, but he now saw clearly that education was the one thing that would keep him from spending his life on the railroad tracks or in a brickyard. He overcame his parents' reluctance to his further schooling by promising to pay his own expenses if they would let him go on to high school.

In 1909, when Frank was still in sixth grade, there were only two high schools in Los Angeles. The older and more prestigious was Los Angeles High School, situated downtown on Bunker Hill, about a mile's walk from where he lived. It was the school he would have expected to attend. There was also Polytechnic, or Poly, farther out on 19th Street and Grand Avenue. The dusty suburb called Hollywood, whose population still was under 4,000, had a high school, too, but it was only for those who lived there.

With the phenomenal population growth of the early 1900s, Los Angeles had an urgent need for a new high school to relieve the overcrowding at the two existing schools and to serve a wider area. Crews working around the clock built a brand-new school in a barley field on the south side of the city at 42nd and Vermont near the University of Southern California, then a sparsely populated area of farms, orange groves, dirt roads, and small middle-class bungalows (today it is a densely populated Latino and black neighborhood). The new school opened in September 1910. It was called Manual Arts High School.

By the second semester, when Capra enrolled there, Manual had 1,054 students, 668 of them in his Winter '15 class of freshmen. The $500,000 school complex was an architectural showpiece, its three long and graceful main buildings connected with arched walkways and opening onto spacious grounds planted with gardens of roses and cacti. But physical conditions otherwise were primitive in the early days. The streets surrounding the school had been laid out, but they were unpaved and lacking storm drains. The streetcars stopped several blocks away, and students had to walk through an open field to get to the school. The schoolyard was dusty in dry weather and a muddy morass in rain; by the time students entered class, their shoes and clothes were filthy. "We were styled the 'Country Cousin,' and the surroundings and our appearance sure did fit the title," student Langdon Smead wrote in 1914.

When Capra was told by a teacher at Griffin Avenue Elementary that if he wanted to go to high school, he would have to go to the "Country Cousin" rather than to Los Angeles High, he experienced it as a slap in the face.

Manual was seven miles and two streetcar rides from his home. He assumed that he was being exiled there because he was considered unfit to be part of the elite at the two established schools: "They were hoity-toity high schools, because only hoity-toity people *went* to high school. High school then was like Harvard or Yale. Only people who had money enough sent their kids to school. It was the moneyed class." Sixty years later, the hurt was still fresh when he told in his autobiography of being rejected from Los Angeles High because he was regarded as "riffraff" and being sent to Manual Arts to join the other "rejects."

But he misunderstood.

The day Capra entered high school, the *Los Angeles Express* reported that several hundred students had been waiting in line for hours—some all night—to be admitted to Los Angeles and Poly highs. But each school could accept only two hundred new students, so the overflow was sent to Manual Arts. That was the only reason they were turned away. The Manual student body was predominantly white and middle-class, even more so, in fact, than the student bodies at the other two schools, which were closer to the ethnic enclaves of downtown and the East Side. Manual Arts was a step *up* the social ladder for students from those areas.

"If Frank had gone to Poly," said Rocky Washington, "I don't think he would have been treated any differently from the way he was treated around the neighborhood. But Manual Arts was a new school, out farther, in a more aristocratic neighborhood. There he would fall into the category of a black [Capra's class had only three black students]. Going to Manual Arts he would have to pass."

One reason Capra may have misremembered Manual as full of "riffraff" was its change in ethnic composition after he left: when he went back to Manual to pass out diplomas at the 1950 commencement, he felt "scared to death" to look into the faces of so many black people. It was a feeling shared by others of his era. Esther Gleason Schlinger, a member of his class, said she and other alumni were proud of having gone to Manual "until it turned black—that was the worst that ever happened—and people dropped it."

Manual Arts' homogeneity in Capra's years was also a reflection of the fact that most poor teenagers in Los Angeles at that time did not go on to high school. High school was voluntary then, and only a youngster of unusually strong motivation, such as Capra, would insist on going in the face of financial hardship and parental opposition. And contrary to Capra's fantasy about high school students representing "the moneyed class," "Anybody who had a good deal of money in Los Angeles at that time always sent their children to private school in the East," said Brigadier General Harold R. Harris, a doctor's son who attended both high school and college with Capra. "I don't think [Manual Arts] discriminated against poor boys, because most of us were poor. Or certainly not affluent," said Capra's schoolmate Lieutenant General James H. Doolittle. Though Capra claimed that "nobody went there by choice—and we knew it," many of the first students at Manual *did* choose to go there. "It was a brand-new high school with everybody who was fed up with the high schools they happened to be going to at the time, and decided they'd try this new one," Harris said. As Capra's classmate Lynford Hess put it, "The people at Manual were the ones who didn't want to be tied to their own community; they wanted to be independent."

However subjective was Capra's feeling of rejection, it cut deep, so deep that it became an enduring part of his personal mythology and a conscious motivation for his tremendous drive toward success. When he experienced actual rejection during his years at Manual Arts, it only seemed to confirm his original feeling of banishment from the citadel of the WASP establishment.

"He was a sticker," said Josie Campisi. "That made him more determine than ever to do something with his life. He wanted to show them."

With their varied backgrounds and reasons for being there, it is little wonder that Capra's fellow students were baffled by his calling them "nogooders" and "rejects." Some were indignant. "That is his opinion of *himself*," said Isabel Martin Campbell, "and I don't think it's fair to put that on the school as a whole." And Virginia Titus Ives said, "He would like to 'downtrodden' the rest of us. He'd like to have it that way because he's elevated himself to the point of being way above us. But at the time he was in school, we didn't rate him up there at all. I don't remember him as an individual."

Ives's failure to remember Capra from the days at Manual Arts was shared by all but eight of his eighteen schoolmates interviewed for this book. And of those eight, only two really knew him. In a revealing contrast, of the eighteen men questioned who went to college with Capra, every one remembered him. Most of those who went to Manual with him did not become aware of who he was until the burst of publicity that followed *It Happened One Night* in 1934.

"When I would read about him in Hollywood," said Lynford Hess, "I'd rack my brain to know if I ever met him. I've asked myself lots of times why I never did." "I knew he was there," said Ruth Hammond, an actress from the preceding class. "He was in some way kind of a figure around school. But if he hadn't become a famous moving picture director I wouldn't remember him at all. He didn't make any impression on me—he didn't even *try* to make an impression—except that I remember he played a very good game of tennis."

In the self-celebratory retrospective haze of his autobiography, Capra wrote affectionately of Manual Arts, but that was far from the truth. Capra's true feelings about Manual were rarely expressed, because they were so painful. In the uncut manuscript he added that the school taught him indelible lessons about the average American his films ostensibly celebrated. The lessons he learned at Manual did stick, but they were far from simple ones, and they help illuminate the complex social attitudes that govern his work.

Throughout his four years at Manual, despite his sporadic and half-hearted attempts to be recognized, he remained for most of the students a faceless John Doe, lost in the crowd, snubbed and ignored and, perhaps most devastating of all for the egotistic Capra, not remembered.

The immigrant, Foerster points out, is forced to recognize that "for the world he is a supremely unimportant person. What is more, he is less to be thought of, after all, as an individual than as a composite." That Capra felt this can be seen in his evaluation of his family's social status in Los Angeles: "We were nobody."

And yet, discussing the motivations that governed his high school years, Capra said, "I had a superiority complex right from the very beginning. . . . I felt superior to everybody I met. That superiority has always been with me."

When he felt himself exiled from the established schools, Capra reflexively protected his ego by maintaining an outraged superiority to the supposed "riffraff" with whom he now found himself. No matter that they were nothing of the sort; his ego demanded that he see them that way.

This was the outsized chip he carried on his shoulder when he arrived at Manual Arts on February 6, 1911, three days after his graduation from grammar school.

Just getting from his home to school every morning was a major undertaking.

To help put himself through Manual Arts, Capra not only continued selling papers downtown after school and took an added job on Saturday nights stuffing the Sunday edition of the *Los Angeles Times,* but he also worked as a janitor at Manual before class each morning. With two other boys, he cleaned blackboards and emptied trashcans, a job that paid a dollar a day. He claimed he had to wake at 3:30 A.M. and leave home at four to catch a yellow streetcar on the North Broadway bridge two blocks from his house for a two-hour ride to school, but he told the *Manual Arts Daily* in 1950 that he woke around five and began his janitorial job at 6:30, which seems more likely.

"Between me and that streetcar there was a dog who didn't like me and who would try to bite my ass off. I had to have a stick with me to fight him off." The streetcar took him downtown to the Plaza Mission, where he waited, still in the dark, for a second trolley. "Oh, boy, it was no time for kids to be out. If you met anybody he'd be a man and he'd be drunk and he'd make a grab for you and try to screw you. I'd fight like hell. There was an awful lot of that. It was terrible, but I had to stick it out, in the open. It was colder than hell in the winter, and when it rained I had to crawl between buildings and try to keep myself dry."

The second streetcar let him off several blocks from school. Often there would be dense fog covering the fields and Capra would have to feel his way along by kicking the curbs: "That walk was the scariest thing of my life. Your heart was in your mouth all the time. It was simply so silent. There was nobody. It was as if you were the last person on earth. Finally you'd see the glow of the school, and you were very happy."

To his classmates, fancy new middle name or not, Frank Russell Capra still smelled of steerage. His janitor's job, he felt, had much to do with the way he was perceived. "They'd see me in the morning cleaning up and wiping the boards, and they'd take me for a workman. I was looked down on as a workman. Oh, kids are cruel. At that age they're crueler than hell."

With his dark complexion, wavy black hair, thick facial features, cheap clothing, and lack of social graces, Capra indeed appeared to be in the same category as a black or a Mexican. Ruth Hammond remembered him as "a very friendly little fella . . . with a little kind of monkey face." Millson (Mitt) Downs had the impression he was "a Spanish type or something." "He *did* look different," his black classmate Evelyn Turner Loftin observed. "No wonder he thought he *was* different." Esther Gleason Schlinger, the official historian of Capra's graduating class, said, "I don't know that anybody really liked him. He was ostracized; people never invited him anywhere. Because he was a foreigner, they didn't think of including him in their parties. He was a nice boy. He was just a terrible wop."

Manual's principal, Dr. Albert Wilson, "ran what the Navy calls 'a tight ship,'" recalled the future General Doolittle, who as a student had more than his share of run-ins with the principal. Dr. Wilson—who grew up in a one-room Nebraska sod house, took his doctorate at the University of Berlin, and was a high school principal and college teacher in Utah before coming to Los Angeles—was, by all accounts, an extraordinary educator. If he was feared by some of his students, they also loved him, and anyone seeking answers to why so many of the early Manual Arts students became so successful can start by acknowledging the influence of Dr. Wilson.

Partly out of necessity and partly by choice, Dr. Wilson lured a young, energetic, and individualistic faculty to his school, giving them unusually free rein in their teaching methods. "All good teachers," he said, "are a bit eccentric in some way. I wouldn't give anything for one who wasn't. Eccentrics—at least the benign kind—are nearly all worth heeding." He even saw no harm in the unorthodox political views to which the students were being exposed by some of the teachers in that era. "All of the best teachers," declared student Eleanor Kimble, "were card-carrying Socialists." Capra's art teacher, Rob Wagner, was among those espousing socialist ideas, "but with a healthy sauce of humor," Manual teacher Florence Sprenger wrote in her history of the school. Girls' Vice Principal Mary Putnam, who taught Capra freshman English, was one of several female teachers who made women's rights a familiar topic of discussion in those years when suffrage was a burning issue. Dr. Wilson also accepted the presence of teachers he knew would be leaving before long to pursue other career ambitions, believing that "the best way to keep alive" is to "strive to be a practitioner of what one teaches." In this atmosphere of intellectual freedom and spontaneity, an array of remarkably talented teachers came to Manual Arts. Yet Capra felt that "they filled it up with surplus [teachers] from the other schools—the people they didn't like, the pains in the ass, the dopes."

To involve the students in their own disciplinary process, Dr. Wilson established a much-imitated student self-government program; in his junior year Capra was one of the "cops" appointed to turn in fellow students for "misdeeds, from smoking and saying naughty words, to throwing garbage on the ground." But Helen Jerome Eddy, whose all-consuming passion for the theater admittedly made her a "rotten" student, recalled that rather than forcing her to take subjects in which she had no interest, Dr. Wilson allowed her to cut classes in order to direct student plays. She also did extra work in movies while in high school and went on to leading roles in silents and character parts in talkies, including Capra's *The Bitter Tea of General Yen* and *Mr. Smith Goes to Washington*. Dr. Wilson's tolerance of Eddy's irregular attendance was typical of his ability to recognize the individual needs of his large student body.

Departing from the standard curriculum prescribed by the Los Angeles school system, he placed equal stress on traditional liberal arts courses and modern technical training, to counteract "the influence of an artificial society and an exclusive book education." He encouraged school spirit on the new campus by making extracurricular clubs a rage. The drama group spearheaded by the young "expression" teacher Maude Howell soon became so accomplished that it attracted critics from the local papers, and girls' gym teacher Marion Morgan's "fancy dancing" group turned professional and went on national tours so the girls could earn money for college.

Capra's classmate Lawrence Tibbett, the illustrious opera singer, sang in the glee club and had the lead in a number of school plays. Another classmate, Goodwin J. (Goody) Knight, with whom Capra sold papers as a boy, was a champion debater and student body president, and served as the Republican governor of California for six years in the 1950s. But, as happens at any school, the students who would become prominent in later life were not necessarily those who shone at Manual Arts. Harold Harris, the first man to save his life by parachuting from an airplane and later the president of Northwest Airlines, laughingly answered "None of your business" when asked about his classroom performance. The two most famous graduates to emerge from that early group were Capra and Doolittle, and neither was a standout at Manual Arts. Doolittle, the pioneer aviator and World War II hero, has a building at the school named after him now, but he was an indifferent student and was regarded as something of a rowdy.

"Neither Doolittle nor Capra was very social," Esther Gleason Schlinger recalled. "It never entered our heads that either one of them would ever amount to a hill of pins."

Capra was an excellent student, however, compensating academically for the low repute in which he was regarded socially. He received straight A's in geometry, plane trigonometry, chemistry, physics, American history, Spanish, and French. He had a harder time with English, receiving A's in the first semester of his freshman year, but B's thereafter. But though Capra would go from Manual Arts to an engineering college, his ultimate orientation toward the humanities was presaged by his strong showing in those subjects in high school and his spottier record in the manual arts courses, in which he pulled mostly B's and C's, with only a single A. In his last two years Capra was a member of the Mimerians, an honor society for the top 10 percent of each class.

Esther Gleason Schlinger recognized an undercurrent in him that others overlooked: "He had his own life, and he didn't care about other people. He was very polite to everybody; they didn't give him a chance. He knew that he wasn't cared for, so he went away by himself. He just tended to business; he didn't have time for anything else. He was interested in lessons, but he had to work so hard after school, I don't know when he studied. He was just busy." And Harold Harris understood how Capra's quiet determination contributed to his ostracism: "Capra was 180 degrees out of phase with lazy guys like me. He was working all the time. He was trying to make a living and trying to do well in his studies. He impressed everybody as being pretty brash, because he not only worked like the mischief, but *he knew* that he worked like the mischief, and it kind of irritated us lazy people."

As he had with Miss McDaniel, Capra again found teachers who recognized his potential. His favorites were Isabelle Willson, a small, vivacious woman who taught him algebra, geometry, and chemistry, and the exacting Eva Farnum, who also taught him algebra and geometry and was his "class teacher" (daily supervisor) in the last two years. Going to college was not unusual for Manual Arts graduates—many went on to neighboring USC, to Stanford, or to Berkeley, the University of California's only campus at that time—but college had seemed to Capra a remote and impractical possibility until Miss Willson and Mrs. Farnum set out to convince him otherwise. He remembered that they invited him to dinner at their homes and never ceased hounding him about going on to college.

No one at Manual knew about Capra's first professional job in show business: playing the guitar on Sunday nights in one of the many brothels in the red-light district downtown on Central Avenue. Central Avenue, in Capra's words, was "where the niggers were." The brothels, mostly storefront nightclubs with a couple of black girls upstairs for the white clientele, had names like the Cadillac Club and the Hummingbird Cafe. Each had a small combo, and at the low-cost brothel where Capra worked, another boy played the piano, and they performed duets of popular songs to entertain the customers. Capra's pay was a dollar a night.

Asked what his parents thought about his job in the brothel, Capra laughed, "They didn't know what the hell I was doing. Neither did I." If Saridda had known, Josie Campisi said, "She would have died."

It was a puritanical time and place. The girls at Manual Arts were not allowed to wear makeup. If they tried to get away with it, they had their faces scrubbed by the stone-faced Miss Putnam ("Old Lady Putt"), who abhorred girlish frivolity. A hair-raising VD lecture given each year by a gym teacher threw the fear of God into the boys. The school dances mostly were genteel afternoon affairs carefully monitored by teachers. There was some sexual activity among the students, naturally, but "it was all just past the chaperone stage," Ruth Hammond said.

Even for that time and place, Capra had an unusually strong degree of sexual inhibition. If it was true, as he claimed, that he had been molested as a young newsboy, that would have been a major reason sex seemed ugly and frightening to him. Working in a whorehouse could only have reinforced that feeling, and his parents' contentious marriage hardly gave him a positive image of mature sexuality. Nor did the regular beatings inflicted on him by his mother and his conviction that she did not love him contribute to the healthy sexual adjustment of a young man passing through puberty.

The girls at Manual Arts barely knew that Frank Capra was alive. "They wouldn't go out with him," said Esther Gleason Schlinger, who did, however, have Capra to her house. "His dress was very sloppy, all the way through. He *did* have very peculiar things to wear at school. He wasn't clean, but he wasn't dirty, either: he was uncouth. His actions were uncouth. He didn't have any manners. He didn't care what went on. People looked down on him. He was very sociable, but nobody seemed to care anything about him except me. I don't think he appreciated it."

Schlinger, who described herself as having been "a pretty common thing," hinted at a thwarted romantic interest in Capra, despite her protestations to the contrary: "He was just another wop to me. I wouldn't have *gone out* with him. I just felt sorry for him. My mother was very glad I didn't go out with him. She wouldn't let me, because he was a derelict, an outcast. Everybody seemed to think that way. But I stuck to it that I liked him."

"I didn't have much to do with the girls—I was ashamed of myself," Capra admitted. "The girls all looked so pretty. I was a little ashamed of my clothes and my big shoes and everything like that." He owned one ill-fitting suit, which cost about ten dollars, and when holes appeared in his shoes, he stuffed them with cardboard. "And I didn't have any money to take them anyplace," Capra continued. "You take a girl out, you've got to have money. Where are you going to get the money? I saw them all at a distance, but I didn't really make any friendship with any girl. I just never bothered."

Capra kept his distance from most of the boys at the school, too. "It was difficult for me to socialize. I didn't have time. When school was over I ran like a squirrel running from a dog—I ran for the streetcar to go downtown to sell papers. And I did try to hide the fact that I came from a poor family, because I wasn't looking for fights. But I was constantly fighting. I was dressed so poorly all the time, and if somebody said a word about my clothes I'd kick him right in the ass or right in the balls. I didn't like to go to other people's houses. I didn't go to those places where I might get into an argument about my clothes or something."

Venting his anger with his fists at rugby games with spectators from the rival schools who taunted him after they "took one look at my clothes" relieved Capra of some of the emotional pressure he felt at school. And, having done so, he found that he could handle the snobbery of his fellow students: "Honestly, it was not as cruel as it sounds. For instance, if you snub me, I'd say, 'Well, you've got to be a jerk. How can you snub *me?*' I thought I was better than any of 'em at anything. My attitude was that *they're* the ones that *I'm* snubbing. If you take those little things to heart, you'll never get anyplace. I thought they all were jerks. I really felt sorry for them. They hadn't had to work. They didn't know how to do this, they didn't know how to do that. They didn't know how to take a punch."

Jimmy Doolittle knew how to take a punch.

Doolittle, Capra said, was his best friend in high school. That in itself tells much about Capra's isolation at Manual. Doolittle was graduated a year before him, and though they were friendly, they never socialized outside of school. Capra never went along when Doolittle and other boys went on hunting and fishing trips. Most of his time with Doolittle was spent on the Boys' Gymnasium Club, also known as the tumbling team or Pyramid Club, which practiced in the gym three afternoons a week and performed stunts at assemblies, as well as for other schools.

Capra was too small for the major competitive sports. He stood only about 5'4" in his first years of high school, and though naturally agile, with wiry muscles, he was the smallest member of the Pyramid Club. Smallness, and the combative spirit that frequently accompanies it, was one of the natural affinities between Capra and Doolittle. "Small guys are used to being kicked around by the big boys," Doolittle observed. "All of us little fellas had to strive a bit more." And Capra said, "I was very conscious that I was small. I envied tall people, of course. I thought I could lick 'em all anyhow. I really did. I knew, as small as I was, that I could lick anybody there, because I'd been fighting all my life. You had to when most people were taller than you were."

Naturally modest and egalitarian, Doolittle was one student who never acted superior to Capra or patronized him. Capra, for his part, idolized the handsome, gregarious brawler.

"He was a hero to us even then," Capra said. "*There's* a biography."

Although Doolittle himself said with a grin, "I didn't get into the hero business until long after that," Capra vividly recalled a schoolyard incident that, for him, exemplified Doolittle's heroism. The boys were doing back flips over a fence. When Doolittle took his turn, he caught his nose as he was going over the fence, tearing a gash up to his forehead. "He was bleeding like hell. We grabbed him and wiped off his face and tried to take him to the school hospital, but he got away from us and jumped up on the fence and did the back flip again. This time he made it. *Then* he went to the hospital."

Doolittle represented a beau ideal to the despised Sicilian immigrant, a Steerforth to Capra's David Copperfield. With his all-American WASP good looks, ready smile, rugged physique, and reckless courage, Jimmy Doolittle had what later would be called star quality. Capra knew he never could hope to have Doolittle's heroic attributes, but he could share them vicariously by being Doolittle's friend and admirer. Through some process of osmosis he could only vaguely understand at the time, he could project himself to the world through his connection with a charismatic figure like Jimmy Doolittle. That process eventually would reveal itself to Capra as the ability to create heroic surrogates on the motion picture screen—heroes who, unlike himself, were handsome WASPs, but through whom he could project his feelings and ideals. Jimmy Doolittle was the real-life prototype of the characters later played for Capra by Gary Cooper and Jimmy Stewart. And when Doolittle himself made a brief screen appearance in one of Capra's World War II documentaries, *Tunisian Victory*, the director gave his boyhood hero a star close-up.

It was at Manual that Capra received his first encouragement in the arts. But he preferred to depict himself as self-taught—"I'm still a bare-assed newcomer," he insisted in 1984—and declined to give Manual any credit for having helped shape his artistic personality, claiming that before directing his first film, "I had never seen a picture, never been in a studio. I didn't know about the stage, I had never been backstage, I didn't know that actors were expected to rehearse."

For all four years at Manual, however, Capra performed with a group called the Adelphic Society, which ran the assembly entertainments in the school auditorium, putting on literary, dramatic, dance, athletic, and musical acts. Doolittle remembered seeing Capra onstage, and Capra's fellow Adelphic Mitt Downs recalled, "He was interested in show business, in acting and things like that. He was quite active in that line." Evelyn Turner Loftin, who became a professional singer and actress, and performed in a number of films including Capra's *Lost Horizon*, remembered Capra acting with the Adelphics: "I knew Frank from seeing him in aud calls. They had little plays, little skits, and he'd be in them. But he didn't stand out."

Capra was facile with the violin, the guitar, the mandolin, and the ukelele, and probably performed on them with the Adelphics. In his senior year he also became a member of the school's Ukelele Club, which performed at assemblies and other gatherings. "We played for anybody who asked us," said Esther Gleason Schlinger. "He did his part well."

He also showed an interest in still photography at Manual. Though he would acknowledge taking pictures in college—his files contain pictures he took as early as 1917, as well as one of him taking a picture of a girl he was dating—he stubbornly denied any involvement with photography in high school. Schlinger, however, found him "wonderfully knowing all about cameras. I had a darkroom at home where I did my own developing, and he helped me. I don't remember whether he had his own camera, but he was interested in printing, and he knew more about it, he was quite cameraminded. He was a student, all right. We talked photography all the time."

Capra showed far less aptitude at drawing and painting, but his art teacher (and intramural wrestling coach), Rob Wagner, was one of the major influences in his life.

Rob Wagner was a flamboyant bohemian who dressed the part in pincenez glasses and flowing four-in-hand tie. He was an artist and journalist who had been on the stage-designing staff of Broadway impresario Florenz Ziegfeld, as well as art editor of *The Criterion* in New York and the *Encyclopaedia Britannica* in London before joining the Manual Arts faculty in 1912, when he was forty years old.

Later described by journalist Gene Fowler as "one of the wisest noodles in Hollywood," Rob Wagner was something of a guru to the students of his art history and drawing classes, who met in the basement of Manual Arts and considered themselves to be the school's intellectual elite. At the start of each class he would appear at the top of the stairs and give the captain's greeting from Gilbert and Sullivan's *HMS Pinafore*—"My gallant crew, good morning!"—and the students would reply:

"Sir, good morning!"

"I hope you're all quite well."

"Quite well; and you, sir?"

If his class was interrupted by an outsider, he would stop what he was doing, line them all up, and have them sing songs, a ploy Capra would remember when the sets of his films were invaded by studio executives.

Wagner's unorthodox pronouncements often got him into trouble with the school administration, and he did nothing to discourage those around Manual who considered him a bit "pink." When Harold Harris asked the teacher to sign his yearbook, Wagner wrote with his bold John Hancock flourish, "Yours for the revolution." (In December 1919, during the Red Scare that followed World War I, *Variety* reported that Wagner, partly because of his close friendship with Charlie Chaplin, was "the chief object of the Federal investigation of parlor Bolshevism" then underway in Los Angeles.)

Wagner championed individualism. When all of the girls in his art history class showed up one day with the same hairstyle, he told them, "If you'll notice Ziegfeld's lineup, he never has two women who look exactly the same. You can be different and attract attention by being yourself instead of being a goddamn sheep." Someone squealed on him for using profanity, and the "goddamn sheep" line almost cost him his job. But the students never forgot the lesson he taught that day.

Capra had never been exposed to anyone like this before. He was intrigued by Wagner's "delightful, enterprising" personality and his conviction that art adds "more to human happiness than all the other professions combined."

Wagner's classes were in charge of painting the scenery for the school plays, which was built by the woodshop classes. Already interested in the theater, Capra worked as a member of Wagner's stage-designing crew. "Whenever a play is put on at Manual," wrote Wagner, "the stagecraft class goes to the director, who gives them the historical setting, with incidents of the plot, showing its influence on the character and action of the play. After the craft class has read the play, each act is taken up and discussed, with attention to the necessary techniques and provisions for the business of the play."

Capra next came to the attention of the drama coach, Maude Howell, who recognized his talents and saw that he needed encouragement. The adventurous young Howell, who was "crazy about the movies" and who later left Manual to become stage manager for the actor George Arliss, ran the school's dramatic activities from the summer of 1913 until June 1914. The plays she directed included Shaw's *You Never Can Tell;* Mary Austin's drama about American Indians, *The Arrowmaker;* and William DeMille's college drama *Strongheart.* Howell quickly became a student favorite, inspiring Tibbett and Doolittle to become actors with the Players' Club.

She also recruited Capra to run the lights on her plays. Manual had a sophisticated switchboard and lighting apparatus in its new auditorium, and the job was good training for the youngster, drawing on both his mechanical and artistic talents. She recalled Capra could "always be entrusted with the lights."

But despite his acting experience with the Adelphics, his work behind the scenes, and his friendship with Howell, Capra never was able to join the ranks of the elite in the thirty-member Players' Club.

"He wasn't a very good one to be involved in the theater there," Hammond explained. "You see, he wasn't very tall, and he wasn't at all good-looking, so he had no outward equipment. There weren't really any parts that suited him. Most of the other boys in the plays were good-looking boys, from well-to-do families—not terribly well-to-do, but I mean they didn't have to work after school or anything. Frank was from a poor family, and he had to work after school."

Just five days before his graduation, however, on the afternoon and evening of January 22, 1915, Capra finally played a noticeable part in a full-scale Manual play. It was the senior class play, *The Crisis,* an adaptation of a popular novel about the Civil War era by the American author Winston Churchill. The costume melodrama, set in St. Louis, was directed by Lillian C. Eby, whose work was considered pedestrian by comparison with that of her brilliant predecessor, Maude Howell. But Mrs. Eby did not have much of a cast to work with: most of them were what the school paper called "amateur actors," not members of the Players' Club. Capra received ninth billing, in the small role of Maurice Rénault, described by the author as an "excitable little man," a "gesticulating" Frenchman who lives across the street from the heroine. Capra may have been cast in the bilingual role as much for his proficiency in French as for any other reason, and it was indicative of how he was viewed at Manual Arts that his only credited appearance in a school play was as a comical, stereotypical immigrant.

* * *

Though his modest theatrical experiences in high school were helpful to his future career, Capra was much more profoundly influenced by Rob Wagner's passion for the movies.

Wagner had become fascinated by the new popular art form of motion pictures after visiting a film set on the East Coast in 1908 at the invitation of an actor friend, Hobart Bosworth, who was appearing in the film under an assumed name (Bosworth later acted for Capra in *Dirigible* and *Lady for a Day*). Wagner was "so impressed that he forgot about all else," wrote the *Los Angeles Times*. After he moved to Los Angeles and began teaching at Manual, he wrote a series of articles for *The Saturday Evening Post* on the then-novel subject of how to break into the movies. They were collected in a 1918 book called *Film Folk*, making him one of the first serious writers to publish a book on Hollywood. Wagner had set his own sights on a career as a motion picture writer and director.

In his youth, Capra insisted, he did not have the money to spend on something so frivolous as going to movies, which he considered "a waste of time. I wasn't interested in movies. I couldn't see that far." By the time he entered Manual Arts, his growing intellectual and social pretensions made him scornful of what then was generally considered a lowbrow form of entertainment for the unwashed, illiterate, and often newly arrived masses. There is no indication that he was impressed by the news in 1914 that his friend Blue Washington had been cast in a bit part in a Civil War movie called *The Clansman*.*

Under its new title of *The Birth of a Nation*, it premiered February 8, 1915, at Clune's Auditorium at Fifth and Spring streets in downtown Los Angeles, shortly after Capra's graduation from high school. The first movie Capra would admit even watching, it excited him as it did everyone else.

"The most important film ever made," as Capra called D. W. Griffith's controversial, ground-breaking epic of the Civil War and the Reconstruction era, made him realize that film was a genuine new art form with profound social impact, an art form open to the daring and the déclassé, one to which he might dedicate his life and find the fame and wealth and artistic expression he craved. Though Capra's resistance to the lure of the movies evidently persisted through much of his high school years, Rob Wagner's enthusiasm had been impinging gradually on his consciousness, helping make him receptive to *The Birth of a Nation*. It was no accident

---

**Blue Washington went on to some success as a silent movie comedian playing servant types before he walked off a picture due to a salary dispute. He later appeared as an extra in some of Capra's films and had occasional small parts in such films as John Ford's* The Long Voyage Home *and Otto Preminger's* Carmen Jones.

that near the end of 1917, when Capra sought advice about a movie career, he turned to Wagner, who by then had embarked on his own career in Hollywood.

Wagner's entrée into the movie business was a film made partly at Manual Arts in April and May 1915, for San Francisco's spectacular Panama-Pacific International Exposition, held that year to celebrate the opening of the Panama Canal. With its sixty theaters offering free movies, the event provided one of the first major culturally prestigious showcases for the new medium. Wagner sold the board of education on the idea of making a film about the Los Angeles school system for display at the Palace of Education.

Made with the help of Griffith's Reliance-Majestic Company, *Our Wonderful Schools* was a prizewinner at the Exposition. A large section of it was shot at Manual, including the stagecraft and scene-painting classes, a wrestling match, and a kite-flying contest.

There is no way of determining with certainty whether Capra worked on the film or appeared in it. It was filmed just after his graduation, when he may have been busy doing other things, but at the very least he might have dropped by to lend Wagner a hand or simply to kibitz along with the large crowd of spectators who watched Wagner directing in his khaki outfit and leather boots. Ruth Hammond was in a segment filmed at Manual on April 19 showing the scene-painting class; the school paper said "the rest of the artistic bunch" also was part of it. Hammond did not recall Capra being there, but she said, "He probably was, because Rob Wagner was fond of him and would have put him in it."

Our Wonderful Schools helped Wagner break into professional film-making in 1920 writing scripts for Charles Ray, the popular star of rustic romances. After writing and directing short comedies starring Walter Hiers at Paramount, Wagner made comedy shorts at the Hal Roach and Mack Sennett studios, helping Capra find work at both studios as a gag man. As a confidant of Charlie Chaplin, Wagner also helped promote Chaplin as a serious artist. He directed one feature, the 1924 Hiers comedy *Fair Week*, but his movie career dissipated when silents turned to sound. He then started a magazine, *Rob Wagner's Script*, published in Beverly Hills and dealing primarily with the movies, and operated a radio station, shepherding Capra through his "frightening" first appearance on the air.

From time to time in his magazine, Wagner, who died in 1942, proudly reminded his readers that Frank Capra had been one of his students. He put Capra on the cover in 1939, with a note about "Our Cover Boy"; "Frank, of course, had grand training when he attended our art classes at

Manual Arts. He got that smile when he entered our Greek History Class and noted The Teacher had to look up and find out where Greece was on the map before he could begin. And that sturdy look and the doormat on his chest (note the few wisps peeking up through the sweater) resulted from the violent physical training he got in our wrestling class. Larry Tibbett could sing better 'n' Frank, but in those days Larry's neck was long, and what Frank did to it with his wicked wop strangleholds nearly cost America a great baritone. In consequence of the above-mentioned training in art and science, Frank became president of the Motion Picture Academy of Arts and Sciences. He is also a pretty good director, but we can take no credit for that; it's his own stuff."

Throughout his high school years, Capra spent as little time as possible at the "house of pain" on Albion Street. He would come back at night after selling papers to eat the dinner his mother left for him, do some quick studying, and go to sleep. The next morning he would run off to school before the rest of the family woke.

"I was just as far away from my family as I could be," he remembered. "It was a day-to-day proposition whether my family kicked me out of the house or let me in. They thought I was a bum. My mother would slap me around; she wanted me to quit school. There was constant, constant, constant, *constant* pressure for me to quit school. My teachers would urge me to keep going. 'Don't ever quit school,' they'd tell me. They're the ones who kept me going. Without them I don't think I could have taken it—my brother [Tony] flipping dimes at me because I didn't have anything. I wasn't going to school because everybody loved school. I was going to school because I had a fight on my hands that I wanted to win."

What was happening to the rest of his family only strengthened his desire to escape.

Frank's sister Giuseppa, called Peppina or Josephine, had left home shortly after arriving in America and was married at the age of thirteen to an immigrant fruit peddler named Luigi (or "Louie") Finochio, whose family owned a fish store. Josephine and her husband planned to return to Italy. Louie's father was supposed to precede them, carrying all of his savings in a money belt, but someone in Los Angeles tipped the information to New York, and the elder Finochio was murdered before he could reach the boat. So Josephine stayed in Los Angeles with Louie and had seven children in rapid succession, until she had a hysterectomy at the age of twenty-eight.

Tony Capra was working in a candy factory on North Broadway. The damp, airless conditions in the basement where he worked damaged his lungs. He cursed his life. He dreamed of fleeing to the San Fernando Valley, to cultivate trees as his father had in Sicily.

Annie contracted rheumatic fever as a child. Even though she went to work, first with Tony in the candy factory and then as a seamstress, she also went to school, at the 19th Avenue Elementary School and then at the new Lincoln High School (despite Frank's later claim that he was the only member of the family who had any schooling after Tony was thrown out for socking the teacher). Since Annie lacked Frank's robust constitution, the grind made her increasingly frail. They had a close bond. Whenever the other members of the family would call Frank a bum, she would stand up for him, insisting he had a great future.

The family was breaking up. Not only Frank and Tony wanted to escape, so did Papa Turiddu. His endless battles with Saridda over his improvidence made him increasingly morose. Ben could see the deeper reason for his father's unhappiness. Papa Turiddu needed to be back on the land. Away from it he was slowly dying. So Ben encouraged him to find work in the citrus ranches north of Los Angeles, in the foothills near Pasadena. In the spring of 1913, when Frank was a junior at Manual Arts, Salvatore Capra took a job as a farmhand at the La Cañada ranch of Edwin T. Earl, the millionaire publisher of the *Los Angeles Express*.

In Earl's lush vineyards, Turiddu could almost imagine himself back in Sicily. This was, indeed, the "Second Italy" he had been told about when he was persuaded to come to America, against his better judgment. But, still, the land was not his. The newspaper baron was a member of the syndicate which had schemed to bring the water of Owens Valley via aqueduct at public expense to enrich their private holdings in the San Fernando Valley (the subject of the movie *Chinatown*), and he was as much a feudal lord as any big rancher in Sicily. The workers who lived on the ranch mostly were Mexicans. Salvatore Capra, now past his sixtieth birthday, looked enviously upon the Italians who owned and leased small ranches nearby.

Frank sometimes came out on the interurban red trolley and stayed with his father on the ranch, sleeping in the bunkhouse with Papa Turiddu and his Mexican coworkers. The days on the ranch were idyllic, much like his memories of Sicily. Frank was allowed to pal around with Emily and Jarvis Earl, the children of the man who published the newspaper he sold in the streets, and to ride their pony. The experience made him more aware than ever before of the vast gulf between rich people and his own family, but he also enjoyed this borrowed taste of affluence. It was a foreshadowing of the life he wanted for himself.

Now he was listening to the teachers who urged him to go on to college. Papa Turiddu thought it was a good idea, too. Frank was a clever talker, a natural battler, a shrewd judge of human foibles. He ought to become a lawyer. Lawyers knew where the money was, where the power was. Lawyers couldn't be shoved around the way farmers were shoved around. Frank should go away to Berkeley and become a lawyer.

Frank considered it. In January 1915, *Manual Arts Weekly* said that he would be attending Berkeley in the fall.

But he had other ideas.

4. "Cap"

"*H*e changed his whole viewpoint on life, from the viewpoint of an alley rat to the viewpoint of a cultured person."

With those words, written in the third person for a 1929 self-portrait, Frank Capra summed up the experience of his college years at Throop College of Technology in Pasadena.

Pasadena, it was said in those days, was where people from Los Angeles went when they died. Only an hour's trolley ride from downtown Los Angeles, the small winter resort town in the San Gabriel Valley, with its orange groves, stately homes, luxury hotels, and transplanted eastern culture, was as close to an earthly Paradise as Southern California offered in the early years of the century. And as Carey McWilliams would later write, Pasadena "could hardly be more carefully insulated from the rest of Los Angeles if [it] were surrounded by Chinese walls."

Those were the walls Frank Capra was determined to climb. Hobnobbing with Southern California's social elite, he groomed himself to become one of them, while shedding his past and the family that so uncomfortably reminded him of it.

The snobbery Capra had encountered at Manual Arts fed his lust to be accepted in mainstream American society. If his looks, his clothing, and his lack of money stood in his way, his brains would give him the leverage he needed to vault over the walls. Capra never read any books by Horatio Alger, but in his autobiography he portrayed himself as a figure from a true-life Alger story—a story that in his mind might have been titled *Ragged Frank, Or, Luck and Pluck.*

His path to success in America, he decided, was to become an engineer.

*   *   *

Throop College of Technology was a small and little-known school which promoted itself as "The College that Prepares MEN for Modern Life." It offered "Training in Electricity and Hydraulics, Construction and Transportation, Industrial Chemistry. . . . Laboratories New and Completely Equipped. A System of Self-Help for Students, including practical wage-earning Experience. Free Lectures by Leaders of Thought. . . . Best Moral Influences." The school had been founded in 1891 by a retired Chicago lumber baron, Amos G. Throop, who wanted to bring low-cost technical education to young people in his adopted community. Originally called Throop Polytechnic Institute (Capra mistakenly called his college by that name in his autobiography, but the name was changed two years before he arrived there), it was in the process of being transformed by its trustees into "an engineering college second to none in the country"—a goal it later achieved after it became the California Institute of Technology.

When Capra entered Throop in September 1915, it still lacked the prestige of the nation's great science schools, Massachusetts Institute of Technology and the University of Chicago, but those august institutions were beyond his resources. Throop, on the other hand, was close, it was affordable, and, since it was new and needed students, it was not as demanding in its admission requirements; nor did entry into Throop require any social pull. Most important, Throop's small enrollment guaranteed "practically individual instruction," as one alumnus put it.

Any hesitancy on Capra's part vanished when three boys ahead of him at Manual—Harold Harris, Reginald Coles, and Clarence Bjerke—enrolled at Throop. They were among the first of many Manual students who would attend the Pasadena school, inspired by their high school teachers Eva Farnum and Isabelle Willson. Capra was particularly impressed that two men such as Harris and Coles—men from upper-middle-class families whom Capra thought of, with considerable exaggeration, as "rich"—would choose Throop over Berkeley, Stanford, or MIT. And if Bjerke, an amiable but plodding fellow who worked with Capra as a janitor at Manual Arts, could get into Throop, Capra knew he would not be the only social "reject" person there.

But still it would not be easy. Tuition was $250 a year, not exorbitant but yet a considerable sum in those days for a young man from a background such as Capra's. In his autobiography, Capra wrote that he finished Manual half a year ahead of schedule and entered Throop in February 1915, but the records show that he spent the full four years at Manual, graduating on schedule with the rest of his class on January 27, 1915, and matriculated at Throop on September 18, 1915. Capra claimed that to finance his first year at Throop he delayed his arrival at college to spend six months working in a backbreaking job at the Western Pipe and Steel Company next door to his home on Albion Street. But after hearing that account, Tony Capra angrily insisted that *he* was the one who worked there.

Frank Capra may have rewritten the history of that period in order to conceal another job he did not want to acknowledge. But his account of his college years also conceals the fact that his family provided him with financial support to attend college. The Capra myth was that he did it all by himself, and his claim in his autobiography that he never received a penny from his mother while attending college but instead gave her ninety dollars a month for much of that time outraged family members who knew the true story. Despite his mother's previous opposition to his schooling, once she realized he could not be deterred from his ambition, she helped him accomplish it. Saridda, Annie, Luigia, and even Tony gave Frank money all through his college years to supplement his jobs and his financial aid from Throop.

"Annie was really the one who influenced him to stay in school," Rocky Washington remembered. "She was younger than the rest of them, and I guess she saw the opportunity. She worked as a seamstress to help put Frank through school. She probably helped him more than anyone else with money, except his mother. That was the part that always impressed us, my mother especially—the fact that the Capras didn't have any money but that his mother and sister had stood behind him and worked hard to help him get where he got. If there was ever a saving feature in his life, that was it."

Another member of the Capra family also was finding his earthly Paradise. In April 1915, Salvatore Capra rented a ranch in Sierra Madre, a citrus-growing community and resort in the foothills of the San Gabriel Mountains, ten miles from Pasadena. The twenty-acre Churchill Ranch (named after its owner, Henry C. Churchill) grew lemon, orange, grapefruit, and avocado trees in an upper canyon later named Marlborough Terrace in a tribute to the celebrated Churchills of England. With the lease went a handsome two-story wooden house, a replica of Henry Churchill's former home in New England, on a peak with a spectacular view of the entire valley.

Papa Turiddu lived there with Annie, Ben and Mary and their children, and a floating assortment of other grandchildren. The spacious white house still stands at Canyon Crest, beautifully preserved, and is sometimes used as a movie location. It was luxurious by the Capras' standards, with its beamed ceilings, stately porticoes, and an observation deck on the rooftop, from which on most days they could see the city where Frank was going to college.

Frank Capra always claimed that his father had *bought* the ranch, but Ben Capra explained what actually happened: Papa Turiddu went to work on the ranch helping with the lemon harvest, and "he find out that this fellow [Churchill] wanted rent this ranch to somebody who understand fruit trees. My father thought he gets this work by rent-a this ranch, and he could have his own farming." Turiddu and Ben made the lease agreement together in order to profit from the citrus crops they raised on it—a common arrangement in those days for farmers of modest means both in Sicily and Southern California. While it is possible that the Capras had some kind of formal or informal arrangement that gave them an option to buy the property—which Churchill bought in the 1890s from a man named Bauker and sold in 1921 to Z. L. Parmalee, who subdivided it for housing—the existing records say nothing about the Capras making any purchase agreement.

Salvatore Capra never was happier in America than he was at Sierra Madre. The land was rich, and he could work only as much as he felt like working, because he had the help of Ben and the Japanese fruit pickers who lived in a bunkhouse on the property. He had plenty of time at the ranch to experiment with methods of his own devising for growing compost, transplanting roots, and grafting branches from one tree to another. He had time to amuse himself with his large rose garden alongside the main house, even managing somehow to grow green roses.

Papa Turiddu would hunt quail in the canyon, and sometimes the others would hear him playing his guitar outside, far away. And at night, they would bring out the jugs of red wine and Turiddu would sing songs and tell his stories, while his children and grandchildren would sit around laughing and eating nuts or roasted and salted pumpkin seeds and *fabbe* (dried lima beans). It was almost like being back in the old country.

Saridda, who helped pay the rent, made an occasional weekend visit to the Churchill Ranch. "Everybody kept trying to talk her into coming out to live," said her grandson Sam Capra, "but she wanted to stay on at the olive factory." The reasons why were obvious when she did come to visit.

One time Turiddu trapped a wildcat that had been killing chickens on the ranch. While Saridda and Annie made a trip to town, he shot the wildcat, skinned and cooked it. He told the women that he was serving them rabbit. But during dinner little Sam turned to Annie and blurted out, "How'd you like your wildcat?"

"The air turned blue," Sam remembered. "Saridda really let him have it. There were no blows struck, but I was scared to death."

Throop was everything Frank Capra hoped it would be.

Most of his fellow students were from economic backgrounds not much better than his, and they were a hardworking, serious bunch, determined to succeed. Though not all were as gifted intellectually as their later Caltech counterparts, and though none ever achieved the fame of some of his classmates at the more eccentric and adventurous Manual Arts, there was a general dedication to learning among the Throop men. They also had a respect and yearning for culture that was not as prevalent among later generations of Caltech engineers, who tended to be more narrowly specialized. It was a congenial intellectual setting for a young man of Capra's varied and still unformed gifts and ambitions.

Socially, too, Throop allowed Capra's personality to flower, without the barriers he had faced at Manual. "I can't overstress that peculiar happy-go-lucky camaraderie we had there," said Philip S. Clarke, who lived in the dormitory with Capra. "There were no girls. We dressed rather terribly. No one had the feeling of putting on the dog, there was no feeling of superiority or higher social position or more money, there was no pretense. It was the most democratic situation you could imagine. I would call our life there a strikingly monastic life. Much as the monks in the Middle Ages were, we were dedicated and devoted to studies, and I think that partly explains the lack of social condescension or superiority."

There were only sixty men in Capra's class when it entered Throop, and by the time of graduation, the combined effects of scholastic attrition, tight finances, and the Great War reduced the class to eighteen. Unlike the Manual alumni, nearly everyone who went to college with Capra remembered him well.

"Everybody liked him," said Earl Mendenhall. "He was a nice fellow, a good mixer. He was always on the go, and he was in on everything." "I knew he had a terrific load, scholastically and financially, and I looked upon him as one of those superior students," said Clarke. "I thought I was pretty quick, but Capra was way ahead of me." "He was a leader in every respect," said E. V. Hounsell. Louis Essick considered him "a person of tremendous ability. His success didn't surprise me at all. He had the ability to do anything."

Capra spent his first year at college commuting between the Sierra Madre ranch and the campus. He took the red trolley at first, later acquiring a belt-driven Flanders motorcycle, which had to be pushed up the hilly road leading to the ranch, a job he often delegated to his adoring nieces and nephews. It would have been much more convenient for him to live in the dorm, and to that end he took a job as a waiter in the dorm's dining room. That gave him three meals a day, but he had to wait a year to be given a room as well (worth six dollars a month).

He also took advantage of an arrangement a professor had made for the students with the Pasadena Light and Power Plant: whenever they needed money, they could report to North Fair Oaks Avenue and do odd jobs such as cleaning the steam generators, replacing boiler tubes, and stoking the fires. Capra sometimes worked the 3 to 7 A.M. shift, dozing on a stool whenever he could.

Capra's was an arduous schedule, but still he could not resist embellishing the facts in *The Name Above the Title*, devoting considerable space to a fanciful timetable of his daily routine during his freshman year. Capra supposedly was busy nineteen hours a day, with eight hours a day allotted for classes, two and a half for waiting tables and eating, four for working at the power plant, one for social activities, two and a half for homework, one for travel to and from school, and only five hours allotted for sleep, from 10 P.M. to 3 A.M. Many readers of the book have adopted the timetable as a cornerstone of the Capra legend, an example of his superhuman determination to succeed.

But a more accurate picture of Capra's daily life was given in a paper titled "Personal Efficiency," which he wrote on January 11, 1916, for a freshman class in engineering problems. In it, Capra admitted that he slept nine hours a day, an hour more than he considered desirable, and said that he spent two and a half hours commuting, time he hoped to put to better use as a dorm resident. He described his study methods as irregular and admitted he did his share of drinking, smoking, and playing cards and billiards.

The paper reflected a growing tension in Capra's own mind between what he saw as the highly disciplined life of a scientist and the freer life of the artist. Expressing his aversion at following a regimented routine—a life that, as he described it, seemed much like his mother's drudgery at the olive oil factory—he wanted to balance his technical studies by frequenting the theater and the concert hall. Yet he displayed a certain guilt over those feelings, berating himself for not studying as hard as he thought he should. His rewriting of history in his book is a manifestation of that insecurity. It was not that he was lazy: on the contrary, according to Josie Campisi, when he would come back to Albion Street on weekends, "We couldn't go to the bathroom because he was always sitting on the toilet reading, with the door locked. We practically had to drag him off with a crowbar." But his increasingly evident artistic tendencies were putting him in danger of becoming more like his dreamy, poetic father, and stirring the antipathy of his hard-headed mother. His mother, whom he never could satisfy, was the one he always had to work to impress. It was never enough that he worked as hard as he did; he had to work harder, and he had to exaggerate the genuine hard work he did do.

Capra's desire to go beyond the narrow confines of an engineer's training was a reflection of Throop's attempt to strike a balance in its curriculum between the humanities and technical studies. That was the most remarkable aspect of Capra's college education. For it was at an engineering school that his latent interest in the arts and humanities was inflamed into a passion.

Capra majored in chemical engineering, and most of the courses he took were technical. But he also took two years of French, a year and a half of German (the "scientific language"), a year and a half of economics, a semester of business law, and, most important, four years of English.

Only one year of English was required at most engineering schools in those days, but Throop's president, Dr. James A. B. Scherer, a minister who had taught English in a Japanese university, believed that to upgrade his school to the level of MIT or the University of Chicago, it was necessary to take it beyond the trade-school mentality. MIT gave its students two years of English, so Dr. Scherer's decision to require four years of English from his students was regarded as a bold step. The Throop *Catalogue* stated in 1918 that "the English language is the chief tool in the engineer's kit," and Capra wrote that year in *The Throop Tech*, the monthly school magazine, that "the English and language courses at Throop are ones for which we should have the deepest regard, otherwise we may tend to become mere thinking machines instead of warm, appreciative human beings."

The man most responsible for the cosmopolitanism of Capra and his classmates was Clinton Kelly Judy, the school's only English teacher in the first six years of its existence. Professor Judy was a Berkeley graduate and a Rhodes scholar, and in Capra's junior year he went to Harvard for his master's degree. Tall, handsome, and possessed of a dry wit that captivated his students, Judy taught at Throop and Caltech from 1910 until his retirement in 1949, becoming the school's first chairman of the Division of Humanities in 1924. By all accounts he was the most beloved teacher at Throop, which was remarkable, because most of the students were, in his words, "laboring men who resisted the seductions of literature."

"He had a office connecting to the classroom," recalled Fred L. Poole, "and he would stroll into the classroom from his office reading a poem and rather casually begin teaching it. I remember he came in once reading 'Gunga Din.' He presented poetry as a man, not as a teacher. He presented it man-to-man, which made all the difference. We were all men there, and we appreciated having a man teach us. If he wanted to read poetry, it was all right with us."

"Once in a while he'd ask us to write some poetry," said Earl Mendenhall. "My God, you never heard such poetry in your life! And he'd have us write short stories. There were some masterpieces. We were writing about stuff we didn't know anything about in the first place. We had more fun in Judy's class than in any other class, just because of those damn things; we'd read 'em and laugh about it."

Always in awe of Professor Judy, whom he found personally somewhat aloof, Capra learned through him to love literature, and through him developed a lifelong interest in history and philosophy. Regarded by Capra as the most important in the succession of remarkable teachers he encountered in his youth, Judy was the one Capra credited with inspiring him to follow an artistic career.

When Judy retired in 1949, Capra wrote him to express his gratitude, and Judy replied, "Sometimes we teachers feel that we pursue an ideal aim without much tangible evidence that we ever come close to hitting the mark, and we are steadied and encouraged by such expressions as yours. . . . May I say that when from a clutch of duck eggs a swan is hatched—your case—it is not the poultry keeper who should receive the credit."

Before entering Throop, Capra had scorned poetry as "some shit that they gave little kids to read—baby stuff." But in Capra's freshman year, Judy introduced the students to Alfred Noyes, the popular British poet known for such Tennysonian romantic ballads as "The Highwayman" and "The Barrel-Organ." Judy, who had met Noyes at Oxford, persuaded him to take a leave from his teaching post at Princeton—where his students in that era included F. Scott Fitzgerald and Edmund Wilson—to be poet in residence at Throop, an unheard-of post for a technical school.

Capra listened in fascination as Noyes recited his own work, as well as Shakespeare's sonnets and the poems of the Brownings.

"It was a great discovery for me," Capra said. "I discovered language. I discovered poetry. I discovered *poetry* at *Caltech*, can you imagine that? That was a big turning point in my life. I didn't know that anything could be so beautiful. There was this other world I had never seen or heard. And I thought I was pretty smart. He gave me the appetite."

After Capra had become successful in movies, he invited Noyes to his home for dinner with the Ronald Colmans and the Charles Boyers. "I gained quite a new impression of Hollywood," Noyes recalled. "Frank Capra had a fascinating library, with first editions of *Paradise Lost* and Ben Jonson. After dinner, to my great surprise, he showed me the framed manuscript of one of my own poems which, although I didn't remember it, I had given to him when he was a young student working his way through Caltech twenty-five years earlier."

Capra took as one of his life's maxims something he heard Noyes say in one of his lectures: "There are times in every man's life when he glimpses the eternal." The line was used in *Lost Horizon*, in which it is attributed to the Ronald Colman character, and again in *State of the Union*, in which Spencer Tracy says that Katharine Hepburn once read it to him.

It was in Judy's class that Capra first attempted to tell a story of his own. Written in May of his freshman year, "The Butler's Failure" was retitled "The Butler's Adventure" when published that November in *The Throop Tech*.

The conflict between rich and poor, a theme that would obsess Capra throughout his film career, is at the heart of this lurid tale of an immigrant English butler driven by poverty to rob and kill his millionaire American employer. Cornered, the butler shoots a police detective and then kills himself. The language is pedestrian, the psychology simplistic, and the social attitudes crudely schematic (the millionaire has a heart of stone, the butler is a deranged animal), but the story does display a nascent gift at bringing a scene to life with bits of "cinematic" business. After killing the detective, the butler, "a picture of utter despair . . . laughing the harsh, metallic laugh of the lunatic[,] put a bullet through his crazed brain. He reeled and turned halfway round, his teeth bared in a horrible grin, [and] fell across the legs of the detective."

The unhinged butler resembles John Wray's memorable vignette as the displaced farmer who tries to kill the millionaire Longfellow Deeds (Gary Cooper) in Capra's Depression-era classic *Mr. Deeds Goes to Town*. But at this stage in Capra's development, perhaps because he was still too close to the real fears he was writing about, there was no happy ending, no deus ex machina rescuing the character from the brink. Capra's early social vision is unrelentingly Darwinian, without the fervent overlay of hope that, in his films, counterbalances the desperation. This cynical story of an immigrant's failure to realize the American Dream demonstrates an understanding of what it means to be poor, but not much real sympathy with poor people. As

Stephen Handzo pointed out in 1972, "Careless critics think Capra sentimentalizes poverty, but real need in his films appears as desperation close to madness. . . . Perhaps Capra, whose book begins, 'I hated being poor,' has created a portrait of The Man I Might Have Been."

At Throop Capra was earnestly engaged in trying to determine what kind of man he could become. And, most decisively, it was not one of the common herd. College papers he wrote on Walt Whitman and Ralph Waldo Emerson found him scolding Whitman for his licentiousness and his subversive belief in universal equality, but responding more favorably (though not without some conformist misgivings) to Emerson's belief that we must "profoundly revere" heroism because "Heroism feels and never reasons, and therefore is always right . . . for the hero that thing he does is the highest deed, and is not open to the censure of philosophers and divines."

That first year at Throop, Capra scored the best grades in his class, winning the Freshman Travel Scholarship Prize.

The prize provided $250 for a six-week trip around the United States and Canada to visit schools, laboratories, and factories, with a concentration on the chemical field, since Capra's intended major was chemical engineering. Among the places he visited in the summer of 1916 were the University of Chicago, MIT, the Bureau of Standards in Washington, D.C., the rapid transit system in Philadelphia, the Westinghouse plant in Pittsburgh, and the Eastman Kodak Company in Rochester, New York. He also visited New York City and Montreal.

The day he spent touring the Eastman plant and watching the manufacture of film stock made an indelible impression on Capra, helping stimulate his growing interest in motion pictures. Another inkling of Capra's future was his ten-day detour to New York City, where he had no official visits scheduled. Since he had to make the $250 last for the duration of the trip, he spent some of his nights sleeping on park benches so he could have enough money to attend concerts and plays.

In an essay published that October in *The Tech*, "Manhattan Island," Capra wrote of seeing "for the second time the Statue of Liberty and Ellis Island" but sounded more like Mr. Deeds on his first trip to town: "You must not regard me too harshly when I say that from the time I entered New York to the time I left it my mouth was continually agape and my eyes continually wanting to leave their comfortable sockets."

He found in New York "the extremes of nearly everything. There is the multimillionaire of Fifth Avenue and Riverside Drive, and the poor laboring man of the Lower East Side. There is the highly educated college professor giving lectures on the nebular hypothesis at Columbia, while at Madison Square the fervent Hebrew still sells a whole library of knowledge for five cents. There is the Broadway boy with bandanna tie, cheesecloth socks and a vacuum above his shoulders. There are the rich children with a couple of acres of beautiful park for their back yard and opposite them are the thousands of children that eagerly try to find amusement and recreation in the filthy streets and sidewalks."

The prizewinner was required to give an oral report in the fall to his fellow students. But before doing so, Capra accepted an invitation from Dr. Wilson to address an assembly at Manual Arts. It was the first time he had ever given a lecture, and what he planned to do with it, he pointed out later, was a foreshadowing of his work in motion pictures.

He wrote out his impressions of the trip in shorthand on index cards and coordinated an elaborate system of cues for slides. A fellow student at Throop, Edison Hoge, was a camera buff, and Capra had borrowed one of his cameras to take photographs on the trip. Hoge went along to Manual Arts to run a slide projector from the balcony of the auditorium. Capra had a button at the lectern for changing the slides, with cues indicated on his index cards. They rehearsed it over and over, "until I could do it with my eyes closed," Capra recalled.

But when the moment came, he found himself paralyzed with stage fright. Sweating and trembling as he went to the lectern to face the large auditorium full of snickering students, he mumbled something about not being a speechmaker. Then he picked up the stack of index cards, "and the friggin' things fell out of my hands." He crawled around on his hands and knees trying to pick up the cards, while the students hooted with laughter. Finally Dr. Wilson came up and told him to forget about the cards and just give the speech.

"I got started talking and I couldn't stop," Capra remembered. "I thought I could speak all day and night. I didn't know I was there. Finally Dr. Wilson comes up and puts his arm around me and says, 'Frank, that's very nice.' I had forgotten all about Edison Hoge. I never did press the button for the slides. They never saw them."

The speech went more smoothly when Capra gave it at Throop during the morning assembly on October 23. Earl Mendenhall was one of the students in the audience. He recalled: "We were so enthusiastic about what Capra said that we never forgot it. Frank gave us a wonderful discussion of what he did. He was an extrovert, and he had a knack of telling things in an interesting way."

*   *   *

"I became kind of popular at Caltech," Capra acknowledged. "I was well liked, and I liked all the kids."

His fraternity brothers in the Gnome (pronounced "Know-me") Club, the major social club at a school that generally frowned on fraternities, affectionately called him "Cap." In his junior and senior years they elected him president. It was quite a social turnaround for a young man who had been a virtual pariah in high school.

"The fraternity brothers had the highest regard for him," said Lois Keener Thome, a Pasadena girl who was pinned to another Gnome, Corliss Bercaw. "The fellows would say, 'Oh, Cap! Cap is such a great boy. Did you know that he used to sell newspapers on the street?' Or they'd say, 'Gee, I don't know what we would do without Cap in the Glee Club.' Or at a dance they'd say, 'So glad Cap could come tonight and didn't have to work.' They never put him up on a pedestal or anything, but he really was admired."

Capra's social life took a quantum jump forward in his sophomore year, when he moved from the ranch into the campus dormitory. The old two-story wood structure stood in the midst of an orange grove at the opposite end of the campus from the school's main building, Pasadena Hall. There was little carousing or rowdiness on the campus in those days, and few of the elaborate pranks for which the school later became renowned, but the dorm was a center of good fellowship, the focus of most of the campus social life. There was always a card game going somewhere, and Capra and his roommate, Bob Sticht, could often be heard harmonizing from room thirteen, Capra on his violin, guitar, ukelele, or mandolin and Sticht on his battered wooden flute.

"Their repertoire seemingly included only one composition," Philip Clarke recalled, "a lengthy, slow-paced and doleful tune entitled, as Frank finally told me, 'The Herd Girl's Dream.' It kind of interfered with our studies. Frank and Sticht were very bright fellows and were very quick learners, so they would put off the start of study until long after the rest of us started to bone up on our assignments. Some of us were in despair."

"We made the lousiest music you ever heard," Capra agreed, "but we loved it."

Robert C. Sticht, Jr., Capra's best friend in college, was from Queenstown, Tasmania. His father, an American-born mining metallurgical engineer, had emigrated there to open a copper mine. He brought his family to California in 1914 in the midst of a vacation which was extended indefinitely, partly due to the outbreak of World War I and also because the elder Sticht wanted to retire from business to dabble in metallurgical research. His son, a chemical engineering major, was tall, slender, fair, and athletic, a member of the Throop track and tennis teams.

Capra met him in the registration line on the first day at college. "I heard a man speaking English in a funny way," Capra recalled. "I turned around, and he was a long-faced guy, taller than I am. He had an accent, but I couldn't figure it out, so I said, 'Where are you from, bub?' He says, 'Austroylya.' " Capra laughed, delighted by the way Bob Sticht talked and by his friendly nonchalance.

Bob Sticht was from another country and as such would not think amiss of Capra being an immigrant. He had another attraction for Capra: in Capra's eyes, at least, Sticht was wealthy. His family had servants, and Bob's younger brothers, Chester and John, had nannies. But the reality was not all that it appeared. Their house on South Marengo Avenue, though comfortable, was no mansion, and the elder Sticht's business was foundering.

"We were not rich," said Chet Sticht, who was seven when he first met Capra at Throop and later became Capra's personal secretary, working for him for thirty-nine years. "My father had a good income, but he didn't have a lot of money piled up."

Nevertheless, Bob Sticht moved in the best circles of Pasadena society, and he provided entrée for Capra to people he otherwise might never have known and to homes from which he might have been excluded. More to crash parties than to make money, Capra, Sticht, and another boy formed a musical combo which played at the homes of wealthy people in Pasadena, Eagle Rock, and Arcadia. Sticht later left the group, but Capra continued it without him.

Asked how he chose his friends at Throop, Capra laughed, "Well, I knew who had money." He explained that he had to tag along with boys from prominent families—such as Jackson (Jack) Kendall, whose father was the city's wealthiest real estate man, or Dudley (Dud) Wheelock, whose father was president of the power company in Riverside—in order to be accepted in Pasadena society, because "I didn't have nice clothes. People whose sons went to Caltech used to come to vacation with their boys, and they usually would stay at the Maryland Hotel. You couldn't get in there without proper credentials. I never went in there without somebody else, because they'd throw me out.

"The best thing about this Sticht fellow was that he never bought anything that I couldn't buy; we never did anything I couldn't afford to do. Wasn't that wonderful? We went to the joints where I could pay my half.

He never paid for anything for me because he knew damn well the friendship would stop if he did that. I wouldn't take it."

Joshed in the school yearbook as "Ragged Castaway Sticht," Bob dressed as casually as the poorest student. He was the owner of the only student automobile on campus, a horrendous-looking rattletrap Ford with no doors and wobbly tires that was known to all as the "Stichtmobile." Bob generously lent the use of his car whenever anyone in the dorm needed a lift. The Stichtmobile transported Capra and Sticht into downtown Los Angeles almost every week so they could usher for the upper crust at the Philharmonic Auditorium (formerly Clune's, where *The Birth of a Nation* premiered), the city's most prestigious showcase for concerts, opera, and ballet. They worked there without pay, Capra said, "to be able to hear all the great singers and musicians, because we were both nuts about music. I was very lucky to get that job—to be able to go to Caltech and then to see an opera, it's a hell of a life."

Before long Capra had worked his way backstage, where the manager let him serve as a gofer for the star performers, receiving tips for bringing them drinks, making phone calls, arranging assignations: "I remember an English tenor who was always looking for girls. In between songs while the other man was playing the piano, he'd say, 'What about the girl in the second row?' "

Meeting the performers and watching the shows from backstage helped pique Capra's interest in the theater, which he found "a wonderful place to be." He soon gravitated to the semiprofessional Pasadena Community Playhouse, then at the beginning of its long and influential history. The Playhouse was already a magnet for the local blue bloods, and it drew heavily on Throop for extras and bit players. "They wanted guys to hold spears—they got 'em for nothing," Capra recalled. "I did it a couple of times with Sticht. One of the plays, I remember, was a Western, something to do with a man from New York who went out West. We were just part of a crowd. I had to stop doing it because I didn't have time to come back night after night. But for a kid, looking out and seeing the audience was a kick in itself."

Saturday morning, November 18, 1916, was cold and windy on the Churchill Ranch.

Salvatore Capra, wearing a long, split-tailed gray overcoat, came out of the ranch house wrapping a round loaf of hot, fresh bread in a dish towel and slipping it inside his shirt. His six-year-old grandson, Sam, speaking Italian to the old man, asked him what he was doing. Turiddu replied that he had a chest cold, and the bread, fresh out of the Dutch oven, would help to cure it. The bread had been cooked by Sam's mother, Mary. She was in the kitchen preparing lunch for the family.

The boy and his grandfather were going out with a two-man saw to cut lemon tree prunings for firewood. Using the big saw with his grandfather always made little Sam feel grown-up, but it frightened his mother. Turiddu ignored her warnings.

The night before there had been a square dance at the house. It was a boisterous, wine-giddy party, but Saridda had come to visit for the weekend, and before long she and Turiddu got into a shouting match. She stormed off and went back to Los Angeles.

Turiddu stopped in the well pump house at the edge of the orchard, before he and the boy started cutting wood. That November was a dry month, and the motor-driven pump was used to fill a reservoir that sent water through pipes to irrigate the orchards. Though Ben, who worried about his aging father's ignorance of machinery, did not like him to go into the pump house, Papa Turiddu had a mind of his own, and as Ben remembered, "That morning he wants me to go get the load of fertilizer and he was gonna start the pump."

Little Sam wandered off toward the orchard. Suddenly the boy heard his grandfather cry out, "*Aiuto!* [Help!]" Little Sam turned back and looked through the half-open door of the pump house. The cold wind was roaring through the door.

"I looked in and saw him sort of fighting something," Sam remembered. "His eyes were bulging. He'd got his coat pulled into the gears, and he was trying to get it out. It was sort of a tug-of-war. He was caught in the gears, caught across the waist. Then I saw two squirts of blood, and there was blood all around the ceiling. I ran away."

Sam remembered going for help, but others who were on the ranch that day said the boy hid in the orchard.

After a while, in the ranch house a quarter of a mile away, Mary became concerned that Papa Turiddu had not come in for lunch. She sent some of the other grandchildren to look for him. Meanwhile, her husband, Ben, working in the orchard, heard a loud noise from the pump house, a kind of high-pitched scream. Ben ran to the pump house and looked inside.

His father's body was cut in half at the waist. Part of him was still stuck in the gears. The engine was racing and the twenty-foot-long belt connecting the motor and the pump shaft was twisted around him grotesquely. "He went to put a little oil in the hotbox or something," Ben realized, "and the wind blew part of the coat between the high gear and the little gear, so the gears pulled him right between, cutting him in half. When I went in, I found half one way and half the other way." The gears had jammed and the engine had thrown the belt. The screaming noise they had heard was the engine racing out of control.

Sam eventually came back to the door and looked in, wide-eyed. "Dad had a long piece of pipe, and he and a Japanese fruit picker were prying him out of the wheel with it. They laid him on a little metal cot. There was just a little thread holding him together. I remember the wind blowing open his overcoat as he lay there, with the fresh bread on his chest. I couldn't see what all the fuss was about. I thought he was sleeping."

Ben's sister Ann, just short of her sixteenth birthday, was on her way home from doing chores for a neighbor family when she, too, heard the shriek of the electric motor. She ran to the pump house and found her father lying on the cot. Mucus was running from his nose. She knew he had a cold, so she went to wipe his nose with a handkerchief. It was then she realized that he was dead. She could not stop screaming. On the way to the main house, she collapsed in hysterics and suffered a slight heart attack.

Frank Capra was in his sophomore year, living at the dorm, when it happened. One of his teachers found him on the campus and told him his family had called, there had been an accident, and they wanted him at the ranch right away.

Back in the old neighborhood, Turiddu's daughter Josephine Finochio also received a telephone call from the ranch. She ran screaming out of the house to find her mother at Grogan's Olive Oil Factory.

When Saridda saw her husband's body, Sam remembered, "She came in and ran around and pulled her hair and fell on the floor and screamed. She tore her hair out by the handful. Later a doctor came, and then they put newspapers over his body. When Frank came home, grandmother was still wailing. They had to give her shots to calm her down. They were all trying to soothe her and Aunt Annie. My dad had to do all the dirty work."

Frank Capra stared at the two inconsolable women. He was too overwhelmed to show much reaction. And for the moment he was too worried about his beloved Annie to think much about his own future.

Papa Turiddu was sixty-four years old. When the coroner filled out the death certificate, he wrote under Cause of Death, "Crushed and mangled in stationary engine accident," and he asked Ben what his father's occupation had been.

"Laborer," Ben replied. Then he had a second thought: "Rancher."

The body was taken to Albion Street, where it was laid out in the middle house. Neighbors streamed in for two days to console Donna Saridda, who sat stoically on a couch near the coffin. The widow refused, as always, to wear black. She was dry-eyed.

"Don't you want to cry?" her daughter Josephine asked as they sat there with the body.

"He's *your* father," Saridda replied. "If you want to cry, cry. He made me cry enough when he was living."

Even though Turiddu had not been a good provider, there was a void in the family now that could not be filled. Tony expressed it most simply and eloquently: "When died Papa Turiddu, we was not all together any more."

In the weeks following the accident, Ben Capra began having more of his visions. While working in the fields, he would see Papa Turiddu's ghost gesturing to him and calling, "Over here! I'm over here!" Terrified, Ben began plotting his escape from the ranch. He developed an ulcer and for the rest of his life would suffer stomach trouble because of the trauma of having to pry his father out of the machinery.

Annie's heart attack made her a semi-invalid. For the next few years she was unable to hold a regular job, and though her health later improved, she never was strong again. She would have a much shorter life than the other Capra children who came to America, living until 1955, when she died at the age of fifty-five.

Saridda stayed home on Albion Street for about a month after the funeral before going back to work at Grogan's. Work had always been her refuge, but now she was noticeably tired, her age showing. She had never wanted to spend much time at the ranch while her husband was alive, but now she clung to it as a center for the family's existence.

Tony was still living in the middle house on Albion Street and working in the candy factory, but he, too, was longing to escape.

Frank was also at a crossroads that fall. His version of subsequent events is more melodramatic than the rest of the family's version, and less credible. What he claimed was this:

"We had one more payment to make on the ranch. We owed $5,000. This was the last of five payments. And my father had the money to pay for it, but with the state of mind my mother was in, my mother forgot about the money, and we lost the place.

"The time passed for the last payment. A few days later, this little guy with four eyes came to take over the ranch. Well, I was never so incensed in my life. So I grabbed that little sonofabitch by the collar, and I knocked him down, and dragged him all the way to the place where my father died, and I threw him in there with my father [who in fact was buried by this time in Los Angeles's Calvary Cemetery], and, well, here come the police."

They took him to court, and the "country judge" told him, "Come on, son. Just forget this. You were late [with the payment], and there's nothing we can do about it. No use to go to jail for this. I know how you feel. Why don't you go and help your mother? Just go home."

"And he let me go," marveled Capra. "I've loved judges ever since. If you'll notice, every judge I've had in a picture has been like that. His kindness saved me. I was going a little bit berserk. I might have killed a policeman.

"I went back to school, and I told them what had happened. I told them I would have to quit school and take care of my mother and my sister. I couldn't pay the $250-a-year tuition. Well, they offered to loan it to me. It took quite a while for me to accept it."

Throop had a student loan fund, underwritten by a benefactor named Olive Cleveland. Capra went to see the school's treasurer, Edward C. Barrett, who administered it. According to a later president of the school, Dr. Lee A. DuBridge, Barrett told Capra, "Frank, you're such a credit to [Throop] that the school will gladly loan you the money so that you can graduate." Capra was loaned his tuition for the last two and a half years. He eventually paid it back, and always expressed profound gratitude for Barrett's support.

The reason for the loan, however, was not that Capra was supporting his widowed mother and his sister but that *they* were helping support *him*. Saridda and Annie were living on a reduced income now, primarily from the olive oil factory and the rental properties. Despite their hardships, they continued to help Frank financially until he finished college. Frank added two more jobs to his already busy schedule, running a campus laundry service for the Royal Laundry and Dry Cleaning Company and, in his junior year, editing *The Tech*. One summer he went to Arizona to work in a copper mine with Bob Sticht and another Throop student (each working a separate eight-hour shift, so they could share a single bed)—but he still needed the loan to finish school.

Capra's claim that the family was thrown off the ranch because of a default on the mortgage seems highly unlikely. They had no mortgage on the Churchill Ranch, which they were only renting. Nor did the weekly column in the *Sierra Madre News* listing sheriff's foreclosures—and there were many in that period—list one involving Churchill or the Capras at any time between Salvatore's death and Frank's graduation from college almost two years later.

According to other family members, rather than evicting the family in the hard-hearted manner of a mustachioed villain in a nineteenth-century melodrama, Churchill pleaded with Ben Capra to stay and run the ranch himself. It was Ben's decision to give it up. He made up his mind while on a visit to his wife's parents in Sacramento. Deciding to remain there, far from the troubling visions of his dead father, he took a job as a mechanic. When Saridda heard of his plans, she was furious. She, too, begged him not to quit. But he remained adamant, and whenever she would see him at family gatherings she would rail at him for giving up the ranch.

As for Frank's supposed arrest, it is impossible to prove that something of the sort did not happen—the Sierra Madre Police Department destroys arrest records after five years. Capra certainly was in an agitated state of mind at the time of his father's death, and perhaps he did take his wrath out on someone. But no one else in the family remembers him being arrested, and there was no mention of any such incident in the *Sierra Madre News*.

Capra's story heightens his sense of himself and his family as helpless victims, their lives governed by fate and economic exploitation, rather than portraying them as people realistically cutting their losses. The story he tells also puts the onus of blame on his mother, whom he always cast as his antagonist, rather than admitting that Ben made the decision to give up the ranch. Portraying Saridda as confused and financially irresponsible is a misrepresentation along the same lines as his claim that she was illiterate. And claiming that Salvatore was on the verge of paying off a fictitious mortgage through his imaginary diligence as a rancher is not only a way of heightening the poignancy of the story but also a means of exalting his father's memory at his mother's expense and further obscuring Ben's importance in the family.

Perhaps most importantly, Frank Capra's emotional allegory may have been conceived as an alibi for the academic problems he began to experience after his father's death—problems that partly were due to the precarious condition in which his family now found itself but that had other causes as well, which Capra was loath to admit.

"Absolutely not," Capra declared when asked if he had any academic problems in that period. Not only did his grades not suffer in the aftermath of his father's death, he said, "They upped 'em, because I was more anxious to get out of there and make some money."

The record shows otherwise.

Capra's sophomore year also saw the declaration of war by the United States against Germany.

When President Wilson signed the declaration on April 6, 1917, Capra marched down to the Army recruiting station with another Throop man and enlisted in what Capra called "the first burst of enthusiasm . . . our wish for spectacular glory." But they were told that the Army needed them to finish their scientific training for the war effort more than it needed them in the trenches. After being sworn in, they were sent back to Throop as privates, to receive their military training in the ROTC.

"Frank was horrified," Chet Sticht recalled. "He wanted to go off and fight with a bayonet."

Wearing a regular Army uniform and drawing the standard $33-a-month domestic duty pay (while nonenlisted ROTC members received only $7.50 per month), Private Capra became the captain of one of the two cadet companies as Throop went on a wartime footing that eventually saw virtually all the students in uniform. When the companies were combined in his senior year, Capra was made supply officer, ranking directly under the adjutant, Captain Eugene Imler, the president of the student body.

Academic life at Throop was "somewhat blighted" by the militarization of the campus, Philip Clarke recalled: "It is very difficult both to get a satisfactory education and to hold up in the military, so it was pretty rough. We weren't able to finish all of our texts." Capra's class—originally scheduled to graduate in June 1919—was rushed through its courses on a year-round, seven-day-a-week schedule in order to finish in September 1918. It was renamed the class of "War '18." Twenty-six of Capra's classmates left for active service before graduation, including his friends Reginald Coles, Clarence Bjerke, and Jack Kendall.

Even more students would have left Throop before graduation had it not been for President Scherer's interruption of his wartime duties organizing scientific research to return to campus and urge the students to remain in school. And Capra wrote in a *Tech* editorial, "We must be prepared to sacrifice everything, including our existence on this earth if we are called into active service. But until America needs [us], our place is here at Throop, working hard and diligently, preparing ourselves to give our nation the best that is in us when the moment comes. It is just as patriotic, in fact more so, to stay in school and train ourselves for the time when we are called or needed, as it is to enlist as a private, when the country has no immediate need of privates. This may sound slightly unpatriotic, but we assure you that all the great men who are directing the destinies of our nation have the same opinion."

Capra's mixed motives for rushing off to enlist at the onset of America's involvement in the war perhaps were suggested by an unsigned parody of

Hamlet's Soliloquy in *The Tech* for December 1917, which has the sound of Capra's voice:

> *For who would bear the whips and scorns of time,*
> *The professor's looks, the khaki's stirring call*
> *The girls' cold shoulders and the dates denied,*
> *The insolence of officers, the name*
> *Of slacker that the college man abhors*
> *When he himself might personal glory gain*
> *By enlisting?*

In his autobiography, Capra did not even mention his early enlistment, but said his enlistment came *after* graduation. He evidently was too embarrassed to admit what really happened as a result of his precipitate burst of patriotism. Ironically, his early enlistment penalized him when he was mobilized upon graduation: while other ROTC members who had not enlisted went in with commissions as second lieutenants, Capra had to go in as a private.

Not only that, but when he enlisted he received a most unpleasant piece of news: he was not an American citizen. His father had been naturalized, and (as many immigrants did in that period) the rest of the family assumed that they shared his citizenship status. Frank did not know until the Army told him that the law had been changed to require individual naturalization. They let him join up, anyway, with his application pending. His final papers as an American citizen did not come through until June 4, 1920, long after his discharge.

There is another possible reason for the timing of his rush to the colors. The Class Prophecy in his graduation yearbook noted that Capra "had planned to join the Army and try to remain there the rest of his life." The comment may not have been entirely facetious. Those who knew him well at Throop said that he was more interested in the military than in anything else at that time, and they confirmed his statement that he was disappointed when the war ended before he could see action overseas. With his academic career beginning to falter, he may have seized on an Army career as a serendipitous alternative, and as an immigrant, he felt the need to demonstrate his eagerness to defend his adopted country. Being sent back to Throop was a setback, but the ROTC officer's post helped reinflate his ego, and the monthly pay didn't hurt, either. He also may have been under the mistaken impression then that being a captain in ROTC would guarantee that he would become an officer upon mobilization. His classmate

Robert W. Flory remembered Capra as having been "a little hustler in ROTC." Not only did he receive good grades in military courses, he "was always on the ball, very well-organized, and he knew what he was doing," said one of his cadets, E. V. Hounsell.

Capra, who saw the war as "this most noble cause . . . the greatest fight for civilization the world has ever known," helped do his bit during his final year at Throop by whipping up a clever new bomb for the government—or so he claimed.

During World War I, Throop became closely tied with the National Research Council, the government agency which coordinated scientific research for the war effort. President Scherer was a member, Dr. Robert Millikan, the University of Chicago physicist on leave to Throop, was its director, and the chemistry professor Arthur A. Noyes, on leave from MIT, became its acting chairman in 1918.

Capra had visited Noyes at MIT during his Freshman Scholarship Prize tour in the summer of 1916, and, as Capra told the story, on a visit to Throop in the spring of 1918, Noyes asked him what he thought of the German policy of *Schrecklichkeit*—the willingness to kill noncombatants if necessary to achieve a military objective, such as the sinking of a ship.

"Theirs or ours?" Capra said he replied. "If you mean theirs, it's all right with me."

Noyes confided that the Germans were using poison gas and said that the Americans had to come up with a defense against it. At the same time, the United States was rushing to develop poison gas of its own, and the Army was recruiting Throop students for its Chemical Warfare Service.

Acting on Noyes's suggestions and under the direction of a chemistry professor, Stuart Bates, Capra worked secretively behind a shatterproof glass shield in the new Gates chemistry laboratory, mixing up a formula for a liquefied gas that, when propelled by an exploding bombshell, would burn holes in the Germans' gas masks.

Capra said he sent the secret bomb formula off to Noyes in Washington, and "fortunately, we didn't have to use it. But it was ready. Had the war gone on another month or two, we would have been using it." He wrote in his autobiography that after the war Noyes sent him an effusive letter of commendation.

There is no such letter in Capra's files. When asked what happened to it, Capra admitted that there never was one—his bomb formula, he said, was simply filed and forgotten.

Capra was beginning to doubt whether he had the ability, or the desire, to become a chemical engineer.

The problems started in the first semester of his sophomore year, the period during which his father died. They intensified during his junior year, when he failed two courses and did not complete several others. His grade-point average (as calculated from the numerical equivalents of Throop's Roman numeral grading system) declined from 3.1 in his freshman year and 3.0 in his sophomore year to 2.1 when he was a junior and 2.4 when he was a senior, for an undistinguished overall average of 2.7.

Throop students had to begin specializing in their junior and senior years, taking more advanced courses in their chosen fields, and it is possible that Capra did not realize he was not cut out to be a chemical engineer until he began taking some of those courses. That would help explain why, in the first semester of his junior year (the fall of 1917), he did not complete three scientific courses (two of them in chemistry), and failed two others (including organic chemistry laboratory). His only strong subjects that semester were English, in which he pulled his usual A, and military and phys. ed., in which he received B's. Allowed to register for the second semester only after being placed on three weeks' probation (there were three terms that academic year, because of the accelerated program), he again started but did not complete theoretical chemistry laboratory, and he received C's in three other chemistry courses and a D in technical analysis. He withdrew from French (a subject in which he previously had received four straight A's), and he even failed to complete his English course.

When asked in later years why he switched fields from science to filmmaking, Capra had a stock answer. After his discharge from the Army he couldn't find a job as an engineer because the war-caused economic boom was over: "Everything was closed down. You don't know how hard it is for a country to switch from being in a war to not being in a war. Here I was, a chemical engineer . . . [and] I couldn't find a job. Of any kind. As wonderful an education as I had, it was a complete loss." While it was true that 1919 was a lean year for engineers and scientists, it also is true that all of Capra's classmates sooner or later managed to get jobs in the field, most of them going to work for power companies, oil companies, or manufacturing firms such as General Electric and Westinghouse. The reason Capra couldn't find a job in that tight job market was, most likely, because his academic record wasn't good enough.

Because of his disastrous showing in the first two-thirds of his junior year and his only partial rebound in subsequent terms, Capra did not graduate with a degree in chemical engineering, despite his claims in *The Name Above the Title* and elsewhere that he possessed such a degree. According to the official record, his college transcript, the degree Capra received was a "general" Bachelor of Science degree. He and another member of his class were the first two Throop students to receive such a degree, which was discontinued by Caltech in 1928. The college *Catalogue* for 1918 described the general course as providing "a thorough collegiate education in which science predominates, but with a generous admixture of other subjects." It was designed for "those who may desire to engage in scientific research, those who plan to become teachers of science, and those who may desire some scientific preparation for a business career." Capra's decision to switch courses most likely was made as a result of his academic trouble in the first semester of his junior year.

There was another reason for Capra's waning interest in studies: his love life.

Few subjects made Capra so uncomfortable to discuss as his love life at college. Although in his autobiography he mentioned an unnamed blond girlfriend from that period, he insisted to the author of this book that he had no girlfriends during his years at Throop: "I couldn't afford one." And he credited Throop's intellectual atmosphere to his and his classmates' lack of interest in the opposite sex: "We didn't screw around with girls, you see, so we didn't get tired that way." There are pictures in his files of Capra with various girls in the Throop years, but when asked to identify them, he tried to pass off all of the girls as Bob Sticht's girlfriends. Sticht was notoriously shy around girls and "didn't have any girlfriends" at Throop, his brother Chet confirmed.

Capra did indeed have trouble finding a steady girlfriend in his early days at college, and he often assumed the role of extra man at social functions.

"He was never able financially to do the things the other fellows could, so when our steady dates couldn't take us to a dance or whatever, they would ask Cap to take us," Lois Keener Thome remembered. "We always loved going with him. He was good company, very well mannered and very dapper, and never pushy. I loved to dance with Cap. He was careful about the little courtesies. And he was a very smooth dancer. He had good rhythm; I think he had music in him."

Capra's charm with the girls irked some of his male friends. "When I went to college, I didn't know how to dance," said Harold Harris. "I had a sweetheart [Grace Clark] whom I later married. She loved to dance, and Frank danced very well, so she and Frank used to dance together. I always used to be very unhappy about that."

Sometimes Lois Keener and Corliss Bercaw would go on a double date in his father's two-seater Ford with Capra and one of the girls he dated. Capra's girls, almost invariably, were petite blondes with what Lois called "that fresh, clean look; they all looked well scrubbed." And Capra always was very busy in the back seat. "Frank was a lover boy," she said.

Josie Campisi remembered Capra as "a womanizer" in his college days. But when asked about his girlfriends, she could remember only one. He almost never introduced any of them to the family, keeping a careful separation between his dual lives in Pasadena and Lincoln Heights. The only one Josie was allowed to meet was Ida Paggi, an Italian from Lincoln Heights who became a teacher at the 19th Avenue Elementary School. Ida developed a terrific crush on Capra. She would come to the house on Albion Street asking after him, but he wriggled away. The Italian and Mexican girls who made themselves available to him in the old neighborhood were nothing more than a diversion for him. He was determined to focus his sights on WASPs.

But when asked how serious he became about the WASP blondes he dated in Pasadena, Capra snapped (unconvincingly), "I was never *stupid*. What the hell could I do with these girls? Who needed 'em?"

The story he was trying to cover up was an embarrassing and painful one, a trauma that affected all of his future dealings with women, helped confirm his perception of himself as a social outcast, and drove him to sublimate his sexuality by concentrating his energy into his work.

"**H**e was the most brilliant student—till he met me," Isabelle Daniels Griffis said in 1986, finally breaking a lifelong silence to speak of her relationship with Capra.

"That sounds so conceited, but the kids at Throop used to say that. I knew I was Frank's first love, and I know he was crazy about me. I had two or three other fellows who were wanting to marry me at the time Frank was. It wasn't as serious with me as it was with Frank. I was awfully fond of Frank, but I was not in love with him. Where I merited all this attention I don't know, except that I was something different—I was blond and not Italian. And I guess I had sex appeal."

They met near the end of 1917, during the disastrous first semester of Capra's junior year, at a dance held for Throop boys by Isabelle's Universalist church in a small hotel on South Marengo Avenue. Frank was in his Army uniform that night, Isabelle was wearing a pink satin evening dress trimmed with black velvet. "Frank had beautiful curly black hair," she remembered. "He was a good-looking fellow. And he was a gentleman." Sixteen years old, a junior at Pasadena High School, she was short, round-faced, with a delicately curved figure and an impish, teasing personality that made the boys flock around her. "I was a conceited little bitch," she later admitted. The man she married called her "the busy little butterfly."

She and Capra went to Throop and Gnome dances together "once in a while" in his junior and senior years. They might have seen each other more often, but "Frank had no car," other than the rattletrap Stichtmobile, in which he and his friends sometimes came to pick her up, doing head-stands on the hood and seat to impress her. "I had lots of other boyfriends who were taking me to real nice places. Not Frank. I don't remember him taking me any place where it cost him anything. I don't think he could afford a lot of girlfriends. And I don't really think he had much time for playing or going out; he was mostly working all the time. He was concen-trating on his career." Aside from dances, they saw each other mostly at church, where he liked to listen to her singing in the choir.

Isabelle's parents were the kind of solid, prosperous Pasadena citizens ("Republicans, of course") Capra later liked to mock in his work. Her mother's genealogy traced their lineage back to the *Mayflower* and to the Pilgrims John and Priscilla Alden; on her father's side they claimed to be descended from Presidents John Adams and John Quincy Adams. Her father, George A. Daniels, who came from Ohio, was co-owner of a planing mill and ran a construction business. He married Laura Packard, a school-teacher and librarian, born in Maine, who was the first curator of the Pasadena Historical Society. They had four children; Isabelle was the only girl.

"Dad hated Frank because he was Italian," she recalled. "He was sure he was up to no good; Dad was making up a grand passion between us. And he was a Mason, and he didn't want me to marry a Catholic. It was a regular *Romeo and Juliet* the way my [father] felt. My mother liked Frank. She thought he had a future. But I was never ready as far as marriage was concerned. He was so poor then, just starting out; he was struggling hard to even live. He was an interesting boy, but just a boy. I figured he was so smart he would be a success doing something, but no one knew *how far* he would go."

When they met, Isabelle listened sympathetically as Frank talked about his father's death and how hard it was for him to make ends meet, how he was trying to take care of his family. "He didn't talk about movies. He didn't talk about books. He didn't talk about politics. I don't think he had any particular soapbox thing he talked about. He was concentrating on his career, and I think he was really interested in the military.

"There were a lot of tensions. He kinda scared you off. He'd get his temper tantrums, and all through our relationship he had a cruel streak. He would say cutting things to me. He would say something real nasty about what a flirt I was. But I guess that's why he was mean, because he cared so much, and he wanted me to be in love with him."

One night toward the end of his college years, Capra borrowed the Stichtmobile and drove Isabelle to a quiet spot near a lake outside of town. "He started to kiss me," she remembered, "and then he pulled himself short and said, 'I'd better leave and go right home. I don't know what will happen if we don't stop.' People didn't *do* that, didn't kiss like that. I let him kiss me that time and I didn't resist him. It was his decision to stop. I think he was afraid he would lose control of himself, that he would lose his head and go all the way. I think he respected me. I wouldn't dare do anything, because if I got pregnant my brothers and my father would have shot me."

"At that time I was clean, but I was scared," Capra recalled. "I didn't know what the hell to do. I'd grown up, but I'd gone so long without it. I was a little worried that I would lay an egg."

Though she continued to see Capra off and on until 1938, Isabelle insisted, "I only kissed him once in all those years. I liked him and I respected him, but we just didn't have that magic, that chemistry."

Despite his growing love for her, which led him to propose marriage in 1920, Capra evidently kept his physical distance for a variety of reasons: his awe of her appearance and social standing, the competition from her other beaus, his sense that she was not sexually attracted to him, and his fear of her father and the social taboos George Daniels represented. Underlying it all was Capra's deep-seated timidity with women, a fear of sexuality, and an exaggerated sense of deference that stemmed from his embattled relationship with his mother and was reinforced by the rejections he frequently suffered in high school and in college before he met Isabelle.

When they went swimming in the ocean off Santa Monica in 1920, Isabelle, thinking she was drowning, clutched at Capra, who told her later that day, "You got frightened in the water and you threw your arms around me—and I almost passed out."

Toward the end of his college years she turned her affections to one of his friends, Robert L. Griffis. Griffis was two years younger than Capra, a fellow Gnome, and a member of his ROTC platoon. Frank liked Bob because Bob could play the violin better than he could. And Bob was from a good social background, he had traveled the world, he was another of the tall, handsome WASPs Capra always wished he resembled.

"Frank introduced me to Bob at a country club dance, a Throop dance.

Neither Bob nor I thought much of the other," Isabelle remembered. Shortly after that, she and Frank went on a picnic with Bob, her brother Foster, and three other young people. Foster captured the moment in a photograph: Frank, nattily dressed in a suit with a high starched collar, beaming as he and Isabelle ride in a swing, her head back, laughing gaily; Bob standing in the background, watching silently.

On the way home, Frank and Isabelle rode in the back seat with Bob and his date. "I was sitting on Frank's lap," Isabelle recalled. "I reached around and put my hand on [Bob's] shoulder. Bob took hold of my hand, and, boy, it was just like an electric shock. Frank told me later, 'I knew it. I knew Bob was holding your hand.' "

Frank salved his wounds in those last months at college by wooing other girls.

On the July 4 weekend, Capra, Sticht, Wilbur Thomas, Milton Weldon, Turner Torgerson, Fritz Karge, and a Pasadena oilman's daughter named Marion (Ellen) Andrews piled into a borrowed Hudson for a camping trip to the Yosemite Valley in Northern California. Ellen, several years older than Capra, was living on her own in Pasadena and working as a clerk. When asked about his relationship with Ellen Andrews, Capra insisted, as usual, that Ellen was Bob Sticht's girlfriend. In an article he wrote about the trip for *The Tech*, Capra discreetly omitted any mention that Ellen had gone with them.

Capra conceived a wild stunt to make an impression on Ellen Andrews: he gave her his still camera and asked her to snap a picture of him standing on the famous Overhanging Rock, balanced improbably on the very tip of Glacier Point, three thousand feet above the valley.

Ellen watched nervously through the viewfinder as Capra scampered onto the rock and started to stand on his head. She snapped the picture and fainted. The picture caught Capra with his legs still rising into the air. He heard a thud but did not know that Ellen had fainted until he completed the headstand and came down safely from the rock.

"Don't ever make *anyone* take a picture of *anyone* standing on that rock at Glacier Point," she wrote Capra seventeen years later. "I still tremble, thinking of it. Do you remember how disgusted you were that I took it when your heels were only at half mast?"

He later paid Ellen a backhanded tribute by giving her name to the Claudette Colbert character in *It Happened One Night*, a snooty socialite who condescends toward Clark Gable's working-class hero before he wins her over. The real Ellen, who it seems was one of the first truly independent women Capra had ever encountered, found the use of her name amusing.

Back in Pasadena, Capra disposed of his relationship with another girl he had been dating, Faith Van Horn, and did so quite cavalierly, according to Faith, who wrote him in 1935, "Well do I remember the last date I had with you, Frank. Was prepared to be all thrilled and you spent the entire evening moaning about some damsel who had left you flat—said you couldn't even shave—tho what that has to do with a broken heart, I don't know. Anyway, I didn't enjoy the 'dear sister' act so much."

Frank's date for the Throop graduation ceremony in September 1918 was Isabelle Daniels. The following month Frank went to San Francisco to begin his regular Army service. Before leaving he told friends at school that he and Isabelle were going to be married. Philip Clarke, who also left for Army duty at that time, remembered hearing the rumor that a secret marriage was in the works, and Lois Keener Thome heard that the girl had followed Capra to San Francisco and married him.

"Wishful thinking," said Isabelle. "When he was up there I fell in love with Bob, I'm embarrassed to say so. We fell madly in love."

The bitterness Capra carried with him from those years can be seen in "Heart Beats," a film treatment he wrote around 1919. The autobiographical overtones are rawly apparent in Capra's tale of Larry Doyle, a poor boy who works his way through Stanford and becomes a world-famous heart specialist.

The son of an impoverished groceryman and a mother who died when he was born, Larry grows up wanting to be well-off like the local doctor. Pursuing an education as a means of seeking revenge for his miserable upbringing through worldly success, he wins a college prize for his academic achievement and astonishes his friends with the ferocity of his ambition. Like Capra, Larry could subscribe to Emerson's precept: "I shun father and mother and wife and brother when my genius calls me." He marries a woman he does not love in a calculating attempt at bettering his social position and ensuring that he won't be sidetracked by sentimental attachments. His career, for a time, brings him the glory he craves, but part of him realizes that it has come at the expense of his humanity.

Dr. Doyle causes his wife's death through neglect, guiltily destroys his career, and winds up despairingly stumbling around a potter's field on a wintry night like Jimmy Stewart in the fantasy sequence of Capra's 1946 film *It's a Wonderful Life*. The ghostly shapes of other great egotists such as Julius Caesar, Napoleon, and Kaiser Wilhelm II come to accuse Capra's alter ego and try to pull him into a grave; his own father, who caused Larry's mother to die of a broken heart on the day of his birth, is the gravedigger. As he falls into the ground, Larry wakes from this nightmare of an anonymous oblivion and realizes how heartless ambition has led him to the brink of self-destruction.

"I'll be damned—sounds like a good story!" said Capra when it was recounted to him in 1985.

Another passion was taking the place of science in Capra's life in his last months at Throop: motion pictures.

He insisted in his autobiography that he had absolutely no interest in a movie career until 1921, when he directed a dramatic short called *Fulta Fisher's Boarding House.* He repeated the claim countless times in interviews and in discussions with film students. It is an important part of his self-created myth that he was a cinematic innocent until he bluffed his way into the directing job because he needed money. But the truth is that Capra probably became seriously interested in movies by 1915, the year *The Birth of a Nation* changed everyone's thinking about the infant medium, and he began considering a career in movies while he was still a student at Throop.

It was common knowledge on campus in his last two years that Capra was fascinated by motion pictures. Recalling Capra's friendship with Edison Hoge, staff photographer for *The Tech,* Earl Mendenhall said Hoge "probably had something to do with Frank Capra getting interested in motion pictures." Capra described Hoge (who made a career out of scientific photography and worked on some of Capra's Bell science films in the 1950s) as "a motion picture nut—he was one of those kind of guys who would say, 'Have you seen this picture? Boy, you ought to.' "

Hoge helped put himself through school by working on the photographic plates at nearby Mount Wilson Observatory. It probably was through Hoge that Capra came to assist a newsreel cameraman, Roy Wiggins, who was photographing Mount Wilson. Wiggins showed him how the mechanism of the camera worked, and they socialized together. That experience was one of the few pre-1921 brushes with the movies Capra would acknowledge in his book.

Capra's 1916 visit to the Eastman plant probably stemmed from more than scientific interest. A 1951 Screen Directors Guild document about the career beginnings of various major directors in the silent era states that Capra entered the industry as a film editor with Mack Sennett's Keystone comedy studio in about 1915; though that could account for the missing six months in Capra's life following his graduation from Manual Arts when he was working to help finance his college education (and when he may also have participated in the filming of Rob Wagner's *Our Wonderful Schools*), the document may place Capra's first Hollywood job a bit early, especially since Wagner at the beginning of 1918 referred to Capra "trying to break in" to the industry. However, Warner Bros.' 1941 publicity biography of Capra said that "During his days at Caltech, Capra had earned a few dollars by selling 'gags' and situations for screen comedies to Mack Sennett" (for whom Capra would become a full-time gag man in 1924). Sennett's sketchy files from the late 1910s offer no documentation on Capra's possible free-lance or full-time employment there, but a "sideline" writing gags for Sennett in his college years also was mentioned in the authorized biography of Paul H. (Scoop) Conlon, Capra's longtime publicist, who started working with him in the late 1920s. Conlon's biographer, John McCallum, wrote that "It was this strange sideline that prompted young Capra to forget engineering in favor of a steady job as a 'gag' writer."

The story could have been Conlon's invention, yet some kind of early, unacknowledged work for Sennett would help explain why Capra became so angry over the Class Prophecy in his college graduation yearbook. The prophecy kidded "Capra and the movie bunch," who it said spent much of their time sunning themselves at the seaside resort of Venice, California, then the Los Angeles equivalent of Coney Island and a place where many film folk lived. It went on to say of Capra that "on graduation he offered his services to the Government in the capacity of Captain. After a short inquiry into his ability he received a reply offering him a position as private in the infantry. The poor fellow's feelings were hurt for he had long felt that he was worthy of at least captaincy. While he was considering whether or not to go into the Army, he received an offer from the Keystone Comedy Company of a captaincy in their military company. He has made quite a success as a film star. I understand that he is now drawing fifteen dollars per week. He is scrappily married, has seven children, and a beautiful home at Venice—the city of his college dreams."

Capra resented the kidding so much so that in 1936, when he was invited back to Caltech to speak for the first time at the alumni club, the Athenaeum, he went out of his way to recall that long-forgotten prophecy, telling his audience that its author, *Tech* editor Retla Alter, had harbored a personal animosity toward him. "He was an ornery guy," Capra elaborated in 1984. "He was a cripple, he had a bum leg and a bad temper, and I had it all: I could run, I was the editor of the paper. He was mentally pretty good but he was sour. Didn't laugh. So the worst thing he could think about saying, the lowest thing that he could possibly think up, was how I became a Keystone Kop."

Others did not see Alter the way Capra did. "If he didn't limp so damn bad," said Earl Mendenhall, "you wouldn't think there was anything wrong with him." What probably caused the friction between Capra and Alter (though Capra denied that it did) was the fact that Alter won a campus election to replace him as editor of *The Tech* in their senior year, costing Capra a lucrative and prestigious job. But what mattered more to Capra, enough to make him seethe for more than sixty-seven years, was that Alter had needled him in his most sensitive spot by publicly reminding him that the profession he was thinking of entering was, despite *The Birth of a Nation*, still considered highly déclassé.

The most striking evidence of Capra's early fascination with the movies is a paper he wrote for his junior English class in December 1917, near the end of his worst academic semester. "A Treatise on Moving Pictures" (which Capra later insisted he had no memory of writing) is a nine-page essay covering the subject from a wide variety of perspectives: historical, scientific, economic, aesthetic, practical, educational, sociological, and moral. Capra's command of facts is impressive, and his enthusiasm is unmistakable. Some of his aesthetic and moral judgments are naive, but there also is much in the essay that is prescient about the future of movies and about the kind of movies he himself would make.

Movies, Capra felt, had outgrown their infancy. Those who formerly looked down on the medium now had to concede that it had become an art form, one already superior to the stage in terms of presenting spectacle and, as in the case of Griffith's epics, a worthy vehicle for important themes.

Capra still found the movies lacking because of the absence of sound. The three-dimensionality of an actor's work on the stage, freedom of movement, and ability to evoke verisimilitude was hampered by the restrictions of movie pantomime. But Capra felt the movies were superior in their wide-ranging visual scope and their ability to peer closely and revealingly into human behavior, both comedically and dramatically.

By ending his essay with reflections on the social and moral value of movies, Capra made it clear that he was no longer an aesthetic elitist, at least where the movies were concerned, and that he embraced the new medium with a quasi-religious fervor. Moving pictures, he felt, had great potential not only for entertainment but also as an informative, educational, and persuasive medium, one that would enlighten and edify the average citizen, making his life richer and happier.

The small crowd sang "America" as it gathered in front of Gates Laboratory building at four o'clock on a sweltering Sunday afternoon, September 15, 1918. Eighteen young men were graduating from Throop College of Technology, and all but two (the German citizen Fritz Karge and the crippled Retla Alter) were going off to military service in the waning days of the war. "There was a feeling of tenseness," recalled Lois Keener Thome, who attended with Corliss Bercaw. "They weren't in uniform but of course they didn't know if they would survive. It was very hurried, and it really was very sad."

Many years later, remembering the impulse that had driven him to this moment, Frank Capra said, "I was out for an education. I wanted an education the worst thing. I knew if I got an education that something would fall." But as he received his diploma, with Isabelle Daniels looking on, Capra's future seemed even more uncertain than it had been when he had left Manual Arts. With his chances for a job as a chemical engineer threatened by his shaky academic record, and with his own doubts about his fitness for a technical career, he did not know what he would do once he left the Army. Like his fellow students at Throop, he had been enlisted since August 1 in the Engineer Enlisted Reserve Corps, but even his final assignment to active Army duty was unknown at the time of his graduation.

A future in the movie business was one of the options Capra was actively considering. While preparing his "Treatise on Moving Pictures," Capra wrote his letter asking career guidance from Rob Wagner. Capra's letter has not survived, but he carefully preserved Wagner's reply, which was dated January 1, 1918:

> *Dear Frank:*
>
> *You'd be one dam* [sic] *fool to give up your scientific work for the movies. There are many reasons; here are a few:*
>
> *Scientific specialists are the rarest animals in the social cosmos. Know more than any other man about the horse-fly, or the color red, or why a hen crosses the road, and you can make a good living.*
>
> *Let science be your vocation and art be your avocation.*
>
> *Even if there was a good chance in the movies—which there isn't—it is about the last place for an artist.*
>
> *Moving pictures are social products, and art is individual. If an artist could own a company, and all the others had to obey his orders there would be some fun in it.*
>
> *As it is, there are twenty men butting in on every picture, and the artist being the most sensitive, gets it in the neck all along the line. The most unhappy artists in the world are in the pictures, struggling against conditions that are absolutely heartbreaking.*

The moving picture business is in a shaking down process. The output this year will be only half of what it has been. Studios that used to work thirty companies are now using five or six. Some have quit entirely.

The great army that has been thrown out because of this condition is standing around with first call on their old jobs.

So even if the work was desirable no worse time could be selected for trying to break in than the present.

I'm sorry, Frank, that I am compelled to be so discouraging but since I've been writing those movie stories I have had to answer hundreds of similar requests and, though I have answered them all the same, I have not been so full.

Stick to your specialized education and some day you will thank me for having so urged you.

> *Cordially your friend,*
> *Rob Wagner*

5. "I'm from Hollywood"

$\mathcal{S}$till recovering from his shock at being mustered into the regular Army as a private, Capra found himself on October 15, 1918, not in European combat but at the Presidio at picturesque Fort Point on San Francisco Bay, headquarters of the coast defenses. He was one of 2,500 prospective officers from eleven western states crammed into the Enlisted Specialists' Preparatory School. From reveille at 5:30 A.M. to taps at 10 P.M., they studied tactics and weaponry, practiced with artillery, and trained in trench warfare with bayonets, hand grenades, and machine guns.

Capra said that to take advantage of his scientific background, the Army made him an instructor in ballistics mathematics. The existing Army records do not say anything about teaching duties at the Presidio, only that Capra was on duty at the school. A journalist visiting the camp noted that it was not unusual for "a stripling" to be made an instructor, "refreshing the memory of some old-timer who drilled under the old manual." The frustrated Capra, however, spent much of his brief service at the Presidio taking classes himself. While the war reached its final days in Europe, he was in a master gunner section, taking a crash course in surveying. On November 11, when the rest of the country was celebrating the Armistice, Capra was plodding through a study of "Chaining Between Two Points, One of Which is Inaccessible."*

---

* Some of Capra's publicity material over the years stated that he was promoted from private to second lieutenant in World War I. Capra told the author that he was promoted from private to technical sergeant before being discharged; he said he was "bumped up to sergeant because I was teaching the big boys." But none of the existing documents from World War I in Capra's Army personnel file indicates a rank above private; and the adjutant general's Official Army Register for December 1, 1918, a week before Capra's discharge, lists every officer in the Coast Artillery Corps of the rank of second lieutenant or above, but it does not list Capra. An Officer Qualifications Record sheet Capra filled out during World War II listed the highest grade he achieved

*   *   *

In the fall and winter of 1918, an epidemic of Spanish influenza swept the world. More than twenty million Americans became ill, and half a million died. Schools were closed for the duration, people wore breathing masks when they ventured out in public, and the Army was devastated by the attack as it spread unchecked through crowded camps, killing 44,270 American soldiers, nearly as many as were killed in battle.

Capra's hardy constitution initially put up a resistance. But he soon felt the symptoms coming upon him. In desperation he fled the post to downtown San Francisco, still wearing his uniform, and fainted in a cafeteria.

"I woke up in a strange room. There was a little bottle of water on a desk. I was in a bed. There was nobody else there. I lay there for a day in a terrible sweat. Nobody came to see me. Finally a couple of Army guys came and took me to a hospital."

At the French Hospital on Geary Boulevard, he was dumped in an "enormous old brick room" with "beds so close together nobody could get between them.

"When somebody died, some old men would come in and put him in a basket, and as they walked this basket made a creaking sound. We heard that sound all night and all day. I never saw a doctor. I was there six days. I saw the guy next to me die. For the first two or three days I wasn't hungry. Then I started getting a little better. I asked one of the guys carrying out caskets if I could have some food. He went out and came back with two eggs. I picked 'em up and they were cold rubber.

"I got an idea. Might as well get these guys laughing, they're going to die anyhow. There was a nail in the brick wall right over my head. So I reached up and stuck those two eggs onto the nail and hung 'em there. There was laughing all over the room. It was so wonderful to hear.

"Those two eggs stayed there until I left."

Capra was sent back to the Presidio, weak from flu and pneumonia but no longer in danger of death. When he was discharged on December 8 after only seven weeks of active service there, he "ran like hell to the train."

---

in World War I as private (he described his duty as "Enlisted Specialist"). The only existing Army document which supports Capra's claim to have been promoted from private is a 1942 memorandum from his superior officer in World War II, Brigadier General Frederick H. Osborn, which stated that Capra served in World War I as a "Master Sergeant, Coast Artillery Corps." "I've always understood that he was just a private," said Chester Sticht, who served as Capra's master sergeant in World War II. "I never heard him mention that he was a sergeant. I doubt it was the case, unless it was done because of his teaching. Sometimes they bumped you up; they may have made him a sort of temporary sergeant and bounced him back at the end of the war."

*   *   *

Before going home he went to visit his brother Ben in Sacramento.

Ben was working in a railway machine shop. For the first time in his life, he had a job that gave him security and time to relax with his wife and three children. Between repair chores, he invented mechanical devices for streetcars. Eventually he held seventeen patents. But good-hearted Ben, whom life always seemed to shortchange, made almost nothing from the inventions he came up with on company time. Undaunted, he continued to tinker in his workshop, trying to build a perpetual motion machine.

When Frank came to visit, he brought along a box of .22 caliber target-practice bullets as an ironic souvenir of his noncombative service in the war. His nephews, Sam and Claude, and his niece, Sarah, were thrilled when he gave each of them one of his bullets. "We idolized him," Sam said. "He was a great guy." Before Frank left he told Ben, "I don't care what you do, but see that the kids stay in school."

After recuperating at Ben's for a week, Frank found a temporary job picking hops for a rancher in the Sacramento Valley. He was short on funds, and working in the open air seemed a good way to recover his health.

Then he heard that a movie company from Hollywood was shooting a Western nearby, along the Sacramento River. The film company put out a call for local people to work as extras. Capra went over to investigate.

The movie was *The Outcasts of Poker Flat*, an ingenious interweaving of the title story by Bret Harte and Harte's "The Luck of Roaring Camp." The star was Harry Carey, a veteran of D. W. Griffith's Biograph stock company, and the director was a twenty-four-year-old with just two years of directing experience, mostly on Carey Westerns for Universal—John Ford. He was billed as "Jack" Ford then, and *The Outcasts of Poker Flat*, released in July 1919, would be his first film to receive much attention from the critics, who usually despised "horse operas."

Olive Carey, Harry's wife and herself a longtime member of the Ford Stock Company, was with them on location. She remembered Frank Capra as "a nutty young man who came along and said he needed money. They paid him five dollars a day as an extra." Capra played a laborer loading a stern-wheeler riverboat in the film-within-a-film based on "The Outcasts"; the scene was filmed at the Front and K streets dock, Sacramento's busiest moorage, now preserved as part of Old Sacramento. It was one of the scenes that made the strongest impression on *Photoplay*, which hailed "director Ford's marvelous river locations and absolutely incomparable photography." (Like all but a handful of the twenty-two Ford-Carey Westerns, it no longer exists today; the negatives of all the films were destroyed in a fire at Universal in 1921.)

Capra had only passing contact with Ford during the making of the film, but he did become acquainted with Harry Carey. He told Carey he was interested in a movie career, and the amiable actor encouraged him, telling him to look him up when they returned to Hollywood. Jim Tully wrote in a 1937 profile of Capra that he "wandered from one studio to the other, obtaining a day's work now and then as an extra. When a 'feature Western' was made at Universal he was given work for three days, Harry Carey was again the star [and Ford again the director]. The extra did not make himself known. 'Why should I inflict myself on Carey?' " Other articles on Capra in the 1930s and 1940s mentioned that he had been an extra in Harry Carey Westerns, and one article said that Carey helped him find a job on "Poverty Row," the haven of fly-by-night producers in Hollywood, where Capra went to work not long after his return from Northern California.

In a 1938 article Capra wrote for a London newspaper, he stated that he had been an extra "fighting Injuns [sic] in a 'Western' picture," but he neglected to mention *Outcasts* or other extra work in his autobiography. According to Ollie Carey, Capra remembered *Outcasts* well, and reminisced with her about it on more than one occasion in the late 1940s. And in 1939, when Capra was making *Mr. Smith Goes to Washington* and Harry Carey was no longer a major star, Capra was able to repay him for his kindness by giving him the key supporting role of the vice president of the United States, which won the veteran actor his only Academy Award nomination.

Capra came home to his mother and sister Ann in the duplex on Albion Street. He claimed in his book that he was confident he would find a job quickly. More likely, given his rocky academic career and the postwar industrial slowdown, he was not totally unprepared for the wave of rejection he experienced from employers as he exhausted local prospects in his field and tried to renew the contacts he had made during his cross-country tour of businesses and laboratories in 1916.

Wearing his uniform because he could not afford to replace it, he became part of the army of unemployed veterans haunting the streets trying to find work. He even looked in Chinatown. "The places I went looking for work would fill a book," he said. He took intermittent employment in the fruit and meat markets, unloading freight or running errands. He also worked as a ditchdigger on a waterline being installed in the downtown area. But mostly he lounged around his mother's house pounding out his frustrations on an old upright piano.

His relatives and neighbors did not hide their disdain.

"Those people with education can't make a living," his brother-in-law Luigi Finochio, the fruit peddler, would say. Frank's sneering brother Tony would flip a dime at him, telling him to go buy himself a pack of cigarettes.

While drinking Saridda's wine, the neighbor ladies would ask her, within Frank's earshot, about his job prospects. Then they would add, more loudly, "Oh, you poor lady—you're stuck again with a bum."

His spirits took another beating when he looked up Isabelle Daniels and learned that in his absence she had begun dating Bob Griffis, who still was enrolled at Throop. But, she said, Frank "wouldn't give up," and she resumed seeing him, chastely as ever.

Isabelle was in her senior year at Pasadena High School when Capra returned from the Army. She was thinking of going to college, but her father opposed it, so she was beginning to take the prospect of marriage more seriously—but to Bob, not to Frank. Still, there was something adventurous and "cocky" about the more experienced Capra that kept her interested in him and made her wonder if he might surprise all of the skeptics.

Then Capra got a break. It didn't seem like much of a break at the time, but it launched him on his life's work: in early 1919, he found his first verifiable full-time job in the movies.

Before he published his autobiography, Capra and his publicists made no attempt to conceal his film jobs prior to the 1921 *Fulta Fisher's Boarding House*. "Frank Capra has been associated with motion picture production since his release from the Army at the close of the World War," a Columbia Pictures pressbook noted in 1931, and many newspaper and magazine profiles of Capra contained references to his pre-1921 film work. The biographies distributed by Capra's personal publicists continued to do so as late as November 1968, almost two years after he began writing the book. Then the references abruptly stopped. Since the book was published in 1971, its misleading account of his early career has been accepted by the vast majority of film historians, who have continued to print the legend that he started without experience as the director of *Fulta*.

There was more than the urge to tell a good story in Capra's decision to ignore his apprenticeship. It was also a form of self-aggrandizement,

Capra's way of showing that he was so brilliant that he could master his complex new medium without training and without the stumbles and false starts and humiliations that actually occurred. The true story of Capra's early film jobs is a story of sheer dogged persistence that shows his fictional story for what it is: a fairy tale.

He went to work in early 1919 with the Christie Film Company, a leading producer of slapstick comedy, in its small Poverty Row studio at 6101 Sunset Boulevard, at Gower Street—catercorner from the future site of Columbia Pictures, where Capra eventually would make his reputation.

The Christie studio, no longer standing, was a historic site, the first movie studio ever opened in Hollywood itself. A former roadhouse with adjacent barn, corral, and outbuildings, it was converted into a movie studio in 1911 after Prohibitionists shut down all the taverns in Hollywood. Two English brothers, David and William Horsley, ran it as the Nestor Film Company until it was taken over in 1916 by a pair of Scotsmen, Al Christie and his older brother, Charles; Al was a cousin of David Horsley's wife and a financial partner of the Horsleys.

When Capra went to work for the Christies, the company was second only to Mack Sennett's Keystone as a comedy factory. Al Christie, who directed most of the company's films, and Charles, who ran the business end, turned out cheap but popular comedies, mostly two-reelers, released through independent exchanges. Their stars in that era included Bobby Vernon, Laura La Plante, and Walter Hiers. *When Bobby Comes Marching Home, Marrying Molly,* and *Oh, What a Night* were some of the films made around the time Capra was on the lot.

"Al Christie was a very good comedy director with a great sense of timing," recalled Colleen Moore, who appeared in several Christie films. "I learned a lot about comedy from him. It was a very small place, everything was done as cheaply as possible, and they made pictures in nothing flat—a month was a long time—but it was a nice atmosphere."

Capra's job there probably lasted no more than a couple of months. But it was mentioned frequently in articles in the 1930s, which reported that he had been a set builder, prop boy, grip, juicer, and assistant director, all at the rock-bottom salary of four dollars a week. One article said that he "made two-reelers" for the Christies, another that he got his job by selling them a script for a two-reel comedy. "I don't remember what the hell I did for them," Capra said in 1985, "but it certainly was not writing a story or anything like that. I'd have been very happy to sell a story to the Christie brothers." While Capra may have gone there hoping to sell a story, he admitted to having done nothing much more on the Christie lot than "cleaning up the horseshit": Rocky Washington said that Capra was a janitor for the Christies, although he added, "It was generally talked about in the neighborhood that Capra was working in a movie studio. It was kind of a glamorous job even though he was only a janitor."

Capra later disparaged the typical scene in a Christie comedy as "two comics plastering wallpaper on a third comic's back." Of his early work in Hollywood, he said in 1985, "I did a lot of little bitty things, but it doesn't mean anything to me. It was just a job. It was just a place to get a few bucks."

However humble the job was, for a young man who had already displayed a keen interest in the movies, it was enough to start his adrenaline rushing. When someone offered Capra a steady job in a bank, he refused it, even though it might have helped him win Isabelle. He said he was a college graduate and he did not want to waste his life in a bank. His mother was furious at his stubbornness. As usual, only Annie sided with him.

Capra's budding movie career was sidetracked while he was with the Christies by another bout of illness. This one appeared at the time to be an outgrowth of his flu and pneumonia. He was bedridden for several weeks on Albion Street. His mother, he claimed, refused to call a doctor: "She didn't believe in doctors. She believed in people living their lives as they should. She had the idea that doctors kill people. Anyway, she didn't have that kind of money. I had a terrific fever, but there wasn't anything I could do. I didn't have money enough to call a doctor."

Every couple of hours, Saridda would come home from the olive oil factory to take care of him. Her cure was folk medicine: she kept a raw potato in cold water, cut slices from it, and wrapped the cool slices in a handkerchief, placing it on his head to reduce the fever. At night, she and Annie would sit in a chair by his bedside. Somehow he pulled through.

Fifteen years later, when he complained of chronic abdominal pains, Capra underwent an appendectomy, and learned the probable cause of his 1919 illness: his doctors discovered that his appendix apparently had ruptured then but had healed itself, leaving only shreds of the burst appendix in his body. Such an attack usually was fatal in those days, but one of Capra's doctors later said that he had a remarkably resilient constitution, a product of his Sicilian heritage.

People who saw Capra during his 1919 illness, not knowing what caused it and knowing of his problems finding his bearings after college and the Army, suspected that he was malingering. He evidently came to share that attitude, reflected in a 1932 newspaper profile describing him as having been "morbidly sensitive" and "stricken by [an] illness which was more mental than physical—a crippling of the will." The profile credited Capra's recovery to an unnamed doctor who "jerked him out of his semi-coma and sent him out job hunting again after two months of idleness and prostration."

This would not be the last time in Capra's life when a serious medical problem coincided with a crisis of the spirit. "A crippling of the will" seems an accurate description of his mental state during that uncertain period. Working as a lowly crewman on the fringes of the film business, mocked by his family and rejected by the woman he loved, he had reason to despair of his ultimate success in life.

When he had recovered enough to get out of bed and dress himself, Saridda packed him a bag of bread and sausages, put a $10 bill into the pocket of his uniform, pointed to the door, and said, "Go!"

"**I** had to stop about every twenty-five steps and sit on the curb," Capra recalled. "I was sweating like crazy. I had no idea where I was going.

"I managed to get downtown, and the red cars were going out to Van Nuys, so I thought, 'I'll go out and see my brother.' I hadn't seen Tony in a long time. So I went out to Van Nuys, and I didn't know which direction to go to find him. I walked about half a block, and I knew I couldn't just keep walking, because I was so tired. I was sitting on the curb, breathing very hard, and here comes my brother in a little truck. I yell at him and he puts on the brakes and says, 'Frank! What the hell are you doin' here?' And I said, 'Well, Mama threw me out.' "

Tony took Frank to his home at 132 Delano Street, where he lived with his second wife, Kate (born Caterina Daniele in Italy), and their infant daughter, Violet, who died of dysentery shortly after Frank moved in with them. There was no room for Frank to sleep inside, so Tony nailed a hammock to a tree alongside the house, next to the chicken yard. The chickens shared the yard with the still in which Tony made bootleg liquor.

Since his father's death, Tony had started a profitable business hiring Mexican crews to pick fruit and prune trees in fields owned by the Fernando Valley Feed Company. After a few days at Tony's, Frank decided he should help to earn his keep. He took a pair of shears and went out to help Tony's crew prune trees. The pay was twenty cents a tree. Frank earned sixty cents that day.

"Boy, it was awful hard for me just to reach up and cut. They laughed at me. As long as I felt like that, I wasn't capable of doing anything. But I was welcome at the house. Tony felt sorry for me. He would always look down on me, you know."

A bantam rooster who wore diamonds and flashy suits, Tony had nothing but scorn for the rules of polite society and no scruples about how he made money. He was taking advantage of Prohibition by getting into bootlegging in a big way. "I was the chief bootlegger," Tony bragged in his old age. He later branched out with a grocery store, a filling station, a laundry, a restaurant, and a bottling company in downtown Los Angeles. Tony claimed to have a special relationship with the police, having cut a high police official in on his bootlegging operations. He admitted to having been jailed "about five times, but I never slept there. I was always out before night."

Tony tried to interest Frank in bootlegging, figuring that Frank's scientific training would be useful in the construction of stills. Frank was tempted, but for the time being he was more interested in pursuing a new passion: writing short stories. He set up shop in a little shack behind the house, writing his stories by the light of an oil lamp in emulation of O. Henry, who had written some of his earliest stories by oil light in an Ohio prison cell.

"The Master Mind," dating from this period, is a bizarre fable about a psychic named Eloysius Spooks who attempts to conceive a child with his wife purely through the use of his mental energy. But the child that results bears an uncanny resemblance to his deformed Filipino manservant. Capra's humor is racist as well as sophomoric, but the sexual themes offer some insight into his puritanical aversion toward sex in his young manhood. Another early story, probably written at Tony's, is called "Tempus Fugit." The central character is a wealthy old man who masquerades as a blind beggar in order to observe people from a park bench in New York's Washington Square. Capra fails to involve his narrator sufficiently in the sketchy plot—which has the old man eavesdropping on two bumbling anarchists plotting to blow up another rich man's home—and his attempt at an O. Henry twist ending is inept.

Capra admitted that those stories were "a pretty amateurish lot, most of them—they were not good enough to sell," either to magazines or to the movies.

That spring of 1919, Katie brought Frank a want ad.

A young man needed a couple of months' tutoring in chemistry and math to help him gain admission to Berkeley. What appealed to Frank even more than the $300 monthly salary was that the young man was Baldwin M. Baldwin, grandson of the fabled E. J. (Lucky) Baldwin, discoverer of the Comstock Lode.

The tutor was to live with the fifteen-year-old and his divorced mother, Anita Baldwin (the former Anita Baldwin McClaughry), on their spectacular twenty-acre estate in Arcadia, just down the hill from Sierra Madre. Lucky Baldwin had named the estate the Santa Anita Rancho in tribute to his daughter, who also lent her name to the Santa Anita Race Track (then part of the estate) and the Little Santa Anita Canyon in the foothills, next to the Churchill Ranch where the Capras had lived. The little musical combo that Frank organized at Throop had performed at Mrs. Baldwin's estate. She shared Capra's love of music, and that earlier contact, made through Bob Sticht, may have helped him win the tutoring job.

The first thing Mrs. Baldwin did when he came to stay was to tell her butler, "Go buy this man three suits." Capra threw his tattered uniform into the Baldwins' incinerator, not heeding Thoreau's admonition in *Walden* to "beware of all enterprises that require new clothes."

He was able to put up with the tedium of the lessons and with young Baldwin's indolent, supercilious manner because he was so enraptured by his surroundings. Mrs. Baldwin called her fifty-room, mostly Italian Renaissance palace "Anoakia," an amalgamation of her name with that of the huge oak trees surrounding it. She later learned that Anoakia was an Indian word meaning "Where No Harm Shall Befall," a phrase Capra borrowed for Mr. Deeds's poem about his hometown of Mandrake Falls ("Where No Harm E'er Befalls"); the poem is displayed on a sign at the local train station, in a scene which Capra shot at the old Arcadia station, not far from Mrs. Baldwin's grounds.

Capra and young Baldwin had a wing of Anoakia all to themselves, with their own music room and rumpus room, and, best of all, Capra had the run of Mrs. Baldwin's library. The pride of her estate, the wood-paneled library was open to writers from all over the country. They would come for weeks to study her rare books and her beautifully bound editions of the classics. "That's where I started to read," Capra recalled in 1985; the experience intensified his desire to become a writer.

As for Capra's lovely and gracious patron, he claimed, "She fell in love with me." There can be no doubt that he, at least, fell in love with her. For the rest of his life he revered Mrs. Baldwin as "one of the most wonderful women I ever met."

She paid him the supreme compliment of letting him eat at their table, "which surprised the hell out of me." In the films he made later, Capra would reserve some of his most pointed satire for the dining rituals of the rich. For even though the Baldwins treated him with respect and without condescension, he still felt that somehow he didn't belong at their table:

"That's where I saw a lot of rich people. And I heard 'em talk. And, Christ, their talk was so inane."

He felt his differences most acutely around Mrs. Baldwin's seventeen-year-old daughter, Dextra. He found her alluring but icy, like other rich girls he had met. Capra was still a virgin at the age of twenty-two and, he insisted later, didn't know "what the hell to do with a girl." Part of Mrs. Baldwin's charge to Capra was to keep her son away from girls. "This crazy kid was so nuts over women that he couldn't think of anything else," Capra explained. "He was smart, but he'd work about five minutes and then say, 'Let's go do something.' I'd say no and he'd say yes. I'd grab him and throw him down and we'd have a wrestling match. I'd had some wrestling experience, so I held him until he yelled 'Ouch.' His mother loved that, of course. He had a great ear for music, and had I been able to stay with him another three or four months I would have turned his mind to music."*

Isabelle visited Anoakia when Capra was living there. "Being with the Baldwins he saw another way of living," she recalled. "He had better clothes when he was with the Baldwins, and somehow those people influenced him. I think that was the germ of the idea that he would like to live that way himself.

"Baldwin would pick up a girl at a hotel, buy her orchids and dinner, and go all the way. He took me over there [to Anoakia]. Frank was there too. While we were dancing, Frank said, 'You know, I could do like Baldwin does—for the money I am spending on you I could get everything I want.' I was shocked. That was so uncalled for, and terribly insulting. I thought, 'He just hates me because I'm decent.' He wouldn't have taken everything he wanted, anyway; he wanted to marry me. He could be real mean, say some real smart-alecky remarks, some cutting things. Frank has a Sicilian temperament. We just had a different way we looked at life."

During the last months of the war, Mrs. Baldwin had made the patriotic gesture of leasing some of her land, cost-free, to the Army. Two hundred acres, including the old racetrack, were pressed into service as Ross Field, the headquarters of the U.S. Army Balloon School. More than a thousand men were training on the grounds at any one time. Balloons were then in vogue for reconnaissance work, and the school remained open even after the Armistice, under Army supervision, as the United States Balloon

---

* Baldwin M. Baldwin died at age sixty-six in 1970. A hard-drinking playboy, he had been married six times and spent much of his time racing yachts. But he also was a prominent art collector and dabbled in real estate, heading a corporation which developed the Baldwin Hills Village in Los Angeles. During World War II he served as a major in the U.S. Army Air Forces in England and received several decorations for valor.

School of Arcadia. In 1930, after it had fallen into disuse, Capra used it as the location for the South Pole scenes in *Dirigible*.

Capra wanted a job to supplement his income, so young Baldwin introduced his tutor to the commanding officer of the Balloon School, who hired him as an instructor. His linguistic skills were more highly valued than his background in science and mathematics, so he taught mostly English. Baldwin chauffeured him to his classes.*

Capra said that he finished tutoring Baldwin that summer when Baldwin passed his college entrance exam, but that Mrs. Baldwin wanted him to watch over her son until he entered Berkeley for the fall term. However, Baldwin did not enter Berkeley until a year later. While it seems likely that Capra's stay with the Baldwins did occur in 1919, he was working in Reno, Nevada, by the end of that summer, and in Hollywood by the spring of 1920; he went to San Francisco by August 1920, perhaps also accompanying Baldwin to Berkeley at that time as a favor to Mrs. Baldwin.

In his book Capra misleadingly summarized this period by writing that he spent from late 1918 to late 1921 "on the 'bum' all over Arizona, Nevada, California; hopping freights, selling photos house-to-house, hustling poker, playing guitars; running, looking, sinking lower." But, in fact, he left the Baldwins to make another attempt at crashing the movie business.

Schools to train aspiring movie actors and writers were proliferating in Southern California. Some were legitimate, but many were dubious operations, in business only to soak their gullible, movie-mad students before tossing them out, jobless and disillusioned. It was perhaps during his stay at Tony's, or while he was with the Baldwins, that Capra enrolled in the Plank Scenario School. It had just been opened in Los Angeles by a former actor named W. M. Plank, described by Capra as a somewhat threadbare but still dashing figure with wavy white hair. Plank's pitch to his students was that he would not only teach them how to write and sell their scripts but that he would actually make a feature film based on one of their outpourings. He did not mention that the money for this venture was to come from the students themselves, principally from a wealthy woman named Ida May Heitmann, who, as Capra would learn, was Plank's mistress and had enrolled in the school in the fervent hope of becoming a star.

---

*The job, which Capra said lasted no more than a month or two, later was inaccurately described in some sources as a position teaching languages or math at Caltech. Capra encouraged the misconception, writing into the Army personnel record in World War II that he had been an "instructor in math at Caltech."

Still having "visions of writing some stories that you could sell," Capra had been making the rounds of the studios with his portfolio, unsuccessfully. Plank "promised everything," Capra remembered. "If you would learn how to write a very good story that could be made into a picture, the whole thing would come true. Who the hell would believe it? But you would believe a school." He saw an advertisement for the scenario school and after submitting samples of his work he not only was admitted but was offered a job as Plank's personal assistant. The student who couldn't sell his scripts soon was helping to teach others how to write and sell scripts.

Eventually Plank's grand moviemaking scheme grew to the point at which he decided to abandon the school and head for Reno to raise the rest of the money he needed to start his production company. Where else was there such an abundance of "sucker" money? The newspapers were full of get-rich-quick pitches for oil and mining operations, and those who struck it rich might easily be parted from their profits in the saloons and casinos. Hollywood studios had discovered the Reno area for its spectacular scenery and that of nearby Truckee, across the California line, which was ideal for Westerns and snow scenes. Plank may have been "just a con man," as Capra later put it, but after striking out with the Hollywood studios, he was desperate enough to try anything, and the scheme seemed crazy enough that it might work.

Capra was driving Plank's big touring car as they pulled into Reno with Ida May Heitmann in August 1919 and checked into the prestigious Overland Hotel, which charged two dollars a night and boasted "rooms equipped with tub baths and showers." Generously bankrolled by Ida May, Plank hit the casinos, and between stints at the gambling tables, he talked up his plans to potential investors and to the local newspapers. The papers described him as "a motion picture director of Los Angeles" and Ida May as a "prominent movie star from Los Angeles . . . backing the undertaking." While Plank was hustling investors, Capra learned to hustle poker. He recalled standing behind Nicholas Dandolos, the original Nick the Greek, at the poker tables, kibitzing and pumping him for technical tips. Soon Capra was good enough to make a few dollars at poker, which would serve him in a pinch whenever he was short on cash.

Capra and his partners took an office at the Fordonia Building and had impressive-looking stationery printed up listing Plank as president, Heitmann as vice president, and Frank R. Capra as secretary and treasurer of the Tri-State Motion Picture Company, a Nevada corporation which proclaimed on its letterhead that it was capitalized at $250,000, although only $1,000 of that actually was put up when the articles of incorporation were signed on September 16 ($400 from Plank and $300 each from Heitmann and Capra). An elaborate advertisement was placed in the *Reno Evening Gazette* and the *Nevada State Journal* three times between October 7 and 13 to announce the company's grandiose plans:

> *To build an up-to-date, modern Motion Picture Studio here in Reno including laboratories, etc., in which to produce motion picture stories by famous authors.*
>
> *To produce Five-reel Semi-Western Motion Pictures bearing our own trade mark.*
>
> *To build an Alaskan and a Western Village and to rent these villages to companies outside of Reno for locations, thus making the overhead expense of our studio, aside from deriving a big profit for the company.*
>
> *This company is putting on the market $50,000 worth of treasury stock at $12.50 per share, par value being $10.00. The construction of studio and laboratories will cost $20,000, and $30,000 will cover the cost of two five-reel semi-western productions. These two pictures will be the means of the company being self-supporting after their respective release.*
>
> *This company is being managed by men of long experience in the production of pictures, and its entire staff consists of trained and tried men with a thorough knowledge of the business.*

The first picture announced for shooting by Tri-State was *The Ranch of the Wolverines*, at the studio which "will probably be located on the Riley ranch on Arlington Road." The plot was not described, but it is possible that it was based on a treatment Capra wrote around this time called "Hearts and Bronchs [*sic*]," a comedy-romance about a ranch waitress who temporarily loses her head over the handsome and arrogant star of a visiting rodeo troupe and spurns her easygoing cowboy fiancé until the cowpunchers run the rodeo fakers out of town. Despite its trite framework, the story has some of the warmth Capra would later bring to his films about small-town people and their romantic dreams. In the waitress's conflict over her true allegiance—with ordinary people or with the big-time phonies (here identified, revealingly, with show business itself)—Capra is roughing out a formula that he would continue to develop throughout his career.

*   *   *

Isabelle also remembered hearing of a "play" Capra and his partners were preparing to stage in Reno. A fragment exists of a stage play Capra wrote around this time, *Don't Change Your Husbands*. It was an awkward attempt at a comedy about an unscrupulous divorce lawyer who habitually seduces his female clients but is forced to reform after being caught trying to bed the wife of his ranch foreman—a subject obviously inspired by the Reno setting, and one that might as well have been planned as a Tri-State film. Capra later used it as the uncredited source of a short comedy he wrote for Mack Sennett in 1924, *A Wild Goose Chaser*.

The Overland Hotel was crawling with what Capra called "loose women" waiting the required two months to obtain Nevada divorces. "All of them were easy pickups," he recalled, "because they had nothing else to do." As he told the story in 1985, he began to cast a knowing eye toward one of those women, whose name he did not remember. She had a sick dog, and he knew that "dogs are the best way to meet women." He offered to take her dog to the veterinarian. When he brought it back, she repaid him by inviting him for dinner, and they wound up in her bed.

Capra wrote to Isabelle about the experience. The letter has been lost, but she remembered what it said: "He started the letter by saying he knew he would be successful, he had a premonition he would be a success, and he wanted me to share it with him. Then he went on to tell me about an affair he had with an actress. He was still a virgin and she led him on; she heard he was a virgin and she wanted to take care of it for him. It was a cut-and-dried sexual thing. He said that nothing could stop him once he got started. He was so excited he had to tell me about it. Maybe he thought it would make me jealous."

The letter was intercepted and opened by her parents. Although Capra personally described the experience to her in 1920, she did not read the letter until many years later, after her parents' deaths, when her brother gave it to her. All she knew at the time was that her father was furious with Capra: "My father asked what kind of relationship Frank had with me. He told me to tell Frank if he did come around he'd shoot him. I don't know if I ever told him. I didn't want to hurt him."

Although Capra described Ida May Heitmann as a "beautiful gal," he said it was not she he slept with. Also present in Reno that fall was Ann Austin, a stage and film actress Tri-State hired in September to play the lead in its first two films. Austin, while in Reno, was accused by her husband of having an affair with "the director of the company." She filed for divorce on the grounds of "extreme cruelty," denying her husband's "imputation of unchastity." The uncontested divorce was granted on December 1, in the same week Tri-State began shooting its first picture, without Ann Austin, who was replaced by Peggy Lawson.

The Pulse of Life—evidently directed by Plank, with a cast that also included W. Montgomery, Denison Standing, and one "Frank Russell"—was rushed into production to capitalize on an unexpected blizzard that dropped twenty-six inches of snow on Reno between the first and third of December. After location work was completed in the area, interiors were shot at the glass-enclosed studio of the California Motion Picture Corporation near San Rafael in Marin County, California. Filming was completed by mid-January, but the company ran into more financial difficulties during postproduction.

Capra wrote Isabelle from Reno on February 28 to bemoan the string of misfortunes he had been experiencing in the last few months, even as he had been hoping to make his fortune. The negative of *The Pulse of Life* was being held by the lab because of a $2,000 bill Tri-State couldn't pay. Worse, the company had been dealing with some unsavory characters, and he even wondered if he might wind up in jail. His emaciated and disheveled appearance echoed his anxiety.

Somehow *The Pulse of Life* was finished, and after being previewed for about fifty invited guests on April 1, 1920, it opened on April 25 at Reno's Grand Theater for a three-day run. Apparently it never was shown publicly again, vanishing into the limbo of unreleased films. Virtually all that is known about it is what was written at the time by the anonymous reviewers in the Reno papers, who concentrated on details of local color but neglected to describe the plot. The *State Journal* commented, "The picture is in six reels and is of great photographic merit, aside from its interest as a film story. The wonderful scenery round about Reno shows up to its best advantage, the big mountains in the west and the Truckee River looking especially well, while many of Reno's fine homes and hotels were shown."

Judging from the title and the details in the newspapers, it is likely that *The Pulse of Life* was the film version of Capra's screen treatment "Heart Beats," his semi-autobiographical tale of Dr. Larry Doyle, who fights his way from poverty to fame as a heart specialist but almost ends up a despairing failure, nightmarishly falling into a pauper's grave—a fitting subject, indeed, for Capra's debut as a screenwriter, with its foreshadowing of *It's a Wonderful Life* and its evocations of the violent swings between success and failure that would mark his own life. His possible presence in the cast, under the pseudonym of "Frank Russell," also would point to the unusually personal nature of the project, even if Capra may have been reluctant to use his last name (a 1941 publicity biography of Capra listed "actor" among the jobs he had in films before becoming a director).

According to an item in *Variety* on January 13, 1920, Plank said that Tri-State recently had completed both *The Pulse of Life* and a five-reel feature called *The Scar of Love*, also starring Peggy Lawson. There were no mentions of the other film in the Reno papers, however, and the author could find no evidence of its being released. Plank may have been engaging in some wishful ballyhoo, but it is possible that the film was made— perhaps it was "Hearts and Bronchs" or *Don't Change Your Husbands* under a different title.

Capra's failure to acknowledge the Reno adventure in his autobiography may have been a measure of the depth of his disappointment over its failure. His 1946 publicity biography dealt with it cryptically, but left no doubt of how it affected him: "His first experiences in Hollywood [*sic*] were a series of disasters with independent producers whose picture projects failed."

Capra returned to Pasadena to see Isabelle, who "just thought my father was wrong, it didn't make any sense to me, so I went out with Frank again." As they rode in the back seat of her brother's car, Capra began reminiscing about his sexual experience in Reno, which he apparently thought she knew about from his letter, and she broke into tears.

"It just knocked me over," she remembered. "I didn't hold it against him, because I thought maybe it was time. I just thought it was so terrible that Frank had lost his virginity, and I was kinda sad that it had happened without any love."

She told Capra that she loved Bob Griffis and that they were engaged to be married. "It seemed to be a terrible blow. He acted very sad. He stood outside the house for a long, long time, standing there looking at the bedroom window."

Capra next found work with a new movie company that was scrabbling for a toehold on the fringes of Hollywood. The job brought him under the employment of a man who later would become his most important patron in Hollywood: Harry Cohn.

The CBC (for Cohn, Brandt, Cohn) Film Sales Company, in which Harry was partnered with his brother, Jack, and Joe Brandt, had been launched in New York with a $100,000 loan from A. H. (Doc) Giannini, head of motion picture lending for his brother A. P.'s Bank of Italy. CBC's first release in July 1919 was a two-reel comedy series called *The Hall Room Boys*, based on H. A. McGill's comic strip about two bums (Neeley Edwards and Edward Flanagan) bluffing their way into high society. When CBC ran into financial problems, William Horsley, who also backed the

Christies, took over the financing of the series. CBC branched out in early 1920 with a series devised by Jack Cohn, *Screen Snapshots*, which was coproduced by former newspaperman Louis Lewyn. Briskly edited, light-hearted newsreels about "stars at work and play . . . a fan magazine on film," the series was an immediate success when the first one-reeler was issued in April 1920.

Although Capra made no mention of *Screen Snapshots* in his autobiography, Columbia publicity material in the 1930s mentioned that Capra had worked on the series, and the 1968 biographical notes distributed by Capra's publicists said that "Harry Cohn hired him at $20 a week to make *Screen Snapshots*." Capra acknowledged to the author that he worked on the series. He probably did not work for CBC longer than four or five months, between March and August of 1920, perhaps on as many as six or seven issues (he also may have worked on *The Hall Room Boys* as an assistant to director Al Santell).

Philip K. Scheuer wrote in a 1938 *Los Angeles Times* profile of Capra that he "directed the first *Screen Snapshots*," and other printed sources also claimed that Capra had been the director or codirector of the series. The most he later would admit doing on *Screen Snapshots* was assisting Lewyn and editing some of the film, but given the impromptu nature of the shooting, he probably did have some directing responsibilities. After he went to San Francisco later that year, he listed himself in the city directory for 1921 as "Capra Frank R mov pic director."

Screen Snapshots was a quick learning experience for Capra, giving him entrée into the major studios and allowing him to observe the working methods of top actors and directors. The first issue, for example, featured scenes of the destruction of the Babylon set used in D. W. Griffith's *Intolerance*, a dance by Alla Nazimova, director Edwin Carewe at work, and demonstrations of the contrasting romantic styles of leading men Charles Ray and Sessue Hayakawa. Subsequent issues featured such stars as Fatty Arbuckle, Viola Dana, and Bessie Love, and such directors as Marshall Neilan and Maurice Tourneur. No doubt his involvement on *Screen Snapshots* helped Capra acquire the veneer of knowledgeability and confidence he needed when he directed his first dramatic film the following year.

Though Capra's book implies that he arrived in San Francisco around December 1921, he was there by August 1920, an ideal time for a young man trying to make a name in the movie business.

The years between 1920 and 1924 saw the last intense flowering of the

Bay Area's attempt to establish itself as a major competitor of Hollywood. Filmmakers had been attracted to the area from the early days of silent pictures, but San Francisco companies never had been able to secure the capital necessary to build an ongoing local industry. Nevertheless, the Bay Area's spectacular and varied scenery and the cosmopolitan atmosphere of San Francisco itself continued to be powerful incentives. Hollywood film-makers continued to come there for location work, and there were a number of thriving independent companies in the area as well.

Those companies typically were maverick outfits receptive to fresh new talents. And a little movie experience in Hollywood and Reno didn't hurt Capra in looking for a job. San Francisco would serve as a back door to Hollywood for the impatient young man whose efforts in the film business up to now had netted him little satisfaction or promise of future success. But even the back door would not open immediately.

Shortly after arriving in San Francisco, he received a cheery letter from Isabelle, which moved him to tears. Replying to her in the early-morning hours, while two roommates were carrying on within earshot with a pair of married women, he made no secret of his despair. The future seemed purposeless; he felt abandoned by his family; he was unable to romance another woman without thinking of her. He professed his love again, but without any expectation that it would be reciprocated.

Soon after that, he recalled, "I met somehow, somewhere, a woman that liked to give parties. She had a lot of girls and she gave a big party and invited me. This party was for a girl who had just come back from Hono-lulu. I started dancing with her and I thought she wouldn't mind, so I says, 'Whaddya say?' and we danced out of the room, down the hall, and into the bedroom.

"A couple days later, my pecker began to itch."

Capra then was living downtown in a six-dollar-a-week room at the Hotel Eddy, and he had made friends with a young pharmacist who worked in a drugstore near the hotel. The pharmacist directed him to a clap shack not far from the elegant St. Francis Hotel on Union Square. It was run by a Scotsman who called himself a doctor but was actually a quack, though Capra did not realize that until it was too late.

Capra went there regularly for an excruciatingly painful treatment. While he sat in the waiting room, he was impressed by the democratizing effect of the clap: "I was not alone—there were rich men, poor men, streetcar conductors, guys that swept streets, men who talked only about stocks, every goddamn kind—and each with his pecker in his hand."

* * *

To support himself during those first desperate months in San Francisco, Capra became "a migratory small-time racketeer . . . a tin-horn gambler and petty financial pirate," Alva Johnston wrote in his 1938 *Saturday Evening Post* profile, "Capra Shoots as He Pleases." The embarrassed Capra told *Time* magazine shortly after Johnston's piece appeared that the story of those escapades was a "legend," but he admitted to the author of this book that the account was accurate.

The job he claimed occupied most of his time during the three years between late 1918 and late 1921 probably kept him busy only intermittently in 1920 and 1921. He met a footloose young Irishman named Frank Dwyer and they rode the rails in the farming valleys of central California. Whenever Dwyer needed money, he would stop in a town and go door-to-door selling coupons for Hartsook Photographs. He would make a dollar each time he persuaded a housewife to take her children to the nearest Hartsook studio and have their portraits taken. Dwyer taught the routine to Capra. And he advised Capra to keep his good suit in a traveling bag while riding in boxcars so that when he was ringing doorbells he would look presentable. In two days, each of them could make ten or twelve dollars, enough to live for the rest of the week. Then Dwyer would look up girls he knew. The amiable drifter seemed to know a telephone operator in every town who would spread the word that he and his buddy Capra were in town. The girls would cook them a meal and throw a party, with the two Franks taking turns serenading them on a ukelele.

"Got a real sense of small towns, got a real sense of America," Capra said of this period. "I found out a lot about Americans. I loved them. . . . I met the farmers, the people, the people who were working and not complaining. It was a great experience. I met a lot of Gary Coopers."

Capra also found a roving commission as a salesman of Elbert Hubbard books. Hubbard's cracker-barrel philosophy and middlebrow cultural pretensions had lost none of their popularity since the author had gone down on the *Lusitania* in 1915. His printing company, The Roycrofters of East Aurora, New York, kept cranking out deluxe fourteen-volume sets of his *Little Journeys to the Homes of the Great*, inspirational accounts of the lives of famous people throughout history.

"Oddly enough, they're great books," Capra claimed, remaining true to his salesman's calling more than sixty years later. "He's not Shakespeare, but they're likable books, and they're about people."

Since the Memorial Edition sold for $120 per set, Hubbard salesmen pitched them only to the prosperous, mainly through office visits to doctors, dentists, lawyers, and others who might be willing to pay that much to display a veneer of culture. For each sale the drummer would pocket $30. Capra averaged a sale every ten days.

He learned the sales pitch from a carny man he had met on his wanderings. Based on Hubbard's own writings, it was a simple but effective con requiring a knack for manipulating people's emotions, as well as a cynical contempt for the emotions evoked by the pitch.

Before Capra would hit a certain town, the Hubbard company would mail cards to potential buyers notifying them that he would be coming to call. The cards did not indicate why he would be calling, nor that he was a salesman. They merely would state that the company would be much obliged if the recipient would hear what Mr. Capra had to say. "They were written very poorly," Capra added. "The very crudeness of it would keep it in these people's minds. So when you showed up they knew who you were."

Unlike his job selling Hartsook Photographs, being a Hubbard salesman required Capra to wear shabby clothes and appear to be a rube.

"The idea was to be completely ignorant of the world, to be so naive, a shy, scared little guy," Capra explained. "You didn't have anything in your hands—you'd put one of the books down the back of your pants and cover it up with your coat. When the guy would call you into his office, you'd look around and marvel at the things he had in his superb office. You'd be so impressed that you wouldn't know what chair to sit on. If the guy got a smell—from even a word—that you were a bookseller, he'd throw you out on your ear."

Then Capra would make his pitch, telling his heart-tugging story: "When I was seven years old, my father and mother died in an accident. And the writer, Mr. Hubbard, came by on a horse and saw me crying. He asked me what was the matter. I said, 'Oh, my father and mother just got killed and I don't know what to do.' 'Well, young man,' he said, 'you just come up here on the back of my horse.' And he took me to this house where they made these books. He took me in and I've been working there ever since.

"He was a great man, this Mr. Hubbard. He saved my life and lots of other lives. We made a series of books in his name and offered them to the public. I don't know how to sell things. I don't know how to tell you about them, but that's what I'm trying to do. I've never been out of the factory before. I want to get back there as soon as I can because I get kind of lost in the city, and I don't know what I'm saying."

Finally, the doctor or lawyer "would get tired of this crap" and ask to see one of the books. Capra would pull it out of his pants and tell him in his most earnest manner, "These are the books that we made with our hearts and our hands. Mr. Hubbard went to all the houses of these great people and wrote about them."

"How much did you say these were?" the doctor or lawyer would ask, and Capra knew he had found another sucker.

Mining stock was Capra's next promotion. The stock was "phony," as Capra later admitted. All there was to show the customers was a glittering sixty-pound rock. Capra's boss was a big Texan who wore flashy clothes, boots, and a broad-brimmed cowboy hat. He ran the operation out of a San Francisco storefront, with Capra and another young man as traveling salesmen.

"Most of their customers were farmers," Johnston reported in his *Post* article. "They always opened the conversation with a farmer by telling him that he had been 'recommended.' Who had recommended him? The answer was always the name of the biggest man in the locality."

While Capra was making his spiel and displaying the sixty-pound rock, he would pick up the rock and hand it to the farmer.

"When the sharp edges were getting painful and the farmer started to put the rock down, Frank would explain, 'Look. Did you notice these pyrites?' As the sharp edges bit deeper and deeper into the customer's hands, the pyrites were examined and their fabulous value explained. The next step was that of inducing the farmer to turn the rock bottomside up in search of platinum. At this point the sucker, in order to save himself from further punishment, was expected to say: 'It looks good to me. I'll sign right now.' . . .

"Capra was only in his early twenties when he was in this racket. He and his partners justified themselves on two grounds. The first was that, after all, the stock might turn out to be worth millions, as some despised securities had done. The second and sounder argument was that, if they did not take the money from suckers, somebody else would."

By this time Capra's stubborn case of gonorrhea had finally gone away. He was jubilant. "The first thing I did, I went to grab some gal I knew and I did it. And here it comes—another dose of clap."

The treatment didn't take as long this time, but the doctor had a suggestion to prevent another recurrence: "What you need is to be circumcised." Capra remembered telling his pharmacist friend, "This guy wants to make a Jew out of me." He finally agreed to undergo the treatment. On a Sunday morning he lay across a table in the makeshift operating room.

As Capra remembered it in 1985, "He gave me a little shot of something, and then he opened my legs and operated on me. He never knew when to stop. He took too much. The son of a bitch cut everything off. He left me with no skin at all. He put a rag around it, a bandage, and I went home walking all hunched over. It hurt like hell. It finally healed up, but it's never been that well. It's still irritable and awfully tender. I've had a hell of a time with it all my life. Well, that finished women for me. Because every time I came close to a woman I got a hard-on, and then, oh God, all the pain, because it was tied tightly. I'd go out with a girl and start dancing with her, and I'd start getting an erection, with absolutely horrible pain. The girl wouldn't know what the hell's the matter. I had to stay away from dames. It practically wrecked my life.

"I've been scared of women since then. I became a lousy lay, I'll tell you. I've had very few women. I've been afraid of that—I've been ashamed of it more than afraid of it. I've had a hell of a time holding back with women. I just go in and bang bang bang—there it goes, I can't hold it back. No woman likes to be fondled and then have somebody squirt all over her. She wants time to do it, too.

"I told my [second] wife [Lucille] about it before I married her. I told her exactly what would happen: 'Just as soon as I touch you, I'll have an erection. There's nothing to hold it back.' We worked it out. She was wonderful, and she was a great help. But it was not pretty. I went to a lot of doctors about it, and I finally learned how to do it and hold back, but it was a job. It took a lot of brainwork. I had to think of everything else for a while. God, it just wrecked me."

Perhaps Capra's account should not be taken at face value, any more than his simultaneous claim in 1985, shortly before his eighty-eighth birthday, that he still was sexually potent. Given his habitual reticence on sexual matters, his volunteering such intimate and embarrassing details could have been a ploy designed to deflect attention from some other kind of sexual dysfunction. Capra's sexual wound may have been as much a psychological trauma as a physical one, and his story about the circumcision, with its horrific suggestion of near-castration, may have been part fact and part metaphor. The sexual problems he experienced with both his wives—and the largely chaste love relationships in his films—tend to suggest that such may have been the case. Given his claims of homosexual molestations in childhood, the abuse he suffered from his mother, and his anguish over Isabelle, it hardly would be surprising.

As Capra later told the story, he was broke and wondering how he could raise his rent money without further recourse to the increasingly dodgy mining stock racket when he was visited by a Los Angeles bootlegger and boyhood acquaintance named "Tuffy." Knowing of Capra's (supposed) degree in chemical engineering, Tuffy offered him $20,000 to make illegal stills. Capra was mightily tempted, but he had to resist because "I'd never get away from them—I knew, I'm a Sicilian." Though there was a hoodlum named Tuffy whom Frank had known as a boy, when Frank's book appeared with the account of that meeting, Tony Capra told his wife that *he*, not Tuffy, was the one Frank was writing about, and that he had gone to San Francisco to bail his brother out of trouble.

In a 1935 profile of Frank Capra for *Collier's* magazine, John Stuart wrote, "Somewhat awed now in the midst of his success, the little wop has been known to say he had a close call from becoming a gangster and racketeer, when he recalls those rough, hard days." Capra had to get into another line of work, but his options were limited because, as Alva Johnston put it, "He had been connected with wildcat promotions too long to handle anything legitimate."

The Name Above the Title tells how precisely at this moment the providential news appeared in the paper about a new motion picture studio opening near Golden Gate Park, how the neophyte Capra barged in, brashly announcing "I'm from Hollywood," and conned an old actor-producer named Walter Montague into letting him direct a film; how he planned to abscond to Reno with the advance money, but was seized with an unexpected enthusiasm for the new medium, and went through with the mad endeavor, bluffing all the way.

Capra claimed it was through a "column" in the newspaper that he found his job as the director of *Fulta Fisher's Boarding House*. As he recalled on *This Is Your Life* in 1959, "It said a motion picture was—motion pictures were going to be made at Golden Gate Park." The column he quotes in his book was an invention, but on December 8, 1920, a brief article appeared in the *Chronicle* under the headline, "Movie Concern to Open Studios in San Francisco." It told of a "new" studio being opened by Columbia Features (no relation to the Columbia Pictures for which Capra later worked) half a block from Golden Gate Park at 1974 Page Street by a producer from Los Angeles, R. C. P. Smith, an associate of William Horsley. Smith was "registering applicants" for a feature film project, *Cinders*, starring Zasu Pitts, on which "as many as 800 people" would be needed. The article probably was what led Capra to Walter Montague, who also was getting ready to make films at the Page Street rental studio, which first was used for filmmaking in 1919.

Capra later liked to pretend that he took the job only for the money, but there was no mistaking the creative ambition of the young man who directed *Fulta Fisher's Boarding House*.

Montague could see through Frank Capra's sharpster's veneer to recognize the earnest college student who had written about his exalted vision of the future of film. They were kindred spirits in hope and frustration, this forty-seven-year-old Shakespearean actor and playwright from Kent (son of Major and Lady Montague Williams) who had been reduced to writing and starring in vaudeville playlets, and the young would-be O. Henry and failed chemical engineer who had been wasting his creativity in sales pitches to suckers. By now Capra was familiar with Montague's type: a newspaper story in 1916 said that Montague was "taking a limited number of pupils—adults only—guaranteeing them an engagement at the end of the course." Montague, Capra told the author, "had something to do with" W. M. Plank. There was yet another connection which helped him get the job: Capra told Chet Sticht that the newsreel cameraman he had assisted at Mount Wilson, Roy Wiggins, who was hired to photograph *Fulta*, recommended him to Montague.

Capra and Montague came together in a visionary, if slightly daft, scheme to make film equivalents of famous poems for a company called Fireside Productions. After filming Rudyard Kipling's 1886 poem about the stabbing of a Danish sailor in a Calcutta grog shop, "The Ballad of Fisher's Boarding-House," they intended to film Whittier's "The Barefoot Boy," Longfellow's "The Village Blacksmith," and Rose Hartwick Thorpe's " 'Curfew Must Not Ring Tonight' " (a tale of a maiden saving her lover from execution in seventeenth-century England), as well as Capra's script of "The Looking Glass," from a story credited to one F. B. Lowe. The filmed poetry idea was a kind of artistic shotgun marriage—an exercise in pseudoculture of the sort that Vladimir Nabokov later would dub "*poshlust*"—but in those days when the movies generally were regarded as a lowbrow amusement for subliterates, putting Kipling or Whittier on the screen in the most literal manner was an aesthetic mission to Montague and Capra, a means of elevating motion pictures to an art form worthy of their high ideals and ambition.

Capra was given a budget of $1,700 for the one-reeler, with a salary of $75 a week. Montague had raised the principal funding from a local investor named David F. Supple, a real estate man and prominent civic benefactor whom Capra never met. Supple also agreed to finance the next four pictures in the Fireside series.

Because of his and Capra's inexperience, Montague brought another man into the production, a theatrical promoter named George F. (Doc) Harris. Harris had the show business expertise and contacts needed to organize the filming and keep it within the budget. He also took charge of the building of the single interior set on which the entire film was made.

With his training from Manual Arts and Throop, Capra was able to help with the design, and he and the producer soon became fast friends.

Because of his own insecurity, Capra decided to cast only actors who had never appeared in films. That way, he reasoned, they would not realize how little he knew. They also would act for peanuts, an equally important consideration.

Capra's first notion for casting his central character, a whore called Anne of Austria, was to go out and find a real Barbary Coast whore. The first one he approached scoffed at the meager wage he offered. Wiggins suggested a chorus girl he knew named Mildred Owens, who was appearing with *King's Queens and Jokers* at Loew's Casino. When Capra talked to her after the show, he was sure she would be perfect as his first leading lady because "she was too dumb to know what I was doing."

She also had the faded, brassy exterior the part demanded. Rather than softening or glamorizing the character, he cast a woman who looked as if she could have lived the kind of part she was playing, just as he would do with the relatively unglamorous leading ladies he favored in his mature work, such as Barbara Stanwyck, who also came from a rough background in the chorus, and Jean Arthur, so utterly credible as a working girl who'd been kicked around.

Most of *Fulta*'s cast were hungry, unemployed, or retired stage performers (from an old actors' home) who had the right "down-and-out" appearance. Some of the atmosphere players were bums he and Wiggins recruited from waterfront dives. Their happiest discovery was a one-eared sailor for the character called Jake-Without-the-Ears.

But when shooting started, "Capra's earnestness nearly spoiled everything," Alva Johnston reported. "His intensity made people afraid of him. At the sight of him, they stiffened up as if in the presence of DeMille or Griffith. He had to counteract this by reassuming the democratic joviality which he formerly used on farmers and villagers before talking them out of money. He coaxed his actors into talking, and roared at their jokes. . . .

"Capra did not, however, have to fake an intense preoccupation with his work. He had, in fact, gone movie-mad. . . . He couldn't sleep for excitement."

Fulta Fisher's Boarding House is peopled with lowlifes, ruffians, and whores, the level of humanity on which Capra often had found himself in the past four years. But his acquired, self-protective cynicism had not obliterated his stubborn streak of romanticism. Nor had his rebellion against the discipline of the Catholic church and his skepticism about its doctrines destroyed his instinctive, almost mystical attachment to the

Christian ethic. The heroine of *Fulta,* in Capra's reworking of Kipling, is a Mary Magdalene figure, brazen and fickle, who nevertheless is transfigured by Christian redemption, filmed luminously at the end "as if she was inspired by heaven."

The characters and setting of the poem are introduced with lines of verse superimposed over stylized tableaus, composed and lit in a rather pretentious painterly style that Capra foreshadowed in his college paper, yet with a degree of sophistication that belies his later protestations of cinematic naiveté. Capra's narrative style is fast-paced and elliptical, his direction of actors broad but balletic, minimizing the obvious deficiencies of his spartan set and his grab-bag cast.

In his intensely romantic mood after filming *Fulta,* Capra made one last attempt to win over Isabelle. On August 24, 1921, from his room at the Hotel Robins on Post Street, Capra wrote an eloquent nine-page plea for her love, comparing himself—in terms of devotion, ambition, and ability to conquer misfortune—to Homer's Ulysses and to Joseph Conrad in his days as a young seaman.

Spelling out candidly for Isabelle his intense erotic desire, Capra declared that he now intended to become the master of his destiny, rather than a passive participant in life. In case she hadn't guessed his true intentions before, he planned to make a formal proposal of marriage on their next meeting, one he knew she would accept.

Despite his obvious drawbacks of social status and appearance, and his uncharacteristic moment of sexual weakness in Reno that hurt her so badly, he wrote, he could assure her of his lifelong fidelity and an illustrious future with her as his partner, once she rid herself of that interloper Bob Griffis. She, Isabelle Daniels, was the woman of Frank Capra's lifetime.

Two months later, on October 23, 1921, in Pasadena, she married Bob Griffis.

Capra edited *Fulta Fisher's Boarding House* that summer under the guidance of Waldon S. (Walt) Ball, a cigar-chewing bachelor from Kansas who loved to tell dirty jokes as he processed film and tinkered with inventions in his small photographic laboratory at 290 Turk Street. The one-man lab processed mostly newsreel, industrial, and amateur film, but it occasionally also did work for local theatrical film producers and for visiting Hollywood companies.

Capra's finished film was shown to a local representative of the Pathé

Exchange, a nationwide distributor based in New York, which bought it for $3,500, more than doubling the initial investment. The film opened on April 2, 1922, at the Strand Theater on Broadway, playing for one week with five other shorts on a program headed by Charlie Chaplin's featurette *Pay Day*.

According to Doc Harris, *Fulta* "played all the big houses" and was regarded as "more or less of an epic." Laurence Reid wrote in *Motion Picture News* that it was "stirring at all times and unusually rich in characterization . . . a masterpiece of realism, carrying dramatic value and a spiritual flavor." *The New York Times* said that it "consists of faithful and vivid illustrations of the poem, with, however, an energetically sentimental ending which surely Kipling never dreamed of."

Capra always had a sentimental spot for *Fulta*. He retrieved a print from Ball in the 1930s and carefully preserved it, eventually donating it to the Library of Congress. He sometimes showed it to his friends, and when interviewed for a *New Yorker* profile in 1940, he commented, "It's a very melodramatic thing—not bad at all."

Capra claimed that Montague was ready to let him go on to shoot *The Village Blacksmith*, but that he resigned because of a guilty conscience. He said he confessed to Montague that he had conned him to get the job, and declared that "I didn't want to make any more pictures until I knew what the hell I was doing. I had my mind on becoming a star, but though I didn't do so badly with the first one, I certainly wasn't ready to direct pictures."

Johnston's 1938 account in his *Saturday Evening Post* profile (probably taken from Capra, since Montague died in 1924) told it another way: after *Fulta*, Montague "became difficult. He objected to going to the classics. 'It isn't necessary,' he said. 'I'll write the poems myself.' Capra argued that the original plan of using the famous poems of famous authors was better. Montague thought otherwise. He had written a ballad about an ill-fated Chinese girl and insisted that it should be the Montague company's next production. Capra resigned. The ballad of the Chinese maiden was filmed. Pathé rejected it. A third film was made and rejected. Then the Montague concern busted."

However, Warner Bros.' 1941 biography of Capra states that after *Fulta*, "He made two or three more short features for Montague." Capra's papers include his highly detailed shooting scripts for *The Looking Glass*, dated 1921—undoubtedly the "ballad of the Chinese maiden" to which Johnston referred, though he misdescribed the plot—and *The Barefoot Boy*, dated September 1921.

The Barefoot Boy script romanticizes a boy's life in rural America with overheated imagery in undramatized tableaus reflecting a longing in Capra for his lost boyhood paradise in Sicily and its brief reflowering in Sierra Madre (he indicates that certain nature shots were to be filmed in the two-strip Prizma Color process). *The Looking Glass* takes a satirical but affectionate tone toward its rustic characters, who are Chinese of the late eighteenth century. This charming vignette tells of the first mirror introduced by a traveling peddler into a peasant village and the social disruption resulting from the simple folks' discovery of vanity and self-consciousness. Capra lightly conveys some of the shock he felt at having been uprooted from a primitive life and thrown uncomprehending into an industrialized society far more advanced than the one he left behind—advanced in knowledge, but not in spirit—a theme to which he would return in such films as *Mr. Deeds Goes to Town* and *Mr. Smith Goes to Washington*. The script also points to classic Capra in its emphasis on what later would be called women's liberation, and on the sexual backwardness of the central male character, the young farmer Sam Sing.

The Village Blacksmith, whose script does not survive, evidently was given a brief release by another company. A short subject of that title (not to be confused with a feature version directed by John Ford and released later that year) was reviewed by *The New York Times* on June 5, 1922: "Also at the Cameo is an impudent film called *The Village Blacksmith*, which not only takes the name of Longfellow's poem but definitely quotes it in places, and then introduces a lot of extraneous matter which Longfellow would never have been guilty of. It is cheaply sentimental, and, among other things, turns the blacksmith into an automobile mechanic!"

When Capra made the rounds of the small film companies that had been springing up in San Francisco, he found that having directed the shorts for Montague did not qualify him as a director.

Nor was there any demand for the feature-length scenarios he was writing on "spec," including *The Child-Woman*, a melodrama about the reformation of a petty crook as a result of his rescue of a suicidal amnesiac woman, and *The Boneyard of the Sea*, a formulaic tale of rum-running set among the abandoned ships of the Oakland estuary. The most "Capraesque" of those early writing efforts was *The Eternal Will*, about an embittered Shakespearean actor living in obscurity in the High Sierras who serves as the local storekeeper, doctor, and minister. The character's quasi-incestuous love for his daughter leads him to shoot her lover, but his basic decency makes him step into his role as a physician to save the young man, and the townsfolk gather in a surprise celebration to express their gratitude. Though Capra was inhibited by the lack of opportunities for humor in these melodramatic plots, with *The Eternal Will*, as with *The Looking Glass*, he was struggling toward the themes of his maturity.

"Living on peanuts," Capra offered his services to Walt Ball, reminding Ball of his scientific training. Ball felt that Capra "already had plenty of know-how," but he told Capra he didn't need an assistant and couldn't afford one anyway.

"I demanded and pleaded," Capra recalled. "I told him, 'I want to learn. I learn fast. I'll help you do your job. You can tell me what to do. I can make your soup [developing mixture] for you, I can do a lot of things.' I practically forced myself on him."

He had gone to the right man to learn. Walt Ball had been involved with motion pictures since 1901, when he ran the projector for Thomas L. Tally's pioneering theater in downtown Los Angeles. After opening his lab in San Francisco around 1912, he invented several new kinds of cameras, including a color wheel camera for Prizma and a slow-motion camera, and he built the printer he used in his own laboratory.

As Walt Ball's assistant, Capra worked intermittently winding film racks and processing film. He learned the mechanics of motion pictures from the inside out, and he acquired an intimate, hands-on knowledge of film itself that would prove invaluable in his directing career, enabling him to talk the language of his technicians: "I could handle negatives. I could make the print. I could cut the print. I found out everything about a laboratory."

But Capra barely made enough to survive. He took his meals at a delicatessen on Powell Street run by "a wonderful man—*Jewish*, by God— who was kind of a philanthropist." The man had a soft heart for people down on their luck, serving good food and not charging much for it. Capra was grateful but "a little bit ashamed" to take what he felt amounted to charity.

To pick up spending money, Capra made a deal with Ball to let him do night work at two dollars an hour. In addition to handling the overflow from feature and newsreel filmmakers, Capra developed a profitable and instructive sideline editing industrial and amateur films. A Berkeley professor hired him to edit his home movie of his daughter's pet in a dog show; a botanist at the school hired Capra to come to the campus each night for a month to take single-frame shots of a flower growing for a time-lapse film. "I did an awful lot of little one-shot things like that," he said.*

---

*Capra also was hired by a group of businessmen to write titles for a scenic documentary promoting San Francisco. He was to receive fifty dollars for the job. But he recalled that after he

*   *   *

The most ambitious of Capra's "little one-shot things" was a short documentary film he directed on November 6 and 7, 1921, sponsored by the Italian Virtus Club in San Francisco to commemorate the two-week visit of the Italian naval cruiser *Libia*, then on a world tour. Although forgotten today, it was the first film Capra directed that received a public exhibition.

Patriotic sentiment ran high among Italians in the Bay Area over the ship's visit, for it had been the first to fire a shot for Italy in the Great War and had participated in many other important engagements against Austria. Capra filmed the welcoming festivities: the *Libia*'s arrival in the harbor, flying the Stars and Stripes and being greeted by dignitaries and a surging, singing, flag-waving crowd of 1,500; a dinner and ball held by the Italian Chamber of Commerce at the Fior d'Italia restaurant; and "an automobile tour through the Italian colony," a parade headed by the ship's commander, Admiral Ernesto Burzagli, and an actress named Dorothy Valerga. As Dorothy Revier, she would be the blond leading lady of two of Capra's films for Columbia Pictures, *Submarine* (1928) and *The Donovan Affair* (1929); she also served as the model for Columbia's trademark "Torch Lady," a glamorized Hollywood equivalent of the Statue of Liberty.

Giulio DeMoro, a playwright and journalist who helped Capra with the titles of the *Libia* documentary, recalled, "It was a magnificent spectacle. I remember the first part perfectly—the boats of the Italian fishermen of San Francisco leaving Fisherman's Wharf . . . in a colorful forest of flags, and escorting the big ship into the harbor, with cannons firing and all the ships' whistles blowing. The whole thing was a masterpiece. Capra's professionalism on this occasion was one of the first proofs of his brilliance as a filmmaker."

The film was shown at the People's Theater on Broadway on December 3, the day before the cruiser sailed from San Francisco; it beat *Fulta Fisher's Boarding House* to the screen by four months, but Capra had the misfortune to see it premiered on the day the French war hero Marshal Ferdinand Foch came to town, parading before 100,000 people on Market Street. The newspapers also were preoccupied with jury deliberations in the Fatty Arbuckle case, and there was not a single mention of the *Libia* film in the three major papers.

*   *   *

wrote the titles, the businessmen decided the film was no good and refused to pay him. He filed a small claims suit on October 5, 1921, against Charles A. Warren, an investment banker and real estate man, to recover his unpaid salary, a suit Capra said was successful, although the court records no longer exist.

Although Capra would not admit it, he owed his next major break in his film career to a young actress named Helen Howell, whom he married in San Francisco.

"When he was up in San Francisco," said Josie Campisi, "he was so desperate I don't think he knew what love was. I think he loved other girls more in his young life. Helen did a lot for my Uncle Frank—got him started. I think that's why he latched onto her—he thought it would help his career."

Helen Edith Howell was a green-eyed, auburn-haired beauty a few months younger than Frank. She was Jewish; her mother was the former Violet Rosengarden, from Albany, New York, and her father was a prosperous New York attorney, Charles F. Howell. Helen was born in Illinois and moved with her family to Los Angeles, where she was educated and found work in vaudeville, also playing small roles in Hollywood movies. She was a divorcée when she met Capra; he said she had been married twice, to cameramen George Barnes and Ben Reynolds (both of whom later photographed Capra features), but when she and Capra took out a marriage license in 1923, she listed only one previous marriage. Helen was related to a producer named William A. Howell. Though the exact relationship is unknown, he was said to have been Helen's uncle. Theirs was a theatrical family. William Howell was a former stage actor who had played supporting roles to Henry Irving and Richard Mansfield; his father, Curtiss Howell, and his grandfather had been actor-producers as well. Leaving the stage in 1910 to produce short comedy films, William also directed films occasionally and made propaganda films on behalf of the United States government during World War I.

Capra claimed in his book that he met Helen while delivering footage from the Ball Laboratory to the location of Erich von Stroheim's *Greed*, in which she was playing a small part; that would place the meeting in April or May of 1923, when *Greed* was being filmed at Laguna and Hayes streets (the cameramen were Ben Reynolds and William Daniels, who also would work with Capra). Capra wrote that he married Helen only five weeks after they met, but the wedding actually took place on November 29, 1923, and Capra conceded to the author, "It was not an overnight marriage."

In fact, Frank and Helen knew each other for two years before they were married. According to Isabelle Griffis, who was living with her husband in San Francisco at the time and occasionally spoke on the phone with Capra, he told her that he had met Helen in the fall of 1921, shortly after he made *Fulta Fisher's Boarding House*. He said Helen had seen *Fulta* and sought him out, impressed by his talent.

Unlike Josie Campisi, Isabelle thought that Frank genuinely loved Helen, at least at the beginning. But it surely was no coincidence that the qualities which attracted Frank to Helen were some of the same qualities which attracted him to Isabelle: Helen was petite and charming, and she combined a generosity of spirit with a sharp, sometimes sarcastic wit. She was fond of music, and she was from an affluent background. "Oh, I *loved* her for that. I liked classy gals."

That fall of 1921 evidently was the time Capra began working as an assistant director for Paul Gerson Pictures Corporation, whose principal financial backer was William A. Howell.

A strikingly handsome Englishman, Paul Gerson had acted with William S. Hart in the original 1899 New York stage production of *Ben-Hur* and later started dramatic schools in Chicago and San Francisco. Like Plank and Montague, in exchange for his teaching fee, Gerson promised his students jobs, first on stage, then with the California Motion Picture Corporation in Marin County, and later with his own film company, whose formation was announced in a *Chronicle* article on February 24, 1921, "Gerson Company to Begin Filming Picture Comedies."

"San Francisco is about to take its rightful place in the moving picture world," Gerson declared, announcing that he was planning to make four features and a series of two-reel comedies, the William A. Howell Comedies. Howell, whose title was "director, Paul Gerson Pictures Corporation," had an office in Gerson's film studio at 353-361 10th Street and also was manager of the Redwood Film Company on Market Street.

Unlike Plank, Gerson actually managed to make releasable movies on a regular basis, but "everything was done on the cheap," recalled Edward Dryhurst, a British writer and editor who worked on several Gerson films. "He paid rock-bottom salaries, about seventy dollars a week, and he would shoot a picture in ten days."

Capra's entry in the San Francisco City Directory for 1922 identified him as "asst dir Paul Gerson Pict Corp." He probably began working for Gerson on *Life's Greatest Question,* an action melodrama directed by Harry Revier, with Roy Stewart playing a Mountie, which was shot in October 1921, with exteriors in Golden Gate Park and interiors at the Page Street studio. It was released by the fledgling CBC through the states' rights market (in which independent producers would lease rights in a film to independent exchanges in each territory, usually a state). Revier followed *Life's Greatest Question* in February with the crime melodrama *The Broadway Madonna.* The leading lady in those two films was the director's wife, Dorothy Valerga Revier.

Production began by early March 1922 on another series of two-reel comedies, the Plum Center Comedies, produced by William A. Howell, with exteriors filmed in the nearby small town of Belmont and interiors at the Gerson studio on 10th Street. The series was presented by Gerson and released by a Hollywood production-distribution company, Film Booking Offices of America (FBO), a predecessor of RKO. Helen Howell was the ingenue in the series, and Capra worked on it in 1922 and 1923 as a prop man, editor, gag man, and finally personal assistant to the series' director, Robert Eddy.

Belmont was a sleepy, old-fashioned hamlet twenty-five miles down the Peninsula. Its Middle American ambience was perfect for the rustic comedy of the Plum Center series, an unofficial knock-off of the Toonerville Comedies made by the Betzwood Film Company in Philadelphia, based on Fontaine Fox's comic strip *Toonerville Folks.* Dan Mason, who starred as the Skipper in those films, played a similar role in the Plum Center Comedies, as goat-whiskered Pop Tuttle, proprietor of a one-horse bus line between the hotel and the railroad station. Besides Helen Howell, the supporting cast included Oliver J. Eckhardt as the town dentist and towering Wilna Hervey, the Powerful Katrinka of the Toonerville Comedies, as the Amazonian baggage smasher Tillie Overton. Judging from two surviving films, *Pop Tuttle The Fire Chief* and *Pop Tuttle, Deteckative,* the Plum Center Comedies were amiable successions of simple slapstick gags, endearingly acted and broadly but well directed. The earliest one Capra remembered working on was *Pop Tuttle The Fire Chief,* the fifth of the twelve films in the series, and he said he worked on all the subsequent ones without having to give up his regular job with Ball. The series ended with *Pop Tuttle's Russian Rumor,* a May 1923 release.

When asked about Helen's involvement in the series, Capra at first claimed she was not even in the films, and then, when shown the proof that she was, said, "She might have been, but I was running too fast to see anything. I was so goddamn busy." But he was photographed looking dapper in a three-piece suit with his arm around Helen on a Belmont street during the shooting of *Pop Tuttle's Lost Nerve.*

During the production of the series, Alva Johnston wrote, Capra "made a bad impression. He was short and swarthy. From under bushy brows, he darted inquiring glances in all directions. He kept watching everything. He did this because he was anxious to learn, but everybody else jumped to the conclusion that he was a spy. In those days the motion picture industry was ravaged by spy fever. The usual notion was that spies were stealing plots and gags for rival companies. Capra, however, was spotted as a front-office spy. He was supposed to be spying out loafing, waste, and graft. The Toonerville troupe gave him the routine spy treatment. Nobody spoke to him. Nobody even swore at him. There was no room for him in the bus in which the company traveled to and from the location. . . . Capra, a genial, sensitive young fellow, suffered horribly, but he would not be hazed out of his vocation. Moreover, he regarded his tormentors as splendid fellows and geniuses. He was lost in hero-worship of the director, who not only never spoke to him but never looked at him."

In Capra's version of events, when the original film editor walked out in a row with Eddy, he volunteered to step in during the emergency, and Eddy promoted him in desperation. But Johnston wrote that it was the company manager who promoted Capra and that "the director almost went mad at having the spy promoted." Three films later, Capra said, he was advanced to gag man (under scenario writer A. H. Giebler) and the director's personal assistant. Capra claimed that was a reward for his work as an editor. Johnston told it differently: Capra was showing rushes to the company manager and a stranger from Hollywood. The stranger inquired about the cost of the scenes he was watching, and then told the manager, "They're robbing you. If you make me director, I'll make the pictures twice as good for half the cost." Capra quietly informed Eddy. Eddy was able to outmaneuver the interloper and keep his job. As a reward, Eddy bought Capra a new suit, they became friends, and Eddy later helped him find work in Hollywood. Only the conclusion of Johnston's story was told in Capra's book.

The series ended acrimoniously, with an exchange of lawsuits in May 1923: Dan Mason suing along with the director for back salary and Gerson countersuing for damages caused by their "temperamental vagaries."

Capra related in his book that Eddy decided to leave town and offered to help him find work at the Hal Roach and Mack Sennett studios, the two leading comedy production companies in Hollywood. That version omits several important facts, among them that Frank and Helen stayed in San Francisco and continued to work for Gerson for nine months after the demise of the Plum Center Comedies.

They were married at 4:30 in the afternoon on Thanksgiving Day 1923 at Helen's apartment at 2135 Sacramento Street, a fashionable address overlooking Sharp Park. They compromised their religious differences and were married by a minister of the First Unitarian Church, the Reverend C. S. S. Dutton.

Bob Eddy was the best man, and the bridesmaid was a friend of

Helen's from Missouri, Dorothy Gellam. Others in attendance included members of the film troupe with whom Helen and Frank were working at the Page Street studio on such crime melodramas as *Waterfront Wolves*, *Three Days to Live*, and *Paying the Limit*: stars Ora Carew and Jay Morley and director Tom Gibson.

A large picture of the couple appeared in the *Chronicle* under the headline "Film Actress, Director Wed," with Helen smiling, her arm linked in her husband's, Capra looking somber, his hands clasped in front of him.

In January 1924, Frank and Helen left for Hollywood. They shared a cramped guest house near the studios with Bob Eddy while they went about looking for work.

Soon after coming back to town, Frank introduced Helen to his family. His mother held a big party in the old neighborhood for the entire clan. Now almost totally Italian, Little Sicily had become a haven of bootlegging and violence. Frank was more appalled than ever before by the surroundings he had left behind, but Helen was delighted by his unpretentious family, and they accepted her wholeheartedly, not fazed (as many other families in Los Angeles would have been) that she was divorced, Jewish, or an actress.

"I liked her very much; we all liked her very much," Sam Capra remembered.

"She was cute, she had a nice personality, she loved kids, and she was really talented, too," said Josie Campisi.

In a passage excised from his autobiography, Frank Capra wrote contemptuously of Helen's rapport with his too-easily-impressed family, putting it down to her fondness for slumming with social inferiors and her taste for his mother's homemade wine.

Helen, he felt, cared more about the kind of life he had left behind than about his future.

6. The Gag Man

"*I*f there is any shortcut to fame and fortune in motion pictures, it is as a gag man," Capra wrote in 1927. "Here you may jump to the top overnight, after the short probationary period, which is long enough to show you whether you have the stuff that makes gag men."

Capra did not "jump to the top overnight," but his period as a Hollywood gag man between 1924 and 1927 was, indeed, a formative and decisive step in his career. He started with the Hal Roach Studios in Culver City. When Capra was working on the lot for $75 a week, the star performer was Will Rogers, who earned $2,000 a week. The witty young director Leo McCarey, whom Capra emulated, was making comedies with Charles Parrott (later known as Charlie Chase), and future director George Stevens was a cameraman. Roach had not yet teamed Stan Laurel and Oliver Hardy, but his *Our Gang* ensemble of "clever street kids" whom he hired in 1922 "to just play themselves in films and show life from a kid's angle" already was a box-office bonanza.

According to the Roach payroll and production records, Capra's job on *Our Gang* began in late January or early February of 1924, several months earlier than his book has it, and he lasted not the six months he claimed but only seven or eight weeks. He implied that he left voluntarily to pursue a break as a director, but when he was discharged after a "'short probationary period," he must have wondered if he did have "the stuff that makes gag men."

He claimed that he got the job through a recommendation by Bob Eddy to *Our Gang* director Robert F. McGowan, but in a 1984 interview, Roach said, "McGowan did *not* hire writers. That was up to me." Roach, however, did not remember Capra working for him: "There was nothing in his working for the Hal Roach Studios that was in any way outstanding. He was just another writer to me in those days." Most likely the person who steered

Capra to Roach and put in a good word for the young gag man was not Eddy but Capra's high school teacher Rob Wagner. Nothing would have been more natural than for Capra to have looked up Wagner when he heard that Wagner was directing Will Rogers comedies for Roach, such as *Two Wagons, Both Covered*, a burlesque of the hit Western *The Covered Wagon*, and *High Brow Stuff*, a satire of little theater groups.

After Capra was assigned to provide gags for the *Our Gang* two-reelers *Cradle Robbers* and *It's a Bear*, the first complete script he wrote for Roach was for *Jubilo, Jr.*, a sentimental short comedy in which Rogers played a takeoff on the philosophical tramp character from his most famous silent feature, the 1919 *Jubilo*. Because it was primarily an *Our Gang* film, with Rogers appearing only in the framing segments, it was directed by McGowan, but for Capra to have landed such a plum assignment so quickly suggests that Wagner was instrumental in getting him on the lot in the first place.

"I never quite lost sight of Rob Wagner," Capra acknowledged. "He got around and he knew most everybody. He was a very sociable guy, very easy to talk to, and he loved all his students. He knew I was pretty good at gags, and he called me in to talk about it. He was a very dear friend of Chaplin's, and we talked a lot about how Chaplin worked, how he got his material, and everything else."

"Bob McGowan was one of the nicest guys I ever knew, the oddest guy I ever knew, and one of the funniest," Roach said of his *Our Gang* director. "He looked and acted serious, but he was quite the reverse, actually. You never knew what was going to happen next with Bob McGowan. McGowan was very good at ad-libbing. And nobody could handle kids any better than he could."

Capra, however, found McGowan dour and unsympathetic. McGowan, he claimed, would not let him come on the set and accepted his work grudgingly and with an obvious lack of enthusiasm. Roach, who took the sole writing credit for himself on the early *Our Gang* pictures, said that while it was highly unusual for a writer to be barred from the set, the writers worked primarily with him, in any case, rather than with the director.

Capra admitted that both he and McGowan quickly realized that he was temperamentally unsuited for the tranquil juvenile comedy the director and Roach expected. The gags Capra wrote for Mickey, Mary, Farina, and the rest of the gang were more suited to the rowdy characters he had known as a boy on the streets of East Los Angeles. When he worked on retakes for

It's a Bear—in which the gang, tired of playing big-game hunter in the city, go to a farm to hunt real animals—Capra suggested having the kids put on a Wild West Show at the farm, and many of the gags in his working notes involved cigarette smoking and knife throwing, as well as what Capra called a "nigger baby act," involving the black kids Ernie (Sunshine Sammy) Morrison and Allen (Farina) Hoskins: "Ernie has Farina behind a canvas and is selling ten shots for a penny to hit the nigger baby."

The amiable and touching *Jubilo, Jr.* was more the kind of thing that Roach and McGowan wanted, with the Rogers character reminiscing on Mother's Day to a group of fellow tramps about his childhood, which is shown in flashbacks using the *Our Gang* kids. Mickey Daniels plays the young Jubilo, trying to raise money to buy his mother a hat by conning other kids into paying for the privilege of digging him a ditch—a borrowing from Mark Twain's celebrated fence-whitewashing scene in *The Adventures of Tom Sawyer.*

The extensive script material in Capra's files on *High Society* indicates that he worked harder on it than on any of the other films he wrote for Roach, and Leonard Maltin and Richard W. Bann, in their book on *Our Gang*, call *High Society* one of the finest of the 211 films in the series. For once the story gave free rein to Capra's best comic instincts, and he was able to rough out some the ideas he would use later in his own films as a director.

Capra put Mickey Daniels in a Huck Finn role, his aunt "offering to raise Mick as a gentleman and not as the roughneck Pat [his poor-but-happy father] is making out of him." Taken by chauffeur-driven limousine to the aunt's mansion, Mickey is, as Huck would put it, "sivilized," and he hates every minute of it, especially when a valet gives him a bubble bath and forces him into a tight-fitting suit and shoes. Although the script is more simply condemnatory of riches than Capra's later films, Mick resembles the central characters in *Platinum Blonde* and *Mr. Deeds Goes to Town*, ordinary men who find themselves living in luxury and finally rebel, longing to return to the simple life.

When the gang comes to the mansion in *High Society* to cheer up Mick, joyously trashing the place in the process, Capra's own feeling of liberation from the restraints of the *Our Gang* series was palpable in the anarchic abandon of his comic imagery. He was given his final paycheck on March 29, midway through the shooting of the picture.

Capra's intense absorption in his work during his Hal Roach period was obvious to everyone around him.

"He would go into sort of a trance, and you couldn't get through to him," his nephew Sam Capra said. "He would get so wound up in his work that he'd forget to shave. One time on the set he only had one sock on. Grandmother and Ann would both jump on him and make him shave and take care of himself. Annie even had a razor in her house for him to use whenever he'd come to visit."

Helen had quit her career not long after they moved to Hollywood, hoping to raise a family. But Frank seemed to be using his work in part to escape from his role as a husband, and she must have wondered whether he had married her for love or to advance his career.

"I spent five years with her, and stayed with her, and never slept with her but once or twice," he claimed, although that seems an exaggeration, given the evidence that they were trying to have children during at least part of their marriage.

"Actually, I was married to my job, not to her. The dedication to the film was all the way. I loved film better than I loved women."

"He certainly wasn't a boy for catching the eye of young ladies," agreed Edward Dryhurst, who worked with Capra as a Sennett gag man in the mid-1920s. "I don't think he was particularly interested in the young ladies; he was interested in his work. He seemed to be a very earnest, very conscientious young man who seemed to be taking life very seriously. He wasn't like the rest of the guys. He always seemed a bit withdrawn. I wouldn't think he socialized very well.

"You'd never take him for a gag man."

"No good gag man is out of work," Capra wrote in his 1927 article "The Gag Man," published in an anthology called *Breaking Into the Movies*. Despite those optimistic words, he did not work as a gag man for about two months after losing the job with Roach. His book does not explain what he was doing during that period, but the Los Angeles City Directory for 1925—based on information compiled the previous year—provides part of the answer, listing Capra as "asst mot pic dir FBO Studio."

The moderate-budget production and distribution company was located at 780 Gower Street, five blocks from the house where Capra was living at 1202½ Gower. The pictures turned out by FBO around the time Capra worked there included such forgettable second features as *Vanity's Price*, a drama with Anna Q. Nilsson on which the young Josef von Sternberg was the assistant director, and *The Fighting Sap* and *Thundering Hoofs*, Westerns with Fred Thomson and his gray Irish stallion Silver King (the horse received top billing).

Capra also worked for a short time that June as a gag man for the

Hollywood Photoplay Company on two college-humor shorts in its *Puppy Love* series starring Gordon White as a fun-loving swimming champion. Then he was offered a six-week tryout as a gag man at the Mack Sennett Studios.

The circumstances of his hiring by Sennett in 1924 have long been obscure. Profiles of Capra in 1937 and 1941 claimed that he had been recommended to Sennett by his boss on the *Screen Snapshots* series, Harry Cohn, but Capra denied it. Nor did Capra acknowledge his possible earlier experience working as a film editor for Sennett and selling gags and "situations" to Sennett during his college years. He claimed that Eddy and McGowan sent him to Sennett's head writer Felix Adler, and that Will Rogers also made Roach call Sennett on his behalf. Roach said he "would have done that" if he had been asked, because he and Sennett often recommended writers to each other, but he did not remember having done so in Capra's case.

Again, there was a simpler explanation: Rob Wagner was working for Sennett.

Wagner had left Roach in May, *Variety* reporting that the studio chief "for the past six months has been dissatisfied with the type of pictures turned out at his plant," and was putting the studio on hiatus until August. At Sennett's, Wagner was "sort of a general catchall fellow at the beck and call of all the directors," said Dryhurst. "They called Rob if they needed a gag or something. He was a very clever comedy man, an amusing character." Sennett eventually let him go because, as he put it, "Rob's brand of humor was several cuts too intellectual and satirical for our burlesque." But he liked Wagner and valued his opinions.

The Sennett lot at 1712 Glendale Boulevard in Edendale, just outside Hollywood, was the home of, among others, the Keystone Kops. But while the Capra of 1918 was embarrassed to write gags for Mack Sennett, the Capra of 1924 was overjoyed. The frenetic, madly inventive Sennett Studio was Hollywood's *commedia dell'arte.*

James Agee described it in his 1949 *Life* magazine article on silent comedy as "a profusion of hearty young women in disconcerting bathing suits, frisking around with a gaggle of insanely incompetent policemen and of equally certifiable male civilians sporting mustaches. All these people zipped and caromed about the pristine world of the screen as jazzily as a convention of water bugs. . . . 'Nice' people, who shunned all movies in the early days, condemned the Sennett comedies as vulgar and naive. But millions of less pretentious people loved their sincerity and sweetness, their wild-animal innocence and glorious vitality."

For Capra, whose training in film up to this point had been wide-ranging but unfocused, the year and a half he spent at Sennett's was his graduate school, the "Custard College" from which he would emerge as an expert in the creation of visual humor. It was a discipline which would never leave him, even after his work grew into a deeper, more dramatic exploration of character. "It was very good training, and we didn't realize how lucky we were," Dryhurst recalled. "If we accept the premise that comedy is satirical drama, then it was a good start in the movie business for a fellow like Capra." There always would be an undercurrent of inventive and irreverent sight gags at work in Capra's human comedies, and a dynamic sense of narrative and editing which were his legacies from the great anarchist of American film, Mack Sennett.

The creative energy bottled up in Capra—and the emotional turmoil underlying his sexual frustrations—would explode at Sennett's in a liberating riot of surrealistic images. With their breakneck pace, physically uproarious style, and bumptious, nose-thumbing anarchy, Sennett's films were refreshingly free of the middle-class attitudes of the *Our Gang* series against which Capra had butted his head with such frustration.

Capra and his fellow gag men were housed in the top floor of a four-story tower in the middle of the lot. Sennett built the tower so he could "keep an eye on my outrageous employees. . . . I was convinced that the entire studio would go Indian-wild if I did not keep persistent and hard-boiled watch on them."

"Working for Sennett was murder," recalled Darryl F. Zanuck, who was employed there as a gag man shortly before Capra arrived, "because he was a real slave driver and he could be a son of a bitch if he thought you were wasting a minute of the time he was paying you for."

Vernon Smith, who collaborated on scripts with Capra and served as Sennett's scenario editor, described how they worked: "Mack Sennett supplied most of the basic ideas. Then he and I would kick these basics around until we were satisfied that we had the springboard for a good comedy. Then I would assign two writers to develop it. All they did was tell a story—no gags. . . .

"When the story was complete I would . . . tell it to the Old Man. When we decided that a yarn was good enough, it went to the gag room. . . . A gag conference consisted of about six gag men, the Old Man, and myself. There was no orderly procedure. The story was attacked from all angles by everybody. Anyone who thought up a funny situation would not only tell it but act it out at the same time. One gag would suggest another and often two jokesmiths would combine their gags into one routine. . . .

"If a stranger had walked in, falling on his face, of course, he might have thought he was in the violent ward of an insane asylum. One of our best young men was Frank Capra. . . . He was an action boy. When he wanted to get over how funny a plumber could be, lying on his back under a kitchen sink, he would sprawl on the floor and make like a plumber."

Edward Dryhurst worked with Capra on Harry Langdon two-reelers, as part of a six-man team headed by gag man Arthur Ripley. "Capra was very literate," Dryhurst remembered. "Few of the other gag men had college backgrounds. Most of them were what the English call 'common.' But Capra was very quiet. I wouldn't say he had a particularly strong personality.

"The work didn't involve writing, it involved talking around the table. We all had notepads, and there were lots of notes made by Ripley. When we finished, a script would be prepared of all the gags he liked; Ripley must have done it. I forget now, but let's say Langdon was supposed to be a sailor. The time would come when Arthur Ripley had to read the story to Mr. Sennett. Mr. Sennett came into the room and leaned his head against the door, cap pushed well down and his eyes half closed, looking like he was falling asleep. He stood there and this went on for a while as Ripley read haltingly. Finally he finished and all eyes turned to Mr. Sennett. After what seemed like a couple minutes of him saying nothing, he would say, 'Not bad. How about making him a cop?' "

"**I**t's the only honest-to-God human tragedy I've ever been up against," Capra said many years later.

In March 1923, Harry Langdon was a $1,500-a-week vaudeville comedian *Billboard* magazine called "one of vaudeville's best-known performers." Harold Lloyd caught Langdon's act at the Orpheum Theater in downtown Los Angeles and advised Hal Roach to hire him for pictures. Roach offered him a contract, but the negotiations broke down and producer Sol Lesser snapped up the suddenly hot Langdon. Lesser sold Langdon's contract to Mack Sennett, whose ads would proclaim, "Mack Sennett Presents His Greatest Comedy 'Find' Since Charlie Chaplin."

Privately Sennett was somewhat baffled by the strange, dough-faced little man, who resembled a slightly depraved baby and worked in a slow, hesitant, delicate style, totally unlike that of the knockabout *farceurs* who ran amok on the Sennett lot. "He had his routines, well learned in vaudeville, and he could do them on demand, but he seldom had the mistiest notion of what his screen stories were about," Sennett wrote in his autobiography. "Like Charlie Chaplin, you had to let him take his time and go through his motions. His twitters and hesitations build up a ridiculous but sympathetic little character. It was difficult for us at first to know how to use Langdon, accustomed as we were to firing the gags and the falls at the audience as fast as possible, but as new talent arrived, we found ways to screen it and to cope with it."

By the summer of 1924, Langdon had made ten two-reel comedies for Sennett, but none had stirred much enthusiasm. "He had kicked around from guy to guy, and nobody wanted him," Capra recalled. "Nobody knew what to do with this guy who took an hour to wink." Langdon did not seem comfortable in slapstick roles that could have been played just as well, if not better, by other comedians. He asked Harold Lloyd's advice. The problem, Lloyd said, was the same one that had hampered Chaplin when he worked for Sennett: Sennett tried to make him move too quickly. Lloyd advised Langdon to slow his pace, regardless of what Sennett told him to do.

Maybe they were missing something, the Old Man agreed. After all, Langdon had been doing his vaudeville act, "Johnny's New Car," for seventeen years with his wife, Rose. He had been playing the big towns on the Keith and Orpheum circuits since 1911, and he was a favorite of sophisticated audiences at the two top vaudeville theaters in the country, the Palace in New York and the Majestic in Chicago. Sol Lesser had committed Langdon's vaudeville act to film. Maybe that would give them a clue.

Sennett ordered Dick Jones—who received credit as supervising director of Sennett's first twelve Langdon films—to show the film of "Johnny's New Car" to every writer on the lot. Finally it was Capra's turn, along with Arthur Ripley and a couple of other gag men. Capra "wanted Langdon as soon as he set eyes on him," Sennett remembered.

The novice gag man seemed to have an intuitive understanding of the odd little man he watched in the vaudeville skit. He spoke excitedly of Langdon's unusual quality of comic innocence. So Capra, who only recently had passed his six-to-eight-week probation period, was assigned to contribute gags (without credit) to a Langdon story being written by Vernon Smith and Hal Conklin.

Langdon played a spectacularly incompetent doughboy in World War I France who miraculously manages to survive combat without a scratch, win the heart of a dazzling French girl, save his commanding officer's life, and come home a hero. Directed by Harry Edwards, *All Night Long* was released on November 9. Meanwhile, Capra was working, still uncredited, on Langdon's next film for Edwards, *Boobs in the Wood.* The Arthur Ripley story cast Harry as a timid lumberjack whose girlfriend cons the other woodsmen into believing he is a famous gunman known as "The Crying Killer." It was first previewed on October 16. The public response to both films was enthusiastic.

Without waiting for the February release of *Boobs in the Wood*, Sennett promoted Capra to Ripley's junior partner on *Plain Clothes*, with Langdon playing a bumbling detective. The team of Ripley and Capra would write six more Langdon pictures for Sennett in little more than a year, all of them directed by Edwards, including a feature, *His First Flame*.

Langdon soon became a major star. But by the summer of 1927, he was a has-been, shunned by audiences and ridiculed by critics. In 1929, broke and beaten, he went back to vaudeville. His film career after that was inconsequential.

Capra's version of these events, laid out at length in his autobiography and in print and television interviews, is generally accepted as the truth, even though Capra was so obviously bitter and scornful toward Langdon, referring to him in conversation simply as "the little bastard." Mack Sennett expressed similar views in his book, *King of Comedy*, published in 1954. Langdon died in 1944, so his voice has remained unheard, aside from a few diplomatic interviews at the time his career collapsed. Only in the last few years have film historians begun to question the Capra/Sennett version of what happened to Harry Langdon.

Capra could see much of himself in Langdon. Langdon was like a crazy mirror of Capra's emotions, comically distorted in such a way that Capra could stand back and observe them from what Rob Wagner liked to call "Mount Detachment."

Both were little men, born into modest circumstances (Langdon the son of Salvation Army workers from Council Bluffs, Iowa). Both went to work at an early age, hustling papers on the street. Both had early show business experience as theater ushers and prop boys. Both were expert tumblers. Both played the banjo and the ukelele. And both were gag writers (Langdon wrote and staged his own act).

But while Capra was pursuing an education, Langdon was acting in Dr. Belcher's Kickapooo Indian Medicine Show, performing in music halls, clowning in the circus, and, from the age of fifteen, making his living in vaudeville. Contrary to what Capra wrote, when Langdon signed with Sennett, he and his wife had long outgrown sleazy theaters in tank towns; they were respected and successful stars. Sennett was equally misleading in describing Langdon's as a "small-town vaudeville act . . . with no money and no fame."

In his stage persona, Langdon was a sort of premental Capra, a creature of seemingly pure instinct, uncomplicated by any brush with mental labor or emotional agony. A creature who somehow seemed to have remained suspended in a world of innocence, a bizarre and blissful state of permanently arrested development that had a dreamlike way of protecting him from harm. He was Capra before the fall—Capra in his imagined Eden as a bumptious five-year-old in Bisacquino—Capra before the rough streets of America took away that innocence and forced him to become a gut-punching little man in order to survive.

And, perhaps most arrestingly for Capra, when he first encountered the comedian in that summer of 1924—a time when he was using his work to escape an intolerable marriage—Harry Langdon's adult babyhood represented a comical embodiment of his sexual anxieties.

In the filmed stage act that Capra and Ripley watched in the Sennett screening room, Langdon struggled helplessly with two equally formidable opponents: a self-destructing automobile and a castrating wife. Both clearly were beyond his capabilities and his understanding. His outgrown pants and jacket and little squashed hat were the clothes of someone who hadn't decided if he was a boy or a man, and his timid look begged women not to hurt him. "Frank Capra's enormous talents," wrote Sennett, "first showed themselves when he saw all this as something that would photograph." Capra said that Ripley gave him the clue about how to deal with Langdon's character when he remarked after seeing the film, "Only God could help that twerp."

"I had just read *The Good Soldier Schweik,* and the connection between the two was immediate," Capra told silent-film historian Kevin Brownlow. "We asked permission to work on it for a while. . . . A new star was born. A new kind of personality. Innocence was his forte. . . . but Langdon did not invent his own character. It was invented for him. And that he never understood."

However, Joyce Rheuban's revisionist study *Harry Langdon: The Comedian as Metteur-en-Scène* makes it clear that neither Capra nor anyone else at the Mack Sennett Studios "invented" Langdon's character. The essence of that character already was firmly established in vaudeville by the time Sennett, Ripley, and Capra came across it: the details of makeup and costuming; the ineptitude with recalcitrant props; the slow pace, befuddled reactions, infantile personality; the melancholia underlying the character's surface cheerfulness; and the distinctive techniques of staging that allowed the character to emerge.

What Ripley, Capra, and Edwards were able to do was to recognize and appreciate what made Langdon unique and to find a way to let him relax on film and be himself rather than trying to force him into being something else, something more conventional. Following the lead of Smith and Conklin, they developed a congenial narrative context for Langdon to inhabit, something for which Langdon, with his vaudeville-sketch background, had little aptitude.

To James Agee, Capra made an often-quoted capsule description of the method of the films he wrote for Langdon. He called it "the principle of the brick": "If there was a rule for writing Langdon material, it was this: his only ally was God. Langdon might be saved by the brick falling on the cop, but it was *verboten* that he in any way motivate the brick's fall." The principle of the brick applies well enough to much of Langdon's humor, but Langdon just as often *did* motivate the brick's fall—though usually unconsciously or with an altogether different purpose in mind. The humor in those cases comes from the way the character saves himself, without deliberation, from the consequences of his own ineptitude: a classic example occurs in *Tramp, Tramp, Tramp,* when Langdon, an escaped convict dragging a ball and chain, sits next to a train track and carelessly drops the chain across the track and a train immediately whizzes past and cuts the chain in half. The principle of the brick also fails to account for the full complexity of the character we see on screen in the Capra-Langdon films. It leaves out what Agee called "a sinister flicker of depravity about the Langdon character." Langdon frequently behaves in a destructive fashion, usually with the heedless abandon of a baby. "Premoral" was the word Agee used for it. In *Plain Clothes,* confronted with a menacing gang of jewel thieves, Langdon turns on a gas jet to asphyxiate them (not stopping to consider that he is also passing out), and in *The Strong Man,* which Capra directed, he fights off the hostile audience for his weightlifting act by firing a cannon into the crowded theater. And sometimes the character did cold-blooded, unmitigated evil—such as his elaborate attempt to murder his sweet, innocent wife in *Long Pants,* which Capra also directed.

Capra seemed unaware on a conscious level of the obsessive undercurrent of sexual perversity in the films he cowrote and directed for Langdon. When asked about the hilarious, yet disturbing, sequence in *The Strong Man* of statuesque Gertrude Astor virtually raping the cringing little Harry at knifepoint (he does not realize that she is actually trying to lift a bankroll she has concealed in his coat), Capra simply noted that having an aggressive woman chase a shy man has always been a source of role-reversal comedy. Perhaps, but one gets the impression that such behavior reverberates on levels whose existence Capra had to deny precisely because they were so personally threatening. Joyce Rheuben observes that "Harry's experiences with sex are almost always associated with violence. . . . Harry's fear of women is a fear of castration. . . . One also finds many comic references to sexual potency and impotence in Langdon's films. Harry's physical inadequacy and inaptitude is often equated with sexual inadequacy."

The darkness of the misogynistic humor in several of the Langdon films stemmed as much from the unhappily married Capra as it did from any other source, yet commentators on the films who mistakenly assume that Capra was an uncomplicated optimist also make the corollary assumption (encouraged by Capra in his book) that Ripley was responsible for all of the dark overtones in the Langdon films.

Capra's simplistic notion that Langdon's "only ally was God" meant that a clash between Capra and Langdon was inevitable, particularly since the saturnine Ripley seemed entirely comfortable with the darker, perverse elements of Langdon's character. Ripley was credited for the extraordinary grim stories of the black comedies Langdon made after Capra left the team (although Capra evidently worked on one of them, too). There is no question that Ripley responded more to Langdon's dark side than to his bright side. But Capra and Ripley, by all indications, shared a remarkably similar outlook during much of their collaboration.

"They were very close friends," said Edward Dryhurst. "Ripley was equally serious, with, of course, flashes of dry humor. He was a very tall, lanky New Englander with a deadpan. He was an introspective sort of chap who took life very seriously. You would think he was an accountant in a bank or a schoolmaster, something like that. My impression was that Ripley and Capra became partners because they just happened to like each other. Ripley was definitely the number-one boy, and he was also very close to Langdon. It didn't surprise me that when Langdon left for First National, Ripley took Capra along with him."

Capra did not write only Harry Langdon films for Sennett.

"I made twenty-five pictures for Sennett," he said in 1984. The Sennett production files indicate that Capra received screen credit as a writer of twenty-one films, seven of those for Langdon. A comparison between script material in Capra's own files and the scripts and synopses in Sennett's files established that Capra worked on at least four other Sennett scripts without credit (including two Langdon films), bringing to twenty-five the number of verifiable Sennett films on which he worked.

Capra was able to try his hand at virtually every kind of film Sennett made: the crazy chase pictures directed by Del Lord and starring such comics as Andy Clyde and Billy Bevan, the burlesque romantic melodramas with cross-eyed Ben Turpin, the tongue-in-cheek adventure sagas with stolidly handsome Ralph Graves, the romantic comedies with winsome Alice Day, the Smith Family situation comedies with Raymond McKee, Ruth Hiatt, and little Mary Ann Jackson, and the "girl pictures" starring the Sennett Bathing Beauties and such comediennes as Daphne Pollard and the leggy young Carole Lombard.

His imagination was allowed to run wild, conjuring up such broad visual images as Ben Turpin, the great hunter in *A Wild Goose Chaser*, firing a rifle whose double barrels spread when he pulls the trigger; jockey Billy Bevan carrying a chloroformed horse to victory on his back after it collapses near the finish line in *The Iron Nag*; and mad scientist Andy Clyde inventing a radio beam that powers automobiles in *Super Hooper-Dyne Lizzies*, causing autos to drive wildly by themselves all over Los Angeles.

The first two scripts that Capra helped write at Sennett's (without credit) were for the Ralph Graves comedies *Little Robinson Corkscrew* and *Riders of the Purple Cows*, directed by Ralph Ceder. Capra's college background may have influenced his assignment to Graves, an engineering graduate who usually played college men or bright but neurotically clumsy go-getters for Sennett. Capra then was teamed with Arthur Ripely to write *The Reel Virginian*, a spoof of Owen Wister's Western classic *The Virginian* with Ben Turpin in the role of the mysterious stranger later played by Gary Cooper. Sennett wrote "very good" at the top of the first page and rewarded Capra with his first screen credit at the studio. Completed by early October 1924, *The Reel Virginian*, directed by Ed Kennedy and Reggie Morris, was released two weeks before *All Night Long*.

But Capra and Sennett quarreled, according to Capra, over a gag in a Turpin comedy involving a loose wagon wheel in a love scene between Turpin and Madeline Hurlock. Hurlock did not remember such a scene, however, and it could not be found in Sennett's script files. Most likely the argument occurred over a gag in *The Reel Virginian*, in which Turpin takes Alice Day for a ride in a covered wagon, loses control of the horses while making a pass at her, then lifts the canvas top and makes it into a sail so he can continue his wooing unhampered.

Sennett rejected the gag, but Capra passed it along to the directors anyway, and it played well when the film was previewed. Sennett peevishly fired him, but soon relented.

Years later Sennett told a journalist about "the dark, determined young man he had around the studio and fired and hired again. Capra stuck to pictures and wouldn't be beat."

As Sennett's confidence in him grew, Capra was able to start going beyond the basically mechanical nature of most of the gags in his early scripts to explore character comedy and express some of his more personal concerns.

His embryonic bent for social satire was evident in three other Ralph Graves comedies—*Cupid's Boots*, *Breaking the Ice*, and *Good Morning, Nurse!*—and in an Alice Day comedy, *Love and Kisses*, all of which satirized the phoniness and enervation of high society. *Love and Kisses* is the most complex, with wholesome Alice playing an Oklahoma heiress who's mistakenly thought to be poor by a family of secretly impoverished eastern snobs; she chooses a wealthy young man who falls for her even though he thinks she's only a scrub girl, suggesting that the wealthy are best able to behave like social democrats, while the worst snobs are those who have nothing but crave the wealth they don't deserve.

Love and Kisses anticipated later Capra romances such as *It Happened One Night* and *You Can't Take It With You* in which the wealthy partner's redemption is accomplished through an attachment to someone from a lower class. But the ambivalence of Capra's ostensibly egalitarian sentiments was shown by the lower-class protagonists' instinctive attraction to wealth in these films, and by the racist gags that continued to blot his writing. In *Love and Kisses*, the wealthy suitor thinks he sees Alice on her hands and knees scrubbing the floor. He "tries to surprise her, but is greatly surprised himself instead, when he discovers a colored girl grinning her biggest Ethiopian smile. Without a word, he leaves." *Cupid's Boots* has an elaborately sadistic "comic" sequence—part of Graves's fantasy of rescuing a wealthy girl and her family—in which the family's black chauffeur (called a "coon" in the script) is covered with white feathers, sent terrified into the woods in the midst of a lightning storm, and tied up and tortured by the villains.

But the most pervasive theme in Capra's work for Sennett—both for Langdon and for the other comedians—was the treachery and duplicity of women. Capra's sexual and marital problems were brought into his work with an increasing ferocity that often makes the scripts seem more tragic than comic.

The essential horror of *The Marriage Circus* (whose title was a pun on the influential Ernst Lubitsch comedy of 1924, *The Marriage Circle*) seemed to be lost on audiences at the time, but the script (which he wrote with Vernon Smith) was a pure, undisguised scream from Capra's heart, an outcry at all the women who had ever mistreated him, beginning, of course, with his mother, and ending with Helen. Pathetic, cockeyed Ben Turpin plays Rodney St. Clair, a mama's boy who has somehow conned the darkly attractive Madeline Hurlock into marrying him. Two of her former suitors still hope she will change her mind. Fifteen minutes before the wedding, she does. Seeing Madeline kissing his best man, Turpin returns to his mother (Louise Carver), "beating himself in rage" as he blames her for his failure with women: "Why did you give me this face and this body? Why must I go through life only to be laughed at and unloved?"

The Marriage Circus, directed by Morris and Kennedy, was so successful (the trade paper *Moving Picture World* called it "a knockout . . . Turpin is at his best") that Sennett let Capra write the next Turpin picture on his own.

Capra must have sold Sennett on doing the story, because whether he admitted it or not at the time, it was based on his unfinished play *Don't Change Your Husbands*, about an unscrupulous divorce lawyer who seduces female clients. *A Wild Goose Chaser*, as the film was called, was directed by Lloyd Bacon. Turpin had the title role of a man whose wife cuckolds him with her lawyer, complaining, "My husband neglects me for wild birds!" More light-hearted then *The Marriage Circus*, *A Wild Goose Chaser* displayed an equally jaundiced view of the relations between the sexes: "Marriage is like a cafeteria," warns the opening title. "You pick what you want and pay for it later."

Harry Langdon's popularity was such by the beginning of 1925 that Sennett ordered Ripley and Capra to write a five-reel feature for him called *His First Flame*. The first feature-length screenplay of Capra's to be filmed in Hollywood, going before the cameras that spring, it turned out to be not so much a comedy about firemen as a soapbox for a tirade against women.

"WOMAN—the eternal question," the screenwriters' synopsis begins. "Many have there been who have championed the potential greatness of the long-haired, soft-skinned, soft-tongued variety of mankind, the female of the species, WOMAN. Many also have there been who have vigorously contradicted the truth of these assertions."

Capra's anger is so extreme that it collides with his comic sense. The outline indicates that the film is to open with a "historical sequence of how women have always dominated and ruined men." In a later draft, Sennett's reluctance to go along with this is indicated, but the writers stick to their explicit theme: "Historical sequence yet to be approved; a prologue to open the story of how a youth who, like all young men, placed woman in a shrine and worshipped her, until he was disillusioned, [with] his transition into a hater of women, and how, after all, Love, the Mistress, directs his steps into that state of bliss called Love."

Harry (whose last name in the film is Howells) is "a rich young boob" and celebrated feminist whose belief in the superiority of the female sex evaporates in a series of traumatic encounters with women, not all of which made it into the considerably watered-down film.

He looks up a married friend from college who does nothing but fight with his wife. He moons over a baby buggy in a store window, fantasizing himself as the baby, and is harassed by a woman and her eight bratty children. He watches a pair of newlyweds having a quarrel and separating immediately after they leave the church. And he blunders into the middle of a jailbreak from a women's prison, convinced that the horde of rampaging women are all after him, for he feels that "women in general had taken a violent dislike for him." A woman thief knocks him out, steals his clothes, and leaves him wearing her dress. Now he has a new problem— *men* are after him.

The outline notes tersely: "Now despondent. Hates all women. Wants to get away from them."

After taking "refuge" in the all-male fire department, Harry finds true love in the end, but the moral of this essentially bitter fable is that, as the opening title puts it, "Love is the only fire against which there is no insurance."

Isabelle and Bob Griffis moved back from San Francisco in 1925, settling in South Pasadena, and they frequently had dinner with Frank and Helen. It was obvious to Isabelle that the Capras were growing more and more estranged.

"I liked Helen," Isabelle said. "She was fun and outgoing. After Frank left her, he told me, 'She was never happier than when she was one step ahead of the sheriff.' I think he meant she was happier when he was having such a struggle to get a foothold in the movie business. After he began to prosper and was gone for such long hours I imagine she became bored and restless. Helen seemed lonesome. She didn't like being alone so much. I heard her talking on the phone to her girlfriend about it. Any wife would feel that way. I don't think I could have adjusted to him being gone all the time."

"Who knows, maybe he drove Helen nuts," said Josie Campisi, who saw them occasionally in Hollywood. "Maybe that was why she started drinking. It was hard for anybody to live with a person who had that much drive, and she didn't have it."

"Fortunately, I was working," Capra said of that period. "I'd rather be at the studio. I went to the studio very early and I stayed late. I worked like hell, I didn't notice what was going on with Helen, because I was too busy. She was a lovely girl. Just a lovely girl. I was too young to get married, shouldn't have been married, didn't have the money to get married with. I really felt sorry for her."

Sennett did not release *His First Flame* in the fall or winter of 1925, as he normally would have done. Langdon was beginning to get restless. He wanted to make his own films, and he wanted full creative control. Other studios were beginning to make offers in anticipation of the November expiration of his Sennett contract. Sennett feared he would lose Langdon, as he had lost so many of his other stars, and he decided to hold back *His First Flame* to release if Langdon moved elsewhere.

While Langdon's lawyer, Jerry Giesler, was weighing the production offers being made to the comedian by virtually every studio in Hollywood, Sennett began putting him into three-reel (about half an hour) comedies designed to capitalize on Langdon's increasing drawing power. The first of these was *There He Goes*, directed that summer by Harry Edwards from a script by Capra and Ripley, with Langdon becoming a burglar in a misguided attempt to demonstrate his toughness to his fiancée's cowboy uncles.

Capra too was getting restless. "He would write everything down in a notebook," his nephew Sam Capra remembered. "He said he was doing it because he knew he'd be a director someday. He'd write down gags and he'd see what the guys he was working with were doing wrong."

But when he asked Sennett to let him direct, the Old Man refused, saying he wouldn't want to "spoil a good gag man."

Undaunted, Capra insinuated himself into Sennett's personal life. Since the breakup of Sennett's romance with Mabel Normand, and the ruin of Normand's career by drug addiction and unfounded rumors of her involvement in the murder of director William Desmond Taylor, Sennett had become a melancholy and isolated figure. Capra went deep-sea fishing with him and was a frequent dinner guest in his twenty-one-room mansion.

The next Langdon three-reeler, written by Capra and Ripley in late July, was a spoof of *The Prisoner of Zenda*, with Harry playing the dual roles of King Strudel the 13th and the impostor put on the throne by plotters against the real monarch. The Sennett version of the oft-filmed Anthony Hope romance was set seventeen months after the end of World War I. Harry is first seen as a confused American doughboy wandering around a deserted battlefield, trying to find his army, when the plotters come across him and take him to the kingdom of Bomania. The working title was *Soldier Boy*.

Probably in an attempt to placate Capra so that he would not leave the studio with Langdon, Sennett finally gave him his chance to direct. The film's editor, William Hornbeck, told Kevin Brownlow that Capra was assigned to direct *Soldier Boy*. Shooting began around August. But Sennett was displeased with the rushes. After the third day of shooting, he told Hornbeck, "No good," and took Capra off the picture.

"This fellow will never make a director," Sennett declared.

Harry Edwards finished the picture, which was released two years later as *Soldier Man*. Capra was lucky, in a sense, to have been fired from the film: with its tired, derivative script, it never could have been first-rate Langdon. When the author asked Capra about the firing, he denied it ever happened, but this, rather than his brief firing over the gag in the Turpin film, may have been what Capra was referring to when he wrote in 1961, "Nothing since has seemed quite so bleak as the day Mack Sennett fired me." The incident gave him the final impetus he needed to leave Sennett with Langdon. "I did have a great ambition to direct," Capra recalled. "To [Sennett], directors didn't mean much."

"Sennett really knew comedy," Hornbeck commented, "but of course he made mistakes. He fired Frank Capra."

Capra now concentrated his campaign on Langdon. They had become tight. Each recognized the other's role in the success of their pictures, and Langdon, unlike Sennett, encouraged Capra's directorial ambitions. So, apparently, did the generous Harry Edwards. The team would escape Sennett's domination together and make their own films, their way.

On September 15, 1925, Harry Langdon signed with First National Pictures.

First National, later absorbed into Warner Bros., was a joint venture of exhibitors who owned first-run theaters in about three dozen major cities, as well as many second-run theaters. They entered into partnerships with stars, advancing them production money in return for being allowed to play the pictures.

Langdon's stunning contract provided for him to produce and star in four features within sixteen months, with an option for four more. He had creative autonomy, a demand that had held up the negotiations until First National finally bowed to (as the contract put it) "Harry Langdon's judgment, management, supervision and control, solely, exclusively and uninterruptedly exercised by him at any and all times and places and in the manner determined by him alone," including the "employment, discharge, control, direction and action of directors." Each film would have an A-picture budget of $250,000, from which Langdon would pay his staff. Langdon would receive a salary of $65,000 per film, plus 25 percent of the net profits. At Sennett's, Langdon's highest salary had been $2,000 a week.

Langdon was to report on November 15 to the lavish bungalow First National was building for him on the United lot in Burbank (later sold to Warner Bros., which still occupies the lot today). His first picture was to be ready for release within five months.

Langdon took with him Arthur Ripley as his scenario editor and two other gag men from Sennett's, Capra and Hal Conklin. His staff writers also included two former writers for Harold Lloyd, Tim Whelan and Gerald Duffy, as well as ex-vaudeville writer J. Frank Holliday.

Langdon fulfilled his contractual obligations to Sennett by delivering two more shorts that fall, *Saturday Afternoon* and *Fiddlesticks*, which delayed his arrival at United until December 3. But the writers were already at work on the script of his first feature for First National, *Mr. Nobody*, by November 1.

Saturday Afternoon and *Fiddlesticks* were a fitting valedictory for Langdon and Capra at Sennett's. A three-reeler written by Ripley and Capra, *Saturday Afternoon* is one of Langdon's most rueful and cynical comedies. The opening title reads: "In 1864 when Lincoln declared all men free and equal, did he, or did he not, intend to include husbands?" Langdon plays a meek husband who is "blissfully ignorant that he is henpecked," the script notes, until "one day he discovers that the world thinks he is a big joke, as the result of which he sets out to assert himself and cease to be henpecked." Harry's wife (chillingly played by Alice Ward) contemptuously suggests he have a fling, so he and Vernon Dent step out for a double date with flappers Ruth Hiatt and Peggy Montgomery. "The result of this is disastrous to him and at last he is very happy to return to his wife and her henpecking, full knowing that he had to have such a wife to be happy."

In *Fiddlesticks*, Ripley and Capra solve the problem of women by the simple expedient of disposing of a love interest altogether. This almost perfect little comedy deals instead with another Capra obsession: ambition. Harry has no interest in life but playing a bass fiddle that's bigger than he is. His loutish father and brothers think he's a "loafer," but his mother says, "Don't be too hasty, father—he may be a great musician some day!" But whenever Harry plays his music on the street, people throw things at him from their windows. Eventually he falls under the patronage of a junk peddler who follows him around collecting the mountains of junk that come cascading down in their direction. Harry comes home to his astonished family a wealthy man, wearing a top hat and tails, smoking a cigar, carrying a cane. When they ask how he did it, he shrugs, "Just fiddling around."

During the making of Langdon's first feature as an actor-producer, *Tramp, Tramp, Tramp* (as *Mr. Nobody* was retitled), *Photoplay* columnist Cal York tried to visit the set. York found Langdon "surrounded by henchmen. An ex-pugilist sits at the door to the set and refuses any and all comers admission unless they have an order from the business manager."

York sent in his card. The doorman emerged after several minutes and told him that Mr. Langdon would not be able to see him until after five o'clock, in his bungalow.

"After five in his dressing room," the columnist said.

"In his *bungalow*," the doorman repeated.

"Harry really has a bungalow with a capital B," wrote York. "This bungalow ought to help Harry make better pictures—perhaps better than Harold Lloyd—for Harold has no bungalow—just a nice little suite of dressing rooms in a building where mere mortals dress."

The columnist found Langdon's bungalow jammed with hangers-on. "My gag men," Langdon indicated, with a wave of his hand. They had to go outside to do the interview, sitting on the running board of an automobile, because there wasn't room in the bungalow—"too many gag men."

Capra, however, was not about to be lost in the crowd. Langdon was grooming him to direct. Capra stayed close to Harry Edwards during the making of *Tramp, Tramp, Tramp,* an amiable but uneven takeoff on the current fad of cross-country walking races. The script sent Harry off on a trek for $25,000 in prize money, to save his father's tiny shoe company from being gobbled up by the national chain sponsoring the race—an early sketch for the David and Goliath theme that would animate later Capra classics. Though it went $50,037 over budget, coming in at $300,037, the film was a box-office success, and the critical response was typified by the review in *Photoplay:* "This picture takes Langdon's doleful face and pathetic figure out of the two-reel class and into the Chaplin and Lloyd screen dimensions. Not that he equals their standing yet, but he is a worthy addition to a group of comedy makers of which we have entirely too few. Langdon has graduated and this picture is his diploma."

Capra claimed in his autobiography that he was the "codirector" of *Tramp, Tramp, Tramp.* His official Columbia biography in the 1930s called him simply the "director." He told Charles Wolfe in 1981 that he directed several scenes when Edwards left the set, exasperated with Langdon's interference with his directorial prerogatives. The fact remains, however, that Edwards gets sole directing credit on screen.

Was Capra codirector? "No," he admitted in 1984. "Just helping him."

Edwards had been instrumental in guiding Langdon to his great success at Sennett's, but now he was coming to a parting of the ways with the comedian. The embittered Sennett suggested that Edwards was being made a scapegoat for Langdon's deficiencies as a producer: "Langdon became important and unfortunately realized it. Suddenly he forgot that all his value lay in being that baby-witted boy on the screen. He decided that he was also a businessman. His cunning as a businessman was about that of a backward kindergarten student. . . . He blew the entire $150,000 [sic] production budget before he got his first story written."

"The film was fine but Langdon's director had taken too much time on it and run him into the red," Katherine Albert wrote in a 1932 *Photoplay* article apparently based in part on an interview with Langdon, "so Harry looked about for another director on the next one."

But *Tramp, Tramp, Tramp* was completed and delivered to First National in less than three months from the date of Langdon's arrival on the United lot, about seven weeks before the release date stipulated in the contract. So Edwards, a veteran trained in the penny-pinching Sennett school, could not have been solely responsible for running Langdon into the red. Langdon's eagerness to demonstrate his artistry in features no doubt contributed to the cost overrun and the clash with his director.

"It was on that picture that [Edwards] talked about quitting and talked to me about going on," Capra said. "He was a very nice guy. He helped me a lot. We had an idea that he would turn that little guy [Langdon] over to me when he quit. I worked more closely with him on that than I normally would, at his request, so I could see how he did it."

Edwards's disenchantment and the resulting lack of a consistently strong directorial hand may help to account for the spottiness of the humor in *Tramp, Tramp, Tramp*. There are several outstanding sequences, particularly the one of Harry dangling from a fence over a cliff (copied in part from *The Reel Virginian*) and a cyclone that anticipated Buster Keaton's similar sequence in his 1928 *Steamboat Bill, Jr.* But *Tramp, Tramp, Tramp* has some dry, unfunny stretches. Capra, Ripley, and the four other writers had not yet mastered the technique of feature-length comedy, using the picaresque framework of the walking race to string together what seems like a series of arbitrarily connected two-reelers. Nor did they manage to make the conflict between the small and large shoe manufacturers anything more than an excuse for involving Harry in the race; Harry's principal motivation is to win the attention of the young Joan Crawford, whose picture is on every billboard advertising her father's shoes. In Capra's mature work, his hero, as he put it, was "not so much chasing the woman as he was chasing ideas."

The relationship between Langdon and Capra was harmonious on *Tramp, Tramp, Tramp,* and Capra accompanied Langdon to the premiere in New York on March 17, 1926. Colleen Moore also remembered Capra being present during the filming of Langdon's two-minute cameo appearance in her First National film *Ella Cinders* (released on June 6), a romantic comedy about a household drudge who wins a fraudulent Hollywood talent contest and still manages to become a star. On the run from a studio cop, Ella blunders into a scene Langdon is shooting, thinking the cops chasing him are also real; their attempts to shield each other from harm are exquisitely timed drollery. Alfred E. Green directed *Ella Cinders,* but Moore had the impression that Capra was directing Langdon in the scene they did together.

Capra worried about Langdon's growing ambition. "I could see it coming. His major villain, the heavy in his life, the dart in his heart, was Chaplin. He wanted to be like Chaplin, and to beat him."

But Capra also was the kind of man who wanted artistic control. He claimed that Langdon "never knew the difference between his own character and Chaplin's. He never knew that Chaplin invented his own character, and could direct himself, because he knew his own character better than anybody else. Chaplin—he was the champ. . . . Langdon did not know his character, did not know why he was funny, did not know that his goodness was his power. But he wanted to be smart. He wanted to be Jack the Giant-Killer, like Chaplin was."

To Frank Capra, *The Strong Man* was "more than a comedy."

In the early frames of his first feature as a director, he declared his artistic independence with a direct evocation of his primal experience—his rebirth as an American. Harry Langdon plays Paul Bergot, a Belgian doughboy who emigrates to America on a giant steamer, passes under the protective gaze of the Statue of Liberty, and disembarks on Ellis Island. The title preceding the sequence calls Paul one of the "immigrants seeking a newer Rainbow in the Land of Promise."

It is worth noting that this film is the only one Capra made with Langdon in which Langdon's character is not named "Harry" or "The Boy" but has a separate identity. This may have been Capra's way of bringing the character closer to himself and infusing him with an unaccustomed depth. Though Ripley received solo story credit, with the adaptation credited to Tim Whelan, Tay Garnett, James Langdon, and Hal Conklin (Bob Eddy and Clarence Hennecke contributing without credit), Capra clearly was the dominant personality on *The Strong Man.* This moral fable, whose working title was *The Yes Man,* treats in comic terms several of the key elements of Capra's life: the gullible immigrant's harsh exposure to the corruption of big-city America as he pounds the streets looking for work; the shock of his first sexual encounter with a rapacious older woman; his entry into show business, as the assistant to a vaudeville strong man, and his sudden rise to stardom in the unmerited role of the strong man; his attempts to overcome the pervasive corruption which has penetrated even the archetypal American small town, Cloverdale (read: Hollywood); and his romantic yearnings for a pure, wholesome woman through whose love the weakling can find the power to become *The Strong Man.*

The extent to which Capra was able to personalize the story helps account for its unusual quality, its adroit blend of comedy and drama, and his instant recognition as an important director with an individual point of view. *The Strong Man* was, acclaimed by the critics with a fervor no one connected with the film had anticipated. "It's a grand and glorious laugh from the start to the finish," wrote *Photoplay.* "It begins with one laugh overlapping the other. Chuckles are swept into howls. Howls creep into tears—and by that time you're ready to be carried out."

Though there is no evidence of *The Strong Man* being chosen as one of the top ten films of 1926 in a survey of critics, as Capra claims in his book, it did rank nineteenth for that year in *The Film Daily* poll of 218 critics, a remarkable showing for a first-time feature director (Edwards's *Tramp, Tramp, Tramp* ranked forty-fourth). Today *The Strong Man* is considered one of the classic silent comedy features, ranked with the best of Chaplin, Keaton, and Lloyd. Even critics and audiences who are indifferent to Langdon's peculiar personality respond favorably to *The Strong Man,* perhaps because, as is often remarked, it seems more like a Frank Capra film than a Harry Langdon film.

Members of the cast and crew recalled that the strength of Capra's personality was immediately apparent on the set. "Capra was a smart little man," said Glenn Kershner, who photographed Capra's first two features with Buster Keaton's cameraman Elgin Lessley. "He didn't clown around. He was a serious thinker, but he always had a smile, and he never lost his temper."

The leading lady of both features was Priscilla Bonner, a young dramatic actress with no comedy experience when she was cast in *The Strong Man.* She played Mary Brown, a preacher's daughter in Cloverdale who corresponded with Paul Bergot during his service in World War I and imagines from his letters that he is a great hero. As her introductory title puts it, "She looked at the world through the eyes of optimism—perhaps because she was blind."

The scene of her meeting with Harry, neither knowing the truth about the other, is one of the tragicomic highlights of the film. Bonner described the scene and Capra's directing method: "She never dreams that she's going to see her dream man. And suddenly he's going to find out that she's a poor little blind girl. She can hardly stand it. Then there he is, this weird-looking little fellow with a little hat on top of his head, and she thinks he's Cary Grant. Actually they're fooling each other, but they're happy, so who cares? It's a lovely thing, charming and very poignant, and it's unusual for a comedy.

"Capra didn't rehearse much. Of course, Langdon was magnificent. Capra responded to the sensitiveness of Langdon. When these things would come into full bloom, Capra just let him go. In emotional scenes, like the ones I was in, we just rehearsed the mechanics, and I didn't act it until the cameras rolled.

"Capra was not a talker. He didn't say a great deal. But he was forceful. He knew what he wanted, and he knew how to create the right feeling with his actors. Mostly it was just the way he looked at you and told you the situation—when he smiled it went all over his face. His smile embraced you. You immediately felt friendly. And it was natural, the warmth that he had. He was a very sensitive man in working with people. Especially in the scenes with me. Oh, my, he was superb."

Capra's delicacy with Bonner, the sincerity with which she plays the scenes, and Langdon's awestruck behavior toward the first woman who did not reject him because of his appearance all help to make a potentially mawkish romance highly effective in the film (and may have inspired or influenced the romance between The Tramp and a blind girl in Chaplin's 1931 silent classic *City Lights*). Another crucial element in the success of *The Strong Man* is the slightly satirical edge Capra brings to the romance, as exemplified in Mary's introductory title and in such bits of visual comedy as the final shot of Mary helping the stumbling Langdon (now the town gendarme) up from the gutter as he walks his patrol. The cynicism of the earlier "love scenes," in which the baffled Harry is physically assaulted by a rough female crook called Gold Tooth (Gertrude Astor), also helps to soften up the audience to accept the sentiment.

In his later work, Capra and his writers would blend these two female types—the sweet and the fraudulent—into a more complex heroine (typified by Barbara Stanwyck and Jean Arthur) whose hardened exterior serves as protective covering for her basic tenderness. But if the division seems overly schematic in *The Strong Man,* a sign of Capra's unresolved conflict over women, the fact that Capra does show both sides indicates that as his work became more ambitious, he recognized that to develop his full potential as an artist he needed to be more generous and understanding toward the opposite sex, rather than continuing to wallow in unalloyed and ultimately sterile misogyny.

The recognizably "Capraesque" social attitudes underlying the Cloverdale sequences were a major departure for the previously asocial Langdon character. Capra's vision of Langdon as a Christian innocent whose "only ally was God" was translated here into a social principle, as he single-handedly cleans up the town, ridding it of the prostitution, gambling, and bootleg liquor dispensed in the local den of iniquity, the Palace. In a sequence graphically revealing the growing conservatism of a young man for whom such amusements had not been unfamiliar, and who had attacked the Prohibition movement in his college paper on motion pictures, Capra depicts the prior transformation of Cloverdale from an idyllic nineteenth-century small town into a modern cesspool with a crashingly literal but nonetheless powerful dissolve showing how its Main Street "had changed overnight—certain interests found it ideally located for a defiance of law" (remarkably similar to Capra's transformation of Bedford Falls in *It's a Wonderful Life* twenty years later). Capra's sympathies in *The Strong Man* are unambiguously with the psalm-singing reform elements led by Mary's father, Parson Brown, whose puritanical conservatism and Prohibitionist platform would make him perfectly at home under the Republican banner then being carried by President Calvin Coolidge (for whom Capra had voted in 1924).

Capra's treatment of the Langdon character does not really fit Richard Griffith's often-quoted but misleading schematic description of the typical Capra movie as a "fantasy of goodwill" in which "a messianic innocent, not unlike the classic simpletons of literature, pits himself against the forces of entrenched greed. His experience defeats him strategically, but his gallant integrity in the face of temptation calls forth the goodwill of the 'little people,' and through their combined protest, he triumphs." Despite explicit references in *The Strong Man* to the David-and-Goliath and Joshua-at-Jericho fables, Langdon is portrayed as a man of limited comprehension, motivated largely by his chivalric instinct to protect Mary (whom the villain wants to put on stage in the Palace) and acting alone in defense of a community largely indifferent or hostile to his cause.

But the degree to which Langdon, however unconsciously, serves as the savior of his community points forward to Capra's later depiction of such reluctant heroes as Gary Cooper in *Mr. Deeds Goes to Town* and Jimmy Stewart in *Mr. Smith Goes to Washington* and *It's a Wonderful Life*. It is unlikely that Capra consciously intended a visual irony by photographing the band of marching psalm singers in *The Strong Man* to resemble a lynch mob, as the "little people" so often do when they come together in his films. But it is no accident that the hero of Capra's first feature starts out as a penniless European immigrant and winds up working as a cop, as the American flag flies once again over Cloverdale, "protected by the majesty of the law."

As in the shorts Langdon made with Harry Edwards, not all of the finest sequences in the film have much to do with the plot. Langdon's desperate clowning as he tries to impersonate the strong man before the utterly impassive dance hall audience is a masterful vignette. Two other sequences are often recalled in anthologies of silent film comedy—the lovingly prolonged pantomime of Langdon doctoring his cold with Limburger cheese in a crowded bus to the disgust of the other passengers, and the exquisitely timed sequence of Langdon carrying the formidable Gertrude Astor, apparently unconscious, up a flight of stairs from a backward seated position, one step at a time, until he unwittingly continues up a stepladder and topples heels over head, sending her crashing to the floor.

Langdon was preoccupied with more than *The Strong Man* during its production that spring and summer of 1926. For it was on June 17 that he broke up with his wife, Rose, a casualty of the growing extravagance of his life-style.

He had "gone Hollywood" with a vengeance, buying an expensive house and fancy cars, surrounding himself with sycophants, and dabbling in what Mack Sennett acidly described as "marital adventures, in which he was about as inept as he was on screen." After more than twenty years of marriage, and partnership with her husband on stage, Rose found herself without work and discarded by a man who, as Capra put it, had "developed an interest in dames. It was a pretty high life for such a little fellow." Langdon himself said years later, "I look back to the time when I was making $7,500 a week, and now I know that I was never so unhappy. Sure, the money was great, but to keep the chiselers away! It was one mad rush."

The rapturous reviews *The Strong Man* received on its release September 5 ironically made Langdon even more unhappy. Though successful at the box office, *The Strong Man* was by no means a runaway hit, its critical standing far outdistancing its popular reception. The film was ranked seventieth commercially out of 202 major feature releases surveyed by the Hollywood magazine *The Film Spectator* for the eighteen months beginning in February 1926 and ending in August 1927. That represented only a slight increase over the box-office performance of *Tramp, Tramp, Tramp*, which was ranked seventy-fifth.

Langdon may well have been perturbed by this situation. He certainly was bothered by what he felt was greater acclaim for the film's direction than for his contribution as its star and producer. His own desire to direct was stimulated by his jealousy toward his twenty-nine-year-old protégé, whom he had elevated from gag man to director.

But all of this did not come until after the next picture began shooting.

The first thing Capra did when he started to make money with Langdon ($750 a week) was what all the Capras did—he bought a piece of land.

Early in 1926 he purchased an empty lot at 6480 Odin Street in Hollywood, in Majestic Heights, a comfortable, hilly residential area adjacent to the present location of the Hollywood Bowl. It was just up the winding street from the four-acre spread of the director he most admired, John Ford. With the money Capra made from the first feature he directed, he built a two-story, Spanish-style house for himself and Helen.

The Capras built a nursery into their new house: Helen was expecting their first child. "Frank was crazy to have children," Isabelle Griffis remembered; the development might have helped account for his kinder attitude toward women in *The Strong Man*. But not long after Frank and Helen moved in, Helen lost the baby. It was an ectopic pregnancy, conceived in one of her Fallopian tubes, a life-threatening condition which accounted for Capra's cryptic remark in his book that "her doctor told her she couldn't have children. Nothing can depress an Italian more than to discover he cannot sire bambinos."

"It was a terrible blow to both of them," said Isabelle, who felt it did more than anything else to destroy the marriage.

The loss of their child made Frank even more distant from Helen both emotionally and physically. His performance anxiety undoubtedly was intensified by feelings of guilt over the nearly fatal consequences for Helen of her impregnation and by his dread of its happening again. In such cases a man can suffer a loss of sexual desire, and even impotence, particularly if, as Capra suggested in his book, he has an aversion to contraception and thinks it lessens his fertility.

Contrary to what he wrote, and perhaps believed, Helen still could have children, although her risk was greatly increased. After their divorce, she came back to see Capra with a child she said was her own, and a man named William Bartlett wrote Capra in 1964 that he was Helen's son.

But when she lost Frank's baby, Helen went to pieces.

"Helen's drinking started after she lost the baby," Isabelle confirmed. "I don't think she did it before. I felt so sorry for them."

"Frank always said it was his own fault," said Sam Capra. "He was so busy getting ahead in the world he didn't spend any time with her, so she took to drink."

When discussing Helen in 1984, Capra made no mention of the loss of their baby, and he tried to shirk responsibility for his neglect by backdating the beginning of her alcoholism to the San Francisco period. "It didn't take me long to find that this girl was a drunkard—I would say two months [after their wedding in 1923]," he claimed. "I thought that she'd take a drink someplace like normal, and I'd have a drink with her, but I did not know that she drank all the time. I couldn't sleep in the same bed with her—I couldn't stand that liquor. The smell of liquor used to drive me crazy. Just drove me completely mad." Because of her drinking, he said, "We didn't go out, couldn't go out." And it was because of her drinking, he contended, that "she could never have a career. Drunkards can't have careers, for Christ's sake. They get a job and nobody wants 'em after that. It's sad. Poor gal. There was nothing I could do about it. She was my wife, and I tried to protect her and do everything I possibly could."

Partly to give Helen some companionship, Capra asked his mother, Annie, and Annie's new husband, a musician named Sam Huffsmith, to move in with them on Odin Street.

The grinding toil of Grogan's and the growing violence in Little Sicily also were among Capra's reasons for wanting to move his mother to Hollywood. In 1926, his sister Josephine's son Sam Finochio was killed when an illegal still exploded, burning him to death in a tunnel the bootleggers had dug beneath several houses in the neighborhood. Three months later, Josephine's husband, Luigi, died after a long illness, making her the third of the Capra women to be widowed since the family's arrival in America. Helen wanted children so badly that she talked with her husband about adopting Josephine's son Frank Finochio.

Saridda resisted the move to Odin Street. Her attachment to the old neighborhood, and to her independence, was still strong. Frank finally talked his mother into staying with Helen, Annie, and Sam whenever he had to be away on location (Saridda kept the houses on Albion Street until

1931). An actor friend of Capra's, Al Roscoe, also moved in with them on Odin Street.

Capra may have wanted his mother to keep an eye on Helen for him; and Saridda had much to report. When Frank came home from location, his mother told him that Helen brought strange men to the house. They had drunken parties, and the men sometimes stayed all night. She and Helen had nasty arguments. Saridda told Frank that when his wife was drunk, she would pick up with anybody. She called Helen "his whore."

His mother's reports had their desired effect. Capra felt humiliated in the worst way an Italian man can feel humiliated—wearing the horns of a *cornuto*, a cuckold.

"She was fast," he said of his first wife many years later.

The charges became common knowledge in the family, though Josie Campisi always gave Helen the benefit of the doubt. "You know how old people are," she said of her grandmother. "They suspect the worst. Maybe when she was drinking Helen would go into the bedroom with somebody. Maybe she was lonely. Maybe it was his fault. It takes two. But *I* never saw her with anybody."

After Capra brought in *The Strong Man* ahead of schedule and $9,368.33 *under* its $250,000 budget, Langdon, according to *Photoplay*'s Katherine Albert, "believed that the troubles he had had—both domestic and professional—were over and that he could take it easy now and things would just sail along on their own momentum."

He decided to take a rare vacation, playing golf for a month and leaving Capra and Ripley behind at the studio to flesh out the story line of the next feature, *Long Pants* (Ripley received story credit, with Bob Eddy receiving credit for the adaptation). The subject matter of the film was announced to the press as "the joys and sorrows of naive adolescence."

Capra and Ripley quarreled in Langdon's absence, Albert reported: "The writer [Ripley] thought there was too much footage [planned] that retarded the action before Langdon's entrance. The director said he knew his stuff and wouldn't be interfered with. . . . When [Langdon] returned, they put their separate cases before him. He strung along with the writer, agreeing with him on almost every point. The director was furious and the picture was completed in all the maddening discord of a schoolgirl squabble."

The friction that now broke into the open between Capra and Ripley had been growing for some time. Priscilla Bonner sensed it on *The Strong Man* and felt that it probably had originated back in the Sennett days.

During the making of *The Strong Man*, Capra recalled, Langdon often turned to Ripley as an ally in his disagreements with the director.

Long Pants is a fascinating, subversive, dark, but not very funny work which, in the words of critic Leland Poague, "is concerned with demonstrating the folly of innocence gone berserk."

Harry plays a naively romantic young man from a small town who is just at the point of receiving his first long pants. Harry is not ready to deal with women, however, because everything he knows about them comes from books. In a series of daydreams (only one of which survives, in part, in the film), he fantasizes himself a great lover. Though his parents want him to settle down with the sweet, innocent Priscilla (Priscilla Bonner), he falls under the spell of Bebe Blair (Alma Bennett), who fits his image of a sultry, sophisticated femme fatale. Not realizing that she is a peddler of "snow" (cocaine or heroin), he allows himself to be duped into following her to San Francisco to work as her unsuspecting accomplice. When he learns the truth, Harry numbly returns to the protection of his small town, his parents, and Priscilla, just in time to say grace at their table.

Though the misogynistic violence of the story reflected the deterioration of Capra's relationship with Helen, and the odd intrusion of drugs into the story may have been a projection of his revulsion over Helen's drinking, Capra felt that Ripley wanted to push the dark elements of the story much further than he was willing to go. There were certain things he believed Langdon should not do on screen: it was important to keep a balance between the comedy and the drama, between the optimism and the pessimism. Capra said he objected with particular vehemence to both Ripley and Langdon about the bizarre black comedy sequence in which Harry, to get out of his forced marriage with Priscilla, sees no alternative but to take her out into the woods and shoot her. In his daydream (no longer in the film today), he succeeded smoothly, but when he actually tries to do it, he is a pathetic failure. To Capra, this scene was a gross violation of Langdon's character: "I don't say it wasn't funny. It *was* funny that he was going to be the villain, that he was going to take the girl out and kill her. And the way he played it, he did it well. I think he had Chaplin in mind. But it was not in character for him that he wanted to kill in the first place. He was not the kind of a man who would want to kill. He might want to kill a fly, but not a human being."

Capra lost every major argument. "Ripley was in command even though I was directing the picture," he admitted. "He was just a guy who wanted my job, that's all. And he couldn't do it. He went to hell. All he could do was talk. He was the one who really tried to talk Langdon into making his own pictures. They went down faster than they went up."

Long Pants began shooting in early September, around the same time as the premiere of *The Strong Man*. One of the main problems on the second picture, Capra felt, was that Langdon paid too much attention to the critics when the reviews started to appear. "He read the wonderful reviews from New York," Capra told Brownlow. "People went crazy about this man, and he just couldn't handle it. He couldn't handle the renown he was getting. So when we made *Long Pants*, he said, 'I want to do more pathos.' I said, 'No, no—the pathos is in your comedy.' 'How the hell do you know?' he said. 'Do you know more than those critics in New York?' "

Priscilla Bonner found the situation extremely uncomfortable, so much so that she never wanted to see *Long Pants*. "Langdon was always nice to me, but he was ornery with Capra. Somehow Mr. Ripley seemed to get the inner ear of Langdon. Ripley was taking over then. I didn't notice at first what was going on, but gradually I did begin to notice it. Things were very, very tense. My feeling was that Harry was more against Capra than Capra was against Harry. Capra was trying very hard to do the best he could for his very gifted and temperamental star. Harry had his back up and he was being difficult and unpleasant. He wasn't normally that kind of a man.

"Of course, I had acquired a very great admiration for Mr. Capra. Also, the reviews had come out on his first picture, simply stunning reviews, so naturally he had my total confidence. He was in control when he directed *The Strong Man*, believe me, and the reviews gave him a great deal of confidence. So that he was really feeling that he knew what he was doing in the second picture. And I would notice that Mr. Langdon and Mr. Ripley would go over in the corner and stand with their backs to everybody and talk. Mr. Capra would not be included.

"I think maybe Ripley was jealous because Capra got a lot of credit for *The Strong Man*. And Ripley won. I must say that Capra had excellent control of himself, because there was never any flare-up on the set. And it seems to me that they gave him plenty of motivation. Ripley was a strange man. In contrast to the warmth Capra had, Ripley was dour. His mouth turned down at the corners. I was weeks and weeks on both pictures, and I don't ever remember Mr. Ripley saying good morning to me.

"Langdon suggested a couple of things for comedy routines, and I was very grateful, because I was in a new field and I was nervous, but it was not done against Capra. Langdon suggested, for instance, that I should follow directly behind him and lift my feet right at the same time he did. I looked over at Capra, and he said, 'Yes, that's a good idea. That's fine. You do that.'

"But, you see, Capra had just as great a talent as Langdon, and

Langdon threw his away with poor advice and turning to the wrong man, whereas Capra went ahead and soared."

Cameraman Glenn Kershner, who had been working in films since 1914, also was impressed by the young director's demeanor on the set. "The first thing I remember was that he was a neat dresser. Very neat. He always had his chair dusted. And he was receptive. He never said, 'Don't bother me, don't bother me.' He had both ears open to hear everything. Sometimes we'd get into a situation that we didn't know how to get out of, and we'd all sit down and talk it over. We were a happy family on *The Strong Man*. We were going along fine until some woman spoiled the whole thing."

The woman was Helen Walton, Langdon's mistress, whom he later married. "She was a very grasping woman," Priscilla Bonner remembered. "She'd go over and sit in Mr. Capra's chair, which of course was inexcusable. She would sit there and say, 'Harry! Oh, Harry, dear!' She was milking him. She wanted his money. I sensed it, and I thought, 'Mr. Langdon is too good for this woman.' But he was completely overwhelmed with her charms.

"When he married her, it was one of the big mistakes of his life. She was spending money like water, and also she was feeding his ego. And she was in with Ripley. Harry was a simple man. He was not shrewd. And when he got in the hands of a designing woman, and the designing woman decided 'Ripley vs. Capra,' she tied in with Ripley. She controlled Harry. I'm sure that she was responsible for his closeness with Ripley. And Ripley finally got him away from Capra. Then, I think, it was a case of 'You're fired'—'I quit.' "

The tension manifested itself in delays and cost overruns. *Long Pants* wound up costing $318,614, and Langdon had to pay the $68,614 overage out of his own pocket after First National refused to do so, threatening on November 22 to exercise its contractual right to take over financial and creative control of the picture, which was scheduled to be delivered to the company (in final cut form) on January 1 but continued shooting until January 16. Capra's nineteen-year-old nephew Tony Finochio, who worked on the production, fetched the lunches each day for the company; he recalled that he had to make sure his Uncle Frank's sandwiches were toasted, because the situation was giving him an ulcer.

The editing was contentious, and Langdon had to ask First National for several more extensions before delivering the picture. Capra was fired on February 23, shortly before the film's first preview and eight days before the finished negative was turned over to the distributor.

Capra made sure that the *Los Angeles Times* put a good face on it for him: "Director Frank Capra, to whom the success of Harry Langdon's comedy *The Strong Man* is largely credited, has severed connections with the Langdon organization." *Long Pants* had its world premiere in New York on March 26 and received its national release on April 10, cut in the interim from seventy to sixty-one minutes.

When Capra saw the final version two days later in Los Angeles, he was unhappy with the pacing and with the way the elaborate structure he had planned for the picture had been altered. Among the scenes dropped after the premiere was the entire prologue Ripley had objected to, showing Frankie Darro as the boy Harry Langdon being pampered by his parents. The fantasy sequences were reduced substantially and all but a brief snippet discarded of a ten-minute romantic daydream, originally filmed in two-strip Technicolor. Tom Waller described the sequence in *Moving Picture World:* "It shows Langdon, gorgeously costumed, as the gallant lover of a beautiful maiden in a fairy castle. [The maiden was played by Alma Bennett, the same actress who plays the vamp.] It depicts Langdon fighting a duel with his fist as the weapon against a long sword wielded by a huge knight. In the end the fist wins and just after Langdon marries the Fairy Princess, amid much pomp and splendor, he wakes up—the adolescent youth on the broken spring bed in the small-town farmhouse of his mother and father."

Capra's low standing in the industry after his firing was graphically demonstrated in a large ad for *Long Pants* placed by Harry Langdon Productions in the March 23 *Variety*. Under the heading "All the World Is Yelling for LANGDON," the comedian's name was mentioned three times—one of the times in type three sizes as big as the film's title—and the director's name was not even listed once.

But Capra had managed to acquire new Hollywood agents, Morris and Eddie Small. Early in April they came up with a job for him with Robert T. Kane, a New York producer of low-budget features distributed through First National. The line given out to the *Los Angeles Times* was that to accept the offer Capra had "canceled negotiations with three other producers who were seeking his services." But in reality, Capra was so desperate that he accepted Kane's project, *Hell's Kitchen*, with the stipulation that he was to have a codirector, Joseph C. Boyle (whom he later managed to subjugate as his assistant). The movie was to be made at the Cosmopolitan Studio rental facilities in Harlem.

On April 12, 1927, his marriage with Helen ended. "The parting was very brutal," he said. The timing of their final argument suggests that Capra may have transferred to Helen some of his feelings of helpless rage toward the other person he felt had betrayed him, Harry Langdon.

Humiliated and finally driven out of Hollywood in order to find work, Capra saw Helen as a living reminder of the slide from opportunity to failure and the price he was paying for his ambition. By punishing her for his own failure in Hollywood and as a husband, he was also punishing a part of himself, a part he feared and hated.

Capra was to leave for New York on the eve of the Los Angeles premiere of *Long Pants*, scheduled for Good Friday, April 15, at the Loew's State downtown. But, he recalled, he wanted to see *Long Pants* before leaving California, and he wanted Helen to see it with him. There was a preview that Tuesday night. One can readily imagine the emotional turmoil both Frank and Helen felt as the time approached for him to see the film that had caused him such anguish.

Capra said that before leaving the house that morning, he asked Helen, "Would you do me the favor of not drinking today and come with me to this preview?" and that she replied, "Well, of course."

The morning was cold and windy. In the afternoon there was a freak hailstorm, pelting the streets with hailstones the size of walnuts. Capra came home to dress for the preview. As he remembered: "I walked in the door, and I said, 'Come on, gotta get your clothes on.' And she was standing next to the piano, blotto. *Blotto!* There was nothing in my mind but 'What a bitch you are!'

"I didn't say a word. I went over to her and hit her. *Really* hit her. I certainly must have knocked a lot of teeth out of her. She ended up in the corner all in a heap. I didn't give a damn what happened to her. I went upstairs, I got a little bag, got a pair of pants and some shirts. I came down the steps. She was still in the corner. I walked out.

"She was lucky I didn't kill her."

Some, if not all, of the violence in their final argument may have been a fantasy on Capra's part, like Langdon's murderous fantasy in *Long Pants*. Capra's rewriting of the other events leading up to their divorce suggests that such may have been the case.

After the argument he moved into the Hollywood Athletic Club, a fashionable bachelor haven at Sunset and Hudson. Two days later he was on the train for New York. Helen left the Odin Street house while Frank was in New York making the Bob Kane picture, and she took an apartment in Culver City.

In his book Capra wrote that Helen filed for divorce that summer. He claimed that he moved out because after buying her a dress shop on

Hollywood Boulevard for $2,500, he became fed up with her friends carousing with her in the shop.

When asked by the author why he really left her, Capra gave Helen's drinking and his suspicions of her infidelity as the reasons.

Under the California law of the time, Helen had to wait at least a year to file for divorce. She did so on July 23, 1928. Although Capra, in his book, remembered the grounds as "mental cruelty," the grounds she gave was desertion.

Helen's lawyer had worked out a property settlement by that time, but the document was removed from the public record after being confirmed by the court. Capra wrote that he could not afford alimony but gave her a cash settlement of $8,000, which he raised by mortgaging the Odin Street house. His account of his finances would have been true if Helen had filed for divorce in July 1927, as he said in the book. In fact, she filed a year later, when he was earning a good, regular salary, which he wanted to protect. He later admitted to his lawyer, before the divorce became final, that he had paid Helen's living expenses in 1928.

To make matters worse, Helen's private life became public in the newspapers, the only time in Capra's life that he was brushed with sexual scandal.

On December 12, 1928, Mrs. Elizabeth L. Coverdill of Culver City filed a $100,000 lawsuit against Helen for alienation of affections, charging that beginning on August 3 (shortly after Helen filed for divorce), Helen had successfully "launched a campaign" to take away her husband, William, "by offers of money and other inducements."

"Helen fell in love with a fellow who worked in a roller-skating rink in Culver City," Isabelle said. "Frank was so insulted that she would fall in love with somebody he felt was inferior to him. Especially after she told him she had never been happier in her life than she was with that man. Frank told me that. That sort of drove Frank wild. You know how Italian men are—when they get mad, they get mad."

Josie Campisi said that the shop Capra referred to in his book, which he claimed he had established *before* the divorce papers were filed in an attempt to save the marriage, actually was part of the property settlement, which involved Frank setting Helen up in a millinery and dress shop in Hollywood with Annie. Helen made the hats and Annie made the dresses.

Capra was not present in court when the divorce was granted by default on August 13, 1928. The final judgment was entered after the mandatory year's wait, on August 16, 1929. Not long after the opening of the shop, Helen Howell left Hollywood. Capra continued to send her small amounts of money from time to time thereafter. Josie Campisi thought he felt guilty: "It's very hard when somebody gives you a lift with your life, and maybe you're using them. There's a resentment there, but it's hard to let them down. I think he really didn't love her, but he still felt obligated to her.

"Maybe that's why she drank, because she realized it. You've got to be realistic about these things. If he had loved her like he should have, he would have gotten help for her or stayed home more. But he was on the road to success and he was not going to let anything stop him. She couldn't take that loneliness. No matter how you slice it, he was selfish."

"After he left Helen," Isabelle said, "for a year or two he was just so down on women. He *hated* women. He would come to see us in South Pasadena, and he said women were not half as attractive as men. I don't think he was homosexual or anything—I remember him telling me, 'I just love those legs in silk stockings, my God! it makes me so excited!'—but he was really off women. He was kind of disgusted on account of his wife and because I didn't marry him.

"He was so terribly bitter."

It was not true, as Capra claimed in his book, that the critics and the public liked *Long Pants* even more than *The Strong Man. Long Pants* marked the beginning of Langdon's plunge from stardom—a fact that Capra did not want to admit, preferring his readers to believe that the decline began only when Langdon started working on his own.

"A bit of a letdown for Langdon," *Variety* reviewer Alfred Rushford Grearson called *Long Pants.* "It hasn't the popular laughing quality of his other full-length productions, principally because the sympathetic element is over-developed at the expense of the gags and the stunts that made *The Strong Man* a riot."

Langdon's fans undoubtedly were baffled and put off by Harry's involvement with dope peddlers and by his attempt to murder his sympathetic leading lady. After a preview in the Los Angeles area, *Variety* reported that "in the past the pictures of the comedian had been greeted with plenty of laughter and applause, but this got very little of either." (It closed in Los Angeles after only one week.)

Langdon defended the picture in an interview with the *Los Angeles Times.* The writer, Marquis Busby, reported, "In discussing the proposed murder, which, of course, never came to pass, Langdon said that many people tried earnestly to dissuade him from introducing any such theme in a comedy. But the same people had voiced objections to a blind girl as heroine of *The Strong Man,* yet this character did much toward making the picture the human document that it was. . . . Consequently Langdon feels that he will secure approbation." Langdon also attempted to shift the blame for the production problems to Capra by acknowledging that while *Long Pants* ran over its twelve-week shooting schedule, his next feature would be made "in six weeks if necessary. Before we start we will have it thought out in every detail."

The box-office returns for *Long Pants* were appalling. It ranked dead last on the *Film Spectator* survey of major theaters. Yet most film historians, taking Capra's account at face value, have failed to mention the role *Long Pants* played in triggering Langdon's decline.

Langdon's box-office problems were compounded by Mack Sennett. All the time that *Tramp, Tramp, Tramp* and *The Strong Man* had been playing, Sennett had been capitalizing on Langdon's growing popularity by reissuing his old shorts, oversaturating the market. Sennett also held back the release of *His First Flame* until May 3, 1927, shortly after *Long Pants* hit the screens. But rather than capitalizing on the expected commercial success of *Long Pants*, the release of the two-year-old, $75,000 feature backfired. "Langdon is, was and always will be funny but it is just a plain low trick to show this to audiences," wrote the *Photoplay* reviewer of *His First Flame*. "The lighting is bad, the girl's clothes are a scream—in fact the picture looks like a number of two-reelers pasted together."

Even more damagingly for all concerned, the feuding between Langdon and Capra became open knowledge. Capra described only part of the situation in *The Name Above the Title:* how when he took on an agent, Demmy Lamson, after the firing by Langdon, he found that Langdon had poisoned the air against him; the comedian claimed that *he* had directed *The Strong Man* and *Long Pants*, and that Capra had been nothing more than a gag man. Lamson dropped him because of the story, Capra wrote; no other agent would touch him, and he quickly became shunned by the studios.

Capra did not mention in his book that the press picked up on Langdon's putdown. Nor did he mention the way he counteracted it.

On March 2, a week after Capra's firing, an item appeared in *Variety* under the headline "LANGDON WILL DIRECT AND TITLE OWN PICTURES": "Harry Langdon has decided he no longer needs a director to lead him through his paces. Langdon, who has been in the films about five years, is going to direct *The Butter and Egg Man* as his next picture for First National.

"The comedian feels no one can interpret his thoughts as well as himself, so he is going to hold the megaphone instead. Langdon is also said to feel that nobody can title his pictures like he can, so he is also going to title same.

"In the past all ideas and gags used in the Langdon pictures were credited with having been conceived by the comedian, with the gag man simply helping out in the construction."

In her February 1932 *Photoplay* article, "What Happened to Harry Langdon," Katherine Albert revealed what happened next, without mentioning Capra by name: "The angry director wrote a letter to all the movie columnists. He said that Harry was impossible to work with, that he wanted to have a finger in every pie, that he was conceited, egotistical and considered himself the biggest shot in pictures. That he gave himself airs and wore the high hat instead of the little battered felt of his films. It was a vitriolic letter from a disgruntled man.

"But the substance of it got printed. The news was flung all over the world that Langdon was impossible on the set and dabbled in everything. Other writers picked up the story. Almost every newspaper carried it and it gathered power as it went spinning into the world. Movie fans saw it, but more important, it was read by producers.

"Those who knew nothing about it added incidents to make it all seem more important. It was talked about by everyone, the principal topic in the smart luncheon places and the athletic club locker rooms.

"So Langdon thought he was somebody now, did he?

"Producing his own pictures had gone to his head.

"Wanted to be a big shot, did he?"

It is almost certain that the *Variety* article was what sparked the battle. Capra's letter must have been written after the article appeared, perhaps immediately following it. For in the next week's issue of *Variety*, an editorial appeared which indicated that while the industry still believed Langdon's claim that Capra did not really direct *Long Pants*, Langdon was also thought to have gone too far. The editorial sounded like a partial retraction: "There was much talk around the West Coast studios that this comedian had let matters get to his head and that he was making a bad move. The last picture he appeared in was previewed around Los Angeles a few days ago.

"Though this man has been known since on the screen as a great bet and his pictures in the past have been highly commended[,] the audience as well as picture wiseacres who saw the picture quickly realized that something was wrong after seeing one of the frames of the sub-title lead with the actor's name in type that covered the entire frame. Then they looked at 6,500 feet of film, which dragged along at a snail's pace and in which the comic saw to it that 95 percent of the celluloid used had him in the scenes as the principal figure.

"Though the comedian had a director on the job for this picture he practically took away the megaphone and personally directed most of the scenes."

When Kevin Brownlow unearthed the long-forgotten Albert article and cited it in his 1967 book, *The Parade's Gone By. . .* , he added, "Frankly, I find this episode hard to believe, for Capra is revered as a kind and considerate colleague as well as a great director. But it is told by the usually reliable Katherine Albert and the evidence of Langdon's collapse is irrefutable. Capra is sure to provide the full explanation when he publishes his autobiography."

But Capra did not.

It was not until 1985 that he finally admitted to the author of this book that he had in fact written the letter. "I had a lot to counteract," he explained. "Unless you defended yourself, what the hell, nobody would know it." Just rebutting the charges personally to studio executives would not have been sufficient, Capra insisted, because "Langdon had achieved a tremendous reputation. Everybody was talking about him. I couldn't find a job. Nobody would believe me. They'd believe *him*, you see, because he spread it around very hard and very fast that I was just a gag man that he brought over, I was no director."

Although Albert wrote that Capra sent the letter to all of the movie columnists, and although she implied that his letter was sent as background and not for direct quotation, Capra said in 1985 that he had sent it only to one of the Hollywood trade papers and that it *was* printed. However, a search of the trade publications of the time—*Variety, The Film Daily, The Film Spectator, Moving Picture World,* and *Motion Picture News*—failed to turn up such a letter. The only item corresponding to Capra's attack at that time was the *Variety* editorial, which set the tone for subsequent commentary on Langdon's decline, although it is possible that other publications also received a copy of the letter and were influenced by it directly.

Hollywood has always been eager to pounce on a star whose films are failing at the box office, particularly if the star has been behaving in a ridiculously overbearing manner. A star can get away with almost anything if his films make money, but once he starts slipping, it is open season. In any case, the unemployed Capra felt he had little to lose by writing his not-for-attribution poison-pen letter, and, to quote a line he had written for Ben Turpin in the script of *The Reel Virginian:*

"Madam, self-preservation is the first law of nature."

* * *

Langdon's decline was swift and brutal.

First National exercised its option for two more films on April 4, six days before *Long Pants* opened. Langdon directed his next picture, a lugubrious Chaplin imitation filmed as *Gratitude* from April 28 through June 22 and released in August as *Three's a Crowd*. Walter Kerr noted in *The Silent Clowns* that Capra may have contributed to the script without credit (Ripley received credit for the story, James Langdon and Bob Eddy for the adaptation). This is supported by the fact that the salaries of the entire Langdon staff were billed to *Gratitude* as of January 17, when Capra was still there; and Capra told Charles Wolfe in 1981 that Langdon fired him after a disagreement over the script for their next project after *Long Pants*. The story cast Harry as the Odd Fellow, a tenement dweller caring for a homeless mother and her baby. Langdon's sense of comedy seemed to have utterly deserted him when Capra left, and the ineptly directed *Three's a Crowd* is oddly lacking in genuine warmth, wallowing in self-pity and heavy-handed symbolism, such as Harry's playing with a doll resembling himself which he has found in a garbage can. Though Langdon brought in the film for only $243,598, it was an even more resounding flop than *Long Pants*.

"For some reason or other Mr. Langdon has gone intensely tragic," wrote Quinn Martin in *The New York World*. ". . . [H]e appears to have forgotten for the time all he has ever learned of the value of movement and life in the making of comic pictures." "A few more like this," added *Photoplay*, "and he'll be sent to that limbo of lost movie souls—vaudeville."

First National, contractually powerless to interfere with Langdon's decisions unless he went over budget, resorted to warning him in the press that his option would be dropped if he did not make "comedy features that meet market requirements and which would obtain wide distribution and grosses." But his next picture, *The Chaser,* a black comedy about a suicidal skirt-chaser, was so poorly received that First National, undergoing a financial crisis because of the coming of sound, carried through with its threat. Langdon went ahead anyway with the final picture on his six-picture contract, *Heart Trouble,* but First National gave it only a perfunctory release. Langdon returned to vaudeville, and, by 1931, he was forced to declare bankruptcy. He was divorced from his second wife, Helen, in 1933, and though he was happily married to Mabel Sheldon in 1934, whenever he found work Helen plagued him with lawsuits to collect unpaid alimony. Until his death in 1944, he worked mostly in cheap two-reel comedies and wrote gags for other comedians.

Katherine Albert described the impact of Capra's letter on Langdon's personality: "Langdon is a highly sensitized fellow. The thing completely got him. It took away his morale, his pep, his enthusiasm. It made him self-conscious. He had a contract to fulfill. He must go on making pictures, but now when he walked on the set he could feel the cold eyes of his co-workers waiting for his interference, already sure that he was going to make himself objectionable.

"Fearful lest he prove true the statements made in the letter, he took anyone's advice. Trying to overcome and live down his undeserved reputation, he would listen to any prop boy's suggestion for a gag and try to use it. He also heeded the advice of one of the other producers who told him he should shoot his stuff fast, turn out pictures and cash in quick. . . .

"He couldn't be funny when he knew that they were all whispering about him, that they all believed the stories of his conceit.

"It ate into him. He didn't want to see people, he didn't want to be watched off the set. He tried being too friendly and managed to be just a little eccentric instead.

"And one letter from an ex-employee of his had done it."

Wherever he went, Capra's letter followed him. When Hal Roach hired Langdon to make two-reel sound comedies in 1929, the producer, who never had met or worked with Langdon before, warned him immediately, "Now, see here, Langdon, none of that high-handed stuff you pulled at First National." Poisoned before it started, Langdon's working relationship with Roach never progressed beyond that initial distrust, and Roach let him go the following year, complaining of the comedian's "slowness," which had become a code word in Hollywood not only for attacking Langdon's bygone conceit and his previously dilatory production methods, but also for attacking the style that made him a great artist.

"He never did understand what hit him," Capra said of Harry Langdon. "He died of a broken heart."

7. "Marrying the harlot"

Capra regarded the picture he made in New York, which was released as *For the Love of Mike,* as the worst of his career (it is now a lost film). A comedy about three New York ethnics (a Jewish tailor, a Dutch delicatessen owner, and an Irish street cleaner) who adopt a baby and raise him together, putting him through Yale, it starred Ben Lyon as Mike, with George Sidney, Ford Sterling, and Hugh Cameron as his godfathers. Other elements in the commercial formula were action (the Yale regatta, filmed on location) and romantic comedy (in the person of Claudette Colbert, a stage actress making her film debut as an Italian girl working in Sterling's delicatessen).

Producer Robert Kane was hard up for cash and hoping to bluff his way through the shooting of *For the Love of Mike,* keeping the company one jump ahead of creditors. Kane went to Europe before the shooting started, leaving production manager Leland Hayward in charge. The actors insisted on being paid every morning, and Capra cut corners all through the production. "It was just so jumbled up that nobody ever paid attention to the picture. I remember every day, waiting, waiting, until the poor guy [Hayward] would come in with a sack full of money, sweating like a son of a bitch. By then the day was gone."

Unlike the cast, Capra had so little bargaining power that he agreed to defer his entire salary until after the completion of shooting. But he was not in it for the money. He was in it to prove to Hollywood he could direct a picture—*any* picture—apart from Harry Langdon and to dispel his own anxiety on that score.

Claudette Colbert was appearing on Broadway in the hit play *The Barker* concurrently with the filming, and her first film made her determined never to make another: "*For the Love of Mike* I hated. It was not the kind of pantomime I knew anything about or was interested in. I was used to acting with my voice. I remember sitting on a stool and Capra telling me to cry and I couldn't do a thing. The way it was made was terrible—they rushed me from the theater, got me in a car, and raced me to the studio."

"The French girl never did understand me," said Capra, who later directed her again in *It Happened One Night*. "She was a new star on Broadway, and I was nothing. She didn't know what a director was. She had no idea of what to do. But I can't blame anything on her on that picture. We were both neophytes. She was very pretty, but she didn't get anything to do. It was horrible."

When he finished the editing in July, Capra discovered that there was no money left to pay his salary. Not only that, there was no money to buy him a return train ticket.

So the director hitchhiked back to Hollywood.

"**F**lat on my ass" again, in the late summer of 1927, Capra considered quitting the movie business. "I was at a crossroads," he said, "and it was a hell of a decision to make. The first good job that came along would have finished it for me."

There was talk of a job as a chemist with a rubber company on an expedition to South America. But more appealing was the idea of going back to Caltech (as Throop was now called) to study for his master's and doctorate in astronomy, so he could work with his then-idol, Dr. Edwin P. Hubble, at Pasadena's Mount Wilson Observatory.

But Capra first had to take care of an embarrassing problem: he still owed $750 on his college loan. His mother advanced him the money, and he went out to Pasadena to return it to the controller, Edward Barrett, who had made him the loan ten years earlier.

Capra recalled that while visiting the campus, he also went to see Dr. Robert A. Millikan, the president of Caltech. The celebrated physicist had taught at Throop during Capra's junior year, while on leave from the University of Chicago. Capra had never forgotten the thrill of watching Millikan demonstrate his famous oil drop experiment, by which he had been able to determine the charge of an electron. Millikan became president of Caltech in 1921, and under his aggressive guidance the school had outgrown its parochial beginnings and was now regarded as the equal of the University of Chicago and MIT. Caltech's prestige received an enormous boost in 1923 when Millikan was awarded the Nobel Prize.

As Capra told it, the great man "pleaded" with Capra to come back. He told him of all the great things that were happening at Caltech and in the world of science and said, "You ought to come back and be part of it."

"The more he talked, the crazier I got thinking that I was doing the wrong thing in trying to make pictures," Capra said.

Capra evidently exaggerated the degree of his intimacy with Millikan. Correspondence between Capra and Millikan in 1934 indicates that even by that date, Millikan hardly knew Capra, if he knew him at all. What probably happened in 1927 is that Capra pleaded with Caltech to let him come back. Caltech may indeed have offered him some encouragement, but it probably also made him aware of the long odds against his resumption of his career in science and academia because of his mediocre undergraduate record.

"These were the kind of people I liked and wanted to be with," Capra remembered. "It sounded just wonderful. I went away from Caltech that day believing that I was coming back. But when I got home, I started to think that I'd have to go back to school for three years, and would it be worth it? I had to make a decision where I could do better."

Capra wrote that he was mulling over his options when he ran into Mack Sennett on the street: appearing like a deus ex machina and knowing of Capra's hard luck as a director, Sennett invited him to lunch and offered him a return engagement as a gag man. But what probably happened was that Capra, uncertain about returning to the academic life, went back to Sennett and asked for a job.

"That was a real comedown," he admitted. "Sure, it bothered me. I knew a lot of gag men there, and they said, 'Couldn't make it, huh?' 'Big time, ha! Big time a little too big for the boy?' All that crap. It really hurt. I just couldn't take this flak. So I thought about Caltech again. I thought, 'Why should I take all this when I can go and spend the rest of my life with gentlemen?' I was about ready to go back to Caltech."

But he needed money. So on September 12 he went to work with another writer, James J. Tynan, on a two-reel comedy. They spent sixteen days cranking out formulaic gags about the shenanigans of a girls' swimming team on a train en route to a match for berths on the 1928 U.S. Olympic team. Directed by Alf Goulding, the film starred the young Carole Lombard and was released as *The Swim Princess*, with some scenes in two-strip Technicolor.

Capra next worked on two installments of Sennett's series on what the studio called "the domestic adventures of this typical American family," the Smiths. It was the kind of bland situation comedy that later would become the province of television. *Smith's Burglar* and *Smith's "Uncle Tom,"* both directed by Phil Whitman in October–November 1927, did not appear on screens for more than a year.

Despite his ambivalence about his future in the movie business, Capra did not sit around during his second stint at Sennett's waiting for another break. He was desperate to escape from the Tower, afraid that if he stayed in the gag room too long he might never get another chance to direct. It was while he was still at Sennett's, evidently, that Capra, with Nick Barrows (a former Roach gag man who also had worked on *The Swim Princess*), wrote a full-length "spec" script called *Hold Your Husband,* hoping that he could persuade some studio to let him direct it.

Hold Your Husband found no takers, but it was a fine piece of work. A twist on Ferenc Molnár's play *The Guardsman,* the romantic comedy about marital neglect and infidelity also shows the influence of the films of Ernst Lubitsch, whose elliptical visual wit and European sexual sophistication were revolutionizing Hollywood's approach to comedy.

Bebe Dale, a young wife whose husband is having an affair with a nightclub dancer, decides to teach him a lesson by masquerading as a suave, mustachioed French aviator. Not only does she manage to lure the dancer away from her husband, she also persuades her husband that she herself is having a torrid affair with the aviator. The androgyny of the protagonist, the feebleness of the husband, and the greed of the golddigging dancer add up to a jaundiced view of the relations between the sexes, but the portrayal of Bebe represented a lightening of Capra's mood on the subject of women now that Helen was fading from his life.

Capra and Barrows touch deftly on some highly risqué material, allowing the viewer to imagine what happens in private between the "aviator" and the dancer. The most explicit scene in the script is one of Bebe and the other woman dancing together in the nightclub, and it is mostly played for comedy. But when coupled with the transvestite plot, even such mild hints of lesbianism may have been enough to make the script unfilmable in the Hollywood of 1927.

In October 1927, Capra went to work for Columbia Pictures, then located at 1438 Gower Street, just off Sunset Boulevard on Poverty Row.

Poverty Row was a jumble of small buildings and stages housing low-budget production companies. Since many specialized in Westerns, cowboy extras and stuntmen hung out at the drugstore on the corner, giving the area its other nickname, "Gower Gulch" (Capra later memorialized the spot in *It's a Wonderful Life* by having the young George Bailey work for Gower's Drugs).

Capra came to Columbia at a critical point in its history. After beginning as CBC with *The Hall Room Boys* and *Screen Snapshots,* the company was renamed in 1924 to stop people from calling it Corned Beef and Cabbage. With financial success and increasing stature in the industry, production chief Harry Cohn and his partners Joe Brandt and Jack Cohn began an expansion program. In 1926, they made their first public stock offering and opened their first distribution exchanges. By selling their own pictures directly to exhibitors rather than leasing them on a flat-fee basis to states' rights distributors, Columbia could make more money if a film became a hit. Also in 1926, Columbia, which had been renting space on Poverty Row, bought the small studio and office building owned by independent producer Sam Bischoff. Brandt, who often served as mediator between the bitterly competitive Cohn brothers, balked only at the idea of buying theaters, considering it too risky.

So Columbia, in that fall of 1927, was just beginning to engage the major studios in serious competition. But since it had only two stages, no theaters, and little available cash, Columbia had to make its battle with cheap program fillers. "Every dollar spent shows on the screen," the studio's trade ads proclaimed. The average cost of a Columbia picture was $18,000; there were two big-budget "specials" a year, each budgeted at $30,000. The studio could not afford to build expensive sets or to make fancy costume pictures, so most Columbia films were contemporary melodramas or comedies with a threadbare visual look. Nor could Columbia afford to compete for top-line stars, so it usually hired slipping or rising stars for a few days in between their other pictures. Columbia pictures had to be short, not only because production resources were tight but also because Columbia usually found its playdates on the bottom half of double bills, where short features always were preferred by exhibitors.

Harry Cohn said in a 1928 interview that exhibitors were "always on the lookout for the picture that can pinch-hit for a mediocre one. We feel that our pictures must be better than the other fellow's to gain a consistent play on the market. That is why we work on our stories a long time before we put them into production. . . . [W]e have concentrated on ideas and we have created most of our pictures right here in the studio."

Though Cohn ran the production arm of the studio as an autocracy and could be rough on mediocre directors, he recognized that a good director needed to be the boss on his own set. "The only supervisor who is any good at all is the man who can tell the director how to direct," Cohn said, "and if he is able to tell the director how to direct, he should be the director himself."

"Anybody who wanted to could demand control," Capra agreed. "It was not difficult to get. Anybody who was silly enough to want it, they gave it to him. Because then [the director] couldn't say, 'Oh, they gave me a bum script. Oh, they're a terrible cast.' No, you had all the responsibility."

Harry Cohn was also a man whom Capra, like many others, described as a "hunch player." But Cohn was not operating on a blind hunch when the Sennett gag man came in for a job interview at Columbia.

Capra claimed that Columbia called him in for the interview because his name appeared at the top of an alphabetical list of unemployed directors. But if Cohn did not already know Capra from his work for CBC on *Screen Snapshots* (a job that was duly noted in Capra's official Columbia biography during the 1930s), he would have heard something about Capra's work at Sennett's (Columbia frequently hired people from Sennett's), and he certainly would have known about Capra's much-heralded feature directing debut on *The Strong Man*. Cohn must have figured that he could get Capra cheaply and that, after two successive flops and his humiliating return to Sennett's, Capra would be trying especially hard to make an impressive comeback picture, on time and on budget.

It also appears that, as so often happened in Capra's early career, he received a well-placed recommendation which he failed to acknowledge in later years.

Ralph Graves, who starred in five films Capra wrote or cowrote at Sennett's, had turned to directing earlier that year—for Harry Cohn. He directed three features at Columbia in 1927, also starring in two of them. Not long before his death in 1977, Graves discussed Capra with silent-film historian Anthony Slide: "He was one of my gag writers at Mack Sennett. He was a very delightful guy. A wonderful director. I brought him over from Mack Sennett to Harry Cohn."

Though Capra denied the story, he also denied having written any of Graves's Sennett films, and the male lead of the first film he directed at Columbia, *That Certain Thing*, was Ralph Graves, who had the same agent as Capra, Eddie Small.

The job interview, Capra recalled, was with Sam Briskin, Cohn's hard-boiled second-in-command. Capra claimed that he immediately accepted Briskin's almost contemptuous initial offer of $1,000 for a single film provided that he could be not only the director but also the writer and producer.

When Briskin ushered him into Harry Cohn's office and Capra repeated his list of demands, Cohn supposedly asked him, "What do I do?" "You, Mr. Cohn, have the greatest job of all," Capra said he replied. "You can fire me."

Capra's imaginatively embellished accounts, in his book and elsewhere, of the job interview that resulted in his "marrying the harlot," to quote his revealing metaphor for his grudging commitment to a film career, were designed to show not that he was not desperate for work but that he was "trading money for power. . . . I thought, 'If I'm going to stick to this, I'm going to get it all right here—*everything*. Or I screw back to Pasadena.'

"It was the climax of my life. I was at a point where I had to shit or get off the pot. So I said if I'm going to be in this, I want to be Mr. Boss. I wouldn't have talked like that if I hadn't [had Caltech to fall back upon]. That kept me going against people. Years later, I always knew that place was open for me."

While Capra may indeed have wanted to be "Mr. Boss," he did not obtain creative freedom simply by asking for it. It was a gradual process, achieved through a combination of stubbornness and box-office clout—and even then he never had complete freedom.

Despite his supposed agreement with Sam Briskin, if Capra did any writing on his first Columbia film, he did so without credit. Elmer Harris was the credited screenwriter on *That Certain Thing*, a fact that Capra's book doesn't mention. Nor did Capra receive a production credit—that was not granted until his fifth picture for Columbia. As for the $1,000 salary, it is unlikely that Capra had any other choice except to reject it and go back to being a gag man. And if Capra did act that cocky, it was his way of hiding the embarrassing fact that he was overjoyed to take anything he could get, and a way of conveying his ambivalence toward the movie business.

One reason Capra was so eager to claim the authorship of *That Certain Thing* was that of all his early Columbia films, its story is the most "Capraesque."

Ralph Graves is a millionaire's son, disinherited for marrying a poor, ambitious Irish girl (Viola Dana). Graves's father (Burr McIntosh) has made his fortune with a chain of restaurants operating on the theory of "Slice the Ham Thin." Dana and Graves start a small company to sell box lunches to working men; *their* motto is "Cut the Ham Thick." They draw so much business away from McIntosh that he snaps up their company for $200,000, not realizing who the owners are. The newly rich young couple are accepted by the crusty old capitalist, who is impressed by their ability to beat him at his own game.

Capra had touched on elements of this plot in some of his previous films, satirizing the hypocrisies of the rich in his Graves and Alice Day films for Sennett and using the big corporation vs. small entrepreneur conflict as a springboard for the plot of *Tramp, Tramp, Tramp*. But never before had he managed to find these concerns crystallized into such a simple and crowd-pleasing dramatic formula. It was one which would serve him, in one way or another, for much of his mature work. The typically Capraesque blurring of class lines in the romantic plot combined with an equally characteristic economic perspective that proposes a method of getting rich without gouging the workingman.

For the first three days of Capra's twelve-day shooting schedule, Harry Cohn was away from the studio on a vacation in Mexico. The first thing he did when he returned was ask to see all of his new director's rushes. Cohn was anxious about Capra because of the lingering suspicions caused by his firing by Langdon and by the rumors that Capra had not really been in charge during the making of *The Strong Man* and *Long Pants*.

Cohn settled into his chair in the studio projection room. The first day's rushes began rolling. He was shocked. Everything was in long shots. Capra had not bothered to shoot any medium shots or close-ups. Cohn ordered the projector stopped and told Eugene De Rue, the assistant director assigned to the production, to go to the set and fire Capra on the spot.

De Rue's first impression of Capra was that he "didn't look like a director. He looked like a young punk trying to get into the business. But I liked that little guy from the start because I realized he had a good education. He was always thinking."

De Rue urged the "frantic" Cohn not to fire Capra until he watched the rest of the rushes. Cohn complied, grudgingly. The second day's rushes were all medium shots. Then the third day's rushes came on the screen: all close-ups.

"If you don't fire Capra, I'll fire *you*," Cohn barked.

But De Rue talked him out of it by convincing Cohn that there was a method in Capra's apparent madness.

Capra explained what he was doing: "I did it for time. It was so easy to be better than [other directors], because they were all dopes. They would shoot a long shot, then they would have to change the setup to shoot a medium shot, then they would take their close-ups. Then they would come back and start over again. You lose time, you see, moving the cameras and the big goddamn lights. I said, 'I'll get all the long shots on that set first, then all the medium shots, and then the close-ups.' I wouldn't shoot the whole scene each way unless it was necessary. If I knew that part of it was going to play in long shot, I wouldn't shoot that part in close-up. But the trick was not to move nine times, just to move three times. This saved a day, maybe two days."

Capra said he never knew that his job was in jeopardy. It was not long, however, before Cohn changed his mind about him.

"Harry Cohn and I watched the rushes together, and I could tell that he was well pleased with the director," Viola Dana recalled. "We sailed along quite easily. It was a cute picture. Harry Cohn said it was the beginning of Columbia making a better quality of pictures."

That Certain Thing also was the first film Capra made with a man who was to become one of his most important collaborators, cameraman Joseph Walker. The heavyset, soft-spoken Walker had been the regular cameraman for director George Seitz, but when Cohn tried to cut the budget of a Seitz picture from $18,000 to $12,000, the director quit.

"Seitz was a dramatic director," Walker said. "I was a dramatic cameraman, I did real stories—not comedy. All I knew about Capra was that he was a comedy director for Harry Langdon. But when I heard Viola Dana was going to be in it, I decided to do it. It's funny how those little accidents decide your life. If Viola Dana hadn't been in the picture I never would have become associated with Frank Capra and done all those pictures with him."

They did twenty pictures together, including all of Capra's classics at Columbia and *It's a Wonderful Life*.

Born in Denver in 1892, the son of a wealthy mining engineer, Joe Walker began as an assistant to radio pioneer Dr. Lee De Forest, and managed De Forest's radio station in Venice, California. He became interested in motion pictures in 1911 when he watched cameraman Billy Bitzer shooting a film on location in Venice, and in 1914 he found a job as an assistant to Bitzer at D. W. Griffith's Reliance-Majestic. Walker also shot newsreels and documentaries before photographing his first feature in 1919. His work was distinguished by soft, diffused lighting and by his extremely sensitive portraiture of female stars. His romantic, subtly fantastic photography set the style for Capra's best work in the 1930s.

Capra also found Walker congenial because of their shared scientific interests. Walker designed and ground his own custom lenses for each female star he worked with (at one time he had ninety-eight different lenses), and he held twelve patents for devices he invented pertaining to motion pictures, including the world's first zoom lens, which he began developing in 1922, and the television zoom, the Walker Electra-Zoom, which he manufactured after retiring as a cinematographer. He also invented lightweight camera blimps which cut down on noise and revolutionized sound filmmaking; follow-focus equipment; and optical diffusion devices. Capra encouraged him by letting him try out his Duomar (dual focal-length) lens on *Dirigible* (1931) and his early zoom lens (then called the "Traveling Telephoto") on *American Madness* (1932), the first films to incorporate those technical innovations.*

Before they worked together for the first time on *That Certain Thing*, Capra had directed three features and Walker had photographed thirty-six. When he met Capra for the first time in Briskin's office, Walker thought, "He's not only a comedy director, he's just a kid!"

Capra took him to his tiny, cell-like office facing the rectangular courtyard in the middle of the Columbia office building. He gave Walker a chair and took a seat on the desk. After telling Walker the story of the picture, Capra praised his work for Seitz, but added, "This is strictly comedy and we have to work fast. There'll be no chance for anything 'arty.' We want clear, sharp lighting, clear all the way to the corners."

Walker bristled. "You understand," he told the young director, "there's more than an attempt to be 'arty' when I use diffusion and tricks of lighting at Columbia. Their sets are cheap and phony; photography has to make them look like something. And most of the stars who come here are asked to play roles much younger than their own age. Well, soft lighting and a light diffusion can work wonders."

The point was not lost on Capra. In time, he would allow Walker great latitude to experiment with lighting. But on *That Certain Thing*, Capra was determined to prove his ability to work efficiently on a tight shooting schedule. Nor did Capra, before meeting Walker, have a highly developed pictorial sense. His sense of composition and lighting on the Langdon pictures was not much more than utilitarian, and after he stopped working with Walker in 1946, his visual style collapsed, becoming flat, pedestrian, and clumsy. His late work in color is particularly weak, reflecting his utter lack of sensitivity to color values.

---

* *During the 1930s and early 1940s, Capra helped finance Walker's invention of several devices they unsuccessfully tried to market to the military, including a cryptography machine and fins designed to set the wheels of big bombers spinning before they touched the ground. Capra claimed in 1984 that he helped on the design of the zoom lens and on other devices Walker invented: "It wasn't my idea[s] that gave him patents, but it was our talks through which he got patents. You know, he got ideas out of them. Sometimes what he'd do, he'd say, 'Why does this do this or this?' So I'd explain it to him in calculus or in some way that he didn't know about. He was a pretty wise guy, but he didn't have any school[ing]. He didn't have the theory of it. He learned by practice, by doing it." Walker indignantly denied that Capra helped him with the design of the zoom lens ("not a particle") or of his other inventions: "He would have if I'd have asked. I had no need for his knowledge. I started working on the zoom in 1922 and after a while I thought I'd better cover myself with a patent, so I applied for one in February 1929 [it was granted in 1933]. I would have sold it to Capra, but I wouldn't have asked him [to buy it], I wouldn't have put him in that position. I was trying to sell it to a picture company, but I couldn't get anyone to buy it, so on one or two Capra pictures I decided to test the lens."*

Capra's awareness of how critical Walker's contribution was to his work perhaps was what made it difficult for the director to give Walker the acknowledgment he deserved. As Elliot Stein wrote in his *Sight and Sound* review of *The Name Above the Title,* "Although Walker's name pops up here and there in passing, we are graced with an ungenerously skimpy amount of real information concerning his contribution to the quality of many of Capra' films." Walker's wife, Juanita, said diplomatically of the book, "We know a different fellow." "I was very disappointed in Capra's not paying a little more attention to Joe Walker in his book," said George J. Folsey, who photographed Capra's *State of the Union.* "I just think that's awful; I don't like that in Capra. Joe was such a wonderful guy, such a perfectly marvelous cameraman. Every shot he did was beautiful, and he gave Capra's work such class."

As disgruntled as he initially was by Capra's lack of interest in visual style, Walker found himself captivated by the director's personality: when the cameraman arrived on the first morning, he was surprised to find that the director was there ahead of him.

"Frank was smiling and confident—like it was fun to make motion pictures," Walker wrote in his autobiography. "I wondered how long that enthusiasm would last. It wasn't sour grapes on my part, but I knew what a beating the spirit could take on Gower Street. Especially an eager, fresh spirit.

"On that first morning his attitude became contagious and [was] picked up by the cast and crew; even dour Burr McIntosh, the veteran actor, joined in robust chuckles. What a change of pace! . . . in his lighthearted 'let's-get-with-it' manner, he knew what he wanted, and in remarkably short time we began clicking off scene after scene. . . .

"I was very much impressed by Frank's enthusiasm, his confidence in himself, the ease with which he was able to tell people what he wanted. He was so different from any other director I'd ever worked with."

Capra, however, had sensed Walker's initial suspicion. "He thought I was a crank—he only knew me as a director who wanted to do everything. He asked me if I knew anything about the camera. I said, 'Very little. The camera is yours.' That cleared the way with Joe. I had to make friends with these guys. Anybody who thinks he knows everything is crazy. If I told 'em, 'Stand back, I'm gonna do everything'—well, I'm not *that* silly.

"It was the first time I met a cameraman who understood his camera. He understood how it worked and he understood *why* it worked. It was a joy to talk with him. He showed me his lenses, told me about them, told me he was making a new kind of lens. When he found out I was from

Caltech, it made a hell of a difference. Immediately he had a changed attitude. He knew he wasn't talking to some jerk. I may not know anything about a camera, but at least he was talking to somebody who'd been through school.

"He was easy to work with. I'd say a couple of words and he knew what the hell I wanted. He knew what I was thinking."

"Capra didn't tell me what to do," Walker said, "but he thoroughly understood what the lens would do and what the angle was. He wouldn't say, 'I want you to use a 75mm or a 150mm lens,' he'd just say, 'I want a couple of big heads,' and he knew what it would look like. But he said, 'I have enough to worry about, I don't want to have to worry about the photography.' He left it to me. Capra wanted to keep close on people."

Though Capra appeared "lighthearted" on the set of *That Certain Thing*, Walker quickly sensed his determination.

They were shooting a crowd scene on a street-corner set at the Columbia Ranch in Burbank. Capra made a frugal request for fifteen extras. Only four people showed up on the set. Capra complained to Eugene De Rue, who said, "I'm sorry, Mr. Capra, that's all the studio's allowed us." "Let's get in the car and go back to the studio," Capra told Walker.

"You don't understand because you're new," Cohn said after hearing Capra's complaint. "We know you directors. We understand how you work. If you order a hundred extras, we give you forty. You order sixty extras, you get maybe twenty-five or thirty. The picture gets made, everything's fine, nobody worries about it. So you got four extras, so run along now and shoot your scene. Try to work fast so you make up for this lost time in coming into the studio."

"O.K., I'll do that, yes," said Capra, and Walker thought, "Well, Columbia's knocked his ears down, but what can you do?"

"Yes, I'll do that," Capra continued, "when I get fifteen people."

"What do you mean fifteen people?" demanded Cohn. "We just told you—"

And Capra replied, "I know what you just told me. You said that's how you work. I'm willing to go along with how you work. I just want to know how many I have to ask for to get fifteen."

All through his years at Columbia, Capra later insisted, with some exaggeration, "It was fight, fight, fight, fight. Even after it was proven that if they left me alone they would get a better picture. I was the toughest bastard you ever knew. I had to be. Because if you give in you've lost your position. You're lost."

Capra's intensity on *That Certain Thing* became too much even for the admiring Walker. Walker went to Sam Briskin at the end of the production and declared, "Never put me with that director again! He's a great guy—but he's a killer when it comes to work. Just do me a favor. See that I get back to Seitz."

When *That Certain Thing* opened on the outskirts of Los Angeles, Walker went to see it, not expecting much. "Surprisingly, it looked good," he wrote. "A couple of shots of Viola Dana in the rain were pleasing and the rest of the stuff seemed all right. Soon I realized I wasn't looking at the photography; I became engrossed in the story. And it dawned on me: This was awful good directing. A simple little tale had become important in the telling of it!"

The next morning Joe Walker was back in Briskin's office. "I've changed my mind," he said. "I want back on the next Capra picture."

"Those who don't think the independents are trying to make good pictures had better take a look at *That Certain Thing*," wrote *Variety*'s Mark Vance. "Here is an indie that gives A-1 entertainment. . . . Directing is splendid and the work of the small cast immense. . . . It's wholesome, full of fun, and has that touch of neighborhood kin that will make it acceptable everywhere."

Capra's first Columbia film opened on New Year's Day 1928. Even though it was an $18,000 programmer, it had such quality that Columbia marketed it separately as a "special" rather than block-booking it with the regular releases. Capra's second Columbia movie was a romantic comedy, *So This Is Love*, released just a month after *That Certain Thing*. Because he was so high on these two films, Harry Cohn in late January rewarded Capra with a one-year contract, tripling his salary to $3,000 per film, with an option for a second year at $4,000 per film.

Cohn kept Capra moving from one picture to another with barely a pause in his first months at Columbia, and Joe Walker did not catch up with the director again until his fifth Columbia picture, *Say It With Sables*, filmed in June of 1928. The story department would offer Capra a choice of several stories, but the ones he chose, he later admitted, were not always as good as *That Certain Thing:* "Every one of those films has got to be taken purely as a lesson. On every picture that I made, good or bad, I learned a hell of a lot. I learned what not to do, I learned what to do. I was making every different kind of picture, because I didn't know what I liked. I found out that I shouldn't direct dramas. The first couple of dramas I made just stunk, because I made the actors cry but not the audience. But I found out that I could do comedy *and* drama."

Elmer Harris again was the screen writer on *So This Is Love*, this time adapting a story by Norman Springer. Viola Dana's sister, Shirley Mason, had the lead role of a delicatessen girl whose infatuation with a prizefighter (Johnnie Walker) forces her timid dress-designer boyfriend (William [Buster] Collier, Jr.) to battle Walker in the ring. Mocking the traditional macho code all the way through the film, Capra directed the David-and-Goliath tale in a breezy, offhand style that makes enjoyable what might otherwise seem a disturbingly masochistic story.

So This Is Love needed all the help it could get from the director, because it has even skimpier production values than *That Certain Thing*. Almost all of the film takes place on a single tiny studio street, and the paucity of extras in the delicatessen, dress shop, and sidewalk scenes is very noticeable, suggesting that the studio was determined to show the rebellious Capra who was boss when it came to budgetary matters. The extreme cheapness of the film probably contributed to its modest reception. *Variety* found it amusing but said condescendingly, "From the angle of second- and third-run box office—not a bad picture."

But Capra was making movies so rapidly now that *That Certain Thing*, *So This Is Love*, and his next Columbia picture, *The Matinee Idol*, released in March, all had their New York openings within a span of six days that April. His hectic shooting pace was reflected in the tempo of the pictures. According to Cohn, the now-lost *Matinee Idol*, a burlesque of the theater centering on the tribulations of a hammy tent company run by Bessie Love, "started the audience laughing in the first fifty feet and never allowed them to stop except for little impressive human touches injected here and there which never failed to register."

The *Variety* reviewer, Sid Silverman, gave resounding approval to what he called a "solid laugh and hoke picture. . . . It's a picture a good organist can have a circus with. The chest-heaving and gesturing drama lays itself open to all kinds of kidding sobs." Columbia was starting to spend more money on Capra's films, and that helped elevate *The Matinee Idol* in status to a movie that *Variety* said could play on its own without a second feature on the bill. "A few more thousands spread between production and cast," the trade paper observed, "would have made this one worthy [of] the deluxe sites around the country."

Cohn first put the credit "A Frank Capra Production" on the July 13 release *Say It With Sables*. He also advanced Capra $7,500 as the first payment on a $45,000 beach house. The small two-story house, which had its own tennis court, was situated at 95 Malibu Beach, in what one day would become the exclusive Malibu Colony. Capra turned the Odin Street house over to his mother and his sister Ann. Ann's husband had left for South America after she had a tubular pregnancy (the operation left her unable to bear children), and she now was working as a designer for Zukin's, a dressmaker downtown. Al Roscoe, who had been living with Capra on Odin Street, joined him in the Malibu house. At different times Capra also maintained quarters at the Hollywood Athletic Club and the Hollywood Roosevelt Hotel, using the Malibu house on weekends and during the brief periods between pictures.

Now that he was more secure in his situation with Columbia, Capra was trying his hand again at drama. Perhaps the decision was more the studio's, attempting to see how much range he had. But though Capra felt that *The Way of the Strong* and *Say It With Sables* "stunk," from a biographical point of view the subject matter of those films is most revealing.

So grotesque it verges on the operatic, *The Way of the Strong*, written by William Counselman and Peter Milne, was described by Columbia as the story of "the world's ugliest man, who can bear anything except the sight of his own face in a mirror." Mitchell Lewis plays "Handsome" Williams, a hulking gangster whose misshapen face is crisscrossed with scars. The beauty underlying his brutish exterior is shown by his tenderness toward Nora (Alice Day), a blind violinist who works in his cafe and falls in love with him, thinking he is truly handsome. But when she realizes for the first time how he looks, she recoils. Handsome sacrifices her to a good-looking rival, then shoots himself in the head as he drives his roadster into the sea. Of the many suicide attempts in Capra films, this is one of only two that succeed (the other is in *The Bitter Tea of General Yen*), and it is a particularly startling ending for a supposedly "optimistic" director.

Capra by this time was cutting a dapper figure in Hollywood. Colleen Moore, the most popular female star in pictures when she worked on the First National lot in the mid-twenties, remembered doing a double take one day when she saw Capra walking along the street past her bungalow. "Who is *that?*" she wondered, thinking the dark young man strikingly handsome.

It was a time when, thanks to Valentino, the Latin look was fashionable, and Capra was appearing on the set fastidiously attired in tastefully cut, relatively subdued three-piece suits, although some of his old habits persisted: Annie would become exasperated when her brother bought expensive cashmere sweaters and let them become torn and moth-eaten. Still there was a confidence, almost a swagger, in his manner now, that women found attractive, a quiet sense of power that emanated from him since he had become a director. Yet Capra (as in Moore's story) seldom seemed to notice women's approbation. In his inner mirror, he was always the ugly, ungainly, ostracized immigrant boy, who habitually disparaged his own appearance to women throughout his lifetime.

Capra and Milne wrote the story of *Say It With Sables*, a throwback to the virulent misogyny of some of his Sennett films; the screenplay was by Columbia's story editor, Dorothy Howell, the first of several she would write for the director. Margaret Livingston starred as a golddigger with a penchant for expensive furs. Banker Francis X. Bushman dumps her to marry the more genteel Helene Chadwick, but years later she takes her revenge by seducing his not-very-bright son (Arthur Rankin). The mother shoots her, and a sympathetic detective lets the death go on the books as a suicide. It was a drearily puritanical "sins of the fathers" melodrama.*

Harry Cohn, the inveterate gambler, recognized that he had a valuable bargaining chip in Frank Capra. He had long been frustrated over his inability to borrow stars from the bigger studios, but he figured he could trade Capra's services for the use of another studio's contract player to enhance a Columbia production. The prime target of Cohn's envy was Metro-Goldwyn-Mayer, which boasted of having "More Stars Than There Are in Heaven."

Capra did not mind being used as a pawn in Cohn's game. Chafing at the low social status Hollywood accorded a Poverty Row studio such as Columbia, he frankly lusted after the prestige of directing an MGM picture. So Cohn made a deal with Louis B. Mayer to loan Capra to direct a prison comedy, *Brotherly Love*, for MGM. Capra said Cohn was sufficiently intimidated by Mayer to make the loan simply as a favor in hope of a future payoff.

In early 1928, Capra went to MGM to work with writers Earl Baldwin and Lew Lipton on *Brotherly Love*, based on a *Liberty* magazine story by Patterson Margoni, "Big-Hearted Jim." The film was to star Karl Dane and George K. Arthur as a prison guard and an inmate who both love the

---

* *All that exists of the film today is a forty-second trailer, preserved by a private collector in Florida and copied by the American Film Institute after it began rescuing old films in the late 1960s. Other Capra silents which have been lost through neglect and nitrate film decay are* For the Love of Mike, The Matinee Idol, *and part of* The Power of the Press. *That Certain Thing exists only because a private collector preserved it in 16mm. So This Is Love was copied from a print found in France, and* The Way of the Strong *was discovered in Denmark. Even such major Capra films as* Lady for a Day, It Happened One Night, Broadway Bill, Lost Horizon, Meet John Doe, *and* It's a Wonderful Life *are missing part or all of their original negatives, and the AFI, the Library of Congress, and various film archives have devoted strenuous effort to restoring them, with help and encouragement from Capra himself.*

warden's daughter. Dane tries to humiliate the diminutive Arthur by having him put on the prison's football team, but Arthur becomes a hero and is released to marry the girl. The script was approved by MGM executive Harry Rapf on March 24, 1928, and was scheduled to begin shooting at the end of May, with a twenty-four-day shooting schedule (twice as long as a typical Columbia comedy). Capra was to make both a silent version and one with some talking sequences.

But as the start of production drew closer, Capra said, he began to feel constricted by the MGM approach to filmmaking. He realized that, despite the minuscule budgets and shabby production values he had become accustomed to at Columbia, he had much more freedom under Harry Cohn's benevolent dictatorship. One way MGM kept its directors in line was by ordering extensive retakes on most pictures, with other directors usually stepping in to shoot them. The result was a finely tooled but relatively impersonal product. The MGM directors were highly paid, but, as Capra often pointed out, they were little known outside the industry because they were not allowed to develop personal styles. Capra mentioned in his book that he had been fired from an MGM picture, but he did not name the picture, and he mistakenly remembered the year as 1931.

The story he told was that three days before the film was to begin shooting, he was asked to direct a retake on the previous Dane-Arthur comedy, with former Sennett comedienne Polly Moran. But, according to Capra, Moran refused to appear scantily dressed as the script indicated, so he made up several alternate scenes on the spot and shot them all so the studio could choose the one it liked. Rapf did not appreciate Capra's inventiveness. He sent him back to Columbia and replaced him with Charles F. Reisner, who was assigned to *Brotherly Love* on May 28 and began shooting the following day.

Whether or not this was the actual reason Capra was fired is not known; most likely it was the last in a series of conflicts over his demands for directorial autonomy. A measure of his lack of creative control on *Brotherly Love* was that he was not allowed to cast the leading lady, and so he never met the young woman chosen by MGM until seven years later, when he cast Jean Arthur in *Mr. Deeds Goes to Town*.

Because of its public stock sale and the increased profits from its pictures (particularly Capra's), Columbia had enough cash on hand in the summer of 1928 to take a gamble. Though the penny-pinching Harry Cohn was nervous about the idea, Jack Cohn persuaded his partners to go head-to-head with the major studios by making an A picture. The $150,000 budget was more than eight times the cost of the quickies Capra was making, but Columbia covered its bets by persuading the U.S. Navy to come aboard as its partner in the production.

The movie was *Submarine*, an adventure story suggested by two actual disasters involving Navy submarines. The Navy, which had come under heavy criticism for losing the two subs, was eager to give Columbia full cooperation in presenting a heroic view of its rescue efforts—Columbia agreed that the ship in *Submarine* would be successfully rescued, unlike its namesake, the S-44. In exchange for this "valuable propaganda," as *Variety* called it, the Navy let Columbia use an actual submarine, as well as the aircraft carrier *Saratoga*, airplanes, battleships, and squads of enlisted men for extras.

Such a large-scale production demanded an experienced action director, so Columbia hired Irvin Willat, best known for his sea pictures, particularly the 1920 submarine tale *Below the Surface*. Jack Holt and Ralph Graves were cast in the lead roles of Navy diver Jack Reagon and submarine officer Bob Mason. Much of Winifred Dunn's formulaic screenplay dealt with the *What Price Glory?* brand of rivalry between the two friends over Jack's sluttish wife, Bessie (Dorothy Revier, who had appeared in Capra's 1921 documentary about the Italian battleship *Libia*).

Joe Walker, who shot *Submarine*, recalled that during preproduction (when the film was alternately titled *Into the Depths* or *Out of the Depths*), "Harry Cohn became fidgety and irritable, more so than usual. For the first time, I detected fear and uncertainty in his ordinarily bullish expression. The New York office put the pressure on him; this picture *had* to be good."

The first few days of shooting in June 1928 did not allay Cohn's anxiety. He found Holt and Graves stiff and unconvincing.

"Can't you make them look tougher?" he asked Walker.

But after three weeks, the executives decided that the problem was not with the actors.

"We were unhappy with the film," Sam Briskin recalled in a 1965 interview with Bob Thomas, "so on a Saturday [July 7] we decided to replace Willat with Frank Capra. It was like replacing Billy Wilder with a TV director. We asked Capra to see the film and read the script on a Saturday, and he went to San Pedro to begin the picture on a Monday."

Variety told its readers that "a nervous breakdown from overwork" had caused Willat's departure. Still smarting over the firing in his old age, Willat attributed his replacement by "a little dago" to studio politics: "Capra at that time was making his way up . . . Mr. Cohn wanted to contract him and hold him." He quoted Harry Cohn as telling him, "I wanted to build Frank Capra."

Despite their many battles, it was the confidence Cohn placed in his young director that made Capra look back and say, "I owed Cohn a lot—I owed him my whole career. So I had respect for him, and a certain amount of love. Despite his crudeness and everything else, he gave me my chance. He took a gamble on me."

Waiting on the dock at San Pedro on Monday morning, July 9, 1928, to see whom the studio was sending out to take over the reins of its biggest production, Walker was surprised and delighted to see Capra step out of the studio limousine.

"I wanted to cheer him outright," he recalled. "This was like the talented understudy taking over for the star. . . . [But] Frank was not his usual smiling self. Solemn-faced and slightly nervous, he tackled this responsibility thrust upon him in a forthright manner as he addressed the crew in clipped words, telling them speed was imperative from now on, that everything to date had to be reshot."

Despite Willat's assertions that Columbia "used every goddamn foot of film I made" and that Capra only shot the ending, Walker confirmed Capra's statement that he reshot all of Willat's footage. Walker agreed with Capra's assessment that what made Holt and Graves seem phony was their makeup and their starchy, immaculate uniforms.

Out of loyalty to Willat, both Holt and Graves threatened to walk off the picture. Recognizing the tenuousness of his position, Capra decided to force them to accept his authority that first morning by issuing an edict that none of the actors would wear makeup. He also persuaded the spit-and-polish Holt to dirty his uniform and leave his hairpiece in the dressing room.

From that point on, Capra was in command. Walker found him "the same on big pictures as he was on small pictures—easygoing, business-like, no pressure."

On August 30, *Submarine* opened in New York at a first-run Broadway theater, the Embassy. The biggest moneymaker in the young company's history, it was also a critical success, decisively rehabilitating Capra's reputation from the lingering effects of the Langdon debacle and establishing him as a versatile and important director.

"Frank R. Capra's direction is especially clever," wrote Mordaunt Hall in *The New York Times*, "for not only has he attended to the action of the story, but he has also obtained from his players infinitely better characterization than one is apt to see on the screen, especially in a melodrama."

Even Irvin Willat had to admit that "it was a hell of a good picture."

*   *   *

Submarine also was Columbia's, and Capra's, first tentative venture into sound. The industry had been in a state of barely controlled panic in the months following Warner Bros.' unexpectedly successful premiere of the part-talking, part-singing *The Jazz Singer*, with Al Jolson, on October 6, 1927, shortly before Capra came to Columbia. Not sure whether talkies were just a passing fad, the other studios adopted a wait-and-see attitude. They were reluctant to undertake the great expense of rebuilding their stages and theaters. There also were many in Hollywood who considered sound a threat to the art of motion pictures and fervently hoped it would go away.

Capra was not one of them. When he first saw *The Jazz Singer*, he later recalled, "It was an absolute shock to hear this man open his mouth and a song come out of it. It was one of those once-in-a-lifetime experiences."

Capra was convinced that sound was "an enormous step forward. I wasn't at home in silent films; I thought it was very strange to stop and put a title on the screen and then come back to the action. It was a very contrived and very mechanical way of doing things. When I got to working with sound, I thought, my, what a wonderful tool has been added. I don't think I could have gone very far in silent pictures—at least not so far as I did go with sound."

The most memorable scene in *Submarine* involved a sound effect. It was added, like the other effects, after the film had finished shooting. Following the lead of Fox, which had added Movietone music and sound effects to its "silent" pictures, Columbia decided to add a musical score, a song, and limited sound effects to increase the box-office chances of its ambitious production.

The dramatic climax of *Submarine* comes when the crew in the disabled sub almost has run out of oxygen. Attempts to reach them fail until a lone diver, Holt, descends four hundred feet to the ocean floor. (Lacking money to shoot the scene on a larger scale, Capra and Walker filmed part of it in a fish tank using a toy submarine and diver. Capra found the diver in a nickel novelty machine in the drugstore at the corner of Sunset and Gower.) Holt, reaching the submarine, taps on its hull, hoping someone inside is still alive to hear him. The audience at the New York premiere cheered when they heard a faint *tap-tap-tap* from inside the submarine. Even today, the effect is chilling.

The public reaction gave Columbia's nervous executives the confidence they needed to order a major retooling for sound. In the meantime, Harry Cohn gave Capra a new contract, with a sizable advance in pay for a period of three years. Almost as an afterthought, Cohn assigned Capra to one last silent film, a newspaper melodrama called *The Power of the Press*, released on October 31. Douglas Fairbanks, Jr., had the lead role of a crusading cub reporter who solves the murder of the district attorney during a political campaign. Shallow and contrived though the story was, it enabled the former paperboy and *Los Angeles Times* stuffer to indulge vicariously his fleeting youthful ambition of becoming a reporter. The best sequence in *The Power of the Press* was a piece of pure directorial bravura, a masterfully filmed and edited documentary interlude depicting the progress of a newspaper story from the reporter's typewriter through all the various mechanical stages of typesetting, layout, composing, and printing. It was a tribute not only to the power of the press but to the power of film.

Capra was relieved, in a way, to be back at Columbia, where his cockiness paid dividends. But the rejection by MGM had made him determined to return one day, when he had more clout in the industry, and make them do it his way. In the meantime, he recognized that he had a valuable power base: "I could have gotten a lot more money outside. I preferred being at Columbia because of my freedom. I paid for my freedom. Freedom to make your picture is freedom to choose—to choose your actors, to choose your story. Nobody else at Columbia had my freedom.

"I had one hammer, and that was that I could leave. That's what made Cohn mad. He needed me."

After his first talkie, *The Younger Generation*, the word got around that his Caltech education had enabled him to adjust quickly to sound, Capra bragged in his book. But his chief cinematographer on that picture, Ted Tetzlaff, who also shot *The Power of the Press* and Capra's second talkie, *The Donovan Affair*, was not even aware that the director *had* a scientific education. "It wasn't something that came up," Tetzlaff said. "You had to bluff to survive. When sound first came in, nobody knew much about it. We were all walking around in the dark. Even the sound man didn't know much about it. Frank lived through it. But he was quite intelligent. He was one of the few directors who knew what the hell they were doing. Most of your directors walked around in a fog—they didn't know where the door was."

Made in late 1928 and early 1929, and released on March 4, the day President Herbert Hoover was inaugurated, *The Younger Generation* was, like *The Jazz Singer*, a part-silent, part-talking picture about a Jewish immigrant family in New York. It was shot first as a silent, but when Columbia belatedly decided to join the rush into talkies, several sequences were reshot with dialogue, with several cameras being used at once to obtain all the necessary angles with the sound in synchronization. Since Columbia was just beginning to retool its stages for sound, it had to rent facilities at Al Christie's Hollywood Metropolitan Studios (now Hollywood Center Studios). The track was recorded on wax discs and played on records in theaters; a symphonic score was used during the nondialogue sections.

"Every day you worked was more or less a test," Tetzlaff said. "If it worked, you kept it. If it didn't work, you did it over again. We had to hide mikes in bouquets of flowers and in people's pockets. That's why everybody would walk up to a spot and talk to it, because that's where the mike was. I remember doing a sound sequence in *The Younger Generation* in which the characters all sat around a dining room table, and we had the mike in a bowl in the center. It was an experience."

When *Variety*'s Alfred Rushford Grearson saw *The Younger Generation* during its premiere engagement in March at New York's Colony Theater, he found that "sound reproduction at this performance was as bad as it could be. Sound and action were way out of step. Lips and machine were ten words apart and dramatic lines inspired only laughs." However, Grearson blamed the problem on the disc sound projection system rather than on Columbia's recording: "Quality of tone production is excellent, and all five principal characters sound well."

Despite all the mechanical encumbrances, *The Younger Generation* (based on Fannie Hurst's 1927 play *It Is to Laugh,* with a screenplay by Sonya Levien and Howard J. Green) has more emotional power than any of Capra's other pictures of the 1920s. Capra obviously felt a strong identification with the story of a Jewish immigrant (Ricardo Cortez) who grows up in the ghetto of New York's Delancey Street and feels he has to deny his ethnic origins to rise to success in America. Changing his name from Morris Goldfish to Maurice Fish, he leaves his father's junk business to trade antiques on Fifth Avenue and becomes ashamed of his parents, Julius and Tilda (Jean Hersholt and Rosa Rosanova). In the film's devastatingly painful climactic scene, the social-climbing Morris, embarrassed when his ritzy friends unexpectedly come face-to-face with his parents, passes off his mother and father as his servants.

One reason *The Younger Generation* is so little known is that Capra never talked or wrote much about it, except as his first experience with talking pictures. When asked by the author of this book whether the story had any personal resonance for him, Capra insisted, "I didn't make it because of the story." He also insisted he had no special interest in immigrants or their problems because (Maurice Fish could not have put it better): "I was practically born in America, so those were the people I associated with."

"That was the trouble with him," Josie Campisi observed of her Uncle Frank. "He had that insecurity about being a peasant. His brothers and sisters were good people. He missed a lot."

Despite his denials, *The Younger Generation* abounds with parallels to Capra's own life. The earthy, convivial, improvident, cigar-smoking Papa Julius (a lovely performance by Hersholt) has much in common with Frank Capra's Papa Turiddu. Julius prefers schmoozing with his friends on the street to selling junk out of his pushcart. His hardworking wife demands, "How can we ever get out of this low-life, Julius, if you only make jokes, and no money?" Young Morris has the indomitable drive and optimism characteristic of the young Frank Capra: when their home burns, the enterprising lad exults, "Now we can have a fire sale!" His subsequent rejection of his parents echoes the shame Capra admitted feeling toward his family as he rose in social status.

The film's most serious flaw is that Morris/Maurice is never allowed to engage the audience's sympathy except in his childhood and at the very end, when he pathetically tries to make amends with his shattered family. Most of the time he is a stick figure, seen from a distance, barely in the movie at all. It is as if Capra felt he could not risk getting too close to his protagonist and had to shift the emotional focus to the father and the other members of the family so that no one would mistake him for Maurice Fish.

Capra followed *The Younger Generation* with his, and Columbia's, first all-talking picture, *The Donovan Affair,* based on a play by Owen Davis, with screen continuity by Dorothy Howell and dialogue by Howard J. Green. The studio selected the property because its murder mystery plot was set inside a country house (mostly in the dining hall) and would present a minimum of sound problems for the five cameras needed to shoot the picture.*

The plot was so ridiculously contrived that Capra had little choice but to treat it tongue-in-cheek. Jack Donovan (John Roche) is a roguish gambler murdered by an unknown person in the darkened dining hall. As is customary in the genre, several of the guests had reasons to wish him dead. Inspector Killian (Jack Holt) restages the scene with the original partici-

---

* *A silent version also was released to theaters not equipped to handle the sound discs. Today this forgotten film can be seen only at the Library of Congress, in a print lacking a sound track. The sound elements exist but a restoration would have to be undertaken to synchronize them with the picture.*

pants, and the atmosphere is full of the usual clichés of howling wind, barking dogs, and sinister servants, all of it adroitly orchestrated by Capra and Tetzlaff in this fast-paced and flamboyantly photographed film, which Capra felt marked an important advance in his development as a director.

"Capra has manipulated his story and people with restraint and intelligence," Robert J. Landry wrote in *Variety*. "Recording and technical details all nicely taken care of. Production looks good. In short, Columbia has rung the bell." And Mordaunt Hall wrote in *The New York Times*, "It is a yarn that sustains the interest, and because of its farcical quality it affords good entertainment."

Now that he was making fewer and more expensive pictures, Capra had more time to relax, whooping it up with Al Roscoe at their Malibu beach house and going on hunting and fishing expeditions to Baja California and to Silver Lake in the High Sierras, near the community of June Lake, with Roscoe's friend Wallace Beery.*

Some, relying on what Capra told them, described Capra as having been a "womanizer" in that period. Though he was loath to form any emotional attachments and felt he was "a lousy lay," he apparently indulged in some uncharacteristic Don Juanism under Roscoe's influence. Josie Campisi said her uncle was "always kind of a square" when it came to women, but while acknowledging that his sexual inhibitions continued to restrain him, he boasted of his relationship in that period with the young actress Ginger Rogers. "I loved her," he said. "I loved her every way. She's funny, she's beautiful, she's clever, but I could not see her as a mother of kids. We were great friends, we knocked around, but I stayed away from getting involved.

"My dedication to film went all the way. I was determined not to marry an actress, because it would interfere with my work. I knew it would be the wrong thing to do, because actresses should never get married. You can't control them. Jesus, she's your wife but she tells *you* what to do! So I stopped at marriage, because I had seen too much of that."

Columbia decided to capitalize on the box-office success of *Submarine* with another military action melodrama starring Holt and Graves, this time as Marine Corps aviators fighting Nicaraguan rebels and battling again over the same woman (Lila Lee). Graves wrote the story, called *Flight*, and Capra was credited with the puerile dialogue. Seldom revived today, the

---

* *Roscoe died of cancer in 1933 at the age of forty-four.*

extremely reactionary *Flight* would cause anyone who considers Capra a liberal to hastily revise that view of his politics.

The 1929 *Flight* is a gung-ho sales job for the Marines, who had been sent to Nicaragua in an unsuccessful attempt to help suppress the first Sandinista rebellion in 1927 (the César Augusto Sandino character is called "the bandit Lobo" in the film, "a cruel, cunning devil"). The film shows Graves and Holt enthusiastically bombing the "gooks" besieging an isolated Marine fort, in a sequence based on the Marines' aerial slaughter of several hundred Sandinistas at the Battle of Ocotal on July 16, 1927. The political situation is little more than an excuse for the Graves character to prove his manhood—an excuse he sorely needs, for this bizarre film takes the character through the wildest extremes of cowardice and blood-crazed abandon.

Although there is an obvious parallel between the Graves character and Conrad's Lord Jim, the story also had a deep personal resonance for Capra, who struggled all his life with fear and cowardice and in his boyhood dreamed of becoming an aviator, like his idol Jimmy Doolittle. He and Graves took the springboard for *Flight* from an incident Capra and Harry Cohn witnessed at the Rose Bowl game between Georgia Tech and the University of California in Pasadena on January 1, 1929. Georgia Tech's 8–7 victory came about because a California lineman, Roy Riegels, grabbing a fumbled ball, ran for sixty-nine yards in the wrong direction before being tackled at California's one-yard line by members of his own team. The unfortunate player became known as "Wrong-Way" Riegels. *Flight* starts with Graves as a Yale football player running the wrong way to win the game for Harvard as the closing gun sounds. Lefty Phelps is a more dramatic, but still intentionally somewhat ridiculous, version of the neurotics Graves played in the comedy scripts Capra wrote for Sennett. Lefty goes to Nicaragua to escape his humiliation, and his redemption as a courageous flyer, under the sympathetic eyes of his superior officer Jack Holt, shows Capra's lifelong fascination with the twin poles of heroism and despair, and their coexistence in the personalities of his manic-depressive heroes.

Columbia again received full government cooperation, with men and planes supplied by the Marine base at San Diego. To play the Nicaraguan rebels, Columbia rounded up American Indians from nearby towns. Most of the picture was shot in the foothills around La Mesa and Fallbrook, just a few miles from the Fallbrook ranch Capra later owned and an hour-and-a-half journey by car from the company's base at the Hotel del Coronado across the bay from San Diego.

The shooting of *Flight* marked a further advance in Capra's use of sound. One of the most fluid of the early talkies, it shows his refusal to be bound by the restrictions of the sound men and their bulky equipment. With Joe Walker as chief cameraman, and Elmer G. Dyer photographing the aerial footage, Capra shot much of the action footage silent, dubbing in the sound tracks later. Taking full advantage of his technical resources and his growing reputation at Columbia, Capra used 100,000 feet of film on the single sequence of the pilots bombing the rebels. It took two or three days just to project the rushes on that sequence, and Columbia had to put three editors on the picture so it could be finished in time for its September premiere. But despite Capra's trumpeting of the film's technical achievements, it is marred, as critic Elliot Stein noted, by being "full of scenes of miniature planes taking off, miniature planes crashing in trick tabletop shots, as Jack Holt and other staunch Marines bomb the hell out of hundreds of scrubby Nicaraguan rebel 'greasers.' "

Flight opened with full ballyhoo in New York on September 13, 1929, and it was, like *Submarine,* a substantial commercial success both in the United States and abroad. Some reviewers objected to its political stance— *The Canadian Forum* called it an "obnoxious film . . . a ridiculous misrepresentation of American activity in Nicaragua"—but most overlooked the message, and the notice that counted for Cohn was the money review by *Variety*'s Sime Silverman, who hailed it as "a crackerjack picture for an independent producer." Silverman called Capra "a most skillful and imaginative director . . . with plenty of guts."

It was during the making of *Flight* that Capra met a young widow named Lucille Warner Reyburn, whom everyone called "Lu."

"The most important person in my life" (as Capra later described her) had come to the location to visit her best friend from college, Alyce Coleman, the wife of his assistant director, C. C. (Buddy) Coleman. "What a lovely voice!" he thought when Lu finally spoke to him. She had been sitting at his crowded dinner table for several nights without catching his eye. The Colemans maneuvered her closer to Capra one night after rushes, and he drove her back from San Diego to the hotel along the Silver Strand, a peninsula favored for nocturnal romantic occasions. As he recalled the moment in his book, at the door of her room, "I kissed her. I knew. She knew."

Lu was one of those "classy gals" for whom Capra had always had such a weakness. Though more handsome than beautiful, she was short, slender, and deceptively delicate looking. Wholesome rather than glamorous, sweet rather than brassy, she was easily overlooked in a roomful of more extroverted people. Those were qualities that appealed to Capra.

When they did notice Lu, people always appreciated her ready, vivacious, sincere smile and the friendliness that flowed from her wide, dark, attentive eyes. "She was a person with a most wonderful sense of humor," Jean Arthur recalled. "She was very pretty and very charming and kinda happy, like she was just going to burst out laughing. She always found a joke in something. You felt good when you were around her."

She was of Welsh and English descent and came from a family background that, at least in Capra's eyes, seemed "classy" indeed. On her mother's side, she claimed descent from Sir Thomas More. Her paternal grandfather, James Warner, came to America from Wales and settled in the San Joaquin Valley in north central California, where he became a successful pioneer rancher. He raised seven sons and two daughters, the family becoming so large and prominent that the small community where they lived, near Ceres, was named after them—Warnerville. One of James Warner's sons, Myron, married Florence Marr, the first-generation American daughter of English immigrant parents living in Oakland; her father was a shipbuilder.

Lucille Florence Warner, the first child of Myron and Florence Warner, was born in Oakland on April 23, 1903, seventeen days before the five-year-old Frank Capra left Italy for America.

She spent her early years in Ceres, where her father was a rancher and farmer, and in the Oakland and Sacramento areas. When she was about twelve, her family, which now included a brother named James, moved to Rochester, Nevada, where her father operated a gold mine. The town consisted of nothing but two saloons, a school, and a handful of other buildings. In that isolated area the children grew up to be both hardy and introspective. One of their favorite amusements was to catch and ride the wild donkeys that roamed the desert around their little town. The Warners returned to the San Joaquin Valley, to a small town near Planada, when Lu was about sixteen. Her father made a comfortable living as the operator and joint owner of a four-hundred-acre ranch that grew Kadota figs.

Lu was a bright enough young woman, though in the end her personal ambition went no further than a good marriage. She attended UC Berkeley between September 1921 and December 1923, majoring in English. "She loved books—she read every book ever written," Capra said, but she enjoyed socializing more than her college studies, and left without a degree. Following her parents to Los Angeles, where her father had gone into the real estate business, she worked as a stenographer, as a clerk for

UCLA, and as a secretary for another real estate man. (Capra denied that Lu ever worked before he met her. "When I met her," he said, "she wasn't anything.")

In 1928 she married a young oil company engineer, Francis Clarke Reyburn, who worked in Long Beach. Clarke was from a wealthy and socially prominent family in St. Louis; his father was a judge. Lu and Clarke lived in Los Angeles and were happily married, planning to have children in the near future. After they had been married about a year, Clarke, who was somewhat overweight but otherwise appeared to be in good health, suffered a ruptured appendix and died of peritonitis. The young widow was left a share of the family trust fund, enough to enable her to live comfortably (at the time of her death in 1984, her share amounted to $277,216). Lu stayed for a while with her late husband's family in St. Louis and then returned to Los Angeles. She did little socializing until a few months later, when Alyce Coleman coaxed her into visiting the location of *Flight*.

Lu was the "perfect" mate for Frank Capra. "She loved what I was doing," he said after her death. "She was a very intelligent girl—she had been graduated [*sic*] from the University of California. She knew a lot about a lot of things. She was fun to be with. She enjoyed the same things I did. She was sunny. Our arguments were very few and very mild."

And, most critically, Lu, unlike Helen, was not jealous of his work. "She was not in show business, but she liked movies. She was a good audience. She enjoyed the whole process as much as I did. I did not have to worry about her, whether she was going to get mad if I was a little late, 'Where have you been?' and all that kind of crap, none of that. She was too smart."

As Josie Campisi put it, "She was just his shadow—whatever he said went."

And yet he resisted her. After his "horrible" first experience, he was wary of marriage.

If Capra needed a reminder, he received a dramatic one in 1930 when Helen made an unannounced appearance at his office on the Columbia lot. She had a small child in tow who she said was her own, which he said surprised him because he thought she could not have children. Evidently only one of her Fallopian tubes had been removed following her ectopic pregnancy, but if Capra's surprise was genuine, it must have intensified his sexual anxieties. Capra said Helen wanted to get back together with him, and that he told her, "I'm sorry, honey, but it's too late." It was the last time he saw his first wife, who died in obscurity around 1960.

But there was another reason for Capra's hesitation over marrying Lu: Barbara Stanwyck.

Columbia assigned Capra to *Ladies of Leisure*, based on a 1924 stage play by Milton Herbert Gropper, *Ladies of the Evening*. Capra wrote the first draft of the screenplay himself. The central character, Kay Arnold, is a New York hooker whose emotions are thrown in turmoil when a wealthy and idealistic young painter hires her as a model and gradually falls in love with her.

Ralph Graves was set to play Jerry Strong, the painter, but Harry Cohn was reluctant about the actress Capra wanted for Kay. He suggested instead that the director interview Stanwyck, who had been successful on the Broadway stage but had fizzled in her first three movies, including a Columbia quickie called *Mexicali Rose* which, she said, "reached what I shall always believe was an all-time low." But Cohn recently had seen her singing and dancing at a Hollywood benefit and thought she might have the right combination of brassiness and vulnerability the role in *Ladies of Leisure* demanded.

"She had appeared in only two [*sic*] pictures—very poor ones at that," Capra wrote in 1941. "At our first meeting I informed her that I had seen the two pictures and frankly told her what I thought of them and of her performances. She took it without a flicker. She frankly admitted her failure, offered no alibis or excuses. That impressed me."

But he also recalled (in his autobiography) that he found her to be a "sullen" and disdainful "drip" he had no interest in hiring. The meeting quickly ended when Stanwyck refused Capra's request to make a screen test. "That was like waving a red flag before a sore bull," she recalled. "I don't know what I said but I do remember his reply: 'No test—no work.' It was not very pleasant. I had decided to quit Hollywood and go back east. I was right on the verge of going back. I was in a bad mood about it, and I didn't like the people I had met. They were all very starry and very important. I thought that was a crock. And they weren't very friendly to people from the East, anyhow. They were all frightened—that was the beginning of talkies—I know that now, but I didn't then."

She was sick of making tests. "He had a right to ask but I also reserved the right to say no. I wasn't really upset. I just thought, 'Screw it. I can't make it here, so I'll go back where I made it.' "

Stanwyck was married at that time to vaudeville star Frank Fay, who also had been trying to make it in Hollywood, without much success. It was an unhappy marriage. The alcoholic Fay was resentful of his wife's career and of his dependence on her to help him win parts.

But if it had not been for Fay, Capra never would have given her a second chance. When she came home from the interview, Fay called Capra and urged him not to give up on her without seeing a test she had made for Warner Bros. An emotional scene she had done on stage in *The Noose*, it was photographed in Technicolor by Ray Rennahan and directed by Alexander Korda, whom Warners also was giving a tryout.

Grudgingly watching the test, Capra found himself electrified by the young woman's intensity and conviction. "I offered her the part and she was the most surprised girl I have ever seen," Capra remembered. "So many directors after my refusal would have forgotten me entirely," said Stanwyck. "But not Frank Capra! He is too big."

Asked by Richard Glatzer to compare Stanwyck with two of his other leading ladies, Jean Arthur and Claudette Colbert, Capra said: "Barbara Stanwyck started out with a pretty hard life. She was a chorus girl at a time when the gangsters ran the nightclubs, and that was pretty rough on the girls. Life was pretty seamy. So she can give you that burst of emotion better than the other two can. She is probably the most interesting of the three. She's also the hardest to define: she's sullen, she's somber, she acts like she's not listening but she hears every word. She's the easiest to direct. She played parts that were a little tougher, yet at the same time you could sense that this girl could suffer from her toughness, and really suffer from the penance she would have to pay."

"True. True," said Stanwyck. "Very astute. But then, that's Mr. Capra. He sensed things that you were trying to keep hidden from people. He'd been kicked around, maybe not as much, but he understood it. And without probing and asking you a lot of intimate questions, he knew. He just knew."

Capra also was fortunate to find a writer who could understand what he saw in his new actress.

In those uncertain early days of talkies, when studios were not sure that writers and directors trained in silent movies could adapt to the new medium, hordes of New York newspapermen and playwrights were brought to Hollywood.

One of them was Jo Swerling, a rumpled, cigar-smoking newspaper veteran. Swerling had fled czarist Russia with his family, barely escaping a pogrom, and settled in New York, where, like Capra, he sold papers on the street to help support his family. But his political views were much different from Capra's.

"Jo was an emotional leftist," said screenwriter Philip Dunne. "He had been a very, very poor boy in New York. He looked as if he had been undernourished. His politics were entirely informal and emotional. He was full of hero worship for whoever his hero was at the moment, and Franklin D. Roosevelt was the greatest hero of his life."

Swerling had run the gamut of newspaper jobs in Chicago, Boston, and New York for twelve years, working as a reporter, a rewrite man, and a reviewer. He was Chicago correspondent for *Variety* and wrote a comic strip called *Gallagher and Shean*, based on the two vaudeville stars. On the side he wrote short stories and tried his hand at vaudeville sketches and plays. His fifth play, *The Kibitzer*, written with Edward G. Robinson, helped make Robinson a star.

During its New York run in 1929, Columbia signed up Swerling and shipped him west with three other writers. Swerling recalled how he met Capra at a story meeting presided over by Harry Cohn: "It seemed to my bewildered gaze that everybody on the lot had been dragged in, from directors to props. Pretty soon someone started reading a script, in a singsong voice, to which no one appeared to be listening. It went on and on. I began to droop, to fidget, to curse. It was, by all odds, the most imposing drivel I had ever heard in my life. . . .

"Finally the script was finished, and Cohn, who had been telephoning, looking out of the window, writing on a pad, asked for questions. He started with the fellow next to him and ran round the circle. Almost without exception he was yessed. The story was fine, the possibilities were great, it was a surefire hit.

"This obvious kowtowing made me ever madder, so when it was my turn I said I thought the piece was terrible. My throat was constricted, I was so angry with the hallelujah chorus. A restrained silence greeted this graceless comment. I noticed a dark little guy I thought was Cohn's secretary staring at me murderously as I read my report.

"In a few minutes we all filed out. I was ready for the dismissal I felt sure would be handed me, when Cohn said:

" 'Hey, you!' indicating me. 'Come back here. Meet Mr. Capra. It was his script you were criticizing.' I felt myself growing smaller and smaller, when Cohn continued: 'Since you think you know so much about pictures, could you take this script and improve it?'

" 'Yes, I think I could,' I replied. After all, I had given my honest opinion. All there was left for me to do was to stand by my guns.

" 'It's the old Camille story, but it needs a new twist,' I said. 'Take it and see what you can make of it,' he replied tersely.

"I went to my hotel, locked myself in my room and for five days pounded out a rewrite story of the plot I'd heard, interrupting the writing only long enough for black coffee, sandwiches and brief snatches of sleep. I was simply writing a newspaper yarn with a longer deadline than usual. The result was *Ladies of Leisure*."

Shooting began on January 14, 1930, just eleven days after Swerling finished his rewrite. The dialogue was now terse and witty, the characters offbeat and unpredictable, the situations equally amusing and touching. Capra continued to work on the script throughout the shooting, but he never disputed the importance of Swerling's contribution.

Ladies of Leisure marked the first time Capra had worked with sophisticated dialogue, and the script brought out qualities in his direction that had not been seen before. It inaugurated a more ambitious stage in Capra's career, in which, for the first time, thanks in part to Stanwyck, he seemed to be turning his full and undivided emotional resources to the conscious exercise of his craft and art.

An equally important element in this awakening was the fact that the social attitudes of Swerling's script carried more bite than Capra's films had shown previously, working up a fine rage against the hypocrisy of "respectable" people who scorn Stanwyck's honest, sympathetic, self-respecting hooker. The film was the beginning of the bond that Capra, with the too infrequently acknowledged help of his writers, forged with his largely working-class audience during the Great Depression.

Capra had an unexpected problem with Stanwyck. She was always best in her first take. Doing a scene a second time diminished her intensity.

"That I think is theater training," she explained. "The curtain goes up at 8:30, and you better be good. You don't get a retake. I have worked with actors who lie back and wait to see what you're going to do, and the fifth or sixth time they come forward. Well, that's a bunch of crap to me. You should shoot for the first time. And if you have an emotional scene you only have so much water in you to come out! About the third or fourth take, you start drying up, not because you want to, but it's a physical thing that happens."

Capra, who liked to rehearse, changed his methods to fit Stanwyck. He gave her only a loose technical run-through, not a formal rehearsal, conferring privately in her dressing room before each scene was shot. "The change from rehearsing to non-rehearsing," he said, "saved all of her pent-up emotion for the time when it went on the screen."

"There were times you felt you were not being directed at all," she said, "but of course you were. You weren't dumb enough to know that wasn't the case. But he would come in the dressing room and he'd say, 'Let's talk about it.' He didn't say, 'Psychologically, do you think she would—?' That always kills me somehow. I don't know why, it usually makes me laugh. That's much too analytical. It has to be from the gut. His role in life was not to probe people, but to watch them.

"We would talk about the character: 'You would speak out?' 'No, I don't think she would.' 'Well, why *don't* you?' If you have a plausible answer, fine, you give it. If he agrees with you, he'll say, 'Yes, that's good, that's the way we'll do it.' It was always 'We.' It was never 'I, I, I.' It was never 'I don't want you to do this.' I never heard him say that.

"He loved actors. That's another great secret of his. Some directors don't like actors, you know, they really don't, and you can almost smell it. But he did. And he liked women—not in a lecherous way, he just liked women, period, which a lot of directors do not. He *did*. He didn't demean them in any way. If you were a hooker, you were a hooker, but you'd better be a good one. That was how you made your living."

"I try to let a person play himself or herself," Capra said in 1931. "Miss Stanwyck is a natural actress. A primitive emotional. I let her play herself, no one else."

Capra quickly fell into the practice of shooting Stanwyck's scenes with two or three cameras so he could get the coverage he needed in one take (the method he had learned by necessity in his early talkies): "I had to use multiple cameras on her, because I'd never get the same scene again if I used different shots, different setups."

In spite of the fact that no one knew exactly what Stanwyck would do when the cameras rolled, Capra insisted that his crew not make any mistakes. "You guys are working for the actors," he told the crew. "They're not working for you!"

"It put a hell of a burden on everybody," said Edward Bernds, who started with Capra as the sound mixer on *Ladies of Leisure* and worked on all but one of Capra's subsequent Columbia pictures. "My God, we were all on our toes to get it the first time. That first take with Stanwyck was sacred."

"It was inspirational to work with Capra because everyone was trying to do his best," recalled Al Keller, who worked as a camera assistant on all of Capra's films from 1930 through 1939. "We were anxious to do things for him. Capra inspired 110 percent from his crew. We felt that working with him, we were the elite. But he wouldn't tolerate anyone who couldn't cut it. Boy, you did it the first time or you weren't there."

Another way Capra preserved Stanwyck's all-important spontaneity was that after the blocking had been roughed out with the actors and the crew, and he knew what shots he planned to take, he would shoot Stanwyck's close-ups first, rather than shooting the establishing shot first and finishing with the close-ups.

"It's all right if you have one or two people, but if you have four or five people in a scene, working backwards is very difficult for a director, because he's got to remember all the places," Stanwyck noted. "But Mr. Capra made it easy for me. He wanted me to be free."

From the trial-and-error of his work with Stanwyck on *Ladies of Leisure*, Capra was beginning to evolve a method of working, a style. As he defined it in 1931, "The audience should never realize that a director has directed the picture."

"Everything mechanical—the dolly tracks and the lenses and everything—he didn't pay any attention to it," said Jimmy Stewart, who first worked with Capra in 1938. "If the scene called for it, he used two cameras, three cameras, the cameras were there, but he didn't move them all over so that you were conscious of them moving all the time. I remember the long filibuster scene in *Mr. Smith*—you know, I talked *forever*—I only found out later that he had six cameras that were taking it. In doing it you became not conscious of where the camera *was* exactly; you forgot about the camera.

"He was capable of getting things on the screen and telling a story on the screen so that it got beyond directing, beyond acting, beyond writing, as far as the audience was concerned. It got above the movie itself; it appeared to the audience as a real experience, as something actually happening that they were viewing, and he had the cameras picking it up."

"If something went wrong he wouldn't blame an actor, he would put the blame on something else," said Joe Finochio, who worked as his uncle's sound recorder from 1934 through 1939. "He never yelled at people or lost his temper."

Once, Edward Bernds remembered, an actor blew a scene, but rather than embarrass the actor, Capra picked up a large spike from the floor and dropped it behind his back, making a loud clattering noise. Then he called "Cut!," turned to the crew, and in a loud voice demanded to know which of them had dropped the spike. "We knew what it was for," said Bernds. "Anything to take the pressure off the actor."

Capra's methods caused more problems for Joe Walker than they did for any other member of his crew, because using multiple cameras and allowing the actors to change the blocking in midshot forces a cameraman to compromise on the quality of his lighting. "I complained," Walker said, "but I realized that was what he wanted, so that was what I tried to give him. Capra worked with other cameramen who didn't want to do what he wanted, and they didn't last long. You can't argue with success. The use of multiple cameras had a lot to do with the feeling you get in Capra's pictures even today, the feeling that they're real people and this is actually happening to them.

"I don't want to give you the impression that Capra's rehearsal methods were some kind of mishmash or free-for-all, however. Capra was thoroughly in charge, and I never heard an actor question his judgment. An actor could read a line any way he felt, or switch it around, but always completely under Capra's control. Sometimes he would catch them off guard and shoot a take when they thought they were practically rehearsing. It made their performances natural.

"Now, anybody can do that—the question is judgment, when to use that or when not to use that. They all ask, 'What's Capra's secret?' I think *that's* Capra's secret."

Capra began to give Walker almost as much freedom as he gave his actors, and the result was an increasing visual sophistication in Capra's films during the early 1930s. The romantic sheen that became characteristic of Capra—the backlighting of actresses and the sculptural modeling of actors, the ability to transform minimal sets into dreamlike images, the delicate beauty of his night scenes and his erotic rain scenes—all of these elements were brought to Capra by Walker.

Before the start of production of *Ladies of Leisure*, Walker shot a lighting test of Stanwyck at Harry Cohn's request. Cohn was worried about her looks and urged the cameraman to do everything he could to glamorize her. But Capra did not agree with Cohn. Like Jerry Strong in the film, he responded to her proletarian beauty and felt that it was a mistake to make her glamorous. He told Walker to bring out Stanwyck's natural, unorthodox appeal.

Ladies of Leisure opened on April 2, 1930. The public reaction was reported in *Photoplay*: "Halfway through, the audience choked up. Something was happening. . . . a real, beautiful, thrilling wonder had been born.

"It was Barbara Stanwyck, whose performance in *Ladies of Leisure* is one of the greatest yet given in the adolescent talkies. It is truly thrilling. A star's been born, and we are proud to cry her welcome . . . this beautiful young girl who possesses emotional power and acting talent that are really amazing."

*   *   *

It was during the making of *Ladies of Leisure*, evidently, that Capra began his affair with Stanwyck.

Though Stanwyck would not discuss the extent of their personal involvement, Capra wrote in his book, "I fell in love with Stanwyck, and had I not been more in love with Lucille Reyburn I would have asked Barbara to marry me after she called it quits with Frank Fay."

But it was Stanwyck who rejected him.

She probably regarded the affair with Capra—which lasted intermittently for about two years, until the fall of 1931—more as an escape from the pressure of her unhappy marriage to the possessive, alcoholic Frank Fay than as a serious involvement.

Capra's sister Ann was the only member of the family to whom Stanwyck was introduced. "He was a very private person," Stanwyck noted. "He didn't go around telling everybody everything." Ann told Josie Campisi about her brother's relationship with Stanwyck: "He likes her, but she doesn't want to marry him." Ann had the impression that remarrying was the last thing Stanwyck wanted to do.

Then, too, Stanwyck must have been shrewd enough to realize, even if Capra did not, that despite their satisfying working relationship, they would not have been compatible in marriage. She must have known that Capra needed a more placid woman, a woman who would stay home and raise children, a woman whose life would revolve around him—not a career woman.

Discussing Capra's mood swings, Stanwyck observed, "I think that's an Italian quality. The Irish go through their black depressions, too. I know, I'm an Irisher. And you can ask that Irish person why and he can't tell you, it's just a black cloud that comes over us. Well, the Italians are a very emotional race. You can say hello to an Italian and they go into an explosion. But that's part of their charm. Mr. Capra was not afraid to show emotion. He understood it."

When asked about their love affair, Capra spoke guardedly: "My relationship with her was very important and very rewarding. We were very close. I wish I could tell you about it, but I can't, I shouldn't, and I won't." Then he added, "But she was delightful."

There is no doubt of the emotional turmoil this new romance created in his life. He made a revealing slip when he recalled, "I didn't want to fall in love with her—I was married."

In fact, he was *not* married then, but his relationship with Lu Reyburn was such that Capra evidently felt that he was betraying her. She had fallen for him wholeheartedly, but he was holding back. Whether or not Lu recognized that his aloofness was due to his fixation on Stanwyck, she could see that he was taking her devotion for granted and she was growing increasingly impatient with his unwillingness to commit himself. In one of a series of abjectly lonely letters she wrote to Capra during the summer of 1930, while he was on a six-week eastern trip to make *Dirigible*, she recounted a visit to Alyce Coleman and her baby daughter, Gay. She forthrightly, even defiantly, expressed her desire for a child and a home. Yet Capra made no comment when he replied nine days later.

When asked if Lu ever brought up the subject of marriage during their courtship, Capra said, "No. But, what the hell, you don't have to spell it out. She wanted to marry me."

8. "The Man in the Street"

*C*apra's rise to fame and material success stemmed from America's descent into the Great Depression, as he somewhat uncomfortably assumed the role of Hollywood's champion of the "common man."

He shared his peasant family's thrifty habits and their instinctual distrust of banks. While making his prudent Hollywood and Malibu land investments in the late 1920s, he kept his extra money in safe-deposit boxes and hoarded at home. As a hedge against the instability of the world currency market, he converted some of his holdings into gold. After his years of struggling, he was not one to squander his savings on needless possessions. But like so many others in that era, he could not resist playing the stock market, twice losing $30,000, in 1929 and 1930.

Capra had voted for Calvin Coolidge in 1924 and Herbert Hoover in 1928, confident that their probusiness policies would keep the country afloat on its wave of apparently unending prosperity. When Hoover made his ringing proclamation in his March 1929 inaugural address that "in no nation are the fruits of accomplishment more secure," Capra could see in himself the living proof of that faith in the American system.

Unlike many other Americans who lost all of their investments in the market crash that October, Capra had a lucrative job and the assurance of a bright future with a prospering company. He could feel certain that his loss was only a temporary setback, and he was shortsighted enough to believe that the same was true for the country.

Hollywood's prosperity encouraged his illusions. After the trauma caused by the conversion to sound, talking pictures had proven to be a bonanza for the studios and theaters. Studio profits rose to record levels in 1929, and again in 1930, at a time when more than four million people were unemployed, more than double the number before the crash. Even as the breadlines in American cities lengthened, so did the lines at movie theaters. Despite the higher ticket prices charged for talkies (fifty cents to a dollar, compared with the thirty-five-cent average for the late silent pictures), eighty million Americans went to the movies each week, seeking a few hours' respite from the troubles of the darkening world outside.

There were warning signs for those in Hollywood who could see them. Because of the cost of remodeling the studios and theaters for sound and the slower and more expensive production process of making talking pictures, the number of productions had dropped from about 600 to 800 a year in the late silent era to 300 to 400 in the early 1930s. The studios cut back their ranks ruthlessly, causing labor unrest and pressure to unionize the industry. Despite their increased profits, the major studios which also owned their own theater chains (Paramount, Fox, Warner Bros., and RKO) had seriously overextended their capital investment in sound equipment and real estate, saddling them with a high overhead that demanded a continued prosperity. It was not long before theater attendance fell sharply, driving them to the brink of bankruptcy. Columbia expanded its operations by establishing its first national distribution organization in 1929, but it would fare better than most of the majors in the Depression because it did not own theaters, thanks to the foresight of Joe Brandt, who had talked his partners out of expanding into exhibition.

But all that seemed remote to Frank Capra in early 1930, when his name was being listed on theater marquees for the first time with *Ladies of Leisure*, and he was about to embark on a picture called *Rain or Shine*.

Rain or Shine was based on a 1928 hit Broadway musical (book by James Gleason and Maurice Marks), starring comedian Joe Cook as Smiley Johnson, a circus manager who keeps his little show together through good times and bad. In retrospect, it is impossible not to read the film version of *Rain or Shine* as an allegory of the Depression, despite its seemingly frivolous subject matter.

Written for the screen by Jo Swerling and Dorothy Howell and stripped of its songs by Capra, *Rain or Shine* gives mixed political signals, probably because of the clash of Capra's fundamentally conservative attitudes with more liberal ideas that were in the air at the time. The precarious financial state of the circus echoes the state of the country, and Cook's Smiley, the indefatigable optimist, can be seen as a Franklin Roosevelt precursor, galvanizing the demoralized troupe with his energy and courage. His black organist, Nero (Clarence Muse), plays an instrumental version of "Happy Days Are Here Again," the Broadway show's pep tune that FDR would adopt as his theme song in the 1932 presidential campaign.

But the film also has a strong antilabor slant. Al Roscoe's villainous ringmaster stirs up a strike among the performers so that the circus will fold and he can buy it for himself. When the performers begin walking out despite Smiley's pleas, the two-faced ringmaster provokes the audience into rioting. The audience within the film (and, by extension, the American public) is portrayed as a fickle, easily manipulated, and easily stampeded herd. The riot causes the circus tent to catch fire, and Smiley's heroism is all that prevents anyone from being killed. Underneath its beguiling "let's pull together" spirit, *Rain or Shine* rebukes the workingman as disorganized and untrustworthy.

That Capra himself recognized the film's ideological confusions is evident from the section in his autobiography recalling how a newfound writer friend, Myles Connolly, berated him for taking the easy way out by making vacuous commercial films and urged him to express deeper thoughts and feelings.

"Connolly hurt because he was right," Capra admitted. But Capra worried that if he made "idea" films he might risk being unsuccessful or, worse, risk persecution. Still, he hungered to make something more meaningful, more important, than the kinds of films he was making. The real problem was that, as he put it, "this director doesn't know what the hell to say."

Myles Connolly's longtime agent, Bill Shiffrin, claimed in 1977 that "Connolly was responsible for most of the marvelous homey philosophy in the Capra pictures which really evolved into the Frank Capra trademark." That is an exaggeration—the contribution of Robert Riskin, the principal writer of most of Capra's major films, was more crucial and salutary—but there is no doubt that as a confidant and shadowy writing collaborator whose role grew more overt in later years, Connolly also exerted a profound influence on the development of Capra's artistic personality.

Before coming to Hollywood, Connolly worked at the *Boston Post* and wrote the religious novel *Mr. Blue* (1928), which Capra greatly admired and which eventually became a best-seller in Catholic circles. It was a seminal, though largely unrecognized, source of ideas Capra would adopt in his films.

An allegory about a modern Christ figure, a humble, celibate, Gary Cooperish man who practices the Christian virtues of poverty and brotherhood in the midst of the modern metropolis, *Mr. Blue* points forward to the messianic innocents of *Mr. Deeds Goes to Town, Mr. Smith Goes to Washington,* and *Meet John Doe* (Connolly contributed to the scripts of all three films), and it is a broadside against agnosticism, scientific rationalism, intellectualism, and liberalism, all of which "isms" would become favorite topics of Capra's scorn. There also are prefigurations of "Capraesque" rhetoric in Connolly's talk of "Christian laughter . . . the laughter that comes from innocence surprised"; of the importance of fighting for "the Lost Cause" (a central idea in *Mr. Smith*); and of Blue's "special way with good common people," though the Connolly surrogate figure who narrates the book tends to equate charity with pity and condescension, and rails against "many an honest fool and dishonest liberal" who would view a man such as Blue as insane, "yet I have never known a saner man in all my life" (compare the insanity trial in *Mr. Deeds*).

Connolly had a messianic view of motion pictures, writing a paean in *Mr. Blue* that Capra would echo for years to come: "If you want to reach the masses you can reach them through pictures. These new children can be bent and molded as they sit in the dark enrapt before the magic of the mobile screen. There, in the dark, they can be lifted out of their daily servitude. There, they can be raised high above their stone-and-steel environment. There, they can be brought to the high places and shown the deeps beyond the hard horizon. . . . Here is a destiny for an art second to none in history. For it is given to the motion picture to save the soul of a civilization!"

Although Capra said in 1984 that John Ford was "the best friend I had in the world," Capra's longtime secretary, Chet Sticht, felt that Capra privately was closest to Myles Connolly. Capra's grief when Connolly died in 1964 was intense, yet in his book, he described their friendship as a complex and volatile one, damaged by what he saw as Connolly's possessiveness: "He wanted to be my only guru; my Edgar Bergen. I resented being anyone's Charley [sic] McCarthy."

After being introduced to Capra by Al Roscoe at the wrap party for *Ladies of Leisure*, the gruff, bibulous Connolly encouraged Capra (with limited success at first) back toward Catholicism and away from the liberal political ideas Swerling and Riskin brought to his work as the Depression deepened. With more than a trace of opportunism, he tempered his insults by buttering up Capra's ego and urging him to leave Harry Cohn to make the truly important pictures he was capable of making.

As Capra recognized in comparing Connolly to a ventriloquist, Connolly saw him through somewhat patronizing eyes, as a gifted but simple soul, a man yearning for something to believe in, a malleable figure Connolly could use both as a meal ticket and a mouthpiece in Hollywood. He saw Capra, in fact, much as he saw his creation Mr. Blue. The novel's businessman narrator says, "You see what I mean about Blue having the human touch that could be capitalized. They say humor sells best nowadays. But I really think that Blue's sincerity, under astute management, could have been made to pay dividends. You meet plenty of witty men but very few sincere ones. I am sure I have an idea here."

Connolly also had a way of putting it in more exalted terms, which helped overcome Capra's skepticism by playing on his guilts, ambitions, and feelings of unrealized self-importance: "Something is wrong with your artists," says Blue. "It is cowardice to blame the age. Perhaps it is their art. Perhaps it is the dryness and dullness of their souls. . . . Tell your artists to immerse themselves in the fresh waters of the Faith and come up, vibrant, clean, alert to the world around them."

During the 1930s the fanatically right-wing Connolly—who later would encourage Capra toward anti-Communist propaganda—served as a conservative counterbalance to the simultaneously rising influence of Swerling and Riskin on Capra, whose moral bedrock was always shifting and who always was susceptible to the influence of collaborators with stronger personalities than his own. Though in the thirties Capra would lean primarily on Riskin, whose worldview was more realistic than Connolly's and more in tune with the mood of the public during the Great Depression, Connolly's well-paid but largely uncredited backstage presence in the thirties and early forties was substantial and helped account for the ideological tensions that make the Capra-Riskin films resist political pigeonholing.

But in 1930, "idea" films had to wait.

Columbia assigned Capra to yet another action-adventure movie with the reliable team of Jack Holt and Ralph Graves. This one was called *Dirigible*, and it was budgeted at $650,000, the biggest investment Columbia had ever made in a film and a real gamble considering the tenuous state of the business. Making *Dirigible* was Harry Cohn's attempt to put Columbia on an equal commercial footing with the major studios and to realize his seven-year ambition to have that status recognized with a premiere at Grauman's Chinese Theater on Hollywood Boulevard.

Dirigible was a pep talk for the U.S. Navy Bureau of Aeronautics' attempt to promote lighter-than-air craft for potential wartime use. Plans were under way at the time for commercial passenger use of the big dirigibles across the Atlantic Ocean, but they were considered too risky by most of the American military establishment—with good reason, as the explosion of the German dirigible *Hindenburg* would prove in 1937. The eerie beauty of the aerial scenes in *Dirigible* is shadowed today by the awareness that much of the film was shot at the same place where the *Hindenburg* later exploded, the U.S. Naval Air Station at Lakehurst, New Jersey. The Navy gave Columbia the full resources of Lakehurst, including the pride of its dirigible fleet, the 650-foot-long *Los Angeles*. As Joe Walker recalled, they were able to spend "many weeks at Lakehurst, comparatively unhurried, seeking only to get the utmost of accuracy and cinematic effectiveness into our scenes."

Capra's enthusiasm for the subject was genuine. He had seen dirigibles at close hand during his brief postwar stint as a teacher at the U.S. Army Balloon School, on Mrs. Baldwin's property in Arcadia. The technical aspects of lighter-than-air flight stirred his scientific interests, as did the challenge of constructing elaborate aerial action scenes with a combination of real airships filmed by Walker and aerial cameraman Elmer G. Dyer, matching studio sets, and miniatures. Walker's integration of all the disparate visual elements was a tour de force, the state of the art for its time.

For the scenes taking place at the South Pole—where Lieutenant Commander Jack Bradon (Holt) takes the *Los Angeles* to rescue a stranded group of explorers, including Navy flyer Lieutenant Frisky Pierce (Ralph Graves)—Capra took over the old Arcadia airfield to film on a set consisting of artificial snow, fake ice mounds, and a painted backdrop attached to the back side of the dilapidated Army barracks. The scenes were filmed convincingly in a blistering September heat wave.

Though the plot of *Dirigible* was in some respects just a carbon copy of Capra's two previous service pictures, it was given more substance and authenticity by Lieutenant Commander Frank Wead, USN, who received story credit (Dorothy Howell did the continuity and Swerling the dialogue). "Spig" Wead was a former Navy flying ace who had become paralyzed below the neck after falling down the stairs of his home in 1927. He regained partial use of his forearms and legs, and at John Ford's suggestion turned to writing aviation and sea stories for Hollywood, including the 1929 MGM film *The Flying Fleet*. While at MGM preparing *Brotherly Love*, Capra was impressed by Wead's courage, and later called on him for *Dirigible*.*

Wead's characteristic theme of the futility of romantic love was one that was particularly suited to Capra in the ambivalent interlude between his two marriages. Frisky's globetrotting aviation exploits make him a hero to everyone but his wife (Fay Wray), whom he thoughtlessly neglects, caus-

* *Wead went on to write films for Ford* (Air Mail, They Were Expendable) *and Howard Hawks* (Ceiling Zero, *based on his own play*). *His life story was told by Ford in the 1957 film* The Wings of Eagles, *with John Wayne.*

ing her to have a flirtation with Bradon. It is no accident that the character's name is Helen. Because of the film's critical attitude toward Frisky's immaturity, and the sympathy developed for Helen—a reflection of Capra's growing distance from the traumas of Isabelle Griffis and Helen Howell—the plot of *Dirigible* is more complex than that of either *Submarine* or *Flight*. By 1930, Capra was only superficially interested in the buddy-buddy aspect of the Holt-Graves team, which made *Submarine* seem so misogynistic and *Flight* so juvenile. But he failed to develop a good working relationship with Fay Wray, who played Helen stiffly. She remembered the filming as "an unpleasant experience" and Capra as "a dark soul."

Dirigible fulfilled both of Harry Cohn's dreams. A major commercial success, it had its Los Angeles premiere at Grauman's Chinese on April 7, 1931, four days after its New York opening. "COHN REJOICES AS AIR DRAMA EARNS TRIUMPH," read the headline on Louella Parsons's column in the *Los Angeles Examiner*. On a scale much grander than that of *Submarine*, *Dirigible* proved that Cohn could entrust Capra with the future of the studio.

But the question remained: what did Capra want to say in his films?

Even with his growing success at Columbia, Capra could not forget the humiliation of having been fired from MGM, his only shot at working for a major studio. So he decided that if he couldn't join 'em, he'd lick 'em. He set his sights, obsessively, on winning an Academy Award.

The Oscar competition was dominated by MGM, which was not surprising, since the Academy of Motion Picture Arts and Sciences had been conceived in 1927 by Louis B. Mayer, whose own lawyer had drawn up its constitution and bylaws. The primary purpose of the organization in those days was not, however, the awarding of Oscars, but, as Mayer put it, to "serve as a convenient mediator and harmonizer in any disputes" involving creative workers. The Academy was a company union, devised and controlled by the moguls to stall off the inevitable organizing of Hollywood actors, writers, and directors (many technicians and laborers already had been organized by the International Alliance of Theatrical Stage Employees, or IATSE). The maneuver worked for more than five years, until even Hollywood could no longer ignore the realities of the Depression.

The Oscar had been an afterthought to the Academy's creation. It served to disarm creative talent further by feeding their egos, luring them under the Academy's supposedly benign banner and blinding them (and the public) to the real purposes of the organization. Limiting the Academy membership and voting ranks mostly to big-name talent from major studios, the moguls ran the Oscar nominations as a back-room operation, doling out rewards to dutiful employees and withholding them from the recalcitrant. The smaller studios, such as Columbia, were tossed occasional crumbs but seldom won major awards.

After finishing *Ladies of Leisure*, Capra predicted to Stanwyck that it would win Oscars for best picture, actress, and director. On the day of the nominations, while Capra paced the floor of a Columbia soundstage waiting for a runner to bring him the trade papers, Harry Cohn said, "I hope to hell he gets nominated. Otherwise we'll never get any work out of him."

But the film failed to receive a single nomination. "I thought Stanwyck would get a nomination for sure," Capra said. "It opened my eyes immediately to the truth about the Oscars."

He sent the Academy an irate letter demanding membership, followed up by a telephone call from Cohn to Jack L. Warner, a member of the executive committee of the Academy producers branch, demanding to know why Columbia's star director was being snubbed. The Academy, apparently hoping to forestall criticism and broaden its base of support, responded on May 8, 1931, by inviting Capra to become one of its 449 members. But that was not enough for Capra, who recognized that he would have to become involved in back-room politics with his fellow directors to become a member of the Academy's board of governors, since each branch nominated its own members. When five vacancies opened up on the Academy board that fall, Capra, with Cohn's backing, maneuvered his way into one of them, first by being appointed on September 8 to the nominating committee of the directors branch, then by having the branch nominate him for the board ten days later, and finally by winning unopposed election by the board on October 17 to fill a three-year post.

Though he had an antilabor bias, when Capra came to his Academy post his primary concern, unlike that of the other board members, was not for labor issues or for the interests of the industry's power structure, except as they applied to him. He thought of the Academy as dealing with "small problems—it dealt with prizes." Considering the Oscars "the most wonderful thing that had ever been thought of for advertising, because we made the front page of every newspaper," he sought Academy membership for only one reason: the aggrandizement of Frank Capra. He hoped to become president of the Academy and to further his Oscar goals by trying once again to vault over the walls of MGM.

When the new board of the Academy posed for a photograph, Capra stood proudly but somewhat uneasily among the older men, holding a cigar and wearing an ill-fitting tuxedo.

*   *   *

He went all out for prestige in his next film, which touched off the most important—and most controversial—creative relationship of his career.

A Broadway playwright and producer named Robert Riskin had written a play with John Meehan called *Bless You, Sister*. A satire of religious hypocrisy, with Alice Brady playing a character based on evangelist Aimee Semple McPherson, it opened on Broadway in 1927 to good reviews but lost money for Riskin and his brother Everett, his producing partner. One of their other plays, however, became a hit, a drama of infidelity called *Illicit*, which Robert Riskin wrote with his then companion and writing partner, Edith Fitzgerald. After Warner Bros. bought *Illicit* as a vehicle for Stanwyck, Columbia snapped up *Bless You, Sister* and asked the suddenly hot Riskin to come to the studio for a story conference.

Riskin arrived late and took an inconspicuous place in a roomful of writers and executives. A small man in a black sweater was telling a story to the group. Riskin turned to the man sitting next to him and asked, "Who's that?"

"Capra," the other man whispered.

Riskin did not share the other's reverential attitude. His first impression of Capra was that "he looked like a mug, and he was telling the story badly—very badly."

The writer had not been told that the conference was being held to discuss the filming of *Bless You, Sister*. "Even so, as he stumbled along I thought I recognized it," Riskin recalled. "The recognition was painful."

Bless You, Sister was the kind of "idea" film Capra was hungering to make, the kind he thought might win him an Oscar. But there was a deeper reason for Capra's response to the play. While lampooning the gullibility of the superstitious followers of Sister Florence Fallon and the cynical commercialism of her mission, Meehan and Riskin also gave the evangelist a streak of latent idealism that ultimately redeemed her. The theme gave Capra a shock of recognition: here was the conflict he had sensed but had only vaguely understood in himself, between his slick con man's ability to make a buck by manipulating mass emotion and his nagging sense that he ought to be devoting his talent to a higher purpose.

When Capra finished telling the story, Cohn said, "Since this was Mr. Riskin's play, we'll call on him first for suggestions."

Riskin rose. "I wrote that play," he admitted. "My brother and I were stupid enough to produce it on Broadway. It cost us almost every cent we had. If you intend to make a picture of it, it proves only one thing: You're even more stupid than we were."

After a stunned silence, Capra jumped up and demanded, "Why?"

Riskin said the play had failed commercially because its theme was too hard for the public to take. And if the Broadway audience found it offensive, he was sure that less sophisticated movie audiences would reject it even more vehemently. (He may have feared, too, that Hollywood would water down the play to make it more palatable for the mass audience.)

Capra argued heatedly against Riskin's position. Riskin did not back down. He told Capra he had no interest in writing the screenplay for a film that was sure to flop.

The spectacle of an author urging a studio *not* to film his work made a strong impression on Capra and Cohn. They did not change their minds about making the film—after *Dirigible*, Capra was in a position to make just about anything he wanted to make, and Cohn was in no mood to stop him—but they could not help marveling at Riskin's honesty and integrity. Nor could they have failed to recognize later, when the film they made of the play did in fact flop, that Riskin was smart enough to have told them so.

Capra had no trouble casting Sister Fallon: Barbara Stanwyck. His continued hope in 1931 that he could persuade Stanwyck to marry him was evident in an oblique item filed from the set by a newspaper columnist: "Saw Barbara Stanwyck over at Columbia Studios yesterday, and here's one movie star who is happily married. Frank Capra, the director, says she was so pleased with her last wedding that she can hardly wait for the next one."

Borrowing from a 1919 Lon Chaney film about faith healing, *The Miracle Man*, which had played in Reno while he was there, Capra retitled the story *The Miracle Woman*. Swerling wrote the screenplay, keeping Riskin's terse, colloquial, witty dialogue largely intact and closely following his briskly paced story construction. But the screenplay did contain an element of compromise, as Capra admitted in his book. The director introduced a con man character named Hornsby (Sam Hardy) who lures Sister Fallon from honest Christianity into hucksterism: "There's only one way to lick a mob. Join 'em." Capra's self-flagellation over this change was somewhat excessive—Richard Koszarski aptly described *The Miracle Woman* as "one of those wonderful films of the early thirties which attacked all the rotten, sacred things the studios could think of"—and despite the director's admitted uncertainty over how to present Sister Fallon, Stanwyck insisted, "*I* never felt that, not at all. I knew the idea was Aimee Semple McPherson and I did it accordingly."

Despite Capra's punch-pulling, *The Miracle Woman* set some of the thematic patterns he and Riskin would later follow and develop in their most important work—and which Capra would continue to use in the films he made with other writers. Sister Fallon's ambivalent public position as a fraudulent savior who confesses her sins to the followers she had deceived is most closely akin to Gary Cooper's moral dilemma as Long John Willoughby in the 1941 *Meet John Doe* (with Stanwyck, in that film, taking a role resembling Hornsby's). More generally, the Capra-Riskin protagonist frequently has to live up to a public trust of which he or she initially feels unworthy; the motifs of fraud, despair, self-redemption, and public confession recur in various forms and characters throughout Capra's subsequent work with or without Riskin. Another Capra-Riskin trademark that first appeared in *The Miracle Woman* was the spiritually redemptive love affair between a cynical woman and a more romantic, idealistic man—in this case David Manners, playing a blind suicidal World War I veteran with none of the mawkishness one would expect from such a part.

Even before the completion of *The Miracle Woman*, Capra told Cohn that he wanted to make another picture with Stanwyck.

Borrowing the plot of Fannie Hurst's novel *Back Street*, the classic weepie about a kept woman living in secret devotion to a married man, Capra whipped up a story called *Forbidden*, which reached the screen seven months before Universal's adaptation of *Back Street*. Derivative though Capra's film was, and usually dismissed as an impersonal genre piece, it in fact was replete with covert autobiographical overtones referring not only to Stanwyck but to the other women in his life, and was a strangely incongruent grab bag of other Capra obsessions, straddling the genres of the soap opera, the newspaper melodrama, and the political exposé. The central character in *Forbidden* is a repressed librarian named Lulu Smith—an obvious reference to Lu Reyburn—who spends her life having a fruitless, masochistic affair with a married politician, Bob Grover (Adolphe Menjou), with whom she has an illegitimate daughter named Roberta—private references to Isabelle Griffis (in 1930, Isabelle and Bob Griffis had a daughter named Roberta; Capra tried to visit Isabelle in the hospital but was turned away, and left a bouquet of flowers).

Swerling wrote the screenplay, and Capra received screen credit for the story, though it was reported during production that "practically the entire Columbia writing staff had a thumb in the composition of the story." Some reviewers blamed the film's muddled viewpoint on Capra's deficiencies as a writer: Mordaunt Hall in *The New York Times* called it "a cumbersome effort at storytelling. . . . It happens invariably when a director tackles his own brainchild that the result is disappointing."

Perhaps it was because the material went through so many hands that

Capra's intentions again seemed rather confused. The odd ambivalence of tone in what Charles J. Maland has called "a study of how a woman's intense romanticism leads to personal self-sacrifice bordering on self-destruction" stemmed from Capra's simultaneous identification with Stanwyck's character and with the domineering, self-loathing politician, who tells her near the end, "I've taken your life away, almost as though I'd murdered you." Capra also expressed some aspects of his convoluted emotional life in the characters of a newspaperman (Ralph Bellamy) who wastes his life in devotion to Lulu and of the politician's crippled wife (Dorothy Peterson), whose name, naturally, is Helen. Helen's infirmity—clearly an equivalent of Helen Howell's alcoholism—is not only her husband's excuse for infidelity but also a source of guilty bonding between them, since he was responsible for the auto accident which crippled her, just as Capra blamed himself for his wife's drinking. Helen in the movie is unable to bear children, as Capra thought his Helen had been, so she adopts the illegitimate daughter Lulu has conceived with her husband.

Forbidden was set to start filming in April 1931, shortly after the completion of *The Miracle Woman.* But Stanwyck was having a contract dispute with Harry Cohn. She was obligated to make three more pictures for Columbia on a nonexclusive basis. Following her success in *Ladies of Leisure,* she also had made a deal with Warner Bros., but she felt she deserved more from Columbia now that her name had more box-office allure. Cohn was paying her $2,000 a week, but only when she was actually making a film (usually about a six-week period). She held out for more, and on July 17 it was announced to the trade press that she had "failed to put in an appearance at the Columbia studio for the production of *Forbidden.* . . . As it stands now, *Forbidden* has been laid aside and Miss Stanwyck claims screen retirement."

According to Stanwyck, her talk of returning to the stage was only a bargaining ploy; she wanted to stay in Hollywood. But it is possible that Frank Fay had reasons of his own for trying to keep her from doing *Forbidden.* His movie career had not been a success; Warner Bros. that June had made an early settlement of his contract. It was the classic *A Star Is Born* situation: the blow to his ego was compounded by his wife's sudden rise to stardom. Trying to keep the marriage together, Stanwyck told the press, "I am Mrs. Frank Fay first, and Barbara Stanwyck second." There was open speculation that Stanwyck's money dispute with Columbia was simply a ploy by Fay to break her contract so that she could go back east with him. "I never did want Barbara to go into pictures," he admitted.

He also may have been trying to keep her away from Capra. When

Forbidden eventually was made, Fay showed up on the set several times in a hostile and suspicious mood. "I can remember vividly how the crew would separate and make way for him," Ralph Bellamy said. "He was a very unpopular guy—and worked at it." Capra and Stanwyck were discreet about their affair, and they were never linked romantically in the increasingly frequent press reports of her marital problems. And though Fay's jealousy was well known in Hollywood, it is not clear whether even he realized exactly what was happening. "Barbara told me afterward that he thought *I* was having something to do with her," Bellamy said.

While Cohn was trying to pressure Stanwyck into returning to work, *Forbidden* was shelved temporarily and Capra went on to a romantic comedy, alternately tilted *The Blonde Lady* and *Gallagher*, which was to have been directed by Eddie Buzzell.

Robert Williams, an experienced young stage actor, was exciting interest in the film industry for his work in his first three films. Columbia had borrowed him from RKO-Pathé for *Forbidden*, but he was cast instead in the new project, playing Stew Smith, a raffish New York City newspaperman who falls in love with a wealthy woman (Jean Harlow) and finds himself living uncomfortably in high society. Loretta Young was cast as Gallagher, Stew's devoted and unpretentious colleague, who loves him for himself and wins him in the end. Like Lulu Smith in *Forbidden*, Gallagher takes an emotional beating from the man she loves. Stew's inability to appreciate or even recognize her feelings for him comes off as incredibly callous, much more so than is required by the script, and a reflection, perhaps, of the way Capra felt about his treatment by Isabelle or about the way he was treating Lu. It also may have reflected the director's personal preference for the earthy Jean Harlow over Loretta Young, who, along with Williams, snubbed Harlow during the shooting.

Even though Harlow's lower-class accent and personality made her wildly unsuited to play a blue blood, she was hot and getting hotter in the wake of such box-office hits as *Hell's Angels* and *The Public Enemy*. Capra's film with her was titled *Gallagher* from the end of shooting until its final preview in Santa Barbara on September 24, 1931, when it was shown as *The Gilded Cage*. But by the time of its trade review in *Motion Picture Daily* six days later, it had received its final title of *Platinum Blonde*, reflecting the commercial pull of Harlow's presence in the cast.

Platinum Blonde firmly established Harlow's stardom, bringing out qualities of humor and relaxed sexiness that had not been evident in her previous appearances, although Capra realized she was not right for the part. When she asks Williams, "Won't you step into the library?," it took

Capra fifteen takes of a complicated tracking shot to get her to say "library" instead of "liberry," and even in the take he finally used she sounds a little uncertain. But the reviewer for the *Los Angeles Express* noted that "Jean Harlow shows a marked improvement as an actress. Credit for this, I believe, should go to Director Frank Capra, who again proves his right to be named with the ten best megaphonists. Capra has a certain style, or knack, for getting just a trifle beyond the cold screen. He has warmth and feeling, subtle gestures that tickle ribs or pull on heartstrings as he desires."

Even more remarkable, though, was the performance by Robert Williams. His Stew Smith is one of the most sophisticated comic performances in all of Capra's work, and he showed unmistakable star potential. "If his succeeding parts are made to fit his personality and his demeanor, it will be eggs in his coffee for this comer," *Variety*'s Roy Chartier wrote in his November 3 review. Shortly before that, Williams had gone on holiday to Catalina Island, where he was stricken with appendicitis. By the time he could be taken to the mainland for medical treatment, peritonitis had set in, and, after two operations, the thirty-three-year-old actor died at Hollywood Hospital on the night of November 3, four days after the premiere of *Platinum Blonde*.

Platinum Blonde has a complicated list of writing credits, which was not uncommon for an early talkie. Though Capra claimed that he and Swerling borrowed the story from the Ben Hecht–Charles MacArthur newspaper comedy *The Front Page*, the fact was that Capra was the second director on the project and came along after the writing was well under way, if not completely finished. His working script contains only a few minor pencil changes; there is nothing else in his files to indicate that he had anything more than that to do with the writing. Harry Chandler and Douglas Churchill received the story credit; credit for the "adaptation" went to Swerling and for the "dialogue" to Robert Riskin.

Since his first meeting with Capra, the outspoken coauthor of *Bless You, Sister* had made no great impact at Columbia, going from assignment to assignment and receiving only one minor screenplay credit, on *Men in Her Life*, directed by William Beaudine. In an article on Riskin in 1937, *The New York Times* reported that Columbia had been close to firing him until "Frank Capra took a dozen or so of assorted scripts home to get ideas for his next picture" and discovered the script Riskin had written for *Gallagher*. After Capra made the film, Harry Cohn, without even waiting for its release, rewarded Riskin with a three-year contract.

The brilliance of Riskin's contribution and of Capra's direction elevated *Platinum Blonde* from a formulaic comedy into a first-rate film, probably the most underrated of Capra's career. Despite its good reviews and box-office success, the film's unpretentiousness has caused it to be ignored in favor of the later and more overtly ambitious Capra-Riskin classics. Though Capra privately was consistent through the years in acknowledging *Platinum Blonde* as the pivotal film in his artistic development, he contributed to its later lack of a reputation by belittling it in his book as an impersonal and undemanding programmer he made to compensate for the box-office failure of *The Miracle Woman.*

Along with his claim to have cowritten the story with Swerling, Capra's downgrading of the film could only have been motivated by a retrospective desire to deflect attention from Riskin. "So little is known of the contribution that the screenwriter makes to the original story," Riskin observed in a 1937 interview. "He puts so much into it, blows up a slim idea into a finished product, and then is dismissed with the ignominious credit line—'dialogue writer.' "

Though *Platinum Blonde* does have precedents in Capra's previous work—notably his script for the *Our Gang* comedy *High Society*—the 1931 film brings together for the first time most of the essential character and thematic elements that would be present in the Capra-Riskin classics, such as *Lady for a Day, It Happened One Night,* and *Mr. Deeds Goes to Town,* the films that established Capra's reputation as the most important American director of the 1930s.

Platinum Blonde's Stew Smith is the prototype of the Capra-Riskin common man protagonist thrust into a situation of great wealth and tempted to forget his true allegiances. Like Gary Cooper in *Mr. Deeds*, he becomes known in the press by the derisory nickname of "The Cinderella Man" after he succumbs to Harlow's charms and moves into her mansion. Like the initially bemused Longfellow Deeds, he ultimately comes to his senses, renouncing both his wealth and the soul-destroying hypocrisies that go along with it. And like Clark Gable's newspaperman in *It Happened One Night,* who also falls in love with an heiress, Stew mocks the pretensions of the snobbish rich, but his attitude cannot dispel his attraction to high society. Some of that attraction was built into the stories themselves; some was purely Capra's way of telling them. As Manny Farber has observed, while in the story of a Capra film "the world is given to the underdog," the director paradoxically tends to make "a plush, elegant movie that subtly eulogizes the world of powerful wealth."

One of the most important things Riskin brought to Capra was a dramatic and moral attitude toward that world.

"Well, if you'll notice," Riskin said in a 1936 interview, "the chief character is always full of something he's trying to express; he has just one idea he's trying to get over. In *Mr. Deeds*, for instance, there was a country boy given twenty million dollars that he didn't want, and he was always trying to express his distaste for it."

Riskin's background was similar to Jo Swerling's, and like Swerling he developed social beliefs very different from Capra's. Riskin's parents were Russian Jews. His father, Jakob, left for America to escape conscription in the czarist army; as he told it, "A couple of army men came in the front door, I went out the back door and kept going." Jakob Riskin was known for his wit and storytelling ability, and he might have become a writer, but the only work he could find in America was as a tailor, making vests. He and his wife Bessie, whom he brought with him to America, lived in the Jewish ghetto of the Lower East Side, later moving to Baltimore and then to Brooklyn. Their five children grew up speaking Yiddish.

Robert Riskin, born in New York City in 1897, six weeks before Frank Capra was born in Sicily, was short and streetwise, developing a satirical tongue as a self-defense against the Irish boys who tormented him and against the equally combative Italians who lived in the adjoining neighborhood. Like his older brother, Everett, he peddled *The Saturday Evening Post* on streetcars to bring in extra money while he was going to grammar school, but he had to drop out after the eighth grade to earn a living as an office boy, and later secretary, for a textile company owned by a man named Joe Golden.

Riskin had already shown a glimmer of writing talent when he composed a satirical poem whose subject, prophetically, was money. Titled "A Dollar Ninety-Three," it was a tongue-in-cheek account of his trip to Coney Island with another boy and two girls. The boys had managed to scrounge up $1.93 between them, and Riskin detailed the diminishing amusements they were able to afford as their money shrunk to a disheartening fifteen cents, just enough for carfare home.

The youngster was also a theater buff. He crashed local playhouses and taught himself shorthand in order to copy down the jokes he heard onstage. Before long he had accumulated a thick pile of notes. "And with a touch of polish on them," he said in 1941, "I'm still using the same gags."

Joe Golden noticed that Riskin used his lunch hours to write poetry on his typewriter. The youngster told his boss he also was trying to sell short stories to magazines. This gave Golden an idea. He had fallen in love with a popular soubrette named Trixie Friganza, whom he knew only slightly. He wanted to propose to her, but felt inadequate to the task, so he asked

Riskin to write him a proposal letter. If the letter had the desired result, he promised, Riskin would be promoted to an executive position.

Riskin wrote the letter. Trixie ignored it. Golden fired him.

After an unsuccessful stint as a traveling salesman peddling shirts in New England, Riskin found another office job in New York City, with the shirtmaking firm of Heidenheim and Levy, two Jewish immigrants who spoke only broken English. Riskin's bright, glib personality made a quick impression on the partners, who made him their office manager.

The shirtmakers had made a side investment in a motion picture company cranking out silent comedy shorts in Florida to be released by Famous Players–Lasky, the predecessor of Paramount Pictures. They showed a few of them to Riskin and asked his opinion. All of the other investors thought the shorts were hilarious, but Riskin said, "They stink. A moron could write better, a blind man could direct better, and as far as the acting is concerned, *I* could be funnier."

His opinion was disregarded until Famous Players–Lasky, seeing the films for the first time, decided not to release them. Heidenheim and Levy, in desperation, sent the seventeen-year-old Riskin to Jacksonville to take over the forlorn little film company. He hired Broadway comedian Victor Moore and his wife, Erma Littlefield, to star in a new series of domestic comedy shorts called Klever Komedies. Getting a crash course in every phase of filmmaking, the young producer soon took over the writing and directing as well, making several dozen two-reelers in 1915 and 1916.

Riskin put movies aside to enlist in the Navy during World War I. After the armistice, he returned to New York with $6,000 he had earned from the Klever Komedies. Everett Riskin was so impressed with his younger brother's success that he quit his job as a salesman for a silk mill and the two of them opened an office in New York City, calling themselves motion picture producers. They had little success, managing to produce only a series of puppet films featuring inflated rubber "Riskinettes" and another series called *Facts and Follies*.

Robert Riskin also was writing magazine stories and trying to become a playwright. Since he was unable to sell his plays to established producers, he and Everett decided to produce the plays themselves. With the exception of *Illicit*, their plays were not particularly successful.

After Robert Riskin went broke in the stock market crash, he tried to get a writing job in Hollywood. Paramount rejected him, but the movie sales of *Illicit* and *Bless You, Sister* finally brought him to Hollywood on a week-to-week deal with Columbia. Everett became a producer at Columbia in 1934 and made such films as *Theodora Goes Wild*, *Holiday*, and *Here Comes Mr. Jordan.*

Though Robert Riskin was making a great deal of money by the standards of the Depression era (his salary rose to $1,500 a week after *It Happened One Night*), it still was much less than Capra was making, and, unlike the director, Riskin had no share in the profits of their films. Partly through his growing realization of his own lack of power as a screenwriter in relation to Capra's power, Riskin's success, unlike Capra's, actually increased his sympathy for the underdog.

Years of struggling in a wide range of occupations had left Riskin with an appreciation of the finer things in life. An elegant dresser, he wore expensively tailored suits and hand-tooled leather shoes that were waxed, not polished. Fellow screenwriter Sidney Buchman described him as "the exact opposite of Capra: Imagine a very cultivated, nonchalant playboy, and you will have an idea of their rapport." Though Riskin was not a natural social activist and was inclined more to armchair political sympathies in the early 1930s, he always had the sensitivity to injustice natural to one raised in a Jewish ghetto and proud of his origins. Perhaps because real success and career stability did not come to him until the Depression, Riskin was able to feel the impact of the Depression more keenly than Capra. When Capra lost all his savings in the crash, he had another film to fall back upon; when Riskin lost all his savings, he had to bum meal money from his friends.

"Bob's social character was that of an extremely cautious, conservative man, but politically he was a natural liberal," said his friend and colleague Philip Dunne. "He was a solid New Deal liberal. He was a Rooseveltian—he was Bob Sherwood. He was not a radical. He was a very pure democrat, with a small 'd.' "

Nothing delineated the complexities of Riskin's politics better than his involvement with the Screen Writers Guild. One of the founders of the SWG in 1933, Riskin admittedly was "apathetic" toward guild affairs in its stormy first three years of existence, a period which paralleled his and Capra's joint rise to eminence in Hollywood. "I just went along minding my own business," as Riskin put it, until the spring of 1936, when the guild was split by a nearly fatal internecine rivalry. Its left wing was trying to enhance its bargaining position by affiliating with the Authors League of America, the New York–based organization which represented playwrights.

"The studios were scared," recalled Dunne, one of the guild's most prominent liberals, "because then they would have no source of strikebreakers, and the writers would control material for the screen. The right-wing writers feared that the guild would fall under the domination of 'Those Eastern Reds,' by whom they meant Elmer Rice and Bob Sherwood."

With the connivance of the studios, a right-wing faction of the guild began to organize an opposition group. The right-wingers, as Riskin put it, "mercilessly shook me out of my pleasant apathy." Playing on his liberal anticommunism, they convinced him that the guild was in danger of being overrun by radicals, or, in Riskin's words, "placing our destinies into the hands of some sort of ogre in New York."

In what he "thought was a movement to insure a sane and practical Writers Guild," Riskin joined "the conservative element" to demand five seats on a restructured fifteen-member board, including one for himself. The liberals in the guild agreed to the compromise. "We also agreed to delay the vote on amalgamation," said Dunne. "It was a big concession on our part. But this board never met. They suckered us."

After winning their concession, three of the conservatives, James Kevin McGuinness, Patterson McNutt, and Bert Kalmar, resigned from the guild board and, four days later, with MGM screenwriter John Lee Mahin, who also had resigned from the guild, they helped form a company union, the Screen Playwrights, taking 122 guild members with them. The four ringleaders attacked the guild as "a dangerous and non-representative instrument," and the venomous battle between the Playwrights and the Screen Writers Guild for recognition would rage for more than two years.

"We were struggling for survival," said Dunne of the aftermath of the conservative revolt. "At one point we could muster only 36 members [of nearly 1,000]. The guild went underground. We were whipped. We met in living rooms.

"It should be known that when the guild got screwed by the right-wing writers, the two guys [from the conservative faction] who did not resign from the guild were Bob Riskin and Sam Raphaelson. I remember at an informal meeting of as many people as were left in the guild, Bob stood up and apologized for ever having been associated with those people. And Sam said, 'I think the guild has just had a bowel movement and is in excellent condition.' After that, Bob was on the guild board."

During the guild's successful studio-by-studio balloting for recognition in 1938, Capra stood with Riskin in support of the SWG. Newly elected to the presidency of the Screen Directors Guild, Capra took time off from the shooting of *You Can't Take It With You* to make a dramatic appearance with Riskin at the crucial caucus of MGM writers, to oppose the Screen Playwrights.

The Playwrights' John Lee Mahin was still shaking his head in 1979 over the fact that the conservative Frank Capra "was against us. So it's very strange bedfellows you got."

Robert Riskin became the social conscience of Frank Capra's films in the 1930s.

Because Capra was not, like Riskin, born in America, he always felt an anxiety about whether or not he truly belonged in his adopted country. He felt compelled to be more American than the Americans. And while, as a child, he had resented wealth, he also saw it as a barometer—*the* barometer—of worth in the dog-eat-dog society in which he found himself. Though he did not particularly enjoy his money or the possessions it could buy him, he cherished it as his protection against his humiliating immigrant past. He spurned his family and his ethnic heritage and scorned other members of the lower classes who were unable to rise as he had risen. He feared the Democratic reformers who, he felt, wanted to take his wealth and redistribute it to people who could not make it on their own, as he wanted to believe he had made it, forgetting the many people who had helped him along the road to success in America.

And yet he could respond, for a time, to the moderate-liberal reformist beliefs of Robert Riskin. At the beginning it may have been that Capra was simply responding to the times: his thirties films sometimes espoused positions which he personally opposed, and under the pressure of the social unrest of the Depression he temporarily softened some of his conservative views, such as his instinctive distrust of organized labor. Capra's championing of what he initially referred to as "The Man in the Street"—or what the press liked to call, in the somewhat condescending phrase that soon became the catchword of Capra criticism, "the common man"—in part was commercial calculation, a canny assessment of what played best at the box office in the age of Roosevelt.

Like the popular artist he was, Capra was being led by his audience. *They* were demanding reform, *they* were demanding social welfare programs and redistribution of wealth, *they* were angry at the shortsightedness and greed of big business and the Republican party. The sense of brotherhood and compassion that came from Riskin's writing and began to open up the narrow vision of Capra's work brought him into closer contact with his audience, giving his work a deeper and more popular resonance, putting him in touch with a sense of community for which he previously had little feeling.

"Someone is going to evolve a great film out of the Depression," Capra told *Variety*'s Ruth Morris in an interview on February 2, 1932, three months after the release of *Platinum Blonde.* "Satirical treatment of a plutocrat, insanely trying to conserve wealth and finding happiness only when he is reduced to a breadline, will strike a responsive note in the mass mind. When that picture is made, it will inaugurate the cycle that follows in the wake of any successful film." Capra also observed that (as *Variety* paraphrased it) such films were just waiting for a director "cagey enough to capitalize on the present state of public mind."

Indeed, it was impossible for anyone to ignore the implications of the Depression any longer. Unemployment doubled in 1931, and it would triple in 1932, until 12,060,000 Americans were out of work. Every day when he came to work at Columbia, Capra saw people begging for money on the sidewalks along Gower Street. President Hoover had claimed in October 1931 that the Depression was just "a passing incident in American life," but few believed him anymore (though Capra would vote for his reelection). Still, by 1932, even to a conservative such as Capra, the necessity for some kind of reform was becoming inevitable, if only to stave off the even worse specter of communism, labor revolt, the Bonus Army, riots in the streets. The system clearly was not working, though Capra seemed to have no idea of what should be done except to blow a raspberry at it. He told *Variety:* "The Man in the Street has had so many dogmas crammed down his throat that he is prepared to revolt against current under-estimation of his intelligence. He's fed up. Politics, Prohibition, patriotism, big business, high-powered advertising are subjects ripe for ridicule."

While Capra was making *Platinum Blonde*, Harry Cohn was putting the screws to Barbara Stanwyck.

First announcing that *Forbidden* was shelved permanently, Columbia then told the press that it was considering it as a vehicle for Helen Hayes. Stanwyck tried to outflank Cohn by announcing that she would make her next picture for Warners. But Warners declared she would not be allowed to work there again until she fulfilled her obligations to Columbia, which took her to court and obtained an injunction forbidding her to work for any other studio. When she gave up four days later and agreed to return to Columbia, Cohn raised her salary to $5,000 a week. She agreed to star in *Forbidden,* and Cohn agreed to let her make three films at Warners.

"Once you got to know what type he was, you didn't argue with him," Stanwyck said in retrospect. "He was a bully toward everybody, or tried to be. But Capra handled him beautifully. You see, Cohn needed Capra, he didn't need any dumb actors. Actors didn't mean anything, they were a dime a dozen. But Mr. Capra was different. He was class. He made Columbia. Cohn wasn't about to let *him* go."

An incident occurred during the shooting of *Forbidden* which so upset Capra that he refused to discuss it more than fifty years later.

On October 4, 1931, the company was filming on location at Emerald Bay, near Laguna Beach. The scene called for Stanwyck and Adolphe Menjou to gallop horses along a moonlit beach. Stanwyck's horse became spooked when a reflector flared into its eyes.

"He reared up," she remembered. "I didn't expect it. He threw me, his head hit mine, and he kicked me in the spine."

Menjou pulled her from under the horse. She had fainted. Someone threw water on her, and she regained consciousness.

The first words she said were: "Hurry—we'll have to finish this scene now. My legs are stiffening."

Capra wanted her to go to the hospital, but she refused. She went ahead with the rest of the scene. She walked into the surf with Menjou, swam fifty yards offshore, came back—and fainted again. She was carried to a nearby cottage, then removed to a hospital. X rays showed that no bones were broken but that her coccyx had been dislocated.

"It hurt," she said in 1984. "It still hurts."

Yet she would not miss any work on *Forbidden*. For two weeks, she returned to the hospital after each day's shooting to spend the night in traction. Capra had the crew build her a slant board to rest against between takes.

"Her courage, to me, was inspirational," said camera assistant Al Keller. "This gal had that much integrity that she wouldn't leave the film. Boy, I thought she was something else."

Though Capra was in no way to blame for Stanwyck's injury, it cast a retrospective shadow over the film for him, one of the reasons he disparaged *Forbidden* in his book. He may have linked her accident in his mind, whether irrationally or not, with Stanwyck's final rejection of his marriage proposal, for it was during the filming of *Forbidden*, or shortly thereafter, that she made it clear to him that she was going to stay with Frank Fay.

Meanwhile, Lu Reyburn was still regarded in Hollywood as "Frank Capra's girl"—even though he was often too busy to take her out and she would have to find other escorts to social events.

After wrapping up *Forbidden*, Capra decided to take a long European vacation—not with Stanwyck or Lu but with Al Roscoe. He claimed that he went to Europe because "I couldn't make up my mind between these gals." But then he added, more honestly, "There was somebody else connected with it [i.e., Frank Fay]. I didn't want to think about it, so I went to Europe."

When he asked Harry Cohn for eight weeks off, Cohn grudgingly agreed, but only with the proviso that the vacation, his first long trip since he had gone to work for Columbia in 1927, would be without pay. Capra's contract, signed in 1929, was to expire in July 1932, but because of the trip the expiration date was extended to September. In addition to his habitual cheapness and his desire to hang on to Capra as long as possible, Cohn needed time to work out problems surrounding Capra's next project.

It was announced that the first film Capra would do upon his return was *Tampico*, from Joseph Hergesheimer's 1926 novel about the corruption of a legendary American oil driller in Mexico. Walter Huston and Jack Holt were considered for the lead after Capra and Columbia unsuccessfully tried to borrow Ronald Colman (from Samuel Goldwyn) and Clark Gable (from MGM). There were political roadblocks as well. The Mexican government not only refused to let the film be made there, but also raised the possibility that all Columbia pictures would be banned in Mexico if the locale of the story was not changed. Columbia considered switching it to North Africa. All of this happened before Capra had a chance to begin working with Swerling on the adaptation.

Before Capra left for Europe, Lu pressed the issue of marriage. He resisted, suggesting that Helen had soured him against marriage. As yet, apparently, Lu still knew nothing about his proposal to Stanwyck or Stanwyck's rejection. But Lu was becoming tired of waiting around for him. Since he wasn't taking her on his vacation, before he sailed from New York she pointedly sent him a photograph of herself to take in her place.

His itinerary, as reported widely in the press, was to include London, Paris, Switzerland, Berlin, Vienna, Rome, and a visit to Sicily for what the *New York Mirror* described as "his first appearance in the role of 'local boy makes good' since he left that town (Palermo) as a child." He had an audience scheduled in Rome with Benito Mussolini, who admired his films and was proud that a fellow Italian had done so well in Hollywood.

Capra and Cohn shared a fondness for Il Duce. Cohn had a fellow tyrant's appreciation of Mussolini's fascistic style, and Capra evidently shared the naive belief many (including Franklin Roosevelt and Winston Churchill) initially had in Mussolini as a champion of the Man in the Street and a bulwark against communism. According to John Lee Mahin, Capra in the 1930s "had a picture of Mussolini on his bedroom wall—a big oil painting—he adored him."

Though Capra, because of unexpected developments on the trip, never kept his appointment with Mussolini, he later attended a private screening at Columbia of a documentary about Mussolini which Columbia was thinking of releasing in the United States. Along with the Bank of America's A. H. (Doc) Giannini, Columbia's most important financial backer and a member of its board, Capra advised Cohn to go ahead with the release of the film, which Columbia put on the market in 1933 as *Mussolini Speaks*, with narration by Lowell Thomas and an ad campaign that asked, "Is this what America needs?" The film grossed more than $1 million, and the delighted Duce summoned Cohn to Rome to give him a medal. Cohn was impressed with the intimidating scale of Mussolini's office, particularly with the way a visitor had to make a long walk from the entrance up to the dictator's desk. When he returned to Hollywood, Cohn had his own office redone to match it, with a desk even bigger than Mussolini's, and for a while he even kept a bust of Il Duce on display.

Emboldened by the success in America of *Mussolini Speaks*, the movie-mad dictator conceived an even grander scheme. In the fall of 1935 he notified Cohn that he wanted to invest $1 million in a Columbia picture to be directed by Capra. It was a princely sum in the Depression era, as much as the studio had ever spent on a single film; only Capra's 1933 film *The Bitter Tea of General Yen* had cost Columbia a million dollars. When the news got around that Columbia was considering the offer, Ethiopia, which had been invaded by Mussolini's troops, slapped a ban on Capra's pictures.

Cohn, undaunted, dispatched Eugene De Rue, the assistant director on Capra's early Columbia silents, to Rome to discuss the proposal. To De Rue's surprise, Mussolini told him that he not only planned to finance the film, he also planned to write the story for it—and that it was to be the story of his own life.

"Maybe all right for Frank," a London newspaper commented, "but imagine what a spot a native Italian director would be in if the premier's story didn't go over at the preview."

The idea was too much for even Harry Cohn to stomach. He might have been willing to accept Il Duce as a silent partner, but a dramatic glorification of the dictator's life was unthinkable. He explained to De Rue why he had to reject Mussolini's offer: "After all, Gene, I'm a Jew. He's mixed up with Hitler and I don't want no part of it."

*　　*　　*

Lu saw Capra and Roscoe off on the train when they left for New York several days before Christmas 1931. She spent the holidays with her parents in Santa Maria while Capra had Christmas dinner in New York at Joe Cook's house and saw some plays before sailing on the *Europa* at midnight on December 28.

One can readily imagine Lu's reaction to Capra's effusive telegrams telling her about all the fun he was having, and sending her New Year's greetings from the ship, with a pro forma expression of romantic longing.

It was with uncharacteristically lurid relish that Capra described in his book how he and Roscoe made a drunken tour of the seamier sections of London and Paris. But he took pains to assure his readers that even their encounters with prostitutes were just innocent diversions.

However dubious those protestations appear, there seems to have been some truth, at least, in his claim that he began to miss Lu; he sent her a similar message from the Hotel Claridge in Paris on January 11.

But Lu had stopped listening. Her replies to Capra are not among the papers he gave to Wesleyan University, but it is clear that at this point she became terribly upset about his behavior, so upset that she was suddenly willing to drop him after almost three years of involvement. Just what occurred is not known, but the unmistakable inference from her actions over the next few days is that she must have learned something that made her reconsider her previously unshakable devotion to Capra—something hurtful and humiliating, such as the fact that, while claiming to her that he never wanted to marry again, he had been trying to persuade Barbara Stanwyck to become his wife. One of their mutual friends may have taken Lu aside and told her what had been happening. In any case, she sent Capra what must have been a withering message, judging from his terse and apologetic reply of January 12.

On the fourteenth, the eve of his planned departure from Paris for Switzerland, he begged her to wire back, but again she did not reply. He began to panic. He sent another message the same day, and delayed his departure, hoping to hear from her. When he finally did, it sent him into a state of shock: Lu informed him that she had decided to marry a "Dr. Brown" in Santa Maria.

Coming so close on the heels of the rejection by Stanwyck, his abandonment by Lu—a woman he so confidently had been taking for granted and whom everyone considered his for the asking—was more than his already shaken ego could bear.

He tried to appear offhand about the situation when he told the story in his book, implying that he did not believe that there really was a Dr.

Brown. His actual response was anything but offhand. In a telegram from Paris at 3:42 P.M. on January 15, 1932, he begged her to reconsider, profusely apologized for his behavior, and proposed a hasty wedding in New York.

Lu's response was immediate and affirmative. Exactly one hour after sending his proposal he was able to wire back with ecstatic relief.

She never made another reference to Dr. Brown as long as she lived. Capra said he never knew whether or not she was bluffing, and admitted, "I never asked her—I was afraid to find out." There *was* a Dr. Brown in Santa Maria—a London-born physician named Dr. Robert Walter Brown— but he was sixty-nine years old and married, a beloved figure who it was said "knows better than anyone else perhaps the joys and sorrows of Santa Maria, for he . . . has introduced scores of this city's young people to the world." Evidently Lu was having a little joke on the unknowing Capra as well as making him sweat.

Capra's messages to Lu from the *Europa* betrayed his anxiety that she still might change her mind if he didn't marry her as soon as possible. The posh German liner was the fastest passenger ship in the world at that time, but on this trip it ran into gale conditions in the mid-Atlantic, with winds blowing between sixty-five and seventy miles per hour and the high seas crashing over the bow. While Capra oscillated between barely controlled panic and elation, keeping Lu abreast of his progress and supervising her travel arrangements, the boat's speed was cut to seven knots and the journey was slowed by two days.

Ten days elapsed between Capra's return on January 22 and the wedding. Against his wishes, the news of the impending marriage had appeared in the trade papers and in the *New York Daily News*. It was announced originally that they would be wed on January 28. But they had to wait at the Waldorf until his divorce papers could be sent east.

They finally went ahead with the quiet ceremony on February 1, in the chambers of Brooklyn Supreme Court Judge Mitchell May. The judge was a friend of Harry Cohn, who had handled all the wedding arrangements.

In his prenuptial interview with the *Daily News*, Capra admitted that he had broken off his European trip because he had become "lonesome." "He talks about [marriage] very shyly," wrote the interviewer, Irene Thirer. "Admits he likes actresses and enjoys working with them, but that when it came to picking a second bride (he's been divorced) he chose a home girl."

His friends agreed he made the right choice. "It was a beautiful marriage," Barbara Stanwyck felt. "Those people were clones. I never saw such love and devotion between two people. In this town that's rather amazing." Doc Harris wrote Capra expressing pleasure that "you are married again and this time a non-pro. Congratulations, dear 'Wop,' for your nature demands a home of peace and quiet."

Frank and Lu were planning a honeymoon cruise to Cuba—the same place where Stanwyck took her romantic boat trip and met Adolphe Menjou in *Forbidden*. Capra was figuring to charge the honeymoon to Columbia by combining it with location scouting for *Tampico* in the Caribbean, but after Cohn loaned him $5,000, the travel plans were changed so that the newlyweds could attend the Winter Olympics in upstate New York and then take a leisurely train ride through Canada.

On the train to the Olympics they ran into character actor Benny Rubin, who had become friendly with Capra after working as a dancing double and gag man on *The Matinee Idol*. Rubin could not afford a sleeping compartment, so the newlyweds let him sleep on the couch in their drawing room; he spent the entire honeymoon week with the Capras at Lake Placid. And at every stop across Canada, Lu had to share Frank with film exhibitors and journalists.

But she did not mind, for she had won the man she loved and now could bask confidently in the reflected glory of being Mrs. Frank Capra, whose husband was described by a Montreal paper as "a famous man, known in every moving picture theater on the continent."

9. American Madness

*W*hile Capra was on his honeymoon, Robert Riskin was putting the finishing touches on an original screenplay called *Faith*.

The subject was a bold and timely one: a run on a bank. More than 3,600 American banks had failed since the end of 1929, one fifth of all the banks in the country, with deposits totaling more than $2.5 billion. In March of 1932, as Columbia put *Faith* into production, faith in the American economic system was a scarce commodity indeed. The Bank Holiday proclaimed by President Roosevelt and his dramatic overhaul of the banking system were a year away; Herbert Hoover was still in office. In the meantime, Americans were hoarding more than $100 million they were afraid to deposit in banks, contributing to a critical deficit in treasury reserves. As *Faith* started filming, the 1932 presidential campaign was just getting under way, with candidate Roosevelt arguing that the only way to end the bank crisis was for people to stop hoarding and to "put their money to work."

Before 1932, the Depression was reflected in movies mostly as a backdrop for the depradations of gangsters, but by that year, when Warners made *I Am a Fugitive from a Chain Gang* and Columbia dealt with the Bonus Army and congressional corruption in *Washington Merry-Go-Round*, Hollywood had been forced to admit that American institutions were in serious trouble. For by then, even the film industry itself was no longer "Depression-proof." With a fourth of the country's workers unemployed, ticket sales had fallen drastically. Paramount and RKO would be in receivership within a year, and Fox and Warners would be close to bankruptcy. Only the mighty MGM and the frugal Columbia were still healthy.

"Every time Capra made another film, Columbia built another sound stage," Al Keller recalled. Capra's films were so much in demand that Columbia was able to use them as spearheads in block-booking deals, forcing theater chains to accept other Columbia films in order to play Capra's—an arrangement that literally meant the difference between life and death for a studio without its own theaters. Columbia was thus in the unique position of being competitive without needing the chains that were dragging down the major studios.

Because of the expenditures involved in the conversion to sound, all of the studios had become heavily indebted to banks, mostly in the East, giving bankers an unprecedented degree of control over the movie industry. Columbia went public with its stock in 1932, when Joe Brandt sold his holdings and Harry Cohn added the presidency to his role as production chief by acquiring a 50 percent ownership, with Jack Cohn becoming vice president and treasurer. Columbia as a result had more capital on hand than other studios, and its lack of theaters kept it relatively independent of Wall Street control, but it still depended greatly on its close ties with the California-based Bank of America and the brothers Giannini.

Starting on a shoestring with his Bank of Italy, which he founded in San Francisco in 1904, Amadeo Peter Giannini had made his reputation as the champion of "the little guy" by loaning money on character rather than on collateral. The Bank of Italy (whose successor, the Bank of America, was created in 1928) pioneered branch banking services, advertised for borrowers, and billed itself as "The Bank for Just Plain Folks." Adventurous and freewheeling, the Italian-Catholic-Democrat–dominated Bank of Italy was viewed by the staid eastern banks with the same suspicion they held for the Jews who dominated the movie business, and A. P. Giannini's bank was one of the first to recognize the potential of motion pictures. At the urging of his younger brother Dr. Attilio H. (Doc) Giannini, a physician who switched to banking and took charge of motion picture lending at the Hollywood office, the Bank of Italy made its first loan to a film company in 1909, and it introduced the practice of accepting motion picture negatives as collateral, a practice that later would enable Capra and Riskin to make *Meet John Doe*, and Capra to make *It's a Wonderful Life*, productions financed primarily by the Bank of America.

Doc Giannini followed the principle of loaning on character when he took a chance in 1919 on Harry Cohn, Joe Brandt, and Jack Cohn, lending them the $100,000 they needed to capitalize their new movie company, which became Columbia Pictures. During Columbia's 1932 ownership struggle, Doc Giannini threw his weight behind Harry Cohn against a coup attempt by Jack, and with the departure of Joe Brandt, the banker became a board member of Columbia and one of the three-man voting trust that controlled the company.

The Bank of America kept faith with the film industry even as the Depression deepened, but in 1932 the bank itself and its parent Transamerica Corporation were also in serious trouble. The previous year the bank had lost deposits totaling $254 million, and as Columbia prepared to roll the cameras on *Faith*, the bank was losing $3 million in deposits each day. There was a real possibility that it could go under and Columbia along with it. Wall Street interests represented by Transamerica's conservative board chairman Elisha Walker were frantically trying to weather the crisis by dismembering and liquidating the corporation's assets, at the expense of small borrowers and depositors, who were leaving the bank en masse. The Walker faction was opposed by the ailing A. P. Giannini, who came out of semiretirement in the fall of 1931 to launch a highly publicized proxy fight to regain control of the bank he had founded. Columbia's decision to make *Faith* was an attempt to propagandize for the liberal lending policies the Gianninis stood for and to help ensure that their bank would survive and maintain its character.

Riskin, assigned to write the screenplay, went to see Doc Giannini and came back with admiration for his banking philosophy. He reportedly used him as the model for the hero of *Faith*, New York City banker Thomas Dickson, who was played by Walter Huston, although Capra later claimed that the character was modeled on A. P. Giannini; no doubt there was some of both men in Dickson.

When the film opened—retitled *American Madness*—some expressed surprise that Hollywood would make a film with a banker for a hero at a time when the public image of the banker was near its lowest ebb. But the film's analysis of the problems of the banking community, while fundamentally optimistic, was not without its critical aspects, and the conflicts between Dickson and his board of directors symbolically reflected the major split in the financial community at that time, which underlay the battle for control of Transamerica. As Arthur Schlesinger, Jr., wrote in his history of the New Deal, "The New York banking group wanted to reinstate the gold standard and return control over interest rates to the private financial community. Representing to a large degree a class which had already made its money, the New York bankers were primarily concerned with protecting the value of the dollar and maintaining high rates of return on savings. . . . Outside New York, the businessmen of the South and West had another set of concerns. They were predominantly men on the make; their desire consequently was for an abundance of cheap money at low interest rates." The Gianninis, Edward Buscombe observed in "Notes on Columbia Pictures Corporation 1926–41," can be seen "as a kind of contradiction in terms: populist bankers. The populists of the nineteenth century had regarded bankers as the physical embodiment of all that was evil, and believed that the agricultural problems of the Midwest were largely caused by a conspiracy of monopolists on Wall Street keeping interest rates up and farm prices down. . . . The little man, the populists contended, stood no chance against those who commanded such resources and used them for selfish purposes. But the Gianninis believed in deliberately aiding such small businessmen and farmers who got no help from Wall Street. . . . This too is Dickson's policy in *American Madness*."

Dickson, though a New York banker, stands firmly in opposition to the conservative policies of the Wall Street interests, and the offbeat casting of the vigorous, raw-boned Walter Huston, shortly after he played the title role in D. W. Griffith's *Abraham Lincoln,* underscores the character's roots in the American heartland. Like Giannini, Dickson believes in loaning money on character, or what he called "hunches," to small businessmen he trusts. "Jones is no risk," he says of one of them, "nor are the thousands of other Joneses throughout the country. It's they who have built up this nation to be the richest in the world, and it's up to the banks to give them a break." Dickson espouses the Rooseveltian belief in a fluid currency, which also was the credo of A. P. Giannini, a supporter of the New Deal's attempts to harness Wall Street control of banking.

When Giannini won his proxy fight on February 15, 1932, he started a "Back to Good Times" campaign, bringing about a dramatic renewal of depositor confidence that reversed the flow of deposits by March 27. "Keep your dollars *moving!*" the bank exhorted the public. ". . . Move your money by banking, sensibly spending or investing it. Banked dollars create credit—credit finances business—business creates *prosperity*."

When Dickson's directors accuse him of being "more liberal than ever" in the face of the growing financial crisis, he declares, "Yes, and I'm going to continue to be liberal. The trouble with this country is that there's too much hoarded cash. Idle money is no good to industry. Where *is* all the money today? In the banks—vaults—socks—old tin cans buried in the ground. I tell you, we've got to get the money in circulation before you'll get this country back to prosperity."

The run on the bank in *American Madness* is a reflection both of public panic and of the bank's internal instability: it is triggered by a robbery committed with the help of a corrupt bank officer. When the bank's telephone operator thoughtlessly spreads the news of the robbery, the $100,000 loss balloons into a rumored $5 million, stampeding the bank's anxious depositors. Dickson barely manages to avert the panic through the force of his own personality, drawing on his private holdings and those of his reluctant directors to keep the bank open until the small businessmen he has helped in the past come through with deposits to demonstrate their faith in him and his bank.

A. P. Giannini, who gave Roosevelt crucial support over Hoover in the election of 1932, often said, "Depressions are the product of fear."

Allan Dwan, a major director in the silent-movie era whose career had peaked in 1922 with Douglas Fairbanks's *Robin Hood* but had slipped into routine assignments with the coming of sound, was given the job of directing *Faith*. Since Capra was tied up with *Tampico*, his regular crew, including cameraman Joe Walker and sound mixer Edward Bernds, were assigned to work with Dwan.

"Dwan didn't seem to know what he wanted out of it," Walker recalled, and Bernds found Dwan "a dead-ass director. The whole thing was turning out to be a dreary mess. Dwan even made Walter Huston look bad, and we wondered how long it would take Cohn and [Sam] Briskin to wake up to the fact."

After three days of shooting in late March, Dwan was replaced by Roy William Neill, who shot for only one day before Capra was taken off *Tampico* and reassigned hastily to *Faith* (*Tampico* was passed to director Irving Cummings, who made it with Jack Holt, the setting changed to North Africa and the title to *The Woman I Stole*). Columbia announced that Dwan had been taken ill suddenly, "but it is known he had difficulties with Harry Cohn," *Variety* reported. Cohn often removed a director after a few days of shooting, Walker said, because "it shook the company up and put everyone on his toes."

Capra insisted on starting over from scratch, and Cohn readily agreed. He also demanded that the set be rebuilt by art director Stephen Goossón. "We shut down for two or three days while we changed the set around," Walker recalled. "Capra built Huston's office way up at the back of the stage," Bernds said, "with the bank activity in the background. It was unusual reasoning: the motive was not just pictorial, but to influence the psychology of the actors."

When Capra took charge of the foundering production, Bernds, who later became a director himself, wrote, "I fully realized, for the first time, what directing really was. Scenes that had been dull became lively, performances that had been dead came alive."

But Capra had no time—or inclination—to make many changes in the screenplay. With one major exception, the addition of the superb and virtually silent bank robbery sequence, Capra followed Riskin's story and dialogue almost to the letter, and he also adhered closely to the screen-play's unusually detailed visual plan. *American Madness* is a classic piece of screenwriting which tells its story with a terseness of dialogue and a fast pace that perfectly expresses the tension and propulsive movement of the theme. Even the elaborate montage showing the spread of the rumor lead-ing to the run on the bank—the film's most brilliant sequence—is fully developed in the script. Capra told Bob Thomas in the 1960s that *American Madness* marked "the first time I developed a style." And he told Richard Schickel in a 1975 interview, "Prior to that I'd been making films that sort of were escape films, entertainment, comedies. But this time I thought, well, why don't we make a picture about the contemporary hangups—you know, bank runs and things?" While it is true that Capra, unlike Dwan, was able to flesh out Riskin's blueprint and give the film the vitality it demanded, it is also true that many of what usually are described as directorial "touches" in *American Madness* actually were the screen-writer's.

The circumstances under which Capra took over the direction of the film disprove one of the most blatantly false claims in his autobiography: that he and Riskin wrote the story of *American Madness* together. In a 1973 interview, Capra overlooked Riskin entirely: "I got the idea for the story from the life of Giannini."

Bernds felt that Capra made no mention in his book of his replacement of Allan Dwan "because he didn't want to put down a revered member of the Directors Guild." But Capra felt no compunction about discussing his takeover of *Submarine* from Irvin Willat, and so it is hard to escape the conclusion that Capra deliberately obscured the situation regarding his takeover of *American Madness* in order to downgrade Riskin's contribution to his career: as he admitted in his book, it was not until he made the film that he found the social themes of his major work. Film historians, taking Capra at his word, have echoed his account. In *Hail, Columbia*, her 1975 history of the studio, Rochelle Larkin wrote that "Capra had thought up the story line, and it was the first foreshadowing of what was to become his major theme in almost all his future work: the celebration of the basic goodness and honesty of most men."

But not only did Capra have nothing to do with writing the story of *American Madness* (nor with the title, which was suggested to Harry Cohn by Capra's old MGM nemesis Harry Rapf after the film had received its trade reviews in May), the theme hardly was one he could have come up with on his own. As critic John Raeburn wrote in his 1975 book on Capra,

"Very little in Capra's early career as a director suggested he was capable of creating a film as sharp in its social observation and as ambitious in its analysis of American values."

Although Capra's confused political beliefs were dominated by his need to identify himself with the Republican philosophy of the wealthy and educated elites, his upbringing also left him with some affinities with the antiurban Populist movement. He exemplified the displaced immigrant who, though he thrived in the competitive atmosphere of the city, shared with the Populists a belief in what Richard Hofstadter in *The Age of Reform* called "the agrarian myth . . . a kind of homage that Americans have paid to the fancied innocence of their origins. . . . [which] perhaps relieved some residual feelings of guilt at having deserted parental homes and childhood attachments." That reactionary idealization of small-town America and suspicion of the cynical city was a central and lasting theme of Capra's films, from his first feature, *The Strong Man*, through *Mr. Deeds Goes to Town*, *Mr. Smith Goes to Washington*, *Meet John Doe*, and *It's a Wonderful Life*.

But Capra's contradictory view of America also exemplified Hofstadter's observation that "the ideal implicit in the myth was contesting the ground with another, even stronger ideal—the notion of opportunity, of career, of the self-made man." Capra shared some of the less attractive biases of Populism, which Hofstadter summarized as "isolationism and the extreme nationalism that usually goes with it, hatred of Europe and Europeans, racial, religious, and nativist phobias, resentment of big business, trade-unionism, intellectuals, the Eastern seaboard and its culture." Most (though not all) of those sentiments would be represented in an uneasy and often contradictory mélange in Capra's films of the thirties, whose politics were further complicated by the influence of his predominantly liberal and leftist screenwriters.

The Frank Capra who directed *American Madness* in 1932 with such apparent (and no doubt partly real) conviction personally belied Thomas Dickson's principles by hoarding most of his savings (some in gold) at his home and in safe-deposit boxes, sharing a distrust of banks with so many of his fellow citizens. The Frank Capra of 1932 also voted against Franklin D. Roosevelt in the presidential election that November. One of Roosevelt's first acts as president was to take the country off the gold standard and to recall private gold hoardings, thus expanding the supply of paper money and curtailing the power of private banks to dominate the economy. During the making of *Forbidden* in the fall of 1931, Capra and Adolphe Menjou privately discussed their vehement opposition to the proposed recall of gold hoardings. A person who overheard their discussions on the set characterized them as "some pretty good hate sessions" in which "Menjou and Capra used to get together and excoriate FDR," who then was governor of New York and the leading candidate for the Democratic presidential nomination.

Because of the kind of pictures he was making, almost everyone assumed in the thirties that Capra was a liberal; the debate then was whether he was a "radical" liberal or only a "moderate" one. But from 1931 onward, Capra's principal political activity was his involvement with the reactionary Academy of Motion Picture Arts and Sciences in its attempt to keep control of Hollywood labor. Because the Academy managed to focus more attention on the Oscars than on its political machinations (partly through the efforts of a public relations committee of which Capra and Louis B. Mayer were members), few people seemed to draw a connection between Capra the filmmaker and the Capra who was, as he later put it, "stooging for producers" on the board of the Academy.

Those who looked closely into the activities of the Academy during that period would have noticed that Capra actively participated in its promanagement labor decisions, serving as a member of the Academy's Arbitration Agreement Committee, which settled employee complaints with the studios, and before that as a member of a special committee appointed to study the agreement.

The Academy had established a basic contract for actors earning above fifteen dollars a day, and on April 21, 1932, the board approved an agreement between writers and producers, but both contracts were biased so blatantly in the studios' favor that they fueled growing agitation for the establishment of actors', writers', and directors' guilds (the directors never had an Academy agreement).

The Academy had "conciliation" procedures to settle labor-management disputes, but compliance was not mandatory, merely left to "the honesty and sincerity of the parties involved" in keeping with "the customs and ethics of the industry." Ralph Block, one of the founders of the Screen Writers Guild, observed that the producers "prefer to make rules where they don't have to abide by them—in the Academy."

To counteract increasing agitation by actors and others in the industry who objected to the studios' maintenance of long-term contracts as a form of virtual servitude, the Academy on July 12, 1932, adopted measures proposed by board member and MGM production chief Irving Thalberg "for the purposes of preventing raids and secret or premature negotiations" with talent. Thalberg's "anti-raiding" scheme was a way for the studios to cooperate in dictating terms to potentially rebellious employees and to keep the employees from playing one studio against another to make more favorable deals. One of the most important challenges to the Academy system came shortly thereafter, when James Cagney took his contract battle with Warner Bros. to the Arbitration Agreement Committee, with Capra serving as chairman for the hearing on September 27.

Cagney was signed by Warners in 1930 and rose to stardom with *The Public Enemy* the following year. The studio rushed him into a series of quickies to capitalize on his stardom, and Cagney felt he was overworked, underpaid, and given no say in his choice of roles. He was not a member of the Academy, but with his contract expiring, he had no choice between legal action and taking his complaints before the committee. The committee's decisions normally were published without names in the Academy *Bulletins*, simply showing the results of an anonymous actor's complaint against an unspecified studio, but the Cagney hearing was publicized by the actor himself, and the specifics emerged in court papers filed in Cagney's subsequent suit against Warners.

Jack L. Warner and the studio's production chief, Darryl F. Zanuck, appeared at the hearing to present the studio's case, and after two hours of testimony, Capra sent representatives of both sides into an adjoining room to work out a compromise. But they came out still deadlocked, Warners offering Cagney a seven-year contract with a starting salary of $3,000 per week and Cagney wanting only a three-year contract at a higher salary. Deciding that "the salary offer of Warner Bros. was fair to Mr. Cagney," as Capra later put it, the committee split the difference on the other issue and fixed the term of Cagney's contract at five years. Displeased, the actor returned to work and continued to press his battle in other ways—through his efforts in helping to found the Screen Actors Guild in 1933 as a means of breaking the Academy's stranglehold on talent, through a holdout and his court case in the late 1930s, and eventually his exit from Warners (it was another Warners star, Olivia de Havilland, who finally managed to emancipate actors from long-term studio contracts).

Such actions as that taken by the Academy in the Cagney dispute did not help "in maintaining and stabilizing the industry during a particularly crucial period," as the special committee of which Capra was a member had insisted the Academy labor agreements would do. Unemployment and labor unrest only became more desperate in Hollywood in the closing months of the Hoover administration.

Most of the men who worked on Capra's crew were rank-and-file Democrats, and most of them assumed that Capra shared their political views.

One of the few who recognized the truth was Edward Bernds. During the 1930s Bernds prodded Capra into a number of talks on the set about politics, and he was shocked by his discovery of Capra's true allegiances. The diaries Bernds kept during the shooting of Capra's films in the Depression years are vivid contemporary evidence of how wrong most people were in their assessment of the director's personal politics.

On April 27, 1936, during the making of *Lost Horizon*, Bernds wrote: "[T]alk long with Fr. C. about Fascism, radicalism, etc.—he rails against big-salary stars who flaunt radicalism. My impression his viewpoint very muddled and reactionary."

On October 31 of the same year—three days before FDR's landslide reelection—Bernds listened to another political diatribe by Capra, and wondered over "F.C.'s malicious sneering at the Administration. . . . Why does F.C. dislike Administration? Income tax?"

During the shooting of a crowd scene for *Mr. Smith Goes to Washington* at Los Angeles's Santa Fe train depot on July 1, 1939, Capra became incensed at the behavior of some extras who were "dogging it—wander off—refuse to listen, etc. F.C.'s burnup at them—'These are the people, the fellows you want to do things for.' Wonder: maybe the mob is so lazy, so stupid, so wrong-headed that only harsh leadership of energetic, able men (fascism) is practical. Sure F.C. feels something like it—his 'dominate' theme."

On August 16, 1938, during a dubbing session for *You Can't Take It With You*, Capra vented more of "his cranky, intolerant attitudes," claiming, "Every politician [is] a crook." Bernds wrote in his diary: "I try [to] draw him out. . . . [H]e apparently bitter Roosevelt hater. Some day spill low-down about it?"

"It actually *hurt* me to hear Capra's anti-Roosevelt talk," Bernds remembered. "Labor was being hit over the head in those days. I know *we* were. For Christ's sake, working eighty-five hours a week without any overtime—it was the Depression, so we had to do it. The hours were terrible and unnecessary. Even during the Depression the studios were making money. They just worked us like dogs out of sheer indifference. When Roosevelt came along, my God, he was a savior. He literally was a savior."

Asked about Capra's politics, Chester Sticht, his closest associate for thirty-nine years, confirmed, "That was sort of a misunderstanding. He was always a Republican."

Capra alluded only obliquely to his Republicanism in *The Name Above the Title.* Describing his first meeting with President Roosevelt during World War II, he claimed that FDR's personal charm and praise of his work "almost converted me into becoming a Democrat." In 1948, on one of the rare occasions he went directly on the public record with his political affiliation, Capra wrote a right-wing Hollywood columnist for Hearst's *New York Daily Mirror*, Lee Mortimer: "I am a Republican. I even voted against FDR right along, not because I didn't agree with all of his ideas, but because I thought he was getting too big for the country's good. I am passionately against dictatorship in any form."

But Capra was not always consistent in his feelings about dictatorships, particularly right-wing dictatorships. In the same period when he thought FDR was getting "too big for the country's good," he was an admirer of Mussolini and Franco, who in that era were seen by many as bulwarks against the international Communist menace, and he stated in 1934 that his favorite historical character was Napoleon. But Capra's view of such figures was changed by World War II: busts of Napoleon are prominently displayed by such Capra villains as *Meet John Doe*'s Edward Arnold, who has ambitions of becoming an American dictator, and *It's a Wonderful Life*'s Lionel Barrymore, who speaks of the working class as "a discontented, lazy rabble."

Despite his occasional flirtations with more liberal ideas, Capra assured the U.S. government in a 1951 document that he had voted for the Republican candidate for President in every election since 1920, the year he became a citizen. Though he admitted to liking Harry S Truman and John F. Kennedy, he still voted for their opponents. He admired Richard Nixon, defending him even on Watergate, arguing in 1981 that Nixon "wasn't stealing any great money, he just was fool enough to try to protect his friends." He golfed with Barry Goldwater and Gerald Ford ("the most interesting guy in the world—very funny—the ball goes all over the place"), and he and Lu sent a wire of congratulations to his old colleague Ronald Reagan when Reagan was elected President of the United States.

Capra's lifelong affiliation with conservative Republicanism was consistent with his basic social beliefs. But Capra in later life did not discourage his admirers from finding liberal sentiments in his films, and it was his liberal admirers, ironically, who brought him back into fashion during the early 1970s. "What continues to amaze," critic Elliott Stein wrote in 1980, "is the durable folly of the received opinion of Capra as some sort of New Deal liberal." Capra offered back to his latter-day admirers a safely vague, noncontroversial, humanist interpretation of his work which would bring no discomfort to those on the left of center: "I wanted to glorify the average man, not the guy at the top, not the politician, not the banker, just the ordinary guy whose strength I admire." When asked to go beyond these woolly abstractions and define his personal political beliefs, he usually evaded the question. Close retrospective scrutiny of the political viewpoint of his old films filled him with anxiety.

On the rare occasions, however, when an interviewer managed to pin him down with a direct question about something as specific as FDR's New Deal policies, he had trouble disguising his distaste: when Richard Glatzer asked him in a 1973 interview if Walter Huston's economic ideas in *American Madness* weren't rather "New Dealish," Capra replied uncomfortably, "Well, yes. But we made the film before Roosevelt was elected" (note the uncharacteristic use of the word "we"). When historian Walter Karp brought up the New Deal in a 1981 *Esquire* interview, Capra admitted he "wasn't terribly impressed" with it. Then he took refuge once again in feigned ignorance and a squidlike burst of obscuring, uplifting rhetoric: "A lot of people said my movies were New Dealish. I didn't know what the New Deal represented. I think the real story of the Depression was the people, what they did when all the props fell and everything hit at once. They were down, very down, but they didn't panic; they never quite lost the faith."

Edward Bernds was partially correct in his observation that Capra, despite the liberal tinge of most of his thirties films, voted Republican because he was simply "voting his pocketbook." Capra was just beginning to make a great deal of money as the Depression hit, and it was during the Roosevelt years that he became a wealthy man. Capra made clear his antipathy toward the Roosevelt era's high corporate taxes in his book's section on *Meet John Doe.* But Capra's Darwinian social beliefs were no new development in his life, even if they were intensified by his heightened social position and by his fierce desire to hold on to his new material gains. As it was said of the Spencer Tracy character in *State of the Union,* he may have talked "like a radical, but any man's made as much money as he has is a good sound American."

Capra admitted that there was an irrational basis to his opposition to FDR and the New Deal: he disliked FDR because of his privileged upbringing. But unlike Roosevelt, who managed to transcend the selfishness of his privilege, Capra rarely transcended the selfishness which grew out of his early deprivation. Capra's basic attitudes, unlike Roosevelt's, allowed him no special concern for the underprivileged—by and large he took a typical Republican view, feeling that if he, a poor immigrant boy, could make it to the top, why couldn't they?

Some critics recognized that there were political ambiguities in Capra's films, that they were considerably more complex politically than just sentimental paeans to the "little guy." But even the most perceptive critics seemed to have a great deal of trouble coming to terms with his films' political implications. Donald Willis, in his critical study of Capra, summarized the dizzying variety of critical viewpoints that have been expressed about the director: "Depending on one's political point of view and on what Capra film or films or parts of Capra films one is talking about, Frank Capra is an advocate of Communism, fascism, Marxism, populism, conservatism, McCarthyism, New-Dealism, anti-Hooverism, jingoism, socialism, capitalism, middle-of-the-road-ism, democracy, or individualism." Faced with this conundrum, Willis simply threw up his hands: "It's no accident that there are so many interpretations of his films: the composite Capra that emerges from those films is almost impossible to pin down politically. I myself think that Capra's films were basically not political."

Capra himself devoted a great deal of effort in his later years to encouraging that misleading notion. It was easier, and safer, to claim that his films were "apolitical" than to talk about them honestly. "If you're a real artist, forget the politics," he urged young filmmakers at a Directors Guild seminar in 1981. "Forget all politics. Because if you politicize yourself, what you do is cut yourself in half."

Capra's general avoidance of political discussions helped ensure that his admirers and his detractors alike assumed that his political beliefs were identical with those of his films, or, even more simplistically, that he was identical with the heroes of his films, with Gary Cooper's Longfellow Deeds or Jimmy Stewart's Jefferson Smith. What was most misleading was that people usually started from the premise that Capra's films expressed his own personal viewpoint, and his alone. The "*auteur*" theory of film criticism, which he did as much as any filmmaker to promote, helped make his egocentrism fashionable, indeed elevated it to the status of a principle. As Capra put it when asked in a 1968 public appearance how he had "hit upon this formula": "I think every man's picture is in a sense an autobiography. The films you make—you put them together and you've got the man's autobiography pretty well there somewhere, if he's the filmmaker and not just an employee. And so this feeling to make pictures about the common people was just my answer. As an immigrant kid coming over here I liked the common people, and, you know, I wanted to sing their songs."

The *auteur* theory—or, as Capra called it, the "one man, one film" concept—did not recognize the degree to which a filmmaker such as Capra could be influenced by conflicting points of view and incorporate them into his work, nor the degree to which a filmmaker might be expressing his times as much as he was expressing himself. And though there was much controversy in the 1970s about how much credit Robert Riskin deserved for Capra's success, not even Riskin's supporters ever pointed out that the crux of the problem was that Capra and Riskin did not have identical sociopolitical views, or that their films could have been a volatile fusion between two conflicting viewpoints rather than a smooth and unified expression of one man's ideas. Nor was there any cognizance of the degree to which Capra in the 1930s acted as a relatively passive sounding board for the political views of his diverse brain trust, which also included the far-right Myles Connolly, the Roosevelt liberal Jo Swerling, and the left-liberal writer and associate producer Joseph Sistrom; Sistrom was so passionate about his beliefs and so looked the part of a radical leftist that he was known affectionately around the office as "The Bomb Thrower." As the moderate conservative Chet Sticht observed, Capra in the prime of his career liked to surround himself with colleagues who were not yes men, and his ability to listen to and absorb such a range of viewpoints "made him an interesting guy," contributing to the complexity of his films. As long as Capra worked with strong writers who were in touch with reality—such as Swerling, Riskin, and Sidney Buchman—his films had some degree of coherence, despite their ambiguities, but when Capra lost his openness of mind, cut himself off from left-of-center influences, and began listening almost exclusively to the blinkered Myles Connolly in the postwar period, his films degenerated into nonsense and his career self-destructed.

But little of this complexity was recognized by the people outside his inner circle. Even among those who were in close contact with him—his coworkers and colleagues in Hollywood—Capra tended to obfuscate his politics out of a chameleonlike, self-protective impulse, like the title character in Woody Allen's *Zelig*, known as "The Chameleon Man."

He even kept Lu in the dark. As Margaret Case Harriman wrote in a 1941 article in *The Ladies' Home Journal*, "Capra enjoys long, amiable discussions with [his] pals on almost any subject, and his willingness to take either side in an argument to promote good talk is so familiar to his wife that once, when someone asked her if she always agreed with her husband, she laughed and said, 'How can I? I never even know from one day to the next whether we're Republicans or Democrats.'"

Katharine Hepburn, his staunchly liberal leading lady in *State of the Union*, was one of those who assumed that Capra was "quite liberal." But when told that he disliked FDR (whom she knew personally and greatly admired), Hepburn exclaimed, "Oh, dear! Well, I think I sort of knew that. He certainly wasn't very left. I figured out pretty much what he was—a real American of the old days. I don't think he was a party man in any violent sense. He was a very fair man. He believed in freedom. I think immigrants know more about what this country means than those of us who were born here and criticize it. Those of us who were born here, we tend to take it for granted. Capra's outlook was that of a fellow from Sicily coming into this country: that was his politics: 'Pleased to be here.' "

Capra's embrace of Riskin's Rooseveltian economic viewpoint in *American Madness* in part was opportunism—he could recognize a good script when he saw it, and the mood of the country was swinging unmistakably in that direction—but it also marked the beginning of a genuine, if short-lived, liberal-leftist influence on his thinking. The enthusiasm and sincerity Capra brought to his direction of *American Madness* (and of later Riskin scripts) tapped into unconscious reserves of goodwill that Capra could not allow himself to express in his off-screen politics and which reflected his belated, reluctant, but nevertheless strongly felt awareness that the country's economic system needed overhauling if the American Dream was to survive. It was a time when, in the words of the historian Arnold Toynbee, "men and women all over the world were seriously contemplating and frankly discussing the possibility that the Western system of society might break down and cease to work."

According to the uncut manuscript of Capra's autobiography, sometime during the early years of the Depression he became alarmed enough to read Karl Marx. The radical solutions of Marxism briefly made him ruminate about the evils of capitalism and wonder whether Marx wasn't on the right track philosophically with his view of the plight of "the common man."

Army Intelligence reports on Capra in 1951, declassified in 1986, indicated that the Los Angeles files of the House Committee on Un-American Activities (HUAC) "contained the following information concerning an individual who may or may not be identical with SUBJECT. . . . One Frank CAPRA, 503 East First St., Los Angeles, Calif. was a signer of the Communist Party Election Petition, No. 105C in 1932." The address listed, in a downtown Los Angeles industrial district, was one which was not otherwise associated with the director Frank Capra. Though there is no way of knowing the accuracy of the HUAC information—considering its source it should be regarded with the highest skepticism, and cases of mistaken identity were frequent with the HUAC witch-hunters—such an action, however bizarre, might not have been entirely uncharacteristic for Capra, particularly in light of his admission of an interest in Marxist philosophy in that period and the fact that in the fall of 1932 he began work on a project at MGM called *Soviet,* a sympathetic treatment of the Marxist social experiment which the studio said it dropped because the "propaganda angle in [the] story is too strong."

Such sentiments were something of an intellectual vogue that year. In the November election for President of the United States, the Communist Party candidate, William Z. Foster, received 103,152 votes, the most ever achieved by the Party in a presidential election, and though there was as yet little Party activity in Hollywood, Foster's candidacy received public support from such prominent writers as John Dos Passos, Erskine Caldwell, Langston Hughes, Sherwood Anderson, Sidney Howard, and Lincoln Steffens. But with his general lack of intellectual sophistication and his limited political education, Capra never progressed beyond a superficial understanding of Marxism. His deep-seated emotional bias against collectivism and in favor of rugged individualism eventually made him recoil from the disturbing insights of Marxism into the struggle of the working class from which he had emerged and made his intellectual flirtation with Marxist ideas a brief aberration in his development, though one which left its traces in his work. Partially, perhaps, in reaction to his earlier interest, and because of his growing awareness of the dangers to which it exposed him, he gradually turned violently anti-Communist.

In the Depression era, it sometimes was hard to distinguish the political solutions offered by the far Left from those offered by the far Right. In response to the desperate world and national situations, and under the influence of his liberal and radical screenwriters, Capra's films in the thirties sometimes seemed to veer uncertainly between one pole and the other. In this he was typical of many Americans, particularly those of the privileged classes; when he made *American Madness,* Capra was earning more in one week than most American families earned in an entire year.

"People who had anything to lose were frightened; they were willing to accept any way out that would leave them in possession," Richard Hofstadter wrote in *The American Political Tradition.* "During the emergency Roosevelt had practically dictatorial powers. He had righted the keel of economic life and had turned politics safely back to its normal course. Although he had adopted many novel, perhaps risky expedients, he had avoided vital disturbances to the interests." Anti–New Deal conservatives were not as concerned with righting fundamental social injustices as they were with keeping the American system solvent and heading off a revolt by the underclass. Despite his ideological confusions, in the last analysis that was Capra's position. In 1975, looking back on those years, he told the author of this book, "We've never known hunger in this country since then, real hunger. And there were people at every street corner urging us to go Fascist or Communist. I'm very proud of the American people—they didn't listen to any of them."

With the hindsight of the late 1960s, critic Raymond Durgnat characterized the Capra-Riskin Depression-era films as "propaganda for a moderate, concerned, Republican point of view," but that statement ignores the impact the films had when the issues were more urgent. While there was nothing truly radical about *American Madness*—whose hero was, after all, a dedicated exponent of the capitalist system, like Roosevelt himself—it was bold for Hollywood. Columbia advertised the film as "a dramatic thunderbolt challenging the nation," and the word "radical" began to appear for the first time in press commentaries on a Capra film when it was released with rousing success on August 14, 1932. An editorial in Hearst's *Milwaukee Sentinel* found in *American Madness* "a tinge of the radical thought of this era," but even that conservative paper could not help conceding that the film's themes were "cleverly insinuated . . . in a way that is apt to arouse sympathy rather than opposition." Abel Green's *Variety* review caught the film's crusading spirit by describing it as "swell propaganda against hoarding, frozen assets and other economic evils which 1932 Hooverism has created." William Boehnel of the *New York World Telegram* described the run on the bank as "one of the most excitingly realistic mob scenes ever pictured on the screen outside of the newsreels. The director, Frank Capra—one of Hollywood's best, incidentally—has found a way of projecting all the pent-up fury of a mob of depositors storming a bank, which looks as if it were the real thing and not something manufactured in a studio. This one will grip you."

Like Robert Riskin, Lu was a steadying influence in Capra's life who helped free him to do his best creative work.

His relationship with Riskin was still a flirtation, not yet a marriage; another writer would do the script for his next film. Capra seemed to feel a need to dance gingerly around a person he sensed would have a transforming impact on him. But now that his maddeningly indecisive courtship of Lu was resolved, he began to pour into his work the emotional energies he had been expending on his fruitless pursuit of Stanwyck. If there seemed to be less passion between Capra and Lu than there had been in his romance with Stanwyck, neither Capra nor Lu seemed to mind. As Capra put it on a public occasion in 1982, in Lu's presence, "No man is going to marry a woman because he's seen her bare ass. . . . He won't marry her until they look each other square in the eye and see something." The positive effects of what he saw in Lu were already apparent on his career:

"I had a *home* to go to. I didn't have to be worried about this, I didn't have to be worried about that. I was not in any way encumbered or beset with arguments or fights. It changed my life. She brought me stability— and ability. I could then pay full attention to what I was doing. I could stay at the studio until one o'clock or three o'clock in the morning, and she would know that I wasn't staying with some dame. I wanted to make good pictures, I wasn't after dames. She knew that was what I wanted, and she was going to help me do it.

"That was the good thing about my wife: She *helped* me."

Thinking of his relationships with Helen Howell and with Stanwyck, Capra said of Lu, "It wouldn't have lasted a week if she had been an actress. Just think of how many wonderful people have their lives ruined by their home lives—some stupid thing they do in their home life and they're ruined forever. They become drunkards, and they become this, they become that. Fortunately, I missed all that. I must say that I missed it purposely."

Asked by a student audience in 1972 if Lu had ever been an actress, Capra turned the question over to his wife, who said, "I don't get involved with the directing of his pictures." Capra added: "She directed *me*."

When he described his wife's personality, he used a word that surprised everyone outside of her immediate family: "Tough. My wife was a tough one. She looked delicate, but she was not delicate, she was tougher than hell."

Few others saw beyond her outward appearance of fragility and deference. But she gave her husband an unquestioning loyalty and enthusiasm that he could always count on when he needed reassurance—which was often. "I think she was the stable one in that family," said their daughter, Lulu. By her constant bucking up, Lu provided the strength of Capra's convictions, such as they were, and the emotional strength he needed to counterbalance his extreme moodiness and frequent bouts of despair. Capra called her "Mama," and, indeed, Lu became the mother he never had.

Lu also provided something else he had never had before: "Kids. I was crazy about my kids. Certainly that's the principal thing she brought into my life. And when I had kids I had what I wanted. I didn't have to go to whorehouses."

To work off pent-up emotion after finishing a picture, Capra developed "a routine for dealing with fatigue—I'd go to the tennis court and bat balls against a wall until I dropped dead, or I'd hoe the ground like a crazy man until I sweated and sweated and sweated and got so tired I couldn't move. Then I'd go back to the studio." He also golfed, went deer and dove hunting, and took fishing trips with Lu and other couples to the High Sierras and the St. Lawrence River. "Lu loved to fish, and she would catch more than anyone else," Chet Sticht recalled. "You'd look out and see a whole circle of boats all around her, and she was hauling in fish and nobody else was."

When he was home and not shooting a film, they went to movies and concerts, largely, Frank said, because Lu liked to do so. But on most nights they were content to sit around the house quietly by themselves, reading; she was a voracious reader. Some nights he would study scripts, and she would do her needlepoint. "Capra didn't have many really close friends," Sticht observed: Frank and Lu were so close that they did not seem to need anybody else. Even after they had children, they would eat alone after the nursemaids put the children to bed by nine o'clock. "She was very plain about the fact that he came first," recalled their oldest child, Frank, Jr. "She had to watch over him, and it wasn't her job just to watch over us."

"His hours were very long and very hard," their daughter Lulu remembered. "He left way before we got up in the morning and he got home much after we were in bed, and we didn't eat with my parents. So from that point of view I guess I didn't [get a great deal of attention from him], but as I look back I never, never once thought that he was away a lot. So the time that he *did* spend with us must have been very well spent, because neither my brothers nor I thought we had an odd upbringing or that we were anything but a very close family."

Frank and Lu enjoyed small gatherings with such friends as the Connollys, the Swerlings, the Sistroms, and the Colemans. Lu and Alyce were so close that Buddy Coleman half-jokingly referred to himself as "Capra's brother-in-law." Capra helped Buddy get a job as a director, but he wound up being fired by Harry Cohn, and the Colemans, who had to move to the unfashionable San Fernando Valley, gradually found themselves excluded from the Capras' social circle. "I love those people," Alyce would say of Frank and Lu, "but I don't really know what they're doing anymore."

Most people in Hollywood envied the Capras' marriage. As *Time* put it in its 1938 cover story on Capra, he was making it fashionable in Hollywood "to have a private telephone number, small car, cottage on the beach, and one wife at a time." *The Ladies' Home Journal* in 1941 praised their "simplicity" and called them "one of the most normal couples in

Hollywood—an accolade in a town where screwiness has become conventional."

The Capras were one of the rare married couples in Hollywood about whom there never was any scandal. John Huston, who lived with Capra in London bachelor quarters during World War II, marveled that he was "the most devoted husband I've ever known. He *adored* Lu."

Lu's graciousness and popularity rubbed off on Frank, smoothing some of his abrasive edges and giving him a new social cachet within the industry.

"I liked what I saw of them," said one of Hollywood's most prominent and respected women, Irene Mayer Selznick, the daughter of Louis B. Mayer and wife of David O. Selznick. "I thought Lu was concerned, caring, sane, attractive, well groomed. Of course she adored him. She wanted no glory for herself." As for Capra, Mrs. Selznick said, "I was crazy about him. He was so down-to-earth, without affectation. I admired the simplicity in his personality, and the solidity. He was a practical man, not full of eccentricities and bad habits. He kept his word, he was a good citizen. The assumption was that he was straight, that he put everything on the table and had no secrets."

Almost everyone saw them that way. Their young Malibu neighbor Budd Schulberg later wrote of them, "Just as we idealize the Girl (or Boy) Next Door, the Capras were the perfect Couple Next Door. Sometimes if the waves were rolling in, I would bodysurf them to the beach for an hour, then run up and down the beach, feeling the salt and sun soaking into my skin. If I saw Frank and Lucille at their picture window, I would wave, and sometimes drop in. They made me feel welcome, they liked me for myself, and not for what my father could do for them."

The stuttering young Hollywood prince found that unlike his philandering father, Paramount executive B. P. Schulberg, and other wealthy movie people who surrounded the Capras in Malibu, including Clara Bow with her drunken all-night parties, the Capras were "serious, productive, and moral citizens." Capra, because of his background, "knew the value of a dollar and he and Lucille lived comfortably but without ostentation. To me, the Capras were symbols of sobriety and sanity for whom all-night drinking or gambling and losing ten thousand dollars a session were inconceivable. It was a comforting thought that right next door lived a man who could be famous, creative, and rich without going crazy."

But it was also true, as Chet Sticht observed, that Capra "wasn't the easiest man in the world to live with. He used to say to me, 'I need to have my ego massaged.' " Chet's wife, Bett, recalled: "When Frank would say,

'We're going to London tomorrow,' [Lu would] say, 'Yes, dear,' and off they'd go. We'd all marvel at her. She was the most devoted wife I've ever seen. His absolutely every whim was gratified. Everything he did was wonderful. She would talk up to other people, but to him it was always, 'Oh, yes, dear, it's wonderful'—that was the word she always used, 'wonderful.' He had to have that. She was always there to roll out the red carpet for him when he walked in the door. She kept a nice house for him. She produced beautiful children; they turned out well. It was a very happy family life, I think, with Frank as majordomo. It would be a good picture for Frank: *It's a Wonderful Wife.*"

He also relied on Lu heavily for advice about his work. When Carol Frink interviewed Capra in 1939 for the *Washington Times-Herald,* she told him, "The talk is that you are a homebody and that you consult your wife about everything you do." Lu was listening, and it was she who answered "firmly" that "The talk is correct." Jimmy Stewart recalled Capra telling him more than once that when he was writing at home and was stuck for a line, "I called Lu in and she gave me the line." *The Ladies' Home Journal* reported, "She reads the script of every picture before Capra starts working on it, and he is continually bringing home bits of film as the picture progresses, and running them for her in the playroom—which is fitted up with a projector, a screen, and deep-cushioned chairs."

Despite Capra's long working hours, Lu "really stuck by him," said Josie Campisi. "She loved him in her own way, but it was not a smothering love. If she felt neglected, she wouldn't let you know it. Some women are glad when their husbands are not around all the time—it's too much to handle. That took her off the hook."

After his marriage, Capra had even less to do with his side of the family, except for Ann, than he had before. In the early thirties he stopped about once a month on his way home from work to visit his mother on Odin Street, but the visits became less frequent "as he got busier and acquired a different living style," as Chet Sticht put it. Frank conversed with her mostly in Italian, and Sticht felt that this "little round peasant lady" did not seem really comfortable when she visited Frank and Lu at their home in fashionable Brentwood, where they moved in 1936, or at the studio parties to which Frank invited her. Although she was "a wonderful lady, very friendly and caring," Frank, Jr., remembered, "she spoke kind of weird, spoke with a heavy accent."

The family as a whole "didn't socialize much, except on special occasions and on Christmas," Sticht said. "They were from different worlds."

Ben was working for the railroad in Sacramento, Frank and Tony seldom spoke to each other (with the repeal of Prohibition, Tony was concentrating on his legitimate businesses), and his sisters Luigia and Josephine still lived in Little Sicily, which had become as alien to Capra as Sicily itself. Josie Campisi blamed his increased distance partly on Lu, whom she considered something of a snob. Since Capra expressed resentment toward his first wife for being too fond of his relatives, he probably responded favorably to the aloofness shown them by his "classy" second wife and at least tacitly encouraged it.

"She never was friendly with the family," Campisi said. "She came from a pretty well-to-do family. She was very sweet, but very introverted. We almost never saw her."

Capra's love for his supportive little sister Ann survived his rise to wealth and fame. "My sister was never jealous," he said. "She was the only one who knew that I'd become recognized."

He helped her find a job in the Columbia wardrobe department, which she gave up in 1932 to marry the Danish-born film editor Folmar Blangsted. Her marriage to Sam Huffsmith had been annulled after he left her (she later had him declared legally dead), and she had turned her back on the Catholic church after Papa Turiddu was killed, repulsed by the parish priest's dunning the family for money to rescue her father's soul from Purgatory. Her second marriage was performed by a Baptist minister at a nondenominational church, with Capra as best man and Lu as an attendant. Capra also gave them the Odin Street house, where they lived with Saridda and their two adopted children, David and Joanne, whom Capra insisted be given Catholic educations. Capra's new brother-in-law soon moved from Paramount to Columbia, where he had a brief shot at directing B Westerns before returning to the cutting room. He eventually went to Warner Bros., where he edited such films as George Cukor's *A Star Is Born* and Howard Hawks's *Rio Bravo*.

When Joe Finochio asked his Uncle Frank to help him get a regular job at Columbia in 1932, Capra agreed to do so, but he made his nephew change his name. Capra renamed him Joe "Fidel," from the Latin root for "faithful," which was the name Finochio used throughout his long career at Columbia. He started in the sound department stockroom for thirty-five dollars a week, became a loader, and then was promoted to sound recorder. He worked on five of his uncle's films, beginning with *It Happened One Night,* as the recorder for Edward Bernds. But he never received screen credit from his uncle, and few at the studio knew that Joe Fidel was related to Frank Capra.

"Uncle Frank was tough," he acknowledged. "He got me the job there, but he told me, 'Keep your nose clean—if you get into trouble, don't come crying to me.' I was a young punk then, nineteen years old, and I listened to what he said. I told him, 'Goddamn, Uncle Frank, if it wasn't for you I'd still be delivering ice in Little Italy.' I kept my nose clean."

Joe rarely saw his uncle off the set and then only in the studio cafeteria or at wrap parties. The nephew tried to be charitable about the situation: "Uncle Frank did not mean to ignore his family. The closeness just wasn't there. He lacked that little something necessary for it. Not that he hated his family, he loved them, but the poor guy never had the time to come around and see them. He devoted his whole life to Hollywood and motion picture making. With most Italian families, it's a big show, but people in Hollywood lead a different life."

Capra claimed that even after he became famous, his family was never proud of him, that their belittling attitude toward him "never ended," that they thought his awards and achievements and his *Time* magazine cover were all "silly." Campisi, however, said that there was misunderstanding and oversensitivity on both sides: "He felt out of place being with them. And they put him on a pedestal. Everybody wanted favors from him; you can't blame them. But he couldn't ask *them* for any favors because he'd have to reciprocate. If you have somebody in your family who's very famous, *you* cut off your relationship to *him*. Maybe they thought he thought he was too good for them."

Campisi felt, as did Capra, that despite his success, his mother still was not impressed by what he was doing: "It wasn't that she wasn't proud of him or anything, but he was just her little son, and I don't think she had the capacity to know at that time how famous he was becoming." Joe Finochio, on the other hand, remembered taking Saridda to visit the Shangri-La set of *Lost Horizon* in 1936; she was dressed in a fur coat, and someone gave her a cigarette holder to make her look more "Hollywood." She had never smoked in her life, but through her coughs she proudly waved her glowing hand toward Capra, shouting, *"Questo è figlio mio!"* ("This is my son!"). Capra came over and took the cigarette holder away from her, upset at the people having fun with his mother, and perhaps a little embarrassed by her peasant exuberance. Chet Sticht, who saw Saridda at Frank's parties and on other social occasions during the thirties, said she always showed interest and excitement over her son's Oscars and other honors: "I *know* she was proud of him. But she may not have shown it to *him*." When *Mr. Smith Goes to Washington* had one of its first screenings at the studio in 1939, Capra brought his mother to see it, figuring that with *this* he finally would impress her. As Saridda came out of the screening, he asked her what she thought. "Well, Frankie," she said, "when are you gonna get a job?"

Frank tried everything he could to win her praise and esteem. He supported her generously at the house on Odin Street. He hired servants to cook and clean for her. He bought her new cars. He sent her on vacations to seaside resorts in California and in the Bahamas, where she could rest her aching legs and find relief from her high blood pressure. He sent his mother and Josephine on a month-long visit to Sicily in 1934 so that Saridda could have a reunion with her daughter Ignazia, whom she hadn't seen for thirty-one years.

But, somehow, even this material largess failed to have its desired effect. It may have given Saridda a certain sadistic pleasure to resist the blandishments of a son for whom she had never shown much emotional regard. Perhaps her pride also prevented her from acknowledging his competence to his face. She had always scorned him as a lazy dreamer like her improvident husband, and to admit freely now that he was such a prodigiously successful breadwinner was too much for her stubborn, dominant nature. Frank said his mother thought he must be a criminal, because he was making so much money and never seemed to be doing anything to earn it except sitting in a chair.

"She never believed it would last," Sticht felt.

She gave Frank nothing but trouble. She drove all of her servants away, refusing to admit that she needed any help running the house. She claimed that one servant was stealing from her, and she claimed that another, a black woman, was trying to poison her.

"I knew she was nuts," Capra said bluntly. "I'd leave the studio and on the way home I'd go by and see how she was doing. One time I'd hired somebody to help her. My mother broke a lot of plates and then took me in and said, 'See, she broke all the plates. You've gotta get rid of her.'"

Despite all the trauma she caused him, Capra never lost his love for his mother. He wondered at the strange fact that even though she would not, or could not, show love for him, she could not help loving humanity in general: "I'd get there at six or seven o'clock, and she'd have four or five bums eating spaghetti. She'd put out a big plate of spaghetti for them. This was during the Depression, you know, and there were so many people walking the streets. Well, I got scared. I said, 'Mama, you can't let these people in, you're all alone here.' 'Oh,' she says, 'they're hungry. Are you crazy? They're *hungry*.' She thought it was no great deal. She thought people would naturally help each other. That was the kind of woman she was."

*   *   *

When asked why she thought there was so little about Capra's family in *The Name Above the Title*, Josie Campisi said, "He didn't have anything good to say about them." There was another important group of people about whom Capra had very little to say in his book. They, too, were close to Capra for years, closer, in fact, than most of his family. They were his crew at Columbia Pictures.

Capra worked with essentially the same group of men (and a few women) throughout most of his twelve years at Columbia. No director had a more loyal, resourceful, and talented bunch of collaborators. In contrast to his attitude toward his family, Capra in conversation did have many good things to say about his crew—"Boy, they were like *gold!*" he acknowledged—yet his treatment of them in his book was strikingly perfunctory and ungenerous, particularly where the indispensable Joe Walker was concerned.

As the very title of Capra's autobiography indicates, the book was an attempt to prove he did it all himself, a demonstration of his latter-day "one man, one film" theory. "The concept of one man, one film is very arguable," he conceded in 1984. "It's not very popular. But it worked for me, and it would work for others if they had guts enough to try it." Yet it was a theory that he himself had to contradict in speaking of his relationship with his crew: "They'd go to hell for me. If I asked something from them, they did it. I say one man should make a film, but that doesn't mean one man. . . . [It means] collaboration but not committee. Not committee responsibility. Collaboration—of course."

The "one man, one film" theory seemed strange indeed to the surviving members of his crew, who read Capra's book with an obvious hurt and embarrassment, though they were reluctant to voice those feelings directly. What baffled them about Capra's new theory was that while they were making the films, Capra did not appear to be the chest-thumping egomaniac revealed to them in *The Name Above the Title*.

"He loved his boys," Barbara Stanwyck said, "and the crew, of course, adored him. He understood their work, he understood their problems. He wasn't a Johnny-come-lately—he wrote, he was an editor, he had a great foundation. He didn't just come in and say, as some of the new ones do, 'I'm the director, now pay attention to me.'"

Jean Arthur remembered how Capra inspired "a feeling of great warmth and protection and a feeling that everyone, cast and crew, was working together toward the goal."

"There was a family spirit," Bernds felt. "He would listen to anybody in the crew. He would listen, period."

Buddy Coleman, Capra's assistant director on eleven films, said in 1937 that he had "never heard Frank refer to a production as '*my* picture, in which *I* did this or that'; it has always been '*our* picture, in which *we* did this or that.' "

Capra knew that if his men thought it was their film, not just his, they would work harder for him. A picture of modesty on the set during the prime of his career, he was never autocratic but a benign, seemingly democratic leader. He seldom raised his voice or lost his temper. He was always polite, he almost always seemed relaxed, he was efficient without being officious. It was not without effort.

"Knowing him, working for him as much as I did, I could see the strains in his jaw line," said Stanwyck. "But he never abused anybody. He was in control."

On the set Capra presented an image almost conspicuously devoid of pomp and pretension. Now that he was becoming wealthy, he lost much of his status anxiety about his clothing and appearance. Explorer Harrison Forman, his technical adviser on *Lost Horizon*, observed, "None of your fancy director's boots, breeches, and megaphones for him—just a plain pullover sweater, or perhaps a simple sweatshirt, a pair of floppy corduroy slacks, and serviceable moccasin oxfords." During the making of *Mr. Deeds Goes to Town*, Bernds recorded in his diary: "Capra very human—cold in nose, unshaven, happy-go-lucky, no dignity, sliding down banister to leading lady [Jean Arthur] on stomach, [wearing a] dinky hat."

"On a Capra set," Gary Cooper said, "you'd never pick Frank as the director."

But for all of the casualness in Capra's demeanor, there was never any question who was in charge. "Capra exuded authority," camera assistant Al Keller said. "But not authority for the sake of authority," added Capra's microphone boom operator Irving (Buster) Libott. "Authority because he knew what he was doing. There's a big difference."

No one on the crew called him "Frank"; he was always "Mr. Capra," even to Joe Walker, whose gentlemanly demeanor "set the tone" for Capra's set, as Bernds put it. Such formal address was part of the rigid Hollywood caste system of the time—Capra called them "Joe" or "Eddie" or "Bus"—but it also was part of Capra's personality to maintain an emotional distance from his coworkers. Though his crew, as Keller put it, felt they were "the elite" to work with Capra, their eliteness did not extend to socializing with the Capras, unless it was at a studio party. But the respect Capra showed for his crew when they were working together was a measure of his own increasing stature as a director. What enabled Capra to reach his artistic maturity, helping to make possible his remarkable achievements in the 1930s, was his realization that it was not bravado or even superior knowledge which would win the respect of his crew but the sense of self-confidence he managed to convey:

"Your crew can kill you. But all they want to know is 'Yes' or 'No.' If you can give 'em a 'Yes' or a 'No' fast, you're in. And even if you're wrong, it's all right. They don't blame you, because they knew you made a decision fast. The director has to decide. He has to take the chances of an idea, and he gets the credit or discredit for it."

Capra also had a boss at Columbia.

He created the impression in his book that he always was locked in mortal, love-hate conflict with Harry Cohn. His success, he implied, was in direct proportion to his ability to outwit, outyell, and outbully the president of Columbia Pictures. The story read like a morality play, with Capra the heroic figure representing Art, and Cohn the venal figure representing Commerce. Colorful and entertaining though it was, Capra's account grossly oversimplified a complex relationship.

Until their friendship began to fall apart in the late 1930s, Capra and Cohn functioned much more like collaborators than like enemies. They had their quarrels, naturally, but hardly on such a regular and vociferous basis as Capra's account would have the reader believe.

"They never had any big arguments," said Joe Walker. "Capra could hold his own with Cohn and Cohn had a lot of respect for Capra."

"They had a sort of mutual admiration society," Jimmy Stewart agreed. "Cohn liked to yell at him, and Frank didn't pay any attention to him. Frank was one of the few people who could do that with Harry Cohn."

There were tensions, of course. Dore Schary, then a young screenwriter at Columbia, witnessed a revealing incident in 1932. Cohn had a trick chair in his executive dining room, wired to give an electric shock to anyone who sat in it unsuspectingly. One hot afternoon, Capra came in, looking exhausted.

As Schary recalled, "He said it was too damn hot, asked for a long cold drink, and plopped down in the chair nearest him. The buzzer sounded. Capra did not jump up. He sat there and quietly sounded off, 'Oh, shit! That stupid son of a bitch Cohn and his goddamn chair.' Then he rose, picked up the chair, and smashed it to the floor, shattering it into an irreparable mess. The waiter brought him his drink. Capra sat down, took a long swig of iced tea, and said to me with his infectious smile, 'How's it going?' I answered, 'Fine.' We exchanged some more small talk about the weather and Harry Cohn." (Cohn had the chair rebuilt and kept using it until it gave director Victor Schertzinger a mild heart seizure.)

That kind of public outburst was rare from Capra. "Nine out of ten arguments they had were in Cohn's office," said Chet Sticht, who was Capra's secretary during his last five years at Columbia. "They got along pretty well together. Harry Cohn, like Sam Goldwyn, loved the movies, he was a good showman, and Capra probably liked him."

Years after Capra left Columbia, Cohn volunteered advice to screenwriter Virginia Van Upp on how best to deal with Capra: "Level with him."

But Capra, in contrast to Cohn's bluntness, tended to be diplomatic, subtle, devious. He recognized that "Cohn was everything everyone called him, but he was no fool." Capra deferred to Cohn as much as Cohn deferred to Capra. Though the director frequently chafed at his lack of independence, he achieved his unusual degree of creative freedom not so much through shouting and making threats as he did by being a clever politician.

However, one of the essential facts about his dealings with Columbia which Capra did not mention in his book was that he never had final cut on any of his pictures at the studio. Even after he made his greatest successes and acquired his strongest bargaining power, Columbia still retained the final authority to recut his work. Capra could argue—and often did—and Cohn always would listen. But when he and Cohn could not reach a compromise, Cohn had the last word. In the contract Capra was able to negotiate in 1935, after *It Happened One Night*—his final and most favorable agreement with the studio, and an extraordinarily liberal one for a studio to grant by the standards of that era—Columbia would only go so far as to agree that it would "consult" with Capra on stories, scripts, casting, and editing and that it would let Capra "supervise" the editing. He would work without any "supervisor" except for Cohn and the other general executive officers of Columbia. But in the event of any disagreement, the contract stated, "the decision of the Producer [Cohn] shall be final and conclusive and binding upon the Director."

Although his lack of ultimate control later became a matter of bitter dispute between Capra and Cohn, most of the time he was able to work in collaboration with the studio on the editing.

After he turned in his cut of *Lady for a Day* in 1933, a young worker in Columbia's New York office, Harry Foster, suggested that the film delayed too long before introducing its central character, the Broadway beggar Apple Annie. He urged the cutting of a pretentiously metaphoric opening scene showing a statue of a woman being discovered in a garbage heap. Better to plunge right in, he said, with the scene of Annie peddling her apples on the street.

"What the fuck do you know about making pictures?" Cohn bellowed at Foster over the phone from Hollywood. "You're full of shit!" Cohn hung up. He resented any creative suggestions from the New York office, which was headed by his hated brother, Jack. But an hour later he called Foster back and said, "You're going to California to talk to Frank Capra."

When he arrived in Hollywood, Foster went straight to the president's office, only to find that Cohn had changed his mind again.

"Hey, you little bastard," Cohn said, "what you doin' here?"

"I came out to talk to Capra," Foster replied.

"You think I'll make those changes, you're out of your fuckin' head!" Cohn barked.

At that point Capra entered Cohn's office. "You really think it would help?" the director asked Foster. They worked until three in the morning recutting the picture. Capra acknowledged to Foster that it was a major improvement.

But Capra wanted the readers of his book to believe that he never listened to anyone at Columbia, not even Harry Cohn, much less a lowly office boy. He obscured the truth by overplaying his stubbornness and defiance in his dealings with Cohn. Still, Capra was a realist, and a large part of him understood that as long as he had Cohn behind him, he had more power than he could find at any other studio. As nationally syndicated Hollywood columnist Sidney Skolsky wrote in 1934, "Frank Capra became a successful director because he didn't object to being a big frog in a small puddle."

The other part of Capra, the part that yearned for independence, also was afraid of it—afraid of taking complete responsibility, afraid of the possibility of failure. Harry Cohn's tyranny was like his mother's tyranny: galling to accept but also strangely comforting, for the enemy Capra knew was better than the enemy he did not know.

It was no accident that Capra made his best and most successful films for Cohn. He needed Cohn in order to function at his full powers. Not only was Cohn shrewd enough to handle Capra with just the right proportion of creative freedom and financial restraint—"Cohn rarely gave in on money matters," said Joe Walker, "but he always said no with a reason"—he also had an intuitive understanding of the psychological dynamic that enabled Capra's personality to function at its maximum effectiveness. Capra drew strength from Cohn's confidence in him and energy from his antagonism. Having Cohn as his boss meant that he had someone to help him make his decisions, someone to rebel against, someone to back him up, someone to share the blame with if things went wrong.

It meant he had a partner.

But despite Capra's admission that he had "a certain amount of love" for the man to whom he owed "my whole career," he refused to concede in later years that Cohn's feelings toward him had anything to do with his success at Columbia: "Freedom to make your picture has nothing to do with friendship. It was a fight."

Nor would he even admit that Cohn gave him freedom because Cohn was smart enough to recognize his ability. "That's not being smart," he insisted. "I *fought* for that."

"Basically it was not difficult to get Harry on your side," said Samuel Marx, Columbia's story editor in 1939–1940. "He wanted to be loved and he didn't know how—and he was embarrassed by it. He had soft spots. It wasn't hard to figure how to touch them. The people he respected the most were the people who fought him the most."

Capra's soft spots—his ambition, his need for creative autonomy, his desire for social acceptance, his hunger for money and fame—were compatible, though not identical, with Cohn's soft spots. Cohn's ambition was as strong, in its way, as Capra's, but it did not spring from a need for a public reputation. He was perfectly content to let Capra get all the publicity, as long as Capra acknowledged privately that Cohn was still in charge and as long as other people in the industry knew it. Cohn was driven more by a need for power—power for its own sake, not as a means to another end—than by a need for fame. While Capra's ambition was totally egocentric, Cohn's was inseparable from his ambition for the company he had helped found and which he now controlled. Cohn had no other goal in life than to make Columbia Pictures successful and respected, to elevate it from its Poverty Row beginnings to major-studio status.

Since Cohn kept control before and after the shooting, his power was not necessarily threatened when Capra demanded autonomy on the set. "Columbia was not an easy place at all for a director to work," Joe Walker said. "It was workable, but not easy. In the first place, they would insist that the director follow the script, and in the second place they would insist that he be on time. Some directors did O.K. because they followed the script and stayed on schedule, but the pictures were not good. Other directors became all wrought up about it. But not Capra. Capra was thoroughly in charge." "Capra was the king of the lot," said Sam Marx. "He dominated Cohn. He was the only director who could. He did it by the simple fact that he made the best pictures. Harry couldn't afford to let him go."

Cohn liked to show up on sets unannounced to bluster at the directors. It was his way of humiliating them in front of their coworkers. But after a few such incidents in the early years, he could not get away with that with Capra, who had a standing rule that Cohn was not permitted to watch him work. As Sticht recalled, "Capra threw him off the set one day—that probably was a first—but when Frank said, 'Get the hell out of here,' Cohn had sense enough to leave." If Cohn did show up, Capra would stop everything and refuse to work, sometimes telling his cast and crew to sing songs until the president of the studio left the stage.

"I was the toughest bastard you ever knew," Capra claimed. "I had to be. Even after it was proven that if they let me alone they would get a better picture. Because if you give in *that* much, you're lost, you've lost your position."

Cohn's humiliations of Capra were more private. They arose over Cohn's legendary tightness with budgets, his veto power of stories and casting, his reediting of Capra's finished work, his belief that Capra was becoming increasingly extravagant in his shooting methods in the late thirties, and over Capra's belief that Cohn was cheating him on his contract. Eventually Capra became so big that he felt he no longer had to operate under such constraints, not realizing that being an independent producer carried its own more subtle constraints.

Though Capra sometimes acknowledged how much he owed Cohn creatively, the one thing he would never admit was that he was well paid at Columbia, even though Cohn did not even balk at paying Capra more money, eventually, than he paid himself for running the studio. What Cohn resented, finally, was not the money he had to pay Capra but the challenge Capra represented to his power. It was only when Capra and Cohn became locked head to head in an irreconcilable power struggle that they could no longer work together.

In the bitterness of his old age, Capra came to see that power struggle in stereotypical ethnic terms: the Italian versus the Jew.

As his 1929 film *The Younger Generation* demonstrates, in his younger days Capra felt a kinship with the drive, ambition, and upward mobility of immigrant Jews like those who grew up near him in the partly Jewish Hollenbeck Heights and the Jewish enclave of Boyle Heights. His first wife was Jewish, and during the thirties he showed no hostility in his dealings with the immigrant Jews who dominated the executive ranks of the movie business nor in his dealings with his three best screenwriters, Swerling, Riskin, and Buchman, who were also Jewish. Capra and Riskin made light of their ethnic differences, according to journalist Geoffrey Hellman, who reported in 1940 that "to keep their relationship from being stereotyped, the two men frequently resorted to calling each other names which reflected on their racial origins and to playing practical jokes on each other."

But in his old age Capra rationalized his problems with Cohn—and the collapse of his career after he left Columbia—by spewing out ethnic names in anger. Falsely claiming he had "made nothing" from Cohn and Columbia, when in fact he was among the most highly paid directors in Hollywood, Capra said in 1985: "I've had a lot of Jewish guys as friends, but no matter how friendly they are, when it comes to money, a Jewish man will never screw another Jewish man. So I've had the fun of making pictures, but I haven't made any money. You have to be Jewish, or you're not going to get a goddamn thing."

And he saw his battle for creative control in stereotypical ethnic terms: "This the Jewish producers will never understand. I say 'Jewish' producers because that's all there were. The Jews should be smarter than they are. See, the Jews are not giving this [creative control], because they want to be the ones that make the picture." In his old age, he viewed the entertainment industry as one big Jewish cabal. While discussing a powerful Hollywood figure in 1984, Capra declared, "All Jews are smart. All Jews are crooks." And while discussing the careers of his sons Frank, Jr., a movie producer, and Tom, a television producer, Capra said that to be more successful, "They need more Jewish." He said to Joe Finochio of Frank, Jr., "He's gotta change his name, number one. Then he's gotta get circumcised."

In the early thirties, when Capra and Columbia still were consolidating their reputations, Capra's differences with Cohn were minimized and their goals were meshed into one single, overriding, shared obsession: to win an Academy Award.

For Cohn, a best-picture Oscar would be the symbol of Columbia's recognition as a major studio. But for Capra, the Oscar would put him "on the front page all over the world."

It was not true, however, that it was his disappointment over not receiving an Oscar nomination for *American Madness* that made him turn from contemporary Americana to a more exotic subject in the hope of winning an Oscar, as he later liked to claim (Harry Cohn supposedly having told him, "They'll never vote for that comedy crap you make. They only vote for that arty crap"). There must have been another reason, because *American Madness* had not even been released when Capra, in June of 1932, decided to make *The Bitter Tea of General Yen*.

Bitter Tea originally was to have been directed by the Dublin-born Herbert Brenon, whose distinguished silent films included *Peter Pan* with Betty Bronson and *Beau Geste* with William Powell and Ronald Colman. Brenon's career had been faltering in talkies before he was borrowed from

RKO by producer Walter Wanger to direct Columbia's film version of a popular 1930 romantic novel by Grace Zaring Stone about the love affair between an American missionary and a Chinese warlord during China's civil war.

But on June 15 it was announced that Brenon had been replaced by Capra, who later recalled how he had lobbied with Wanger for the job. *Variety* reported a "mutual dislike" between Brenon and Columbia, caused by squabbling over money and his "ditching" of story conferences. Brenon left for England soon after his firing, and he never had the chance to make another important picture.

There is no reason to doubt Capra's claim that he was desperate for an Oscar nor that he could have seen *Bitter Tea* as his means to that end. It was daring material for Hollywood at that time, and it was even more outré coming from Capra, who was known for his contemporary American comedies and dramas and his male adventure sagas. If he wanted people to sit up and pay attention to him, what better means than a story that gave a director ample opportunity for Sternbergian visual flourishes, of the kind he usually scorned, and a story that also was sure to lift eyebrows because of its controversial subject matter? But, as usually was the case when Capra went out of his way to parade his candor, all his talk about Oscars helped to conceal (whether consciously or not in this case) another, even more compelling, motive for making a film about a forbidden, unrequited interracial love affair.

Though Constance Cummings, who had appeared in *American Madness*, originally was set to play the lead female role of the missionary Megan Davis, Capra gave the part instead to Barbara Stanwyck. *Bitter Tea* was the first film he had made with Stanwyck since she had rejected him and he married Lu on the rebound. For both actress and director, the story must have had deep emotional resonance.

Stanwyck's character is simultaneously repelled by and attracted to the Chinese general, whose pride demands that she come to his bed willingly or not at all. When he realizes at the end that she can never fully overcome her instinctive sexual revulsion toward him, he arranges for her safety and then takes poison.

In the novel, the "bitter tea" of the title is only metaphoric: the general is stabbed to death by his enemies while helping Megan escape. The screenplay, written for Wanger and Brenon by Edward Paramore, kept that ending but added an earlier scene of the doomed general preparing a cup of poisoned tea, then throwing it away when Megan surrenders herself to him. But when Capra took over the project, he changed the ending so that the general has no false hope of winning Megan, and he had the general commit suicide rather than live with the ultimate humiliation of sexual rejection by the woman he loves.

Through his direction of Stanwyck and Walker's luminously erotic photography, Capra also intensified at every point the sexual longing Megan feels for General Yen, and he mocked her feelings of revulsion in the remarkable sequence of Megan's erotic nightmare, which has no equivalent in the novel. In the script, Megan is seduced by a handsome masked stranger who she realizes too late is General Yen. Capra added the expressionistic details of Yen's grotesquely exaggerated teeth and fingernails, which turn him into a rapacious monster. As Stanwyck explained her approach to her character, "Any revulsion would be within herself, at least that's how I felt—'How could I be attracted? How *could* I?' " Capra's addition of the monstrous details demonstrates the absurdity of her racist fears at the same time that he gives them visual expression.

The film's complex viewpoint toward racism—a complexity unique in Capra's otherwise racially insensitive body of work—is also a reflection of Capra's ambivalence toward his own sexuality. It is given full expression here, for once, by his overwhelming need to deal with his repressed feelings toward the now definitely unattainable Stanwyck, and to exorcise those feelings by killing off the part of himself (represented by General Yen) that wanted her. What makes *Bitter Tea* such a rich and subtle film is the way that Capra manages to identify equally with the yearning, fatalistic general and with the ambivalent Megan. Although the pessimism of Capra's ending and his depiction of China as a land of nightmarish barbarism certainly reflect a conservative, if not bigoted, viewpoint, Capra also was able, this one time, to reach beyond his usual racial prejudices by dealing with them forthrightly and critically through Megan. Apparently what enabled him to do so was his recognition that in his affair with Stanwyck, he had played a role similar to that of the doomed General Yen.

Capra's sense of empathy with the man of another race was aided, no doubt, by the fact that the general was a cultured, exotic Chinese, ruthless toward his enemies but also a non-Communist representative of a people esteemed by many Americans of that era. Capra could find no real Chinese he considered suitable for the part, casting instead the tall and elegant Swedish actor Nils Asther. Despite his moments of casual savagery, which seem to lend credence to Megan's moments of revulsion, and despite his protective façade of cynicism ("Life at its best is hardly endurable"), Capra's General Yen is overwhelmingly a romantic, a sensitive and poetic dreamer, a lover of the most exquisite refinement—or, as Stanwyck herself put it, "a marshmallow."

No stronger proof of Capra's emotional identification with General Yen exists than the fact that, despite the film's failure at the box office and its failure to win even an Academy Award nomination (his supposed motive for making it), Capra's enthusiasm for the film was undiminished. In the late thirties he described it to Edward Bernds as his favorite of all his films: "I know it didn't make money, but it has more real *movie* in it than any other I did."

Bitter Tea was the first film ever to play at New York's Radio City Music Hall, the world's largest movie theater. The Music Hall had opened on December 27, 1932, exclusively as a vaudeville house, but the timing was disastrous. It was the nadir of the Depression, and few people could afford to buy tickets at $2.50 a head for the expensively produced live show. To cut costs, the Music Hall hastily went to a policy of alternating a movie with a scaled-down live program, at a top ticket price of seventy-five cents.

Perhaps anticipating just such an opportunity, Columbia had postponed *Bitter Tea*'s nationwide release date, originally set for December 20. The Music Hall, with all of its attendant prestige and publicity, seemed the perfect showcase for the most ambitious and expensive film Columbia had yet made—*Bitter Tea* reportedly cost about $1 million and, as *Variety* noted, was intended to be "the nucleus around which the whole Columbia program this year [1933] will be sold." But Columbia also may have feared that *General Yen* would be a box-office failure and hoped that a Music Hall premiere would buoy its chances.

So on January 11, 1933, *Bitter Tea* opened simultaneously at the Music Hall and in other major cities throughout the country. Scheduled for at least a two-week run in the New York showcase, it was pulled after only eight days. The program had grossed only $80,000, which meant that even with its reduced operating budget, the Music Hall still lost $20,000.

Bitter Tea had no better luck elsewhere. Modern audiences find it much easier to accept the film and its interrracial theme, but the contemporary reception was indicated by the *Variety* reviewer Sam Shain, who called it "a queer story. . . . Seeing a Chinaman attempting to romance with a pretty and supposedly decent young American white woman is bound to evoke adverse reaction."

Like Capra, Stanwyck had no doubt that the racist backlash to the film caused its commercial failure: "The women's clubs came out very strongly against it, because the white woman was in love with the yellow man and kissed his hand. So *what!* I was so shocked [by the reaction]. It never occurred to me, and I don't think it occurred to Mr. Capra when we were doing it. I accepted it, believed in it, loved it."

But Capra, who did not mention in his book that the film played only eight days at the Music Hall, claimed the film failed because it was "banned" in Great Britain and the British Commonwealth.

Bitter Tea in fact was not banned, but was passed by the British Board of Censors after a few cuts were made, and also was approved by the Commonwealth Film Censorship Board. Some measure of the negative reaction it encountered overseas, however, can be gathered from the attack on the film in an Australian scandal sheet called *Truth*, which Columbia passed along to Capra: "A loathsome Chinese bandit pawing and mauling a white woman in White Australia. The mere thought is revolting. Yet this degrading spectacle was witnessed in a leading Sydney theatre this week. . . . The fact that he does not achieve the whole of his intention is immaterial beside the point that a seemingly well-nurtured American girl is willing to become his darling. . . . Yet, detestable as the story is, weird and gross as it is in its sentimental flummery, it has been passed by the Commonwealth Film Censorship Board without the slightest misgiving, apparently."

Controversy, as Capra was fast learning, was part of the price of "prestige."

Shortly after finishing *Bitter Tea*, he was loaned to MGM to make *Soviet*. The project, about an American engineer and a Russian commissar joining hands to build a dam in the U.S.S.R., had already defeated several writers and one director (George Hill, best known for the 1930 prison movie *The Big House*) before the deal for Capra was made on October 18, 1932. Jules Furthman was assigned to write a fresh script for Capra.

Capra was hungry for another shot at Hollywood's leading studio. With his increased stature in the industry, he expected to have more control over the new project, budgeted at $750,000, than he had been able to exert over the modest *Brotherly Love* before his firing in 1928. In exchange for the loan of Capra, MGM agreed to pay Cohn $50,000 and send Robert Montgomery to Columbia to star in Robert Riskin's adaptation of a Damon Runyon story, "Madame La Gimp," which Capra was scheduled to direct after *Soviet*. Capra also hoped that Mayer could be persuaded to loan him Marie Dressler for the title role in his Columbia film. One of Metro's most jealously hoarded properties, Dressler was among the stars Capra was promised for *Soviet*.

Soviet was a pet project of MGM's youthful production chief Irving Thalberg. "I was always a little surprised that Irving was making it," admitted Sam Marx, the author of *Mayer and Thalberg: The Make-Believe Saints* and the head of MGM's story department at the time Capra worked on *Soviet*. "Mayer and Thalberg were outright capitalists. But Irving had been interested in the socialist movement when he was a boy. And he wanted to do a movie about the people of the Soviet Union. *Soviet* was a story of the hardships of the common man in Russia, a story of the survival of the fittest. We didn't know that much about the Soviet revolution, and we didn't have the enmity for the Soviet Union that we had later. Frank Capra was always interested in the human side of world events, so he was a natural selection to make *Soviet*."

Capra spent four months working on *Soviet* before the project fell apart. MGM's worries over its political content regularly found their way into the press. There was a sign of trouble less than six weeks after Capra's hiring, when *Variety* reported that the film's start date was "indefinite owing to story difficulties." An early March start was later set, but on February 21 the trade paper said that MGM was becoming worried because "the story still needs considerable cleansing of Soviet propaganda and will possibly have another rewrite before camerawork starts." Within a week, MGM postponed the project, announcing that the "propaganda angle in [the] story is too strong." The *Los Angeles Times* added that the story was too "depressing" and the production "hugely expensive."

"Capra says the best thing he ever worked on was *Soviet*," Alva Johnston wrote in his 1938 *Saturday Evening Post* profile of the director. ". . . He was getting ready to shoot it for Metro-Goldwyn-Mayer when the company decided it was full of controversial dynamite and put it on the shelf."

Though Capra, like Thalberg, had a romantic infatuation with the spirit of the Russian peasantry, Capra later took pains to sidestep any implication that *Soviet* amounted to Communist propaganda. As Capra described the story, it was to have been a dialectic between the values of American free enterprise and Russian collectivism, with old-fashioned American know-how emerging victorious: "It was a tremendous melodrama, and I had the dream cast of all time," he told Richard Glatzer in 1973. ". . . Wally Beery was going to play the role of a commissar who was given the job of building this great dam. He didn't know anything about engineering, but was a man in charge who had made his way up from the bottom of the Bolshevik regime. Marie Dressler was his wife, and a very patient, loving wife she was. Joan Crawford was to play a very, very politically minded gal who was the assistant commissar. Clark Gable was an American engineer, sent over to help them build this dam.

"The conflicts were personal and ideological: the American wants to get things done and the commissar wants to get them done in his own way. Gable falls in love with Joan Crawford, and they have a running battle: she hates anything American and anything that is not communistic, and he hates anything that is communistic—all this plus the drama of building this dam."

According to Sam Marx, political insecurities may well have contributed to MGM's decision to scuttle *Soviet*, but the overriding reason was that the film became a pawn in the rivalry between Thalberg and Louis B. Mayer. The studio boss had long nurtured a hatred of his younger second-in-command, a former protégé whose immense reputation was now threatening his power. On Christmas Day, 1932, while *Soviet* was in preproduction, the frail, overworked Thalberg suffered his second heart attack, and his doctors ordered several months' convalescence. Taking advantage of his absence, Mayer brought his son-in-law David O. Selznick into MGM as an unofficial replacement for Thalberg, relieved Thalberg of his title "in charge of production," demoted him to the status of independent producer, and canceled most of Thalberg's personal projects. Among them was *Soviet*, which the deeply conservative Mayer found politically dangerous.*

Capra took it hard. In his book he tried to minimize his hurt over his second failure to succeed at the top studio in Hollywood by claiming that he had not wanted Cohn to loan him to that impersonal factory.

And while discussing the *Soviet* experience in 1984, he started to say, "I got scared . . . ," but his mood quickly shifted to belligerence: "I got kicked out before I got started. Oh, they don't want *this* guy around—'He knows it all.' *They* didn't know a goddamned thing. They were so stupid and so dumb. It was run by Jewish people at the top. It was right because *they said* it was right."

On Friday, March 3, 1933, the day before President Roosevelt's inauguration, the Depression reached its crisis point, with panicked investors making runs on banks throughout the country. The film industry was near collapse as empty theaters and diminished production, coupled with the drying up of Wall Street investment capital, caused a cash crisis that threatened to shut down Hollywood. (Capra had managed to keep personally insulated from the crisis, since he had been working at the only two studios that remained relatively healthy, Columbia and MGM.)

"The only thing we have to fear is fear itself," Roosevelt declared in his

---

* *Capra also failed to persuade MGM to let him direct its planned film version of Franz Werfel's 1933 novel* The Forty Days of Musa Dagh, *based on the forty-day resistance of seven Armenian villages under siege by the Turks. Thalberg was eager to make the film, but Mayer balked for fear of antagonizing the Turkish government.*

inaugural address that dark Saturday, and he moved swiftly to meet the crisis with a series of emergency declarations, the most important of which was his proclamation on March 5 of a four-day national Bank Holiday to halt the panic while crucial reforms were begun in the banking system. His New Deal also promised temporary relief for the unemployed and vowed to "put the country back to work" with government job programs and mandatory, government-supervised agreements between management and labor on fair employment practices.

The Hollywood studios reacted to the Bank Holiday in a manner not in keeping with the spirit of the New Deal. The Association of Motion Picture Producers (AMPP) proposed an industrywide pay cut, without which, it said, "the studios no longer can exist." Blanket pay cuts had been proposed before: in 1927 and 1931, the producers had asked the Academy of Motion Picture Arts and Sciences to approve 10-percent cuts, but the Academy had balked because the studio chiefs would not promise to cut their own huge salaries accordingly, and the studios pulled back, using the tool of massive layoffs when they felt it necessary to reduce overhead. But now that the film industry was feeling the full brunt of the Depression, the producers "privately reached an understanding to ignore the [labor] pact" they had made with the Academy, *Daily Variety* had reported on February 24.

"Everybody got scared," Capra recalled, "and the Academy was the only institution that could touch all the bases. The Academy board thought of an idea. We said, 'O.K., we'll come back on half salary.' Everybody agreed to cut it in half."

The "immediate and radical steps" announced by Capra and his fellow board members after their emergency meeting on March 7 with the AMPP in the Academy's offices at the Hollywood Roosevelt amounted to a cut of 50 percent for any studio employee earning more than $50 a week and 25 percent for those earning less than that amount. Blaming it on the freezing of company assets by the Bank Holiday and on falling theater receipts, the Academy said the cut was only temporary, but many feared it would become permanent.

Despite what Capra thought, Jack L. Warner later admitted that the pay cut had only been "arranged" by the Academy after having been decided at an earlier meeting by the studio heads. The qualms the Academy had once had about the studio chiefs' salaries had been allayed when the producers falsely led the industry to believe that the cuts would apply to everyone in the film business, even to the top brass. "We finally realized how the producers were using the Academy and us," said director King

Vidor, who later spearheaded the founding of the Screen Directors Guild. "What a lot of people didn't know was the fact that many producers and executives were subtracting the cuts from their employees' checks but not from their own."

"The events of March 1933 finally shattered the Academy's moral and professional stature in the eyes of Hollywood artists," Larry Ceplair and Steven Englund wrote in *The Inquisition in Hollywood: Politics in the Film Community, 1930–1960*. The furor that resulted from the pay cut was the spark that ignited the smoldering labor movement in Hollywood, leading to the formation of the guilds and gradually stripping the Academy of its role as the "company union."

The pay cut almost collapsed on March 12 when IATSE, which represented most Hollywood laborers and also controlled theater projectionists, refused to accept it. The following day, for the first time in the history of Hollywood, every studio had to stop production. The Academy board hastily reached an unsatisfactory compromise: the 50-percent cut would apply to those nonunion employees earning more that $100 a week, those making between $50 and $100 would have their salaries cut by 25 percent, and those making below $50 would not receive a cut. IATSE agreed to let its members return to work, but they would not accept pay cuts.

Production resumed on March 14 and 15 in an atmosphere of anger and distrust. After mid-April, with the national crisis somewhat abated by Roosevelt's reforms, full salaries were restored at most of the studios, but only the independent producer Samuel Goldwyn retroactively paid his employees the wages they had lost. Warners' production chief Darryl F. Zanuck had made similar assurances to his employees, but when the studio refused to comply and kept the pay cut in force for another week, Zanuck resigned in protest.

"He was quite a hero," Capra thought, "because he was the only one who had guts enough to say 'Fuck you.' The Academy had no punch, no power. It took Zanuck to do it from outside. The Academy lost face, because it was never meant to be involved in these problems. But since the Academy had taken leadership of this thing, everybody began yelling at the Academy. People said the Academy was not strong enough to handle [the pay cut issue], let's handle it by ourselves.

"Now come the guilds. I stayed with the Academy. I had nothing to gain from it. But I said, 'We can't let this wonderful thing, the Academy prize, die from lack of interest. Let's keep it alive until we know what to do.' I kept saying, 'No, killing the Academy is not the way.' "

What had begun as a lust for an Oscar and a desire to advance his own career by becoming a Hollywood insider had led Capra into an unexpectedly difficult position. Capra rationalized his involvement with the Academy by telling himself that he had tried to help arbitrate an equitable arrangement that would keep the industry prosperous. But his acquiescence in the pay cut hurt his reputation in Hollywood, and for remaining involved with the Academy, he ruefully remembered, "I was called more names—'scab' and all that shit. The petty guys!" Even he had to admit that what he was doing amounted to "stooging for producers."

Rather than quit the Academy, as hundreds of others did in the months that followed, Capra stubbornly clung to it as his personal power base, accepting the trade-off of being scorned by most of his colleagues for the rewards of being on a first-name basis with the small group of power brokers who ran the industry. While the guilds were being formed, Capra saw his chance to begin moving up in the hierarchy of the disarrayed Academy. In October 1933 he made an unsuccessful try for the presidency and was nominated for vice president and second vice president but settled for secretary. He was nominated for president again in October 1934 but lost to fellow director Frank Lloyd. When Lloyd was nominated again on October 9, 1935, he declined and nominated Capra instead. Cecil B. DeMille moved that the vote be made by acclamation, and Capra was elected Academy president.

The drive to replace the Academy as bargaining agent for talent was led by 173 writers who formed the Screen Writers Guild (SWG) on April 6, 1933, and the organizing of Hollywood labor gathered force with the signing into law on June 16 of the National Industrial Recovery Act (NIRA), which guaranteed collective bargaining by representatives chosen by employees and provided for the drawing up of codes of fair practice for each industry under the National Recovery Administration (NRA).

But the battle was only beginning: the producers refused to recognize the SWG and the Screen Actors Guild (SAG), which was organized on June 30, and they heavily influenced the drafting of the NRA Motion Picture Industry Code, causing dissent even within the Academy over proposed salary-limiting provisions. Public objections were raised in August by the Academy Code Committee, of which Capra was a member, at a meeting of more than four hundred Academy members. After the code was enacted, Eddie Cantor, the newly elected SAG president, persuaded President Roosevelt to suspend the controversial provisions by executive order.

But talks to resolve the issues broke down, primarily over the issue of recognition for the SWG and SAG. The Hollywood guilds were dealt an-

other setback when the U.S. Supreme Court declared the NIRA unconstitutional in May 1935, but the passage that July of the National Labor
Relations Act (commonly known as the Wagner Act) and its upholding
in April 1937 by the Supreme Court made recognition inevitable. Still,
SAG did not win recognition until it threatened to strike in 1937, and it
took until 1938 for the SWG to be recognized, after the divisive attempt
by the producers to encourage the formation of the rival Screen Playwrights.

The Screen Directors Guild, the last of the three major guilds to be
organized, was not incorporated until January 1936, but its original impetus also stemmed from the 1933 pay cut. Recalling the meeting at the
Hollywood Roosevelt in which the pay cut was approved "in the name of
the Academy," King Vidor said, "The feeling was very strong there that
anyone who got up and objected to taking this cut was fired, that maybe
he'd find himself without a job, any individual. A few fellows had courage
enough to do it, to get up and talk. You could see the anger growing that
these men were objecting to what they wanted to do. The realization was
very strong that we must have an organization to speak for us, and not the
individual alone. After the meeting was over, about six or eight directors
stood on the sidewalk on the street by the Hotel Roosevelt, and it was
bluntly stated, 'We must have a guild.' "

Though Capra claimed, "I was with them from the very start," he was
not among the group on the sidewalk that day, nor was Capra, the newly
elected Academy president, one of the twelve directors who met in Vidor's
home on December 23, 1935, to found the SDG, with Vidor as its first
president.*

"I wouldn't put the Academy above the Directors Guild," Capra later
insisted, "because that wouldn't be kosher."

But he did so for more than a year and a half.

Harry Cohn was anxious to get Capra back to work. With *Soviet* postponed
at MGM, Columbia set a start date on *Madame La Gimp* for early May of
1933. But as it drew near, Capra took to his bed, worn out and demoralized
by the Academy negotiations over the salary cut and by the double blow of
the failures of *Bitter Tea* and *Soviet*. Now he began to worry about the new
picture, too.

Late one night he sat up in bed and picked up his telephone. "Harry,"
he said, "I've got a problem."

*The other eleven were Frank Borzage, Lloyd Corrigan, John Ford, William K. Howard, Gregory
La Cava, Rowland V. Lee, Lewis Milestone, A. Edward Sutherland, Frank Tuttle, Richard
Wallace, and William Wellman.*

Ellis Island, the immigrant's gateway to America, was "a lot of noise and a lot of chairs and we sat on the chairs and waited for two days," Frank Capra remembered. He and his family entered the waiting room on May 24, 1903, the morning after their arrival in New York Harbor in steerage from Sicily on the SS *Germania*. This is Capra's memory image of Ellis Island, a frame enlargement from the first feature he directed, *The Strong Man* (1926). (*Kevin Brownlow Collection / First National Pictures*)

Capra's parents, the stalwart Rosaria Nicolosi Capra, known as Saridda, and the charming ne'er-do-well Salvatore Capra, known as Papa Turiddu. They posed for this portrait not long after coming to Los Angeles in 1903, when she was forty-three and he was fifty-one. (*Joe Finochio*)

Capra's neighborhood of East Los Angeles, Lincoln Heights, around 1910, when he was living there as a boy. Not the "ghetto" that he remembered it being, it was a working-class neighborhood with modest but well-kept homes and mostly paved streets. (*Security Pacific National Bank Photograph Collection / Los Angeles Public Library*)

One of the street corners on which Capra sold papers as a boy—Broadway and Fifth Street in downtown Los Angeles in the early 1900s. (*Security Pacific National Bank Photograph Collection / Los Angeles Public Library*)

Young Frank Capra (FRONT ROW, FAR LEFT) on Manual Arts' Pyramid Team shortly after entering high school in 1911. (*Manual Arts High School*)

Rob Wagner, seen here in 1914 while a faculty member of Manual Arts, was Capra's first artistic mentor. He opened Capra's eyes to the potential of the infant film medium. (*Manual Arts High School*)

Before he settled on the movies, Capra considered a career as a U.S. Army officer. Though he enlisted in April 1917 while a student at Throop College of Technology in Pasadena, he was sent back for ROTC training at Throop, where he is shown in early 1918 (FRONT ROW, FAR LEFT) wearing his regular Army uniform. (*The Archives, California Institute of Technology*)

Capra as a September 1918 college graduate. He set out to be a chemical engineer, but it was at Throop that his latent interest in the arts and humanities was inflamed into a passion. (*Isabelle Daniels Griffis*)

Capra's first love, Isabelle Daniels (SECOND FROM LEFT), with Capra (FAR RIGHT) on a jaunt in Santa Monica when he was working on the *Screen Snapshots* series in 1920. (*Isabelle Daniels Griffis*)

WALTER MONTAGUE Playwright and Producer

Walter Montague, the British-born San Francisco actor and playwright who hired Capra to direct the short film *Fulta Fisher's Boarding House* in 1921. (*San Francisco Chronicle / California State Library*)

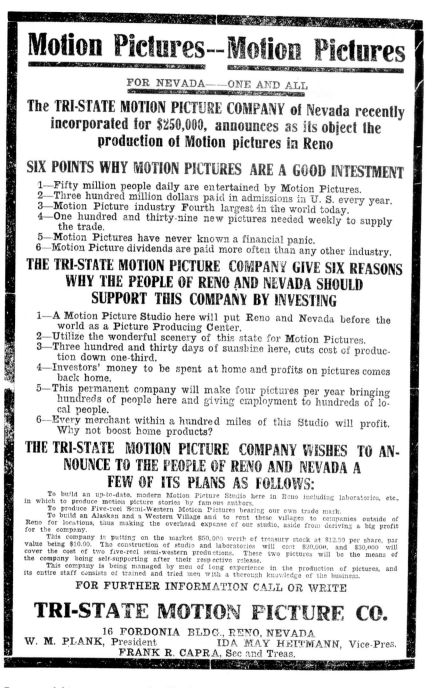

Motion Pictures--Motion Pictures

FOR NEVADA——ONE AND ALL

The TRI-STATE MOTION PICTURE COMPANY of Nevada recently incorporated for $250,000, announces as its object the production of Motion pictures in Reno

SIX POINTS WHY MOTION PICTURES ARE A GOOD INTESTMENT

1—Fifty million people daily are entertained by Motion Pictures.
2—Three hundred million dollars paid in admissions in U. S. every year.
3—Motion Picture industry Fourth largest in the world today.
4—One hundred and thirty-nine new pictures needed weekly to supply the trade.
5—Motion Pictures have never known a financial panic.
6—Motion Picture dividends are paid more often than any other industry.

THE TRI-STATE MOTION PICTURE COMPANY GIVE SIX REASONS WHY THE PEOPLE OF RENO AND NEVADA SHOULD SUPPORT THIS COMPANY BY INVESTING

1—A Motion Picture Studio here will put Reno and Nevada before the world as a Picture Producing Center.
2—Utilize the wonderful scenery of this state for Motion Pictures.
3—Three hundred and thirty days of sunshine here, cuts cost of production down one-third.
4—Investors' money to be spent at home and profits on pictures comes back home.
5—This permanent company will make four pictures per year bringing hundreds of people here and giving employment to hundreds of local people.
6—Every merchant within a hundred miles of this Studio will profit. Why not boost home products?

THE TRI-STATE MOTION PICTURE COMPANY WISHES TO ANNOUNCE TO THE PEOPLE OF RENO AND NEVADA A FEW OF ITS PLANS AS FOLLOWS:

To build an up-to-date, modern Motion Picture Studio here in Reno including laboratories, etc., in which to produce motion picture stories by famous authors.

To produce Five-reel Semi-Western Motion Pictures bearing our own trade mark.

To build an Alaskan and a Western Village and to rent these villages to companies outside of Reno for locations, thus making the overhead expense of our studio, aside from deriving a big profit for the company.

This company is putting on the market $50,000 worth of treasury stock at $12.50 per share, par value being $10.00. The construction of studio and laboratories will cost $20,000, and $30,000 will cover the cost of two five-reel semi-western productions. These two pictures will be the means of the company being self-supporting after their respective release.

This company is being managed by men of long experience in the production of pictures, and its entire staff consists of trained and tried men with a thorough knowledge of the business.

FOR FURTHER INFORMATION CALL OR WRITE

TRI-STATE MOTION PICTURE CO.

16 FORDONIA BLDG., RENO, NEVADA
W. M. PLANK, President   IDA MAY HEITMANN, Vice-Pres.
FRANK R. CAPRA, Sec and Treas.

Capra and his partners in the Tri-State Motion Picture Company placed this grandiose advertisement in the *Reno Evening Gazette* and the *Nevada State Journal* three times between October 7 and 13, 1919. (*Nevada Historical Society / Nevada State Journal*)

Helen Howell, whom Capra later married, was the ingenue in *Pop Tuttle's Lost Nerve* (1922), one of the two-reel Plum Center Comedies on which Capra worked. She is seen here with Oliver J. Eckhardt (LEFT) and series star Dan Mason. (*The Museum of Modern Art / Film Stills Archive*)

The *San Francisco Chronicle* gave prominent play to the November 29, 1923, wedding of Helen Howell and Frank Capra, calling it "a romance of the movie studio." (*San Francisco Chronicle / California State Library*)

Film Actress, Director Wed

Helene Howell and Frank Russell Capra, members of Gerson Productions, who were married Thanksgiving day.

"King of Comedy" Mack Sennett, who taught his "dark, determined" gag man much he needed to know about visual humor, but declared, "This fellow will never make a director." (*Mack Sennett Studios*)

Capra demonstrated an intense emotional affinity with cockeyed Sennett star Ben Turpin and his grotesque screen relationships with the opposite sex. In the burlesque melodrama *The Marriage Circus* (1924), which Capra wrote with Vernon Smith, Louise Carver played Turpin's domineering mother. (*The Academy of Motion Picture Arts and Sciences / Mack Sennett Studios*)

Child-man Harry Langdon, whose film career blossomed after Capra began writing for him at Sennett's, played gullible Belgian immigrant Paul Bergot in Capra's highly successful feature directing debut, *The Strong Man* (1926). (*First National Pictures*)

Capra went to work for Columbia in 1927, near the end of the silent movie period. Standing directly behind him at one of the hand-cranked cameras is cinematographer Joseph Walker, who worked on twenty of Capra's films. (*Columbia Pictures*)

That Certain Thing (1928), a romantic comedy with Ralph Graves and Viola Dana, was Capra's first film for Columbia. (*Columbia Pictures*)

10. "The catastrophe of Success"

*I*t was just a few days before the start of shooting on *Madame La Gimp*.

"Harry," Capra told Cohn when they met at the studio, "I want you to face the fact that you're spending three hundred thousand dollars on a picture in which the heroine is seventy years old."

Cohn rose from his desk and stared out his window onto Gower Street. Then he turned back to Capra: "All I know is the thing's got a wallop. Go ahead."

Thus was made *Lady for a Day*, the first film for which Capra received an Academy Award nomination for best director. Also the first Columbia film to receive a best-picture nomination, it was a stunning artistic and financial success that sealed the thirty-six-year-old Capra's status as one of Hollywood's master directors. And yet he almost had not made the film. His doubts contrasted starkly with the enthusiasm Cohn and Riskin always had for the project.

Capra's autobiography contains a revealing "error" regarding the chronology of events leading to *Lady for a Day*. He seemed to think that his four-month stay at MGM working on *Soviet* came after the making of *Lady for a Day*, not before it. Such a significant misplacing of time is hard to accept as a simple memory lapse, and indeed other evidence suggests it may have been a deliberate attempt to obscure the extent of Riskin's contribution to *Lady for a Day*.

Capra discussed the genesis of *Lady for a Day* in a September 1934 interview with Eileen Creelman of the *New York Sun:* "I'd read the Runyon story for years before we made it. I'd never thought of it as a picture. I used to tell it all the time, to anyone who would listen, just as an amusing story. Then someone at the studio started to tell it to me. I stopped him and said I knew it. I can't remember who the fellow was, but it was he who suggested filming it. Then I began thinking about it as a picture. The more I thought, the better I liked it."

Harry Cohn's memory, in an interview the previous March with the *New York Telegraph*, was more precise: "We believe here that writers are more important than either star or director," the studio chief said, "because the story is the whole foundation of the film. A weak story with the greatest cast ever assembled cannot produce a great picture. Look at *Lady for a Day.* . . . More credit is due to Riskin for that picture than to Damon Runyon, who wrote it as a magazine story. Another studio [Fox], which has first call on the stories in that magazine [*Cosmopolitan*], passed it up. But Riskin saw something in it—the basic story idea—and liked it. He showed it to Frank Capra, who also liked it, and they went to work."

Riskin, despite his own Oscar nomination for *Lady for a Day*, made no public claim to being the prime mover. At first he may have accepted Capra's egotism as part of the Hollywood system that enabled directors to hog the glory they should have shared with screenwriters. But his resentment grew, and in time it would break up their highly successful collaboration.

Runyon, like Cohn, recognized where the central credit lay for the film. He wired profuse appreciation to Riskin for his manifold improvements in the story, and after reading press commentaries describing himself as the "author" of *Lady for a Day*, Runyon went on public record in a February 1935 interview: "I wish you would quote me that *Lady for a Day* was no more my picture than *Little Miss Marker*, which, like the former picture, was almost entirely the result of the genius of the scenario writers [*sic*] and the director who worked on it. . . . How the hell, then, could I be called the author of the picture? . . . I hope I have too keen a sense of literary ethics to assume the role of 'fly catcher' or the applause from something that was not mine."

Capra's sense of ethics was more flexible. His reluctance to share credit for *Lady for a Day* with Riskin by name in the Creelman interview ("I can't remember who the fellow was") was the first public sign of a carefully cultivated amnesia which eventually would lead to a major controversy over the degree of credit Riskin deserved for the success of "Capra's" films.

It was a battle that went beyond simple questions of fairness into complex philosophical issues about the "authorship" of a film, issues that would be lumped together into an acrimonious debate over the *auteur* theory. The debate began in 1954 with the proposal in the French film magazine *Cahiers du Cinéma* by critic (and later director) François Truffaut of "*un cinéma des auteurs*," which included among its tenets the primary role of the director in determining the thematic content of a film.

Truffaut designed *Cahiers'* "*politique des auteurs*" partially to account for a situation like that of *Lady for a Day*, in which the director is not the screenwriter but still exerts his personality over the material. However, in the translation of the *politique* to American criticism, and even more so in its bastardization by its Hollywood detractors, the distinction between writer-director *auteurs* and nonwriter *auteur* directors largely became lost, and the debate degenerated into hopeless and irresolvable battles between the defenders of the director and the defenders of the writer. Little would be said in those battles, except polemically, about the collaborative nature of film, which makes it possible to claim joint (or, indeed, multiple) authorship for a film, which still making it possible to maintain distinctions about individual contributions.

Thus, to say that Capra never could (or would) have made *Lady for a Day* without Riskin—and that, as Runyon himself insisted, the screen story was more Riskin's than Runyon's—is not to say that *Lady for a Day* cannot be considered "a Frank Capra film" or that the characters and situations do not bear the unmistakable mark of being what was later dubbed "Capraesque." But the distinction not often made by Capra's admirers, and conveniently overlooked by Capra himself, is that *Lady for a Day*, and the other films written for him by Riskin, could just as well be called "Riskinesque."

A probably apocryphal story has Riskin, angered in the late thirties by all the talk about "The Capra Touch," marching into Capra's office, dropping 120 pages of blank paper on the director's desk, and demanding, "Here! Give that 'The Capra Touch'!" According to Riskin's friend and fellow screenwriter Philip Dunne, the story was spread by Riskin's brother Everett but was denied by Robert Riskin himself. Capra insisted that "Bob was too much of a gentleman to come up with that corny scene."

"It was pretty evident just by the nature of the work that a lot of the polish in the Capra pictures was put there by Riskin," said Thomas M. Pryor, a friend of both men, who covered Hollywood for *The New York Times* and later was editor of *Daily Variety*. "After Capra stopped working with Riskin, some of the sparks seemed to disappear. But there's no question that Capra's pictures apart from Riskin were better than Riskin's pictures apart from Capra. Riskin was more brittle than Capra but Capra gave it the heart, wrapped the flesh around it."

"Frank provided the schmaltz and Bob provided the acid," said Dunne. "It was an unbeatable combination. What they had together was better than *either* of them had separately."

In attempting to prove his case for authorship, Capra and his admirers staked much of their claim on the undeniable fact that, as Capra put it, Riskin was "a giant among scriptwriters—at least when he worked with me." But Capra muddied his own case by pointing to *Mr. Smith Goes to Washington* (screenplay by Sidney Buchman, with Myles Connolly uncredited, from a story by Lewis R. Foster) and *It's a Wonderful Life* (story by Philip Van Doren Stern, screenplay by nine writers, four of whom were credited, including Capra himself) as proof that he made "better films with other screenwriters." That not only raises an arguable question of quality (there are those who believe that *Mr. Deeds Goes to Town* is Capra's best film, including Edward Bernds, who called it "the perfect motion picture story"; John Ford's favorite among Capra's work was *Lady for a Day*; and *It Happened One Night* remains a popular favorite), but it also overlooks the simple but critical fact that *Mr. Smith* and *It's a Wonderful Life*, like everything else Capra did after he and Riskin dissolved their partnership, were strongly influenced by Riskin's work for Capra.

Despite some foreshadowings of his mature themes in Capra's early film treatment "Heart Beats" and his unproduced script *The Eternal Will*, and in his early films *The Strong Man* and *That Certain Thing*, what Capra called his "formula" did not emerge until he began working with Riskin material in the early 1930s. His career before that point was scattershot and uncertain, that of a director in search of something to say. But once the formula had been established, Capra was content to repeat it, with minor embellishments, for the rest of his career, eventually to diminishing effect. Despite the brilliance of Buchman's screenplay for *Mr. Smith* (which Capra called "one of the best scripts I ever had"), it is obvious to even the most casual viewer that Buchman and Capra were following the character and plot patterns established by Riskin's script for *Mr. Deeds Goes to Town*, which in turn had brought to perfection the themes introduced to Capra by Riskin in *The Miracle Woman* and *Platinum Blonde*. And while *It's a Wonderful Life*, despite its complicated writing pedigree, unfolds like a compendium of quintessential Capraesque scenes and themes, most of them can be traced back to antecedents in one or another of the Capra-Riskin films. After that final high point, Capra's career degenerated into poor remakes of earlier Riskin scripts (*Riding High, Pocketful of Miracles*), an adaptation of a third-rate story from Riskin's dustbin (*Here Comes the Groom*), and lackluster adaptations of Broadway plays that had some Capraesque elements (*State of the Union, A Hole in the Head*). Without Riskin, the formula became a straitjacket for Capra, one in which he struggled uncomfortably for years but could never manage to escape.

Though Riskin always received sole screenplay credit when he worked with Capra, the director insisted, "It was a constant collaboration really on the part of the script. So much so that when I started shooting on the picture I never looked at the script because I knew every inch by heart." When they worked together on the script, Capra told a college class, "I would sort of think ahead and think of the next sequence in terms of visual things . . . and then we'd discuss it. He'd walk and write and while he was writing then I would think ahead to the next sequence to try to figure it out . . . what would happen with the relationships between the people. . . . Then I'd read what he wrote. I'd rewrite . . . he'd rewrite." But in his book, while acknowledging that Riskin was responsible for the dialogue, Capra implied that he deserved more credit than Riskin for the conception of scenes and insisted that Riskin's scripts provided "only the basic guidelines" for his films.

Capra stated his case even more bluntly in a 1977 debate on the issue in the *Los Angeles Times* with screenwriter and Writers Guild of America president David Rintels. Rintels attacked Capra for spreading his "one man, one film" theory at Riskin's expense in his writings, interviews, and college lectures, and wrote that "it is indecent of Capra to call Riskin one of his dearest friends while doing everything possible to undermine his reputation." (Rintels later married Riskin's daughter Victoria, whom he had known only slightly at the time of the debate.)

Capra insisted that it didn't matter who wrote his films, because "they expressed dreams, hopes, and *angsts* that came out of my guts," and so it was "one man, one film." That was Capra's polite, public response. After the paper chose to end the debate, he wrote an unpublished letter to the *Times* venting his apoplectic wrath against Rintels and vaguely threatening him for daring to question the foundations of his reputation.

But before he embarked on his crusade to deny Riskin his due credit, retroactively, for the films they had made together between 1931 and 1941, Capra privately acknowledged his awareness of how much he owed Riskin. Capra made the admission in a confidential 1949 letter to the Screen Writers Guild—for the purpose, ironically, of trying to win joint screenplay credit with Riskin on *Riding High*, Capra's remake of Riskin's 1934 screenplay *Broadway Bill*. Since Riskin had declined to work on *Riding High* because he didn't think Paramount's offer was good enough, Capra said, he had to tackle the job himself, though he soon enlisted help from other writers. (Riskin's widow, Fay Wray, said he had asked to work on *Riding High*, but that Capra refused him.) Capra acknowledged that though he would have made his usual verbal and written suggestions to Riskin, Riskin would have written the script on his own, just as had been the case on Capra's earlier films written by Swerling, Buchman, and Riskin, and that in each instance the sole screen credit belonged to the writer. Though Capra's true purpose here may have been to appear generous toward the writers of his old pictures (on which the credit was now a moot point) in order to wrest a screenplay credit from the actual writers of his new picture, the fact remains that Capra's 1949 statement was a more accurate account of their collaboration than the self-serving accounts Capra gave in later years.

"Riskin brought to Capra a slangy, down-to-earth humor, almost a cracker-barrel philosophy, which worked well with Capra's style," said Sidney Buchman. "But Bob was a soloist—neither Jo Swerling nor he could take the fact that Capra was boss. Bob finally wanted to get out and be a celebrity on his own."

Riskin wrote nine screenplays for Capra, and Capra made four other films from Riskin material (including the two remakes). The films Riskin wrote for Capra prior to *Lady for a Day* do not offer any general insight into their method of collaboration, because it was not until *Lady* that Riskin and Capra had much, if any, opportunity to confer on a script before it was filmed. Before *Lady*, Capra had filmed a Riskin play, with a screenplay written by Swerling after Riskin declined to become involved (*The Miracle Woman*); he had picked a finished Riskin script out of a pile and replaced the director who had been assigned to it (*Platinum Blonde*); and he had been assigned to another finished Riskin script (*American Madness*) after the director who had started shooting it was fired.

But what happened on the script of *Lady for a Day* gave the first real illustration of Riskin's screenwriting autonomy when he worked with Capra.

"Madame La Gimp," published in the October 1929 issue of *Cosmopolitan*, was purchased for filming by Columbia on September 29, 1932. This was during the brief period between the completion of filming on *Bitter Tea* and Capra's departure for MGM on October 18 to begin preparation on *Soviet*. Riskin wrote four drafts of *Madame La Gimp* between that September and May of 1933, as well as a last-minute rewrite of the first forty-seven pages of the screenplay, which was finished on May 6, just three days before the start of shooting.

Capra undoubtedly contributed ideas to the screenplay in discussions with Riskin before leaving for MGM and after returning to Columbia, but the evidence indicates that Riskin worked on his own for most, if not all, of the four months Capra was off working with Jules Furthman on *Soviet*. According to press accounts, Capra returned to Columbia in early April

1933 to begin preproduction on *Madame La Gimp*. His exhaustion kept him away from the studio for part of that month until he returned on April 30. Riskin turned in his fourth draft the following day. This draft—aside from the minor revisions in the first forty-seven pages—was filmed virtually intact. Capra's working script contains the fewest number of pencil changes of any working script in his files, except for the silent scripts. Riskin's was a masterful job of screenplay construction and dialogue which Capra transferred faithfully to the screen in just twenty-four days of shooting. The only major change in postproduction was the dropping of the brief prologue involving the statue. If, as Capra wrote in his debate with Rintels, the film "expressed dreams, hopes, and *angsts* that came out of my guts," it was also true that, as Rintels insisted, "they came out of someone else's guts first."

This is the point that Capra was trying to obscure when he pretended in his autobiography that he and Riskin wrote *Lady for a Day* in six weeks in Palm Springs before he went to MGM, ignoring the months Riskin labored on the script alone while Capra was preparing *Soviet*.

Capra began to give out statements about his own writing contributions shortly before the opening of *It Happened One Night*. After an interview with the director in February 1934, Hollywood columnist Sidney Skolsky helped establish what was fast becoming the Capra line on the authorship of his films:

"Capra and Riskin will go away to write the movie scenario. Capra insists on working on the script with the writer. . . . Strangely, while shooting the flicker he seldom looks at the script on which he worked so hard. He doesn't follow it, but films it according to the way it plays. . . . He will insert pieces of business while directing that he didn't place in the script. . . . He will work with the actor as he goes along, even changing the script to bring out a good performance."

On February 16, 1934, ten days after the interview appeared in print, and a week before the opening of *It Happened One Night*, a qualification of sorts was filed by W. R. (Billy) Wilkerson, editor of *The Hollywood Reporter*, in his regular column: "Just where Bob Riskin started and finished with his work on that story [*It Happened One Night*] and how much Capra had to do with the actual writing or the inspiration for it will never be known. Capra will tell you that he had nothing to do with the writing other than to agree or disagree with any part of its treatment. Riskin will say that 'without Frank, it could not have been.' . . .

"BUT—

"That story in hands other than Frank Capra's would have been as nothing, even worse, probably than MGM's *Fugitive Lovers* or Universal's *Cross Country Cruise,* both subjects around the same idea."

"Bob felt he wasn't getting his fair share of the recognition," said journalist Tom Pryor. "He never got it from the critics—it was always Capra, *Capra.* To a large extent that came from the critics' tendency to attribute everything to the director. There is no question that writers were slighted terribly. The writers were really nothing."

In contemporary interviews, Riskin generously acknowledged that Capra was "a great help" to him.

"Once we get the theme of our story," he explained, "it is usually a simple process. Frank and I take the original story and single out the one unusual situation with its characters. Then we decide upon our line of attack. . . . After we extract the motion picture wheat from it, I write a script. When it is finished Mr. Capra and I go over it and make revisions. It then goes to the front office for official endorsement and then to Capra, who has a positive genius in applying his 'magic touch' to the finished film.

"The reason Frank and I get along so well is that we have the same basic story ideas. We have some awful battles over how the story should be developed, but we never argue over what constitutes a story. He's a great editor. He'll walk into the office, give his opinion of a scene, and in doing so toss off an idea from which I can take a dozen successful steps. . . . I write a first draft, and then we get together and fight it out over changes."

Riskin said he usually needed "four months to think out the conception of the scenario." Then he wrote his first draft quickly while sitting in the sun on the veranda outside his office in the courtyard of Columbia's office building. After he finished his typically "long as hell" first draft, he and Capra usually went to the La Quinta Hotel, a quiet and luxurious desert retreat twenty miles from Palm Springs, for a period of intensive revision. They first worked at the hotel on *It Happened One Night,* and after that film's great success they considered it their "lucky" writing spot. "From one and a half to two months are spent on this," Riskin said. "After that I need a month more to work out the dialogue and finish the scenario."

Chet Sticht visited them regularly during their trips to the desert, and he would type the script pages as Capra and Riskin revised Riskin's first draft.

"They'd talk a blue streak," Sticht said of the revising process. "Riskin used to put it into words and Capra had the idea. Frank would scribble some things down, too, but Riskin would do the final writing. He would write on a yellow pad in longhand, and when he would get a bunch of stuff written, I'd go down to the Desert Inn in Palm Springs and I'd type my tail off, day or night, in long concentrated sessions. They were always breathing down my neck—they couldn't wait to see how long it was, how it looked when it was typed up.

"Riskin had the faculty of putting the words down on paper the way Capra wanted to see them. Capra couldn't keep it all in his head. His idea of a story line was excellent, he knew right from the jump where it was going to go, but he would not always know how to get there. In the technical aspects of putting it on paper, Riskin was better than Capra."

The work on the script usually continued throughout the shooting. "The actors used to hate Capra for that," Sticht said. "He would bring in new things every morning when the scene was being shot. You know how you use different colored paper for scene changes, well, there were so many pink pages, blue pages, the studio never knew what was being shot. Almost invariably the changes were for the better."

"It used to drive me crazy," acknowledged Barbara Stanwyck. "Sometimes he would change two or three pages of nothing but talk, talk, talk. Some of them were bastards to learn on the spot. But I never said anything about it, he was the boss."

Some of those changes emanated from Capra. "Robert Riskin had a saying: 'When Capra works on a film, it is impossible for him to sleep,' " Sidney Buchman recalled. "In the morning, Capra would arrive with twenty-or-so pages in which he'd written down all of his ideas. Most were terrible, then all of a sudden there would be one which was astounding."

Some of "Capra's" nocturnal ideas also emanated from other people, such as the ghostly Myles Connolly. But whatever influence Connolly exerted when Capra worked with Riskin, with very rare exceptions Riskin was always involved in the final drafting of each scene. "Capra always wanted a screenwriter with him, even on the soundstage," Buchman said. "The writer had to be there at his side." By the time each scene was filmed, Riskin had rewritten it at least three or four times, Sticht said (only the later versions of most of the scripts he wrote for Capra survive among both men's papers). Then, once the final pages reached the set, Capra, as the working scripts in his files demonstrate, made only minor dialogue changes or additions, usually with the writer involved.

"A singular experience for a writer is to see his characters come to life on the screen in their true and unmarred form," Riskin pointedly wrote after *Meet John Doe*. "This, Frank Capra accomplishes for you in his masterful and individual way—and generally, just for good measure, throws in some little tidbit of his own, to heighten and clarify your original conception."

Though Capra in his later interviews liked to give the impression that he encouraged his actors to improvise—"An actor would run away with something, and when an actor would run away I'd let him run," he told an American Film Institute seminar in 1971—that was not really the case. Claiming otherwise was another of Capra's not-so-subtle barbs at Riskin and writers in general.

When asked in 1978 how his writers felt about his changes in their scripts, Capra said, "I don't give a damn how the writer feels." But, in fact, once Riskin and Capra had settled on a scene, the actors were not allowed to have their will with the meticulously written and polished screenplay. "The pictures I direct are practically finished before I go on the set," Capra wrote in a 1934 article for *The New York Times*. "I work right along with the writer, Robert Riskin. . . . It takes three times as long to complete a workable script as it does to shoot the picture."

"Capra was very well prepared, and he stuck to the script," recalled Lionel Stander, who played Gary Cooper's press agent in *Mr. Deeds Goes to Town*. "Of course, if you had any trouble and couldn't say the line, if it made you feel more comfortable and didn't interfere with the sense of it, he'd let you change it, but if you're a skilled actor you rarely have to change the actual lines unless they're badly written. And Capra was too good a director to have a bad script."

Jean Arthur, who appeared in two Capra-Riskin films, *Mr. Deeds* and *You Can't Take It With You*, as well as in *Mr. Smith*, said, "I don't think Mr. Capra ever insisted on something being read exactly the way it was written, but I never fooled around with lines or scenes or anything."

"I knew the stuff," said Jimmy Stewart, who acted in *You Can't Take It With You* and in two Capra films written by others, *Mr. Smith* and *Wonderful Life*. "You can't see improvisation. Sure, it's happening lots of times, but it's just the fine points; the basic points are right there, they're not improvised. Capra was absolutely prepared."

Until the late thirties, Capra's relationship with Riskin was outwardly harmonious. As journalist Dudley Early put it in a 1936 feature on the two men, "When you interview Capra, all he will talk about is Riskin, and when you interview Riskin, all he wants to talk about is Capra."

"We've been married for a long time," Riskin agreed.

In *Lady for a Day*, Riskin took Runyon's slender plot—a hard-boiled fairy tale about a bunch of Broadway hoodlums conniving to turn a drunken old harridan into a society dame for the sake of her unsuspecting, convent-reared daughter—and made it into a *Pygmalion* for the Depression era, a joyous and heartening reaffirmation of communal spirit that was embraced as such by its battered audience in that fall of 1933. If even the gangsters and corrupt politicians of America's most heartless metropolis could put aside their selfish grievances to give a wretched old derelict like Apple Annie a New Deal from life, there just might be some hope for the rest of the country.

Riskin touched the themes lightly and ironically, for the metaphor was so fanciful that any trace of heavy-handedness would make it seem ludicrous or even offensive. He brought to it just the right blend of sarcasm and sentiment, a skeptical, wise-guy veneer perfectly balancing, but not canceling out, the story's essentially schmaltzy heart. Stephen Handzo observed that this distinctive balance, which Capra adopted as an integral part of his style, "anticipates audience skepticism and enables Capra to undercut his own sentimentality (and perhaps express his own qualms). Whenever things get too marshmallowy, there is always an insert of an abrasive Lionel Stander or Peter Falk [or in *Lady for a Day*, the prototypical Ned Sparks] to object. As Capra puts it, 'The *world* objects.' "

Lady for a Day was a perfectly judged blend of comedy and drama, shot with an economy and precision that shows the hand of a director fully in command of his craft. But before he began shooting, Capra seemed to be struggling to understand what made the screenplay unique. It was not so much that the story had a seventy-year-old heroine but that it was not a conventional star vehicle. It was a truly democratic story. Each character was equally important. Even the nominal lead role of Apple Annie was merely the centerpiece of a fragile fairy tale that to an unusual extent depended for its credibility on the interaction of an entire community of characters.

Yet almost until the first moment of shooting, Capra desperately cast around for star names for insurance—from Marie Dressler to James Cagney to W. C. Fields—before being forced to settle for a cast of has-beens, hand-me-downs, and also-rans, each of whom rose to the magnificent occasion and gave the performance of a lifetime. Any director could have drawn colorful performances from Dressler, Cagney, or Fields. But such overpowering personalities might have swamped the film and destroyed the very point of the story, which rested in the ordinariness of Apple Annie and the shared understanding among the other characters of the secret beauty of the lowly, the despised, the mundane.

Edward Bernds, who felt that Capra "really hit his stride with *Lady for a Day*," remembered how the director obtained his results: "Capra cast on hunches, and most of the time it worked. For example, he cast Wallis

Clark to play the commissioner of police. I had worked with Clark on a B picture, and he was so hammy it was brutal. But Capra said, 'Well, most politicians are hams. Maybe we can use this quality to our advantage.' I listened intently to what he did with Wallis Clark.

"By God if Capra didn't do what he said he was going to do. Without telling him to tone down, he gave Wallis Clark a background, telling him about his wife and his family, supplying him with the character. His performance is hammy, but in the way that politicians are hammy. Capra shaped it in a very deft way."

By the time Capra returned from MGM in the spring of 1933, his unhappy experience there had made him give up on his hope of obtaining Marie Dressler for Apple Annie. Robert Montgomery, the MGM player for whom Capra had been traded, also was no longer being considered for the role of the gangster Dave the Dude, though in July Columbia announced that Montgomery would star in a Capra film called *Hello, Big Boy* as "a society playboy who is penniless, but who gets by on account of his personality." After unsuccessful attempts to obtain Warner Bros.' James Cagney or Metro's William Powell for *Lady for a Day*, Capra settled on Warren William, a run-of-the-mill leading man who, as it turned out, played the role with a unexpected authority and charm, although Capra felt he made the gangster too likable: "That's always the trouble with actors—they've read the end of the script, so they always want to play the last scene."

About a month before shooting, Capra made a pitch to Paramount for W. C. Fields for the role of "Judge" Blake, the elderly con man with a soft spot for Apple Annie. He settled, somewhat predictably, for the perennially flustered blowhard Guy Kibbee. Kibbee was perfection in the role, transcending his stereotyped persona under Capra's expert guidance to provide some of the film's most touching moments while masquerading as Annie's aristocratic husband, "E. Worthington Manville"—as well as putting on a memorably comic exhibition with a pool cue that even Fields could not have equaled.

Capra quickly lined up a number of other familiar character actors, such as Walter Connolly, Ned Sparks, Nat Pendleton, Robert Emmett O'Connor, Halliwell Hobbes, Irving Bacon, and Hobart Bosworth, as well as a host of well-chosen bit players whose names did not appear on the screen. The director returned to his old haunts as a newsboy in downtown Los Angeles to round up some street people he had known to play Annie's friends in Shubert Alley, including a legless man who scooted about on a board with roller-skate wheels.

Their presence was one of Capra's shrewd stratagems to add verisimilitude to his fairy tale, which helped make it emotionally credible to the audience. One reason his 1961 remake of *Lady for a Day*, *Pocketful of Miracles*, failed was that it was a period piece, set in 1933, and thus emotionally distant from its audience. Those who saw *Lady for a Day* in 1933 were drawn into the screen by frequent evocations of their shared Depression experiences. In updating Runyon's story to the current economic crisis, Riskin stressed Annie's common link with millions of other Americans, old and young, male and female, urban and rural, who had to beg for a living and were torn between suicidal despair and hopeful dreams. Madame La Gimp sold discarded flowers and sometimes newspapers in the original Runyon story. Riskin transformed the character into a symbol of Depression poverty with the simple device of having her sell apples, as so many were doing on the streets of America in those days. From that inspired change came many of the film's plot developments, more organic than those in the story, including the motivation for Dave the Dude, who considers Annie's apples lucky and has to keep her in business in order to prosper against his competition.

Riskin's social satire was more pointed than Runyon's. In the film as in the original story, the gangsters masquerade as socialites at a party staged by Dave the Dude to bamboozle the Spanish count (Walter Connolly), whose son is engaged to Annie's daughter. But in Runyon's story, the gangsters and their molls pull off their ruse with ridiculous ease, mocking the "none too bright" count by passing themselves off as celebrities. Riskin's count is no dope. Dave the Dude manages to coach his mugs into acceptable facsimiles of blue bloods—demonstrating, like Shaw's Professor Higgins, that social aristocracy is but a collection of counterfeit mannerisms—but in the final crunch the count's skepticism can only be overcome when Dave the Dude produces the genuine articles, blackmailing the governor, the mayor, the police commissioner, and their entourage into attending the party. Capra admitted that he initially did not understand the pivotal importance of the count's character in keeping the story suspenseful and believable until Walter Connolly convinced him otherwise.

Capra's most inspired piece of casting, Apple Annie herself, turned out to be a real-life Cinderella story. But it was not until a week before the start of shooting that he gave the role to the seventy-year-old May Robson.

The Australian-born Robson was a minor member of the MGM stock company and had played supporting roles in a few movies, including *If I Had a Million* and *Strange Interlude*. But most of her fifty-year career had been in the theater, so she brought to *Lady for a Day* not only her experience but also her unfamiliarity to movie audiences, which helped make her character's transformation from harridan to lady breathtakingly believable. The spectacle of the little-known Robson being elevated to momentary "stardom" by Columbia made a satisfying analogy to the story being enacted on screen. Robson was rewarded with an Academy Award nomination for best actress.

After going through production as *Madame La Gimp* and receiving its Hollywood preview in early July as *Beggars' Holiday*, the film was hastily retitled *Lady for a Day* for a convention of Columbia salesmen in late July, and the title remained for the September 7 premiere at Radio City Music Hall.

Both a critical and commercial hit, *Lady for a Day* brought in $600,000 in rentals to Columbia, double its production cost and a substantial sum in that grim year of 1933. "*Lady for a Day* made so much money," Al Keller remembered, "that a very short time later pencils and paper clips became available all over Columbia, as many as you wanted. Before that you had to requisition them. Not any more."

Despite its contemporary reputation, *Lady for a Day* until its recent reissue was the hardest to see of Capra's classics. The original negative was lost in the early 1950s in transit between two Hollywood laboratories, but Capra owned a 35mm print. Columbia sold *Lady for a Day* to United Artists for $200,000 when Capra remade it as *Pocketful of Miracles*, a bloated, unfunny, maudlin, miscast, and thoroughly insincere film which, incredibly, he claimed to prefer to the original. Although he made a dupe negative from his print of *Lady for a Day*, donated a preservation copy to the Library of Congress, and on a few occasions over the years loaned a print for retrospective screenings, he claimed to be afraid that contemporary audiences would not like the film if it were reissued. More likely what he really feared was that if the public saw the original, they *would* like it, and that in comparing it with *Pocketful of Miracles* they would realize how badly he had declined.

Capra's next project after *Lady for a Day* was *Night Bus*, about a runaway heiress falling in love with an out-of-work newspaper reporter on the road from New York to Miami. "Aside from Capra," Joe Walker admitted, "most of us were unhappy about doing this one." Joe Finochio said, "We were all joking with one another, 'Hell, let's get this stinking picture over with.'"

Riskin remembered: "We wanted them to buy *Mutiny on the Bounty*. They said it was too much money. We were behind schedule. We were desperate for a story for Capra. We grabbed the first thing that came along. It turned into a miracle.

"Somebody came into the office and asked Capra, 'Did you read that story?' Capra said yes, he had; it was one of the six he'd taken home the night before. 'What story?' I asked him. ' "Night Bus," ' he said, a bit dubiously. 'It's about a runaway couple.' He told me a little of it. 'Sounds cute,' I said.

"Later he came in to see me. 'O.K.,' says he, 'we'll do it.' I'd already forgotten. 'What?' I said. 'That thing I was just telling you,' said Capra.

"That's how we came to make *It Happened One Night*."

Samuel Hopkins Adams's story "Night Bus," like "Madame La Gimp," had first appeared in *Cosmopolitan*. Adams received hardly any recognition, least of all from Capra, for his contribution to the director's most celebrated and most influential film, but many elements of his story were retained in *It Happened One Night*.

Remembering his first encounter with Capra when the director was trying to explain the plot of *The Miracle Woman* to the studio brass, Riskin felt that Capra still told a story "abominably," and he was afraid that Capra's "enthusiastic but halting storytelling powers" might sink *Night Bus* at its inception. So before they went in to pitch the story to Cohn and other studio executives, Riskin suggested, "Let me tell this one." Columbia accepted it, but barely.

There was something, indeed, about *It Happened One Night* that defied description or analysis, even after Capra made the film. For all the merits of its story and screenplay, and Capra's masterful direction, *It Happened One Night* might never have achieved its great success without Clark Gable and Claudette Colbert. They are so apt a team that it is impossible to imagine anyone else in those roles. Yet the characters were written with other actors in mind.

Capra's first choice for the male lead was Robert Montgomery, whom Louis B. Mayer refused to loan to Columbia. Though Mayer was obliged to give Columbia a star in exchange for Capra's loan-out for *Soviet*, he did not want it to be Montgomery. MGM was planning its own bus picture, *Fugitive Lovers*, in which Mayer planned to cast Montgomery.

After MGM's Myrna Loy rejected the lead female role (she explained later that "they sent me the worst script ever, completely different from the one they shot"), Miriam Hopkins and Margaret Sullavan also turned it down. Then Capra went to Constance Bennett, who wanted to buy it for herself, and to Bette Davis, who wanted to do it but was not allowed to by Warners, which was punishing her for insisting on being loaned to RKO for *Of Human Bondage*. Cohn suggested Loretta Young, but Capra was not interested. Then the studio chief urged him to cast Carole Lombard, whose name he had brought up at the beginning. Capra offered her the role, through Riskin, her current beau. She turned it down, however, because of a conflict with the schedule of her next film, *Bolero*.

For a while, the future of the film seemed to hang in the balance. MGM's *Fugitive Lovers* and Universal's bus picture, *Cross Country Cruise*, were under way while Capra was still trying to find a cast. "Nobody wanted to play in *It Happened One Night*," Capra said. "Actors don't like comedies much. They're not dynamic like melodramas—nobody gets hurt, nobody gets killed, nobody gets raped." Rattled by the stars' turndowns, Capra began to listen to Columbia executives who belittled the story. As he had done with *Lady for a Day*, he made a last-minute appeal to Cohn to scuttle the film, but by then the deal had been made for the male lead and it was too late to turn back. Cohn did insist on changing the title to distinguish the film from the rival bus pictures. Capra objected to the new title Cohn came up with at the end of shooting, but he was overruled.

It Happened One Night was rescued from the limbo of unmade scripts by Louis B. Mayer. After he refused to lend Montgomery, Capra asked for Gable. Cohn complained that Gable was not the "first-class" kind of actor Mayer had promised Columbia, but Mayer and Capra prevailed. Gable's career had been faltering, and Mayer wanted to teach him a lesson for making what the MGM chief considered extravagant money demands. So he sent him to Columbia for a mere $10,000.

Casting Colbert was Cohn's idea. After making *For the Love of Mike* in 1927, Colbert and Capra had "ended up hating each other," Joe Walker recalled. Colbert turned up her nose at Columbia's offer. She had just finished a picture and was planning a skiing vacation in Sun Valley, Idaho. She also found the script unappealing. She was accustomed to Paramount's glamorous settings and gowns and did not relish the prospect of roughing it on a bus at such a déclassé studio as Columbia.

They were desperate enough to agree to pay her $50,000 for a film whose total production cost was about $325,000. Not only that, her contract called for additional payments if the film went into overtime. Colbert insisted that she took the part "mostly to work with Clark." But Gable complained afterward, "She made more in overtime than I made for the picture."

It was worth it. Gable and Colbert were a fresh romantic team that would guarantee box-office interest even if the studio thought the story would not. Announcing the Gable-Colbert teaming to exhibitors on November 22, 1933, Columbia proclaimed, "What this means to the exhibitor is that COLUMBIA IS GETTING THE STARS! They're none of 'em too big for a Columbia picture now."

Though *It Happened One Night* was criticized by some for its supposed lack of social consciousness, it hardly could have been such an enormous success if it had been nothing but escapism. The appeal of the film for the mass audience in America of 1934 was the profoundly satisfying and encouraging spectacle of the proletarian hero humbling, educating, and finally winning over the "spoiled brat" heiress, a story that not only provided a fantasy of upward mobility, both sexual and economic, but, more important, represented the leveling of class barriers in the Depression.

Though Peter Warne in the Adams story shares a common touch with Gable's character in the movie, he is not an out-of-work reporter in the story but a college-educated chemist reduced to odd jobs and frequent unemployment. He is secretly one of nature's aristocrats, which blurs the class distinctions in his romantic pursuit of the runaway heiress. According to Capra, the script initially changed Peter to a highbrow artist, but after several of the actresses turned it down, Myles Connolly (a former newspaper reporter himself) suggested transforming Peter into the hardboiled but idealistic reporter desperate to win back his job. Riskin, however, had used a similar character in his first script for Capra, *Platinum Blonde*, which also had the situation of a reporter falling for a spoiled society dame.

Gable's Peter is exasperated by the snobbery of Colbert's Ellen Andrews and too intimidated by class barriers to make anything more than a tentative romantic move until her Wall Street tycoon father (Walter Connolly) gives his approval. Burned before by his romantic view of women, he tries to protect himself emotionally by thinking of Ellie as "just a headline," a ticket back to his old job in New York. He spends most of the film criticizing her for her wealth and privilege (teaching her how to dunk doughnuts, he scolds, "Twenty millions and you don't know how to dunk!"), but he also is criticizing himself for being attracted to someone from her class. And he is blind to the rebellious Ellie's true personality, which is closer to his feminine ideal ("somebody that's real—somebody that's alive") than he wants to admit.

Riskin and Capra portrayed the rich much more sympathetically in *It Happened One Night* than they did in *Platinum Blonde*, perhaps because they themselves were becoming wealthy men. As Robert Stebbins wrote in his *New Theatre* review, *It Happened One Night* "was based on a notion dear to the hearts of a people reared in the school of wish fulfillment—that if you stepped up to a grumpy plutocrat, who, of course, had a heart of gold despite it all, bawled him out, told him his daughter was a spoiled brat, he'd at once grow enamored of you and you'd come into his millions." There was an element of truth in that, yet the film's real dramatic climax is not the wedding scene in which Ellie deserts her decadent fiancé at the altar to rejoin Peter but the preceding scene between Peter and her father, in which Peter presents the old man with a bill for $39.60, the exact sum it cost him to bring her from Miami to New York. Her father is astounded, and delighted, when Peter disclaims any interest in the $10,000 reward offered for her return. This demonstration of integrity is what makes Ellie finally realize that he is sincere in his feelings toward her. She yearns for the simpler life Peter offers ("I'd change places with a plumber's daughter any day"), and much of the humor in *It Happened One Night* comes from watching the heiress being reduced to living on a subsistence allowance, strictly regulated by Peter, whose ability to stretch a dollar struck a sympathetic chord with the Depression audience. While derived from the Adams story, this theme was anticipated by Riskin's very first writing effort, his poem "A Dollar Ninety-Three," which similarly satirized the difficulties of financing a romantic trip with an increasingly empty pocket.

Despite their growing intimacy and partnership on the journey, they continually suspect each other of deceit, Ellie that Peter is only after her money or the reward, Peter that Ellie is just using him to get back to New York. The root of their distrust is their class difference, which Peter symbolizes with the Walls of Jericho, the blanket he pins up to separate their beds in the motel room. Though he does so sarcastically, he erects the Walls more in self-protection than for any other reason: he is too insecure about his class status to believe that a woman from Ellie's background could love him or that their romance could last if she did.

This was a theme Capra knew well.

It Happened One Night, like *The Bitter Tea of General Yen*, deals with the tantalizing lure of forbidden sexuality. Capra saw Colbert's character as the personification of all the rich, "classy," stuck-up women who ever gave him the brush-off. "She wasn't looking for any man, she wasn't looking for any romance," said Capra, who renamed the character after one of the girls he knew when he was trying to crash Pasadena society, Ellen Andrews (in the story the character's name is Elspeth Andrews).

But he thought Colbert had "the best figure of any actress in Hollywood," and demonstrated his appreciation of it by showing her stopping traffic with a shapely leg in the hitchhiking scene and by having her do a discreet striptease behind the Walls of Jericho. She had to be coaxed into displaying her leg, and she did not want to strip as far as he wanted for the Walls of Jericho. Capra later recognized the scene he filmed was more suggestive as a result of her discretion. In an article published shortly after the film's release, he wrote, "I do not argue against sex in pictures, provided it is handled cleverly. But there is more sex in a flash of a pair of pretty ankles than there is in a scene of a thousand bare legs; more allurement in what is not shown than in that which is blatantly and crudely smeared on the screen to the point of nausea."

There were some revealingly adolescent high jinks on the set during the shooting of the Walls of Jericho scene. "Colbert was in bed, and Uncle Frank hollered that he was going to attack her," Joe Finochio remembered. "He jumped on her jokingly and rolled over her."

When there was a delay in the shooting of the scene, Colbert, waiting on her side of the blanket, asked what was wrong.

"Well, there seems to be a slight problem here," Capra said, as she came around the Walls. "Clark wants to know what can be done about this."

Gable lay on his back under the covers, smirking, with a large bulge rising from between his legs. He had taken a prop potato masher and propped it under the blanket.

"Awww!" Colbert laughed. *You guys!*

Such moments were rare. Colbert fought with Capra throughout the thirty-six days of shooting. She admitted, "Clark and I kept wondering, 'What kind of reception can this kind of picture actually get?' This was right in the middle of the Depression. People needed fantasy, they needed a dream of splendor and glamour, and Hollywood gave it to them. And here we were, looking a little seedy, riding our bus."

Colbert's combativeness made her unpopular with the crew. Edward Bernds found her "bitchy" and "snooty." Joe Walker, the consummate gentleman, called her "standoffish" and resented her "angry sulking."

Gable, on the other hand, thoroughly enjoyed himself while making *It Happened One Night*, and it showed in his performance. "You know, I think this wop's got something," he remarked to Colbert about two weeks into the shooting.

"Gable, I believe, idolized Capra," said Bernds. "Capra says that Gable's approach to the picture was one of hostility at first, but that certainly was gone by the time the picture started. We started the film with a night scene downtown at the Greyhound Bus Depot, and Gable was already friendly with the crew. I think that what Gable felt when he came to Columbia was, 'Jesus Christ, picture making can be fun!' "

The likable, egalitarian character Gable found in the film—a change from the gangster types and sinister romantic leads into which MGM had been forcing him—established his image for the rest of his career. Capra's greatest contribution to Gable was to give him a sense of sexual reticence and emotional vulnerability, but the biggest sensation Gable caused in the role came when he stripped off his shirt in the motel and revealed that he was not wearing an undershirt.

Another celebrated scene, the rainy night on the bus when everyone sings "The Man on the Flying Trapeze," also created something of a national fad, and it was the kind of scene which was becoming a trademark with Capra—a joyous, seemingly spontaneous interlude that creates a warm fellow feeling between the characters and the audience. Colbert, however, was mystified by the scene when it was being shot, thinking it was "a little corny," as she recalled in a 1965 interview with Bob Thomas.

"How could everyone in the bus know all the words to the song?" Colbert asked Capra.

"Don't worry about it," he told her. "If the scene doesn't work, it can come right out of the picture without interfering with the plot."

Colbert remained skeptical until she noticed that her black maid was "beside herself watching the scene. Then I knew we had something."

"Sometimes your story has got to stop and you let the audience just look at your people," Capra told interviewer Richard Glatzer in 1973. "You want the audience to like them. The characters have no great worries for the moment—they like each other's company and that's it. The less guarded they are, the more silly it is, the better. These scenes are quite important to a film. When the audience rests and they look at the people, they begin to smile. They begin to love the characters, and then they'll be worried about what happens to them. If the audience doesn't like your people, they won't laugh at them and they won't cry with them."

The reaction of the audience to the preview at Pasadena's Colorado Theater on January 28, 1934, attended by Capra, Gable, and Colbert, was only a modest indication of what lay ahead. But the word spread quickly around Hollywood, and nine days later columnist Sidney Skolsky began his nationally syndicated two-part profile of the director, who could "name his own salary with any company now." It was the first wave in a flood of publicity that eventually would stagger even Capra.

It Happened One Night set a house record for an opening day at the Radio City Music Hall on February 23. The New York reviews generally were favorable (William Boehnel of the *World-Telegram* thought it Capra's best film to date), but the story was often described as "improbable" or "preposterous" and ticket sales did not live up to the early expectations. After grossing $90,000 in its first week at the Music Hall, the film slipped to $75,000 before being pulled after its second week. Results from other major cities, where it opened simultaneously, were equally disappointing.

"That put it way down into the third class," Capra remembered. "We said, 'Oh, all right, to hell with it.' " But in smaller markets all over the country, it was a different story. "It stayed one week, and then it stayed another week, and another. They began to talk about it—'Let's go see the Gable picture again and take so-and-so.' The *people* discovered that picture."

It Happened One Night made 1934 the most profitable year for Columbia since 1929, the year of the mass conversion to sound. At a time when as many as one third of the nation's theaters were dark and other studios were barely managing to stay alive, Columbia reported net earnings of $1,008,870 for the fiscal year ending June 30, 1934, a gain of $268,630 over the previous year. The bonanza continued in the following quarter, with net profits of $235,712, and the film continued to play repeat engagements well into 1935. According to the studio's books, *It Happened One Night* brought in $1 million in film rentals during its initial release, but as Joe Walker pointed out, the figure would have been much larger if the film had not been sold to theaters on a block-booking basis in a package with more than two dozen lesser Columbia films, and the total rentals of the package spread among them all, as was customary in that era, since it minimized the risk and allowed the major studios to dominate the marketplace.

In the terms of the contract he had negotiated before making *Lady for a Day*, Capra was to receive 10 percent of the net profits on his films, and though no figures are available on the profits he actually received from the two films, he was outraged by the block-booking of *It Happened One Night*, which he felt encouraged Cohn to coast on his success. The situation only increased his desire for independence from Columbia.

Capra's downbeat mood was deepened on March 16 by the Academy Awards. *Lady for a Day* had been nominated for best picture, actress, director, and screenplay adaptation. Though *Cavalcade* was predicted as the winner of the best picture award in a *Variety* survey of Academy voters published three days before the ceremony, Capra was listed as the favorite for the directing prize and May Robson for best actress (Katharine Hepburn was considered a close second in *Morning Glory*).

Capra, however, "thought we were going to get the whole thing." He campaigned strenuously for the Oscar and even "practiced shy humility before the mirror" in anticipation of the great moment. But *Lady for a Day* did not win a single Oscar. *Cavalcade* won for best picture and director (Frank Lloyd), Hepburn was named best actress, and Victor Heerman and Sarah Y. Mason took the screenplay award for *Little Women.*

Capra often retold the story of his humiliation at the Oscar ceremony, when he hastened to the stage after master of ceremonies Will Rogers called out, "Come up and get it, Frank!" but realized, too late, that Rogers meant Frank Lloyd. The way it really happened was that after Rogers gave Lloyd his Oscar, he called Capra *and* George Cukor to the stage to share in the applause: Capra had come in second in the balloting and Cukor third (for *Little Women*), in what in those days was a three-nomination race in major categories, except for best picture. If Capra was momentarily confused by Rogers's gesture and thought he actually had won, his reaction apparently went unnoticed. None of the press accounts mentioned such an embarrassing incident, and, indeed, Edwin Shallert reported in the *Los Angeles Times*, "Proceedings at the Academy dinner, especially with reference to losers, were handled with even more grace than ordinarily. And Will Rogers seemed largely responsible. Even though he ribbed nearly everybody at some time or another, he was very successful in imbuing the whole affair with a cheerful spirit. Inviting the directors, Capra and George Cukor, to step up for bows, after he had awarded the prize to Frank Lloyd, and presenting [acting nominees] Miss [May] Robson, Diana Wynyard, [Leslie] Howard and Paul Muni to the assemblage, was effective tactics, and nobody in this group could have felt otherwise than that he or she had also been virtually a prize-winner."

Capra's need for the Oscar was so overwhelming that he perceived Rogers calling him before the Hollywood community in defeat as a slap in the face rather than as the compliment it was intended to be. And though his desire to "sire bambinos" had taken more than a decade to reach fruition, he seemed to take little solace from the birth four days later of their first child. When he received the news that Lu was about to deliver, he said to Harry Cohn, "Fifty bucks it's a girl!" "You're on," said Cohn, ever the shrewd gambler.

They named the child Frank Warner Capra, but called him Frank, Jr.

The manic-depressive mood swings Capra experienced in the wake of *It Happened One Night*, which he described as "the torture of constantly *proving* [I] was number one," were part of the phenomenon Tennessee

Williams experienced after *The Glass Menagerie* and described as "the catastrophe of Success." Capra had schemed and sweated since childhood for the fame that was now his—"That's what you're working for," he acknowledged—but when it came, it left him feeling strangely unworthy: "Well, how do you figure that out? It doesn't make sense."

The barrage of publicity he was receiving was enormous for a director, and it did not just happen. Though he claimed in his book that he never had a personal publicist, throughout his years at Columbia he employed as his publicist Paul H. (Scoop) Conlon, the former drama editor of the *Los Angeles Times*, who specialized in directors and whose clients also included Howard Hawks, Leo McCarey, and Lewis Milestone. According to Conlon's biographer, John McCallum, when Capra met Conlon in the 1920s, "together they cooked up a plan to restore the director to his rightful status as 'the man who makes the picture.' "

Capra's friends also helped oil the bandwagon in 1934. One of the first to jump aboard was the fawning Myles Connolly, with an open letter to *The Hollywood Reporter*'s Billy Wilkerson, published on March 2: "Any praise for [Capra] is a slam at Pseudoism, and a boost for genuine entertainment and genuineness all around. . . . His simplicity is really an idiosyncrasy here—and there is a comment on our sunny town, Bill, and its product."

An only slightly less fulsome profile of Capra by the hobo author Jim Tully appeared the following day in *Rob Wagner's Script* ("In his jaw is determination, and in his eyes is pity"). Not only were magazine writers beginning the process of turning the facts of his dogged rise into mythic Americana, he was even being sought after for commercial endorsements. On March 13, less than three weeks after the premiere of *It Happened One Night*, Capra's scowling mug looked out at readers of *Variety* in an ad for Philip Morris cigarettes: "Frank Capra, whose directing genius produced *It Happened One Night*, says this about Philip Morris: 'I smoke quite a lot when directing a picture. So do a good many of the cast. I like to smoke Philip Morris because of their throat ease, so noticeable when one's voice is important. Ordinarily I can recognize a smoker's voice the moment I hear it, but I have no trouble with my cast when they smoke Philip Morris.' "*

---

* *That ad seems grimly ironic in retrospect, for cigarettes eventually caused Lu's slow and agonizing death from emphysema. She smoked as many as five packs a day, while Capra, who had smoked "since I was a baby, since I was five," alternated between cigarettes and a pipe, with little noticeable effect on his health. He quit smoking when Lu was ordered to quit in 1963. "Now when I see somebody with a cigarette," he said, "I want to run over and grab it out of their mouth."*

Becoming famous gave Capra little real satisfaction but only brought out the bitterness and rage that was festering below the surface of his combative personality. His first impulse was not to feel grateful toward those who had helped him succeed, but to feel revengeful—now he could rub it in on his family for what he perceived as their lack of belief in him when he was struggling to make it in the world.

He could not help feeling that the success of *It Happened One Night* was some kind of "accident." And when he won an Academy Award for the film, it only deepened his self-doubt and insecurity: "What happens to you overnight is incredible," he said of the Oscar in 1982. "Suddenly, you're on the front page all over the world; people in the interior of Asia know who you are; it's pretty heady stuff, and it can be a very shocking thing. It affects different people in different ways. It can affect your work, and you can go downhill afterward."

His basic self-doubt was multiplied by his anxiety over the fact that he had to share his success with someone else. The question raised by Billy Wilkerson about the authorship of *It Happened One Night*—"Just where Rob Riskin started and finished with his work on that story and how much Capra had to do with the actual writing or the inspiration for it"—was one that would bedevil him for the rest of his life. It was a question that went to the heart of the collaborative nature of his chosen profession, and to the darkest undercurrents of doubt underlying Capra's egotism: how much did he have to do with his own success?

"One of the things I've noticed is that certain pictures will live forever, and they're beyond you," he mused late in life. "I look at 'em and they don't seem to be mine. It's difficult for me to understand."

Capra may have suffered from what would be described in 1978 by psychologists Pauline Clance and Suzanne Imes as "the impostor phenomenon," the fear common to many high achievers that their success is actually based on a fraud. Another psychologist who studied the phenomenon, Joan Harvey, has said that the sufferer also has the "obsessive fear that sooner or later some humiliating failure would reveal his secret and unmask him as a fraud. Some very famous people have suffered from the feeling all their lives, despite their obvious abilities." In such people, "because each success is experienced as either a fluke, or as the result of Herculean efforts, a pattern of self-doubt, rather than self-confidence, develops," and each success actually intensifies those feelings of fraudulence.

In Capra's case, the need to appropriate credit belonging to his writers stemmed from his insecurity about the nature of his own abilities and achievements: like his mother, he was never sure that he deserved all of that money and all of that acclaim just for sitting in a director's chair. That feeling was intensified because he had failed in his previous ambitions of being a scientist or a writer and as a third-best option had turned to the new, unformulated, and less socially prestigious profession of directing. Some psychologists trace the impostor phenomenon to unresolved Oedipal tensions, which certainly could apply to Capra, who attributed much of his drive for success to a need to impress his defiantly unimpressed mother. "First-generation professionals are very prone to feeling like impostors," Harvey noted. "When people perceive themselves as having risen above their roots, it can evoke deep anxieties in them about separation. Unconsciously, they equate success with betraying their loyalties to their family."

"Consciously," she explained, those who suffer from the impostor phenomenon "fear failure, a fear they keep secret. Unconsciously, they fear success."

After *It Happened One Night*, the man who impressed most people as supremely self-confident fell into a trough of indecision. "I chickened out," Capra said. "I didn't want to make any more pictures. Every story I thought of doing seemed very poor. How could I top *this?*"

The film's sleeper success not only created expectations that were too high for any director to fulfill but also created an all but insoluble problem in Capra's working relationship with Columbia Pictures. On the one hand, it gave him a tremendously increased stature within the industry, which would translate into more leverage with Harry Cohn: higher budgets, more autonomy, and a bigger share of the profits. But the irony was that Capra's new power in Hollywood made it all that much harder for him to coexist with Cohn. The more creative freedom he was granted, the more money he earned, the more of a threat he would become to Cohn's fiefdom. Eventually, Capra knew, he could become too big for Columbia.

And yet, having tried and failed twice to succeed on his own terms at the mighty MGM, Capra was afraid to leave the security of Cohn's little world to take his chances elsewhere. Two days after the Pasadena preview of *It Happened One Night*, MGM announced Capra again for *Soviet*, but that was the last ever heard of his involvement with the project. In later years Capra described the dilemma he faced after 1934 as a choice between more money or more creative freedom, with the latter winning out, but it was such a gross oversimplification that it had little to do with the truth. The truth was that after *It Happened One Night*, with only one picture remaining on his old contract, Capra gambled that he could win both more money *and* more independence from Cohn.

But at this critical point in his career, Capra faced his future secretly crippled by fear.

When he arrived at the new Tanforan Race Track near San Francisco on June 11, 1934, to begin shooting a sentimental horseracing comedy called *Broadway Bill,* starring Warner Baxter and Myrna Loy, Capra needed something to rescue it from being just a formula picture and, as such, a resounding anticlimax to the magical *It Happened One Night.* Before he finished the location shooting two months later, he came up with a daring and bizarre solution: he would have his title character, a handsome black thoroughbred, drop dead of a heart attack as he crosses the finish line.

The script Capra took to Tanforan was an amiable but lightweight adaptation by Robert Riskin of an unpublished story, "On the Nose," by *New York Daily Mirror* columnist Mark Hellinger. Capra, as usual, filmed the script mostly intact; even the brilliant Doughboy sequence, a montage showing the odds of a race changing as a result of a phony tip spread by word of mouth, was fully blueprinted in the script, like its precursor, the run on the bank in *American Madness.* But as shooting began on the racetrack scenes at Tanforan, the director was dissatisfied with the predictable happy ending of Riskin's script. It was a Cinderella story, in which the long shot, Broadway Bill, urged back from illness by his small-time owner Dan Brooks (Baxter), outlegs the big stables' thoroughbreds to win the race after the favorite, Gallant Lady, stumbles. His taste in endings was much darker than critics generally recognized, and in his troubled mood that summer, anxious that he would not live up to his reputation, Capra wanted to say something more bittersweet, more ambivalent about the American success ethic, though he wasn't sure just *what* it was he wanted to say.

Riskin, however, was not available for any more rewrites: shortly before the start of shooting the screenwriter had departed on a European vacation. So Capra summoned Sidney Buchman to the location to write the new scenes of Broadway Bill's death and the burial of the horse at the racetrack's infield.

The thirty-one-year-old Buchman had just finished his first script for Columbia after three years at Paramount, where his most important credit was on Cecil B. DeMille's *The Sign of the Cross.* Born in Minnesota, Buchman was an Oxford graduate who had worked as assistant stage director at the Old Vic before becoming a playwright and screenwriter. Harry Cohn had an unusually high regard for the young man, who would write *Mr. Smith Goes to Washington* and be elevated to Cohn's executive producer and heir apparent. Capra and Buchman discussed the changes over dinner in Palo Alto, the director explaining that the emotion generated by the horse's death also would provide a stronger motivation for Baxter to throw over his wife, Margaret (Helen Vinson), for her younger sister, Alice (Myrna Loy), who had helped him care for the ailing horse before the race. Buchman felt that having the horse die was one of Capra's "astounding" ideas, with which the director "saved" the film.

Buchman finished the four pages of new scenes at two in the morning, a few hours before Capra filmed the death of the horse. He received no credit for his work on *Broadway Bill*, which was not unusual in those days before the Screen Writers Guild won the right to watch over such matters. But when Capra remade *Broadway Bill* in 1949 as *Riding High*, the director used the changes that were made in Riskin's 1934 script during shooting as one of the key points in his attempt to persuade the SWG that *he* deserved to share credit with Riskin for *Riding High*. He claimed that he had thought up the idea of having the horse die, and that he had written the new scenes himself in Riskin's absence.

Capra not only failed to mention Buchman's contribution to *Broadway Bill* and that Riskin's script had a horse fall in the climactic race, he also did not mention to the guild (as he obviously had not to Buchman) that the idea of having Broadway Bill fall and die had been suggested to him by somebody else. Although there was a foreshadowing of that idea in the 1925 script by Capra and Jefferson Moffitt for the Sennett short *The Iron Nag* (in which a chloroformed horse collapses a hundred feet from the finish line), the climax of *Broadway Bill* was suggested by Capra's friend Albert Lewin, then a producer at MGM, as Capra acknowledged in a January 18, 1935, letter to Lewin. Lewin evidently was under the impression that Capra would give him some kind of credit for the suggestion, and reacted with hostility when he ran into Capra at a college football game in San Francisco. Capra wrote to reassure Lewin of his undying gratitude and to promise that he would never fail to recognize Lewin's crucial contribution to the film.

Broadway Bill was written with Clark Gable in mind for Dan Brooks, but *It Happened One Night* had made him too valuable for MGM to loan a second time to Columbia. So Capra was saddled unhappily with Warner Baxter, who tended to be dour and hammy, but as Otis Ferguson wrote in his *New Republic* review, "Anyone familiar with Warner Baxter's sad succession of recent duds might suspect the hand of God in his present transformation; those who saw Clark Gable in *It Happened One Night* will recognize, in Baxter's quick, breezy, offhand naturalness, the hand of Mr. Capra." Ferguson was being overly generous, as most reviewers were to *Broadway Bill*, now that everyone was leaping on the Capra bandwagon.

Bernds felt that Myrna Loy, like Colbert, gave the impression she was "slumming" when she came to Columbia from MGM, which was happy to loan her to Capra this time, but Capra seemed fond of her and there was no trace of hauteur in her work. She gave her role in *Broadway Bill* much the same boldness, warmth, and vulnerability that Jean Arthur later brought to Capra's heroines.

Loy's Alice Higgins resembles *It Happened One Night*'s Ellen Andrews in her rebellion against her wealth and privilege, represented by the ubiquitous Higgins clan of Higginsville and its patriarch, J. L. Higgins (Walter Connolly again). But Baxter's Dan Brooks is drawn to wealth and status in much more insidious ways than Peter was through his love for Ellie in *It Happened One Night*.

Dan initially works for the J. L. Higgins Paper Box Company before giving it up to race Broadway Bill, much to the horror of his unadventurous wife. He tells his father-in-law (unfairly, as it turns out), "You're only interested in one thing—accumulating money, expanding the Higgins enterprises, and gobbling up the little fella." This was the first time the phrase "the little fella" was used in a Capra-Riskin film, and it marked the advent of a new self-consciousness, and perhaps a touch of glibness, in their social consciousness.

Capra personally had a closer identification with Dan than with the little fella, however much both of them wanted to empathize with that abstract concept. Capra too had married into a wealthy family who had their own community (Warnerville), and he viewed Lu's father with some of the same mixture of fondness and insecurity Dan feels around J. L. Higgins. Capra sought Myron Warner's advice on business matters and eventually hired his father-in-law to supervise his land holdings, yet in his book he blamed his fear of marrying Lu partly on the fact that her conservative father was biased against foreigners and Catholics. Capra and the Warners, like Dan and the Higgins clan, were from different worlds, but Capra desperately wanted the wealthy to accept him on his own terms, as an equal rather than a lackey. Marrying into the family was not enough to make his status secure, nor was financial success; Capra had to achieve fame to transcend his class and compel his social acceptance by his wife's family. His Oscar would equal Dan's racing trophy. But the ultimate sign of Capra's acceptance would come when he was important enough to persuade Myron Warner to work for him, just as Dan Brooks, by winning the race, persuades J. L. Higgins to chuck big business and become his racing partner.

Dan's rebelliousness is more a matter of style than of substance; he is not above financing his shoestring venture with money spirited away from her family by the adoring Alice, whom he treats in an exasperatingly cold and obtuse manner until the obligatory romantic finale ("This was really a love story between a man and a horse," Capra admitted). *Broadway Bill*'s ostensible democratic themes are further qualified by its undisguised racism, which is nasty even by the standards of 1934 Hollywood. Dan lords it over his black stablehand, Whitey (Clarence Muse), kicking and hitting and throwing things at the shrewd but submissive fellow, whose defensive demeanor throughout is expressed in his line, "Boss, you mind if I have an idea?"

When Capra remade the story fifteen years later, the treatment of Whitey (played again by Muse) became more polite in keeping with the changing times—Dan no longer abuses him physically—but, as Manny Farber observed, even in the remake Whitey's "happy slave personality, Sambo dialect (hallelujah), rapid expressions of unctuous love are derived from an old stencil cut out of the deepest kind of prejudice." Capra, who considered his depiction of Whitey in *Riding High* to be enlightened and progressive, was outraged by Farber's attack. Though there is no doubt that Capra had a genuine fondness for Muse, a fine actor who appeared in four of his films and who always managed to keep a measure of dignity no matter how demeaning the part, Capra's attitude toward black people would never progress beyond his shy, sadly tentative relationship with Muse, whom he called "a wonderful guy, I think the only Negro who invited me to his house."

Shortly before the opening of *Broadway Bill* in November 1934, Capra's life took a morbid and unexpected twist that echoed the collapse of his title character at the moment of victory.

His version of what happened is the strangest section in his book. He skipped over the making of *Broadway Bill* entirely and wrote that he became ill after receiving his Oscar for *It Happened One Night* in February 1935. The illness began, he claimed, as a self-pitying psychosomatic episode and slowly turned into a serious affliction that was variously diagnosed as pneumonia or tuberculosis. He thought he was going to die.

Then, he wrote, a friend brought an anonymous "little man" to see him. The little man called him a "coward" for abandoning, in a time of world turmoil, his responsibility to spread a message of hope, a special and divinely inspired responsibility: "You can talk to *hundreds* of millions, for two hours—and in the dark."

The little man left. Capra never saw him again, and never knew his name. But the little man had given him the courage to rise from his sickbed and go back to work.

Most, if not all, of this fantastic story is an invention.

When Capra first rehearsed it publicly, to UCLA professor Arthur B. Friedman in an oral history conducted for Columbia University in the late 1950s, he placed the illness and the little man incident not in 1934–1935, but in 1936, after *Mr. Deeds Goes to Town:* "As often happens to creative people in this profession, they get frightened about making any more pictures. It happens to everybody. You make two or three hits and then you're just so scared that you can't go on making hits that you don't want to make anything anymore. Some people go on a bat. Some people just retire. Some people go to Europe. My defense against that feeling of fear of not being able to come up to the standards of the past was that I got sick."

But he added, "I never was sick at all. It was just a perverse state of mind, a defense mechanism, some way to avoid work."

The fact was that in the fall of 1934, Capra became very sick indeed, so sick that he almost died. His hospitalization was reported in the press, but the public knew little about the gravity of his illness.

It began with sharp pains in his abdomen. He had felt abdominal pain intermittently for years, but when it worsened he thought it might have something to do with the illness which had laid him up for several weeks in 1919, when his mother nursed him back to health on Albion Street. When he complained to his doctor in November 1934, the doctor diagnosed chronic appendicitis and recommended an exploratory operation. Capra entered Cedars of Lebanon Hospital on the night of November 11, and was operated on the next morning. He was reported by *Daily Variety* to be "resting comfortably" after the operation, and a week later was said to be "steadily gaining." After going home late in the month to recuperate, he suffered a reversal, and reentered the hospital on the night of December 1, undergoing a second operation. *Daily Variety* subsequently told its readers that he had been "seriously ill" and had returned to Cedars "after going home too soon following [an] appendectomy."

"I thought I was gone many times," Capra admitted when confronted with the evidence.

When Capra was opened up, the doctor found that his appendix had burst long before, undoubtedly during his previous unexplained illness in

1919. "My mother was right about doctors: Keep the hell away from them," Capra said in 1984. "I'd cured myself. They found a big ball of fat around where the break had taken place. It was perfectly safe." The complications in 1934 began, he said, when the doctor cut off the ball of fat, thinking it was an obstruction. Eventually peritonitis and other complications set in. An emergency operation had to be performed to save his life.

"We almost lost Frank," Joe Finochio recalled. "When he was operated on the second time, it was almost too much for his system." Capra was near death for several days, said Chet Sticht, who visited his boss in the hospital and found him under heavy sedation from the "tremendous shock" of the second operation, which, nevertheless, repaired the damage and cleaned up the infection.

Capra was in the hospital when *Broadway Bill* opened at the Radio City Music Hall on Thanksgiving Day. Though the reviews were favorable, the film was only a modest commercial success, bearing out Capra's anxiety about not being able to "top" *It Happened One Night*. But Columbia, which promoted him as "The World's Foremost Director," had more faith in Capra than he had in himself. While he was in the hospital Columbia's stock hit a new high on the New York Stock Exchange, largely due to the continuing success of *It Happened One Night*. Harry Cohn and Sam Briskin meanwhile "drove the [hospital] staff half frantic with their telephone calls at five-minute intervals," *Collier's* reported in its profile of Capra the following August. " . . . Much of this arose out of affection for Frank. But a great deal, too, arose out of the fact that while his appendix was getting impossible Frank Capra was becoming one of the most valuable single individuals in this community of super-valuable individuals."

Lu, who had lost her first husband to a burst appendix, was "going crazy" with worry, Capra remembered. She was about four months pregnant with her second child when Capra became ill, and, while visiting him in the hospital, she fell down a staircase. They feared that the child might have been injured.

"I lost weight, I lost interest, I lost everything," Capra recalled.

To recuperate further he went with Lu, Frank, Jr., and the boy's nurse to the La Quinta Hotel after being released from the hospital on December 15. On Christmas Eve he sent a batch of reassuring telegrams to worried friends, admitting he had been very ill but professing defiant optimism.

He returned to Columbia in early February, but was still so weak that in mid-March he went home ill, and a doctor found "a spot on my right lung." Though tuberculosis was feared, it probably was pneumonia; *Daily Variety* reported on April 4, "His heavy cold hanging on, Frank Capra will stay at [La Quinta] for a week or more in an attempt to shake it. Robert Riskin with him talking story." By April 22, in a letter to a friend, Capra was able to proclaim himself recovered, but he admitted that it had been a close call.

On the night of April 24, Lu gave birth at Cedars of Lebanon Hospital to a six-pound, thirteen-ounce boy they named John. He was strong-looking but did not seem mentally sound. Later they realized he had been born deaf, and as time went on he displayed symptoms which then were often identified with mental retardation but which today probably would be diagnosed as autism. The Capras covered their anxiety about John with forced gaiety in reporting the birth to friends. Nor did Capra admit in his book that there was anything seriously wrong with John at the beginning. But the subject was so painful that it might help explain why Capra could not deal honestly with the events surrounding his own illness.

When his health worsened early in 1935, Capra recalled fifty years later, "I thought, 'Well, that's perfect. I'll go out with flags flying.' I was gonna die. What better time to die? Gosh, it would be wonderful to die right now. I would have died just by talking myself into it."

This is where the business about the little man comes in.

"It doesn't make sense to me," Chet Sticht said. "I never met the little man. It could have been true—but it also could have been an imaginative thing." Even if the character was invented, Capra was telling a kind of metaphorical truth when he had the little man accuse him of being a "coward" and abandoning his responsibilities both as a man and as a filmmaker. Whether or not someone pointed the finger at him, the quasi-suicidal Capra certainly was pointing it at himself in those "terrible" months.

"Boy, it hit me right square in the stomach, this 'cowardly' stuff," he admitted, drawing yet another connection between his spiritual and gastrointestinal problems.

"People had said" he was a coward. "I told my wife what people had said. She said, 'They could be right.' "

Were they right?

"Well, at that moment, yeah, damn right."

Capra said nothing in his book about the 1934 appendicitis attack, though he did refer to it briefly in the uncut manuscript. The reasons for his fictionalizing these events were complex and in themselves revealing of what Capra saw as the underlying causes of his spiritual and physical crisis.

One motive could have been purely literary, to enhance the dramatic impact of his illness by having its onset follow rather than predate the Academy Awards of February 1935, thus underscoring the trauma of success. The little man also stood for several people, including Lu, who helped Capra achieve a new philosophical and religious attitude that helped him return from the depths. An important reason for changing the date of the onset of his illness from November 1934 to early 1935 could have been to avoid dealing in the book with Lu's fall during her pregnancy.

Capra's involvement with Christian Science may help account for his later stress on the psychosomatic nature of his illness. His first wife, although she was Jewish, had become a believer in Christian Science, and Capra, estranged from Catholicism, had flirted with her new religion while they were married. At the time of his 1934–1935 illness, Capra found support from Max Winslow, a brother-in-law of Harry Cohn who was producing musicals at Columbia and who, claimed Capra, brought the little man to see him. As part of his recuperation, Capra and Lu took a fishing vacation at Max and Tillie Winslow's lodge on the Saint Lawrence River. While Capra was there, Winslow reintroduced him to Christian Science. "Their theory that you are just what you think is pretty good," Capra continued to believe. "There's no doubt about it, it saved my life."

The teachings of Christian Science about the interrelationship of the body and the spirit no doubt contributed to Capra's willingness to believe that his illness stemmed entirely from his spiritual malaise. Christian Science helped him survive his crisis, when he was no longer sure just who or what he was, by giving him a temporary surge of optimism, a novel and reassuring sense of personal integration, a feeling of being in control of his life, which Catholicism, with its debilitating emphasis on sin and guilt, had been unable to give him. Myles Connolly frequently visited Capra during that period and Capra also consulted a priest, but he remained skeptical about the Catholic church.

"He was a very complicated guy," said Chet Sticht. "He was a brilliant guy in many ways, and yet subject to depressions. Being somewhat of an idealist, he may not have had enough faith in himself. He may have worried every time about his next picture not being a smash hit; he may have doubted it every time. But he was fine as soon as he started working on a film—there usually was no problem then, because he was too busy to worry about anything else. *Between* films was when it was a problem."

During the crisis of 1934–1935, Lu "was a great help, of course," Sticht said. "She was optimistic. She was an outgoing person, with a cheerful nature. She liked people. He was more complicated than she was."

Further help came from Dr. Verne Mason, a physician friend of Capra's who spent long hours at his bedside discussing his problems. Dr. Mason "seemed to understand Capra," said Sticht, "and he was a great help in bucking him up."

But Dr. Mason's ministrations and Capra's temporary religious deliverance were only a distraction from his fundamental problems, not a solution to them. Wrestling with the "shocking" advent of fame and success for which he felt so unworthy, Capra at that juncture in his life was engaged in a desperate search for a social message big enough to justify, to himself and to the world, his new status as something more than a mere commercial director.

There was an element of guilt in that search.

"I guess he figured he wasn't worth what he was getting, that it was sort of a fairy story," Sticht said. "He had such a hard beginning, and had to scrimp and save and fight other boys on the street corner for money, and all of a sudden he had tremendous wealth. It probably was due to his upbringing that he did not live ostentatiously. He would buy good cars and things, but he would use them until they wore out. It was only *after* he retired that he switched from Buicks to Lincoln Continentals."

But in 1934 Capra faced the prospect of a social message with great trepidation, for, as he told Philip K. Scheuer of the *Los Angeles Times* shortly after he made *Broadway Bill*, "People don't want to think." He worried that he would lose his audience, his money, and his newly achieved social status if he said too much in his films or if he said things the audience did not want to hear. Nevertheless, he decided, from now on his films would "*say* something." He now believed that he no longer should devote his talents just to self-aggrandizement but to improving the lot of humanity.

Yet when he found what he wanted to say to audiences "for two hours—and in the dark," it was written by somebody else—Robert Riskin.

A flirtation with death would be enough to make anyone more conscious of social obligations, but the "little man" incident provided Capra's readers with an explanation for his transformation into a socially conscious director without giving any credit for it to Riskin (who was himself a little man). Since Capra could not do that, he credited the little man as the heaven-sent messenger who brought him his inspiration and his message, which was defined in the anecdote as anti-Fascist and pro–common man, a vaguely New Dealish formula that had nothing to do with Capra's own political or social opinions before he started working with Riskin.

A socially conscious Capra did not mean a more generous or less self-centered Capra. On the contrary, after *It Happened One Night* he began to take the "one man, one film" concept more seriously, regardless of what Riskin or anybody else thought of it. But wishing did not make it so. It is fitting, in that light, that Capra probably borrowed the little man incident from his writers.

Connolly, who berated Capra for his lack of a social conscience, sent him a copy of St. Francis of Assisi's poem "The Canticle of Brother Sun" as a birthday present in the mid-1930s, unctuously comparing Capra to the saint, whom Connolly referred to as "the Little Man" (Connolly's *Mr. Blue* was the source of Capra's "little man's" idea about movies providing spiritual inspiration to the masses sitting enrapt for two hours—and "in the dark"). Riskin not only wrote in praise of the little fella in *Broadway Bill*, he also wrote a little man into *Mr. Deeds Goes to Town*, in the scene of the anonymous farmer bursting into Deeds's mansion to force on the hero a social conscience. But most striking of all, a character virtually identical to Capra's little man appeared in "The Flying Yorkshireman," a 1937 short story by British author Eric Knight to which Capra bought the screen rights in 1941.

Knight's story is an allegory of faith, dealing with a humble Yorkshireman named Sam Small who, on a visit to Hollywood, discovers that he has an inexplicable gift for flying. Though his family are not impressed, he soon becomes celebrated and wealthy, but before a scheduled appearance at Madison Square Garden he loses faith in his gift. At this point he is visited by "the little man," as Knight calls him, a little old man who appears to Sam without warning, sitting on the edge of the bed in his hotel room.

"There is no more faith, simple and blessed," the little man tells Sam. ". . . [W]e have lost the faculty of having faith in the incomprehensible. . . . the world will do anything but believe. Although they see, they won't believe." The little man urges Sam to have faith in himself and tells him that "if you find it gets harder than usual . . . just say to yourself: 'I can fly. I can! I *can!*' and don't ever disbelieve it."

Capra must have seen this as a vivid imaginary rendering of his lack of faith in his own gifts, and he probably adapted the incident for his own purposes in *The Name Above the Title*, even though he had long since sold the film rights to "The Flying Yorkshireman." By taking this apparition and combining it with the urgent social message written by Riskin for the farmer in *Mr. Deeds*, and then inserting them retroactively into his own life story, Capra not only could claim divine inspiration for his work but also could render his own life more Capraesque than it really was, thereby laying a spurious "autobiographical" framework for his films which would diminish the contribution of his writers.

Leaving his sickbed for the Academy Awards ceremony on February 27, 1935, at the Biltmore Hotel, Capra was an appalling sight. His eyes and cheeks were sunken and dark, his hair was disheveled, his tuxedo hung loosely on his scrawny frame. He could barely force a smile when he arrived, but he became so excited that he kissed Harry Cohn after *It Happened One Night* won an unprecedented five major Oscars—for best picture, actor, actress, writer, and director, the only such sweep until *One Flew Over the Cuckoo's Nest* in 1976.

Capra received what was described as "tremendous applause" when he accepted his long-anticipated prize, winning over Victor Schertzinger (*One Night of Love*) and W. S. Van Dyke II (*The Thin Man*), but he was too emotional to say anything. One journalist covering the event, noting Capra's ill-fitting clothes but apparently knowing nothing of his sickness, wrote that "he is unlike Hollywood, too, in that he acknowledges congratulations with a seriousness that is so apparent it seems a secret and very sly amusement."

His triumph was shadowed, however, by the political tensions surrounding the Academy. Both the Screen Writers Guild and the Screen Actors Guild discouraged their members from attending the ceremony, and many stayed home, including Robert Riskin. Much to Harry Cohn's irritation, Riskin later made conspicuous use of his Oscar as an office doorstop. Since the pay-cut controversy, the Academy membership had been severely depleted, with only 46 writers and 94 actors left on its rolls, although *Daily Variety* reported it still had 666 voting members at the time of the 1935 Oscars (today the Academy says it does not have membership figures for that period). The SWG then had more than 750 members and SAG had 2,375, but the guilds had not yet won recognition, and the Academy still was trying to maintain control of labor contracts. The labor-management committees appointed to renegotiate the NRA Motion Picture Industry Code had reached a stalemate, largely over the issue of a guild shop, and, with the NRA scheduled to expire in June, both sides were waiting for Congress to act before making further moves.

The best-actress award that year became a symbolic battleground for the greater issues and a further embarrassment to Capra. Bette Davis's performance in RKO's *Of Human Bondage* had received sweeping critical acclaim, but it was a role she had fought her own studio, Warner Bros., to let her play, and Warners punished her rebelliousness not only by denying her the chance to appear in *It Happened One Night* but also by not supporting her for an Oscar in *Of Human Bondage*. Nor did she receive much support from RKO, which had little stake in her career. Her fans and many colleagues were outraged when she was not included among the three nominees: Colbert, Grace Moore for Columbia's *One Night of Love*, and Norma Shearer for MGM's *The Barretts of Wimpole Street*. Davis's exclusion spotlighted the blatant studio politics that controlled the Academy and its voting process.

Joan Blondell and Dick Powell mounted a campaign to force the Academy to reconsider. "The whole town seems to be talking about the failure to include Miss Davis," the *Examiner* observed. Though the Academy rules did not permit write-ins, Davis's supporters urged the voters to do so anyway, as a protest. In a face-saving maneuver twelve days before the ceremony, Capra, Riskin, and three other nominees (Shearer, William Powell, and writer Norman Krasna) lent their support to a rule change opening the ballot to write-in candidates, "feeling that it is only fair to all entries that the winners shall be unquestioned." Despite what was reported to be a sizable write-in vote for Davis, it came too late; she was given a consolation Oscar the following year for a potboiler called *Dangerous*. The controversy further undercut the Academy's waning stature in the Hollywood community. As Blondell put it, "I suppose there was no chance for any part of the process to be fair because everybody had quit the Academy. But when they left Bette out, we all began taking a closer look and decided, 'Hey, something's rotten in Beverly Hills.' "

"Positive I wouldn't get it," Colbert decided to skip the Oscar ceremony. She made plans to depart on the Super Chief that night for a New York vacation.

As was the custom in those days, the winners were informed of their awards about an hour before the ceremony and were paraded before the newsreel cameras to make acceptance speeches. While Gable was expressing "my thanks and sincere gratitude to Mr. Frank Capra, the director of *It Happened One Night*, and Miss Claudette Colbert, who was gracious enough to costar with me in that same picture," Academy PR man LeRoy Johnston was on the phone to the train station, having Colbert pulled off the train and begging her to come back to accept her Oscar. "It's the Nobel Prize of motion pictures," he pleaded into the phone as reporters eavesdropped. Colbert protested that she was not dressed for the occasion (she was wearing a tan traveling suit, a fur, and a brown felt hat). "But nobody will see you," promised Johnston. "I'll meet you and get you in privately."

They rushed her to the banquet with a police motorcycle escort. She arrived at 11:01 P.M. and accepted her award two minutes later. "I feel a little foolish," she said, "and I'm afraid I'm going to cry." She left the podium, but on her way out the door she stopped, dashing back to add an afterthought, "I owe Frank Capra for this."

Harry Cohn accepted the award for best picture. It was the culmination of his eleven-year dream for Columbia's recognition as a major studio. Yet in his acceptance he was remarkably generous and selfless: "I want to thank Frank Capra. I want to thank Robert Riskin. I was only an innocent bystander."

11. "A sense of responsibility"

"**S**omething to say" was proving elusive.

Before his illness, Capra had been thinking of making a musical. His thoughts went to the opera star Grace Moore, a surprise success in Columbia's 1934 *One Night of Love*. After the visit from the little man, however, such a project may have seemed too fluffy for "The World's Foremost Director."

The first project announced for Capra when he made his abortive return to the studio in February 1935 was an adaptation of Maxwell Anderson's play *Valley Forge*. The inspirational saga of George Washington's refusal to surrender to the snow and the Redcoats appealed to Capra's newfound obsession with courage and to his budding interest in patriotic Americana. He claimed he dropped the project because he felt uncomfortable about doing a period piece, but commercial considerations probably were the prevailing factor.*

Around this time he also considered making films of *Crime and Punishment* and *Anna Karenina*. "I have always hankered to make classics as films or do more ambitious productions but have usually ended up doing a comedy," he said when he tried to revive the *Anna Karenina* project in 1962 with Sophia Loren. A more fitting excursion into high culture was Capra's attempt in July 1935 to obtain the film rights to Leoncavallo's opera *Pagliacci*. The tragicomedy of the circus clown who kills his un-

---

Capra proposed it again in the fall of 1938, with Gary Cooper as Washington, but Cohn vetoed it as inappropriate to make at a time when Hitler's shadow was falling over England. In 1971 Capra and John Ford tried to obtain the film rights from Columbia, intending to codirect it (Capra doing the exteriors and the ailing Ford the interiors) to benefit the Motion Picture and Television Country House and Hospital, with John Wayne or George C. Scott as Washington. Columbia, however, was preparing to make what Capra called "that awful goddamn thing, that musical about the Revolutionary War [1776]," and refused to part with the Anderson play for fear of competition. Four years later, Columbia made Valley Forge as a movie for television.

faithful wife may have struck an emotional chord in the Italian director, with its echo of his violent anguish over his first wife's supposed infidelity. As late as 1938 he was still talking about making it.

The story Capra was most eager to film, however, was James Hilton's mystical novel *Lost Horizon*, first published in English in 1933. Capra said he read it that fall while making *It Happened One Night*, and that his interest in Hilton's fantasy had been roused by Alexander Woollcott, whose radio interview helped make it a best-seller in the United States. But Riskin explained it differently: "Every studio in town had turned it down. I had read it in London, and I talked it over with Frank on getting back here. He read it and liked it. We mentioned it to Cohn, sure that after reading it he'd say we were crazy. But he surprised us by agreeing. So we went to work [in March 1935, after *Valley Forge* was dropped]."

Hilton's appealing but rather sophomoric vision of Shangri-La, an escapist paradise in which the problems of the real world are blandly dismissed with advice to "be gentle and patient," struck Capra as the perfect vehicle for the kind of philosophical statement he so earnestly yearned to make. "With men and women the world over groping for a solution to the turmoil and terror in their lives," he wrote while making the film in 1936, "I saw in the book one of the most important pieces of literature in the last decade. The story had bigness. It held a mirror up to the thoughts of every human being on earth. It held something of greatness. The fact that it did not conform to Hollywood formulas interested me even more." But Ronald Colman, the ideal choice for the lead role of the British diplomat Conway, was unavailable until the following year, so on June 4, 1935, Capra decided to wait for Colman and began looking for another picture. By July 1 he had found it.

Mr. Deeds Goes to Town began as an *American Magazine* serial, "Opera Hat," by Clarence Budington Kelland.* There was nothing remotely of what Capra called "bigness" about Kelland's tediously protracted murder mystery. But Riskin and Capra saw something of value in the story's springboard about a greeting-card poet from Mandrake Falls, Vermont, who inherits a New York City opera house and millions of dollars along with it—and the film they made from the story would be described as "a genuine PR contribution to the New Deal," as "boosting NRA ideas," even

---

*Opera Hat *was the film's title during principal photography. For a while it was called* A Gentleman Goes to Town *or* Cinderella Man. Columbia *offered its publicity staff a fifty-dollar bonus for a better title, and Fanya Graham Carter won with the aptly allegorical, John Bunyanesque* Mr. Deeds Goes to Town. *"Fifty dollars in the middle of the Depression," she recalled, "was a fortune."*

as giving vent to "quasi-communistic" ideas. Gary Cooper's Longfellow Deeds, who in the Riskin-Capra version is accused of insanity for trying to give away his fortune, would be seen as "a kind of Roosevelt accused by his opponents of instituting the New Deal and 'wasting millions' in helping the poor and unemployed." In the Soviet Union—which in later years retitled the film *Grip of the Dollar*—Capra, in the words of the 1938 *Saturday Evening Post* profile, was "hailed as a comrade, a world improver, and a Red propagandist."

Capra was no stranger to social issues when he made *Mr. Deeds,* but for those few who knew him well, the depth of the film's concern for the poor and unemployed was surprising, coming as it did from a Roosevelt hater who, by the middle of 1935, was on his way to becoming a very wealthy man.

After FDR took office and banned the hoarding of gold, the director of *American Madness* had no choice but to rely on a bank rather than continuing to squirrel away his earnings. In September 1934 he opened an investment trust fund with Chase Manhattan. "Capra had enough sense when he got up to $3,000 a week that he was sticking $1,000 a week in the trust," said Chet Sticht, who began working for him that September. "They were investing it for him in blue-chip stocks. They never paid much in annual yields, but there were incredible stock dividends and splits." Capra's Columbia earnings and his stock proceeds were not squandered on chancy business propositions but were safely invested in land and more blue-chip stocks, which helped make him a millionaire before the end of the decade. "He never owned Columbia stock," Sticht noted. "He probably didn't think the stock was any good." Capra confirmed that he was "afraid" to tie up his holdings in such a dicey proposition.

Capra's new contract with Columbia of June 6, 1935, was one of the most favorable ever negotiated by a creative artist in Hollywood up to that time. It provided for him to produce and direct four pictures over a two-year period and guaranteed him a salary of $100,000 per picture and 25 percent of the net profits, with each picture separately accounted. The contract was amended on November 25 of that year to include a fifth picture, *Mr. Deeds,* which was about to begin shooting, with Capra to receive a salary of $159,500, of which $59,500 was a bonus; *Mr. Deeds* replaced his option to make a picture outside Columbia. Capra erroneously stated in his book that the June 6 contract was for six pictures, but a second option to make an outside picture had been deleted in the final negotiations. His salary was to be paid in weekly installments of $5,000 while he was working, with any remaining part of his $100,000 per picture to be paid when production was completed. A crucial clause provided that if Columbia did not let Capra make a picture in either of the contract's two one-year periods, he was to receive his full $200,000 salary anyway.

The creative terms were, for that time, almost as generous, although contrary to Capra's later claims, the contract did not guarantee him full creative autonomy or final cut, something no director in Hollywood could hope to receive unless he bankrolled his own pictures as Charlie Chaplin did.

And despite his boast in *The Name Above the Title* that *Mr. Deeds* marked the first time he had "my name above the title," that simply was not true.

His contract at that time said nothing about having his name above the title, only that his directing credit would appear on a separate card on the screen (then a matter of negotiation, later mandatory for all directors) and that each of his films would be announced as "A Frank Capra Production"—the kind of credit he already had been receiving since the late twenties. The phrase "A Frank Capra Production" appeared on the main title card of *Mr. Deeds below* the names of the stars, Gary Cooper and Jean Arthur, and only Cooper's name was listed above the title. The same was true of the advertisements for the film. It was not until *You Can't Take It With You* in 1938—the twenty-fourth of his twenty-five pictures for Columbia—that his name appeared above the title on screen and in the ads. Pretending that his name was above the title of *Mr. Deeds* was part of Capra's strategy in his book of trying to prove the film was entirely his, not Riskin's or even Columbia's—a crucial point after the visit of the little man.

"I never asked for a penny during all the years at Columbia," Capra told Bob Thomas in the 1960s, claiming he received "complete control of the picture in return." He told *Money* magazine in 1979, "I never saved anything from the money I made directing movies." And he insisted to the author of this book that he made "nothing" from his profit percentages on the films he made for Columbia between 1933 and 1939. Since it was central to his self-cultivated public image to appear to be a modest-living champion of the common man, Capra continued to claim, even when challenged on the issue in 1985, that he "never did get" any of his profits from the Columbia pictures, because according to Columbia's books, "the pictures don't show a profit yet."

Figures for Capra's profits from *Lady for a Day* and *It Happened One Night* (on which he had a 10 percent share) are not available, but through

October 1985 Columbia's books showed that Capra had earned $299,406 in profits from *Mr. Deeds*, $262,084 from *Lost Horizon*, $212,043 from *You Can't Take It With You*, and $42,125 from *Mr. Smith Goes to Washington*—a total of $815,658. (These figures also do not include the $100,000 supplementary settlement Capra received when his contract was renegotiated after a legal dispute with the studio in 1937, at which time Columbia also agreed to drop his obligation to make a fifth picture.)

While $815,658 over the period of half a century may not compare with the huge profits some filmmakers receive today, it is by no means a negligible sum, especially considering what a dollar was worth when Capra received much of that amount. Not only that, but as of 1985 (the last year for which figures were made available by a confidential source at the studio) Capra still was receiving fairly sizable amounts of money from his old movies, and he was the only filmmaker from that era to be earning continued profits from Columbia. For the five-year period from 1980 through 1984, Capra received $133,807 from Columbia, of which $74,467 came in 1984 alone, primarily reflecting the cable television sales of *Lost Horizon*.

When he started to become wealthy after *It Happened One Night*, Capra built a second home for his rapidly growing family. The Malibu house was too small and isolated, so the Capras decided to use it only on weekends and holidays and to close it during the winter months. For just over $30,000 in March 1936, they bought two and a half undeveloped acres in Brentwood, then a sparsely populated, semirural area of sprawling, lavish estates. The Capras' hilltop property at 215 North Barrington Avenue was across the road from the estate of Gary and Rocky Cooper and next door to that of director William Wellman and his wife, Dorothy, with whom they became close friends. With the purchase of adjoining land, the Capras eventually increased their property to eight acres, and in 1936 they commissioned the prominent Los Angeles architect Roland Coate to build them a two-story, fifteen-room contemporary house with a screening room but no swimming pool. The estate's total value was then between $175,000 and $200,000. Keeping two homes was costly. They had five full-time, live-in servants, including an English butler whose name was Frank Chaplin and whose nickname, naturally, was "Charlie"; a Danish cook and nanny, Rosa Haspang; two other nursemaids; and a Mexican gardener named Joe Lozano, who was an illegal immigrant.

Capra's only other extravagance during the 1930s was his magnificent collection of rare books, which included first editions of *The Divine Comedy*, *The Canterbury Tales*, *The Federalist Papers*, and *Adventures of*

Huckleberry Finn, as well as such other rarities as a copy of Shakespeare's Fourth Folio, Queen Elizabeth I's copy of Montaigne's *Essays,* and a proof copy of *A Christmas Carol.* Capra began collecting in 1933 and purchased most of the major items by 1935, when his collection was valued at $84,230. He handled his treasures with a tactile delight and revered them with a passion that came from a yearning to overcome a semiliterate upbringing. *Collier's* writer John Stuart described—no doubt with some exaggeration—what happened between Capra and the only man in Hollywood reputed to have a better collection of rare books, screenwriter Jules Furthman: "Furthman recently bid against Capra and made him pay $10,000 for a Dante's *Divine Comedy.* Capra coldly announced that he'd kill Furthman rather than let him have it, and an injudicious friend of the old days in the Italian quarter, overhearing the threat, asked where he could find Furthman. Capra just stopped him in time."

Capra was learning from such articles that wealth and fame had their distasteful side effects.

Stuart's August 17, 1935, profile in *Collier's,* "Fine Italian Hand," dwelled on precisely those aspects of Capra's background the director had tried hardest to live down: "Somewhat awed now in the midst of his success, the little wop has been known to say he had a close call from becoming a gangster and racketeer, when he recalls those rough, hard days. But somehow or other Frank got the education bug. . . . [T]here is a sensitiveness about that Italian mind of his, wop or not." Stuart lavished praise on Capra as a filmmaker and as a family man, but the writer kept harping obsessively on Italian stereotypes: "The snarl, the potential gangster trait, comes out in Frank when he plays bridge."

Being called a "potential gangster" in an era when J. Edgar Hoover's G-men were shooting it out on the front pages with the likes of John Dillinger and "Baby Face" Nelson was no joke. The stunned Capra, while complimenting Stuart on the portrait's verisimilitude, also expressed anger over it.

Capra soon launched an intensified campaign to upgrade his image. That September he began writing the first in a series of essays to demonstrate his thoughtfulness and responsibility as a filmmaker. In the first seven months of 1936, he had pieces published in *Esquire* about the commercial factors inhibiting creativity in Hollywood, in *The New York Times* about the primary importance of actors in movies, and in *Stage* about *Lost Horizon* and his growing need to inject something more than mere "entertainment" into his pictures.

The most revealing was the *Esquire* article, "A Sick Dog Tells Where

It Hurts," a bizarre mixture of self-promotion and self-flagellation. "It takes a strong stomach to digest 'success' in Hollywood," he wrote, attacking the studio system for holding back the artistic potential of motion pictures by rewarding conformity and artificiality.

He called for some radical changes in the film industry, including a deemphasis of business concerns, the divorcement of studios from their theater chains, and a tougher stand against censorship. But he also blamed himself and other filmmakers: "Although I've been called a 'giant' in my particular kind of work by some overly kind critics, I'm really just a pigmy among pigmies."

He urged writers, actors, and directors "to refuse to be high-pressured and blackjacked into signing long-term contracts, and have the artistic guts to make only the pictures they want to make, or go into the business of making pictures for themselves."

And he concluded: "To prove that I have refused to join the dollar dance, I've just signed a new long-term contract. Pardon me while I look for my intestinal fortitude. Darn thing, I'm always misplacing it."

Clarence Budington Kelland had more modest aspirations. He wrote "to satisfy the homely, decent emotions and give pleasure to millions." In his Scattergood Baines stories, and in "Opera Hat," the cracker-barrel humorist reassured his conservative *Saturday Evening Post* and *American Magazine* readership by trumpeting old-fashioned, small-town Vermont values over the slimy sophistication of New York and other big modern cities. He was a prominent Republican and opponent of the New Deal.

"Opera Hat" provided Riskin and Capra with the basic character of Longfellow Deeds, with his poetry, his tuba playing, his native intelligence, his shrewdness with money ("he was a surprisingly good businessman for a poet"), his shyness around women, and his essential innocence. Kelland's story set up the situation of Deeds inheriting a fortune from a distant relative who dies in an Italian automobile accident, and it also provided the initial conflict between Deeds and the snobbish, greedy New York opera crowd who try to bilk the hayseed out of his fortune. But there the film story radically diverged from the magazine serial.

Riskin and Capra did away with Kelland's tiresome plot about Longfellow becoming a patsy in a crime of passion committed by a member of his opera company. Deeds's primary romantic interest in the Kelland story is the diva Madame Pomponi's pallidly sweet secretary. But Riskin and Capra, in a more cynical twist on the plot of *It Happened One Night*, involved Deeds with a duplicitous newspaper reporter, Babe Bennett (Jean Arthur), who feigns affection for him to get material for exposés of the "Cinderella Man" (a phrase they borrowed from the similar-themed *Platinum Blonde*).

Another critical change in the film was Deeds's attitude toward his sudden riches. In Kelland's story, when Longfellow is told of his inheritance, his response is simply "Gosh!" The murder plot serves to distract Deeds—and the reader—from the personal and social consequences of sudden wealth. But Riskin saw that as the whole point, calling *Mr. Deeds* the story of "a country boy given twenty million dollars that he didn't want, and . . . always trying to express his distaste for it." When he is told of his inheritance in Riskin's script, Longfellow says, "I wonder why he left me all that money. I don't need it."

The film evolved into a meditation on "the catastrophe of Success" that had descended upon both Riskin and Capra in the wake of *It Happened One Night*. Like Deeds when he is wrenched from the familiar moral values of Mandrake Falls and the modest success of his greeting-card homilies into great fame and wealth, Riskin and Capra, in different ways, felt marked by their success and by their awareness of the heightened social responsibilities that went along with it.

While Riskin remained a staunch supporter of FDR, Capra voted for Alf Landon in the 1936 presidential election, fuming over what he saw as an encroachment on his own growing wealth by the social and economic policies of the New Deal. While Riskin tried (unsuccessfully) to get into Spain in 1937 to observe the Civil War, telling the press that Spain was "the focal center of the world, and I would like to be where things are happening," Capra's anti-Communist, pro-Catholic sympathies led him to favor the Fascist revolt led by General Francisco Franco.

And while Riskin was becoming more active in the struggle of the Screen Writers Guild for recognition, Capra was becoming more deeply entangled in the reactionary politics of the Academy of Motion Picture Arts and Sciences.

He had little success trying to persuade fellow directors to support the Academy. Turning down Capra's invitation to join on July 31, 1935, director Frank Tuttle told him that the studios had too much influence in the Academy to make it a legitimate all-industry organization. Capra in his reply on August 14 contended that the Academy was merely a forum for bringing both sides together, and claimed that it had been more useful to the rank-and-file than to the studio bosses, toward whom he professed distaste.

Capra's election to the Academy presidency on October 9, 1935, came

at a time when the moribund organization was largely discredited among
the ranks of the Hollywood creative community. It was on December 23
that twelve of his fellow directors (including Frank Tuttle) met in King
Vidor's house and contributed $100 each to form the Screen Directors
Guild, over the bitter opposition of the studio bosses, who had tried to use
the Academy to co-opt the Hollywood labor movement.

"It was tough to get important directors in because they had a lot to
lose, big salaries to lose—the bigger the directors, the more reluctant they
were," said Rouben Mamoulian, who joined the guild and its board the
following month. Vidor, who was elected as the guild's first president,
recalled in a 1977 interview with Hollywood labor historian Mitch Tuchman, "When you'd talk to somebody, they'd say, 'Well, this is a
Communist-inspired thing.' That's what you hear a lot of—'Communist-
inspired.' . . . [T]here were certain directors who were being such rugged
individualists that they were holding out, key directors."

Capra, who prided himself in his defiance toward what he felt were
communistic tendencies in the Hollywood labor movement, was instinctively antipathetic to organized labor, and he did not identify his interests
with those of other directors in the formative days of the SDG when the
founders were trying to sign up enough members to force the producers to
the bargaining table. He was already rich and successful, and he wanted
to protect his position in the Hollywood establishment, to curry favor with
the studio bosses by running a company union. In the uncut manuscript of
his autobiography, he even drew a comparison between himself and Sammy
Glick in Budd Schulberg's archetypal Hollywood novel *What Makes Sammy
Run?*

The purpose of the SDG, in Mamoulian's words, was "to lift the position of the average director." The average director in those days was
handed a script a day or two before the start of shooting and was kept out
of the cutting room. The guild wanted the director to have more voice in the
preparation of the script and participation in the entire cutting process. It
also sought to curtail the increasingly common "unit" system of assigning
more than one director to a picture, and to counteract the growing role of
the associate producer as a buffer between the director and the studio
head, a trend which spurred the realization of the guild's founders that the
director's authority was being eroded.

A standard minimum contract establishing wages and working conditions and arbitration procedures was the guild's objective. Most of the
founders of the guild, Mamoulian said, "did not need that contract because
their compensation was way beyond any minimums and their authority was

close to independent at the big studios. But the rest of the directors were all underpaid because we had no minimum salary and no union. And not only were they underpaid, but because they were underpaid, their authority was very limited in making films. . . . The ultimate purpose was better films. We were thinking about the quality of films."

On January 28, Capra, the archconservative Cecil B. DeMille, and three other members of the Academy's directors branch held an executive committee meeting to discuss a proposal by the branch's "conservative wing" to preempt the SDG by formulating, for the first time, a code of working conditions for directors, similar to the code the Academy had tried to persuade the writers to accept. The idea failed to achieve a majority. The individual votes are not recorded, but of the other three participants in the meeting, two (Clarence Brown and W. S. Van Dyke II) joined the SDG that month, and a third (Norman Taurog) joined in April. Like Vidor, the three dissidents also were MGM directors, yet Capra claimed in 1985, "The MGM guys, all of 'em, were against the Directors Guild, because they had great big salaries. Those people I held in complete disdain."

The Academy was in "bad repute," Vidor recalled, so with "every membership application that was signed, we also gave them an application to resign from the Academy. [Eventually] we had about 150 to 200 resignations from the Academy in the safe-deposit box which we never used, we finally destroyed. We didn't have to use them."

The new president of the Academy wrote in his memoirs that he took the job because the "little man" had inspired him to put the good of the community ahead of his personal ambition. But the fact was that having worked so hard to win his Oscar, which he considered his passport to equality with the lords of Hollywood, Capra was not about to stand by and see it mocked and rendered worthless along with the Academy's archaic labor agreements: "I took it upon myself to keep it going." Grim as the situation seemed at the time, however, Capra's memory exaggerated it.

"It was a one-man show," he claimed. "It sounds so ridiculous, too me-meish to tell you. There's also a point at which people get tired of hearing this—'Jesus, did he do everything?' The truth is that I *did* everything."

He further stated that there were only forty members left in the Academy when he became president, and that the studios had virtually abandoned the Academy after it proved ineffective at keeping Hollywood labor in line.

The Academy claimed about 800 members shortly after Capra became president, and the same number at the time of the 1937 Academy Awards. That number probably was somewhat inflated, but in his history of the

Academy, Pierre Norman Sands wrote that the membership never fell below 400 during Capra's five years as president. The studios did cut back on their financial support of the embattled Academy, but largely through Capra's urging they never entirely failed to recognize the publicity value of the Oscars.

Although Capra called the Academy "a one-man show," the executive secretary during Capra's presidency, who handled many of the day-to-day functions, was Donald Gledhill. His wife, Margaret Buck Gledhill (later Margaret Herrick), was an unpaid staff volunteer in the Capra years, running, among other things, the Academy library, which now bears her name. "She was the one," Capra declared in a less egocentric moment. "We counted on her."

The Academy still arbitrated its actors' agreement, and it adopted a new writers' agreement at the same board meeting at which Capra was elected president. That agreement did little to challenge the status quo (it still allowed producers the final control over screen credits, a key issue for the writers), and the stubborn move only widened the schism between the Academy and the SWG, which called for writers to boycott the 1936 Academy Awards ceremony.

The guilds were not mollified by such changes in the Oscar voting procedures as taking the best-picture nominations from the hands of the producers and giving them to the entire membership or by the Academy's hiring of the accounting firm of Price Waterhouse to count the ballots. Two days before the March 5 banquet, James Cagney, Paul Muni, and Gary Cooper sent telegrams to their fellow performers asking them to stay home. "It was either that or give the group some tacit recognition," Cagney explained. Capra scrambled frantically behind the scenes to talk the studios into pressuring their contract personnel to defy the boycott, which an Academy spokesman blasted as "childish and petty." The studio bosses sent telegrams ordering their stars to attend, but the tactic backfired by causing more to support the boycott.

Faced with disaster, Capra pulled a rabbit out of the hat. He suggested giving an honorary Oscar to D. W. Griffith, who had been languishing in alcoholic obscurity, virtually forgotten by the industry he had almost singlehandedly created. "We used him," Capra admitted. "But we had to have a hell of a drawing card to keep the Academy alive, to keep the lights burning. We didn't know where he was. We finally found him in a Kentucky saloon. It took a little doing but he finally agreed. And strangely enough, he did bring the crowd in. Everybody was anxious to see D. W. Griffith and pay homage to him."

But Capra's claim that the boycott failed was a considerable overstatement. The Academy managed to turn out a crowd of about 1,000 at the Biltmore Hotel, with tickets "liberally distributed to secretaries and others on the various lots," *Variety* reported. Capra packed his own table with friends and colleagues, including Robert Millikan, Myles Connolly, Jo Swerling, and Robert Riskin. But few stars or other prominent writers and directors attended. The only major stars there were Norma Shearer, brought by her husband, Irving Thalberg, whose studio collected the best-picture Oscar for *Mutiny on the Bounty*; Bette Davis, placated with an Oscar for *Dangerous*; and Victor McLaglen, honored for his performance in *The Informer*. But the screenwriter of *The Informer*, Dudley Nichols, and its director, John Ford, both prominent in their guilds, failed to appear to accept their Oscars, although Ford later accepted his in private and denied that he had intended to snub the Academy.

A few days later Nichols explained in an open letter to the Academy: "I am aware that to bestow awards for cinematic achievement is a most academic and praiseworthy function. . . . But three years ago I resigned from the Academy and, with others, devoted myself to organizing the guild because I had become convinced that the Academy was at root political, that it would not be made to function for the purposes to which it had been dedicated, and that in any major disagreement between employed talent and the studios it would operate against the best interests of talent."

"If that's the way they felt about it," Capra shrugged in 1985, "I'm not going to argue about it. It was not a thing to press people about."

But in his public reply to Nichols at the time, Capra's anger barely could be contained: "Membership has no connection with the Academy Awards and never has had during the eight years they have been conferred. . . . The balloting does not in any way take into account the personal, political or economic views of the nominees nor the graciousness with which they may be expected to receive the recognition."

The handwriting was on the wall for the Academy. To buttress its sagging membership ranks, and to counter demands by SAG, the SWG, and the Screen Playwrights for the sole right to vote on the awards in their categories, it set up a fifty-member committee from its five branches to make the major nominations, and the final Oscar voting was thrown open to the entire membership of the unions and guilds, including the Screen Playwrights, about 15,000 people in all (a change that would not be rescinded until 1946). Still, Capra had to overcome the guilds' resistance to cooperate in distributing ballots: "We practically kissed their asses to get them to stay in the Academy, writers and everyone else."

But another threatened boycott of the Academy Awards in 1937 was averted only by the Academy's decision to remove itself from labor-management affairs. With IATSE craftsmen now covered by a five-year closed-shop agreement, SAG on the verge of winning recognition, and the SWG and the Screen Playwrights approaching their final showdown, the Academy was bowing to the inevitable. Now that it truly "dealt with small problems—it dealt with prizes," as Capra had claimed it had all along, he was reduced to being what Chet Sticht called "a figurehead." But he clung to the presidency, which still had its uses. Following his reelection on October 22, 1936, virtually by royal fiat—the nominations were made by secret ballot, and the minutes stated simply, "Frank Capra was declared elected president"—elections were suspended entirely in 1937 and 1938, and he remained in his post.

Despite the open balloting for the 1937 Oscars, the studios still managed to control the awards. Gary Cooper in *Mr. Deeds* seemed a strong candidate for the best-actor award, but his own studio, Paramount, did not want to promote his chances in a Columbia picture, and Columbia did not have "sufficient trading power among the ballotees to garner the 'Oscar' for him," *Variety* reported. The two studios with the heaviest employee representation in the Academy were MGM and Warner Bros., so the best-acting awards went to Luise Rainer for Metro's *The Great Ziegfeld* and Paul Muni for Warners' *The Story of Louis Pasteur*, with *The Great Ziegfeld* taking the best-picture Oscar.

No one seemed surprised, least of all Capra, when he won his second Oscar on March 4, 1937, for *Mr. Deeds.*

When master of ceremonies George Jessel facetiously called Capra up to assist him with the presentation of the directing award, Capra deadpanned, "I don't see how anybody could look over these nominees for the director of the best picture and pick one out."

"Well," retorted Jessel, "they all may be presidents of the Academy some day and then they can select whom they please."

It was despite his political views, not because of them, that Capra was capable of responding emotionally to the plight of the poor and unemployed in *Mr. Deeds*. The theme of his films, he said later, was that "every person should help those who are below them." But the better part of Capra, the part that was freed when he was directing Riskin's scripts, the part that made him an artist, still retained a visceral sense of empathy with those he thought he had risen above. In his book he confessed to have had "a guilty conscience" in that era because of the disparity between his work and his way of living.

Mr. Deeds always remained Riskin's favorite of the films he wrote for Capra, and it completed the Capra-Riskin formula by adding the element of overt social protest. By portraying Riskin in his book as little more than his stenographer in the writing of *Mr. Deeds,* and the "little man" as their guiding eminence, Capra betrayed the urgency of his need to claim *Mr. Deeds* totally for himself, when everything about his life and Riskin's indicates that the social values of the film stemmed not from him but from Riskin.

But what does *Mr. Deeds* actually "say"? Was it "a genuine PR contribution to the New Deal," as Leif Furhammer and Folke Isaksson wrote in their 1971 *Politics and Film,* or was it, as Raymond Durgnat wrote in 1969, "propaganda for a moderate, concerned, Republican point of view"?

Longfellow Deeds's disdain for riches is partly a reluctance to disturb his comfortable status quo: he is co-owner of a tallow works, has a housekeeper and plenty of free time to play his tuba and write poetry, and he never seems to have given a thought to the Depression outside the Norman Rockwellian village of Mandrake Falls. But Deeds is no one's fool; during his first meeting with the opera's smugly patronizing board of directors, he surprises them by demanding to inspect their books. His eccentricities— his artistic streak, his fascination with fire engines, his tendency to punch out people he doesn't like (a trait he did not possess in the original story)—are signs of what the neighbor ladies at his insanity hearing call the "pixilated" side of Longfellow's personality. Deeds has a strong natural egalitarianism—he objects to his valet helping him put on his pants, ordering, "Don't ever get on your knees again"—yet he is intoxicated by his newfound luxury when he goes to the big city. He displays a childish delight in his surroundings, sliding down the banister of the huge staircase in his mansion and leading a chorus of echoes with three servants in the grand hall (scenes improvised by Capra during the shooting). Up to this point the film is not much different from the many other escapist fantasies of overnight riches with which Hollywood distracted its audience during the Depression.

But the real world forcibly irrupts into Longfellow's fairy-tale existence just as it does into the previous escapist world of Capra's films—in the person of the deranged little man, the farmer (John Wray) who breaks into the mansion to shoot him: "I just wanted to see what a man looked like that could spend thousands of dollars on a party when people around him were hungry. . . . You money-grabbing hick! You never gave a thought to all of those starving people standing in the breadlines not knowing where their next meal was coming from—not able to feed their wife and kids." The farmer breaks down, dropping his gun: "I'm glad I didn't hurt nobody. . . . You get all kinds of crazy ideas. . . . standing there in the breadlines."

Deeds's compassion for the farmer, reflected in several moving close-ups as he watches the man wolf down a meal, is responsible for his impulsive decision to give away most of his fortune (eighteen of his twenty million dollars) to impoverished farmers in ten-acre parcels, providing they work the land for three years—an idea clearly inspired by the social programs of the New Deal.

This recognition by Riskin and Capra that the upper class in America has a responsibility to share the wealth with the lower classes does not mean that the filmmakers are "quasi-communistic," as *Variety*'s Abel Green labeled the viewpoint of the John Wray character. American plutocrats in the twentieth century, typified by John D. Rockefeller, had long recognized the advantage of distributing part of their holdings in charitable enterprises, both as public relations maneuvers and as a means of pacifying the working class. In the same way, the wealthy aristocrat Franklin D. Roosevelt's programs to help the unemployed were the best means of preventing a socialist or Communist revolution in America during the Depression. Longfellow Deeds, then, was no Communist (he still intends to hold on to two million of his dollars), but an unusually enlightened plutocrat, like Roosevelt in the genuineness of his feelings for the poor but like Rockefeller in his stubborn preference for private charity over governmental welfare programs.

Initially reduced to a near-catatonic despair by the insanity charges brought against him by his grasping lawyer, John Cedar (Douglass Dumbrille)—who insists, "If this man is permitted to carry out his plan, repercussions will be felt that will rock the foundation of our entire governmental system"—Deeds finally speaks in his own defense and puts forth a philosophy that President Ronald Reagan would quote before the National Alliance of Business on October 5, 1981, to defend his administration's economic policies and their emphasis on "volunteerism," policies designed to dismantle the social programs created by the New Deal.

"Personally I don't know what Mr. Cedar's raving about," Deeds tells the court. "From what I can see, no matter what system of government we have, there'll always be leaders and always be followers. It's like the road out in front of my house. It's on a steep hill. Every day I watch the cars coming up. Some go lickety-split up that hill on high, some have to shift into second, and some sputter and shake and slip back to the bottom again. Same cars—same gasoline—yet some make it and some can't. And I say the fellows who can make the hill on high should stop once in a while to help those who can't. That's all I'm trying to do with this money—help the fellows who can't make the hill on high."

Gary Cooper was Capra's first and only choice for Longfellow Deeds, but the role of Babe Bennett was trickier to cast.

Despite Capra's claim that actresses were clamoring for the role, three days before the start of shooting in December 1935, Carole Lombard turned it down to do *My Man Godfrey*, and shortly thereafter she also refused a final marriage proposal from Riskin. Capra's message of regret pointedly reminded her that she and other actresses had passed on *It Happened One Night*. A week into the shooting, in near-desperation, Capra gave the role to Jean Arthur, a Columbia contract player who had been drifting from studio to studio since making her feature film debut in John Ford's 1923 *Cameo Kirby*.

A native New Yorker who had started as a photographer's model and had taken her acting name from Jeanne d'Arc and King Arthur (her real name was Gladys Greene), she was a quirky thirty-five-year-old woman who identified emotionally with Peter Pan ("because he was a rebel"), fought for unconventional roles ("I didn't play just a wife who made everything nice for the fellow when he came home"), fiercely guarded her private life, and was cursed with insecurities that eventually cut short her career. Despite her lovely voice, an indescribable blend of huskiness and girlish vibrato that reminded Capra of Lu's, she had been stagnating in Hollywood since the coming of sound, appearing mostly in programmers, and had fled to the New York stage before Harry Cohn lured her back with a promise of better parts. Before making *Mr. Deeds*, she had appeared in a sparkling gangster comedy written by Riskin and Swerling and directed by Ford, *The Whole Town's Talking*, which prompted *Daily Variety* to write of her in January 1935, "Jean Arthur has a screen personality to be reckoned with. She has plenty of appeal plus a grand comedy sense and handles lines expertly." But her image still seemed amorphous and she had yet to reach true stardom.

Capra had almost directed her once before, in the 1928 MGM silent *Brotherly Love*, but they still had never met until she reported to work on *Mr. Deeds*. Capra wrote that he cast her after chancing to see rushes of a scene she was playing in a Columbia Western with Jack Holt, but that was an impossibility, since the only films she did with Holt, *Whirlpool* and *The Defense Rests*, both were released in 1934, and neither was a Western. Most likely he cast her because of her performance in *The Whole Town's Talking*.

When Capra told Harry Cohn he wanted her, Cohn, according to both Capra and Arthur, scoffed that she was a has-been. But, as Stanwyck had before, Arthur bloomed under Capra's firm but quiet authority, becoming a major star as she released previously untapped qualities in her personality, qualities best described by the other of her two favorite directors, George Stevens (*The More the Merrier* and *Shane*): "Jean Arthur was terribly vulnerable and exposed even under the most ordinary of circumstances, even if she had to stick her hand out into traffic to make a left-hand turn." She became Capra's quintessential leading lady, appearing in three of his last four Columbia films, *Mr. Deeds Goes to Town*, *You Can't Take It With You*, and *Mr. Smith Goes to Washington*.

"Kick her in the ass!" Capra laughed when asked how to direct Jean Arthur. "She's a funny combination of things. You can't get her out of the dressing room without using force. You can't get her in front of the camera without her crying, whining, vomiting, all that shit she does. But then when she *does* get in front of a camera, and you turn on the lights— wow! All of that disappears and out comes a strong-minded woman. Then when she finishes the scene, she runs back to the dressing room and hides."

Joe Walker confirmed that "she stalled and just couldn't bring herself on set to do it. There was nothing wrong with her except insecurity. She couldn't take charge of herself, so Capra would take charge and make her do it, mainly through the tone of his voice. She became the person he wanted her to be on screen."

Arthur admitted that she had such little confidence in herself that though she watched the rushes, she never saw *Mr. Deeds* in its entirety until she watched it with Capra in 1972 at the USA Film Festival in Dallas, when, as he reported, "She cried and thought it a lovely picture."

"Maybe I thought I wasn't any good, but I certainly knew that it was a great picture," she told the author of this book. "The crew felt the same way. We were all just walking on air. On Mr. Capra's set you always thought, 'Something wonderful is going to happen.' When I was crying and working so hard at the end in the courtroom in *Mr. Deeds*, well, it's funny, but I forgot about it being a picture. I mean completely. Now I look up at the screen and my face starts to do the same things. I feel the feeling all over again."

But Capra insisted, "She thought I was the worst director in the world! I didn't look the way she thought a director should look. She thought a director should look like Cecil B. DeMille."

When told of Capra's comment, Arthur exclaimed with an embarrassed grin, "That's crazy! Tell him to shut his big lying mouth or I'll punch his nose in! I think he's making up these stories to make himself happy."

"*Now* she doesn't think I'm the world's worst director," Capra retorted. "She's seen the pictures."

The essential difference between Capra and other directors, she said, was that "he lets you alone more. You never know he's on the set. And you don't hear him, he never raises his voice. Sometimes he'll ask a bunch of electricians up there, 'How did it look?' But he's invisible. He's so tiny you could almost not see him. He's a great director, and he does it seemingly without any effort. He's a very pleasant, good-looking, agreeable man."

"She needs new glasses," Capra responded.

"He seems very modest," Arthur went on. "He understands what you're trying to do, and what you're doing, and if you need some help. He lets you do what you want—he might make a suggestion here and there—but somehow he gets what he wants. His set was free of Cohn and all the other people that bothered us. If anyone showed up, Mr. Capra would call a coffee break and say, 'Come back in half an hour.' Well, half an hour means a tremendous amount of money, so the creeps went. Mr. Capra whittled *me* down three or four times real sharp. Sometimes when I think I'm being funny, nobody thinks so but me, and Mr. Capra would say, 'Come on!' One time I went over and stood up next to him and I said, 'I'm *taller* than you!' I don't think I am, but I puffed myself up when I stood beside him. He was awful mad at that."

Capra usually appeared "unself-conscious" about his shortness and was "almost brash" about it, said the lanky (6'3") Edward Bernds, who felt embarrassed because he towered over the director, who stood 5'7" in his maturity. During the making of *Mr. Deeds*, however, perhaps because of Capra's obvious attraction to Arthur and the sexual tension that her jibe expressed, Capra's latent insecurities about his shortness came pouring out. He called attention to it by posing for a gag photo standing eye to eye with Gary Cooper on a New York street corner, a feat he accomplished by standing on the curb of the set while Cooper stood in the street. "Short men," Capra told Arthur and actress Ruth Donnelly, "try to make themselves attractive to women by doing things." And Capra told Bernds on another occasion, "If Napoleon had been a handsome, six-foot lieutenant of cavalry on the island of Corsica, history would have been different. The girls would have been after him, and he would have stayed there."

Near the end of his life, Cooper thanked Capra for inspiring his finest performances. But at the time they made *Mr. Deeds*, Cooper did not display the warmth toward Capra and the crew which they had been shown by

Gable. "Cooper certainly respected Capra, but he was just taking it as another job, another director," Bernds felt. "He was a cold fish."

Jean Arthur, however, saw beyond his reserve. Even though she thought *Mr. Smith* was a greater film than *Mr. Deeds*, she said, "Jimmy Stewart is marvelous, but Cooper's better. You get to know Stewart too well, and with Gary there are always wonderful hidden depths that you haven't found yet. Stewart is almost too much when he acts; I get tired of his 'uh, uh . . .'—his cute quality. With Cooper it just seems to *happen*. I can't remember Cooper saying much of anything. But it's very comfortable working with him. You feel like you're resting on the Rock of Gibraltar."

Longfellow Deeds's sexual reticence, which Riskin and Capra considerably intensified from the original story, marked a departure for Cooper, whose previous roles had allowed free rein to his natural sexual swagger. Capra would not acknowledge the extent to which he had transformed the actor in his own image, claiming that he simply was following Cooper's own personality: though Cooper was a notorious ladies' man, Capra contended that he seduced women through his apparent shyness (*"They* came to *him"*). *Mr. Deeds* set the pattern for Cooper's subsequent roles, a development which enhanced his public appeal but disturbed critic Pauline Kael, who observed: "Frank Capra destroyed Gary Cooper's early sex appeal when he made him childish as Mr. Deeds. Cooper, once devastatingly lean and charming, the man Tallulah and Marlene had swooned over, began to act like an old woman and went on to a long sexless career— fumbling, homey, mealymouthed." But Capra also was sensitive to deeper feelings than Cooper previously had been allowed to express, and the audience responded to the vulnerability shown by both characters when Babe reads aloud a poem Deeds has written about her, a scene whose emotional power, Riskin said, reflected the director's "Italian sentimentality."

"I knew when I first read the scene that it was corny," Arthur recalled, "and I thought, 'I'm gonna make it so it isn't corny.' I worked and worked on it, and on the day we were going to shoot it, Frank took me aside and said, 'This scene's too corny. It won't go. We might as well cut it out.' I said, 'I've been working on it for three weeks. I wish you would just do it once and see if it's any good.' " She felt the scene avoided corniness partly because she wept while she read Cooper's poem, "because I had abused him so terribly and here was his heart laid out in front of me, and the way I had treated him made me cry, I couldn't help it." Though she remembered her tears coming spontaneously while she rehearsed the scene, the tears were not only in the script but in the original story as well. Capra, however, added a gag that both Arthur and Riskin credited with removing any lingering trace of corn. In the script, after Arthur embraces him, Cooper was to have run off, jumped over an ash can, and hitched a ride on a horse-drawn garbage wagon, singing a joyous duet with the Italian garbageman. Capra eliminated the wagon and had Cooper *trip* over the ash can, making Arthur laugh through her tears on the fade-out.

"No one but [Capra] would have had the nerve to shoot that scene and then have [Cooper] do an old-time Sennett fall over an ash can!" Riskin remarked. "Reading poetry on the screen is dangerous business. Unless it is perfectly done, your audience is likely to laugh. They didn't laugh at that scene, though."

Capra did little other tinkering with the shooting script for *Mr. Deeds* aside from tightening it and changing the locales of a couple of scenes, in one case moving the deranged farmer episode from Deeds's bedroom to the grand hall, underscoring the contrast between Deeds's luxury and the farmer's desperation. He kept enough of the 200-page script to make a 115-minute film, the longest in his career up to that time. Now that he had an Academy Award behind him and was becoming more ambitious in what he wanted to say in his films, he began to loosen some of his former constraints and to abandon the economy he had formerly maintained in his working methods. He no longer took pride in his ability to set 'em up and knock 'em out; he wanted quality, and quality took time and cost money.

"It is difficult to make a good picture quickly anymore," he admitted in 1937, though he probably felt his candor would not hurt him in Hollywood, since the interview was printed only in the Moscow newspaper *Izvestia*. But it was a course that was bound to bring him into head-on collision with Harry Cohn.

Capra boasted that he never went over budget on any of his films, but Chet Sticht laughed at that claim: "He was *always* over budget!" *Mr. Deeds* went 5 percent over budget, by $38,936, coming in at a negative cost of $806,774. Much of the (still modest) overrun resulted from Capra's new penchant for shooting multiple angles and takes, which added five days to the forty-day shooting schedule and used up 150,000 feet of film, a shooting ratio of about fifteen feet of film shot to each foot used in the final cut.

Edward Bernds, who had been with Capra since 1930, immediately noticed this change in the director's shooting habits, describing it in his diary on the second day of shooting: "The Capra method: mechanical— very full coverage of angles, from master shot to individuals—partial to angles shooting *over* foreground people to other (featured) people. Very crisp and decisive in setting up and shooting. His direction: continual emphasis on tempo. Over and over rehearsals, more in the nature of 'drill,' but informalized so that there is no sense of 'ten rehearsals,' 'twenty rehearsals,' or rehearsed until stale.

"Fine use of joking little comments to put players at ease: to [Arthur] Hoyt [playing the lawyer Budington in the firm of Cedar, Cedar, Cedar, and Budington], explaining meekness: 'You're probably the guy who put up all the money for this firm, too.' Capra clichés: 'Think of what we're saying, folks'—'Let it flow a little more smoothly'—or 'Didn't quite have the flow.' Capra never 'acts out' a scene—when he does give an inflection, he gives it diffidently, which is soothing to the actorly ego.

"Outstanding: the way he puts his actors at ease (avoids mental hazards for them) and efficient way he organizes mechanics of shooting."

Bernds added five days later: "Marvel at number of angles Capra can find. He puts his faith in repetition [like William] Wyler, [Josef] von Sternberg. . . . Not much 'direction'—only effort to keep up tempo. When actors blow—hearty laugh puts them at ease." George Bancroft was playing the part of the city editor, and Bernds observed that he was "very declamatory and overprecise in speech. Tell Capra and he says actors 'press' with him. He devises elaborate schemes for making them feel at ease. That's one of the reasons for his many angles."

Compare these precise contemporary descriptions with Capra's later analysis of his method with actors: "I lead people, not direct them. My part is to excite people to do what they can do. The word 'actor' is anathema to me. I'm shooting people who are alive—they don't know what's ahead of them or behind them—I'm shooting people who haven't read their parts.

"The principal reason my pictures are good is that they were *not* rehearsed. Actors like to rehearse, because they like to be called actors, and they think that actors must rehearse. I think actors must *not* rehearse.

"We get around a table, four or five actors, and I say, 'Read your part, just read it, don't try to act it.' I notice that some of their words do not fit, so I change them. Sometimes I take the words all out of a scene, and I do it silent. We keep reading until they are more or less settled into who they are. Then I take them on a set that's already lit up, and we go through a first rehearsal of the scene, and that first rehearsal becomes the picture. Certainly I never take more than a rehearsal and one take, unless something goes dastardly wrong—but never a retake."

Capra's stated policy against rehearsals bore some rough resemblance to what Bernds described as his "informalized" rehearsal methods, but the director's claim that he rarely reshot a scene was designed to cover up a sensitive fact about his career after 1935: his growing reputation for self-indulgence, which escalated with his next film, *Lost Horizon,* when, as Sticht put it, "He shot more film than almost any other director ever did." Though Capra's cost overrun on *Mr. Deeds* was not serious, the warning sighs were plain for the frugal Harry Cohn. Shooting fifteen times as much film as he used in the picture and going five days over schedule was Capra's declaration of independence, a forcible test of his power within the Columbia system. Would Cohn continue to allow Capra these special privileges, or would Capra be forced to go elsewhere?

The remarkable new contract he had wrested from Columbia disproved Capra's later claim that "whatever they wanted to pay me, I didn't give a damn," and he was telling only a half-truth when he said that the relative creative freedom he enjoyed under Cohn was worth "much more than any money." His freedom was the tie that continued to bind him to Columbia despite the fact that he was "being offered an awful lot of money else-where," but he still chafed under Cohn's control, loose as it was, and he was torn between his desire for quality and his desire for big money. The proof that his concern for quality was greater was that with his profit participation, cost overruns put his own financial interests in jeopardy, but it was a gamble Capra was willing to take to further his leaping ambitions.

Mr. Deeds was released on April 12, 1936, to great popular and critical acclaim. Unlike his previous Columbia pictures, it was sold separately to exhibitors, not lumped in with other studio releases, and it was carried on the books as an even bigger hit than *It Happened One Night,* bringing in film rentals of $1,040,767 in its first release and $102,504 in its reissue (total rentals as of October 1985 amounted to $3,524,926). But Capra fumed over what he thought was Columbia's practice of charging items against the costs of his pictures which should have been absorbed in studio overhead. "Columbia would refloor a stage and charge it to Capra," Joe Walker said. "There always were little things like that going on," Chet Sticht agreed. "But that's how all those companies did business." A more serious disagreement over the *Mr. Deeds* money occurred a few months after the film's release, when Capra was shooting *Lost Horizon.* One day at rushes Al Keller witnessed a shouting match between Capra and Cohn in a projection room after Capra accused Columbia of underreporting the rentals on *Deeds,* a charge the director was never able to prove.

"Get rich, get famous—and then get even," says a character in *The Miracle Woman.*

Capra and Riskin followed the last part of that formula in *Mr. Deeds* by venting their spleen against the New York intelligentsia. Though their films generally had been treated rather well by the critics, if not as seriously as they would have liked, they had been stung by the faint praise some New York critics gave *It Happened One Night*, and they found *Mr. Deeds* an ideal vehicle to get some of their own back. In addition to the film's satire of the snobbish opera crowd and its scathing attack on the unscrupulousness of the New York press, Riskin and Capra gave Longfellow Deeds an impassioned defense of the notion of popular culture, and, by implication, their own work. After the writers at the round table in Tullio's posh Italian restaurant ("Eat with the Literati") mock his writing of greeting-card verse that "wrings the great American heart," he tells them: "It's easy to make fun of somebody if you don't care how much you hurt him. . . . I know I must look funny to you, but maybe if you went to Mandrake Falls, you'd look just as funny to us, only we wouldn't laugh at you and make you feel ridiculous, because that wouldn't be good manners. I guess maybe it *is* comical to write poems for postcards, but a lot of people think they're good. Anyway, it's the best I can do."

Deeds bashes a couple of his detractors on the way out the door, and if the attack on the highbrows was partially calculated to beat the New York critics into submission, it only partially succeeded. The New York Film Critics picked *Mr. Deeds* as best picture of 1936, on the second ballot, over Fritz Lang's *Fury*, but snubbed Capra himself, who received only one vote on the first ballot for best director before the prize was given to Rouben Mamoulian for *The Gay Desperado*. The New York reviews failed to reflect a consensus on *Mr. Deeds*: Frank S. Nugent of the *Times* called it "another shrewd and lively comedy," but Bland Johaneson in the *Daily Mirror* inexplicably called it "a program picture" and the *American*'s anonymous reviewer objected to the mixture of comedy and "some pretty serious business about the Depression"; Kate Cameron of the *Daily News*, on the other hand, said it was a "wholly delightful story" with "social implications that give the tale grip and substance."

Some of the most ardent praise for the film must have sounded a little foreign to Capra. The left-wing publication *New Theatre*, which had disparaged *It Happened One Night*, hailed *Mr. Deeds* as "a tremendous advance" in the social consciousness of Hollywood. Writing of John Wray's farmer, Robert Stebbins called it "the first time in the movies we have been given a sympathetic, credible portrait of a worker, speaking the language of workers, saying the things workers all over the country say." When the film reached London in September, Paul Holt of the *Daily Express* placed the director between a pair of strange bedfellows: "Frank Capra of Hollywood is as big potentially a political force in the States as Father Coughlin and Franklin Delano Roosevelt."

It remained for Graham Greene, then film critic of *The Spectator*, to write the most eloquent assessment of the virtues of *Mr. Deeds* and of the Capra-Riskin films in general—though Greene, an early auteurist, neglected the screenwriter's contribution: "*Mr. Deeds* is Capra's finest film (it is on quite a different intellectual level from the spirited and delightful *It Happened One Night*), and that means it is a comedy quite unmatched on the screen. For Capra has what Lubitsch, the witty playboy, has not: a sense of responsibility, and what Clair, whimsical, poetic, a little precious and *à la mode*, has not, a kinship with his audience, a sense of common life, a morality: he has what even Chaplin has not, complete mastery of his medium, and that medium the sound-film, not the film with sound attached to it. . . . I do not think anyone can watch *Mr. Deeds* for long without being aware of a technician as great as Lang employed on a theme which profoundly moves him: the theme of goodness and simplicity manhandled in a deeply selfish and brutal world."

Those few critics who grumbled about the film's politics made no impact on its popularity. Capra showed no sign of alarm over being accused of Communist sympathies; on a trip to the U.S.S.R. with Riskin in 1937, Capra blithely accepted the Soviet praise of what *Izvestia*'s translator called *Mr. Dietz Goes to Town*. And whether in England or America, the director made no public objection to being taken as a New Deal propagandist. Doing so would have been inopportune while *Mr. Deeds* was being swept along by the same emotional landslide FDR enjoyed in 1936 over Alf Landon.

Hardly anyone, least of all Capra, paid much attention to a lone British voice, that of the BBC and NBC journalist and film critic Alistair Cooke, who told his radio audience: "Capra's is a great talent all right, but I have the uneasy feeling he's on his way out. He's starting to make movies about themes instead of about people."

*L*ost Horizon was a colossal act of hubris, a self-inflicted wound that caused lasting damage to Capra's career.

The man who claimed in 1985 that he had "*never* gone over budget—not one penny" shot for ten months and spent $2,026,337.01 of Columbia's money ($776,337.01 in excess of the original budget authorized by Harry Cohn) producing a film that took more than five years to earn back its cost, which, including prints and advertising, came to $2,626,620, by far the most Columbia had ever spent on a film. The *Lost Horizon* debacle caused a grave financial crisis for the studio, and the tensions it engendered broke the partnership not only between Capra and Cohn but between Capra and Riskin as well. Their film was little more successful aesthetically than financially. They lost sight of the characters and the wispy plot in a haze of debatable but unexplored philosophic abstractions and in a distracting succession of handsome but vacuous images.

"Nothing reveals men's characters more than their Utopias," wrote Graham Greene in his *Spectator* review. ". . . This Utopia closely resembles a film star's luxurious estate in Beverly Hills; flirtatious pursuits through grape arbors, splashings and divings in blossomy pools under improbable waterfalls, and rich and enormous meals. . . . It is a very long picture, this disappointing successor to *Mr. Deeds*, and a very dull one as soon as the opening scenes are over."

Columbia gritted its teeth and advertised the white elephant as "Frank Capra's Greatest Production," even as Cohn heavily cut the picture against Capra's wishes, precipitating a bitter, months-long legal struggle. After its uneventful general release, Capra added a complaint that Columbia was no longer even mentioning his name in the trade ads. The myth Capra later concocted, however, was that it was his own brilliant recutting that had saved "a completely unreleasable picture."

"My independence is an extremely relative conception," a chastened Capra admitted to *Izvestia* on his Russian trip in the uneasy period after the opening of *Lost Horizon* but before its general release. "So long as I make pictures which have great success and bring large profits to our 'bosses,' I enjoy relative freedom in selection of themes, stories, actors. They let me spend more money on my pictures than they do other directors. But I have only to make one unsuccessful or even mediocre picture, and my 'independence' will be lost."

When he quoted from that interview in his autobiography, Capra eliminated the sentence about his freedom to spend money.

The budget Harry Cohn first authorized on *Lost Horizon* was $1.25 million, and even that would have made it the most expensive film in Columbia's history. Principal photography began on March 23, 1936, and by the time that phase was completed on July 17, the production cost was reported in the trade press to have risen to $1.6 million. "Hope we make a picture again, sometime," Capra joked to his crew when they parted. His first cut was nearly six hours long, and neither he nor the studio knew quite what to do about it. There was talk of releasing the film in two parts, but the idea was deemed impractical. Capra whittled it down to about three and a half hours for the first public preview at Santa Barbara's Granada Theatre on November 22, but a disappointing reception led to more cuts and retakes, the last of which was shot on January 12, 1937. When the film had its premiere in San Francisco on March 2 (a month later than scheduled), Cohn had cut it down to 132 minutes. "Capra objected, but he couldn't do anything about it," recalled Dimitri Tiomkin, who composed the score for the film. "He walked out. He didn't even attend the premiere." While Capra was overseas, Cohn cut it by another 14 minutes for the general release in September—making that version about 90 minutes shorter than Capra's first preview cut.

Capra wrote that Cohn *originally* authorized a budget of $2 million on *Lost Horizon* and that he did so without even reading the Hilton novel, making his decision on the director's verbal outline. Capra's account did not mention that Riskin had first brought him the novel or that they had showed it to Cohn. According to Capra, Cohn's nearly blind faith proved him to be almost recklessly daring, since $2 million was "about half of Columbia's whole budget for the year." Columbia's total expenses in fiscal 1937, however, totaled $17,546,000. Cohn was not as reckless as Capra made him seem, though for the head of a small studio which was trying to remain economical while still competing for major status, he was taking a considerable risk. Once Capra began shooting, Cohn had little choice but to keep pouring more money into the film and hope that Capra's artistry would justify the mounting expense, which Chet Sticht aptly characterized as "outrageous."

Though *Lost Horizon* eventually turned a profit, with rentals amounting to $5,295,546 and net proceeds of $1,048,337 through October 1985, it was in the red until its 1942 reissue. Its impact on Columbia's overall performance was reflected in the studio's $1,134,607 drop in net profits between fiscal 1937 and fiscal 1938 (the period during which it went into general release), from $1,318,000 to $183,393, and Columbia's subsequent decline in fiscal 1939 to net profits of just $2,046. Not only was *Lost Horizon* itself disappointing, but the fact that it was Capra's only new film for the twenty-nine-month period between April 1936 and September 1938 effectively deprived Columbia of its most dependable moneymaker, the one person who, as Bob Thomas wrote in *King Cohn*, could produce "that magical attraction which could buoy a whole season of Columbia films."

The shooting of *Lost Horizon* took one hundred days and nights, thirty-four days in excess of the original schedule. Joe Walker and the rest of Capra's crew shot an entire picture, *Theodora Goes Wild*, for director Richard Boleslawski during one of the breaks in the production of *Lost Horizon*, while Capra was resting in the High Sierras, and another picture, *When You're in Love*, directed by Robert Riskin, while Capra was editing *Lost Horizon*.

Capra's filming of snow scenes and airplane interiors inside the downtown Los Angeles Ice and Cold Storage Warehouse, using machine-made snow, helped bring a level of physical credibility to the fantastic tale in combination with the documentary footage taken in the Himalayas, the Alps, and the High Sierras, but the ice house shooting proceeded with exasperating slowness (one shot of an avalanche required four hours to refill the snow bins), and the cold caused havoc with the film and equipment. Most of the exteriors on Stephen Goossón's lavish Shangri-La set, built on Columbia's Burbank Ranch smack up against the traffic and telephone poles of Hollywood Way, had to be shot at night, so that the background would not show (glass shots were used to create the illusion of a mountain setting). The Tibetan village scenes were filmed on the MGM back lot, but Capra also took his company on location to Tahquitz Canyon in the mountains above Palm Springs, for the horseback-riding scene; the Lucerne Dry Lake near Victorville, for the refueling scene; and Sherwood

Forest, now Westlake Village, forty miles north of Los Angeles, for the scenes taking place in the Valley of the Blue Moon.

The new tendency Capra had exhibited on *Mr. Deeds* to shoot multiple takes and angles escalated into a near mania for perfection on *Lost Horizon*. The records kept by Al Keller, Joe Walker's first assistant cameraman, show that Capra used about 1.1 million feet of film—a shooting ratio of about 93 to 1, and more than seven times the footage Capra had used on *Mr. Deeds*. "Frank used to say 'Film is cheap,' " Sticht recalled, "and *Lost Horizon* was a beautiful picture visually, but sometimes you'd wonder why the hell he was doing it so many times. Maybe it was overprotecting himself, overinsuring that he would get a good scene. There were constant confrontations with Cohn about it."

Capra covered almost every scene from several angles, often using multiple cameras. "Shoot in true Capra style," Edward Bernds noted in his diary of a dinner table scene involving Ronald Colman and four other actors on May 5: Capra filmed the entire four-minute scene from eight different angles, using two cameras each time, consuming about 6,000 feet, more than one hour, of film. On another day alone, July 15, Capra shot 17,000 feet of film (more than three hours) of Sam Jaffe doing his monologues as the High Lama, which took a total of six days to shoot and which Capra later reshot in their entirety two more times (once with Walter Connolly playing the role). The Lama scenes accounted for about forty minutes of the film's six-hour assembly, though they were trimmed to twelve minutes in the original release print. Such profligacy seldom had been seen in Hollywood since the wildest days of Erich von Stroheim, whose directing career had been terminated as a result.

While Capra was making his intended masterpiece, Harry Cohn was slowly going crazy.

"Right from the jump when I was there," said Sticht, "Capra could do whatever he wanted, and Cohn had sense enough to leave him alone. But Cohn would beef about the cost, because Capra's movies cost more than Cohn had agreed." "When Frank Capra made a film, money was no object to him," said Joe Finochio, who recorded the sound for *Lost Horizon*, "but they were always saying, 'Oh, my God, they're going over budget.' And after they put all that money into *Lost Horizon*, they were afraid they were going to go broke." Capra knew that *Lost Horizon* "could have meant [Cohn's] downfall," since it so drastically intensified the ongoing arguments between Jack Cohn's fiscally conservative New York head office and Harry's more adventurous Hollywood operation, which had gone so far out on a limb to gratify the director's artistic ambitions. At one point, Finochio recalled, Harry Cohn had to assemble all of the studio employees on a soundstage and ask them not to cash their paychecks for a week: "He said that the Bank of America was going to take over. They blamed it on Capra because Capra spent a lot of money, and there was no money left. Everybody cooperated, because we were one big family, and Harry Cohn was the whole damn studio. If it wasn't for him the place would still have been Gower Gulch."

Cohn was torn by *Lost Horizon* because of his respect for Capra, because the two of them had had such a long roll of the dice together. "Talent being left alone—reliance on the man—that was Cohn's gambling instinct," said Cohn's protégé Sidney Buchman, who contributed to the script of *Lost Horizon*.

Capra liked to boast that *Lost Horizon* was "one of my great films," but in a more candid moment during the late 1950s, in a Columbia University oral history conducted by Arthur B. Friedman, he put his finger squarely on what was wrong with it: "Although it's been said that it's one of my best pictures, I thought that the main part of the film should have been done better somehow. I got lost in architecture, in Utopia, in the never-never land, and it was only toward the end of the picture that I got back on the track with human beings. . . . This is common for one who wants to exploit a theme, and gives the theme too much a part in the story. I wavered several times. I shot several endings before I decided how to end it."

The previous Capra-Riskin films had thrived on conflict, on clashes between individuals from different social classes, and, when they were at their best, on the inner battle between self-interest and social responsibility. But these elements were submerged in their depiction of Shangri-La. Avoidance of conflict was its raison d'être, an attitude that Hilton proposed as a contemplative alternative to the bellicosity of the modern world but in the film seemed more like escapist avoidance of the urgent issues of the times. The essentially static nature of life in the Capra-Riskin Utopia dictated a series of lifeless conversations and compositions, which the director desperately tried to enliven with his endless reshooting.

Some of the more thoughtful overtones of the *Lost Horizon* script were, however, lost on the cutting room floor. Capra refused to discuss the changes imposed on the film before the premiere—he claimed that the disagreements with Cohn arose only over the recutting of the general release version, not the version that was premiered on March 2—but from the director's comments on the film's recutting it was clear that his most painful losses had to do with Colman's character, Robert Conway.

Both Riskin and Capra identified strongly with the character, who underwent significant changes from the Hugh Conway of the book. Once again they wanted to deal with the "catastrophe of Success." In Hilton's tale, Conway is a relatively insignificant figure on the world stage, a British consul in the Far East, but in the film he is inflated into a world-famous soldier and statesman, an indispensable man, the man next in line for the post of foreign secretary, "Churchill and all the other great Englishmen rolled into one," as Joe Walker put it. Riskin and Capra had planned also to depict Conway as a man profoundly disillusioned with political life and British imperialism, giving him a much deeper reason for welcoming the refuge of Shangri-La.

In the script, there was a repeated emphasis on the duality of Conway's character, on the unreconciled clash between his idealistic sentiments and the cold sterility of his public duties. Conway had a drunken speech on the airplane during his and the others' abduction to Tibet in which he railed against the hypocrisy of his life and against the racism of the British Empire: "Did you make that report out yet? Did you say we saved ninety white people? Good. Hooray for us! Did you say that we left ten thousand natives down there to be annihilated? No. No, you wouldn't say that. They don't count." Though the scene was included in the original and general release versions, it was cut by Columbia when the film was reissued in 1942 as *Lost Horizon of Shangri-La*, at a time when the world war made unacceptable Conway's cynicism and his mockery of war and diplomacy ("Everybody wants something for nothing—if you can't get it with smooth talk, you send your army in"). Capra later remarked that the whole story was contained in that speech on the airplane by Conway, and that the film made little sense to him without it. (When the American Film Institute undertook its 1973–1986 restoration of the film, it located a 16mm print of the scene, among others, and put it back where it belongs.)

The evacuation from the burning city of Baskul, which opens the film in its post-preview versions, seems so effective partly because it contains what most of the other scenes lack—a sense of dynamism and conflict, a powerful visual metaphor for the chaotic world Conway is leaving behind. Where the film founders is in the philosophical alternative it proposes to that chaos; Conway's superficial attraction to Oriental mysticism is more a vague desire to escape the excesses of Western life than a true desire to explore an alternate set of cultural and moral values. The film's Shangri-La is hardly an alternative at all, only a prettified, tidied-up reflection of Western values.

Despite Conway's avowed distaste for British imperialism, *Lost Horizon* is essentially an imperialist fantasy. Shangri-La is a white-run aristocracy (the High Lama is actually a Belgian priest, Father Perrault) supported by the labor of the Tibetan peasants in the Valley of the Blue Moon below the lamasery. There are locks on the doors inside Shangri-La, and no one who enters from the outside world is permitted to leave without the approval of the High Lama or his assistant Chang (H. B. Warner). Conway is brought there not by chance, as in the book, but is kidnapped to take the place of the dying High Lama; in the original cut of the film, it was done at the instigation of Shangri-La's white schoolmarm, Sondra (Jane Wyatt).

Conway's alacrity in accepting his role as head of the little kingdom in the original cut stemmed from his disenchantment with the inequity of Western society and its colonial life, but in the shortened versions seems to reflect merely a dislike for his culture's messiness and ungovernability: his ethics are not those of a mystic but rather those of an efficient and relatively humane colonial administrator. Since life in Shangri-La contains so little dramatic conflict, Riskin and Capra felt compelled to overemphasize the clash between Conway and his younger brother, George, who hates the place, finally persuading Robert to leave with him. In the book the character is not Conway's brother but an immature young colleague named Mallinson. The family ties were added to make more plausible the idea that, after becoming so enraptured over Shangri-La, Robert Conway would leave it, a serious dramatic flaw in the story that Capra and Colman barely managed to skirt with a scene which Riskin built up by rewriting during production and which Capra shot and reshot. Though he tested David Niven for the part of George, Capra mistakenly thought him too shallow and gave it to the American actor John Howard, who played the role unconvincingly and with a strident monotony.

Riskin and Capra gave George a love interest, Maria, played by the Mexican dancer Margo (Capra also tested Rita Cansino, later known as Rita Hayworth). Maria appears young but is actually an old woman, a fact that becomes appallingly clear to George only after they leave Shangri-La's protective environment. In a speech Riskin considerably expanded from his original, Maria's hatred for Shangri-La convinces George and then Robert Conway to leave: she says the High Lama has been "insane for years," and accuses the apparently benevolent Chang of harboring pathological sexual jealousy. This scene offers an unintentionally provocative glimpse into another viewpoint on this dubious Utopia, and it suggests a dramatic idea which, if explored more fully, might have rescued the film from its simple-minded concept. Instead, Riskin and Capra accounted for Maria's subversion and deceit simply by making her a Russian.

*   *   *

The aspect of the script, and of the shooting, which caused the most trouble was the High Lama. His part originally was planned as one enormously protracted scene, but at the very end of production it was broken into two scenes between Sam Jaffe and Colman; an expository interlude was added, in one of the final retakes, of H. B. Warner, rather than Jaffe, telling Colman of the High Lama's background. Those scenes were rewritten several times during the shooting, more than any other scenes in the film, and Capra not only employed two actors as the High Lama but at least two writers on those scenes as well.

Riskin wanted Capra to cast Walter Connolly, the versatile character actor who had served them so well in *Lady for a Day, It Happened One Night,* and *Broadway Bill,* as the High Lama. The gruff, portly Connolly was an offbeat casting choice for a monk more than two hundred years old, but Riskin argued that the Lama should seem well preserved and hearty rather than shrunken and feeble and not so much ascetic as "a kindly Franciscan sort of fellow, gently and indulgently appreciating the wayward world," as a *New York Times* interviewer explained Riskin's conception. But Capra, according to the *Times,* "wanted a sterner sort, a little more positive in his concern about the way of the world, a Paul of the Himalayas. Capra had his way." (One suspects the hand of the dogmatic Myles Connolly, who contributed to the script.)

The part was offered to two veteran actors, A. E. Anson and Henry B. Walthall, but both died that June, before they could film it. Sam Jaffe, who was younger, was unsuccessful in his first go at the High Lama, both because the makeup was unconvincing and because his voice was barely audible, though his delivery of the lines was letter-perfect. Before the first public preview, Capra listened to Riskin, who now had Cohn firmly on his side, and reshot the High Lama scenes on October 9 and on October 29 through November 2 with Connolly, who wore little makeup other than long white hair and beard, looking "like Santa Claus," editor Gene Milford told Capra. Capra told Bernds on the set that it was his idea to recast the Lama as "hearty, healthy, cheerful" instead of "aged, spiritual [and] feeble." But Keller learned otherwise: "Capra didn't want to do it at all. It was *Cohn* who wanted him to do it." Capra's resentment of this fiat ran so deep that he always denied vigorously that he had shot the part with Connolly, even though photographs exist of him directing Connolly in the scene. Both versions were tested with studio preview audiences, and the negative reaction enabled Capra to talk Cohn into letting him shoot it again with Jaffe, using more crepuscular lighting and more realistic makeup (by MGM's

Jack Dawn), on December 21 through 23, barely two months before the world premiere.

Riskin was angered by Capra's refusal to take his advice on the High Lama. The argument crystallized his awareness of how little say he had over their films, and it caused the first open rift between the two men after more than four years of collaboration.

The problem had been welling up since *It Happened One Night,* when Capra began to dominate the limelight and make public statements implying that he deserved almost as much credit for the writing of their films as Riskin did. Riskin made no such claims about Capra's directing credit, but he was turning an increasingly jaundiced eye toward the director's grandstanding and, according to Fay Wray, he told Capra the films should carry a "Capra-Riskin Films" logo or something similar. It was shortly after the opening of *Lost Horizon* that Riskin told an interviewer, "So little is known of the contribution that the screenwriter makes to the original story." But Capra thought Riskin should be satisfied with his screenwriting credit, and Riskin decided it was time to direct his own scripts.

Shortly before Capra shot the High Lama scenes with Sam Jaffe for the first time, Riskin insisted that Cohn honor a clause in his contract providing for him to direct his first feature. Cohn, who had been reluctant to break up the team, previously had offered Riskin only quickies to direct, and Riskin had refused, waiting for a better opportunity. Cohn handed him Grace Moore, who had proved to be temperamental, overweight, and a growing box-office liability. Riskin was unenthusiastic about the idea, but he nevertheless pushed ahead with the film, which he started that fall. Cary Grant was Moore's costar in the romantic comedy, released as *When You're in Love.*

Although Capra and Riskin remained outwardly cordial, such as on the occasion of Capra's visit to the set of *When You're in Love,* the split between them was public knowledge as early as June 1936, when it was announced that Riskin would produce and direct his own scripts. Columnist Cameron Shipp, an old friend of Riskin's, predicted that "within a year Riskin will be a better-known director than Capra and that Capra will fade unless he hurries to discover another writing partner as smart as Bob Riskin."

Sidney Buchman was pressed into service in revising the Lama scenes for the retakes with Jaffe in December. After the Santa Barbara preview, Buchman recalled in a 1965 interview with Bob Thomas, "Frank went to the desert to bring *Lost Horizon* back to order. He recast the High Lama with Sam Jaffe. Bob refused, and went east." Capra sent for Buchman and they discussed the new scenes, which the highly politicized Buchman rewrote with a more pointed emphasis on the desperation of the current world situation. Buchman received no credit for his work, but it helped cement his relationship as Capra's new number-one writer.'*

Riskin never directed another film after *When You're in Love*. It was not a success, and Capra could not help gloating about it in his book, implying that Riskin had made a mistake in leaving him. Joe Walker felt that Riskin did "a good job, but not an outstanding one. It's pretty hard to assess the direction from one picture. You learn by experience, and Riskin didn't have enough experience." Buchman, like Capra, had a harsher assessment: "Riskin went into directing and made a film with Cary Grant which applied to the letter all the ideas which had made his comedies famous. It had everything except that little something—and the film was a failure."

Columbia had announced in October 1936 that Capra's next film after *Lost Horizon* would be the life of the Polish composer Frédéric Chopin, with a script by Buchman and Riskin, but now Riskin's name no longer appeared in the announcements of the project. Knowing of Capra's interest in music, Harry Cohn had suggested that he remake a German film about Chopin, *Abschiedswalzer* (*Farewell Waltz*), an idea originally proposed to Cohn by William Wyler, who had not been able to come to terms with Columbia. Capra could see reflections of his own inner conflicts in Chopin's struggles with exile, political responsibility, and artistic ambition, as well as in the composer's ambivalence toward success and his resulting illness, reminiscent of the director's after *It Happened One Night*.

The young Czechoslovakian actor Francis Lederer was proposed by Cohn for the title role in *Frédéric Chopin*. Capra wanted Paul Muni as Chopin's teacher, Joseph Elsner, and the child piano prodigy Leonard Pennario was set to play the ten-year-old Chopin in the opening scenes. Buchman wrote the screenplay while Capra was editing and reshooting *Lost Horizon*. The screenplay was in final form by January 1937, the month it first was scheduled to begin shooting. But the project, which Capra insisted on shooting in color, was held in abeyance during his fight with the studio.

Capra's choice of Buchman to write *Frédéric Chopin*, though partially influenced by studio politics, also reflected the growing influence on the director of the Hollywood Left. Buchman testified before the House Committee on Un-American Activities (HUAC) in 1951 that he became a member of the Communist Party "sometime [in] late '38 or late '37."

---

* *Herbert J. Biberman, a writer-director under contract to Columbia, also contributed to the script of* Lost Horizon.

Although he was not a Party member when he wrote it, Buchman brought his political convictions to the *Chopin* script, responding eloquently to the composer's commitment to the cause of Polish independence. Capra, at the time, did not seem to be bothered by Buchman's politics. He clearly felt the need to deal in his work with the theme of the artist's social responsibility. As a filmmaker wrestling with the necessity of finding "something to say" and as a man who in the late 1930s would become increasingly active in the political arena through his involvement with the Screen Directors Guild, Capra, like Chopin, was feeling an unresolved tension between the demands of art and the demands of politics. With Riskin's help, he had begun to bring the two together in *Mr. Deeds* and *Lost Horizon* before planning to dramatize the conflict with Buchman's help in *Frédéric Chopin*.

Capra regaled many audiences with the story of how he supposedly saved *Lost Horizon* after the Santa Barbara preview simply by throwing the first two reels into the studio incinerator. He said he came to the bold and momentous decision while pacing through the woods around Lake Arrowhead in solitude for two days after the preview audience shocked him by laughing at the picture.

However, according to William H. Rosar's carefully documented 1978 study of the postproduction and Tiomkin's musical score, the opening sequences probably ran no more than a single reel and the preview version probably was shortened not by two reels but by *six reels* (about an hour). Rather than being incinerated, some of the footage in the first reel of the preview version—the montage of Londoners learning of Conway being discovered alive after his escape from Shangri-La and the scene in the London club of Lord Gainsford (Hugh Buckler) telling the story of Conway's attempt to return to the lamasery—wound up being incorporated in the closing sequences of the film. Furthermore, there were numerous cuts made all through the more than three-hour version previewed November 22 in Santa Barbara; the High Lama scenes were reshot for the third time and tightened considerably in the editing; and two endings were filmed before a third and final one was patched together from the existing footage. Capra's account of the preview aftermath, which Keller called a "figment of his imagination," covered up what in fact was a massive overhauling job, of which shortening the opening was but a single, though crucial, part. And that decision may not even have been Capra's.

Columbia's publicity chief Lou Smith recalled the preview: "Capra drove up in Cohn's limo, and they left their coats in the car. The picture went badly, with many walkouts. Capra was so distraught he walked out and went to the train station without his coat, took the train to Los Angeles, and went to Lake Arrowhead to hide out. Cohn returned to the studio and took out the first reel and a half [*sic*]."

Gene Milford had been put on *Lost Horizon* near the end of principal photography to help Gene Havlick cut the mass of film Capra had shot; the editors won Academy Awards for their work on a film of which Havlick despaired at first, saying, "I don't know how I can make it go together." Milford recalled the circumstances of the recutting somewhat differently from both Smith's and Capra's accounts. The decision to drop most of the opening was made on the night of the preview, Milford said, at an impromptu conference held in Cohn's office back at the studio. Smith, who was not present at the meeting, thought the director was not involved in the decision, but Milford clearly remembered Capra being present at the lengthy session, along with Cohn and Riskin. The editor did not recall which of those present had suggested cutting the opening, but he was certain that the final decision was made jointly by Capra *and* Cohn (Cohn, of course, having the right of final cut).

The fact that *Lost Horizon* was previewed with the screwball comedy *Theodora Goes Wild* could not have helped put the Santa Barbara audience into a receptive mood, but "the length was the primary factor," Milford felt. "The audience could have been restless because of the length of the film. I argued desperately against [cutting the opening], because I felt it set the stage better. The entire picture was in retrospect, and it created an excitement, a suspense. I guess I was the only one against cutting it."

Capra claimed to have forgotten how the film originally opened, but both the original assembly and the version at the Santa Barbara preview opened with the first part of what is now the penultimate scene of the film, Gainsford's narrative in the London club. Following the montage of London reactions and newspaper headlines (evidently longer originally), there was an elaborate sequence on board a ship, with the amnesiac Conway being returned to England. Overhearing a pianist (Max Rabinovitz) playing Chopin in the ship's bar, Conway sits at the piano and plays an unknown piece he says he learned from a pupil of Chopin's. When Rabinovitz questions his story, pointing out that Chopin died in 1849, Conway becomes agitated, muttering about Shangri-La, and tries to leave the ship, desperate to recover his lost dream. Gainsford then listens to Conway start to tell him and several others the story of Shangri-La. This dissolved to what is now the beginning of the film, the evacuation from Baskul.

The discarded framing story was to have picked up at the end to show

Conway finishing the tale, saddened by his listeners' disbelief; being locked in his cabin by Gainsford; crawling out a window and jumping ship, running off into the distance. *Then* was to have concluded Gainsford's recounting of Conway's adventures, ending with his famous lines, "Yes, I believe it. I believe it, because I *want* to believe it. Gentlemen, I give you a toast—Here's my hope that Robert Conway will find his Shangri-La! Here's my hope that we *all* find our Shangri-La."

As for the legend of the director throwing the first two reels into the incinerator three days after the preview, "You wouldn't throw nitrate film into an incinerator," Milford observed. "Nitrate film could explode even if it was rolled tightly. It seems unlikely." Whatever the director might have wanted to do, Milford said, "The negative would have been in the vault. And I had the first two reels [of positive print from the preview version] sitting in one of the cabinets in my cutting room for a long time, thinking they might reinstate it."

"Capra kept on changing the picture" all during postproduction, recalled conductor Max Steiner. But Capra and Cohn could not reach agreement on the length of the film. Capra's desperate reshuffling was part of his hope that they could reach a compromise. Another preview, he hoped, would placate the studio chief and settle their differences. But though the second public preview (in San Pedro) was more successful than the first, it was not successful enough for Capra to keep control of the editing.

Cohn "knew it wouldn't work" at more than three hours, recalled MGM screenwriter Frances Marion, whom Cohn called in to suggest ways of tightening the story. In January, Cohn cancelled the film's scheduled February 1 opening and recut the picture. "Cohn thought he was a great cutter," said Buchman. "He often said, 'I'll tell you what's wrong with it. I'll snap it up.'" Apparently disinclined to concede his adversary such power, Capra was reluctant to admit in later years that Cohn had done any cutting before the film's release. *Variety* and *Motion Picture Daily*, however, said the studio chief's recutting was the principal reason behind the lawsuit Capra filed against Columbia that August, ostensibly over other contractual disagreements, and Chet Sticht said the suit was "partly" over the recutting. Cohn, as Marion's account suggests, may have based his objections to the film's length as much on aesthetic grounds as on financial considerations—and as the man responsible to Columbia's stockholders, Cohn could not have ignored his obligation at least to *try* to make a profit with *Lost Horizon*—but Capra did not see it that way.

"The Jewish producers" sabotaged his intended masterpiece, Capra said in 1985, contending that Columbia's decision to cut it in order to give theaters more shows per day, and thus to increase its chances of turning a profit, was purely a show of greed: "They wanted to be the ones to make this picture. I wasn't shooting *lengths*, I was shooting a *picture*. It was a little longer than the usual picture, but it was the best that I could do [in cutting it down]. It wasn't a two-hour picture, but when it played well in the theaters, why fool with it? This the Jewish producers will never understand."

When he lost that fight to Cohn, Capra said, "I could have cut his balls off."

One of the key artistic battlegrounds was the ending. In Hilton's book, Conway turns his back on Shangri-La, becoming one of those who, in the author's memorable line, are "doomed to flee from wisdom and become a hero," but then changes his mind and sets out again to find it. The preview version of the film ended with Conway struggling up a snowy hill as a glow on the horizon seems to guide him toward Shangri-La. That was deemed too indefinite a finale for a film with such doubtful box-office prospects, so Capra on January 12 shot another ending in which a haggard Conway finds Shangri-La, with Jane Wyatt beckoning him onward to the accompaniment of a montage of ringing bells. That version was used in the film's opening engagements, but Riskin argued against such a soppy fade-out, and he and Capra prevailed on Columbia to let them recut it after the film had been playing for several weeks. The final ending dropped Wyatt and simply showed Conway looking toward Shangri-La, concluding with a shot of the lamasery and the orgasmic bell montage (a ringing bell would become Capra's trademark, ending several of his later pictures as well).

Capra's problems with the editing of *Lost Horizon* were the subject of an expert postmortem that November by David O. Selznick. In a New York lecture addressing the question of "just where the directing producer is different from the producer," Selznick used Capra as an example: "The great danger in a producing setup is that the director, being close to the picture, on the set day by day and in the cutting room day by day, has no perspective on the picture as a whole, on its story values, entertainment values, or, least of all, its commercial values. Frank Capra told me recently that he was dissatisfied with *Lost Horizon*. I don't know how many of you saw it, but he felt that if he had had someone to lean on or someone to guide him, someone he could have respected, many of the faults of the picture would have been remedied and the picture would have been much better."

Capra's dispute with Cohn became so bitter that Columbia failed to pay Capra the semiannual $100,000 in salary that was due him on February 6,

1937, Capra charged in his suit. After Columbia ignored his demand for payment, he said, he informed the studio on February 16 that he considered it in breach of contract. Columbia, however, replied in a letter four days later (the day after the film was first shown to the press) that it had *not* refused to make the payment, and a studio lawyer later told the press that Capra had spurned repeated offers of payment to settle the dispute. The studio also contended that it did not owe Capra the money if he would not agree to make another film, as his contract required.

Rumors spread quickly that Capra and Columbia were "at loggerheads," as *The Hollywood Reporter* suggested the day before the world premiere. *Frédéric Chopin* originally had been set to begin shooting that January, but Capra's friend Sidney Skolsky wrote on March 22 that it could not begin until the "feud" was settled; *Chopin* itself was one of the causes of the feud. Columbia's New York office already was alarmed by the potential cost of Capra's next project. Given his new proclivity for high spending in the pursuit of high art, and his insistence that *Chopin* be filmed in color, it was understandable that Columbia worried about letting him loose on a period piece about the largely unhappy life of a classical composer, a subject without obvious box-office potential.* Withholding Capra's salary may have been both a punitive measure to express the studio's wrath over the budget overrun on *Lost Horizon*, and, by linking the refusal to pay the money with the delay in authorizing the start of production on another film, a maneuver to force him back into line.

Nor was Cohn willing to heed Capra's plea to buy him the film rights to the George S. Kaufman–Moss Hart play *You Can't Take It With You*, which Capra saw while in New York for the opening of *Lost Horizon*. Producer Sam H. Harris was demanding $200,000 for the rights to the hit comedy about a family of lovable eccentrics, which won that season's Pulitzer Prize.

Capra took no further action for the moment, letting his lawyers ponder the case and stalling for time in hope that the public response to *Lost*

---

*Despite the claim made to Daily Variety in 1986 by Frank Capra, Jr., that his father had wanted to shoot Lost Horizon in color but had been refused by Columbia, Capra made a public statement to the contrary in 1985. When asked at a screening of Lost Horizon if he had considered making it in color, the director said he had, but then had decided that "it's not going to get any better by somebody squirting ink all over it." "I don't think there was any serious consideration of it," Al Keller confirmed. "Three-strip color was all new, and Capra was having his problems with Columbia over the budget anyway. Joe Walker didn't think it should be photographed in color because this was a fantasy and color would make it too real." Frank, Jr., said his father would approve of the film being colorized, but Frank, Sr., said, "If you'd try to colorize such a picture as this I don't know what the hell you'd get."

Horizon would vindicate him. The early reviews, for the most part, were respectful (*The Hollywood Reporter* calling it "an artistic *tour de force* . . . in all ways a triumph for Frank Capra"; Frank S. Nugent in *The New York Times* hailing it as "a great picture . . . intoxicatingly romantic"), but there were frequent objections to the slow and static nature of the Shangri-La sequences, the overly "modernistic" decor of the lamasery, the liberties taken with Hilton's characterizations, the insipid performances of John Howard and Jane Wyatt, and the makeup of Sam Jaffe, which Nugent found "grotesque." Though most reviewers were duly impressed by the film's physical scope and its aesthetic ambitions, there was an undertone in some reviews of damning with faint praise, and some had harsh criticisms of Capra's pretensions. Otis Ferguson wrote in the *National Board of Review Magazine*, "This film was made with obvious care and expense, but it will be notable in the future only as the first wrong step in a career that till now has been a denial of the very tendencies in pictures which this film represents." *Lost Horizon* opened as a road show—only two performances a day, and tickets sold on a reserved-seat basis, the first Columbia film shown that way—but the early box-office returns were not encouraging.

With the London opening set for late April, Capra decided to take a trip overseas. He felt it would be a good opportunity to promote the film and to distract himself from his unresolved status at the studio while mulling over his future plans. Riskin already was planning to pass through London en route to Spain. They hoped to extend their trip with a visit to the Soviet Union. Sergei Eisenstein and other Soviet filmmakers visiting Hollywood had issued Capra a standing invitation, and the intellectual interest focused on the U.S.S.R. by the Popular Front movement piqued his curiosity as well as Riskin's. Capra wanted to see at firsthand the social experiment he had viewed with ambivalent fascination in his unrealized *Soviet* project.

On March 31 Frank and Lu boarded a train for New York, where they would rendezvous with Riskin before sailing on the *Normandie*. It was reported that Capra would return to Columbia in six weeks to begin production on *Chopin*, and *Variety* reassured Hollywood that while he and Cohn "have had personal differences away from business . . . it is understood these have been patched since."

But in fact Capra felt that he was "in the doghouse" and that his legal differences with the studio "barred" him from working there, at least temporarily. He was afraid it might be forever: "The trouble was that *I* was becoming Columbia Pictures, not Cohn. I knew that I was getting too big. I could see it coming, and I didn't know what the hell to do about it. I thought of many ways in which I could give him the torch—giving him previews and so forth, putting this guy on a pedestal, 'Mr. Cohn' this and 'Mr. Cohn' that—I was trying to build up his ego, because *I* didn't need it. But I couldn't do it without giving away the making of the picture.

"Well, it had to come to a showdown. It had to be Columbia or Frank Capra.

"This was silly, because everything was going fine. They were beautiful pictures, and all the pictures were making money. But ego stepped in. Inevitable. And I knew it had to happen, because he was that kind of a guy. I just could not think of a way out."

It was night when Capra and Riskin crossed the border into Nazi Germany on the train en route to the U.S.S.R. (Lu, pregnant with Lulu, who would be born on September 16, stayed behind in London). In a passage cut from his autobiography, Capra claimed that he brazenly mocked a German soldier who tried to stop him filming from the train with his 16mm camera, while Riskin, who was Jewish, cowered in terror. When told this story, Riskin's friend Philip Dunne commented, "I don't think Bob would have cowered. He flew in B-17s."

During his three weeks in the U.S.S.R., Capra displayed a naive view of Stalin's regime, from most of whose excesses his hosts carefully shielded him. He was impressed by the May Day parade in Red Square and with the spirit of the Russian people. He was delighted by the respect shown to him and his work by Soviet directors. And despite his book's pro forma criticisms of the people's standard of living and of the state disrespect for religion, there was something about the regimented life of the U.S.S.R. toward which Capra in his memoir revealed a strange attraction. Part of it stemmed from his disenchantment with the capitalistic system as exemplified by Harry Cohn, but part of Capra's infatuation with Soviet life was a latent distrust of democracy, for he believed that the regime's authoritarianism was part of the price of progress in the U.S.S.R.

Capra's contemporaneous remarks were even more favorable. On May 16, 1937, two days before his fortieth birthday, *Izvestia* quoted favorable remarks about the Soviet filmmaking system he and Riskin made in an interview near the end of their stay. Capra quoted from the interview in his book thirty-four years later without qualification. But he discreetly omitted from the book a fervent passage in which he said, "Above all I am astonished by the enthusiasm which I see not only in Soviet cinema, but literally in all persons whom I have met in the U.S.S.R. Your country is young and talented. It seems to me that the future of cinema art undoubtedly lies with you, and not in America, where the bosses of cinema think only of profits and not of art."

The anxiety Capra expressed in the interview about the "extremely relative" nature of his supposed creative freedom in Hollywood, which he felt his Soviet interviewers exaggerated, was reflected in his book's bizarre account of a meeting with the disgraced Eisenstein. Capra claimed they met in a Moscow dive, but Eisenstein's biographer, Marie Seton, reported that Capra "met him at a public gathering . . . [and] had the impression that Eisenstein was entirely isolated from his colleagues." In the first edition of *The Name Above the Title*, Capra quoted Eisenstein lamenting what the government had done to *Ivan the Terrible*, not letting him complete the final part of the trilogy and banishing him to "the doghouse." Elliott Stein, whose *Sight and Sound* review observed that the pidgin English dialogue Capra put into the mouth of the cosmopolitan Eisenstein sounded like that of "a demented Apache chief," met Capra at a Museum of Modern Art reception for the book in 1971 and suggested that Capra must have been confusing *Ivan the Terrible* with Eisenstein's unfinished film *Bezhin Lug* (*Bezhin Meadow*), which had been suppressed for ideological "errors" shortly before Capra went to Moscow. Eisenstein did not begin work on *Ivan* until 1941 and completed the second part of the unfinished trilogy in 1946, almost nine years after Capra's visit to Moscow.

"You have *your* dates wrong, young man," Capra snapped. "*Ivan* was in '37 when I was there. That story's for real!"

A few days later, Stein reported, Capra appeared at MOMA's Film Study Center and asked if "there is anything here on Eisenstein."

In the first paperback edition of his book, published the following year, Capra substituted *Bezhin Meadow* for *Ivan*—and made up new pidgin English dialogue for Eisenstein to fit the change of films.

Whatever the substance of his conversation with Eisenstein was, the true significance of the meeting for Capra was metaphorical. He felt a kinship with the great Soviet director who had run afoul of Stalin, just as he himself had run afoul of Harry Cohn and later (more to the point) would run afoul of political repression in Hollywood. Viewed through the prism of history, whether the system was Communist or capitalist, the end result was the same to Capra: the artist who did not want to compromise with the power structure was "in the doghouse." The Capra of 1937 (as the book had it) saw Eisenstein as a nightmare image of his own possible future— broke, unemployed, discouraged, living in a disreputable part of town, and (the ultimate Capra nightmare) a man who officially had "ceased to exist."

* * *

On May 12 in London, Capra had witnessed the coronation parade of King George VI, filming it in color with his 16mm camera. He took Lu on a frenzied round of socializing, bedazzled by the pomp of British society and thrilled to find himself lionized by the upper crust. His most satisfying moment came when Alexander Korda introduced him at a studio luncheon to Winston Churchill, who expressed admiration for *Mr. Deeds*.

And, according to his book, it was in London that he received the rude shock of learning that Columbia was currently trying to wring some extra profits from a 1935 film called *If You Could Only Cook*, starring Jean Arthur, by labeling it as his production, even though it had been produced by Everett Riskin and directed by William A. Seiter. The lawsuit Capra later filed against Columbia, according to press reports, accused the studio of "unlawfully using his name with pictures distributed in the British Isles," and said Columbia had used his name on the screen and in advertising as supervisor of a "Frank Capra production."

Chet Sticht said that the sequence of events was quite different from what was reported in Capra's book. Capra's clipping service sent him the British reviews of *If You Could Only Cook before* he left Hollywood for London, and Capra made no immediate protest but went to London partly for the purpose of gathering information for use in the lawsuit he was planning against Columbia. Apparently the reason Capra pretended otherwise in his book was to help disguise the fact that the real bone of contention with Cohn was the recutting of *Lost Horizon*. Furthermore, the idea of using Capra's name as supervisor of *If You Could Only Cook* may have been suggested to Columbia in talks Capra had with the studio in 1935 about supervising two films a year which he would not direct. Though Columbia announced the plan that July, no such agreement was ever concluded, and Jean Arthur said that Capra "was never involved whatsoever in *If You Could Only Cook*—as far as I know." In his amended complaint, Capra alleged that Cohn had offered him 25 percent of the profits for use of his name as supervisor, and that he had rejected the offer because he was not involved with the picture. But *The New York Times* had commented that "there is something of *It Happened One Night*" in the story of a homeless blonde involved with a forlorn automobile millionaire (Herbert Marshall), and Columbia, according to Capra, thought it could use his name with impunity on the film overseas. When he received the clippings, Capra quickly recognized that Columbia's action had handed him some unexpected ammunition that might restore the balance in his power struggle with Harry Cohn. "It was incredibly stupid of Columbia," Sticht said. "He had an open-and-shut case, particularly because most of the reviewers were saying the picture was 'not up to Capra's usual standards.'"

While brooding over his next move, Capra motored through Mussolini's Italy that June with Lu, stopping in Genoa, Florence, Rome, and Naples. He showed no interest, however, in making the brief trip to his humble birthplace in Sicily before they boarded the Italian luxury liner *Rex* to retrace the journey which had brought him from Naples to America by steerage in 1903.

He had been away from Hollywood for more than three months when he returned on July 12. Columbia dropped a hint in the trade press two days later that it might be willing to buy *You Can't Take It With You* for him and even to let him make *Chopin* if he would do another film first. But Capra did not go back to work—he went fishing.

In Capra's absence, Cohn had been making more cuts in *Lost Horizon* for the general release, severely reducing the scenes involving Jane Wyatt (who had been the object of so much critical derision) and also dropping other scenes, including one of questionable value in which H. B. Warner consoled the consumptive prostitute Isabel Jewell upon her arrival at Shangri-La, and a tedious comedy interlude of Edward Everett Horton and Thomas Mitchell cavorting with native girls in the Valley of the Blue Moon. When the director learned that fourteen more minutes were missing from the film, he was outraged anew, though he later laid the primary blame not on Cohn but on the exhibitors: "The people who owned these theaters would call up and say, 'Harry, you want us to go broke? Please, Harry, cut a little bit out of it and we'll get five shows a day.' " Walker recalled, however, that "Cohn polled the exhibitors, and they wouldn't go for the long version." Since Cohn had final cut, and since Capra was "barred" from the studio because of his salary dispute, the director was powerless to do anything about the changes.*

---

*Long after Capra left Columbia, the film was cut again by ten minutes for its 1942 release as Lost Horizon of Shangri-La, *in which the setting was updated to the Sino-Japanese War in 1937. Ironically, it was Capra's old friend Jimmy Doolittle who triggered that reissue, for when the press asked President Roosevelt after Doolittle's April raid on Tokyo where the bombers had been based, the President cryptically replied, "I think they came from a new secret base at Shangri-La" (a name FDR also borrowed for his retreat in the Maryland mountains, renamed Camp David by President Eisenhower). The 1952 reissue of* Lost Horizon *was shorn of another thirteen and a half minutes, bringing the film down to just ninety-five minutes, less than half the length of the version Capra first previewed. By 1967, the negative had deteriorated completely, but when the American Film Institute began its restoration in 1973, Columbia came up with a nitrate print of the general release version and the British Film Institute supplied a complete sound track from the original release, as well as three minutes of footage long missing from American prints, most crucially Conway's drunk scene on the airplane. The only picture available on some of the missing scenes, however, was a French-dubbed 16mm print found in Canada, which the AFI blew up to 35mm,*

After his return from overseas, Capra confronted Cohn about the re-cutting and about *If You Could Only Cook*. According to Capra, to make amends for using his name on *If You Could Only Cook*, Cohn not only offered him a share of its profits but also suggested that Columbia continue the practice on two films a year. "That kind of thinking I just don't understand, that it was all right to make a few extra bucks on fooling the public," Capra commented, failing to mention that two years earlier he had considered just such a deal. The director's new pose of moral rectitude was an expediency now that he "had [Cohn] by the balls" over the Jean Arthur picture and was using it as leverage to be freed from his contract.

Cohn remained intractable to Capra's protests, reminding the director that he could not work elsewhere while he remained under contract to Columbia. Capra recalled raving at Cohn, "Go fuck yourself, you fucking lousy cheap son of a bitch!" before storming out of Cohn's office, certain now that he would never return to Columbia.

During the ensuing period, Buchman said, "Capra went into a plunge. He couldn't believe that after all those years, any man, especially Harry Cohn, could say 'You have or have not $100,000 or $200,000.' Capra stayed in Malibu for months and shut out the world. His wife helped him get back from his depression.

"Harry was tough, but he knew immediately that he had made a major mistake. He tried every means to bring Capra back. The East [Columbia's business office] complained bitterly about the loss of Capra. But Frank was in such a state that he couldn't be reconciled. Cohn thought that he could woo Capra back, but Capra resolved *not* to be wooed."

One of Cohn's not-so-subtle ploys was to groom producer-director Leo McCarey as Capra's successor. McCarey began shooting *The Awful Truth* for Columbia just a few days before Capra returned to Hollywood. Cohn minced no words with McCarey, telling him, "I got you here to teach Capra a lesson. Now you're letting me down. I hired you to make a great comedy, but the only one who'll laugh at this picture is Frank Capra." *The Awful Truth* went on to win McCarey an Oscar as best director, but McCarey, who considered Capra his "hero," refused to work for Cohn again. Before the Academy Award ceremony, Capra, who was not nominated for directing

---

matching the blurred and grainy scenes with the original sound track. The AFI staged a gala revival of its "restoration in progress" (7 of the 132 minutes had no picture, only sound) at Mann's Chinese Theater in Hollywood on October 18, 1979, with Capra in attendance. The final version released by Columbia in 1986 has stills in place of the missing footage.

Lost Horizon, was filmed playfully wrestling with McCarey for the Oscar in front of the newsreel cameras.

During Capra's holdout, Jean Arthur and Robert Riskin also joined in what was amounting to a palace rebellion. Arthur felt that after *Mr. Deeds,* Cohn had reneged on his promise to give her better parts. She walked out and filed suit against Columbia. Riskin was being tempted by substantial offers from other companies, but with the failure of *When You're in Love* and the uncertainty over Capra's situation, he decided not to sign a new contract with Columbia until he knew what would happen with Capra.

Dimitri Tiomkin remembered Capra during his holdout as "bursting with ideas and unable to put them on film. He went fishing day after day. He went deer hunting and sent Albertina and me joints of venison, until he had a revulsion against killing and went hunting no more. One day I went to his house and found him laboring mightily, moving a tree. He was shifting the tree on the grounds for want of anything better to do." As the summer wore on, Capra indulged in murderous fantasies about Harry Cohn, and once again sought counseling from Dr. Verne Mason.

He also remembered that he had vowed not to "compromise" with Cohn. Yet it is impossible to see Capra's subsequent reconciliation with Cohn as anything but a compromise—on both sides.

Capra filed his suit in Los Angeles Superior Court on August 28, asking the court to release him from the contract and to award him the disputed $100,000. Four days later Columbia issued a statement to the press: "We regret that a difference has arisen between ourselves and a valued employee of the organization, and we trust the difference will eventually be cleared up either legally or through a clarification of the present misunderstanding."

Answering studio charges of ambiguity in the grounds of his lawsuit, Capra filed an amended complaint in September separating the salary and *If You Could Only Cook* issues and adding the charge about Columbia leaving his name off trade ads promoting the current general release of *Lost Horizon.*

But Cohn too was playing hardball. Capra found to his surprise that the rest of Hollywood had little interest in hiring him. He had tentative discussions with MGM, and talked about forming an independent production company with directors William Wellman, Gregory La Cava, and Wesley Ruggles to release through United Artists, but nothing came of either proposition. He found that he was on what he called a "blacklist" informally enforced among the studio chiefs against rebellious talent. Like

Eisenstein under Stalin, Capra realized that by bucking the Hollywood system he had "ceased to exist."

Columbia won a dismissal of his case on the grounds that it should have been filed in New York, the location of its corporate headquarters. So Capra sued in New York, but the complaint pertaining to *If You Could Only Cook* was thrown out because the film had not played in the United States with Capra's name attached to it. The increasingly desperate Capra then hired a barrister in London who filed suit there, and that, he said, was what made Columbia agree to discuss a settlement. But since Capra had "resolved *not* to be wooed," as Buchman put it, the pressure of the blacklist also must have played a decisive part in bringing the adversaries back together.

Capra took elaborate pains in his book to make it seem that Cohn abased himself in making the first peace overture, that he agreed to return only to save Cohn's job, and that it was only then that Cohn, out of gratitude and relief, offered him a financial settlement. *The Name Above the Title* claims that Cohn came to Capra's Malibu house on November 11 to plead with him to come back, but according to the following day's *Hollywood Reporter*, "Gower Street habitués were agog yesterday seeing Frank Capra duck into Columbia Studios"; and Louella Parsons reported that Capra had visited the studio with his lawyer. Perhaps to save face for both of them, *Daily Variety* said that Capra and Cohn were back on speaking terms, "not across the table but over the telephone wires. . . . Cohn yesterday talked with Capra for almost an hour and inquired why the director had walked. Capra then spilled forth his story and grievances. Cohn summed it up that someone in his organization had done Capra wrong for he said: 'Frank, I'm not responsible for what other people around here do or say. You always got a square shake from me and can get it again.' "

In the settlement announced on November 27, which Chet Sticht described as "a moral victory" for Capra, Columbia agreed to give Capra the disputed $100,000. Capra agreed to release Columbia from any obligations on the *Frédéric Chopin* project (though he still hoped he could persuade them to make it), and Columbia waived his obligation to make one of the five pictures required under his amended 1935 contract. A new agreement was reached for Capra to direct two more films, the first to be *You Can't Take It With You*, which Cohn reluctantly had agreed to buy to keep it and Capra out of the hands of other studios. Riskin, who had settled his dispute with Columbia a week earlier, agreed to write the adaptation despite his own battles with Capra over *Lost Horizon*.

If Cohn felt he was eating dirt by accepting Capra back, he also could take satisfaction in realizing that Capra was publicly humbled by return-ing. Cohn also got what *he* wanted: another Frank Capra picture, without losing him to the competition and without surrendering to Capra any of his own executive power. Cohn's distaste was assuaged further by making peace with his skittish New York office and by the hope that the shaken Capra might return to his old efficient, moneymaking self, thereby renew-ing the glory of Columbia and Cohn.

The showdown thus ended in an uneasy truce. But something had gone forever from the Capra-Cohn relationship—an element of trust, of part-nership, of shared commercial and artistic goals, the likes of which Capra would never see again—and it was replaced with a barely repressed hos-tility. "Cohn needed Capra, so he used him," said Columbia writer Lewis Meltzer, "but Cohn resented Capra's changing from what he was to aloof-ness." Some of the fun had gone out of moviemaking for Capra. When *You Can't Take It With You* started filming the following April—more than fifteen months after the cameras last rolled on *Lost Horizon*—Edward Bernds was disturbed to see signs that Capra was beginning to rush through his work, seeming to care more about cost than about quality, shooting with "hints of quickie pressure and irritation." Wondering if Cohn or someone else had put the "fear of God" into him, Bernds, who was not privy to the whole story of Capra's legal battle with Columbia, wrote in his diary: "Surprised. Not like old F.C. Why?"

13. "Columbia's Gem"

*B*efore July 1937, when the producers agreed to hold contract talks with the Screen Directors Guild, the guild had been limping along with a membership of only ninety directors, but that month another seventy-one agreed to come aboard, including Frank Capra.

Capra signed his membership application on August 8, eighteen months after the formation of the SDG. Despite his later claim that "I wouldn't put the Academy above the Directors Guild, because that wouldn't be kosher," his six prior years of promanagement activity with the Academy had helped the studios stall recognition of the actors', writers', and directors' guilds. But once the actors became powerful enough to force the producers' hand and the Academy removed itself from labor-management issues, Capra lost most of his power base. Seeing events turning inexorably in labor's direction, he began listening to the arguments of his fellow directors.

Before that time, King Vidor recalled, "All our activities were concentrated on getting these directors who were holdouts as members, slowly and with great difficulty." As Rouben Mamoulian put it, "We started taking different directors to lunch or dinner and shaming them into joining us."

After the U.S. Supreme Court upheld the constitutionality of the Wagner Act on April 12, 1937, the Hollywood guilds acquired momentum. SAG signed its first contract in May, and by June 1 the SWG mustered about 400 writers in support of its certification petition to the National Labor Relations Board. That May the directors formulated their contract demands and decided to admit assistant directors and unit production managers as Junior Guild members, swelling the SDG's total strength to about 550 by the end of the summer.

In a 1985 interview, Capra said the pressure on him to become a member had intensified in December 1936, when he asked the SDG to send Oscar ballots to its members. It was to win the guilds' pledge not to boycott the 1937 ceremony that the Academy promised to stay out of labor-management issues.

When he met with the guild board members at their modest office in the Crossroads of the World building at 6671 Sunset Boulevard, "they hopped on me," Capra recalled, with Vidor demanding, "Frank, what the hell are you breaking your ass about the Academy for? Why don't you want to do anything for the directors?"

According to Vidor, the conspicuous absence of Capra and other big names from the SDG's membership was one of the factors that had prevented the start of negotiations with Joseph Schenck, president of the Association of Motion Picture Producers: "We were working to get 100 percent membership of at least all the important directors before going after a contract. I went to England to do a film for MGM, then Frank Capra came in and was the president when we had enough important directors as members, when we went after the original recognition and contract. It was just by the unified strength of all the directors getting together that we succeeded in getting recognition."

Capra said he came in because he felt, "What the hell, my heart's more here than it is any other place."

"The guild needed him more than the Academy did," Chet Sticht said. "The Academy job was a figurehead, a pat-on-the-back kind of thing. There wasn't a hell of a lot to it except for presiding over the Academy Awards ceremony and a few meetings. The guild had a fight on its hands."

His troubles with Harry Cohn over *Lost Horizon* and his placement on the Hollywood "blacklist" contributed to Capra's new militancy on behalf of his fellow directors, he admitted in his book. The month Capra agreed to join the SDG was the month he returned to Hollywood from his trip to Europe and the U.S.S.R., and he signed his SDG membership form twenty days before filing his lawsuit to win his freedom from Columbia. It was during his holdout from the studio that he was elected to the guild's board on October 4.

Though Mamoulian said the studios had attempted to blacklist directors who belonged to the guild, Capra, joining as late as he did, felt no such intimidation: "Fuck, *I* didn't get worried about being blacklisted. How could they blacklist me? I'd blacklist *them*. Everybody wanted to give me jobs. My career was made by them. When the [SDG] contract was in, I turned down the best contract that was ever offered anybody—and it was offered to me by Schenck."

But despite his bravado and his enviable position in the industry,

Capra was anxious about facing the prospect of leaving his once-safe Columbia haven to go back onto the open market. In his new insecurity he was able to empathize with lesser directors who were relying on the guild to help them win better wages and working conditions. The guild also was seeking more creative authority for all directors, and creative authority was the overriding issue in his power struggle with Harry Cohn.

"Only half a dozen" Hollywood directors had creative control of their work, Capra wrote in an April 2, 1939, letter to *The New York Times*, during the last stages of negotiations with the producers. ". . . Truly a sad situation for a medium that is supposed to be a director's medium." He blamed not only the studios but also his fellow directors, for their complacency and lack of "guts" in failing to demand the kind of "producer-director setups" which he felt could give them more independence. He wanted to help lead the way with such a setup for himself, but he wasn't getting "much encouragement" from Hollywood.

When he joined the guild, Capra was the most prominent name among Hollywood directors. Winner of the last three Oscars and a major power at the box office (even if *Lost Horizon* had tarnished his record), he was riding the crest of a wave of publicity that would peak in 1938 with a profile in *The Saturday Evening Post* and a cover story in *Time* magazine. It was also a major coup for the SDG to lure the Academy's president into its ranks; even if the Academy position was now largely a figurehead, by winning Capra's loyalties, the guild had managed to place a Trojan horse inside the producers' citadel.

The prestige Capra wielded, the honing of his gut-fighting talents through years of involvement in the Academy's labor negotiations, and the respect he had earned from studio bosses would prove to be powerful assets for the SDG in the climactic period of its fight for recognition. "An awful lot of people think I take all the bows, but I'm proud of having saved the Academy and having saved the guild," Capra said in 1985. "I'm proud of these goddamn things."

Such boasts by Capra, however, provoked indignation from Mamoulian: "Anybody who could claim he was 'the guy who made the guild accepted' is just wrong. What were *we* all doing then?" Unlike Capra, the ninety members who joined before July 1937 put their careers on the line to stand up for the guild. And their leaders did much of the necessary spadework with the producers. The committee that opened talks with the producers on August 4, 1937, included Howard Hawks, its chairman; Eddie Sutherland; John Ford; Herbert Biberman; and Mamoulian, all of whom were important figures in the early history of the guild. But the guild did not win its contract until after Capra took over the chairmanship of the negotiating committee that fall and the guild presidency the following May, forcing the stalled negotiations to a successful conclusion. Capra took a harsh view of the guild's original bargaining committee, contending that they failed to win a contract "because they had no balls. Because they got scared off. Because they thought they were too big to go begging. They talked to each other big but they didn't talk to the producers big. These guys didn't want to work."

For all the courage displayed by its founders, there is no doubt that the Directors Guild was the least militant of the three major guilds, "a company of gentlemen adventuring in unionism," in Philip Dunne's phrase. According to the minutes of SDG board meetings and other guild documents, Capra's role indeed was crucial in winning the basic agreement from the producers, but it was not a one-man show: the guild recognized that at least as much credit belonged to its legal counsel, Mabel Walker Willebrandt.

She was a prominent Washington attorney and staunch Republican who had served as an assistant attorney general in the Harding administration and had been a vocal supporter of Prohibition and Herbert Hoover. Her recommendation was credited with being a key factor in the selection of J. Edgar Hoover to head the Federal Bureau of Investigation. After her death in 1963, her friend Judge John J. Sirica observed, "If Mabel had worn trousers she could have been President." Willebrandt was hired by Capra's negotiating committee on October 3, 1938, on the recommendation of W. S. (Woody) Van Dyke, to represent the SDG in negotiating and drafting the basic agreement. Two days before she was hired, Capra told his fellow board members that she would be more militant than they were. A 1949 guild document summarizing the history of the subsequent negotiations gave Willebrandt first-position credit ahead of Capra for the attainment of the basic agreement in 1939, and Capra himself gave her the entire credit in a June 1, 1939, letter to Willebrandt on the board's behalf.

The victory was not easy.

Within a week after the producers decided to talk with the SDG in July 1937, the NLRB ruled that high-salaried design workers at Chrysler's Detroit plant were not eligible for protection under the Wagner Act because they had hiring and firing power over other employees. That gave the producers an excuse to withdraw from negotiations with the directors on August 12, only eight days after the single meeting with Hawks's committee, and even though Hawks had reported to Vidor on August 5 that the only remaining impediment to striking a deal with the producers was the SDG's continuing insistence on keeping the assistant directors and unit production managers in the guild.

Darryl F. Zanuck, then production chief of Twentieth Century–Fox and the chairman of the producers' negotiating committee, which also included Jack L. Warner and MGM's Eddie Mannix, declared: "Directors perform a service which is fundamentally creative. The rate of compensation, character of service, and the authority of a director will demonstrate that he has no 'inequality of bargaining power' such as is contemplated by the Wagner Labor Relations Act."

And in what Mamoulian warned his fellow board members was a move to undermine the solidarity of the guild in future bargaining, the producers contended that the assistants and unit managers were management personnel and refused to negotiate with the SDG unless it represented only directors, claiming further negotiations would be "destructive of the basis upon which successful motion picture making has been carried on."

Hawks's negotiating committee wrote Zanuck on August 24 that what the producers proposed was "nothing less than the dissolution of the guild!" But the producers refused to budge, and the guild petitioned the NLRB for certification.

When elected to the board in October, Capra also was appointed to represent the SDG, along with Herbert Biberman and Lewis Milestone, on the Inter-Talent Council, a small group that coordinated the activities of SAG, the SWG, and the SDG. After his behind-the-scenes maneuvering helped pave the way for a resumption of contract negotiations in April 1938, he was named chairman of the negotiating committee, and, with his sights on the guild presidency, he maneuvered himself onto the SDG's election board to supervise the choice of new officers in the May balloting.

Shortly after Capra's return to Columbia, it was announced that his *Chopin* project was back in the works, with Charles Boyer replacing Francis Lederer in the title role and Marlene Dietrich playing George Sand, the pants-wearing, cigar-smoking novelist who in Buchman's script was portrayed as a temptress whose hedonism distracts Chopin temporarily from his true mission as the patriotic composer of "The Heroic Polonaise." In April 1938, when Columbia signed a contract with Dietrich, the project was retitled *George Sand*. In the meantime, Columbia announced on January 18, 1938, that Capra first would make *You Can't Take It With You*.*

---

* *When Capra tried after* You Can't Take It With You *to launch* Chopin *with Spencer Tracy and Dietrich, Columbia refused unless he would agree to add two more pictures to his contract, which he would not do. He gave up on the project, and Buchman's script finally reached the screen in 1945 as* A Song to Remember, *directed by Charles Vidor (in Technicolor), with Cornel Wilde as Chopin, Muni as Elsner, and Merle Oberon as George Sand. The script was little altered except for the inclusion of Chopin's death, and the film was a hit, bringing in rentals of $7,430,468*

Sandwiched between such weighty and ambitious projects as *Lost Horizon* and *Chopin*, Capra's *You Can't Take It With You* seemed a light-hearted interlude. Working again with Riskin, Capra tried his best to find something to say in the midst of the comedy. But as they ran for cover after the commercial debacle of *Lost Horizon* by packaging a sure-fire property, their adaptation of the Kaufman-Hart play was an artistic regression, glibly reworking the utopian themes of *Lost Horizon* in a middle-class American setting, glossing them over with proven ingredients from their previous hits. It inaugurated a pattern that would become increasingly evident in Capra's career, as he turned more and more to adapting Broadway plays (*Arsenic and Old Lace, State of the Union, A Hole in the Head*) and remaking his own successes rather than staking out fresh ground.

With the expertly but somewhat cynically crafted *You Can't Take It With You*, which turned the now-familiar *Capraesque* formula into a commodity, Capra set out to prove not only that he had not lost his touch at the box office but also that he could bring in a picture reasonably close to schedule and at a reasonable cost. It began production on April 25, 1938, was filmed in fifty-six days, only four days over schedule, and its negative cost was $1,644,736, only $64,937 over budget. Capra used 329,000 feet of film, a 28-to-1 shooting ratio but far from the 1.1 million feet exposed on *Lost Horizon* and less than the amount allotted in the budget. Capra's preoccupation with the budget—and, thought Edward Bernds, with Academy and Directors Guild problems—caused drastic changes in his shooting methods.

Bernds recorded his dismay over Capra's "incomplete coverage [and] sloppy shooting . . . [a] complete reversal of his many-angle technique." Capra often seemed pressured and moody; he employed the "worst of quickie tactics" to cut corners and save time. Rather than patiently working for perfection, as he had been accustomed to doing, he now showed a penchant for printing the first take of an important scene. "I don't want to shoot a lot of shots I don't need," Capra explained one day, his face looking "drawn and tired."

But on other days, Capra unexpectedly reverted to his old methods. Shooting the courtroom scene, Capra used a "tremendous number of angles and wild footage" but with no positive effect on the quality of the scene. "Where wasted?" wrote Bernds. "In long 'reactions' with full dialogue—in

(through October 1985) on a negative cost of $1,607,953. The irate Capra filed suit against Columbia in February 1946, claiming he was legally entitled to share the profits. But the November 1937 amendment to his contract had allocated to Columbia the profit percentage he otherwise would have received, so he withdrew the suit in 1947.

long 'master shots' [with] two cameras grinding. . . . In repetitious medium shots. Scandalous—truly inefficient, because effort wasted, photography sacrificed, action sometimes sloughed."

Nevertheless, *You Can't Take It With You* was a resounding box-office success, bringing in domestic rentals of $2,137,575 in its first year of release, the highest sum for any of Capra's pictures for Columbia up to that time, though *Lost Horizon* eventually passed it in rentals, and both *Mr. Deeds* and *Lost Horizon* wound up with higher net proceeds; total rentals on *You Can't Take It With You* through October 1985 amounted to $4,272,560.

For 1938, the year *You Can't Take It With You* was released, Capra's income was reported to be nearly $1 million which included his earnings from that film, his stock earnings, his profits from earlier pictures, and his $100,000 settlement for *Chopin*. Capra denied in 1985 that his income had reached that level, but the figure emerged during testimony before the NLRB during the certification hearings for the SDG in September 1938 and received wide attention in the press. Chet Sticht, who kept his books, confirmed that Capra's income was in the seven-figure range. And Capra admitted to an interviewer in 1972 that he *had* made a million dollars in 1938, though he claimed "the money never meant a thing. I never had any respect for it and spent it like water . . . until World War II. That changed me, and I decided the crazy spending was a lot of chichi."

The irony was becoming inescapable. A man whose films attacked the selfish rich, glorified "the common man" (at least superficially), and preached that "the only thing you can take with you is the love of your friends" had become a millionaire from those very films. Sidney Skolsky, previously an uncritical Capra adulator, acidly noted during the making of *You Can't Take It With You* that Capra evidently believed "that money isn't everything—especially if you have enough." And after his income became public knowledge, a Boston newspaper scolded, "As a good director he ought to know that happiness lies in simple things. The taxes, though—ah, there's the hitch. When all the taxes have been paid . . . does Mr. Capra worry badly about the rent? If so it serves him right."

Capra stopped publicizing his wealth after that sudden flurry of astonished publicity, and whenever he had to discuss his holdings he scaled them downward. Lionel Barrymore's Grandpa Vanderhof in *You Can't Take It With You* tells Edward Arnold's banker Anthony P. Kirby, "What if all your deals fall through? Might be a good thing for you," and Capra was beginning to feel that his way of living was undercutting the values he espoused in his work. When Saridda came to Brentwood for one of her increasingly infrequent visits, she would scold him for the way he had changed. Philosophically, if not practically, he had come to agree with Thoreau's observation in *Walden* (his favorite book) that "with respect to luxuries and comforts, the wisest have ever lived a more simple and meager life than the poor."

Inevitably these conflicts seeped into *You Can't Take It With You.* Riskin said its "underlying theme" was that "the accumulation of gold beyond a man's needs is idiotic." But his script and Capra's direction also showed ambivalence toward that idea.

Like *Lost Horizon, You Can't Take It With You* presents a small utopian community with a nearly miraculous lack of need for money (only Jean Arthur has a job, and she works because she wants to) and a leisurely life-style made possible by the labor of the lower classes, in this case the family's black servants (Eddie "Rochester" Anderson and Lillian Yarbo). The story shrewdly combined elements of economic fantasy with elements of economic reality, in a contemporary New York setting with which Depression era audiences could identify more easily than they could with Shangri-La. Befitting Manny Farber's description of Capra as "a smooth blend of iconoclast and sheep," *You Can't Take It With You* balances its Republican economic principles with a democratic fantasy of noncomformity (Grandpa spends his days collecting stamps, Mrs. Sycamore paints and writes unproduced plays, Essie practices ballet, Mr. Poppins makes Halloween masks, Ed and Mr. Sycamore make fireworks) in an isolated world in which doing one's thing is elevated to a spiritual value. But it is, by and large, a safe nonconformity, without risk of adverse economic or social consequences and therefore a meaningless form of pseudo-revolt. The real down-and-outers—the Vanderhofs' dispossessed neighbors, the prisoners in the jail—are, as usual with Capra, depicted with a mixture of sympathy and distaste: the neighbors helplessly look to Grandpa Vanderhof to save them from eviction, the prisoners react angrily when Kirby calls them "scum" but then dive en masse for his discarded cigar butt, Capra's favorite symbol of arrogant wealth.

One way the film pulled its punches was to take the bite out of the play's satire of the Red Menace. Like the play, the film raises the specter of communism by having the naive Ed (Dub Taylor) design fireworks to celebrate the Russian Revolution. Ed also puts messages in candy boxes reading "Watch for the revolution—it's coming soon" and "The red flag is sweeping the country—get your red flag at the Sycamores," bringing a squad of "G-men" onto the scene to march everyone off to jail (Ward Bond, who later would become one of the ringleaders of the Hollywood blacklist as an officer of the militantly anti-Communist Motion Picture Alliance for the Preservation of American Ideals, appears here as one of the Red hunters). But the film fudges slightly by having the agents say they are from the "police department," not the FBI, and it drops the line in the play that gives the scene its real point: banker Kirby's charge that the values of the Vanderhof family are "un-American." It is remarkable that Riskin and Capra kept any of the Red Menace satire at all—1938 was the year that the newly created House Committee on Un-American Activities (HUAC) and its chairman, Martin Dies (D-Texas), began their investigation of alleged Communist influence in Hollywood—but the filmmakers fell far short of the target by relegating it to just another element in the overall zaniness.

The film's level of political sophistication is summed up in Grandpa's speech to Mrs. Sycamore (Spring Byington) advising her to keep the heroine of a play she is writing free from foreign "isms": "Communism—Fascism—voodooism—everybody's got an 'ism' these days. . . . Only give her Americanism, and let her know something about Americans. John Paul Jones. Patrick Henry. Samuel Adams. Washington. Jefferson. Monroe. Lincoln. Grant. Lee. Edison. Mark Twain. When things got tough with those boys they didn't run around looking for 'isms.' " The final version of the first line evidently was written by Capra himself.

You Can't Take It With You also poked some sour fun at the New Deal's relief programs by having Rochester say things like "I don't go no place much—I'm on relief." Riskin's script kept that and two other relief jokes from the play, and Capra restored more of them during the shooting, only to find when he previewed the film that the audiences didn't laugh much at the "colored servants." He told the *New York Sun,* "Guess a lot of people just don't think relief is funny."

Capra's erstwhile admirer Graham Greene again said it best: "The director emerges as a rather muddled and sentimental idealist who feels—vaguely—that something is wrong with the social system. Mr. Deeds started distributing his money, and the hero of *Lost Horizon* settled down in a Tibetan monastery—equipped with all the luxury devices of the best American hotels—and Grandpa Vanderhof persuades, in this new picture, the Wall Street magnate who has made the *coup* of his career and cornered the armaments industry to throw everything up and play the harmonica. This presumably means a crash in Wall Street and the ruin of thousands of small investors, but it is useless trying to analyse the idea behind Capra films: there *is* no idea that you'd notice, only a sense of dissatisfaction, an urge to escape—on to the open road with the daughter of a millionaire, back to small-town simplicity on a safe income."

Yet, as Greene admitted of *You Can't Take It With You*, "it isn't as awful as all that." Simplistic and rough and uneven though it may be, it is an infectious, all but irresistible film whose virtues are in the broad but delightful playing of its ensemble cast and in the director's often masterful orchestration of comic business.

According to Josie Campisi, of all her uncle's films, *You Can't Take It With You* is most reminiscent of the "crazy" family in which Frank Capra grew up. Capra also showed an unusually strong identification with James Stewart's Tony Kirby, the rebellious banker's son carrying on a romance with Vanderhof's granddaughter, Alice Sycamore (Jean Arthur). Like Capra, Tony is scorned by his family as an idle dreamer, and though Tony marries "down" while Capra married "up" the social ladder, Tony similarly seeks his identity in revolt from a stifling upbringing, from a domineering mother and a father he sees as a failure. Capra wrote into the script Grandpa Vanderhof's description of Mr. Kirby as a "failure as a man, failure as a human being, even a failure as a father" and the moving scene in which Tony tells Alice of his thwarted college dream to develop solar energy (later the subject of Capra's 1956 television science show *Our Mr. Sun*). Though in the film the elder Kirby is trying to buy the Vanderhof home and its surrounding neighborhood as part of a ruthless business deal, he is less of a caricature than in the play: much more emphasis is given to the father-son relationship in the film, stressing the banker's underlying decency, brought out by his son's idealism and by Alice's desire to bridge the social barriers. The banker's improbable but emotionally satisfying change of heart becomes the primary dramatic focus.

You Can't Take It With You marked the emergence of Jimmy Stewart as the quintessential Capra hero, in the first of his three films for the director. When Capra hired him he was a minor MGM contract player, thirty years old, with Princeton, Broadway, and only three years of Hollywood experience behind him. The director had spotted Stewart in *Navy Blue and Gold*, directed by Sam Wood, in which Stewart had played a midshipman at the U.S. Naval Academy. "He had a minor part, he wasn't the star. He did a little something defending a fellow naval student. When I saw him I thought, 'Oh, my land, *there's* a guy.' "

The scene actually had Stewart rising in class to defend his father, a Navy officer who had been court-martialed and dismissed from the service after being unfairly accused of a breach of duty. It closely resembles the scene in Capra's *It's a Wonderful Life* in which Stewart defends the memory of his father before Lionel Barrymore and the board of the failing Bailey

Building & Loan Association. Defending a misunderstood father was a theme that had personal resonance for Capra, who felt a similar bond with Papa Turiddu, and Stewart's earnestness was perfectly suited for the complex father-son relationship in *You Can't Take It With You*.

"He grabbed you as a human being," Capra said. "You were looking at the man, not an actor. You could see this man's soul. He was the one. . . . When you're dealing in the world of ideas and you want your character to be on a higher intellectual plane than just a simple man, you turn to persons like Jimmy Stewart because he has a look of the intellectual about him. And he can be an idealist. . . . a pretty fine combination."

The admiration was reciprocated. "I just had complete confidence in Frank Capra," said Stewart. "I always had, from the very first day I worked with him. He's a classic example of what a motion picture director should be. He had this tremendous sense of story, and underneath everything that happened was a basic, wonderful humor, an awful lot of it visual humor. I think he was born with it. He doesn't bowl you over the head by preaching to you, he does it with humor and warmth and understanding. I just hung on every word Frank Capra said."

"He's the easiest man to direct I've ever seen," said Capra. "A man who gets what you're talking about in just a few words. You wonder if you've told him enough about the scene, and yet when he does it, there it is. He knew by looking at me, and I can look at him and know him. It's not because I've worked with him so much; I think he's probably the best actor who's ever hit the screen."

Edward Arnold—whose performance both Stewart and Capra especially admired—also was making his first film for the director. He would become Capra's stock heavy, growing progressively more sinister in *Mr. Smith Goes to Washington* and *Meet John Doe*. Arnold fit Capra's need for a "stronger" heavy, "not just cardboard—he makes sure your opposition is not feeble, that it has an idea of its own, something they believe in."

Because of Jean Arthur's holdout against Columbia, she almost did not appear in *You Can't Take It With You*. Though she was Capra's first choice, he had to look elsewhere, and he made a deal with Warner Bros. to borrow Olivia de Havilland for the part. But the deal fell apart because of Capra's political maneuverings between the Academy and the Screen Directors Guild.

After the premature death of Irving Thalberg on September 14, 1936, the Academy decided to honor the MGM producer (and longtime Academy power broker) by giving an annual Irving Thalberg Memorial Award to a producer for work of consistently high quality. But the award, first presented in 1938, inevitably became a political football.

As chairman of the Thalberg Award Committee, Capra steered the first one to Zanuck, who was both an Academy board member and the chairman of the committee handling the producers' negotiations with the SDG. The choice of Zanuck was a transparent attempt by Capra to bring the producers back to the bargaining table and to make Zanuck more receptive to the directors' demands. It also was a slap in the face to Jack Warner, who resented Zanuck's departure from Warner Bros. in the midst of the Academy's salary-cut crisis in 1933, when Zanuck's support of restoring the cuts made him "quite a hero" in Capra's eyes.

When word leaked out that Zanuck was being considered for the award, Capra and his committee were besieged with demands by Warner Bros.' production chief Hal Wallis and others who either wanted it for themselves or simply did not want it to go to Zanuck. On the eve of the March 10 ceremony, Jack Warner sent a telegram to Capra at the Biltmore Hotel, vehemently protesting the decision to honor Zanuck, and threatening to ruin the Academy's reputation by revealing the way it came about. Capra resisted Warner's demand to cancel Zanuck's honor, and Warner fumed while the evening went ahead as planned. His mood was lightened somewhat by the three Oscars, including one for best picture, given to his company's *The Life of Emile Zola*, perhaps as a gesture of consolation by the Academy (which nominated *Lost Horizon* for seven Oscars, including best picture, but gave it only two, art direction and editing).

Capra, who was acting as master of ceremonies, thought that the acceptance speeches were starting to become soporific, and suggested that the winners should loosen up and speak as though they were talking to their wives. At that Jack Warner rose and announced exuberantly, "Well, from now on all awards will be won by Warner."

"It sounds as though Mr. Warner was talking to his wife all right," Capra quipped.

The next morning Warner told Columbia he had changed his mind about loaning Olivia de Havilland for *You Can't Take It With You*.

With the start of shooting set for the following month, Capra managed to patch up Jean Arthur's differences with Columbia. He persuaded Harry Cohn to sweeten the deal by buying the film rights to Clifford Odets's *Golden Boy* for himself and Arthur to make after *You Can't Take It With You*.

The hit Group Theatre play dealt explicitly with the "catastrophe of Success"; Capra could find much to identify with in the character of Joe

Bonaparte, the Italian-American boy who turns his back on his talents as a violinist to pursue fame, wealth, and self-destruction as a prizefighter. Capra's interest in *Golden Boy* reflected the increasingly leftward pull of his dramatic interests. He was becoming more sensitive to the mood of the times through his growing discontent with wealth and success, and with his switch to the side of labor with the SDG. Odets, who later made uncredited contributions to *It's a Wonderful Life*, testified before HUAC in 1952 that he had been a member of the Communist Party in 1934–1935.

Because of the brouhaha caused by his political maneuvering over the Thalberg Award, Capra told Zanuck that he had decided to resign as Academy president.

Zanuck urged him to reconsider, suggesting he was too easily rattled by such incidents and reminding Capra how badly the Academy needed him as it evolved into what Zanuck saw as its newly depoliticized role. Embittered as he said he was about his position in the middle of the seesaw between labor and management, by now Capra also must have recognized—if, indeed, that was not always his scheme—that his threat to resign (which he did not carry out) could be used as a potent bargaining chip to force the producers back to the bargaining table. Zanuck played right into his hands.

With John Ford and AMPP attorney Mendel Silberberg acting as go-betweens, Joseph Schenck agreed to meet on April 12 with Capra and Howard Hawks, who formally requested a resumption of talks with the SDG's new negotiating committee, headed by Capra (the other members were Eddie Sutherland and Gregory La Cava). Zanuck again headed the producers' committee, which also included Eddie Mannix of MGM and Pandro S. Berman of RKO. But only one negotiating session was held, on April 22, before the talks broke down again.

According to Zanuck, it was Capra, "and not one of us, who then suggested the possibility of eliminating the unit managers from your group and retaining the assistant directors." Zanuck and Capra subsequently differed about whether an understanding had been reached on the issue, and Zanuck, at Schenck's direction, canceled the next negotiating session scheduled for May 3. Zanuck told Capra "there was no sense in our meeting and wasting each other's time unless you and your committee could see some way of divorcing the assistant directors and unit managers."

Capra's committee wrote Schenck accusing the producers of not bargaining in good faith. The letter was published in the trade press on

May 7 with a letter from the SDG board to its membership contending that the producers wanted "to break up the maximum strength of the guild in order to be able to use the parts to their own advantage against each other." The board, most of whom were up for reelection on May 15 along with the other officers, added that "rumors have been started against the unity and integrity of the guild."

Answering Capra publicly, Zanuck accused him of having gone public with the charges "in an effort to keep the forces of your guild intact." He insisted that "nothing was agreed upon at our meeting" and criticized Capra for implying "that our views are always taken in bad faith and that those of your group are always honest. This attitude will always prevent any successful discussion or determination of our mutual problems."

On May 15, forty-five members of the guild (with eighty proxies) met at the Hollywood Athletic Club to choose a new president to succeed King Vidor, who had gone to London to direct *The Citadel*. Capra was elected by a show of hands over Woody Van Dyke and Howard Hawks, who were chosen as first and second vice presidents. *Daily Variety* called Capra's victory "a complete vote of confidence" in his handling of the contract negotiations.

The new guild president vented his personal feelings on the impasse in drafting a polemic published in *The New York Times* on August 7, in somewhat toned-down form, as an unsigned statement by the SDG. It clearly showed how Capra's militance on the behalf of the SDG had become an outlet for his own growing sense of creative impotence.

"Today the system offers a virtual proscription against originality and freshness in pictures," he wrote, ". . . and many directors who, until recently, were offered creative opportunities are finding the doors progressively closed to them."

The worst aspect of the system, wrote Capra, was that the director usually had "nothing to do with the preparation of the material," but was forced to shoot a mediocre script "without changing a line." The director of *Lost Horizon* also attacked the "uncertainty, duplication and waste" endemic in the Hollywood system. Capra admitted that directors were partly to blame, but added, "[W]e must emphasize that the larger responsibility rests with those in executive positions of power."

Capra and the guild were venturing into dangerous ground by going so public with their manifesto. The *Times* commented that the "bitter" document was "ill-timed" from the producers' standpoint, because it was in that month that a five-year FBI investigation had led the Justice Department to file an antitrust suit against the major studios, attempting to break their monopoly by ending the practice of block-booking and by divorcing the studios from their own chains of theaters—actions Capra had been urging vociferously for several years and would continue to advocate. The *Times* added that the Capra-SDG document, "prepared as it was by an important segment of the business," had "an authoritative ring and easily can be used as ammunition in the trust suit."

Ten days after taking charge of the SDG, Capra became involved in a political issue that seemed innocuous enough at the time but which would have serious ramifications in his later life.

The film community, and particularly the guilds, mobilized an outpouring of support for the Los Angeles Newspaper Guild's strike of the *Hollywood Citizen-News.* "It had been more liberal than the *Los Angeles Times,* but anything was more liberal than the *Times*," recalled Philip Dunne, then a board member of the SWG. "It wasn't much of a paper. But this was a union time, and these were our fellow writers." The strike, which began on May 17, had been caused by publisher Harlan G. Palmer's firing of five staff members in retaliation for the Newspaper Guild's attempt to unionize his paper with the support of the NLRB. The SDG *Bulletin* invited members to join the picket line outside the *Citizen-News* building on North Wilcox Avenue, near Hollywood Boulevard, and on May 23 the board of the Directors Guild voted to support the strike.

Capra joined the picket line on the first day of the strike, along with John Ford and Herbert Biberman. Dunne and Robert Montgomery, the president of SAG, also were there representing their guilds. "We spent about five minutes walking up and down the picket lines and had our pictures taken," Dunne recalled. A photo of Capra, Ford, and Biberman standing in front of the newspaper building "as they joined the picket line" appeared in the *Hollywood Citizen-News Striker* (an ad hoc publication by the striking employees) on June 1 under the heading "Film Directors Give Aid." Capra also was invited to speak at a June 1 strike rally by the Newspaper Guild's publicity committee chairman, Frank Scully; he replied on May 26 that though he was prevented from doing so by the shooting of *You Can't Take It With You,* he strongly supported the strike.

There was a mild backlash within the Directors Guild. At a board meeting on June 6, Howard Hawks criticized the publication of the picketing invitation in the *Bulletin,* and the board reserved the right to approve such action in the future. Capra's involvement in the picketing also was noted with alarm by HUAC, which was created on May 26, just nine days after he appeared on the picket line, and was already turning its sights on

Hollywood as part of its mandate to investigate "the extent, character, and objects of un-American propaganda activities in the United States." Referring to a report in the West Coast Communist Party newspaper *People's World*, HUAC placed an item in a file on Capra indicating that: "The 30 May 1938 issue of the *People's World* described CAPRA as a member of the picket line in the Hollywood Citizen's [*sic*] News Strike which was Communist inspired. . . ."

With his own films being viewed in some quarters as communistic, and having recently gone on record in *Izvestia* favorably comparing the Soviet system of filmmaking with Hollywood's, Capra showed an immediate defensive reaction to HUAC's first public charges of widespread Communist influence in Hollywood, though he finally decided not to go public with his concerns.

On August 12, HUAC's chairman, Martin Dies, began holding hearings in Washington at which witnesses made charges against movie stars (as well as against labor leaders and New Deal politicians). Dies and his special investigator, Edward F. Sullivan, accused the Hollywood Anti-Nazi League—whose supporters spanned the entire political spectrum of Hollywood—of being a Communist front. The committee labeled Hollywood a "Hotbed of Communism," and Dies warned that he was planning further hearings "at which members of the film colony will be afforded an opportunity to reply to charges that they were participating in communistic activities."

Donald Ogden Stewart, the MGM screenwriter who was chairman of the Anti-Nazi League, on August 15 called the charges "an ominous sign that the Dies investigating committee has adopted the practice of making accusations without possessing the facts to substantiate them. . . . [Sullivan] seems to have incorporated into his story all the Hollywood rumors collected from the various antilabor, anti-Roosevelt sources."

The Dies committee became a laughingstock to many when it was revealed that one of the members of the film colony who had come under its scrutiny was Shirley Temple. She and other stars had sent greetings to a French newspaper which the committee alleged was owned by the Communist Party. *Variety* acidly observed that "about everybody in Hollywood except Mickey Mouse, Charlie McCarthy and Snow White has been signed up" as a Communist dupe.

Capra, however, was not laughing, particularly after the investigation pointed the finger at the "foreign-born" in Hollywood.

The statements by Sullivan which triggered Capra's response were printed in the *Hollywood Citizen-News* on August 15. "Evidence tends to show that all phases of radical and communistic activities are rampant among the studios of Hollywood and, although well known, [it] is a matter which the movie moguls desire to keep from the public," the investigator declared. Referring to the "ease" with which groups he considered communistic raised their funds, Sullivan said that "no small part of these funds had been obtained from those engaged in the motion picture industry, evidence shows, and the American public should be informed as to the individuals, both native and foreign-born, who use the large salaries paid to them which come from the American public, engaged in supplying these radicals with funds."

Two days later, the Academy's Reorganization Committee (which had been appointed to clean up the Academy's image by making it over into a more purely "cultural" organization) requested authority from the Academy board to send a rebuttal to the Dies committee in Capra's name denying the charge of "rampant" communistic activities in Hollywood. Though the proposed telegram defended Hollywood in general against such accusations, it was carefully phrased to imply that there were some Communist sympathizers in Hollywood, some whose patriotism could be considered suspect, and to disassociate the majority from them.

One board member, Zanuck, thought it would be precipitous to send the telegram until the full character of the attack on Hollywood became known, and individuals accused, before involving the Academy. Capra agreed to hold his fire. Shortly thereafter, he learned that several board members were afraid that there was some basis in fact for such accusations against important Hollywood figures. There is no record in Capra's papers or the Academy's files that the telegram was ever sent, and it was not mentioned in the partially declassified Army Intelligence file on Capra, which includes allegations against him from the files of HUAC.

The following month brought the American Legion's "Americanization" campaign to Hollywood. The Legion had endorsed Dies's efforts to form HUAC and in years to come would become a leading force behind the Hollywood blacklist. Its power in 1938 was demonstrated by the long roster of studio executives and other Hollywood leaders—including Capra, Cohn, and Riskin—attending a luncheon at Twentieth Century–Fox on September 20 honoring the director of the Legion campaign, Homer Chaillaux. The campaign featured what was called a "war on 'isms,' " and the line Capra wrote for Grandpa Vanderhof in *You Can't Take It With You* attacking all "isms" except Americanism may have been inspired by that campaign. At the luncheon, Zanuck gave a defense of Hollywood similar to the unsent Academy telegram but without its attack on the Dies committee. He said that there was "an infinitesimal minority" in Hollywood who "get out the pink shirt now and then" but that "the vast majority" of people in Hollywood were devoted to "American principles, in mind, spirit, and action."

Capra made a public statement of his own patriotism on December 14 when he directed his first radio broadcast, a short play about the Pilgrims' landing entitled *Ship Forever Sailing,* on the special NBC program *America Calling.* Part of the National Rededication Day observances celebrating the Bill of Rights, *America Calling* was a one-hour patriotic extravaganza featuring songs, speeches, and skits by Hollywood stars. Capra's contribution featured James Cagney, Pat O'Brien, Edward G. Robinson, Walter Connolly, Lionel Barrymore, Edward Arnold, and Donald Crisp. It seemed to have been conceived with one eye on the Bill of Rights and one eye on the Dies committee, for Walter Wanger subsequently commended Capra for demonstrating Hollywood's true allegiance to the American people.

The initial charges made by Dies and Sullivan shocked Hollywood into recognizing the vulnerability of the radicals within its ranks, spurring "the retreat of the fence-sitters and moderates," as Ceplair and Englund put it in *The Inquisition in Hollywood.* Capra's initial righteous anger gradually gave way to a cautious silence on the subject as Dies and his fellow reactionaries stepped up their crusade. But Capra remained in the front lines of Hollywood politics in his posts with the Directors Guild and the Academy, and he was not yet intimidated enough to refrain from any involvement in larger political issues.

When the Hollywood Anti-Nazi League held a mass meeting attended by 2,000 people at the Philharmonic Auditorium in downtown Los Angeles on November 18, 1938, to protest the persecution of Jews and to urge a U.S. trade embargo against Germany, Capra was one of the featured speakers, along with Donald Ogden Stewart, John Garfield, and Luise Rainer.

Recognizing the threat Nazi Germany posed to the very existence of his adopted country, Capra was concerned enough to make a common front with President Roosevelt in preparing for possible war against the enemies of democracy. He made a stirring plea for Christians throughout the world to stand up in opposition to the treatment of Jews in Nazi Germany— although he equally decried the persecution of Catholics in Germany, Mexico, and Spain.

Reminding the audience of his own humble background, he passionately contrasted Nazism with the American principles of religious freedom, freedom of the press, and freedom of speech for all people, and in so doing made what seemed a pointed allusion to the Dies committee as he urged the audience to help defend those principles against any enemy, foreign *or* domestic.

"**H**is stories cannot match his story" read the caption underneath the color photograph of Capra on the cover of *Time* on August 8, 1938.

The "genial, stocky, 41-year-old son of Sicilian immigrants" was pictured in a brown tweed suit, yellow sweater, and red tie, with a pipe in his mouth, a script under his arm, and a bemused grin on his face—"I look like an author!" he exclaimed when he was handed a copy of the magazine forty-four years later.

Appearing shortly before the opening of *You Can't Take It With You*, the article trumpeted Capra as Hollywood's master of "a certain kind of peculiarly American, peculiarly kinetic humor" and said that he was regarded "not only as the mainstay of his company but as the top director of his industry."

Time's sentimentalized portrait, typical enough of the magazine's tendency toward hagiography of its cover subjects in that era, also marked the climactic step in Capra's lifelong rehabilitation of his past. The "little wop" who "had a close call from becoming a gangster and racketeer" was now "Columbia's Gem"; the more dubious aspects of his past were discreetly omitted or flatly denied. His picaresque job as a salesman for phony mining stock, recounted that May by Alva Johnston in his rowdy and more lifelike *Saturday Evening Post* profile, "Capra Shoots as He Pleases," now was said to be "apocryphal."

The basic outlines of Capra's mythic personality were starting to take shape as well: his arrival in America, his job selling papers with Tony on the streets of Los Angeles, and his other printable early jobs in and out of Hollywood led into a streamlined account of his rise in the film business (with emphasis on his mentor Walter Montague) and a down-scaling of his wealth (estimating his income from motion pictures as "roughly $350,000 a year" but not mentioning the rest of his million-dollar income that year, and listing his "vacation cottage" in Malibu but not the Brentwood estate). The article stressed his democratic nature, his lack of "ego-parading," and his happy marriage (making it fashionable in Hollywood to have "one wife at a time").

Capra's apotheosis by *Time*, which concluded with a question mark about his future (would he follow Riskin, who had left Columbia to work for Sam Goldwyn?), marked an end as well as a beginning. While catching him at the peak of his fame and influence, it also caught him on the cusp of decline and failure, poised between public triumph and private doubt, at the moment when the man was starting to run for cover into his myth.

Early in the morning of July 11, as the Capras slept in their Brentwood home, Lu was awakened by a noise from the hallway outside her bedroom. As she stepped through the door, a man brushed past her in the dark, coming from the nursery where Frankie, Johnny, and the nine-month-old baby, Lulu, were sleeping. Lu started to cry out, but the man flashed a gun and said: "If you scream, I'll kill you."

Hearing the commotion, Capra dashed out of his bedroom with a pistol and chased the intruder downstairs and out the back door, where the young man disappeared. The children were undisturbed, but the Capras were badly shaken by the incident. Since the intruder had taken nothing of value, and since he had come on the only night of the week when the children slept without their nanny guarding them, Frank and Lu feared that he was a kidnapper. In an era haunted by the kidnapping of the Lindbergh baby, it was a fear shared by many celebrities. The FBI was called into the case, investigating "what they believed to be a plot aimed at the three children," it was reported the next day. For months the Capra children were closely protected; a man with a machine gun sat near them when they played on the beach outside their home in Malibu.

The mystery remained unsolved until the following March, when a young ex-salesman named Ralph Graham was arrested in San Francisco and admitted being the notorious "Bel-Air Burglar" who had broken into the homes of many Hollywood figures over a five-year period, making off with jewels valued at more than two million dollars. The Bel-Air burglar turned out to be a character who could have come from a Frank Capra movie.

"I got a conscience about kids and old ladies," Graham told detectives. "More than one time when I came prowling into a room where a kid was sleeping, I just turned around and left without taking a thing."

That was what happened when he came upon three-year-old John Capra. "When I saw the kid, I just couldn't work anymore that night. A minute later I met Mrs. Capra in an upstairs hall. I had to point my gun at her, but I just did it to frighten her. I wouldn't have harmed her. . . . I left with only a few trinkets, and I could have, if I had wanted, taken maybe twenty-five grand in jewels."

The burglar added: "Not long after that I read about the death of the little Capra boy, and I certainly was sorry to hear about it."

*　　*　　*

John Capra died at 12:20 P.M. on August 23, after undergoing what was described as a routine tonsillectomy at Children's Hospital in Los Angeles.

Frank and Lu had decided to have him undergo the operation in the hope that it might relieve his deafness, which they thought might be caused by chronic infections of his tonsils and adenoids; Frank, Jr., remembered seeing his younger brother walking around before the operation with a bandage over his ear, stained with blood from tests. There seemed to be little else that could be done to stimulate the development of the boy whom Capra, four days before John's death, had described to Edward Bernds as "a lone wolf."

"They noticed his deafness when the time came for him to talk," Josie Campisi remembered. "He would always be by himself, and when other kids would talk to him, he wouldn't look at them unless he happened to turn his head and see them."

"The poor little guy was never all there," Chet Sticht said. "He would stare at the sun and not move. You got the impression he had headaches; he used to bang his head against the wall. You knew there was something wrong in there. But what happened was a hell of a thing—a complete surprise."

The day of Johnny's tonsillectomy was also the day of the first press preview of *You Can't Take It With You*. The operation was finished shortly after 8 A.M. without apparent complications, and at 11:30 Capra left Lu, the sleeping boy, and his nursemaid at the hospital and drove to Columbia, ten minutes away.

The studio lot was decorated with banners heralding Capra and his new film. Three hundred and fifty members of the press had drinks and lunch on a Columbia soundstage before the screening. Capra remembered the studio gate man telling him to return to the hospital as he was driving onto the lot, but in fact he received the message from Sticht in the screening room during the second reel of the film.

"I got this phone call from a nurse that the kid had died, and I had to tell him," Sticht remembered. "Tough thing. I told him, 'Something's gone wrong at the hospital.'"

Capra arrived to find Johnny lying peacefully in his bed; the boy simply had stopped breathing. It was reported that Capra "wept unashamedly at the side of his son's bed."

You Can't Take It With You was still screening to enthusiastic laughter and applause. No one realized that Capra had left until the end of the screening, when the director failed to appear to receive his congratulations.

The hospital told the press that the tonsillectomy could not be the direct cause of death, because there had been no hemorrhage, so an autopsy was performed on August 24 by a hospital pathologist, Dr. Lucille Anderson. The death certificate said the cause was determined at the autopsy to be "Leptomeningitis (type unknown)," a disease which had not been diagnosed while the boy was living. Also mentioned as a contributing cause was "acute enterocolitis with lymphoid hyperplasia," an inflammation of the small intestine and the colon and a lymphoid swelling. Dr. J. Mackenzie Brown, who had performed the tonsillectomy, said in a statement based on Dr. Anderson's findings that the death was due to "chronic inflammation of the brain. . . . On the left side of the brain, there was a growth the size of a human hand affecting both the brain covering and the brain. Any shock or even the administering of an anesthetic might have caused death. It is possible the condition may have existed since birth." Sticht said the growth "was increasing in size, and he wouldn't have had a chance. In a way it was a release for them, because the boy would never have been normal."

Following Johnny's cremation at Forest Lawn Memorial Park on August 25, Capra told Sticht that he and Lu were going away to be alone for a few days. He was back to work by the early part of the following week, hurriedly completing the cutting of *You Can't Take It With You*, whose premiere at the Radio City Music Hall had been set for September 2 and could not be changed.

Joe Walker's wife, Juanita, recalled in 1984 that Capra seemed to be a different man after his son's death—a less cheerful man, less confident of life, with a deeper streak of melancholia. He was able to express his feelings about Johnny's death many years later in the moving, though somewhat evasive, account in his autobiography and in a magazine article in which he wrote of lying on his back in the High Sierras and hearing "voices from the past. . . . a cheery greeting from my long-departed three-year-old: 'Hi, Daddy,' and you smile back, 'Hi, Johnny.' " And after Lu died, he displayed pictures of the cherubic Johnny prominently in his living room.

Deploring the fact that Johnny had never been baptized into the Catholic church, Saridda told Frank and Lu that Johnny would not be allowed into heaven. Lu quietly began taking Catholic instruction and at Christmas 1940 she told her husband she was having Frank, Jr., and Lulu baptized. In time she even would manage to persuade her husband to return to the faith he had scorned as a child.

*   *   *

On August 22, the night before his son's death, Capra had been at Twentieth Century–Fox past eleven o'clock in a last-minute bargaining session with the producers.

The NLRB hearings on the certification of the Directors Guild had been scheduled to begin that morning, but after the SWG was certified by the NLRB on August 10, the producers knew that the directors were almost certain to prevail. They asked for a week's delay in the hearings to see if a settlement could be achieved without government intervention. The SDG agreed, and talks resumed on the nineteenth.

The meeting on the night of Monday the twenty-second lasted more than six hours, with Capra, Hawks, and Van Dyke reiterating the guild demands to Zanuck, Mannix, and Sam Briskin. The producers still insisted on the severance of the unit production managers from the guild, though Hawks had the impression that the producers were not as strongly opposed to the inclusion of assistant directors.

With Capra absent from the SDG board meeting on the following night because of his son's death, the board voted to continue pressing for the inclusion of unit managers, and Mamoulian was appointed to fill the temporary vacancy left by Capra on the bargaining committee, Van Dyke filling in as chairman. Capra remained absent from the negotiating sessions held over the next four days.

At 2 P.M. on Saturday, the talks broke down, primarily over the unit manager issue.

Capra was monitoring the negotiations in his absence, and that Saturday he dropped a bombshell which went unreported in the press: because of his unhappiness with the way the negotiations had been handled, and perhaps also because of his distress over his son's death, he sent a telegram threatening to resign as president of the guild.

The negotiating committee replied quickly and with undisguised alarm. Admitting that the negotiations had been going badly, Van Dyke, Hawks, and Mamoulian said they had resisted splitting the ranks of the guild and other capitulations that would have negated the original reasons for forming the guild. Capra's resignation, they told him, not only would deprive the guild of his talents, but it also would deal a severe blow to the SDG cause.

Capra relented. Asked later why he chose that moment to threaten resignation, he said, "Got to give them a kick in the ass. They weren't able to do it."

The NLRB hearings began on August 29. Capra denied in his book that they ever took place. Taking the case to the government evidently seemed to him a sign of failure, a surrender of his guild's fate to the hated New Deal. It was also an escalation of the stakes beyond the cozy realm of gentlemen's agreements which had been his experience with labor-management dealings in the Academy. Going to the government was a bigger gamble than Capra wanted to take.

The pressure of editing his film caused Capra to drop his plans to testify in the opening rounds of the hearings (perhaps to his relief); Hawks and Mamoulian took the stand instead to describe the formation of the guild and the functions of the director, the assistant director, and the unit manager. The hearings before trial examiner William R. Ringer turned on the question of whether directors were employees, as they contended, or part of management, as the producers insisted.

Capra's salary—the highest of any director in the industry—and those of other top directors were introduced by a battery of studio lawyers in their argument that the director did not suffer from "inequality of bargaining power" and hence was ineligible for protection under the Wagner Act. But under cross-examination by NLRB counsel William Walsh and guild attorney Barry Brannen, studio executives conceded that they retained the ultimate power to hire and fire actors and other filmmaking personnel nominally under the director's command.

"That point really won our case," Rouben Mamoulian felt.

The main part of the hearings was completed on October 6, and final arguments were made a week later. The examiner was to prepare a report for decision by the national board in Washington, but the case would not be decided by the government. The producers, sensing that they could not prevail with the NLRB, reopened negotiations shortly after the hearings.

The contradictions of Capra's dual presidencies of the SDG and the Academy required some deft maneuvering.

Woody Van Dyke, like Capra, was juggling a dual allegiance. The director of such MGM films as *The Thin Man* and *San Francisco*, dubbed "One-Shot Woody" because of his breezy working methods, he was the first vice president of the SDG and also a board member of the Academy and chairman of its Reorganization Committee. Furious at the behavior of Zanuck and the other producers in the latest futile round of negotiations, Van Dyke resigned from the Academy two days after the start of the NLRB hearings, telling the Academy board in an open letter, "I feel that my first allegiance is due to my economic colleagues."

After conferring with Van Dyke—who may have been serving as his stalking horse—Capra emerged on September 14 with a bold maneuver: he gave the producers ten days to resign from the Academy.

"[Writer] Howard Estabrook, Van Dyke, and I have found it tough sledding selling the Academy to the guilds," Capra wrote in asking the Reorganization Committee's approval for the purge. "In fact we have met with downright opposition. Always the same cry—mistrust of the presence of the producers."

The guild leaders, he noted, "feel the Academy setup is a red herring being dragged across the trail to make the talent groups less guild-conscious. Of course we know that isn't so but nevertheless the feeling exists.

"From our present observations we cannot get anything but opposition to the Academy as long as the producers are members. I personally am disinclined to carry this torch any further."

Following through on the threat he had first made privately to Zanuck that March, Capra said he would resign from the Academy along with Van Dyke and Estabrook if the producers refused to leave. "I can see no other way out or no other way to preserve and advance the Academy for the big and worthwhile activities it should carry on in this industry."

The letter, which soon became public, created the intended uproar, primarily from its main target, Darryl F. Zanuck.

"I sincerely mean it when I say that I was never more astonished in my life," Zanuck wrote Capra the following day. "The request for resignation is so basically unfair and the tone of the letter itself is so unreasonable that I cannot help but come to the conclusion that the actual desire for harmony and peace in our industry is nothing but a fantasy. . . .

"I certainly must refuse to resign even though, as you say, it will mean your resignation if I do not. I also will do my best to convince other producers that after our years of service to the Academy we are entitled to more consideration than what amounts to an ultimatum to get out."

Zanuck urged Capra to "recognize that the Academy must come first. It is bigger than all of us and it should continue to be. It must not be destroyed. It has done great good for our industry throughout the world in the past and it can continue to do so in the future—but it must represent every branch of creative talent."

The Academy board on September 22 refused to accept the resignations of Capra, Van Dyke, and Estabrook, as well as the retaliatory resignations of Zanuck, Mannix, and David O. Selznick. Nor would the board go along with the idea of asking the members of the producers branch to resign. Because there was so much antagonism between the guilds and the producers, everyone agreed that plans to reorganize the Academy would be postponed indefinitely, until "a more harmonious condition shall exist in the industry" and until the Academy could be made "completely free from economic or political problems, confining itself solely to the advancement of the arts and sciences of motion pictures."

By attempting a purge and then backing down, the Academy had bought itself a reprieve from extinction and Capra had managed to keep both of his presidencies. It had worked—barely.

14. "My ancestors couldn't; I can"

*T*he film Capra and Cohn chose to end their twelve years of partnership was *Mr. Smith Goes to Washington.*

It began with a screen story by Lewis R. Foster called "The Gentleman from Montana," the story of the disillusionment of a wide-eyed idealist after his appointment to the United States Senate. Columbia producer William Perlberg had optioned it in 1937, but Cohn decided against making the film after the Production Code Administration, run by Joseph I. Breen, expressed its disapproval. When renewed interest was shown by Paramount and MGM, Breen responded in January 1938 by criticizing Foster's "general unflattering portrayal of our system of government, which might well lead to the picture being considered, both here and particularly abroad, as a covert attack on the democratic form of government. . . . It looks to us like it might be loaded with dynamite . . . for the motion picture industry."

Paramount and MGM passed on the story, but the Columbia story department gave it to Rouben Mamoulian, whom Cohn had been trying to lure to the studio. When he read "The Gentleman from Montana," the native of Soviet Georgia, who had been living in the United States since 1923, found it a powerful dramatization of American democracy: "I have nothing but gratitude for this country. I owe it so much. That's why I've always had the credo of trying to add to the goodness of our lives here, the dignity of our people, and faith in the future of our country. And in America we make fun of ourselves and criticize ourselves more than anybody else."

When he told Cohn he wanted to do the story, Cohn said, "Oh, that's no good. It's been turned down."

"If you don't buy it for me," said Mamoulian, "I'm going to do it anyway."

Though Capra claimed otherwise, Mamoulian said that Capra had been one of those who had read the story and had passed on it: "Capra was talking to a story guy at Columbia, and the guy told him I had optioned 'The Gentleman from Montana.' Capra said, 'Let me read it again.' He came to see me and said, 'My God, I didn't like this story, but it's good, isn't it? I'd like to do it. Is there anything you'd like to do at the studio?' I went to Cohn and said, 'The one thing I like here is *Golden Boy.*' "

"Jesus, I wanted that story!" Capra said in 1984 of "The Gentleman from Montana." "I didn't give a damn whether whatchamacallim [Mamoulian] had that. I traded him *Golden Boy* for it."

Lewis R. Foster, who won the only Oscar awarded to *Mr. Smith* in a year dominated by *Gone With the Wind,* was, like Capra, a graduate of the Hal Roach and Mack Sennett comedy schools. But his career faltered when he left the short comedy field, and his fourteen other writing credits and four directing credits on features in the 1930s were undistinguished. After *Mr. Smith,* he received another Oscar nomination as cowriter of George Stevens's 1943 comedy about wartime Washington, *The More the Merrier,* then sank back into obscurity as a writer and director of potboiler adventure films.

Both Capra and Breen referred to Foster's "The Gentleman from Montana" as a "novel," but evidently what Capra bought was an unpublished novelistic treatment. In a 1979 letter to Mrs. Philip Van Doren Stern, whose husband's story "The Greatest Gift" was adapted into *It's a Wonderful Life,* Capra staked his claim to authorship of both that film and *Mr. Smith* by insisting that they were only loosely based on the original stories. But Mamoulian said Foster's story essentially was "the same story" as *Mr. Smith Goes to Washington,* and Breen's synopsis confirms that. Before making the film, Capra told an interviewer, "The fellow's mechanics are excellent," though he misidentified the author as "someone named Mason."

Some of Capra's vagueness about the story and its authorship may have stemmed from reasons other than his usual egotism. Shortly before the film's release, Columbia discovered that Maxwell Anderson had written a play with a remarkably similar plot, *Both Your Houses,* which had won the Pulitzer Prize in 1933. *Both Your Houses* is the story of an idealistic young Nevada college teacher named McClean ("Serious. Wears mail-order clothes. Reads Thomas Jefferson") who is elected to the House of Representatives to serve as the stooge for a crooked political machine. Congressman McClean discovers that the respected chairman of the House Appropriations Committee is part of a pork-barreling scheme to push a graft-ridden deficiency bill through Congress in order to steal money by building an unnecessary dam in their state. Like Senator Jefferson Smith, Congressman McClean is the son of a newspaper editor, socializes with the corrupt politician's daughter, relies heavily on the coaching of his cynical female secretary, finds all of his colleagues turning against him, and is deluged with telegrams protesting his crusade. The major difference between the play and the film is that in *Both Your Houses* the young idealist *loses* his fight, vowing at the end to take it to the people via the press, while in the Capra film he stages a filibuster and wins a satisfying, if improbable, victory when the corrupt politician is moved to confess his wrongdoing.

After discovering the similarities with Anderson's play while *Mr. Smith* was having its previews, Columbia bought the film rights to *Both Your Houses* in late September 1939 to avoid any legal problems, Hollywood columnist Sidney Skolsky reported; the final production cost report on *Mr. Smith* shows that $23,093 was charged for story rights above the $1,506 charged for "The Gentleman from Montana." When *Mr. Smith* came under attack from senators and members of the press after its Washington invitational preview on October 17, Capra issued a statement noting, "To the many books and plays written about Washington no objections have been raised. A play called *Both Your Houses* called all congressmen crooks in no uncertain terms and yet it won the Pulitzer Prize." *

Capra claimed that when he read "The Gentleman from Montana," he immediately envisioned Jimmy Stewart and Jean Arthur in the leading roles. Arthur indeed had been cast from the start as Miss Saunders, the cynical secretary who puts the new senator wise to Washington, but Stewart was not Capra's first choice for the senator.

The film was announced on August 10, 1938, and in the early press reports was titled either *The Gentleman from Montana* or *Mr. Deeds Goes to Washington*, with Montana native Gary Cooper to play the lead. Negotiations were begun with Samuel Goldwyn for a loan of the actor. The title was not changed to *Mr. Smith Goes to Washington* until January 26, 1939, shortly before it was announced that Goldwyn had decided not to loan Cooper and that Capra was borrowing Stewart from MGM instead.

---

*Mr. Smith *also has a number of similarities to* Washington Merry-Go-Round, *a 1932 Columbia film based on a story by Maxwell Anderson, with a screenplay by Jo Swerling. In that film, directed by James Cruze, an idealistic young ex-serviceman named Button Gwinnett Brown (Lee Tracy) is sent to Congress by a corrupt political machine and defeats a pork-barreling bill with the help of Constance Cummings, the cynical granddaughter of a crooked but sympathetic senator played by Walter Connolly. The discouraged Tracy renews his determination by paying a nocturnal visit to the Lincoln Memorial, just as Senator Smith does in Capra's film.*

Capra later recognized that Stewart was much better suited for the role: "Gary Cooper was an honest man, but he wouldn't know an idealist if one came up and hit him. He had a native honesty and decency about him, but it was on a lower level than Jimmy Stewart. Jimmy could deal with an idea."

While Capra was trying to persuade Goldwyn to lend him Cooper, Goldwyn was trying to persuade Capra to join his company. One of the carrots he held out was Robert Riskin.

After finishing his work on *You Can't Take It With You*, Riskin in August 1938 became Goldwyn's executive assistant, as well as a scriptwriter and script "doctor," with a $500,000 annual salary and a profit percentage (at Columbia he had been making $100,000 a year and no percentage). "It is Goldwyn's plan to give him individual buildup," Katherine Smith wrote in the *Washington Daily News* on September 26. ". . . [F]rom now on, nobody will need to wonder what Riskin wrote or didn't write. 'The Riskin Touch' is being publicized. . . . As collaborators, Riskin [had] as much hand in the directing as Capra in the screen writing—Riskin admirers say more—and now that Riskin has deserted the Lady with the Torch for Sam Goldwyn's lion, some Hollywood schools of thought are clucking that Capra had better follow, for what can a director do without a good scenario?"

If Goldwyn had wanted to play on Capra's insecurities, such publicity was just the thing. He added another carrot by hiring Jo Swerling away from Columbia in October. But Capra had already jumped at Goldwyn's overtures. As early as August 21, it was rumored in the press that Capra would follow Riskin to Goldwyn's studio after making *The Gentleman from Montana*. During the negotiations for Cooper that fall, Capra openly discussed his own future with Goldwyn, and he would continue to do so even after the deal for Cooper fell through. On February 17 a deal between Capra and Goldwyn was reported in *Daily Variety* as a fait accompli.

But Capra was biding his time in making a final decision. He was hoping to persuade David O. Selznick to let him direct *Gone With the Wind*. Selznick was already having friction with its appointed director, George Cukor, but he was reluctant to replace him with such an independent-minded director as Capra. Although Capra was "dying to do *Gone With the Wind* . . . I don't think we need him on it, and I mention this only to show the buying power of a directorial assignment on *Gone With the Wind*," Selznick wrote his lawyer on September 21, 1938. Cukor kept the job until February 13, 1939, shortly after the start of shooting, when he was replaced by Victor Fleming.

Capra had not yet given up on his dream of forming his own independent production company, though the idea of going independent and leaving the security of a studio made him anxious. "Year after year Capra threatened to leave," recalled Columbia writer Lewis Meltzer. "Finally Cohn let him." The security of working for Goldwyn appealed to Capra; the idea of leaving Harry Cohn only to put himself under another man's thumb did not. Goldwyn was a giant in the industry, a relatively tasteful and intelligent man, and a producer known for his respect for writers. But he was also, like Selznick, an autocratic man who liked to have his way with directors. It would be a hard choice.

First Capra would make *Mr. Smith*. And before settling on his own future, he wanted to bring the Directors Guild negotiations to fruition.

With a little help from Sam Goldwyn.

Goldwyn, who had rejoined the producers' organization in August 1938 after several years of going it alone, realized that the government almost certainly would support the guild's right to organize, as the NLRB had decided in the case of the Writers Guild, and he was willing to make a separate peace with the guild if need be. He approached Capra that October, at the end of the NLRB hearings on the certification of the SDG. He and Capra came up with a formula for breaking the impasse, predicated on the guild's acquiescence in breaking ranks with the unit managers after negotiating a pact for that group (although Capra later maintained, "We didn't give away a goddamn thing, we *didn't* back down").

The compromise was accepted by the guild's board and by the producers, and what the guild considered an outline of an agreement was reached on November 8. Negotiations resumed between Mabel Walker Willebrandt and Edwin Loeb, a prominent Hollywood attorney representing the producers.

Capra helped promote interguild unity by directing a radio program, *Can We Forget?*, on January 22, 1939, for CBS's *Screen Guild Show*, a joint effort of the guilds to benefit the Motion Picture Relief Fund. The radio play by SWG activist Mary McCall, Jr., foreshadowed *It's a Wonderful Life* in its story of a lonely New York society woman (Bette Davis) who plans to kill herself on Christmas to join her late husband (Robert Montgomery) but is talked out of it by her husband's ghost, who urges her to marry his former rival (Basil Rathbone). *Variety* called it "absorbing. . . . [T]he scenes moved swiftly and were extremely effective."

By mid-January the only major stumbling block remaining in the SDG negotiations appeared to be the guild's demand that directors be given "reasonable" time for script preparation and for cutting, including the right to a first cut. With the producers amenable to keeping the assistants in the guild and promising a boost in minimum wages for assistants and unit managers, Capra felt that the major issues appeared to have been resolved.

But after appointing a new negotiating committee on February 6, Schenck failed to keep a Saturday appointment five days later for a one-on-one session with Capra. Capra, who "took it as a terrific affront," pursued Schenck to his box at the Santa Anita Race Track. Schenck informed him that the new committee now wanted the guild to drop the assistant directors from its ranks.

The SDG board the following Monday received Capra's report on the meeting with consternation, and Rowland V. Lee, a member of the guild's negotiating committee, blamed the guild for failing to press the producers hard enough for a solution. Prompted by Van Dyke, Capra—the man who later would claim he single-handedly won an agreement for the SDG because he had more "balls" than anyone else in the guild—went to the phone and placed an SOS to Mabel Walker Willebrandt in Washington.

She returned to Los Angeles, while the board demanded that the producers send her a telegram by February 16 promising to conclude negotiations for a basic agreement without further delay. No such telegram was forthcoming, and on the night before the deadline, emboldened by Willebrandt's presence, Capra suggested to the board that the guild stop negotiating with the producers and make a public issue of their duplicitous behavior.

The Academy Awards were scheduled to be presented in eight days, on February 23. Capra was to be the master of ceremonies, and *You Can't Take It With You* was up for seven Oscars, including best picture and best director. But he told the board he was willing to quit his post as Academy president and lead a boycott of the ceremonies. He drafted a statement blaming the producers for their high-handed lack of good faith in their dealings with the guild.

Guild members were summoned by telegram to the Hollywood Athletic Club on Thursday night, February 16. Capra told the 92 senior and 168 junior members attending the meeting that his resignation as Academy president would take effect at 6 P.M. Friday unless the AMPP came to terms with the guild.

"If they refused this time," Capra recalled in 1985, "they would kill the Academy, and, brother, the last thing I wanted to kill was the Academy, but if that's what meant [achieving recognition for] the Directors Guild, that was it, we'd kill the Academy. I had to sacrifice the Academy I'd saved."

But when Wesley Ruggles urged that his statement be given to the press immediately, Capra convinced him that doing so would be precipitous and might backfire on the guild. MGM's Norman Taurog suggested extending the deadline by two hours, and the membership agreed. The line finally was drawn. Capra managed to hold off those who wanted an immediate strike, but rumors of a possible strike were leaked as a warning to the producers.

Even the *idea* of a strike made Capra nervous. He admitted in his book that he was not sure whether he would honor a strike if it meant not making *Mr. Smith.*

Capra's threat to resign as Academy president also was leaked to the press. Schenck hurried back from Palm Springs for an emergency meeting at Fox that Friday afternoon at 2:30 with the executive committee of the AMPP, including Zanuck, Goldwyn, Harry Cohn, Louis B. Mayer, Jack and Harry Warner, Paramount's Y. Frank Freeman, and RKO's Pandro S. Berman and J. R. McDonough, as well as six attorneys representing the producers.

After an hour and a half, they called for Capra, who, as *Daily Variety* reported, "discussed [the] pending negotiations for two hours, at the end of which the producers agreed to recognize the guild and asked for three weeks additional time in which to work out the details" on remaining issues. Though Capra said later that Schenck "gave us every damn thing we asked for," the understanding they reached at the meeting was much more modest. Despite Capra's urging, the producers refused to make any proposal on pay scales and working hours for assistant directors and unit managers, nor could Capra and the producers come to terms on the issues of a first cut and time for preparation and cutting.

Capra did succeed, however, in getting an agreement on the other basic points: recognition of the SDG, inclusion of the assistant directors, an 80-percent guild shop, and conciliation and arbitration procedures. The producers, as previously agreed, would let the guild negotiate a separate agreement for the unit managers but only on the condition that the unit managers would then be dropped from the guild—a concession the original SDG negotiating committee had called non-negotiable and which Capra insisted in 1985 the guild had never made. Capra left with a letter from Schenck confirming the terms of the agreement.

"Jesus Christ, what a moment it was for me!" Capra remembered. "We'd saved the Academy Awards and saved the Directors Guild. My heart just flittered."

As a reward for Capra's help in restoring industry peace, Schenck also sent him out of the room with a promise of a lucrative future deal to make films for Twentieth Century–Fox.

There would be no strike, and Capra would not have to resign from his Academy presidency. He asked Schenck to present the Thalberg Award to Hal Wallis at the Oscar ceremony, and the grateful Academy gave Capra his third Oscar for best director, in addition to choosing *You Can't Take It With You* as best picture.*

After resolving other issues with the producers, Willebrandt removed the last obstacle in the negotiations by proposing a compromise on the key creative issue of the director's first cut. The final agreement, reached on March 13, provided only that every director would be "consulted" on the editing of the rushes and the producer's first rough cut, and it gave freelance directors six days of paid cutting time on pictures budgeted at more than $200,000, and three days for less expensive pictures, but the guild conceded the producers the final cut.†

Capra was reelected to the guild presidency on May 21 and again in 1940. He finally stepped down on May 19, 1941 ("Tired? I should say I was tired"), turning over the presidency to George Stevens. At that night's annual meeting of the guild, in response to a proposal by William Wyler, Capra was unanimously voted an honorary life membership.

"I'll tell you," Capra said later, "I've never had good relations with the Writers Guild—the Writers Guild hates me—but I've got friends *one* place, and that's the Directors Guild."

When Capra and his screenwriter, Sidney Buchman, went to Washington to prepare *Mr. Smith* in October 1938, they toured the capital by bus and visited the Lincoln Memorial, like the young senator in their film. They also visited the White House, attending President Roosevelt's press conference late on a hot Indian summer afternoon, October 11.

Standing in the back row of reporters clustered around the desk in the President's office, Capra was too short to see over their heads and could only listen to FDR bantering with reporters on a day when the President admitted, "I don't believe there is any particular news." But after shaking hands with the President, Capra came away unexpectedly impressed by his first personal encounter with a man for whom he had never voted (and never would). "What a voice! What a personality!" Capra exclaimed as he

---

* *Before retiring as Academy president in December 1940, Capra supervised the production of a promotional short,* Cavalcade of the Academy Awards, *released that April, which promoted Capra almost as much as it did the Academy, while featuring clips from past Oscar-winning films and footage of that year's ceremony.*

† *The guild did not win the right to a first cut for directors until 1964. Capra, who had served as president again from 1959 through 1961, was called back to conduct those negotiations with the producers.*

left. Asked if his new film would depict a presidential press conference, Capra said, "Nobody could do a thing as good as this."

Capra's new stirrings of admiration for FDR, and public statement in support of the President's interventionist policies that November, did not mean that he had been converted from his long-held view of Roosevelt as a man who "was getting too big for the country's good." He was incensed by FDR's failed effort to pack the Supreme Court in 1938, seeing it as an attempt at a dangerous and unconstitutional usurpation of power. And despite the approach of World War II, a note in his shooting script for *Mr. Smith* indicates that Capra was enraged by the prospect of the President winning an unprecedented third term in 1940; he voted for the Republican Wendell Willkie, who would serve as the model for the Spencer Tracy character in his 1948 film, *State of the Union*.

While in Washington Capra scouted other locations for *Mr. Smith*, arranged for government cooperation, and visited the FBI. On October 13, he was photographed firing a Thompson submachine gun in the agents' pistol range, and the photo was sent to his room at the Mayflower Hotel two days later by FBI Director J. Edgar Hoover "as a memento of your tour of inspection of our facilities." Always eager to court celebrities for publicity purposes, Hoover also may have wanted to establish contact with Capra in light of the interest shown in him by the recently created HUAC, and possibly because of Capra's attempt to protest HUAC's investigation of Hollywood and his ongoing associations with various liberals and leftists. The continuing scrutiny of Capra's political views was demonstrated by the fact that U.S. Army Intelligence opened its file on Capra on October 14, indicating that he was an "Additional mbr [member] of 6.100 [code for an unspecified organization]." It surely also did not escape notice that he was in Washington working on a political story with Sidney Buchman, who was a Screen Writers Guild activist and became a member of the Communist Party by late 1938; Buchman's wife, Beatrice, was prominent in the Hollywood Anti-Nazi League, which HUAC called a "Communist front organization" and whose mass meeting Capra addressed in November, shortly after he and the writer returned from Washington.

"**H**ere is Capra, without the help of Riskin, back to his finest form—the form of *Mr. Deeds*," wrote Graham Greene of *Mr. Smith Goes to Washington*. Greene, who in his previous reviews had seemed curiously indifferent to Riskin's contribution, added, "It has always been an interesting question, how much Capra owed to his faithful scenario writer. Now it is difficult to believe that Riskin's part was ever very important, for all the familiar qualities are here."

Capra and his latter-day loyalists have made similar arguments, contending that the quality of *Mr. Smith* and *It's a Wonderful Life* prove that Capra, not Riskin, was the *auteur* of his pre-1939 classics. But, despite its complicated authorship (Buchman and Foster were the only writers credited on screen, but Myles Connolly was credited in the Academy *Bulletin* as "contributor to screenplay and dialogue" and Capra also did some rewriting), *Mr. Smith*, as its interim title *Mr. Deeds Goes to Washington* made evident, adhered closely to what Greene called "the form of *Mr. Deeds*" and to what Capra called his "formula." The mold had been set by Riskin, and though Capra made two of his best films without Riskin, he never made another good film (or a bad film, for that matter) that deviated essentially from the formula. Yet there was an important difference between *Mr. Deeds* and *Mr. Smith:* while the liberal belief that an honest, principled individual could stand up and change the system had been brought to Capra's work by Riskin, the leftist Sidney Buchman intensified the idea and made the lone-man-against-the-system, Senator Jefferson Smith, much more of an active, fighting, articulate force for social change than Longfellow Deeds had been.

Jefferson Smith is an amateur politician from the stronghold of populism, the great American heartland; he is "a young patriot who recites Lincoln and Jefferson, turned loose in our nation's capital." But as the film shows, populism and innocence have their dangerous sides. Smith is a Boy Ranger leader, a political appointee chosen as an "honorary stooge" to fill a desk in the Senate while the corrupt political machine headed by Boss Jim Taylor (Edward Arnold) and senior Senator Joseph Harrison Paine (Claude Rains) sneak their dam construction project through as part of the deficiency bill. Smith naively chooses the dam site—Willet Creek—for his pet project, a camp for "boys of all nationalities and ways of living . . . to educate them in American ideals," and winds up being accused of secretly buying up the land for his own profit. The climax of the film is Smith's challenge to the machine, and to the Senate itself, in the form of his impassioned twenty-three-hour filibuster, hoping to appeal via press and radio to the folks back home.*

Capra's fundamental conservatism was being tempered by the changes in the world around him when he made *Mr. Smith;* World War II began

*Though the senator's state was Montana in the original story, it is not identified in the film; Capra said he thought of Smith as being from downstate Illinois (Lincoln country), with Taylor's machine based upstate (Cook County). The film does not use the words "Democrat" or "Republican," but since Stewart and Rains sit on the right side of the Senate from the vantage point of the president pro tem, that means they are Democrats.

while he was editing the film, when Hitler invaded Poland on September 1, 1939. His "kinship with his audience," as Greene called it, had grown with his understanding of the Depression, even as those years had made him a wealthy man. His growing labor militancy, while it did not extend to sympathy for the average workingman, also contributed to making him, at that moment, more open to progressive ideas than at any other time in his life. And as an immigrant from a country that had become a Fascist dictatorship and would soon be at war with his adopted country, Capra was concerned enough about the spread of fascism that he found himself publicly agreeing with the interventionist FDR rather than with the isolationist "America Firsters." The reactionary side of Capra was overshadowed by an urgent burst of idealism in the late 1930s that enabled him to bring forth, at the end of the decade, a ringing patriotic work that celebrated the American political system without flinching from a realistic depiction of its flaws and corruption.

Capra did not see *Mr. Smith* as a radical statement. When the film's patriotism was questioned, he issued a defensive statement calling it "a very mild motion picture" whose motive "was to idealize American democracy, not to attack it." Even the stirring apogee of Senator Smith's filibuster—"You fight for the lost causes harder than for any others; yes, you even die for them"—was a sentiment that could well have stemmed from the Catholic conservative Myles Connolly, who wrote in *Mr. Blue:* "No great battle for a great cause can ever be forgotten . . . [for] up there is a hearth and home for the Lost Cause that is never lost, the citadel of a strength that shall outlast the hill and rocks it stands upon."

From Capra's later political vantage point, the most uncomfortable irony of *Mr. Smith,* however, was that its chief screenwriter was an active member of the Communist Party.

"The best writer of all, in my estimation, was the guy who got credit for *Mr. Smith Goes to Washington,*" Capra said of Sidney Buchman in 1984. "Some of his words were just perfect. Now, mind you, he was a Communist, and that he should write *that* picture—you see how you can . . . he didn't *want* to write that kind of show.

"He knew what he was doing. I knew it [that he was a Communist]. He *said* it. I didn't give a shit who was a Communist or who wasn't. I had control of the picture, and nothing I didn't like could go in there. I wasn't worried in the slightest."

But though Capra and Connolly made their contributions to the script of *Mr. Smith,* most of it *was* Buchman's, a fact which Capra sometimes denied ("Nobody can take credit for those films as writers—I changed the goddamn things back and forth") and sometimes acknowledged with a rare degree of generosity, as if he were eager to disclaim responsibility for the film. That ambivalence was reflected in another statement Capra made in 1984: "One of the best scripts I ever had—with some of the best speeches, and they were *his*, and they *weren't* 'his' in my movies—was written by a Communist, Sidney Buchman."

In the uncut version of his autobiography, Capra professed ignorance of Buchman's Communist Party membership at the time they made *Mr. Smith*, which was filmed from April 3 through July 7, 1939. He wrote that Buchman did not reveal his true colors to him until that August 24, the day after the signing of the Hitler-Stalin nonaggression pact, when he shocked Capra by turning against President Roosevelt. In Capra's view, Buchman's Communist allegiance now made the writer turn a blind eye (as Roosevelt did not) to the evil of Adolf Hitler, although Buchman was Jewish and until then had admired FDR. Capra wrote that he fell apart with Buchman as a result of that revelation, which he implied also helped sour his view of the many writers who shared Buchman's expedient view of the Hitler-Stalin pact, the event that precipitated the rupture of the Popular Front coalition between Hollywood liberals and leftists.

But Capra's story is disingenuous. "During the making of *Mr. Smith*, Capra was terribly suspicious of me," Buchman, who died in 1975, recalled in a 1969 interview with Bertrand Tavernier. "He knew that I had joined the Party and figured that I wanted to slip in a hidden message, an allusion, an ambiguous sentence. He had the impression that I wanted to betray him." Capra's account of his supposed 1939 split with Buchman differs from his explanation in 1951, when he told John Ford that though he had inklings Buchman was a Communist, the schism had to do with Buchman's opposition to Roosevelt's Lend-Lease plan in aid of Great Britain. But this explanation doesn't wash, for President Roosevelt did not announce the Lend-Lease plan until December 17, 1940,* and Capra remained on speaking terms with Buchman at least as late as 1942, taking his advice to hire writer John Sanford for the U.S. Army's *Why We Fight* films. Furthermore, two of the *Why We Fight* films contain justifications of the Hitler-Stalin pact, a fact which Capra later tried to ignore and which may have led him to point the finger at Buchman, hoping it would not be pointed at himself.

* *Roosevelt formulated the plan during a cruise to the West Indies on the battle cruiser USS Tuscaloosa. On the last day of the cruise, December 16, the President watched* Mr. Smith Goes to Washington *for the first time; afterward he not only expressed his appreciation of the film to the aides and sailors who watched it with him, he also used it as a springboard for a pep talk on each citizen's responsibility in a democracy.*

Capra's attempts to distance himself from Buchman were inconsistent not only because of the shifts in the political climate but also because to disclaim Buchman entirely would mean that he would also have to disavow *Mr. Smith*, as in fact he tried to do during the Vietnam War period, telling a college audience in 1966, "Today I wouldn't consider producing such a picture, because enough people are degrading our country with derogatory remarks. One can't poke fun at what he loves if it is bleeding." Yet five years later, in his autobiography, he conceded that *Mr. Smith* was his masterpiece. In later years, Capra usually called *It's a Wonderful Life* his favorite film, but in 1984 he acknowledged that he considered *Mr. Smith* a better film: "It's a stronger story and a story about our government, a lot of the internal workings of our government are revealed. I suppose that's why I like it better than the other ones—it's *big*."

And as hard as it was for Capra to face in retrospect, there may have been an irony but there was no fundamental inconsistency in *Mr. Smith* being written by a Communist, for, as journalist Tom Pryor put it, Buchman "was an *American* Communist." Ceplair and Englund observed in *The Inquisition in Hollywood* that "virtually all leftists" in America during the 1930s "shared their conservative opponents' ideological underpinnings: loyalty to, and faith in, the American democratic tradition and its possibilities." But while the Right developed "an exclusivist and highly class-conscious definition of nationality through its doctrine of Americanism," the Left "stressed the 'revolutionary' and 'original democratic' impulses of the Founding Fathers and documents."

"I joined the Party when the world was troubled by fascism, the rising tide of fascism abroad," Buchman testified before the House Committee on Un-American Activities in 1951. "We in America were worried about many problems dealing with economic inequality, and political inequality. The Communist Party seemed to be the only political force both concerned and willing to take action to stop the threat of fascism abroad and to work for economic and political reform in this country." Buchman remained in the Party until 1945, when the Duclos Letter appeared, in which French Communist Jacques Duclos condemned the CPUSA for its policy of working with democratic capitalism for the sake of the wartime Soviet-American alliance. After the CPUSA set about "flagellating itself" over the Duclos Letter, Buchman said, he left the Party because of "a lack of freedom of thought. . . . I repudiated communism as a philosophy for myself. I consider the philosophy of the Communist Party as not applicable to our American way of life." But he refused to name anyone but himself to HUAC as a Party member and was blacklisted as a result.

When he wrote *Mr. Smith*, Buchman, unlike Capra, admired President

Roosevelt's personality *and* his policies, and rather than cynically cloaking his communism with flag-waving patriotism, as Capra suggested in retrospect, Buchman managed to put the stamp of his political beliefs on Capra's work. *Mr. Smith Goes to Washington* became a bold frontal assault on political corruption in the nation's capital and a protest against the perversion of traditional American values and institutions. Buchman also gave an explicit warning in *Mr. Smith* about the threat to those values from both foreign and domestic fascism. CBS radio commentator H. V. Kaltenborn appears in the film to call Smith's filibuster "the American privilege of free speech in its most dramatic form. . . . In the diplomatic gallery are the envoys of two dictator powers. They have come here to see what they can't see at home—democracy in action." And Jimmy Stewart tells Jean Arthur, "Liberty's too precious a thing to be buried in books, Miss Saunders—men should hold it up in front of them every single day of their lives and say, 'I'm free, to think and to speak. My ancestors couldn't; I can. And my children will.' "

Capra publicly seemed to have had no trouble accommodating himself to the urgency of Buchman's political thinking. As Geoffrey Hellman reported in his 1940 *New Yorker* profile of the director, "Capra's feeling that the meek will inherit the earth from the rich, or possibly wrench it away from them, is not confined to his pictures, and it often crops up in his conversation. When he airs his social and economic theories, and he does this during most of his spare time, his face lights up, his handsome black eyes sparkle, and he looks like an unusually animated freshman at a college bull session. He likes to tell his friends that money is the curse of Hollywood and that trade and profit are ruining the world."

Buchman questioned the depth of Capra's beliefs, telling Tavernier: "Intellectually he was a very simplistic man. His view of the world came down to that of a fairy tale: at the end the good people had to be rewarded and the evil ones punished. There was no political or social point of view in this. . . . [H]e believed in Shangri-La, but he didn't believe in applying the moral to real life. . . . For him a politician or a capitalist were simply marionettes representing good or evil. . . . Their meaning didn't exist for him, and I really believe that he never knew what *Mr. Smith* actually was saying.

"Capra's great passion was Dickens. As soon as he had some money, he bought some of the rarest and most extraordinary editions of Dickens's work, and he was very proud of his collection. One day he came to see me in my room and we talked about *Smith.* I tried to show him what I meant to say, that it is necessary to maintain a vigilant attitude even when you think you are living in a democracy, that you should refuse to surrender even on the smallest things, because their importance can be enormous. I ended by saying, 'There, that's my theme.' He looked at me and suddenly said: 'Go get fucked with your theme!' It was so sudden that I was dumb-struck. He tried to catch himself by saying that he didn't believe that an artist had to have political or social preoccupations, that he should content himself with entertaining the public, etc. I told him, 'How can you say that, you who claim to admire Dickens? The slightest line of Dickens has a precise social meaning. O.K., he was anti-Semitic, but apart from that, he tried to fight poverty, the exploitation of the poor.' He looked at me and said: 'Are you a Communist?' I answered him: 'Are you a Fascist?' And we left it at that."

Many of Capra's own contributions to the script of *Mr. Smith* involved the relationship between Jefferson Smith and his fallen idol, Senator Paine, whom Capra described as "the good man who has sold himself out."

If seen from Paine's viewpoint, the film is a tragedy, ending in a failed suicide attempt, with the presidential aspirant shouting to his colleagues in the Senate, "I'm not fit to be a Senator. I am not fit to *live!* . . . I'm not fit for any place of honor or trust. Expel *me!*" If Jefferson Smith represented the idealistic side of Capra, the side which saw America's promise, Paine was his more pragmatic and ambitious side, the side which saw America's failure and represented the "catastrophe of Success." The theme of be-trayal runs throughout *Mr. Smith*—betrayal both by Paine and by the American system. It was Capra, not Buchman, who first reworked the scene of Smith weeping at the Lincoln Memorial to include his expression to Saunders of disillusionment over what he calls "the whole rotten show . . . a lot of junk about American ideals."

Smith's final disillusionment comes in a powerful exchange of close-ups when Paine lies to a Senate committee to smear Smith for the very crime of graft he himself committed. He is a false father figure, represent-ing a symbolic opposition to Smith's martyred father, the small-town news-paper editor who died defending the claim of one lone miner against a mining syndicate ("Dad always used to say the only causes worth fighting for *were* the lost causes"). But the lesson Jefferson Smith draws from his father's death is ambivalent and, in light of later events in the film, ironic: "I suppose, Mr. Paine, when a fellow bucks up against a big organization like that—one man by himself can't get very far, can he?" To which Paine, despite the qualms of conscience he will later reveal, answers with a blunt "No," then explains to the despairing Smith, in a speech to which Capra contributed: "This is a man's world, Jeff, and you've got to check your ideals outside the door like your rubbers. Now, thirty years ago, I had your ideals. I was *you*. I had to make the same decision you were asked to make today, and I made it. I compromised. Yes—so that all those years I could sit in that Senate and serve the people in a thousand honest ways."

"For that time, what was in the film was pretty courageous," Buchman felt. "But Capra unfortunately oversimplified a few things. When I watch the film again, I always leave before the end. I detest the [attempted] suicide of Claude Rains; it was an idiotic idea and I fought against it, without success. All of a sudden you're in a totally unreal situation. Capra wasn't able to avoid falling into moments of violence. He really liked that scene, but at the same time he lessened the political impact of the film."

Jimmy Stewart knew he was playing the part of a lifetime. As Jean Arthur remembered: "He was so serious when he was working in that picture, he used to get up at five o'clock in the morning and drive five miles an hour to get himself to the studio. He was so terrified that something was going to happen to him, he wouldn't go any faster."

"Frank gave me this chance, this tremendous, wonderful role, which really started me rolling," said Stewart. Stewart's performance is such a tour de force, one of the richest and most moving in American film history, that Jean Arthur's more self-effacing work is seldom mentioned, but she, too, did some of her best work in *Mr. Smith*. "Well," she said, "I had some good lines. It was very impressive, a lot of those speeches. The *story* was the most important thing in *Mr. Deeds* and *Mr. Smith*. They were *saying* something."

One of the most satisfying ironies of *Mr. Smith* from a contemporary perspective is its commentary on sexual politics—Smith is helpless without his secretary telling him what to do, and her manipulation of the senator becomes her revenge at the system which has all but squashed her own idealism. Arthur's expert comedic playing carries the film along in the early sections, when Stewart has little to do except look wide-eyed and ask questions. Miss Saunders's long monologue explaining how a bill is passed through Congress not only serves as the exposition for the rest of the film, but also sets the film's delicately balanced tone of surface cynicism and underlying emotion, laying the framework for Stewart to let out all emotional stops with his filibuster.

Her most memorable piece of acting, however, is her virtuoso drunk scene with Thomas Mitchell at the National Press Club. As Howard Hawks, who helped Capra with the scene, explained it, "Jean Arthur was in love with Jimmy Stewart, and she was trying to persuade Thomas Mitchell to marry her because she was in love with Stewart." Staging the scene in an unbroken two-shot, Capra allowed his actors to set the tempo of the scene. Mitchell had little to say, but his seriocomic reactions skillfully punctuated Arthur's manic-depressive mood changes.

"I defy any other actress to play that scene," Capra marveled. "She's a great actress, much better than she knows. She made it believable with little things, like the way she tried to pick up her glass and didn't know which glass she was picking up. Her mind was so confused because she was so hurt inside—here was this punk from the country who had gotten to her and she didn't like it. She didn't know what to do about it, whether or not to tell him the truth about all the dirty tricks that the other people were pulling, because she was beginning to fall in love with him. Well, that's not an actress, that's a gal in trouble, that's a human being we can understand."

The role of the vice president gave Capra a chance to work with Harry Carey, who had encouraged him during the shooting of John Ford's *The Outcasts of Poker Flat*, when Capra was a five-dollar-a-day extra.

"Here's a good American face," Joe Sistrom said of Carey while they were looking through a casting directory.

But the old cowboy actor was nervous. "What do I do but damn near muff the part," he told a reporter. "Me, who's been in pictures since 1908. In my first scene I have to administer the oath of office to Jim Stewart. It was no good and I knew it. Capra ordered a retake, and again I muff it. Another retake, another muff. 'Print it,' Capra said. But I knew it was terrible, and so did he, because he left the camera set up exactly as it was while we went to lunch."

"Harry Carey did his lines, but he was tight," Capra recalled. "I could see the sweat pouring from his forehead. There were lots of people watching. I told him, 'Let's try it again when our bellies are full.' I avoided him at lunch, afraid I might say the wrong word. One word could ruin it.

"When we came back from lunch, I leaned over his desk and said, 'Who are you?' 'Harry Carey.' 'No. Who are you?' 'The vice president of the United States.' 'That's right, I don't want Harry Carey, the cowboy actor; when you swear in that young punk senator I want you to remember that you're one heartbeat away from being President—you're swearing him in as the vice president of the United States.' "

Carey followed that piece of direction, and, Capra felt, "He stole the show." Whenever the director needed a reaction shot for Jimmy Stewart's speeches, and when he had trouble deciding how to end the picture, he simply cut to Harry Carey's good American face.

*　　　*　　　*

Mr. *Smith* finished shooting on July 7, eight days over schedule; the negative cost was $1,963,354, exceeding the budget by $288,660. Capra's party for the cast and crew on July 8 was tinged with melancholy, for he and the others realized, as Edward Bernds wrote in his diary, that *Mr. Smith* probably marked his "farewell to Columbia."

Fred W. Perkins of the Washington bureau of Scripps-Howard wrote Capra that month to suggest that the film be given a gala preview at the National Press Club in honor of Jim Preston, the film's technical adviser. Preston, who had been superintendent of the Senate Press Gallery for thirty-five years, was a dead ringer for British Prime Minister Neville Chamberlain, down to the mustache and rolled-up umbrella. He gave Capra valuable advice on Senate procedure and on details of Lionel Banks's magnificent set, a photographic replica of the Senate chamber which filled the two largest stages at Columbia. But Preston was horrified by Capra's jibes at the press, whom the director constantly called "gravy spillers," and he was upset over the director's unwillingness to let him read and critique the script during preproduction, as well as by such scenes as Arthur shouting and giving orders to Stewart in sign language from the press gallery. Preston went back to Washington before the film finished shooting, "completely disillusioned" and feeling that Capra had "misled" him about the nature of the film. Reports of his unhappiness (which he made public only after the film's release) apparently had not hit Washington when the Press Club offered to sponsor the preview.

While visiting the Press Club during preproduction research, Capra shared some beers in its Tap Room with Washington correspondents, and he received permission to re-create the Tap Room for the film. He assured the club's president, Arthur Hachten of the International News Service, that he would not indulge in the usual stereotyping of reporters, but after attending the White House press conference, he was quoted as saying that the Washington press corps were "terrible," a bunch of "yes men" who used handouts to write their stories: "That's not the way I used to picture newspapermen when I thought I would like to be one, years ago." Capra did not warn Hachten that Diz Moore, the reporter played by Thomas Mitchell, would be drunk throughout much of the film or that the scenes in the Tap Room would include a brawl between Smith and jeering, cynical members of the fourth estate. Nor did he mention that the film would show Boss Taylor muzzling the press and radio in his state to stop the people from hearing the truth about what Smith is saying on the floor of the Senate and that the only paper able to print the truth is Smith's own *Boy Stuff*, before the Boy Rangers printing and distributing it are stopped by Taylor's goons.

"The picture took some of the shine off the Washington reporter, who was supposed to be the god of all times," Capra acknowledged in 1984. "I knew trouble was coming."

The rave reviews for *Mr. Smith* in the trade papers (*Daily Variety* calling it "the most vital and stirring drama of contemporary American life yet told in film") emboldened the previously hesitant Capra to accept the offer to preview the film for Jim Preston and his gravy spillers. As a precaution, he invited Hachten, Perkins, and Walter Karig, Washington correspondent of the *Newark Evening News*, to a sneak preview on October 3 at the Dyckman Street Theatre in New York City. "We gave them the chance to say no. I said I'd play it for them in front of an audience, not show it to them alone, and then if they still wanted to play it, fine. But it was not the *Washington* audience." The journalists liked the film, and agreed to sponsor the gala preview, which was set for October 17 at Washington's Constitution Hall, preceded by a Press Club luncheon for Capra.

The preview was a dazzling social event, attended by 4,000 guests, among them 45 senators, including Majority Leader Alben W. Barkley; 250 congressmen, including Speaker of the House William Bankhead and Majority Leader Sam Rayburn; Secretary of State Cordell Hull; Attorney General Frank Murphy; Postmaster General Jim Farley; several justices of the U.S. Supreme Court; and many members of the press. Columbia was represented by Harry Cohn, Joe Brandt, Jack Cohn, and Capra (Jimmy Stewart was busy in Hollywood making *Destry Rides Again*, and Jean Arthur also was absent).

The audience was greeted with searchlights and a National Guard band playing patriotic tunes. The Capras sat in a box with Senator Burton K. Wheeler, the prominent isolationist Republican from Montana (who was not, however, the model for Jefferson Smith, as some assumed), Wheeler's wife and daughter, and the Hachtens. The *Washington Times-Herald* put out a special edition, with a banner headline reading "4,000 WELCOME MR. SMITH TO WASHINGTON" over photos of the audience and the Capras; newsboys were selling copies as the crowd exited the hall.

"Frank Capra had been terrified of this showing," wrote Eileen Creelman in the *New York Sun* the following day. "He admitted it. He admitted, too, that he would rather like it if some senator did publicly protest and try to stop the show.

"But nobody protested."

The account of the preview in Capra's book was overdramatized. The audience reaction, according to Creelman and other reporters, was at least superficially polite. Though members of the Senate and the Washington press corps "came out looking as if they'd been through a tough session with a traffic cop," those who did not like the film "tactfully kept quiet or joined in the tumultuous applause." No one reported a third of the audience walking out, as Capra claimed had happened, nor did anyone report the exiting dignitaries bad-mouthing the film. Columbia officials were "on the professional lookout for any opinionated words that might be dropped" by members of Congress after the preview, but "no adverse political criticisms were heard."

Richard L. Strout of the *Christian Science Monitor* reported that the film soon became "a subject of amused discussion all over official Washington," but there were some who took it more seriously. The trouble really began on October 21, two days after the film began its opening engagements, when the ultraconservative *Chicago Tribune*'s press service blasted the film in a newsletter sent to about twenty subscribing papers. Washington columnist Willard Edwards wrote that members of the Senate were "writhing in their seats" at the preview and that "resentment in Congress was high the following day. The indignation might have produced nothing but violent conversation if some legislator had not remembered the anti-block-booking bill."

Named after its author, Senator Matthew Mansfield Neely (D–West Virginia), the Neely bill was one of the antitrust measures pending in the government against the film industry. It would have outlawed compulsory block-booking of films, allowing exhibitors to bid on each film individually. After twelve years of futile effort by various senators against block-booking, the Neely bill had passed the Senate on July 17, 1939, and was pending before the House Committee on Interstate Commerce, "where it might have lain idle throughout the next session due to the tremendous pressure put on by the motion picture lobby," Edwards wrote. "The Senate, which believes itself to have been maligned by the motion picture industry in a current production, is preparing to strike back at Hollywood. The movie moguls are to be wounded where it hurts most—in the pocketbook."

The journal of independent exhibitors, *Harrison's Reports,* joined the chorus, describing *Mr. Smith* as "a sample of the impotence of the exhibitors to reject a picture that has been sold on the block-booking system . . . Congress must, therefore, make it possible for them to reject such a picture, and similar other pictures, which may offend the sensibilities of the American public." Columbia issued a press release pointing out that Capra's films since *Mr. Deeds* had been sold separately, not block-booked, but the studio admitted, "Our regular established customers have, of course, had the first opportunity to negotiate for *Mr. Smith Goes to Washington.*" Va-

riety observed on October 25 that the threats to revive the Neely bill had "caused industry observers to wonder if releasing *Mr. Smith Goes to Washington* at the present time may not turn out to have been a grave political blunder." Capra consistently welcomed the idea of an anti–block-booking bill, because he thought it would help break up the monopoly of the major studios and thus open the way for his dream of independent production. Despite the anger kindled by *Mr. Smith*, the Neely bill still failed to pass the House, but the controversy helped rally those forces in Washington determined to bring antitrust actions against the film industry. As Capra said, "That brought to a head a lot of things that they had just been talking about."

The floodgates for public attacks on *Mr. Smith* were opened by the *Chicago Tribune* blast. "Hollywood lobbyists quaked," *Time* reported, when House Majority Leader Rayburn said of the film, "It won't do the movies any good." The most vocal opposition came from Senate Majority Leader Barkley, who held an impromptu press conference with reporters in a Senate corridor on October 23.

"It was as grotesque as anything I have ever seen!" Barkley spluttered. "Imagine the vice president of the United States winking up at a pretty girl in the gallery in order to encourage a filibuster! . . . And it showed the Senate as the biggest aggregation of nincompoops on record! At one place the picture shows the senators walking out on Mr. Smith as a body when he is attacked by a corrupt member. The very idea of the Senate walking out at the behest of that old crook! . . .

"I'm sure Mr. Capra's purpose was good and that there was nothing intentionally offensive in the film. But such a travesty of facts is likely to do untold harm among innocent people."

Barkley's comments were reported widely by the *Christian Science Monitor, The New York Times,* and the Associated Press. Other senators jumped into the fray. James F. Byrnes (D–South Carolina) told the press: "Halfway through the picture I said to myself, 'This is a masterpiece, a film that will go out to the nation as an inspiration for democracy.' But when it was over, I said, here is a picture that is going to the country to tell the people that 95 out of 96 senators are corrupt; that the federal, state, and municipal governments are corrupt; that one corrupt boss can control the press of a state; that the newspapers are corrupt; the radio corrupt; reporters are corrupt; that the trucks will intentionally run down boys in the streets. The thing was outrageous, exactly the kind of picture that dictators of totalitarian governments would like to have their subjects believe exists in a democracy."

"Can you imagine that?" Capra said to a New York reporter on October 27. "With all those things they've got to do down there, with the neutrality bill, and social legislation, with war breaking loose in Europe . . . the whole majesty of the United States Senate has to move against one moving picture. It's amazing!"

Criticism of the film's political viewpoint spread across the country in newspaper and magazine reviews, columns, and editorials. Frederic William Wile of the *Washington Star* wrote that it "shows up the democratic system and our vaunted free press in exactly the colors Hitler, Mussolini, and Stalin are fond of painting them." "We have enough political corruption in the country without laying it on that thick," wrote John M. Cummings in the *Philadelphia Inquirer. Editor and Publisher* called the film "a gross libel" both on the Senate and on Washington correspondents, depicting "an atmosphere of damnable cynicism and corruption such as the Congress has not seen since the Teapot Dome days." Even *Rob Wagner's Script*, in an article by former Screen Writers Guild president Ralph Block, incensed Capra by declaring, "It is highly effective propaganda and support, however unintentional, for all the things that unfriendly people, in and out of Hollywood, and in and out of America, are saying about the institutions of these United States."

Columbia began running ads simply quoting lines from the picture under the heading "Liberty Is Too Precious a Thing to Be Buried in Books." The film found as many defenders as attackers throughout the country, with New York critics and editorial writers leading the way: "There is delicious humor in the very humorlessness of [the] implication that Mr. Capra will be the responsible man if the United States fails to stop the war," wrote Frank S. Nugent in *The New York Times*. ". . . Mr. Capra's *Mr. Smith* has come to Washington, and to the nation, at a perfect time: the Senate needs a session on first principles again." William Boehnel of the *New York World-Telegram* called it "a stirring, patriotic document. . . . Perhaps only a man who has acquired liberty rather than inherited it could have made a picture like *Mr. Smith Goes to Washington*. For to [Capra] the meaning of democracy is real and vivid and precious—not something to be taken for granted."

It has become part of Capra folklore that as a result of the public controversy, the other Hollywood studios "thought that picture should be killed," and they offered to buy the negative of the film from Columbia in order to destroy it. Capra's accounts of the offer, however, were contradictory.

If an offer was made for *Mr. Smith*, what may have transpired was a closely held matter between Capra and Harry Cohn. On most occasions Capra said the offer was brought to Cohn by MGM's Louis B. Mayer, but he told *The Washington Post* in 1982 that it was a personal offer by Joseph P. Kennedy, who was then United States ambassador to the Court of St. James's. The amount of the offer, Capra said, was $2 million, which was almost exactly the film's negative cost, though he told Richard Schickel, "that was much more than the picture cost, it cost about $1.5 million, so it would have been a fine profit for Columbia."

According to Capra, Kennedy sent Cohn a cable urging Columbia not to show the film in Europe. No copy of the cable exists in Capra's files, and Ambassador Kennedy's papers are not open to researchers at the John F. Kennedy Library. But Capra's book quotes a letter from Kennedy to Cohn, dated November 17, 1939, in which Kennedy alluded to previous correspondence between them and contended that *Mr. Smith* would cause "inestimable harm to American prestige."

Columbia may have taken into account the fact that Kennedy's own credibility as a spokesman for American values was shaky when he attacked the film. The ambassador was under attack for his isolationist attitude toward American involvement in the war, and many considered him an appeaser. Though Cohn's reaction to Kennedy's initial message had been to defend *Mr. Smith*, Capra claimed that "Cohn was scared shitless." In fact, it was Capra who doubted his own film. As he put it in 1984, "When a prominent man like the ambassador to England says this is going to hurt the war effort, *that* was serious. *Would* it do that? I wanted to do what was right."

Capra said that when he read Kennedy's subsequent letter, "That's when I got mad, when he said not to play it. It was a time in which I had to stand up for everybody, for liberty and freedom. Boy, I made speeches! I told Cohn, 'Nobody should be able to buy a book and burn all the copies. Nobody has the right to stop a picture no matter how much he hates it. You should never allow anybody with money to say what they wish to put on the screen or not put on the screen, and you should never pay attention to what any politician tells you, because if a politician gets the idea that he can have you not show a picture, where's the freedom of the press?'

"I said, 'I'll burn your goddamn place down if you sell this picture to anybody.' I would have! I *would* have burned his place down and *admitted* it. I was all alone. I was alone with these guys, trying to fight, being attacked by big shots. Cohn had to make a decision. In a sense he knew I was right, but this American idea of freedom, that was not his—money talks with those guys. But he did finally say no to them."

If Cohn needed convincing, the public's support of *Mr. Smith* would have been enough. The film opened strongly at the box office, and *Showmen's Trade Review* said on November 11, "We are beginning to wonder whether the whole [controversy] wasn't a smart publicity gag in the first place." The film amassed rentals of $3,860,808 through October 1985, ranking it higher than *Mr. Deeds* and lower than *You Can't Take It With You*, but because of its relatively high negative cost, it earned only a small profit, with net proceeds (rentals less negative cost and distribution expenses) totaling $168,501. But the studio's overall net profits rose from $2,046 in fiscal 1939 to $512,000 in fiscal 1940; Columbia finally was growing bigger than Capra.

And despite Ambassador Kennedy's warnings, *Mr. Smith* was warmly embraced overseas. James Hilton wrote in London's *Sunday Graphic* on November 19: "I doubt if any government in the world today would allow itself to be so freely criticized in the press, in pictures, and on the air, as does the American. And Capra, Italian-born immigrant who once sold newspapers, is exercising every American's privilege in lambasting certain phases of life in the country of his adoption.

"That doesn't mean, however, that Capra isn't a thoroughly patriotic American.

"On the contrary.

"I'd call *Mr. Smith Goes to Washington* just about the best American patriotic film ever made. There's only one that might equal it, if Frank could ever be persuaded to make it, and that is *Mr. Capra Goes to America*."

15. "We're the front office"

*N*ever did Capra have it so good again. His twelve years at Columbia, which ended in October 1939, were the most productive of his life. The freedom he craved would turn out to be a subtle trap.

At the time his options seemed unlimited. In his last months at Columbia, there was great competition in Hollywood for Capra's services, studio offers in which "the financial obligations run into millions," as his would-be partner David O. Selznick put it. The most attractive offers were the ones that seemed to promise the most creative freedom and independence within the Hollywood system—offers from Samuel Goldwyn, Selznick, and United Artists. There also were suggestions, from Goldwyn and Selznick, of possible partnerships involving Howard Hughes in a new production-distribution company similar to UA. There was talk of Capra being financed independently by Doc Giannini of the Bank of America, and there even was talk of Capra, Selznick, and Giannini buying Columbia Pictures.

But Capra cautiously bided his time. He was reluctant to enter into a long-term contract again, but he knew that he was risking everything by striking out from Columbia on his own. He considered approaching Sidney Buchman to become his partner, but Buchman was happy at Columbia in his new role as Harry Cohn's heir apparent. Capra turned to Robert Riskin.

Riskin had not found the creative power he expected to have with Goldwyn, receiving only two associate producer credits, and less than a year into his five-year contract was "weary of the constant harangues that working for Mr. Goldwyn entails," *Time* reported. With a little distance from Capra, he had begun to look back on their years together more fondly, and he surprised Capra by accepting the offer.

"It was the sense of freedom, rather than actual freedom, which led us to do it," Riskin explained. "Also there was the adventurous side to it, which one doesn't feel when working on a stated salary. We were just a pair of dice-shooters at heart."

Capra and Riskin talked with UA about becoming partners in the company, but after those negotiations stalled, Riskin left Goldwyn to join Capra in July 1939 as vice president of Frank Capra Productions, Inc. (FCP), which tentatively planned to release its pictures through UA. Capra owned the controlling 65 percent of FCP's stock and Riskin the other 35 percent.

So, as *Time* put it, "baldish Robert Riskin" was reunited with "hairy little Frank Capra."

Even after Capra announced he was forming the new company, Cohn made a last-ditch attempt to persuade him to stay on the lot. He summoned Joe Walker and said, "You see Frank. Tell him we'll give him a fifty-fifty deal. We'll pay the costs and split the profits." But Capra was in no mood to listen, even to such a stunning and unprecedented offer. He was determined to prove he could make it without Harry Cohn.

"The day I left, everybody, the least person in the studio, came to my office to say good-bye," Capra remembered, "except for Cohn and the five or six guys he had running the place—they locked themselves behind their doors and never came out. After everybody else had said good-bye, I still waited in my office. I waited another half hour, hoping that he would come out and say 'Good luck' or something. And then I realized that I was *persona non wanted.*

"I went by the alley and saw that everything was locked. I walked across the street, got in my car, and that was my good-bye."

It was in early April, around the time *Mr. Smith* began shooting, that Capra fulfilled his father's failed dream and bought himself a ranch.

He asked his father-in-law, Myron Warner, to scout property for him. "Pop" Warner traveled around Southern California and found what they were looking for in Fallbrook, a small agricultural community fifty miles from San Diego and a hundred miles from Los Angeles. A quiet, isolated area of low, rolling hills and valleys, with a dry but temperate climate, Fallbrook closely resembled the land in Sierra Madre where Salvatore Capra had died.

The historic Red Mountain Ranch was one of the oldest and largest ranches in Fallbrook. Established in 1879 by William Hicks, it covered 536 acres, including part of the mountain after which it was named. On the property was a picturesque, gingerbread-style two-story wooden house, built in 1887 and attributed to the architect Stanford White. Most of the land was idle when Capra bought it, but it contained 105 acres of olive trees, an olive oil press, some citrus trees, and a new half-million-gallon reservoir, as well as a garden with a maze and an ancient monkey puzzle tree. The ranchers in the area were lobbying with Washington to build a dam to use the water of the Santa Margarita River and relieve the chronic dryness of the land. Pop Warner thought the ranch ideal both for development as farming land and as an investment; the price was $70,000, which included $50,000 for the house and outbuildings and only $20,000 for the land.

Since Capra was busy with *Mr. Smith,* he bought the ranch sight unseen. In 1943, again on his father-in-law's advice, he bought an adjoining 520 acres of steep, rocky land around Red Mountain for $6,000, primarily as an investment. When he sold the 940 acres that remained of his ranch in 1977, at the beginning of the real estate development boom in Fallbrook, the property went for $2.05 million.

Capra did not have time for more than occasional visits to Red Mountain Ranch in the first years of his ownership. Pop Warner and his wife, Florence, moved down from central California so he could manage the property. In the first two years, he and Capra planted thirty acres of lemon trees, four acres of lime trees, and fifty-two acres of avocados, and they also rehabilitated the olive trees (during World War II, when the Italian and Greek export markets closed, Capra started a mail-order business selling bottles of olive oil labeled "Produced by Frank Capra"). When Geoffrey Hellman's *New Yorker* profile on Capra appeared in February 1940, Capra's land holdings in Fallbrook were substantially underreported, in keeping with his new public austerity program. He was said to own a "forty-acre citrus ranch . . . a sort of memorial to his father."

To Chet Sticht and to Selznick, Capra sometimes spoke wistfully of retiring to Fallbrook within the next few years, if he could strike a good enough deal on his upcoming films to provide for his future. It was not an idle dream but one that carried with it a strong desire to escape from the tensions of life in Hollywood. Like his father before him, and Robert Conway in *Lost Horizon,* Capra fervently was hoping to find his own Shangri-La, and he thought Fallbrook might be the place.

Frank Capra Productions opened up shop in October 1939 on the Selznick International lot in Culver City.

Selznick then was struggling to complete the postproduction of *Gone With the Wind* for its December 15 release by MGM. Although he recently had renewed his deal with United Artists to distribute his other pictures, Selznick was increasingly dissatisfied with the management of UA and sought more power in the company by becoming a partner in association with Capra.

But despite the debacle of *Lost Horizon* and the anxieties attendant upon leaving Columbia, Capra was not willing to surrender his sense of independence as a producing director, even to the insistent Selznick. After the Directors Guild protested the publicity given the producer on *Gone With the Wind,* Selznick wrote Capra on January 22, 1940: "The growing obsession of the one-man jobs is based on vanity, as some men who are attempting to write, direct, and produce will to their sorrow learn, and, in fact, have in some cases already learned. The reaction is already setting in, and two or three splendid directors have had the good sense to give up their vanity, rather than let it destroy them, and return to direction, working in collaboration with fine producers."

UA had been founded in 1919 by Charles Chaplin, Douglas Fairbanks, D. W. Griffith, and Mary Pickford to distribute their pictures collectively, but it had slipped badly by the late thirties. Of the original partners, Griffith had sold his interests, Pickford had retired from the screen, and Fairbanks died in 1939; only Chaplin still made pictures, but with increasing rarity. Samuel Goldwyn, whose productions had become the mainstay of the company, was suing to be released from his distribution contract, and though producer Alexander Korda had come aboard as a partner, most of UA's releases were programmers bought from the less prestigious independent producers. The partners did not work harmoniously together, and Selznick saw an opening in the company's precarious condition.

The earlier talks Capra and Riskin had held with UA brought them close to entering into a partnership agreement, but dissension within UA caused the collapse of the deal worked out between their attorney, Loyd Wright (who also was the secretary of UA's board), and UA managing director Murray Silverstone. Fairbanks and Korda were in favor of giving Capra and Riskin a full partnership, but Chaplin was reluctant and Goldwyn's unresolved status cast doubts about the legal advisability of the deal.

Pickford, in a letter to UA attorney Dennis O'Brien, called it "a source of great disappointment to Douglas, Murray and me that we could not clinch the Capra contract. There is no question about it, the acquiring of a six-year contract with him would be a turning point in the life of United Artists. We are sorely in need of leaders with Goldwyn out, the possibility of our losing Selznick in the near future, and Korda's affairs so uncertain.

Capra is highly rated in Hollywood and undoubtedly he would have attracted to the company many of the leaders—both stars and producers.
. . . [The collapse of the deal] places Murray and United Artists in a very
embarrassing position; in fact, I go on record in saying we are morally
obligated to go through with our proposition with Capra providing it is
legally possible."

But the deal was held in abeyance, and in the interim, as Tino Balio
wrote in his history of UA, "both Capra's and Selznick's value to the
company had gone up and the two producers were in an excellent bargaining position."

Capra, Riskin, and Wright filed incorporation papers in Sacramento on
October 2, 1939, for Frank Capra Productions. Before *Mr. Smith* was
released later that month, Capra and Riskin began discussing in earnest
what their company's first picture should be.

Riskin wanted to do a film on the life of Shakespeare, but Capra leaned
toward comic romances of chivalry, Edmond Rostand's *Cyrano de Bergerac*
with Ronald Colman or Cervantes's *Don Quixote* with John Barrymore as
Quixote and Wallace Beery as Sancho Panza. Capra tried unsuccessfully
to purchase the film rights to British author Eric Knight's whimsical 1937
tale "The Flying Yorkshireman" from director Frank Lloyd. Then Riskin
remembered a story by Richard Connell, "A Reputation," which he had
read when it was first published in *Century Magazine* in 1922.

The story was about an obscure man named Saunders Rook, a clerk
living in New York City, who crashes a Park Avenue party to announce
that he is going to commit suicide in protest over the state of the world. The
incident creates such a sensation that the man feels compelled to go
through with his threat by jumping into the Central Park Reservoir on the
Fourth of July. Jo Swerling in 1937 had written an uncompleted stage
adaptation of the story, *The World Is an Eightball*, before abandoning the
project. A 1939 screen treatment by Connell and Robert Presnell, "The
Life and Death of John Doe," was supplied to Riskin, who sent the material
to Capra in the East, where he was opening *Mr. Smith*, and asked him to
read it immediately. Capra read it on the train back to Los Angeles, and
at the first stop he wired Riskin to begin work on the screenplay.

The Life and Death of John Doe—later shortened to *The Life of John
Doe* and finally retitled *Meet John Doe*—was announced on November 4 as
the next Capra-Riskin film, to be made on the Selznick International lot.
Jimmy Stewart and Jean Arthur were discussed for the lead roles.

On February 21, 1940, however, Capra and Riskin signed a deal with

Warner Bros. Jack Warner agreed to advance $500,000 of the cost of the film, which was not to exceed $1.25 million before Warners' billing for the use of its facilities (Warners' outlay was to be recouped from box-office returns). Doc Giannini and Joe Rosenberg of the Bank of America agreed to loan $750,000 to FCP at 6-percent interest, secured by the negative of the picture and assignment of box-office returns in first position ahead of Warners. FCP's investment, from its bank loan, would include the story and the salaries of Capra ($250,000), the lead actor ($150,000), and the writers ($100,000). Warners originally agreed to take a modest 20 percent of the gross receipts as its distribution fee, with FCP taking 80 percent after the film went into profit; after five years in distribution, the film would be owned outright by FCP. But Warners had second thoughts, and the deal was amended on March 31 to give the studio an additional 25 percent of FCP's net revenue after the gross exceeded $2 million.

"If it's a good show," Capra said shortly before its release, "we'll be back in the money. If it isn't, we'll be back where we started."

They were based on Warners' Burbank lot, the former First National Studios where Capra had worked as a gag man and had directed Harry Langdon in *The Strong Man* and *Long Pants*. When they moved there in January, Capra was thinking of Ronald Colman to star in the film, a curious choice for the quintessential "common man." But on February 23 it was decided that Gary Cooper would play Long John Willoughby, also known as "John Doe." Goldwyn, who had refused to loan Cooper to Columbia for *Mr. Smith,* exacted a heavy price: $200,000 and the loan of Warners' Bette Davis for his upcoming UA production of Lillian Hellman's *The Little Foxes.* Capra did not cast the female lead until May 31, five weeks before the start of shooting. He tested several actresses, including Ann Sheridan and Olivia de Havilland. His first choice was Sheridan, whose casting was announced on May 9, but Warners vetoed her because she was involved in a contract dispute with the studio. Finally Capra settled on Barbara Stanwyck, with whom he had not worked since *The Bitter Tea of General Yen.*

Principal photography on *Meet John Doe* took place between July 8 and September 18, 1940. Riskin, whose own production experience went back to the silent days, had the job of keeping Capra on schedule. He was only partly successful: they brought in the film five days behind its fifty-eight-day shooting schedule, using 386,350 feet of film, a shooting ratio of 34 to 1.

"What is the front office up to *this* time?" Capra exploded on one occasion. "How do they expect us to make a picture if they keep slashing the budget?"

"You're forgetting, Frank," said Riskin. "*We're* the front office."

*   *   *

Even more than *Lost Horizon*, *Meet John Doe* bore out Alistair Cooke's warning about the dangers of Capra making movies "about themes instead of about people."

Capra and Riskin borrowed frequently, and glibly, from their formula in making *Meet John Doe*, but they also made a significant change in their protagonist. "One of the reasons that we got mixed up," Capra felt, "was that we started out not with an innately good man, but with a drifter who didn't give a damn whether he was good or bad." Cooper's Long John Willoughby is a starving hobo who becomes the willing victim of a publicity stunt concocted by a cynical newspaper columnist, Ann Mitchell (Stanwyck), in order to save her own job. She writes a letter to the paper in the name of John Doe, "a disgruntled American citizen," unemployed for four years, who threatens to jump from the roof of City Hall on Christmas Eve to "protest . . . slimy politics" and to demonstrate how "the whole world's gone to pot." Hiring Willoughby to play the role of John Doe, the paper exploits public sympathy by running a daily column in his name, "I Protest," which Ann ghostwrites. Her publisher, D. B. Norton (Edward Arnold), a Hearst-like media baron who has ambitions for the White House and believes that "what the American people need is an iron hand," sponsors nationwide John Doe Clubs as an "apolitical" front for his third-party campaign. Seized with a new sense of purpose, Willoughby makes a nationwide radio speech and tours the country in a membership drive before he realizes how he is being used. He decides that the only way to redeem the John Doe Movement is to commit suicide—then changes his mind.

The problems Capra and Riskin had in coming up with a satisfactory ending were only a symptom of the film's overall confusions. It was a strange mixture of demagoguery and attacks on demagoguery; its anti-Fascist rhetoric is delivered by a muddled, corrupt central character whom critic Andrew Sarris described with some accuracy as "a barefoot Fascist, suspicious of all ideas and all doctrines, but believing in the innate conformism of the common man." While preaching the theme of "Love thy neighbor" and cloaking its characters in explicit Christian symbolism (Myles Connolly was credited in the Academy *Bulletin* as "contributor to screenplay construction and dialogue"), *Meet John Doe* also shows a deep distrust of the "common man," portraying the public as mindless, fickle, and dangerously malleable. While attacking politicians in general and New Deal relief and job programs in particular, *Meet John Doe* can offer as an alternative only a scheme to decentralize the functions of representative democracy, which plays straight into the hands of right-wing radicals who want to turn the country into a dictatorship. Yet though it lacks the overall political clarity and consistency Buchman brought to *Mr. Smith*, *Meet John Doe* contains some of Riskin and Capra's sharpest satire of politics and the media, and, in Arnold's D. B. Norton, a startlingly believable portrayal of an American Fascist.

The film's ideological tensions stemmed in large part from the unusually self-reflective nature of its narrative. *Meet John Doe* finds Capra critically examining his own role as a manipulator of the mass audience and the interplay between sincerity and cynicism in his own feelings toward the public. As Charles J. Maland observed, "Doe's picture appears on the cover of *Time*, just as Capra's had in 1938. Both were getting recognition, and both wondered if they deserved it. When Doe tells Ann in the airport waiting room that he's beginning to see the true meaning of the platitudes he had heard for years and been spouting for weeks, one senses that Capra is also speaking. Yet Capra, like Doe, seems to be torn: who is he (the Sicilian immigrant, the ex-ballplayer) to be a national spokesman of values, communicating to millions through the media?"

Underlying those doubts was Capra's fear that he was an "impostor," as the voice of an anonymous member of the public calls John Doe, and the fear that he would be exposed before his audience and vilified by them, as happens to John Doe in the rain-drenched convention sequence, one of Capra's most powerful visions of American madness. No other sequence in Capra's work more clearly reveals his latent fear of the "common man" and his awareness of how easily the public can be manipulated by the media, including the cinema itself.

"I never cease to thrill at an audience seeing a picture," Capra told Geoffrey Hellman shortly before making *Meet John Doe*. "For two hours you've got 'em. Hitler can't keep 'em that long. You eventually reach even more people than Roosevelt does on the radio. Imagine what Shakespeare would have given for an audience like that!"

It is Capra's awareness of the fragility of his hold over his audience, and his doubts about his own worthiness for such an important role, that give the convention scene its extraordinary tension. The United States Senate could not stop Jefferson Smith's filibuster, yet D. B. Norton can stop John Doe from speaking simply by cutting the radio wires he controls. But this time the flaw is in the "Capra hero" as well as in the system. Unlike the charges brought to discredit Deeds and Smith, the charges made against John Doe are essentially true. As Norton tells him, "*You're* the fake. We believe in what we're doing." Though the crowd, despite everything, is still willing to believe in him, John Doe loses their goodwill when he confesses his deceit. No one wants to listen when he insists, "This thing's bigger than whether I'm a fake!" (After the film opened, however, Capra added a scene in which John Doe follower Ann Doran insists, "Anyway, what he stood for wasn't a fake.")

"If you get their hopes up and they open their hearts to you and then they find out you are a fake, well, you'd better watch out for those people," Capra told Richard Schickel. "They don't like to be disturbed and opened up like that and then be double-crossed. And this is what made *John Doe* such an interesting picture, showing that people can become mobs, and one of the occasions they can become mobs is when they become disillusioned, when somebody has tricked them."

It is John Doe's awakening to the truth about his role in the American cultural-political system that, as Maland put it, "helped to make the demands of *Meet John Doe* absolutely irreconcilable" for Capra, whose own public role contained similar elements of fakery and contradiction. And like John Doe, Capra lived with anxiety about what would happen if the public came to realize that he was not the man they thought he was: "You can be a great filmmaker," Capra said in 1984, "but if they don't like you behind it, they don't give a damn about your films."

What is perhaps most interesting about *Meet John Doe* in the light of Capra's artistic and political personality is that the plot revolves around a question of authorship. Echoing Capra's dependence on Swerling, Riskin, Buchman, and Connolly in his rise to fame and in the formulation of his public political stance, John Doe literally is the creation of a writer, Ann Mitchell, the writer of the suicide letter, his column, and his speeches (which he doesn't even bother to read before he delivers them, because "I get more of a kick out of it that way"). The ghostwriter's role in the deception no doubt reflected Riskin's satirical take on his creative relationship with Capra; it was only after Riskin began adapting the material that the suicide threat was put into John Doe's mouth by somebody else, and Riskin had one of John Doe's bodyguards tell Ann, "He's beginning to believe he really wrote that original suicide letter that you made up." But, as Capra later would do when accused of leftist sympathies, John Doe tries to pass all the responsibility for what he says onto his writer: "What happened . . . was on account of Miss Mitchell here—she wrote the stuff." The irreconcilable irony of the situation is that without a writer, John Doe is (as Capra would be) helpless: when John Doe rebels and tries to speak for himself, Norton does not allow him to do so, and at the end all he can write for himself is a genuine suicide letter.

The temptation to suicide is a major theme of Capra's work. The heroes of two of his most personal (and least commercially successful) films before *Meet John Doe—The Way of the Strong* and *The Bitter Tea of General Yen*—actually do commit suicide. Failed suicide attempts figure in several other Capra films, and almost every Capra film takes its central character on violent mood swings between elation and despair before reaching its fragile happy ending. At his best, as François Truffaut put it, Capra was "a navigator who knew how to steer his characters into the deepest dimensions of desperate human situations (I have often wept during the tragic moments of Capra's comedies) before he reestablished a balance and brought off the miracle that let us leave the theater with a renewed confidence in life." Capra's supposed optimism was a cover for his more fundamental pessimism, and his happy endings which seem tacked on, as in *Meet John Doe*, represent an inability to reestablish the emotional balance.

Capra often said that there were "five different endings" to the film. This has given rise to the misunderstanding that he reshot the ending four times during postproduction. Barbara Stanwyck insisted, "I remember a couple of endings, but I don't remember five." Actually, only two of Capra's alternate endings involved reshooting during postproduction. The others simply were edited differently, from a wealth of material Capra filmed during principal photography, unsure about what to do: "I thought it would come during the making of the show. It didn't." Two of the alternate endings were used only on preview versions of the film, and the other three in the first few weeks of major-city engagements before the film went into national release with the ending it now has.

In one of the preview versions, the film ended with the convention and the comment by Norton's newspaper editor Henry Connell (James Gleason), "Well, boys, you can chalk up another one to the Pontius Pilates." But the audience found this bleak ending unsatisfying.

Before small studio audiences, Capra also previewed the suicide ending, showing Willoughby's hobo friend The Colonel (Walter Brennan) rushing toward City Hall when the body falls onto the street, cradling the dead man as in a Pietà. Riskin argued for this ending, but Capra vacillated.

Edgar (Pete) Peterson II, a young filmmaker who was recording the narration for a documentary at Warners, met Capra when he was trying to decide how to end *Meet John Doe*. "Frank was arguing with the Catholic church about whether man had the right to end his own life," recalled Peterson, who listened to some of the arguments. "Frank had several prominent Catholics who were friends of his [no doubt including Myles

Connolly] look at the ending. He was not a strong Catholic himself, but he had the Italian background. Frank didn't know what to do, but he had the feeling that if Gary Cooper jumped, out of it would come redemption. Eventually Frank saw the light and felt that the guy who had led this fight should not be the one who's the victim. Of course, in Dostoevsky the guy would have killed himself."

In later years, Capra flip-flopped between defending and regretting his choice of endings. Commercial considerations undoubtedly contributed as much as religious scruples to his ambivalence about the suicide in 1941, particularly since the film was his first independent production and his own money was on the line for the first time. Even though he claimed that his primary motive for choosing the story was "to convince important critics that not every Capra film was written by Pollyanna," he ultimately backed away from the darker implications of his chosen theme, laying off much of the blame on his public. "The audience told us" that they didn't like the suicide. "You can't kill Gary Cooper," he rationalized. "He had not done anything to deserve this kind of death. . . . Sure, the intellectual critics would have raved over that end, but it doesn't make sense."

In the end, despite his attempts to put the decision in other hands, what decided the question was Capra's own uncertainty, in the wake of *Mr. Smith*, about social commitment and the lengths to which one should go to defend a principle. He shaped the final ending of *Meet John Doe* so that Cooper's final decision, like his own, would not seem to be his responsibility. As Elliott Stein wrote in 1980, "The last reel of *Doe* was Capra's Waterloo as an artist"; it was the decisive moment in which he abandoned his troublesome role as a progressive political force in American films.

The ending which appeared on the film when it opened on March 12, 1941, was filmed on January 3. As a shouting crowd waits on the street in front of City Hall for John Doe to jump, Norton on the rooftop tries unsuccessfully to dissuade him; Ann makes an emotional appeal, telling him she'll die too because she loves him. As she passes out in John Doe's arms, he decides to live, and Norton orders Connell to print his real suicide letter in the *New Bulletin*, saying, "I want all the John Does to know the truth."

The ending featuring Norton's recantation was not well received at the press screening in Beverly Hills on the afternoon of the premiere, or by the New York critics (Eileen Creelman of the *New York Sun* called it "painfully bad, giving the entire film a phony air"), or by the paying public. Capra and Riskin, as a result, changed the ending again. On March 14 they dropped Norton's recantation from all prints in circulation and had him remain obdurate as John Doe walks past, carrying Ann.

But Capra had to grapple with a deeper source of audience resentment, communicated in letters he received from members of the public who were stung by the sight of the John Doe Clubs turning on their hero. The day after the opening, M. Gluck from Hollywood, writing to Capra and Riskin on behalf of a group of friends, excoriated the filmmakers for depicting John Doe's followers as a spineless and fickle herd who allow themselves to be manipulated by newspapers and politicians. Gluck accused the filmmakers of failing to live up to their images as defenders of the average citizen at a time when Hitler was threatening the survival of John Does everywhere. Capra replied that he was only being realistic in his view of contemporary humanity, but he took the criticism to heart in filming the final ending.

The idea for that ending came from another letter. Capra claimed that it was signed "John Doe" and that it told him, "There's only one thing that will keep that man from jumping . . . and that is if the John Does ask him not to jump." Capra's files contain several letters from members of the public commenting on the ending, but only one makes such a suggestion. It was signed "EGF" and was sent to Riskin, not Capra. The letter proposed that Norton's servants—earlier seen applauding as John Doe stood up to their boss—appear outside City Hall urging him not to jump; one previously disgruntled follower of John Doe joins their chorus, and then others, and together they persuade him to go on living.

Above the letter's reference to the outspoken, previously disgruntled John Doe follower, someone (not Capra) jotted the name of Regis Toomey, whose speech as a small-town soda jerk urging John Doe to continue his crusade received an ovation at the press preview, as it had from his fellow actors when the scene was shot. "He, and not Gary Cooper, was the real John Doe of the picture—the average guy—the little man," wrote John Chapman in *Boxoffice*. Capra shot new footage on March 23 of Toomey's character driving through the snow to City Hall with his wife (Ann Doran) and their neighbor (J. Farrell MacDonald). "We're with you, Mr. Doe," says Toomey. "We just lost our heads and acted like a mob." James Gleason then turns to Edward Arnold and says, "There you are, Norton— the people. Try and lick that." That ending was added to the film by April 15, in time for the national release on May 3; the footage of the shouting crowd on the street was deleted.

Because of the disappointing public and critical reception to *Meet John Doe*, Capra and Riskin dropped plans for a sequel, *The Further Adventures of John Doe*. By early May they were openly discussing the possibility that they might abandon their independent company, which they finally dissolved on December 29, 1941. Capra's share of the box-office returns from *Meet John Doe* would amount to $363,774, over and above his salary, but corporation taxes on estimated profits had to be amortized before all the profits were received. His and Riskin's tax bite for the eighteen months of production, including income tax, was 90 percent, according to Capra. As a result, he reopened talks with Selznick and United Artists and also discussed making more films for Warners, this time as a contract producer-director.*

While Capra was in postproduction on *Meet John Doe*, the Justice Department asked him to appear on its radio program *I'm an American!*, an NBC series in which "distinguished naturalized citizens" discussed their adopted country. As a naturalized citizen whose native country soon would be at war with the United States, Capra was feeling pressure to demonstrate his loyalty.

"Hollywood has been attacked as un-American," the Justice Department's scriptwriter, Dorothy Donnell, wrote Capra on February 4, 1941 (the Dies committee had held a highly publicized series of hearings in Los Angeles in August 1940, grilling Fredric March, James Cagney, Humphrey Bogart, and Philip Dunne before publicly "clearing" those prominent liberals of Communist sympathies). "Please give a defense of Hollywood and its people, showing their strong sense of Americanism and loyalty to democratic ideals."

Capra in his February 11 reply defended Hollywood in general against the "un-American" charges, as he had attempted to do in the 1938 draft of the telegram to the Dies committee, but this time he took more pains to point the finger at those in Hollywood who, he felt, had been led by charitable impulses into being Communist sympathizers or dupes of disloyal groups. He singled out screenwriters, deriding the sincerity of their sympathy for the underprivileged, and he stigmatized émigrés from central Europe as being among the film colony's most disloyal members. But he

---

* *Capra and Riskin sold all rights to* Meet John Doe *in December 1945 for a reported $150,000 to the New York independent distributor Sherman K. Krellberg's Goodwill Pictures, bringing Capra's total gross earnings from* Doe *to $711,274. The camera negative deteriorated while in Krellberg's possession and was junked, and the copyright was allowed to expire, bringing the film into the public domain by 1969. Most existing prints were in poor condition, but in the mid-1970s the American Film Institute undertook a partial restoration of the film. Robert Gitt combined two of Krellberg's nitrate 35mm prints with the Warners studio print to serve as the basis for a duplicate negative, which was deposited with the Library of Congress.*

was insistent that living in America eventually would convert any immigrant into a loyal American.

To Donnell's question "What is the screen doing to defend the democratic institutions?" Capra disclaimed any interest in making message films, claiming they were uncommercial, a reply that showed how far he had retreated since *Mr. Smith* from believing that the screen should be used for social criticism. But she nevertheless put into his mouth a defense of *Mr. Smith*, describing it as "American in spirit" because criticism of government is an "old and well-established American custom."

Capra took a carefully equivocal position when Donnell asked his views on the war issue. He told her he was against war, yet made it clear that if he had to go to war to defend his country, he would go.

In the script Capra was allowed to say that "Democracy glorifies the individual, while war means mass production applied to human beings for the purpose of mass murder. It destroys victor and loser alike. Although at times democracies are forced to resort to war to preserve themselves, it is nevertheless abhorrent to them." But he declared: "Our obligation to the world is to show that democracy will work. We may have to do this at the risk of our lives."

Donnell watered down Capra's attack on the Hollywood Left and his defense of the industry's patriotism.

When the interviewer, William A. Carmichael, district director of the Los Angeles office of the Immigration and Naturalization Service, asked about allegations of "communism, fascism, or some other 'ism,'" the script had Capra reply: "That's rubbish, Mr. Carmichael. Hollywood is no more an offender on this score than any other community. We have lefts, rights, middles, and ups and downs, mostly ups and downs, but not more than any other place. Hollywood is just under the searchlight, that's all. I assure you the great majority of Hollywood people are militantly American and militantly democratic. . . .

"And let me tell you, Mr. Carmichael, if a picture fails to measure up to the ideals and tastes of Americans, they stay away in droves—in other words, it flops! Even if un-Americans did try to creep in in Hollywood, they wouldn't get far. For economic reasons, if for no other."

"That is reassuring, Mr. Capra," said Carmichael, "but from the more constructive side, don't you think that the screen could be more of an instrument to defend our democratic institutions?"

"Personally, I refuse to believe the American public needs educating in democracy," was Capra's response. The screen's foremost populist cut the scriptwriter's next three lines: "I have a profound faith in the American people. It's the leaders who need the educating. The people are way ahead of them."

At the end of the March 23 program, the announcer told Capra, "Your faith in America is an inspiration to all Americans—those who count their ancestry from the *Mayflower* and those who came by way of Ellis Island."

As war came closer to America, the government began putting out more feelers to Hollywood. The production of military training films was being stepped up dramatically. At the end of May 1940, President Roosevelt's son James (then an independent film producer) set up a meeting on the Paramount lot between U.S. Army representatives and executives of the studios and the Academy. The Academy's Research Council, originally established to coordinate technical standards for the film industry, had cooperated in the production of Army training films and the training of Signal Corps officers for ten years under an informal agreement. Capra was at the meeting, along with the man who would succeed him as Academy president that December, producer Walter Wanger.

Major Richard T. Schlosberg, chief of the Photographic Division of the Signal Corps, and Major Mason Wright, Jr., of the Adjutant General's Department, asked the Hollywood brass to formalize the industry's cooperation. The studios agreed to produce training films at cost, and the Research Council was delegated the task of coordinating the Hollywood war effort. Capra appointed Darryl Zanuck as chairman of the council, and Zanuck met in Washington with President Roosevelt and the Army Chief of Staff, General George C. Marshall, returning with a commission as a lieutenant colonel in the Signal Corps and a mandate to incorporate Hollywood talent into the Army film program. But Zanuck went one better than that. The Fox executive's July 1941 study of Army training films, undertaken at Marshall's request, suggested that Hollywood take over all production from the Signal Corps, which had been in charge of Army photography since the Civil War and whose films tended to be dry and soporific. Signal Corps bureaucrats were outraged by Zanuck's presumption, and Lieutenant Colonel Melvin E. Gillette, the top officer in photography, proposed that the Signal Corps establish its own office in Hollywood, independent of the studios.

While the jurisdictional battle dragged on, the most urgent need, once the draft was reestablished in September 1940, was for basic training films, including *Sex Hygiene*, the graphic Army VD film, which John Ford directed in early 1941 at Twentieth Century–Fox. Ford had organized his own group of about two hundred writers, directors, and technicians he was training for combat photography as part of the Naval Reserve. They were making secret reconnaissance films even before the United States entered the war and later became the Field Photographic Branch of the Office of Strategic Services (OSS). Other Hollywood cronies of Capra's, including Jimmy Stewart, were already in military service by early 1941; Stewart had left MGM to join the Army Air Corps.

After President Roosevelt addressed the Oscar banquet by radio hookup on February 28, 1941, praising Hollywood for helping raise defense money and for promoting "the American way of life," Capra, then the Academy's vice president, sent an enthusiastic telegram of support to the President, telling him Hollywood was willing to serve the country as needed. The President was "deeply touched" by the message, his secretary replied.

Yet Capra was not eager to reenlist. The dullness of his desk job in the Army during World War I, he explained later, had soured him on military life. Nor, as a middle-aged married man with three children (a son, Thomas, was born on February 12, 1941), was he under any obligation to join the Army. He was at the peak of his professional earning power and just starting to try his wings as an independent producer.

Training films held no inherent interest for Capra—by his standards they were hackwork—but he felt it his patriotic duty to listen to the Army's proposals. In October 1938, during his Washington research trip for *Mr. Smith,* it was reported that he discussed making an unspecified "service picture" as a joint venture between the government and Columbia. Between September and November 1941 he was said to have been preparing a short Army training film (or films) entitled *Espionage* or *Combat Counterintelligence,* but when the latter was made at Columbia in March 1942, it was directed by Charles Vidor. Capra later would write that long before Pearl Harbor, Captain Sy Bartlett, a former Columbia screenwriter, and Major Schlosberg had brought him into the Signal Corps, but from Capra's official military records it is evident that any understanding he had with the Signal Corps before the war must have been informal.

Until Pearl Harbor, Capra's sights were set on Hollywood—and in the spring and summer of 1941, on a long-term contract with United Artists.

Capra wanted Riskin to join him in the pending deal, which was negotiated by Selznick and Korda, and the press still mentioned Capra and Riskin as partners, but by mid-June, Riskin decided against continuing his professional involvement with Capra. Since the outbreak of war in Europe, he had been chafing to leave Hollywood, telling his friends that he found it impossible to keep his attention on movies any longer. On August 20 he arrived in London, ostensibly on assignment with *Liberty* magazine, and volunteered his services to the Ministry of Information to work on war propaganda films.

"I get homesick once in a while," Riskin wrote Capra on October 1, "but wouldn't think of being anywhere else but here. The whole atmosphere is electric and there are things I have seen and places I have been to which I cannot write about because of censorship, but which makes the thought of going home fantastic. I may think differently when I have gone through a few raids—and then again I may not."

Capra was bitter about Riskin's decision to end their partnership at this critical moment of his career. "Those damn writers shouldn't be making pictures," he said when Riskin returned after Pearl Harbor to make propaganda films with Philip Dunne in the Office of War Information (OWI). He complained to Lu in 1943 that Swerling, Riskin, and Buchman, in wanting to strike out on their own, had deluded themselves into the belief that they could have had their great successes of the past without him. But Capra and Riskin "superficially went on being good friends," said Fay Wray, who married Riskin in 1942. "There was plenty of contact socially. Bob Riskin kept things to himself a great deal. If he was hurt he wouldn't reveal it. He held those feelings close to himself, and I think he was more vulnerable than most people realized."

"Even after they broke up, Bob never spoke critically to me about Frank," said journalist Tom Pryor. "He wasn't that kind of a guy. I think it was more pointed that Frank didn't come up in Bob's conversation as he did before. It was something you would feel, something you would gather yourself. The one time Bob clearly did mention it was when he told me that he had done more on *Meet John Doe* than I realized."

The immediate project Riskin left behind in Hollywood when he went to England was *The Flying Yorkshireman*. When Capra bought the rights to Knight's story from Frank Lloyd on June 20, 1941, he planned to make it as his first film for United Artists. He hoped to persuade Chaplin to play the title role, but he was unable to reach Chaplin to make a formal offer. Capra also bought a story by Hugh Wedlock and Howard Snyder, "Tomorrow Never Comes," as a UA project. It, too, was a fantasy, about a young reporter who predicts the future by receiving the next day's newspaper in advance (for legal protection Capra purchased the screen rights to a 1927 play by Lord Dunsany with a similar plot, *The Jest of Hahalaba*). And he still hoped to film *Don Quixote*.

The death of Douglas Fairbanks on December 12, 1939, and the departure from UA of Samuel Goldwyn, whose stock had been reacquired by the company, rekindled talk of a partnership deal for Capra and Selznick. They joined forces again in May 1941 and resumed negotiations. Korda's persuasiveness soon brought them close to a deal. But it bogged down in haggling between Selznick and Korda over the fine points.

The terms of the offer fluctuated that summer, but essentially UA was to allow Selznick and Capra to become partners in the company with Pickford, Chaplin, and Korda over a period of several years. Working separately (though they were considering a joint lease of Fox's neglected Western Avenue studio), Selznick was to make three pictures and Capra two. The average budget of the films was to be $1 million, financed partially through a revolving fund supplied by UA, which was to receive 10 percent of the profits. Fairbanks's and Goldwyn's combined total of 8,000 shares of company stock, whose market value that June was $720,000, were to be sold to Selznick and Capra in installments as they delivered each picture.

The ostensible sticking points in the deal were the complicated sliding-scale distribution terms. Though the relative independence offered by UA was alluring, Selznick, in a sixteen-page letter to Korda, denounced the deal as unworthy of his and Capra's eminence in the industry, and inferior to deals they had been offered elsewhere. Furthermore, the prospect of becoming voting partners in UA even before the stock purchase was completed was outweighed, Selznick felt, by the step-deal arrangement for purchasing the stock, which would bind him and Capra to UA at the peak of their careers without the certainty that they would earn enough profits to buy the stock.

"The negotiations with Selznick," Tino Balio wrote in his history of UA, "boiled down to an argument over who was going to direct the reorganization of the company. . . . Korda, it seemed, fancied himself as the new UA leader now that he was out of production, but Selznick convinced him otherwise after two more months of haggling. So Korda stepped aside." Selznick finally became a UA partner on October 4, but he did so without Capra; and though Selznick's ten-picture deal included the more favorable distribution fees he wanted, his involvement with UA ended in 1946 after only three films, with Selznick and his partners suing each other.

Capra claimed in his book that he abandoned the UA deal because he wanted to go into the Army instead, but his enlistment in the Army still was several months away when, in midsummer 1941, he began to reconsider the wisdom of the whole arrangement. Frustrated by the delays in the negotiations, he was anxious to get back to work and make up for the relative box-office disappointment of *Meet John Doe*. Like Selznick, he worried about the pressure he would be under with UA to carry a tottering company on his back. But most of all he worried about becoming part of such a contentious company, in which no one person had the clear decision-making powers, unlike Columbia or Warners.

On August 1 he signed a deal with Jack Warner to direct the film version of Joseph Kesselring's black comedy *Arsenic and Old Lace*, which had been running on Broadway since January 10. The play was produced on stage by Howard Lindsay and Russel Crouse, who had rewritten Kesselring's original version, *Bodies in Our Cellar*, without credit.

"I am in the business of making pictures," Capra told the press when he announced in mid-August that he was pulling out of the UA talks. "I can't afford to deal forever. . . . Another contributing factor was the fact that it was almost impossible to meet the people who were supposed to be my future partners."

By which he meant Charles Chaplin. Chaplin had long been one of his idols. But Capra was deeply hurt by Chaplin's refusal to meet with him and deal with him as an equal on the UA partnership and on *The Flying Yorkshireman*. "The only person I can say is a complete shit is Charlie Chaplin," Capra declared in 1984. "Great actor, funny man, I grant him everything, but as a human being—a shit. A plain, ordinary shit."

Arsenic and Old Lace, a comedy about two lovable old ladies who actually are mass murderers, was one of the oddest choices of material Capra had ever made, a complete reversal from the socially conscious work which had become his trademark. On one level of Capra's thinking, that was the whole point. "Hell, I owe myself a picture like this," he declared on a trip to New York to see the play a second time. "I'm not going to try to reform anybody. It'll be a picture without a sermon, and I'm going to have a lot of fun. . . . For a long time now I've been preaching one thing or another. Why, I haven't had a real good time since *It Happened One Night*."

By 1941, even *It Happened One Night* had become controversial. In *Berlin Diary*, journalist William L. Shirer reported that it was one of Adolf Hitler's favorite films and that the Führer had screened it several times. "That was the first bad thing I'd heard about [*It Happened One Night*]," Capra said in 1941. "I was shocked and started to analyze it, but I gave it up. But I resent it like the devil."

That spring Capra briefly toyed with columnist R. Wesley Baxter's suggestion of a Runyonesque film about a Capone-like gangster sprung from the penitentiary to rub out Hitler, but he dropped it upon learning that Warners was making a melodrama about gangsters fighting Fascism, *All Through the Night*. "Wouldn't it be a case of beating the same old drum?" he asked. "Everyone, or nearly everyone except the isolationists, agree[s Hitler] is a menace. Can you make a million people sit still while you editorialize at them in pictures? I don't think so. . . . With the world in its present state, what's the good of a message?"

Capra's retreat from significance helped drive him back under the protective cover of a studio contract, and, as with *You Can't Take It With You*, back into safe, pretested, noncontroversial material. He earlier had made an offer to Lindsay and Crouse for their long-running play of Clarence Day's *Life with Father*, which opened on Broadway in November 1939 and was still playing, with Lindsay in the lead role of the crusty patriarch Father Day. But the playwrights had rejected the offer because Capra demanded script control, a concession they felt they would not have to make if they held out longer (when the play reached the screen in 1947, directed for Warners by Michael Curtiz, it was filmed intact but was disappointingly stodgy and long-winded). Nor was Capra the first choice of Lindsay and Crouse to direct *Arsenic:* they preferred René Clair but went with Capra because he had a more commercial reputation.

Capra admitted to Lindsay and Crouse that he took on *Arsenic* partly as a way of persuading them to let him make *Life with Father*. But he also needed cash to help pay his taxes on *Meet John Doe*. Jack Warner agreed to pay him $100,000 in twenty weekly installments, in addition to $25,000 for five weeks of editing and 10 percent of the gross receipts in excess of $1.25 million. The film was budgeted at $1.22 million.

The deal for the film rights stipulated that it could not be released to the paying public until after the play had closed on Broadway. The play ran for 1,444 performances, and, as a result, though Capra shot the film between October 20 and December 16, 1941, it was not shown until 1943, when it was released to the military around the world, and it did not receive its theatrical release until September 1, 1944—much to Capra's regret, for it missed some of the most lucrative box-office periods of the war years, as he had his lawyer, Martin Gang, complain to Warners in January 1944. Warners had to absorb interest charges on the production cost while waiting for the release, but the studio wanted to make it while Cary Grant was available for the lead role, and Capra promised Jack Warner he would make the film economically, shooting it almost entirely on Max Parker's studio set of the old ladies' Brooklyn house and the adjacent graveyard.

Lindsay and Crouse also were interested in an efficient production.

After failing to convince Warners to wait until the summer of 1942 so they could keep their cast together, they agreed to loan Capra their two lead actresses, Josephine Hull and Jean Adair, for only eight weeks, including two weeks of travel time by train. When Andy Devine, whom Capra wanted for the bugle-blowing "Teddy," was unavailable, they also agreed to let him have the actor who played the role on stage, John Alexander.

The producers balked, however, at Capra's request for Boris Karloff. Karloff was playing Jonathan, the old ladies' criminal nephew who had been turned into a replica of Karloff's Frankenstein monster by his drunken plastic surgeon, Dr. Einstein. An investor in the play, Karloff was its star attraction, and the producers were counting on him to continue bringing in capacity audiences while the other regulars were in Hollywood. Lindsay and Crouse told Capra they would give him Karloff if Warners agreed to let them borrow Humphrey Bogart, but Capra was unable to persuade Warners to make the swap. After considering Sam Jaffe for the part, Capra decided to use Raymond Massey (whom he had tested for the High Lama in *Lost Horizon*) in Karloff-like makeup, to the dismay of Lindsay and Crouse. Peter Lorre was cast as Einstein.

For the role of the drama critic Mortimer Brewster, the single "normal" member of the family, who comes to doubt his own sanity in the course of the story (Allyn Joslyn played the role on stage), Capra considered Bob Hope, Jack Benny, and Ronald Reagan before settling on Cary Grant. "This is something new for me," Grant told a reporter on the set. "I always play the calm, hands-in-the-pocket guy who tosses the answers off to the excited people. But here I'm the one who is always bouncing around. It's an entirely different side of comedy. If it weren't for Frank's helping me, I wouldn't know what I am doing half the time."

Capra convinced Grant to play Mortimer by offering him a salary higher than his own, $160,000, of which the actor donated $100,000 to wartime charities. Though he found Capra "a dear, dear man," Grant never liked the film, and his performance consists largely of hysterical shouting and extremely broad double takes. He said it was "not my kind of humor" and considered it his worst performance.

"I thought he mugged too much," said Julius Epstein, who wrote the screenplay of the film with his identical twin, Philip. "To be fair to Capra, when we told him around the end of shooting that we thought it was too broad, he said, 'I'll get it right next time around, like I always do.' By that he meant when he finished shooting he would always reshoot until he was satisfied. He was planning to do that, but then came Pearl Harbor and he ran off to Washington [to join the Signal Corps]."

Though Capra's enlistment caused him to rush through the editing, the time pressures under which he found himself during production were dictated not by Pearl Harbor but by the actors' schedules. Not only the New York actors but also Grant had to finish *Arsenic* by mid-December. Capra's grudging willingness to shoot in unaccustomed haste for reasons of commercial expediency was the principal reason for the film's frenzied pace and its exhausting overanxiety to please.

In his book Capra bragged that he had filmed *Arsenic* in four weeks. Though he completed the film one day ahead of schedule, the shooting actually took more than eight weeks, and by mid-November Capra was requesting a two-week extension of the actors' contracts. This prompted a frantic plea from Lindsay and Crouse to Jack Warner that their actors be returned before Christmas, as planned, because box-office receipts were slipping in their absence.

Capra suggested suspending production and resuming in the spring, but Warner refused. He begged Lindsay and Crouse for more time, telling them he could improve Hull's and Adair's performances by reshooting some of their early scenes, but they insisted he keep to the schedule. Capra accelerated his pace and managed to finish with Grant, Hull, and Adair by December 13, bringing the somewhat slapdash picture to a halt three days later at a cost of $1,120,175—or $99,825 under budget.

There may have been a subconscious cause for Capra's attraction to *Arsenic and Old Lace*: making the film may have been his way of trying to work out his complex emotions about his mother—who died on May 23 at the age of eighty-one, shortly before he decided to make it—and his way of expressing his compulsive need to escape from his family. Much of the film's underlying emotional frenzy turns on Mortimer's fear of inheriting his family's psychoses: he tells his new bride, Elaine Harper (Priscilla Lane), "Insanity runs in my family—it practically gallops!" Josie Campisi described the Capra family as "crazy," and Capra described his own mother as having been "nuts."

The two superficially lovable little old ladies in *Arsenic*, Abby (Josephine Hull) and Martha (Jean Adair), who resemble the celebrated "pixilated sisters" of *Mr. Deeds Goes to Town*, have poisoned twelve lonely old men with elderberry wine laced with arsenic, strychnine, and cyanide. The comedy comes from their utter inability to see that, as Mortimer puts it, what they are doing is "not only against the law, it's *wrong*." In almost every other conventional sense they are principled Yankee ladies and pillars of society, a class toward which Capra had reason to be ambivalent—Abby has a disturbing tendency to disparage "foreigners," and she says she is happy to go to a mental institution at the end because the neighborhood has "changed."

Behind the façade is a comic, American Gothic version of the House of Atreus, a legacy of family lunacy and violence which, as Mortimer puts it, "goes back to the first Brewster, the one who came over on the *Mayflower*." The Brewsters' Yankeedom has a sly appeal to Capra, who similarly relishes the film's implications of insanity in the Roosevelt lineage: Teddy Brewster, who thinks he is President Theodore Roosevelt, confides that he is planning to run for a third term, like his distant relative FDR, "if the country insists"; Mortimer even tells him, "The name Brewster is code for Roosevelt."

Like Aunt Abby and Aunt Martha, Capra's mother was a woman with many obviously respectable qualities, a lovable figure to people who did not know her well, but a "hard woman" to her family and a figure of terror to her son Frank, who called the house in which he grew up "a house of pain." And, like the Brewster ladies, she made her own wine in the basement. Frank Capra, like Mortimer, felt estranged from his family from an early age, and he had a brother (Tony) who, like Massey's Jonathan Brewster, tormented him and grew up to become a criminal. "As a boy I couldn't wait to escape from this house," Jonathan tells Mortimer, whose entire life has been an escape, from his home and family, from reality (his absorption in the theater), and, like Capra before he married Lu, from emotional involvement with women (before his marriage Mortimer was a notorious Don Juan, the author of such books as *The Bachelor's Bible* and *Mind over Matrimony*).

"The crux of the play," said Julius Epstein, "was that Mortimer couldn't marry the girl because he thought there was insanity in his family. But at the end, when his aunts tell him he's illegitimate, he says with great relief, 'Darling, I'm a bastard!' " In the film, the undercurrent of sexual frustration is intensified by having the couple sneak off to marry at the *beginning* but being prevented from leaving for their honeymoon and consummating their marriage until the aunts, Jonathan, and Teddy are safely packed away to the asylum and Mortimer resolves the question of his lineage.

"We had very little personal contact with Capra in writing the script, because it was abnormally such a good situation," Epstein said. "The only big challenge was that you couldn't say 'bastard' on screen in those days; you couldn't even say 'hell.' We couldn't use the line 'Darling, I'm a bastard!,' but when I saw it in the theater it brought down the house. For a while we didn't think we'd get it, but my brother came up with a solution.

Mortimer's father was a cook on a tramp steamer, and Mortimer told the girl, 'I'm not really a Brewster, I'm a son of a sea cook!' I don't know why, but that line was almost as effective in the picture as 'Darling, I'm a bastard!' was in the play."

The giddy, out-of-control tone of *Arsenic and Old Lace,* with its feeling of helplessness and abandon in the face of irrational impulses toward sex and violence, its mockery of death, and its ultimate sense of catharsis, is a dark celebration, perhaps, of Capra's feeling of release from his mother and from his family, and his exorcism of the guilt stemming from that forbidden feeling.

Capra and his newly acquired agents, Phil Berg and Bert Allenberg, were busy fielding contract offers in the fall of 1941, with Fox, United Artists, Goldwyn, and Universal competing for his services. His old antagonist in the SDG contract talks, Joseph Schenck, held true to his 1939 overture and made Capra an offer the director later described as the best he ever received: a three-year contract with a salary of $250,000 per film, or 15 percent of the gross, on films he both produced and directed, and $50,000 or up to 10 percent of the gross for films he only produced. But the deal contained a crippling clause which Capra did not care to remember: Capra had autonomy in choosing his projects only as long as they did not have themes that dealt with politics or were otherwise likely to cause controversy. The nonthreatening *Flying Yorkshireman* was to be his first picture, with Victor Moore replacing Chaplin in Capra's mental casting process, followed by *Tomorrow Never Comes.* Nothing as topical as *Mr. Smith* or *Meet John Doe* was on his Fox agenda.

Fox announced on November 26 that it had signed the Capra deal. Though an agreement in principle had been reached and the papers were being prepared for signing, Capra was angry over what he considered a premature announcement of an "enslaving" deal to which he had not yet given his final consent. Mostly he was angered because he was trying to use the Fox negotiations as leverage to swing a long-term deal with the more liberal but also more dilatory Warner Bros., which accused him of duplicity when it heard the Fox announcement, but accepted his reassurances that he would wait until completing *Arsenic* to make further plans.

Both the Fox and Warners offers were still on the table on December 7, 1941.

A biographical sketch issued by Capra after he returned to civilian life in 1945 gave the date of his application for a U.S. Army commission as

December 8, 1941, the day after Pearl Harbor. In his autobiography, he wrote that he took his Army oath that day on a Warner Bros. soundstage. He also wrote that he was not given his specific assignment until he arrived in Washington in February 1942.

However, it was on December 9, 1941, that Lieutenant Colonel Schlosberg and Captain Sy Bartlett arrived in Hollywood from Washington on a one-day visit to discuss wartime expansion of the training film program with Zanuck and others and to begin recruiting "top names of the industry into the [Signal] Corps." That day Schlosberg received a telephone call from Brigadier General Frederick H. Osborn, the chief of the Army's Morale Branch, to discuss a series of films General Marshall had ordered them to make to show American soldiers why they were fighting. According to the official Army history of the war, in that conversation with Osborn, Schlosberg "agreed to try to find a qualified person from the motion picture industry to be commissioned in the Signal Corps to direct a series of orientation films. Frank Capra, a successful Hollywood producer-director, agreed to undertake the job." When questioned in 1984 about his enlistment, Capra said that while Schlosberg was making his talent search in Hollywood, John Ford recommended him to Marshall. But there is no documentation on that; the Army history indicates only that Osborn called Capra and asked him to take the job.

It was on December 12, five days after Pearl Harbor, that Capra agreed to join the Signal Corps with a major's commission and announced his decision to the press. He was ordered to report for active duty on January 15, but he later received an extension of almost a month so he could complete the editing of *Arsenic* before reporting to Washington. The date he finally took his Army oath was January 29, 1942, and it was not on a film set but at the Southern California Military District Headquarters in Los Angeles.

At the end of December, shortly after *Arsenic* finished shooting, Capra went to Washington to discuss his assignment with his new boss, General Osborn.

The imposing Frederick Osborn stood more than a foot taller than Capra. He was not a professional soldier but a wealthy Republican blue blood, a Princeton man who had trained as an anthropologist before entering business as a railroad executive and management consultant. An old friend of FDR's, Osborn was commissioned as a brigadier general by Marshall in 1941 to work under his direct supervision as chief of the reactivated Morale Branch.

In their first meeting, Osborn promised to give Capra whatever he required to make the series of morale films, unimpeded. By the first weekend in January Capra was back in Hollywood to complete the last film he would make as a civilian for more than four years. After a preview of *Arsenic* on January 30 and some frantic recutting, he left for active duty with the Signal Corps on February 11.

"The Army was a welcome out for me," Capra would later write. Not only did joining the Army enable him to avoid signing "enslaving" Hollywood deals, it also "gave one a superior aura of patriotism and self-sacrifice."

If he needed any more incentive to prove his loyalty, his sister Ann's experience in 1941 provided it. The Alien Registration Act, commonly called the Smith Act, which had been passed in 1940 to forbid a wide range of "subversive activities," also strengthened the federal government's powers of deportation and required the fingerprinting of all aliens in the United States. Antoinette Capra Blangsted (as she was now known) had lived in the U.S. since 1903, but found herself classified in 1941 as an "enemy alien."

When she had married her first husband, Sam Huffsmith, she was under the mistaken impression that by marrying a native-born American she became an American citizen. Her second husband, Folmar Blangsted, was a naturalized American of Danish birth. But when she registered under the Smith Act in 1941, she learned she was still a citizen of her native Italy. Her experience no doubt reminded Capra of his own discovery that he was not an American citizen when he enlisted in the Army in 1917.

Ann received her preliminary U.S. citizenship papers in November 1941, but Pearl Harbor put all pending naturalizations on hold. When the United States went to war against Italy, Ann became an enemy alien, subject to travel and curfew restrictions which even made it hard for her to visit her relatives.

In August 1942, Frank Capra, by then an Army major, wrote a letter to the government on her behalf, attesting to her loyalty to the United States and explaining that her failure to apply for citizenship before 1941 was caused by her misunderstanding of the law. He pulled the right strings, and she was granted citizenship. But her experience probably influenced his decision to enlist.

However complex Capra's motives for reenlisting may have been, the fact remains that he was one of the few major directors in Hollywood to give up his career to spend the war in active military service during World War II. The trade papers reported Capra's enlistment along with those of William Wyler and John Huston. They were the first major directors since

Ford and Woody Van Dyke to enter the service, although 350 other film industry workers were already in uniform. Most directors concentrated on making escapist entertainment films in Hollywood, which underwent a boom during the war. If not the best years of his life, what Capra gave up for a peak monthly salary of $333.33 was a lucrative and eminent position in the film industry that he never would recapture. He may have enlisted partly because he felt he had more to prove than American-born directors did, and he apparently felt guilty about not enlisting earlier, but the evidence of his enthusiastic involvement in the service of his adopted country cannot be disputed, even if he seemed oddly reluctant in his book to admit that patriotism was his motivation.

There also may have been an element of rivalry with Riskin behind Capra's decision to join the war effort. When Riskin wrote Capra on October 1 from London to describe the bombed-out British cities he had seen and the first air raid he had experienced, Capra was so impressed that, without asking Riskin, he gave the letter to both *Daily Variety* and *The Hollywood Reporter* for publication.

Like Jimmy Stewart in *It's a Wonderful Life*, who chafed at having to stay home during the war to "fight The Battle of Bedford Falls," Capra was beginning to feel a longing to be where the action was. Before Pearl Harbor his contribution to the war effort had consisted of membership in the Motion Picture Red Cross Committee and contributions to relief drives, including those for the British, French, Greek, and Russian peoples. Lu had been more active than her husband, working with the war relief efforts of the Hollywood Women's Red Cross Coordinating Committee and Bundles for Britain.

After his enlistment, Lu and the children spent most of the war at Red Mountain Ranch (Lu helped in the Marine hospital at nearby Camp Pendleton after the base opened in 1942) while Capra, when he was in California, bunked in Brentwood. He wanted the family in Fallbrook partly because he thought they would be safer from Japanese air raids there than in the Los Angeles area, although on March 1, 1942, he wrote Lu to be on alert to escape with the children to Arizona or Reno, Nevada.

Riskin had left London on December 7, after two and a half months' work with the Ministry of Information, to return to the United States. While waiting for a government position, he took a Hollywood assignment, writing the screenplay of *The Thin Man Goes Home* for MGM. In August 1942 he was appointed to the prestigious job of chief of the Overseas Motion Picture Bureau of the newly created Office of War Information, based in New York.

"There was a bit of jealousy on Frank's part that Bob Riskin got this on his own, and as a civilian," said Tom Pryor. "During the war Frank couldn't even fall back on his old friend Riskin." At one point, hurting for writers, Capra swallowed his pride and asked Riskin to come back to Hollywood and help him, but Riskin was too busy.

In the first months of 1942, as Capra was battling with recalcitrant officers in the Signal Corps and struggling to comprehend his mission, he was beginning to feel like "a fool who's turned his back on Camelot."

16. "That fellow Capra"

"*M*ost of you were individuals in civilian life," Capra wrote the officers under his command in 1942. "Forget that. You are working for a common cause. Your personal egos and idiosyncrasies are unimportant. There will be no personal credit for your work, either on the screen or in the press. The only press notices we are anxious to read are those of American victories!"

The films Capra produced during his Army service in World War II, including the *Why We Fight* series of troop indoctrination films, won him great praise and honor, yet his own name never appeared on the screen. He was deeply moved when Winston Churchill privately complimented him on September 29, 1943, for making those films. But when Churchill recorded a foreword to the series for British audiences under Capra's direction, declaring that "I have never seen or read any more powerful statement of our cause or of our rightful case against the Nazi tyranny than these films portray," he gave the public credit not to Capra himself but to "the American Army under the authority of General Marshall, their famous chief of staff."

To a degree that seemed remarkable to those who had known only his public braggadocio and had not known him as a quiet and doubt-plagued craftsman, Capra accepted his wartime anonymity, managing to subordinate his ego to a higher loyalty. "Capra was a team player," recalled Brigadier General Frank McCarthy, Marshall's secretary during the war. "He displayed no self-interest at all." Though disappointed over having to accept a desk job in Hollywood rather than heading a combat photography unit like John Ford's, he covered his disappointment well, in many ways thriving under military discipline. His immediate superior, Colonel Edward Lyman Munson, Jr., told the Army he considered Capra "one of the best-rounded officers I have ever seen; he would succeed at any assignment in the Army."

Relieved of the burden of thinking for himself, Capra performed brilliantly in carrying out official policy, surrendering his increasingly troublesome creative independence and transforming himself into a cog in the American propaganda machine. As General Osborn wrote Marshall in 1943, "[B]eyond his undoubted technical genius, [Capra] has a sincerity of purpose and a loyal simplicity of character which have enabled him to get the help of innumerable people in Government and in the Army and in Hollywood; and he has an indomitable energy and belief in the cause, and has worked unbelievable hours to get his results." Endorsing Osborn's recommendation of Capra for the Legion of Merit, Marshall added a note at the bottom of the letter, "Capra has done an outstanding job, unobtrusively and without the usual prima donna complications."

"The war was a very significant change for Capra, a very revealing part of his character," said Paul Horgan, the Pulitzer Prize–winning historian and biographer, who worked in Capra's unit and served as a liaison between the Pentagon and Capra's creative staff. "I always thought that Capra's smiling ego—which was so utterly detached from other people, like Caruso's—was part of his great power: with utter charm he would be above the battle at all times. But I don't think his ego impinged on his work in the war. No one worked more patriotically or threw all of himself into his work in the war more than Capra did. He was 1,000 percent in agreement with policy directives. Nobody [above him] ever suggested an artistic or technical change, but a message or policy would be directly uttered and Frank would accept it."

"Capra was proving to [the top brass] that he was 100 percent American," said Carlton Moss, a civilian writer in his unit. "If they had told him to stand out at Hollywood and Vine and let them take potshots at him, he would have done it, because he was grateful, because he had come here and been given the opportunity."

Capra often recalled his early wartime skirmishes with Signal Corps bureaucrats—those residual tokens of his individuality he displayed so proudly in later years—and he insisted, "It was difficult for me to function. I felt very uneasy in the military. Any kind of a dictatorship, I'm uneasy." Yet Pete Peterson, who worked with Capra throughout the war as a writer-producer, said, "I never once saw him blow his top. I would see fires building up in him, but he would take care of them within himself." Theodor S. Geisel (Dr. Seuss), who also worked in Capra's unit, observed that following orders so assiduously "must have cost Capra a great deal."

Capra acknowledged late in life that the war had left him "kind of burned out. . . . I left a lot of myself in the war."

* * *

"Do they know what is going on and why?" Marshall asked of his troops in the spring of 1941.

To the average GI, Marshall knew, the causes of the war seemed remote and obscure, and he urgently needed an effective way of motivating his troops for sacrifices that most Americans faced with great reluctance. The series of *Why We Fight* films for which Marshall recruited Capra was an outgrowth of the Army Orientation Course, a series of fifteen lectures on the history and current status of the war, which had been started in 1940. As Marshall recalled in a 1957 interview with his biographer Forrest C. Pogue, "At first they prepared pamphlets—very well prepared by experts from the colleges and all—but I found as a rule, they were presented after lunch and the man was tired and he went to sleep, and the company officer who was explaining the thing was a very poor actor or performer. And I called in Frank Capra, the leading motion picture director at that time, and had him prepare the films, which were a complete education, I think, on the war to civilians as well as to the recruits in the Army."

Marshall's thinking on the subject took shape in the summer of 1941. His young aide Frank McCarthy, a 1933 graduate of Marshall's own alma mater, the Virginia Military Institute, had been technical adviser on the 1938 film version of *Brother Rat*, a comedy set at VMI; after the war he became a Hollywood producer (*Patton, MacArthur*). While Marshall was searching for an alternative to the dry factual approach of the troop orientation lectures, McCarthy read a pair of articles by two young Ivy Leaguers in *The Atlantic Monthly*.

The first was Stewart Alsop's article in May 1941, "Wanted: A Faith to Fight For." Most young American men, wrote Alsop, were "searching for a faith, for something to believe in, to live for and die for. . . . The young men of Germany today have found such a faith; however vicious we on the outside know it to be, to them it remains something for which they would gladly die. The Americans who went abroad to fight in 1917 had such a faith. The Americans of today have not."

Cleveland Amory, McCarthy's Army roommate and a member of G-2 (the Army's Intelligence Division), replied in June with "What We Fight For": "We have no fanatical, wild-eyed faith—no panacea, no total, complete goal. . . . Perhaps we should not use the word 'faith' for what we have. . . . There is, though, an idea in America. It is a very simple and undramatic idea. It is an idea that cannot be spread by force because it has nothing to do with fear. It is an idea that plain, ordinary people, free people . . . can in time and with tolerance work out for themselves a better government than has ever been worked out for any people in any country. That idea is what we have."

"I showed Marshall these two articles," McCarthy remembered, "and he said, 'We ought to have a series of films to indoctrinate the troops about the reasons why they're fighting. And we ought to get somebody to do this who knows how to make entertainment films.' General Marshall loved the movies. He used to go quite often at Fort Myer [Virginia, where he lived] to see movies with the troops—he liked sheer entertainment, he liked the pretty girls. He also realized that film was the best medium in the world for imparting information and influencing people, so he got the best storyteller in films to do the job."

Capra arrived in Washington on February 15, 1942, finding a pervasive despondency in the capital about the United States' chances of winning the war. Vocal in his scorn for such defeatism, he spewed out ideas for films, but found stubborn resistance from Signal Corps bureaucracy and red tape. The Signal Corps officers considered themselves the experts in making films for military audiences, and Capra felt that despite his mandate from General Marshall they intended to push him aside in taking over the making of morale films.

Capra's scorn for the low quality of Signal Corps training films was shared by other officers with whom he worked. McCarthy felt the films "usually were a terrible bore, doctrinaire, with no creative quality at all. They imparted information, but had nothing that would grab a soldier and involve him emotionally. Capra was General Marshall's favorite son as far as film went because Capra knew more about film than anyone in the Signal Corps."

Capra later declared, "I never bothered to deal with a colonel—always with the top man," but McCarthy said, "I don't remember them being together much. I'm sure they weren't. General Marshall was a great delegator. Once he got someone who was responsible, and started him off on the right foot, he would leave him alone to do his job. General Marshall would say, 'Better let Frank Capra do what he wants, because he knows what he's doing.'

"General Marshall would refer to him as 'That fellow Capra.' And 'that fellow' was a term I knew he reserved for people he admired. Capra had the blessing of General Marshall all the way through, and he relied on that when he needed something done. That made it sacrosanct, that was what made it possible for him to get his way."

Though Capra heaped invective on his principal Signal Corps antagonist, Colonel Schlosberg, he also wondered later whether, as he had done with Hollywood moguls, he had set up Schlosberg as something of a straw man in his characteristic need for a test of wills against a powerful antagonist. Capra's resentment of the Signal Corps bureaucracy was so intense at the time that he failed to understand the complexity of the situation— that he was only a pawn in an ongoing battle between Osborn and the Signal Corps for control of morale films.

When Capra was transferred, six days after his arrival, to the Information Division of General Osborn's Special Services—the Information Division was the new name of the Morale Branch, which later underwent another name change, to the Information and Education Division, or I&E—he felt that the Signal Corps had shunted him over to Osborn in an attempt to get rid of him, but Osborn told the War Department that Capra's transfer was at "my specific request for the purpose of assignment to his present duties," those of the officer in charge of the Film Production Section.

Two months later, after Capra was well under way in the production of the *Why We Fight* films, the Signal Corps tried to reassert control over Capra, intending to relegate him to advisory status. Capra threw down the gauntlet in a meeting with Osborn and several other officers, including Colonel Schlosberg and Zanuck, whom the Signal Corps had enlisted on its side. "Schlosberg was talking and Capra was silent," Horgan remembered. "They had all been talking as if over his head, as if unaware of his presence. Then when they got down to Capra's end of the table, General Osborn asked, 'What do you think, Major?' And Frank, with his very droll, rather hesitant speech, said, 'In any discussion of film, where *I* sit is the head of the table.' "

Osborn was directed to return Capra's unit to the Signal Corps, but he appealed to Lieutenant General Brehon B. Somervell, the chief of Army Services of Supply, arguing that Capra had a superior knowledge of film-making and that he had given Capra his word that no one would tell him how to make films. Somervell issued a directive on June 6, 1942, setting up the 834th Signal Service Photographic Detachment, Special Services Division, Film Production Section, consisting of 8 officers and 35 enlisted men under Capra's command (his staff would grow to about 150 by late 1943).

On a day-to-day basis Capra relied most heavily on the support and counsel of the head of Special Services' Information Division, Lyman Munson. Like Frank McCarthy, Munson had Hollywood ambitions; after the war they both became executives under Zanuck at Twentieth Century-

Fox, though Munson proved less suited to Hollywood than to the Army. "Lyman Munson was one of the most imaginative men I have ever known to have come out of West Point and into the regular Army," Horgan said. "The genius of a man like Munson was that he had the imagination to want the very best from civilian life. Munson, Osborn, and Capra had to be unanimous on policy, and Frank understood that perfectly. On the other hand, they understood that Capra had to be in charge on the technical end."

Although Capra sometimes gave the impression that he was the only propaganda filmmaker working for the American government during World War II, his unit of Special Services was only one of many government film units competing for money, personnel, and film, including those of the various military services and the Office of War Information's Motion Picture Bureaus, Domestic and Overseas Branches. The total cost of the *Why We Fight* series was only about $400,000, which was less than one percent of the $50 million the War Department spent on films during the war. Most of the Army's filmmaking budget went to combat photography and to training films, which were produced either in New York at the former Paramount studios in Astoria, Queens (on Long Island), a facility which was converted for use as the Signal Corps Photographic Center (SCPC), or (like most of Capra's films) at the Hollywood studios.

Capra's gradual decision to make the *Why We Fight* films mostly out of found footage—taken from newsreels, from Allied and enemy propaganda and combat films, and from entertainment films—was more or less forced on him by his budgetary limitations, which were reminiscent of his early days on Poverty Row. "Struggling on a shoelace" was particularly hard in the "dreary" first few months, when he was sweating out the congressional appropriation for Army morale films, which did not come through until the summer of 1942. All seven *Why We Fight* films had to be made for about one-fifth the cost of *Mr. Smith Goes to Washington*.

Dismayed by the ramshackle Special Services offices, Capra wasted little time in finding new quarters for his unit in the capital. Within four days he had commandeered space in the Cooling Tower of the North Interior Building, a courtyard which served as a heating and ventilating shaft and also housed the Department of Interior's 16mm film production and storage facilities. "This is our new studio, boys," Capra told his handful of staff members, including Pete Peterson, his first civilian employee, who found it for him. "He called me because I knew where all the film was," said Peterson, who had worked for *The March of Time* newsreel. "We started collecting film and getting ideas."

* * *

Capra's first plan was to outline the morale films in Washington and have them written and produced in Hollywood, but everything was so uncertain in the early days and he was so homesick that he rented a house in Bethesda, Maryland, and moved Lu, the children, and their servants Rosa Haspang and Helga Kelly there in early May for what would turn out to be a much briefer stay than expected.

Almost immediately after his arrival in Washington, he had the War Department telephone the Academy Research Council (the official clearing agency for recruiting Hollywood talent) to send for writers whose names he had drawn from a list of volunteers compiled by the Screen Writers Guild's Hollywood Writers' Mobilization group. Some of those he originally wanted (including Herman J. Mankiewicz and Jack Moffitt) were working, but Leonard Spigelgass, John Sanford, Jerome Chodorov, Edward Paramore, and S. K. Lauren were available, and Capra also made a personal call to Julius and Philip Epstein, persuading them to interrupt work on the script of Warners' *Casablanca* (a move that outraged *The Hollywood Reporter*'s Billy Wilkerson, who wrote, "What right has Major Capra to call writers to Washington?").

Within five days Capra's group of seven writers was in the capital as "expert consultants" to the War Department on twenty dollars per diem, writing scripts in tiny cubicles at the Library of Congress under what Julius Epstein remembered as "chaotic" conditions. They spent several weeks writing short scripts on different aspects of the war, based on the lectures in the Army Orientation Course. When they turned in their drafts, Capra wrote in his book, he was "aghast" to find them full of "Communist propaganda."

"Frank thought *everything* was full of Communist propaganda," said Leonard Spigelgass, an outspoken anti-Communist and the only one of the seven writers who remained with Capra throughout the war. "If you said 'Hello' to Frank, you were a Communist. I thought that was idiotic of him to write that. *I* didn't write Communist propaganda, at least I think I didn't."

But Capra's personal feelings at the time were more closely guarded, and much less simplistic, than his book would indicate. Capra's political point of view, John Sanford felt at the time, was "absolutely nonexistent—he was in favor of America winning the war, and that was it. Capra, as I knew him, was rather timid and rather an inarticulate fellow. He did not do much in terms of leading or directing what we were to do in the scripts. I don't think a single one of us knew exactly what to do, but being, for the most part, experienced screenwriters, we could work from a hint or a word or two without any problem."

Julius Epstein considered Capra "a right-wing populist. That was my feeling, but I couldn't tell you how he voted or even if he was registered to vote. My impression was that he was a strange combination of being for the little man in his pictures and I was not sure how he felt outside his pictures." Epstein said that Capra never told him or his brother that he considered their work "Communist propaganda." "This is news to me," Epstein said in 1984. "It was kind of a hectic experience, but there were no confrontations, and he didn't say that to us. Possibly he didn't like what we wrote." Capra wrote that he "quietly dismissed" the writers and replaced them with "controllable men in uniform." The Epsteins were dismissed so quietly that they thought they were leaving voluntarily: "We had to go back to *Casablanca*," Julius Epstein recalled, "and when we told him we were leaving, he didn't raise any objections."

By 1977 Capra seemed less certain of how to characterize the original group of writers, describing them as propagandists for both the far Left and the far Right. But in his book he remembered his fear that if Congress thought the scripts being prepared were "Communist propaganda," the entire *Why We Fight* program might be cut by those in the Army who were waiting for just such an opportunity. When asked later what he thought was "Communist propaganda" in the scripts, Capra said, "There is a Party line that you can smell. We smelled these guys."

"I think he was referring indirectly to the Spanish Civil War," Spigelgass commented. "He was a big Francoite, and he always felt we were for the radicals. That was what was killing him. All the writers were for the Spanish Republic. Frank occasionally closed his eyes to reality. I'm afraid Capra was very conservative. I was a big New Dealer, and Capra and I had very serious problems about interpretation from time to time."

But Capra's retrospective allegation against the group of seven writers (his book did not name their names, which the author identified from documents in his files and from interviews with the survivors) had less to do with his personal opinion of the scripts they wrote for him than with political pressures exerted on him early in the war by the Dies committee and the Army and with later events in the blacklist era. Sanford was dropped from the Capra unit for political reasons, and he, like three more of Capra's original seven writers—Julius and Philip Epstein and Jerome Chodorov—was publicly accused before HUAC of being a Communist.

Capra's three other writers caused him no public embarrassment. Spigelgass was a self-described "moderate" who helped lead the campaign to purge the SWG of suspected Communists after the war; Lauren was a moderate whose work for Capra, included in the final script of one of the *Why We Fight* films, *The Battle of Britain*, could not even remotely be considered "Communist propaganda"; and Paramore, who had written the script of *The Bitter Tea of General Yen*, was described by his son, Ted, as "a liberal capitalist who liked to call himself a Trotskyite."

Sanford, a novelist and sometime screenwriter, was named as a Communist before HUAC in 1951 by screenwriter and former Communist Party member Martin Berkeley; blacklisted after taking the Fifth Amendment before the committee, Sanford left Hollywood to devote all of his time to writing books. The Epsteins were labeled as Communists by Jack Warner before HUAC in 1947. Warner said their work was "un-American" because "the rich man is always the villain." Warner's charges were not taken seriously in Hollywood because, as Ceplair and Englund put it, the liberal Epsteins "had not only never been Communists, but were known for their criticism of communism." Chodorov, a playwright, stage director, and screenwriter, was another of the 161 people named as Communists by Martin Berkeley before HUAC in 1951; he left the movie business and returned to Broadway. And the Hollywood Writers' Mobilization, which had supplied five of the seven writers to Capra (all but the Epsteins), was accused by U.S. Attorney General Tom Clark in 1947–1948 of being "subversive and Communist."

When asked for a specific instance of "Communist propaganda" in the scripts turned in by his original *Why We Fight* writers, Capra said that he detected the influence of the CPUSA line favoring the Nazi-Soviet pact of 1939, which he also claimed had been the cause of his break with Sidney Buchman. But if that charge applied to anybody, it applied equally to Capra himself, because the *Why We Fight* films, for whose production he was responsible, did attempt to provide a rationale for the pact. *The Nazis Strike* (1943), whose final script, according to Capra's files, was written by Eric Knight and Anthony Veiller, says of the pact: "It was too fantastic to make any sense. It didn't. The Germans hoped they could lull Russia into a false sense of security, and the Russians needed time to prepare for the fight they knew was coming. They'd read Hitler's book *Mein Kampf*, too, and knew he had his eyes on the rich Russian land." The original prints of *The Battle of Russia*, released later in 1943 (final script by Veiller), contained a similar apology for the pact, which was missing from some copies of the film.

Since the U.S.S.R. was an American ally during the war, providing a rationale for the pact was also a pragmatic part of U.S. policy, however embarrassing that stance would seem later. The lecture on *The Battle of Russia* in the Army Orientation Course, which Capra gave to Sanford before he started writing the script for the film, stated that the Soviets "knew that at best they could only postpone war until Russia might better be prepared. . . . Russia during the 1930s offered to sign treaties and guarantees beyond the point where any other nation in Europe was willing to go. . . . Russia was ruthless in her preparation for the days of reckoning with Germany."

Capra's attempt to fix blame on the original writers and on his other colleagues for his films' pro-Soviet stance may have stemmed more from postwar reaction than from anything else. Pro-Soviet films made in Hollywood during the war brought retrospective suspicion on their makers during the cold war, and Capra felt vulnerable for having made *The Battle of Russia,* which not only had nothing critical to say about the Soviet political system but even went so far as to call the Soviets a "free and united people" and to claim that Stalin's U.S.S.R. represented the triumph of "the cross of Christ over the Fascist swastika."

Asked about this in 1975, Capra said, "Well, you understand these were our allies. We were fighting a common enemy at the time, not each other. Unless you get into that, you won't understand the simplifications. . . . [W]e had to *eliminate* things. It didn't matter to us whether the priests were having trouble in Russia. The immediate thing was the destruction of the war machine."

Sanford had been recommended to Capra by Buchman; the two writers had become friends when Sanford wrote Buchman "the only fan letter of my life" in 1939 after seeing *Mr. Smith Goes to Washington.* For Capra, Sanford not only wrote the original script of *The Battle of Russia* but also a script about the U.S.S.R. intended for the *Know Your Ally* series (originally called *America's Friends*). (*Know Your Ally: Russia* never was completed—nor was another project of Capra's unit entitled *Know Your Enemy: Russia.*)

After his original seven writers read their drafts aloud, Capra singled out Sanford, asking him to accept a place in the unit and an officer's commission. A few days later, when Sanford was in Hollywood settling his affairs as Capra had instructed, he received a letter from Capra "saying that I was unacceptable" for political reasons.

Sanford said in 1986 that in his two scripts for Capra about the U.S.S.R., "I extolled the fighting powers of the Russian troops, their vast resources, and their experience in previous wars, establishing the fact that theirs were redoubtable forces and encouraging the [U.S.] military to regard them as a full-fledged ally. It was absolutely necessary to write a film that was favorable to our Allies. But the idea that I would have sneaked in a line saying that 'Karl Marx was a great fellow' or something like that is one of the most ridiculous things I've ever heard. I did not see any of the other scripts, to the best of my knowledge, but I know mine and mine had nothing of that nature in it."

Sanford's scripts bear out the truth of what he said.

After Sanford was rejected for Capra's outfit, he wrote the director on May 2, ". . . I know all about your having put me on the shelf because you suspect that I am a communist.

"If this were a time for gags, I might suspect that I'd been made the butt of one of the very best: The United States Government asked me to devote six weeks of my life to writing a pair of scripts establishing Russia as an indispensable ally, as a result of which effort I am said to have sold myself for thirty pieces of Moscow gold! . . .

"I shall not enter into the question of whether I am a communist, except to state plainly that I am not.* What concerns me, and what should concern my country, is whether I shall be used in the war effort if I am *reputed* to be a Communist.

"In the language of my time, I've been given 'the finger,' but what finger is it, Frank? What finger on what hand? What hand on what arm? What arm on what body? *What body is it, Frank?* . . . But don't get me wrong. I don't want to know its actual name—I detest it unknown, for it can belong to no one but a traitor, and a traitor, marked or unmarked, is always and only the one untouchable in the human race.

"No, Frank, I don't want to know the owner of the finger. I want you to know him! I want you to know the nature and intention of the voice that you have listened to.

"I don't propose to tell you how this war can be won. You know that as well as I do—better, perhaps, for you've beaten me to the punch and put on the only clothes (aside from overalls) that the day recognizes as respectable. I do propose, however, to tell you a rattling good way that this war can be *lost*.

"It can be lost if we are divided against ourselves. It can be lost if Gentile is played off against Jew, black against white, rich against poor,

* *Sanford wrote the author in 1991, "When I told Capra I was not a Communist, I wasn't telling the truth, as anyone who has read my Autobiography must surely know. My only excuse for the lie, if a lie can ever be excused, is that Capra had no legal right to inquire. Nor did the House Committee later on."*

labor against capital, hammer-and-sickle against stars-and-stripes. . . .

"I am a Jewish-American—I am not an American Jew. As a Jewish-American, I am an American first, last, and all the time. . . .

"To silence one anti-fascist voice today (whether it be the voice of a communist, a reputed communist, or no communist at all) is to spike one gun at a time when all guns—good, poor, and obsolete—should be shooting till their barrels get too hot to be held. . . ."

Capra replied: "I know this is quite a painful subject to both of us. You are wrong about one thing: that *I* have put you on the shelf because I suspect you're a Communist. I don't give two hoots in Hell what you are, as long as you're an American first. And as for your being Jewish, that is equally absurd. If we aren't fighting for the elimination of all these discriminations, what the Hell are we fighting for?

"No, John, don't get me wrong. You'd be my first choice on this program, both for your grand ability as a writer and for your intense interest.

"But I've been brought practically to a complete stop by several things. First, the motion picture industry is moving heaven and earth to get all government production stopped. Secondly, some Army quarters are trying to kill it because they finally realized how big this thing could grow. And lastly, the one that concerns you most, Congress has yet to vote the appropriations. Biggest hurdle is that two Dies committee members are on the [House] Appropriation[s] Committee [actually, there were three: Harry P. Beam (D-Illinois), Joseph E. Casey (D-Massachusetts), and Joe Starnes (D-Alabama)].

"The last few days you were here, the Dies committee descended on us about who and what was telling the soldiers what to think. They demanded the names of all concerned. We were notified not long ago that you were too 'red,' and G-2 sent a memorandum advising against using you.

"My whole program is still on the brink. Hollywood, the Army, and Congress are sniping at it. If it wasn't that I have faith in the opportunity to strike a hard blow for democracy, I wouldn't take this beating for all the tea in China.

"So, please, John, don't try to convince me that you should be used. . . . I've been ordered by my immediate superiors to let G-2 make a thorough report on everyone we hire, at least until we get the appropriation from Congress.

"Recently Congress cut off all appropriations for government films. If they carry this policy into the Army, we're sunk.

"I haven't told any of my friends about this because I was afraid they would try to do something about it. Publicity would hurt the program right now.

"Let me get this thing going, then I can move more freely. Right now we're hanging by a thread. It's not what I want that counts now, it's what I have to do to get what I want. One more thing, your letter is just as fascinating as your scripts."

On May 15, Sanford replied, "I'm no dope, and therefore I understand the hole you're in regarding freedom of choice and action. I'm aware of the forces that are bucking you and your project, and to find that you know them for what they are, to find that you needed no warning from me to put you on your guard against defeatists, appeasers, and Fifth Columnists in general, is a matter of the utmost satisfaction. I'd had you pegged as one who knew the bloody score, and my having written as I did sprang from an urge to leave no stone unturned in my private fight to defeat Fascism; it did not spring from distrust. Keep bucking those bastards right back, Frank. I'm behind you, and so is all of America that really counts."

In September, when Sanford heard that Capra had moved his Army operations to the West Coast, he paid a call on Capra, who (now that his appropriation had been approved by Congress) again asked him to join the unit. Sanford filled out an application form, but on the next day he was notified that he was still "unacceptable."

In April 1944, frustrated over "getting kicked in the belly every time I've hopefully tendered my miserable little talent to the Government" (he also had been rejected for officer candidate school as overage), Sanford sent what he called "a hard letter to write," asking Capra, "the only man I know who will listen," to help him find an assignment with the Psychological Warfare Division of the OSS.

Capra did not reply.*

While looking for writers who were politically moderate and "controllable," Capra also was struggling to find a device to unify the series, to give

---

* Also found unacceptable by the Army was director Edward Dmytryk, who wrote in his autobiography that he went to see Capra early in the war "and volunteered my services as a cutter, or in any other useful capacity. My offer was warmly accepted. I was told to go home and wait for the word. It never came. Some years later, I was to learn that the Signal Corps had turned me down as a security risk; I had been a premature antifascist." In his 1951 HUAC testimony, Dmytryk said that although he did not join the Communist Party until 1944, "Probably as early as 1942 I had begun to be interested in what later became, although I didn't know it at the time, Communist fronts." Dmytryk was one of the blacklisted Hollywood Ten who went to jail in 1950 for contempt of Congress, but unlike the others he resumed his career after naming names to HUAC.

emotional life to Marshall's broad mandate of showing "what they were fighting for and what the enemy had done."

Capra found part of his device in April, when he, Peterson, and the Russian-born director Anatole Litvak, a new member of the unit, went to New York's Museum of Modern Art and watched all of the Nazi propaganda films in MOMA's collection. "Tola" Litvak, who had fought with the Russian army in World War I, had directed films in Germany from 1927 until 1933 and had made one of the few Hollywood films dealing explicitly with the Fascist threat, Warners' 1939 *Confessions of a Nazi Spy.*

The most important film the three men watched was *Triumph des Willens (Triumph of the Will)*, Leni Riefenstahl's film of the Nazis' 1934 Nuremberg Party Congress. The Signal Corps earlier had denied Capra admission to a screening of *Triumph of the Will* because his application for a security clearance still was being reviewed. There is no explanation in Capra's Army records or in his Army Intelligence file why it was held up, but material in HUAC's files might have required some explaining. According to Army Intelligence reports in 1951, HUAC's files on Capra included the allegations about the 1932 Communist Party election petition and about his involvement in what HUAC called the "Communist inspired" strike at the *Hollywood Citizen-News* in 1938. In time, however, Capra and his staff obtained what Chet Sticht, his master sergeant and chief film librarian, described as "extremely high security clearances."

When Capra first saw *Triumph of the Will* at MOMA, he recalled, "It scared the hell out of me. My first reaction was that we were dead, we couldn't win the war. [I responded] just exactly as the Austrians did and the Czechoslovakians did and the Channel countries did. That picture just won them over. . . . When I saw it, I just thought, 'How can we possibly cope with this enormous machine and enormous will to fight?' Surrender or you're dead—that was what the film was saying to you. I sat there and I was a very unhappy man. How can I possibly top *this?*"

When asked what they did after the screening, Peterson replied, "We went out and got drunk."

As a filmmaker, Capra was impressed by Riefenstahl's orchestration of the spectacle, which had been staged specifically for the film itself—by her grandiose, mythic imagery, by the hypnotic rhythm of her editing and her use of music to add a further dimension of barbarian emotional power to the endless marching, flag-waving, and speechmaking. He considered *Triumph of the Will* "the greatest propaganda film anyone has ever made."

"I could see that it promised superman stuff to them," he told Bill Moyers in a 1982 television interview. "I could see that the kids of Germany would go anyplace and die for this guy. The power of the film itself showed that they knew what they were doing. They understood propaganda, and they understood how to reach the mind.

"So how do I tell the kid down the street—the American kid riding his bike—what he's got in front of him? How do I reach him?

"The thought hit me, 'Well, how did it reach me? *They* told me.' "*

As he watched more German films at MOMA, Capra began to realize that he could build the first films in the *Why We Fight* series—the ones which told of the coming of war in Europe, laying the foundation for the others—around the footage taken by the Germans, using large amounts of footage from *Triumph of the Will*, from Fritz Hippler's war propaganda documentaries *Feldzug in Polen* (*Campaign in Poland*) and *Sieg im Westen* (*Victory in the West*), and from German newsreels.

"Let their own films kill them," Capra told Peterson.

The basic shape of the *Why We Fight* series was decided between April and August 1942, with a crucial contribution from the British-born writer Eric Knight, a captain in the U.S. Army who had lived in the United States since the age of thirteen.

After he was asked to join the unit, Knight told Capra in an April 15 letter that he found his ideas much too negative, too much concerned with demonstrating the odds against victory. Knight worried that such a one-sided emphasis as Capra's would only reinforce the despair and defeatism afflicting many in the United States. Reminding Capra that in the days when Britain had fought alone, Winston Churchill's speeches had rallied his countrymen's fighting spirit, Knight urged Capra that the *Why We Fight* films similarly evoke the ideas underlying American democratic traditions while also stressing the need for a joint international effort among the Allies.

Throughout the series Capra would employ the basic rhetorical device of contrasting the American Dream with the ideology of the Axis powers.

"This isn't just a war," declares *Prelude to War*, the first *Why We Fight*

---

* *That thought, which Peterson said was not a spontaneous inspiration of Capra's but "a distillation that came from everything we looked at," was anticipated in 1940 by propaganda filmmakers in Great Britain, including Alberto Cavalcanti in his film about Mussolini,* Yellow Caesar; *by Len Lye in* Swinging the Lambeth Walk, *which mocked the Nazis by orchestrating footage from* Triumph of the Will *to a British popular tune; and by Fred Watts in the anti-Nazi compilation* The Curse of the Swastika. *It also was anticipated in the United States in 1940 by* The Ramparts We Watch, *Lothar Wolff's feature-length* March of Time *compilation on life in an American community between 1914 and 1939, which received widespread publicity for turning a Nazi film about Poland,* Feuertaufe *(Baptism of Fire), against its original purpose.*

film, on which Knight collaborated with Veiller and Robert Heller. "This is a common man's life-and-death struggle against those who would put him back into slavery. We lose it—and we lose everything. Our homes, the jobs we want to go back to, the books we read, the very food we eat, the hopes we have for our kids, the kids themselves—they won't be ours anymore. That's what's at stake. It's us or them. The chips are down."

The "us or them" dialectic gave the films the emotional power Capra sought, simplifying the enormously complex historical and political issues underlying the war into a single, quickly grasped black-and-white concept. It was a simplification which caused some tricky problems in dealing with America's allies, particularly in *The Battle of Russia* and *The Battle of China*. Both films would cause Capra considerable political embarrassment.

Capra's war films are severely limited as historical analyses of the events leading up to the war. They say little about the effects of World War I on Germany or about the other reasons for the acceptance of fascism by the German people, aside from the most generalized statements about their "inborn national love of regimentation and harsh discipline." Except for *Your Job in Germany* and *Here Is Germany*, which were released at the war's end, Capra's war films focus the blame primarily on Hitler, rather than on the German people. But with the Japanese, the films take a different focus. The viewer is offered little explanation for Japan's belligerence other than a racist and xenophobic view of Hitler's "bucktoothed pals . . . the blood-crazed Japs . . . a fantastic people . . . a fanatic nation" launched on a mission of world conquest by their "diabolical" religion of Shintoism, which dictates to the individual "Jap" that "where his flag leads he follows in a blind emotional rush."

The films were released abroad by the OWI, and Philip Dunne, Robert Riskin's chief of production in its Overseas Motion Picture Bureau, recalled, "We had to rewrite Frank's troop indoctrination films, because we couldn't send to the Far East pictures which referred to the Japanese as bucktoothed, sawed-off little yellow bastards. We had to put it in our more diplomatic language." *

When asked by Moyers if he intended the *Why We Fight* films to be

---

* *The third Axis power usually seems like an afterthought in Capra's war films, and Mussolini, seen as a buffoonish "stooge" of Hitler, is described as a leader who "betrayed those who first supported him." In light of Capra's ethnic background and his previous mutual admiration society with Mussolini, it is significant that though the other films he made for the Army included* Know Your Enemy: Germany *(revised and released as* Here Is Germany*) and* Know Your Enemy—Japan, *the unit's* Know Your Enemy: Italy *never got beyond the planning stages.*

"hate" films, Capra replied, "I don't want people to hate. I wanted [them] to knock off people that hated. I wanted to stop that hatred." But he conceded on another, less prominent occasion (an appearance before the Community Film Association of Columbus, Ohio, in 1979), "We tried to make them as logical as possible, without hate, but that's difficult in wartime. You'll see it creeps into the dialogue. . . . At the time there was a need for these films. I'm glad and I'm proud that I was able to satisfy that need, but now I don't like to see these films because of the memories they bring back."

Though the emotional power of the *Why We Fight* films is diminished today by the crudity of their rhetoric, they also must be seen in the perspective of the time when they were made and the primary uses for which they were designed.

Although a few of the films made by Capra's unit were shown in American commercial theaters and all seven of the *Why We Fight* films were widely seen abroad both by military and civilian audiences (versions were produced in several foreign languages), they were made principally to indoctrinate the American GI. Marshall issued an order making the entire series required viewing for every soldier. As the last film in the series, *War Comes to America*, states, 37 percent of American fighting men had less than a high school education. The average GI, Capra believed, was "so uninformed [that] this 'free-world, slave-world' [approach was] the only way you could reach that guy at that moment. You give him a lot of 'but-on-the-other-hands' and you confuse him completely."

Having been criticized in some quarters for the alleged "anti-Americanism" of the films of social criticism he made before the war, Capra during the war felt compelled to proclaim his patriotism in the most vociferous manner. Much of it, no doubt, was deeply felt, but there is also an element of overcompensation evident in the stridency of the *Why We Fight* films. His abandonment of his prewar Hollywood "independence" for the regimentation of propaganda filmmaking was "a welcome out" for Capra because it gave him an excuse to avoid the increasingly complex problems he had been facing in making such films as *Mr. Smith* and *Meet John Doe*. Exchanging his role as gadfly for the role of government mouthpiece caused him new kinds of problems, but they were problems which could be resolved (at least for the moment) simply by following orders. In that sense the *Why We Fight* series was a logical outgrowth of the flight from ideas Capra had begun in earnest with *Arsenic and Old Lace*, and which, by the war's end, would leave him virtually bereft of his creative personality.

*   *   *

"**E**verybody from top to bottom deserves equal credit for anything we've done," Capra declared during the war. The sheer volume of work he supervised would have precluded total control by one man in any case.

Between June 1942 and September 1945 his 834th Signal Service Photographic Detachment produced the seven *Why We Fight* films (*Prelude to War, The Nazis Strike, Divide and Conquer, The Battle of Britain, The Battle of Russia, The Battle of China,* and *War Comes to America*), and the unit made ten other films which have been released (*Substitution and Conversion, Know Your Ally Britain, The Negro Soldier, Your Job in Germany, Two Down and One to Go!, On to Tokyo, The Stilwell Road, Know Your Enemy—Japan, Here Is Germany,* and *Our Job in Japan*). The unit also made fifty issues of the biweekly newsreel titled *The War* when first released in May 1943 and, after ten issues, retitled the *Army-Navy Screen Magazine;* and forty-six issues of the *Staff Film Report,* begun in June 1944, a weekly assembly of classified battle, reconnaissance, weapons testing, and enemy footage for viewing by the President, the Joint Chiefs of Staff, American commanders throughout the world, Allied commanders, and the service and command schools. The official Army history of the war states that "at high levels, the *Staff Film Report* was rated the most valuable of all the film projects APS [the Army Pictorial Service] undertook during the war." The *Reports* were reedited for viewing by the troops in thirty-four *Combat Bulletins.* Capra's unit also worked on a number of uncompleted and/or unreleased projects and assisted in the processing of other secret footage, including that of the first atomic bomb test.

Capra also worked for the War Department's Bureau of Public Relations (BPR) and the British Ministry of Information on the joint English-American feature *Tunisian Victory.* In August 1943 he turned over command of the 834th to Litvak, though he continued to supervise projects which had been begun earlier. In the latter years of the war Capra was commanding officer of the Signal Corps' Special Coverage Section, Western Division, APS, supervising combat photography, and served as assistant to the chief for Motion Picture Planning and as assistant chief of the APS.

Like other government films made during the war, those made by Capra's unit do not contain any personal screen credits, an ostensibly equitable policy which actually had the effect of making it seem as if Capra had done everything himself. Some recent Capra filmographies, and some companies which televise and distribute copies of the public-domain *Why We Fight* films, misleadingly call Capra (or others) the "director" of the films, for which little new footage was shot. As Peterson observed, "You don't direct 500,000 Chinese evacuating the city of Shanghai." Capra more accurately called himself the "executive producer" of those films (a few of the other films Capra produced involved extensive shooting of new footage, but of them only *Tunisian Victory, Two Down and One to Go!*, and *On to Tokyo* were directed in part by Capra). Serving under Capra as "project officers" with responsibility for individual films were such men as Litvak, Peterson, Geisel, and Joseph Sistrom; writer Anthony Veiller also acted as a general production aide; and former Columbia executive Sam Briskin was Capra's second-in-command and production manager before he suffered a heart attack. Spigelgass ran the Washington office after Capra moved back to Hollywood, and he also supervised the production of the *Army-Navy Screen Magazine*.

A definitive determination of writing credit for the films is impossible, for the scripts of most films were reworked by numerous hands, and, as Peterson said, "Nobody knew exactly who did what except for the guys who worked on them." The writers on whom Capra relied most heavily included Veiller, Spigelgass, Allen Rivkin, and Knight (who died in January 1943 when the U.S. transport plane in which he was riding on an assignment for the Armed Forces Radio Service was shot down over Dutch Guiana).* Of the scripts in Capra's files, the only ones which bear his own name are *War Comes to America, Two Down and One to Go!, On to Tokyo*, and *Know Your Enemy—Japan*, on all of which he had collaborators.

Rivkin described the production process: "We'd sit around at the beginning of a project and try to establish a point of view. Usually two writers would work on a script at the same time, with one fellow writing the narration. We would prepare a rough outline without knowing what film we had available, and then production would begin on the film. We would try to make the bits and pieces of film fit in, and figure out what gaps we had to cover with animation and supers. Frank was always the arbiter of what went into the script. He'd say, 'It needs punching up here, would you do that?' When we had a script, Bill Hornbeck would put the film together with his assistants. Frank would watch the rough cut and someone would read the narration aloud. Next it was looked at again by Frank and his staff,

---

* *Others who worked on scripts for Capra's unit included Geisel, John Huston, Jo Swerling, Ben Hecht, William Saroyan, Lillian Hellman, Marc Connelly, James Hilton, John Cheever, Janet Flanner, Irwin Shaw, Irving Wallace, Robert Heller, Frances Goodrich and Albert Hackett, William L. Shirer, John Gunther, Gilbert Seldes, Gene Fowler, Bill Henry, Valentine Davies, Claude Binyon, Herbert Baker, John Whittaker, Leopold Atlas, Carl Foreman, and Robert Stevenson.*

all of them talking during the picture. Eventually Frank would take it to Washington."

It has become a cliché that editing is the essence of filmmaking, yet nowhere is that truth more evident than in Capra's war films. As historian William Thomas Murphy has observed, "little credit has been given to those who viewed miles of footage to select the perfect shot and who arranged and edited thousands of shots to present a powerful reconstruction of the past and present." Hornbeck and his staff of editors numbered twenty-five at its peak strength—including Henry Berman, John Hoffman, Merrill White, Rex McAdam, and Arthur Kramer—and sometimes as many as a dozen would be working on a single film at the same time.*

Richard Griffith, a researcher for the unit and head of its New York office, best described Capra's overall role in the making of the films: "It was he who gave them their distinctive shape, based on the editing principle as the defining factor in the conception and execution of every film. Many times, when a film had been virtually completed by others of his staff, he would take it away to the cutting rooms for a few days. Screened again, it would seem on the surface much the same, yet invariably it had acquired a magical coherence and cogency which testified eloquently to Capra's editing capacity."

Capra boasted in his book that he had virtually a free hand in determining the content of the films. Especially in the chaotic first few months of the war, Capra was left largely to his own devices during production in carrying out the policy directives sketched out for him by his superiors. But he was not happy about it.

"What you say about the need for frequent and periodical meetings on the content of projects is, of course, very true," Osborn wrote him on September 23, 1942. "I realize that under all the pressures of last winter, and with my own lack of realization of what you were up against, we have really failed you on this matter to date."

In response to Capra's plea for guidance, the Army prepared a "bible" for the *Why We Fight* series, which Capra told Munson on November 12 was "just what the doctor ordered to keep everybody thinking along the same lines." From that point on, the work of Capra's unit was scrutinized by Army officers at every stage, and changes frequently were imposed. As

---

The music of Dimitri Tiomkin, Alfred Newman, and Meredith Willson, and the narration delivered by Walter Huston, Veiller, Lloyd Nolan, John Litel, and Paul Stewart, among others, also were important elements in unifying the highly diverse footage and intensifying the films' emotional impact.

Capra told the Army in 1954 when the U.S. Senate Internal Security Subcommittee was investigating World War II films, each film in the *Why We Fight* series also had to be approved by Marshall, Osborn, Secretary of War Henry L. Stimson, and Major General Alexander D. Surles, chief of the BPR. Capra neglected to mention the involvement of President Roosevelt.

The President at first was kept out of the loop by Marshall, who decided to make *Prelude to War* "on the q.t." to avoid delays and interference from higher authorities: "I never allowed the secretary of war to see it, or the White House to see it until we had it finished. And [Roosevelt] was thrilled by it, but still he had a great many ideas. . . . I had to get it out to the troops in two weeks. . . . And they kept it four months. But meanwhile, three million troops had seen it. I would not let it go until three million men had seen it. . . . [T]ime was golden with me. And I was perfectly confident with what I had that Capra in each case had done a superb job."

Roosevelt did not see every other film made by Capra's unit before it was released, but the President did take time for private screenings whenever possible. Paul Horgan remembered those occasions when "Frank took the rough cut to Washington, actually carrying the cans with him to the White House in the evening after screening them at the Pentagon in the afternoon. The discussions after those screenings were fascinating, because you felt in the air the policy of the nation being formulated. Every detail was checked, not so much for factual errors, though those would come up, but for emphasis and nuances. Frank was always in an extreme state of excitement when going to the White House to see them with the President and the secretary of war."

Though Capra does not mention in his book that his films ran into any internal censorship, *The Battle of China* and *Know Your Enemy—Japan* were withdrawn from distribution after strenuous objections were made within the Army to their political content. Also for policy reasons, one completed film, Paul Horgan's *Fast Company* (about officer candidate schools), was never released, and another, *Our Job in Japan*, was not released for decades. *The Negro Soldier* underwent extensive revisions and cuts before its release, *The Stilwell Road* (the story of the Burma and Ledo Roads, originally titled *The Campaign in Burma*) almost was abandoned because of conflicts between British and American brass, and *Know Your Enemy: Germany* (*Here Is Germany*) was almost entirely reshot.

In the final analysis, the credit on each film to the Army and the War Department was more accurate than any individual credit or credits would have been, because the films that finally emerged from the chain of command could be considered "Frank Capra films" only in the loosest sense. "If we do discover some of Capra's social vision in the *Why We Fight* series," Charles Maland commented, "it is probably because his vision coincided with and followed American policy and not vice versa."

Capra moved the unit to Hollywood on July 13 "both for production and for political reasons," Peterson said. "You never could have made those pictures in Washington."

After working out of temporary production quarters in the General Service Studios (now Hollywood Center Studios), Capra found a permanent base that fall at the vacant Fox Studio at 1421 North Western Avenue in Hollywood, supplied by Zanuck to the Army for only the costs of renovation and a lease of one dollar a year. Equipment for the Western Division of the Signal Corps Photographic Center, or "Fort Fox," as it was called by his men (though never by Capra himself), had to be wheedled unofficially from people Capra knew in the craft departments of Hollywood studios.

Though he was promoted to lieutenant colonel on August 12, the hand-me-down operation was galling to Capra's pride, and he was sensitive to the fact that he was far from combat. But in his memo to his officers, he covered his anxieties with bravado: "Some carping individuals will accuse you of fighting 'The Battle of Hollywood.' Don't argue with them. This is a total war fought with every conceivable weapon. Your weapon is film! Your bombs are ideas! Hollywood is a war plant! Hitler has taken over whole countries on film. Your job is to counterattack and take them back. . . .

"In case any of you feel that you are making any personal sacrifice in coming into the Army, forget it. The wives and mothers of the heroes of Bataan would not think that you are sacrificing much. You have been selected because of your ability, not because of your martyrdom.

"THE GREATEST GLORY THAT CAN COME TO ANY MAN IS TO JOIN THE SERVICE WHILE HIS COUNTRY IS IN DANGER."

"I became more and more respectful of the climate that was established by Capra in his unit," said Horgan. "The innate quality of Capra's leadership was so implicit that he never had to exert it—it came from the power of that man's character, from his kindness, his decency, his feeling for other people, and also he worked harder than anyone else, which made everyone want to work as hard as he did. You never saw such industry—people working way, way into the nights. Everybody was his ally, uncritically devoted to him. And yet he managed to maintain a certain detachment through it all. I don't think he had any intimates in the outfit. Of course, that detachment is probably necessary for a commander."

"The secret of Capra is his patience," Ted Geisel observed. "He's always been a good teacher. I never heard him cuss anybody out or embarrass anybody. One of the reasons I love Capra is that when I arrived at Fort Fox, he gave me the tour, and the last thing he said was, 'Here, Captain, are the Moviolas.' I said, 'What is a Moviola?' He looked at me rather suddenly and said, 'You will learn.' The average guy would have thrown me out."

The *Why We Fight* series originally was not intended for screening to the general public. But exceptions were made during the war for *Prelude to War* and *The Battle of Russia,* which were released to American theaters through the Hollywood War Activities Committee (WAC), a group of industry executives formed to supervise the theatrical distribution of war documentaries. Marshall, after seeing the rough cut of *Prelude to War* in August 1942, told Capra the film should be shown to the public as well as to the troops, and when Roosevelt finally saw it, he told Osborn that he wanted the public to see it as soon as possible.

However, companies which had supplied footage with the understanding that the films were for nontheatrical use resented the idea of a theatrical release for *Prelude to War*. The OWI and Lowell Mellett, chief of its Bureau of Motion Pictures, also felt betrayed. The OWI had persuaded reluctant commercial exhibitors to show short subjects about the war, half of them made by the government and half by Hollywood, by promising that they would not be asked to show longer war documentaries, with one exception, the OWI's own *The World at War,* released in August 1942. Mellett told OWI chief Elmer Davis that he had been assured repeatedly by Capra and Munson that they were not planning a theatrical release of any of their films.

The OWI was most sensitive to fears of a congressional backlash if it appeared that government propaganda films were being used for partisan purposes, and it raised strong objections to the public release of *Prelude to War*. Mellett wrote Roosevelt on November 9, 1942, "I feel that it is a bad picture in some respects, possibly even a dangerous picture. . . . One of the most skillful jobs of moviemaking I ever have seen, the picture makes a terrific attack on the emotions. . . . Engendering nervous hysteria in the Army or in the civil population might help to win the war, although I doubt it. It won't help in the business of making a saner world after the armistice."

In his elation over finishing *Prelude to War* (it was released to the troops on October 30), Capra showed it privately to some of his civilian friends in Hollywood, but he was ordered to stop doing so by the OWI. The Academy of Motion Picture Arts and Sciences then asked the OWI for permission to show the film to an industry audience.

"APPRECIATE DESIRE OF COLONEL CAPRA'S ACADEMY FRIENDS," Mellett replied in a wire to the Academy on November 9, "BUT SUGGEST IN ALL SINCERITY THAT THEY REFRAIN FROM EMBARRASSING HIM AND OTHER ABLE DIRECTORS WHO HAVE ENTERED ARMED SERVICES BY CONFUSING THEIR PRESENT SERVICE AS SOLDIERS WITH THEIR PRIVATE CAREERS."

Calling the ban "ridiculous," the irate Capra suggested to Munson that Mellett and the OWI simply "don't want competition with their own product." Osborn wrote Mellett that Capra "was following out my instructions that he should obtain the utmost cooperation from the motion picture industry in order to get the finest results and reduce the cost of the picture in every way possible. . . . I am deeply concerned over an unwarranted statement regarding an officer whose integrity and personal character are beyond question. . . . I would appreciate your retraction of this statement."

"I share your opinion of Capra," Mellett replied, "and am resentful, on my part, that anyone should have indicated to you that I had ever questioned his integrity and personal character."

Capra resumed his Hollywood screenings with Osborn's blessings. He submitted *Prelude to War* for Oscar consideration, and at the March 4, 1943, Academy Awards, it was one of four films awarded Oscars for best documentary film: the others were John Ford's *The Battle of Midway*, the Soviets' *Moscow Strikes Back*, and the Australians' *Kokoda Front Line*.*

While the OWI continued to stall the public release of *Prelude to War* by demanding changes in the film, its fears that Congress would attack government propaganda as pro–Democratic Party became a reality on February 8, when Oregon Republican Rufus C. Holman rose in the Senate to denounce *Prelude to War* and the OWI's *Victory* magazine as "personal political propaganda" promoting a fourth term for President Roosevelt. The senator urged an investigation of government propaganda and its cost to the taxpayer, which he called "a waste of political funds."

Telling the press that he would welcome such an investigation, Mellett tried to shift the blame to Capra. He aired the previously secret controversy over a public release for *Prelude to War* and said that "Capra has pulled the stops and played too many notes of hate for general audiences."

---

* *The Oscar was given to the Army and accepted by Capra.* The Battle of Russia *received an Oscar nomination the following year. The New York film critics gave a special award in 1944 to the* Why We Fight *films and John Huston's* Report from the Aleutians, *but that award too was given to the Army, rather than to Capra, as he later claimed.*

After Marshall personally assured Holman that Roosevelt had nothing to do with the making of the film, and after its modest cost was disclosed (the final figure was $60,974), congressional anger against Capra abated. But conservative resentment of the OWI and of Roosevelt's close friendships with Elmer Davis and Mellett had been exacerbated by the incident. As of June 1943, Congress cut the budget for the OWI's domestic branch from $7 million to $2 million, of which only $50,000 was allotted to the Bureau of Motion Pictures, effectively ending its filmmaking program.

Capra's personal finances and those of other Hollywood personalities in military service also came under congressional scrutiny in February 1943, when Senator Harry S Truman's Special Committee Investigating the National Defense Program looked into the allegation that, as Capra put it, "I was under salary during the time I have been in the Army." The broader focuses of the Truman committee's investigation of Army filmmaking were on waste and inefficiency, alleged favoritism on the part of Zanuck and the Academy Research Council in allocating production contracts to the studios, and allegations that studios were profiting from the "nonprofit" contracts.

The committee also cast a cold eye on the commissions that had been granted to Capra, Ford, Zanuck, Sam Briskin, and other Hollywood celebrities, and in alleged conflicts of interest between their military and Hollywood activities, such as Capra and Ford receiving profit percentages from their old films while in uniform, Zanuck's remaining on the Fox payroll at $5,000 a week while on active Army duty, and Briskin receiving $300 a week from Columbia Pictures while serving in Capra's unit. Although some of the questions raised were legitimate (Colonel Kirke B. Lawton, then head of the Army Pictorial Service, conceded that Zanuck "was not putting full time on duty with the Signal Corps"), the investigation tended to spread overly broad innuendos, blurring the facts of individual cases and displaying a biased attitude toward the Hollywood soldiers. After a member of the public who claimed to know Capra personally wrote the committee impugning the patriotism of such Hollywood figures as Capra, Zanuck, Briskin, and Jack Warner for receiving commissions to stay in the U.S. to make films while others were off fighting, the committee's chief counsel, Hugh A. Fulton, responded, "Senator Truman feels that these men could better be hired as civilians, and that the uniforms should be reserved for their original purpose, namely, to distinguish the combatants."

Capra had little problem deflecting the charges of financial conflict raised against him. "I was commissioned on February 11, 1942, at which time I was not under contract or working for any company or receiving any salary," he reported to Lawton. His final paycheck on *Arsenic and Old Lace* had been on January 22, 1942, when he received the last $20,000 of his $125,000 salary. He added that in 1942 he had received $135,910 in net profits from *Meet John Doe*, that profits on the film still were accruing "in ever-dwindling amounts," and that since entering the service he also had received profits from his Columbia films. He made no mention of the income from Red Mountain Ranch and its mail-order olive oil business nor from any of his stock holdings. He later claimed he had withdrawn more than $150,000 from his savings during the war years, and had a $205,000 tax bite taken from his first profit participation payment of $232,000 from *Arsenic* after its theatrical release in 1944. But his book misleadingly implies that his family lived during the war entirely on his income from *Arsenic*, with their total expenses amounting to only about $25,000 per year. Capra's obfuscations not only exaggerated the degree of his wartime financial sacrifice but also reflected a genuine anxiety he felt about his reduced income level, even though the war had made him see that "the crazy spending was a lot of chichi."

The Senate investigation helped bring about a major reorganization of Army filmmaking, eventually resulting in the Academy Research Council being dropped as the middleman for production contracts, Zanuck being relieved of duty after a meeting with Marshall, and Capra's unit being brought back into the Signal Corps for reasons of "economy." Capra personally escaped the investigation with little damage, and he felt grateful to Zanuck for taking the heat that might otherwise have been concentrated on himself and Ford.

Capra's receipt of profit percentages was not, however, his only involvement with Hollywood enterprises during his war service. Though shortly after joining the Army he had sold the story "Tomorrow Never Comes" and the play *The Jest of Hahalaba* to producer Arnold Pressburger (who made the film version in 1944 for United Artists as *It Happened Tomorrow*, with René Clair directing), Capra retained an active interest in filming Eric Knight's short story "The Flying Yorkshireman." On September 7, 1944, while still in the Army, he made an option agreement with RKO to produce the film with Barry Fitzgerald starring and hired a prominent team of married screenwriters, Frances Goodrich and Albert Hackett, to write the screenplay. Their first draft, retitled *The Flying Irishman*, was completed that December; after Fitzgerald turned it down for fear of the flying scenes, the story rights reverted to Capra on February 4, 1945.

*   *   *

Frustrated by the continuing inaction over the theatrical release of *Prelude to War*, Capra in the spring of 1943 enlisted the support of several senators and Undersecretary of War Patterson, who noted that it had been months since the President had said he wanted the film shown to the public.

"Not particularly relishing the dog-in-the-manger role I was alleged to occupy," Mellett was "persuaded to break faith with the industry to the extent of submitting the first three" of the *Why We Fight* series without further changes to the Hollywood War Activities Committee, but the industry committee turned them down, feeling that they would "fail to interest huge sections of the regular motion picture audience which had already seen this material in varying forms."

Capra collected letters from Hollywood executives, including Joseph Schenck and Jack Cohn, who were sympathetic to a public release of *Prelude to War*, and forwarded them to General Surles of the War Department Bureau of Public Relations. He also received support from Assistant Secretary of War John J. McCloy, who told Mellett that the *Why We Fight* films "belong to the public, not to the government nor to the industry," and finally from Secretary of War Stimson.

A compromise was reached in which the grumbling WAC agreed to distribute *Prelude to War* through Twentieth Century–Fox as a supposed "test" of the series' theatrical potential. *Prelude to War* was advertised as "The Greatest Gangster Picture Ever Made" when it was released on May 13, but there was not much public interest. Critical reaction was largely respectful, however. James Agee wrote in *The Nation* that it was "the sort of thing one can expect when capable filmmakers work for a great and many-leveled audience—the best, I suspect, which this country has ever had—under no obligation to baby or cajole, and for a serious purpose." Agee particularly admired its redeployment of Nazi footage into what he called "the grimmest image of fascism I have seen on a screen," but he deplored the "overdrawn" nature of some of the rhetoric, and found "repeated references to a Mr. John Q. Public embarrassing, for I felt they betrayed an underestimation of the audience of which the picture as a whole is hearteningly free."

A more troubling criticism frequently made of the *Why We Fight* films both in their own time and in the years following was that they contained too much fabrication. It was a charge that Capra, in later years, indignantly denied, insisting his unit had fabricated nothing except for animation and other graphics, and claiming that all the film footage was of actual historical events. But such statements bear little relation to what appears on the screen.

Many shots in Capra's war "documentaries" are taken from fictional films, and the sources of such material are pinpointed by shot lists in the production files at the National Archives. At the insistence of the OWI, a foreword was added to the Capra films for their public release covering this practice and other fakery: "Use has been made of certain motion pictures with historical backgrounds. When necessary for purposes of clarity, a few reenactments have been made under War Department Supervision."

Most obvious to the viewer are the scenes depicting historical events that occurred before the invention of motion pictures, such as the American Revolutionary War (taken from such films as D. W. Griffith's *America* and John Ford's *Drums Along the Mohawk*) and the storming of the Bastille (*A Tale of Two Cities*). More subtle is the employment of fictional footage from films depicting modern history, particularly in smoothly fabricated scenes purporting to show the activities of the enemy. Footage of a German soldier kicking a prisoner in the face in *Here Is Germany* turns out to be a scene from a 1944 MGM feature, *The Cross of Lorraine*. Other scenes of German life shown in *Here Is Germany* are lifted from such Hollywood movies as *All Quiet on the Western Front* and *The Hitler Gang*, and from such prewar German entertainment features as *Emil und Die Detektive* and *Kuhle Wampe*. *Prelude to War* uses staged footage of German, Italian, and Japanese schoolchildren hailing Hitler, Mussolini, and Hirohito. In various Capra documentaries, battle footage from Hollywood war movies such as *Sergeant York*, *Air Force*, and *Wake Island* is passed off as the real thing.* Footage of the Pearl Harbor bombing in *The Negro Soldier* and a sequence on Japanese spies in Hawaii in *Know Your Enemy—Japan* come from the 1943 Gregg Toland–John Ford reenactment for the Navy, *December 7th*. Even the 1923 Tokyo earthquake, glimpsed in *Know Your Enemy—Japan*, was filmed on a Hollywood soundstage by George Stevens for his 1941 weepie *Penny Serenade*.

An even more pervasive characteristic of Capra's war films is their unquestioning reliance on staged "documentary" material from a broad variety of sources, including enemy propaganda, which is presented to the viewer as fact—though what facts the shots are supposed to represent vary even from film to film in the *Why We Fight* series.

---

* *It is ironic in that light that Capra, while in London on September 25, 1943, publicly criticized Hollywood for, out of "ignorance," making "flag-waving" war movies "that are embarrassing the boys over here and make them squirm. I hold no brief for Hollywood because I don't think they've done a very good job. They are a long way from the war."*

Capra echoed his own immigrant experience in the part-talking *The Younger Generation* (1929), with Rosa Rosanova and Jean Hersholt as Jewish immigrants on New York's Lower East Side. (*Kevin Brownlow Collection / Columbia Pictures*)

Columbia Pictures rose from a Poverty Row quickie studio to a major because of the twenty-five films Capra made there from 1927 through 1939. (*Security Pacific National Bank Photograph Collection / Los Angeles Public Library*)

Columbia president Harry Cohn congratulates Capra on his third best-director Oscar, for *You Can't Take It With You*, at the February 23, 1939, ceremony. Despite their many battles, Capra would concede in later years, "I owed Cohn a lot—I owed him my whole career. So I had respect for him, and a certain amount of love." (*International Museum of Photography at George Eastman House / Columbia Pictures*)

Jean Harlow as the wealthy seductress and Robert Williams as the raffish reporter in Capra's sparkling romantic comedy *Platinum Blonde* (1931), the first of his films with a screenplay by Robert Riskin. (*The Academy of Motion Picture Arts and Sciences / Columbia Pictures*)

Barbara Stanwyck's emotional incandescence brought out a new depth in Capra's direction of actors. Their affair was over by the time they made the commercial flop *The Bitter Tea of General Yen* (1933), but this film's interracial romance (with Nils Asther as the Chinese general in love with Stanwyck and Toshia Mori as his servant) always remained close to Capra's heart. (*Columbia Pictures*)

When Capra made *American Madness* (1932) from Riskin's original screenplay about an unconventional bank president (Walter Huston) coping with Depression-era hysteria, the director began to assume his role as a spokesman for "the common man." (*Columbia Pictures*)

The question of the authorship of the Capra-Riskin films would lead to heated debate, but Capra and his principal screenwriter (seen here in 1933, rehearsing *Lady for a Day* with Warren William and May Robson) were close friends and collaborators when they were making their 1930s classics. (*The Academy of Motion Picture Arts and Sciences / Columbia Pictures*)

Joe Walker and Capra working together in the early 1930s. The romantic sheen that Walker brought to Capra's films made him an indispensable collaborator. (*The Academy of Motion Picture Arts and Sciences / Columbia Pictures*)

"Behold the Walls of Jericho"—one of the screen's most famous romantic scenes, with only a motel blanket separating the snobbish runaway heiress (Colbert) from her proletarian traveling companion (Gable). (*Columbia Pictures*)

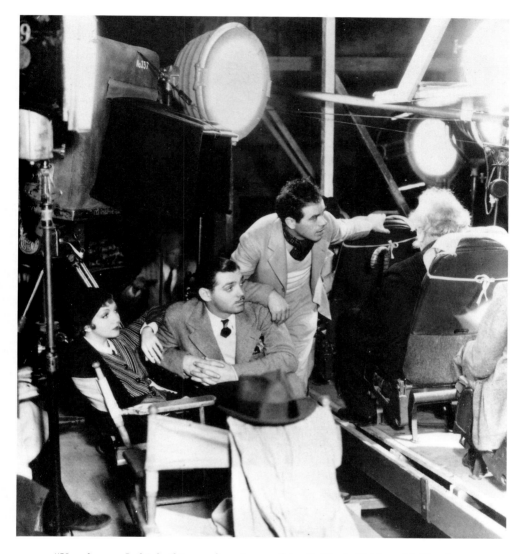

"You know, I think this wop's got something," Clark Gable told Claudette Colbert early in the making of *It Happened One Night* (1934), but she remained skeptical until Capra filmed the joyous scene of the bus passengers singing "The Daring Young Man on the Flying Trapeze." Then she "knew we had something." A sleeper hit, the film won all five major Oscars. (*Marc Wanamaker–Bison Archives / Columbia Pictures*)

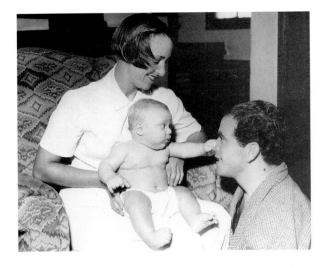

Capra the contented family man, with one of his four children and "the most important person in my life," his second wife, the former Lucille Warner Reyburn, whom he married in 1932. (*Columbia Pictures*)

"Sometimes your story has got to stop and you let the audience just look at your people"—Jean Arthur as the cynical New York reporter who succumbs to the guileless charms of Gary Cooper's smalltown millionaire in *Mr. Deeds Goes to Town* (1936). Graham Greene called this socially conscious film "a comedy quite unmatched on the screen." (*Columbia Pictures*)

MIGHTIEST OF ALL MOTION PICTURES!

FRANK CAPRA'S GREATEST PRODUCTION
RONALD COLMAN
in
LOST HORIZON

JANE WYATT · JOHN HOWARD
MARGO · THOMAS MITCHELL
EDWARD EVERETT HORTON · ISABEL JEWELL
H. B. WARNER · SAM JAFFE
From the novel by JAMES HILTON
Screen Play by ROBERT RISKIN
A COLUMBIA PICTURE

Columbia didn't believe its own advertising claims for *Lost Horizon* (1937), but tried its best to put a good face on what it considered a white elephant. (*Columbia Pictures*)

As president of the Screen Directors Guild during the late 1930s, Capra presented honorary life memberships in the SDG to pioneering director D. W. Griffith and guild counsel Mabel Walker Willebrandt. With them (FROM LEFT): John Ford, Frank Strayer, Rouben Mamoulian, J. P. McGowan, W. S. Van Dyke II, William Wyler, Leo McCarey, and George Marshall. (*UCLA Theater Arts Library [William Wyler Collection]*)

Capra's great capacity for enjoyment of his actors made him an ideal audience surrogate and was one of the keys to his success as a director. He is seen here rehearsing *You Can't Take It With You* (1938) with Lionel Barrymore and Jean Arthur. (*The Academy of Motion Picture Arts and Sciences / Columbia Pictures*)

The director preparing a scene on the U.S. Senate set for *Mr. Smith Goes to Washington* (1939), his passionate defense of the American democratic system, warts and all. (*The Academy of Motion Picture Arts and Sciences / Columbia Pictures*)

"Dad always used to say the only causes worth fighting for *were* the lost causes"—James Stewart as Senator Jefferson Smith. (*Columbia Pictures*)

Robert Riskin and Capra in a publicity shot taken when the longtime partners were making *Meet John Doe* (1941), their first and only film for their jointly owned Frank Capra Productions. (*USC Cinema-Television Library and Archives of Performing Arts [Fay Wray Collection] / Warner Bros.*)

The silhouetted figure in the slouch hat on the camera boom is Capra, directing one of his most powerful visions of American madness, the rain-drenched political convention filmed at Los Angeles's Wrigley Field for *Meet John Doe. (The Academy of Motion Picture Arts and Sciences / Warner Bros.*)

Capra claimed his primary motive for making *Meet John Doe* was "to convince important critics that not every Capra film was written by Pollyanna," but he ultimately backed away from the darker implications of his chosen theme. Seen here are Barbara Stanwyck, Gary Cooper, and James Gleason. (*Warner Bros.*)

Cary Grant in his least favorite film part, as drama critic Mortimer Brewster in Capra's frenzied comedy *Arsenic and Old Lace*, filmed in 1941 when the director was beginning his flight from his 1930s role as a social critic. (*Warner Bros.*)

TOP LEFT: Following orders as a U.S. Army film propagandist in World War II was not easy for Capra, who acknowledged late in life that the war had left him "kind of burned out. . . . I left a lot of myself in the war." (*UCLA Special Collections / Los Angeles Daily News*)

TOP RIGHT: Capra and the man he called his "Negro consultant," writer Carlton Moss, who was primarily responsible for the ground-breaking 1944 U.S. Army documentary *The Negro Soldier*, which Capra cautiously supervised. (*Carlton Moss / U.S. Army*)

CENTER: U.S. Army Chief of Staff General George C. Marshall, who recruited Capra to make World War II morale films, awards him the Distinguished Service Medal on June 14, 1945. (*National Archives / U.S. Army*)

BOTTOM: General of the Army Omar N. Bradley joins Liberty Films partners William Wyler, Capra, and George Stevens, and their wives, at a postwar Hollywood party for Bradley. TOP ROW, FROM LEFT: Wyler, Capra, Bradley, Stevens; BOTTOM ROW, FROM LEFT: Margaret Tallichet (Talli) Wyler, Lu Capra, Mary Bradley, Yvonne Stevens. (*UCLA Theater Arts Library [William Wyler Collection] / Picture Surveys, Inc., Photo by Schuyler Crail*)

"I just hung on every word Frank Capra said"—Jimmy Stewart with Capra during the making of their third film together, *It's a Wonderful Life* (1946). For both men, returning from World War II to an uncertain future in Hollywood, the film became a personal favorite, despite its disappointing reception at the time. (*Marc Wanamaker–Bison Archives / Liberty Films / RKO*)

In *It's a Wonderful Life*, George Bailey blames his wife (Donna Reed) and children (Larry Simms, Jimmy Hawkins, Carol Coomes) for their role in keeping him in Bedford Falls and curbing his ambitions. (*Liberty Films / RKO*)

Spencer Tracy's speech renouncing his presidential aspirations in *State of the Union* (1948) was the bitter conclusion of Capra's elegy for his own abandonment of socially conscious filmmaking. (*MCA / Universal*)

Capra's tension is obvious as he listens to Paramount president Barney Balaban at a studio party in 1949 (with Capra's *Riding High* ingenue Coleen Gray). Capra blamed Balaban's cost-cutting strictures for much of his frustration at Paramount, but the causes of his postwar career problems ran much deeper than that. (*The Academy of Motion Picture Arts and Sciences / Paramount Pictures*)

Of his 1951 Paramount film *Here Comes the Groom*, Capra said, "I used the walk down the wedding aisle that was straight out of *It Happened One Night*, and I decided that if I was having to steal from my own pictures, it was time to take a long rest." Seen here are Franchot Tone and Jane Wyman. (*Paramount Pictures*)

G2-SOD 201   Personnel Action on Officer - CAPRA
AGPB   62   21 November 1950
                                          Major Cortes/75027/mq

1. It is requested that the Chief, Operations Branch, Security and Training Division, Office of the Assistant Chief of Staff, G-2, Intelligence, be consulted before the following-described officer is appointed to the Officers' Reserve Corps, the National Guard of the United States or called to active duty:

NAME G-2/ 201	RANK	ASN	ARM OR SERVICE
CAPRA, Frank	Col	0-900209	Sig C, AUS

ADDRESS   DATE AND PLACE OF BIRTH
215 No Barrington St   18 May 1897
Los Angeles, California   Italy

2. Sixth Army has been notified of this action.

FOR THE ASSISTANT CHIEF OF STAFF, G-2:

                              C. S. CAMPBELL
                         EGON R. TAUSCH, Colonel, GSC
                         Chief, Security & Training Division

MEMO FOR RECORD: Case opened on basis of FBI rept alleging Comm sympathies.

No Ref.

This cmt flags Subj in TAG.   83119

Approp files reveal CAPRA was associated with The National Federation for Constitutional Liberties in 1941 (cited by Atty Gen). "People's World," dtd 15 Apr 44 quoted "Hollywood Reporter," dtd 7 Apr 44 as having stated that Russia had a plan for a series of programs to be given at The House of Cinema Workers in Moscow which programs were to include productions by Frank Capra. Subj was reported to have associated with left-wing groups, and to have been one of several motion picture directors who were plotting a line of attack on the Congressional Investigation of Communism in motion picture industry. Subj considered possibly subversive.

No coord or concurr believed necess.
Concurrent action: Flag in 6th Army.

Auth: Cmt 2, AGCM-M dtd 26 Oct 48; ltr, AGAO-S 201.3 (30 July 47) WDGID 4 Aug

REGRADED UNCLASSIFIED
ON 18 FEB 1986   202
BY CDR USAINSSCOM FOIPO
Auth Para 1-603 2 5200.1-R   PERMANENT RECORD

"Subj considered possibly subversive"—a 1950 document from the 226-page U.S. Army Intelligence file on Capra, which was partially declassified in 1986 as a result of the author's request under the Freedom of Information Act (DETAIL BELOW). The elements of social criticism in Capra's films and his personal and professional associations with leftists and liberals cast suspicion on him during the postwar Red Scare, despite his record of deeply felt patriotism. (*U.S. Army Intelligence and Security Command*)

NAME G-2/ 201	RANK	ASN	ARM OR SERVICE
CAPRA, Frank	Col	0-900209	Sig C, AUS

ADDRESS   DATE AND PLACE OF BIRTH
215 No Barrington St   18 May 1897
Los Angeles, California   Italy

2. Sixth Army has been notified of this action.

FOR THE ASSISTANT CHIEF OF STAFF, G-2:

                              C. S. CAMPBELL
                         Lt Colonel, GSC
                         EGON R. TAUSCH, Colonel, GSC
                         Chief, Security & Training Division

MEMO FOR RECORD: Case opened on basis of FBI rept alleging Comm sympathies.

No Ref.

This cmt flags Subj in TAG.   83119

Approp files reveal CAPRA was associated with The National Federation for Constitutional Liberties in 1941 (cited by Atty Gen). "People's World," dtd 15 Apr 44 quoted "Hollywood Reporter," dtd 7 Apr 44 as having stated that Russia had a plan for a series of programs to be given at The House of Cinema Workers in Moscow which programs were to include productions by Frank Capra. Subj was reported to have associated with left-wing groups, and to have been one of several motion picture directors who were plotting a line of attack on the Congressional Investigation of Communism in motion picture industry. Subj considered possibly subversive.

No coord or concurr believed necess.
Concurrent action: Flag in 6th Army.

Auth: Cmt 2, AGCM-M dtd 26 Oct 48; ltr, AGAO-S 201.3 (30 July 47) WDGID 4 Aug

When Capra returned to feature film-making in 1958 after a seven-year absence to direct the Frank Sinatra vehicle *A Hole in the Head*, he was dismayed to find that the stars were calling the shots. (*The Academy of Motion Picture Arts and Sciences / United Artists*)

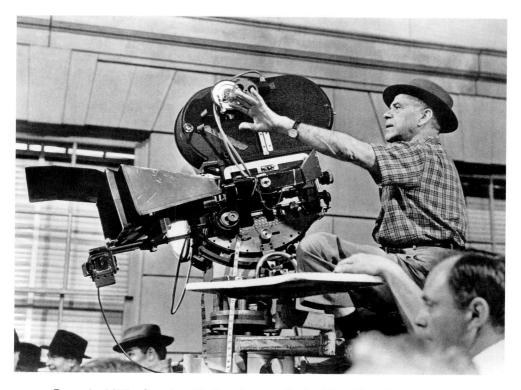

Capra in 1961, directing his last feature, *Pocketful of Miracles*, which Gore Vidal called "one of the all-time bad pictures." (*The Academy of Motion Picture Arts and Sciences / United Artists*)

Three generations of Frank Capras—assistant director Frank Capra III, Frank Capra, Sr., and producer Frank Capra, Jr.—at a tribute to the paterfamilias held by Columbia Pictures at Chasen's restaurant in Beverly Hills on January 23, 1985. One of many such honors accorded to Capra in his later years, the event also was one of his last public appearances. (*Columbia Pictures*)

Capra in his old age enjoyed the adulation of young, antiestablishment idealists, who helped him re-create his reputation, but he couldn't help feeling that their hero-worship stemmed from "what I stand for rather than what I am." (*The Academy of Motion Picture Arts and Sciences*)

Before the war Capra had scorned documentaries as "films about polar bears sliding on their asses down mountainsides," and during the war he never hesitated to heighten reality with the use of dramatized footage, or, if he thought it necessary, to have his unit shoot new material which could be passed off as newsreel footage. William Thomas Murphy points out in his study of the *Why We Fight* films that Capra was following a tradition established in the 1930s by the *March of Time* newsreels, which made liberal use of recreations, and by such documentary masters of that decade are Joris Ivens, Pare Lorentz, and Robert Flaherty, whose films often blurred the line between what was "real" and what was rearranged for the camera (as, indeed, did Riefenstahl's *Triumph of the Will*). Some footage for Capra's war films came from their documentaries, including Ivens's *The Four Hundred Million*, Lorentz's *The River*, and Flaherty's *The Land* (Capra also commissioned new footage from Flaherty of ordinary Americans, used in *War Comes to America*), and as Murphy observes, "This misunderstood tradition, in the context of war exigencies, made the use of staged footage a plausible alternative to no footage at all."

But, as the documentary film historian Jay Leyda put it, "As little as five fictional feet in an otherwise scrupulous compilation can shake a spectator's belief in the whole film, *including its ideas.*"

Capra's redeployment of Nazi propaganda footage, in some ways such a powerful aspect of his war films, in other ways undermines their credibility. Footage of Hitler's speeches from *Triumph of the Will* and other German sources was used with disregard for its original chronology and historical context. Other Nazi films, whose authenticity should have been regarded with the utmost skepticism, were presented as factual records of events, and Capra's unit sometimes manipulated Nazi footage with a cynicism approaching that of the originals. For instance, a sequence presented by Nazi propagandist Fritz Hippler in his 1940 film *Campaign in Poland* as showing "Polish murderers . . . being confronted with their tortured victims in one of the large prisoners' camps" is presented in Capra's *The Nazis Strike* as showing "in village after village, local Judases point[ing] out loyal Polish neighbors." Asked about the use of Nazi films in *Here Is Germany*, Gottfried Reinhardt, its production supervisor, said, "We used their footage, but we wrote the text, so it didn't matter, really, why these things were shot. We took whatever we could find; the footage only illustrated our message. That's all you can do in war."

Describing *The Battle of China* to Marshall as "the least satisfactory of the *Why We Fight* series," Osborn cited among his reasons the fact that "many of the sequences are not actually pictures of historical events, but scenes taken from entertainment or other film to produce the desired effect." Capra replied to Osborn on November 21, 1944: "I was quite disturbed by your memorandum. . . . The statement that it is the *only* one of the series containing film not of historical events is not literally true. There is much more of this type of film in *Battle of Russia*, and *Battle of Britain*, than there is in the China picture. Also in *Nazis Strike* and *Divide and Conquer* we made free use of German film specially shot for propaganda purposes.

"The particular film you must have reference to in *Battle of China* is documentary film shot by MGM cameramen in China for *The Good Earth* several years ago. MGM had thousands of feet of this actual material shot in China which they did not use in *The Good Earth*. It was from this unused film that we selected a few hundred feet of material to visually aid us in portraying the migration. There was a heartbreaking dearth of Chinese material, and we had to resort to any and all known sources to be able to visualize what we were attempting to say about China. . . .

"I'm not trying to alibi for the Chinese film. I know there are people in the War Department who claim we have put too much 'emotion' in these films. They may be right. A dry recitation of facts might have been a 'safer' way to present them. But my experiences with audiences has [*sic*] long ago taught me that if you want facts to stick, you must present them in an interesting manner. The teacher who can excite and stimulate the imagination will, in the long run, impart more lasting knowledge to his students. . . .

"If to create dramatic interest is wrong, then all our pictures have been wrongly presented."

A postwar study of the *Why We Fight* series supervised by Osborn, based on surveys of soldiers conducted during the war, suggested that Capra's method indeed had serious drawbacks. Although the survey found that the films had "marked effects on the men's knowledge of factual material concerning the events leading up to the war," the films were frequently criticized by GIs for being one-sided and for using staged material, and the survey concluded that they had little influence on soldiers' opinions about the war in general and "no effects . . . on the men's motivation to serve as soldiers, which was considered the ultimate objective of the orientation program." The films actually may have had the opposite effect, since "the largest opinion change produced by *Prelude to War* was an increase in men's estimate of enemy strength, which was a factor *negatively* correlated with motivation for active service. This suggests that the effect to be expected from the film would be *decrease* in motivation."

* * *

Anxious to see some genuine combat himself and weary of fighting The Battle of Hollywood, Capra saw an opening in April 1943, when the Army Pictorial Service was removed temporarily from the control of the Signal Corps while being reorganized. At the same time, the Signal Corps was in the process of prying Capra's unit back from the Army's Special Services Division. Despite efforts by Osborn and Munson to hold on to the unit, Capra realized it was a losing battle, and he viewed it with equanimity.

He was bored with making orientation films and, as he confided to Lu in a letter that August, he wanted to do something more important. Capra's ambitions meshed with one of the most pressing concerns of the new APS head, Brigadier General William H. Harrison—the need to improve Army combat photography. The outbreak of war had found Signal Corps combat units ill-trained, understaffed, restricted by distracted and shortsighted company commanders and Signal Officers, and unaccustomed to the role of historical chroniclers. Capra found Harrison sympathetic to his request to have him transferred from Special Services into the War Department Bureau of Public Relations, under General Surles, so he could organize "special coverage" combat photography units whose heads could function more autonomously, as Ford had with his Navy unit in making *The Battle of Midway* and as William Wyler was doing with his Army Air Forces unit in making *The Memphis Belle*. The decision was delayed while Harrison, Osborn, and the Signal Corps argued over the fate of Capra's 834th Signal Service Photographic Detachment. Though Capra predicted in April that all of the orientation films would be finished within two months, work on some of them would drag on for two more years.

The inadequacy of American combat photography was glaringly spotlighted by what had happened with the coverage of the Allied invasion in North Africa following the British victory at El Alamein in November 1942. Darryl Zanuck had been dispatched to organize the American coverage, which was shot by Ford and four Signal Corps crews. But filming conditions were difficult and Zanuck returned with material the Army received with a "lack of enthusiasm" and Capra considered dismayingly weak by comparison with *Desert Victory*, the Academy Award–winning British documentary on the African campaign against Rommel, which supplemented its impressive battle footage with liberal use of night battle scenes staged in a studio. Zanuck made matters worse when he assembled his footage into a self-serving documentary released by Fox in 1943 as *At the Front*, which contained so many shots of Zanuck himself that it became known to his colleagues as *Alone in Africa*.

When President Roosevelt asked to see the American film on the North African landings, Harrison could not bring himself to admit what had happened to that footage. Litvak had been detached from Capra's unit to head the camera crew filming the landings, but the ship carrying his exposed footage was sunk before it could even leave port. So, early in the summer of 1943, the Army and the BPR came up with another idea.

Capra, John Huston, and George Stevens, who had been commissioned as a major in the Signal Corps to head a combat photography unit, were assigned to stage what Huston called "a huge counterfeit operation simply to deceive the President." Capra and Huston were sent to an Army training camp in the Mojave Desert to reenact parts of the North African campaign with cameraman Joseph Valentine, assistant director Jules Buck, and officers involved in the original desert fighting in Tunisia; Stevens was sent to North Africa to fake footage of tank warfare with cameraman William Mellor. Huston also went to Orlando, Florida, to simulate aerial combat for the film, which was released with an end title stating that "a few authentic reenactments" were included (those presumably were more believable than the mere "reenactments" in other Capra war films). The film's working title was *Operation Acrobat*, but the release title was *Tunisian Victory*. Huston laughed when he heard it.

"I regarded the whole thing in rather a more frivolous light than Frank did," Huston admitted. "The whole thing was a fraud and a frost, and funny as hell. Looking back on it, it was absurd, and I was also aware of its absurdity at the time, I'm afraid. But Frank was undertaking it in all seriousness to make a proper picture out of it, and finally succeeded in doing what was required. He was very skillful at concealing his deceit.

"Frank is a man with an enormous sense of responsibility. There is a kind of dignity that Frank has that is impressive, and a reserve—Frank is a charming companion, I enjoy his company enormously, but he doesn't wear his heart on his sleeve."

The fact that the battle footage had to be faked, Capra felt, proved the need for "special coverage" units. But he forged ahead with *Tunisian Victory*.

Huston remembered, "We all met back in Washington and looked at the material, which was so obviously false that it was just disgraceful. Then somebody had a great notion. England was also making a picture about the North African campaign [then titled *Africa Freed*]. Why not pool our material with what the English were doing? The English were told that we had North African material, and since we were allies and so on, wouldn't it be a great gesture of friendship, making the bonds even stronger, if this was a joint English-American production? They were very receptive to this idea. [On August 12] Frank, Tony Veiller, and I then proceeded to England—where they saw what we had, and their faces fell a yard. They had some wonderful material, and Frank won't admit this, I'm sure, but my God, it was terrible what we were doing to them, putting our fraudulent stuff in with their real stuff."

Despite that inauspicious beginning, Capra's "single-minded" dedication to the film, as Huston called it, helped persuade their British colleagues Hugh Stewart (production supervisor of *Africa Freed*), Roy Boulting (who had directed *Desert Victory*), war correspondent and author J. L. Hodson, and novelist Eric Ambler to cooperate (Robert Riskin, now based in London with the OWI, also lent his help).

On September 1, while Capra was in London, his 834th was transferred from Special Services back to the APS. The last two films in the *Why We Fight* series—*The Battle of China* and *War Comes to America*—still remained to be completed. The unit virtually had finished *Know Your Ally Britain* and *Substitution and Conversion**, and it was struggling to complete *The Negro Soldier*, *Know Your Enemy: Germany*, and *Know Your Enemy— Japan*. Some of the unit remained at Fort Fox, under Litvak's supervision, but the rest were shifted to Astoria. Litvak and others complained vociferously to Capra, but from a distance Capra could see that such concerns meant little in the context of the overall war effort, and he felt they would all be better off covering actual combat rather than staying at home.

Capra and Huston had a flat at 49 Hill Street, off Berkeley Square, but Capra spent most of his nights on a cot outside the city in a tiny dressing room at Pinewood Studios, which had been converted into an RAF base. "I'm afraid I socialized and had a good time while Frank kept his nose to the grindstone," Huston recalled. Capra's frequent V-mail letters to Red Mountain Ranch reflected acute homesickness and an awareness of how precious family life had become in a world riven by war.

"The war was a terrible shock to me," Capra told historian Walter Karp in 1981. "I hated the unnecessary brutality. Women and children being killed, terrified, huddling in fear. Going around dropping bombs on women and children. *What the hell is wrong with us?* I used to think. . . . I thought that perhaps I had put too much faith in the human race—you know, in the pictures I made. Maybe they were too much as things should be. I began to think that maybe I really was a Pollyanna."

* *An industrial film about the changeover from peacetime to wartime production, directed by David Miller and written by Lester Cohen, Robert Lees, and Fred Rinaldo.*

The fact that two of the men he most admired, Jimmy Doolittle and Jimmy Stewart, were instrumental in bombing raids—Doolittle bombing Tokyo and later commanding the Eighth Air Force in Germany; Stewart, one of his fliers, leading as many as a thousand heavy bombers on raids over German cities and being awarded the Distinguished Flying Cross by Doolittle himself for one of those missions—must have contributed mightily to Capra's confusion. Capra, who confessed to no such qualms about his claimed laboratory work on chemical warfare for the government during World War I, insisted that he came back from World War II "a fighting pacifist . . . the whole fucking idea of war took another shape for me . . . and the idea of making a hero out of a guy that bombed just made me sick. I would have talked to Jimmy Stewart the same way."

But though such postures played well with his latter-day audience, which Capra recognized often disapproved of his wartime propaganda, Capra was unwilling, or unable, to express such doubts during the war itself, when any ambivalence he may have felt about the morality of Allied bombing raids had to be suppressed in his work, which urged that the "concentrated fury" of the Allies be turned on the Germans "to give the apostles of power an education in the use of it" and that Japan "must be totally crushed before we turn to the ways of peace." To borrow John Dos Passos's description of Andrew Carnegie, Capra "was a dedicated man of peace—except in time of war."

When bombs fell during his stay in London, Capra recalled in 1984, "I happened to run into a little piece of it. I'd just come down from the apartment where I was, and the Germans were bombing the town. And over in a corner I saw a huddled bunch of women and children, on their knees praying." But at the time he was so preoccupied with working on his film—or perhaps too constrained by his sense of duty and by military censorship of V-mail to express his full range of feelings—that his only brief comment to Lu conveyed not dismay but excitement that he finally was an eyewitness to the war.

When the U.S. Senate Internal Security Subcommittee investigated Army World War II films in 1954, the Army asked Capra for the names of the people responsible for the *Why We Fight* films, and he disclaimed any responsibility for the production of *The Battle of Russia*, purporting that *Tunisian Victory* had kept him in London during the entire period that Litvak was supervising the production of *The Battle of Russia*. As late as 1985, Capra was still uncomfortable about being publicly associated with the film, bowing out of a scheduled appearance at the "40th Anniversary

Allied Victory Film Festival" held in New York and Washington, cosponsored by Sovexportfilm, after telling *The New York Times*, "I hope I'm not being used."

Despite what Capra told the Army in 1954, *The Battle of Russia* was all but completed *before* he left for England, and it was screened in Hollywood by the Academy on September 28, 1943, only six weeks after he left. Although Capra's Army associates confirmed that it was primarily the work of Litvak, its project officer, and Veiller, its writer-narrator, Capra was involved with the policy and execution of the passionate and ambitious film (the longest in the series, originally released in two parts) from its beginning in John Sanford's script of February–April 1942. Even as Sanford was writing, Capra's involvements with the Soviets were being monitored by G-2.

The file kept on Capra by Army Intelligence records what apparently was Capra's first contact with the Soviets: as summarized by G-2 on March 11, 1942, it was a "Presentation of Major Frank Capra to Col. Berezin, Acting Russian M/A [military attaché] with object of cooperating with Russians in use of some of their war films. [Berezin was] Pleased that elements of American Army should take interest in films demonstrating Russian Military methods." Nothing more about Capra's dealings with the Soviets that year appears in the heavily censored file (the material still classified includes information from the State Department and the FBI), but Capra wrote in his book that later in 1942, after bypassing official channels to deal directly with Soviet ambassador to the United States Maxim Litvinov, he had been accused by G-2 of "a major breach of the Articles of War."

Capra's oversimplified account of his wartime dealings with the Soviets, which landed him in such trouble both then and later, appears to have combined events of 1944 with events of 1942, when he was beginning work on *The Battle of Russia* (also known during production as *The People's War in Russia*). Capra wrote that he approached Litvinov in an attempt to obtain Soviet war films and film documenting the flow of American materiel into the U.S.S.R. Though it would have been 1942 when Capra needed the Soviet war films, it was not until May 27, 1944, according to his Army Intelligence file, that he formally requested permission from the U.S.S.R. "to photograph the activities of the Lend-Lease Supply Line into the Soviet Union" for a film Osborn described as covering "both Lend-Lease to Russia and the full operation of the Persian Gulf Service Command." George Stevens and writer Joel Sayre took a camera crew from London to the Soviet border of Iran; they sent back footage but were denied permission to film the materiel arriving at its final destination. Despite subsequent attempts, the project had to be abandoned.

It was in 1942, according to Capra, that a G-2 officer showed him a photograph of himself at the doorway of the Soviet Embassy in Washington. "I thought, Jesus Christ, I'd always heard about 'security risks,' " Capra recalled. "Now I know."

As Capra recounted his explanation of his unauthorized approach to the Soviets, he had presented himself unannounced at the embassy and asked to see Ambassador Litvinov. In two subsequent lunches, he and Litvinov arranged for the 834th to receive Soviet films, including raw combat footage, for only the laboratory costs. He claimed he had offered American raw combat footage in return but had rebuffed Litvinov's request for script approval on Soviet subjects, while assuring him that the U.S.S.R. would be treated in an evenhanded manner. When called on the carpet by G-2 for what he later admitted was a highly ill-advised maneuver, Capra claimed he had been acting on Marshall's orders and threatened to go public in Drew Pearson's column. He escaped punishment, and arrangements were made to have subsequent exchanges of film between the U.S. and U.S.S.R. go through official channels.

Despite Capra's difficulties, *The Battle of Russia*—with its stirring footage of the defense of Leningrad and Stalingrad, mostly shot by the Soviets themselves and brilliantly edited under Litvak's supervision by Hornbeck, William Lyon, and Marcel Cohen—was regarded as a triumph for Capra's unit during the war. Agee wrote in *The Nation* that "next to the tearful magnificence of *The Birth of a Nation* [it] is, I believe, the best and most important war film ever assembled in this country." Jay Leyda reported that it was "studied and greatly admired in the Soviet Union—the only American film reflection of the Soviet front that required no apology." Except from Capra.

Shortly before the end of the war, Vsevolod Pudovkin and most of the other leading Soviet directors met in Moscow to discuss *The Battle of Russia* and the other *Why We Fight* films. Pudovkin, a leading montage theorist, called those films' creative editing of "actuality" footage a method that would "gain ever-increasing significance in the postwar period, . . . because . . . it can be widely used for fully and profoundly acquainting peoples with one another, and can serve to a very considerable degree in expressing universal ideas in a graphic and striking way." Pudovkin sent Capra the minutes of the discussion, which Capra felt compelled to disparage and strip of political significance when his wartime dealings with the Soviets were questioned by the U.S. government in 1951. And though

Capra noted in his book that Stalin had ordered the film shown in every Russian theater (Roosevelt told Marshall on March 3, 1944, that he was "very pleased to learn of Mr. Stalin's decision"), Capra did not mention that Stalin had filmed his own foreword to *The Battle of Russia*.

"The Russian leaders, including Stalin, appreciated greatly the war documentary," recalled Averell Harriman, then the American ambassador to Moscow. "Stalin personally expressed himself favorably on the film. This whole thing was rather rare for Stalin."

While in Cairo for the Allied strategy conferences in late November and early December 1943, General Marshall mentioned to Frank McCarthy that he was thinking of promoting Capra to lieutenant colonel, "not realizing, of course, that you already held that grade," McCarthy wrote Capra. "On the flight home, I had a chance to tell General Marshall that you had been in grade for fifteen months, and to recommend to him that you be promoted to the grade of colonel. He immediately concurred." The promotion was made official on Christmas Eve. On Christmas morning, when he unwrapped a package at Munson's home and found the eagles of a "chicken colonel," Capra wept.

Colonel Capra officially began his new job as commanding officer of the Special Coverage Section, Western Division, Army Pictorial Service, on December 26, although he had been functioning in that capacity since returning to the United States on November 15 to complete the postproduction of *Tunisian Victory*. (When it received its British and American theatrical premieres in March 1944, *Tunisian Victory* received praise for its entertainment values and contribution to Anglo-American unity but was criticized for its historical inadequacy and lack of genuine emotional power.)

Despite his ambitious plans for Special Coverage, Capra quickly found that he was doomed to go on fighting The Battle of Hollywood.

"Would like more direct control and command over combat photographers," he told the Army on November 16, 1943, "so as to give better transportation, better overall direction. Present method of turning over cameramen to CO of overseas theater has not produced good results." On November 25 he reiterated his request for a roving assignment with "personal command over all Special Coverage personnel," but APS head Lawton two days later gave him what Capra called "everybody's poor second choice," command of Special Coverage, Western Division. "He wanted to be active out in the field, but he was doing too good a job where he was," said Chet Sticht. Lawton assured Capra that after completion of the two remaining *Why We Fight* films and *The Negro Soldier,* there would be no more films for Special Services. But Marshall and the APS added to his frustration by giving Capra new orientation projects which would preoccupy him until his discharge from the service.*

Capra's role in Special Coverage turned out to be mostly bureaucratic: recruiting and organizing personnel for the overseas units and lobbying with Pentagon and overseas officers for more favorable treatment of the units he sent into combat. "In some vague way, I'm supposed to be in charge of all overseas combat photographers too," he wrote George Stevens on January 14, 1944. "This, as you can well imagine, is purely a redundant title as we have no direct communication or control over cameramen at the front." Stevens and Huston, meanwhile, were doing what Capra longed to do: recording actual combat for history.

While in London Capra had helped lay the groundwork for Stevens's Special Coverage unit with European commanders (including General Doolittle), and he told Stevens in January 1944, "Don't be too surprised if a lot of us come bouncing in on you one day." But he never did, and Stevens essentially was on his own in coordinating photographic coverage of the Normandy invasion and the subsequent Allied advance through France and Germany.

"I know you haven't been given much guidance or advice as to just what you're supposed to get," Capra wrote Stevens that November. ". . . Unfortunately, I've been so swamped with top-priority work that I haven't been able to pay much attention to what is going on in the Theaters. Stick to it, George, and please know that you have some guys here that are pulling and pitching for you, even though it must seem to you that at times you and your gang are forgotten men."

Capra also helped organize Huston's coverage of the Italian campaign, which was used both in the *Army-Navy Screen Magazine* and in the most celebrated of all World War II documentaries, *San Pietro,* Huston's un-

---

* *They included* Two Down and One to Go! *and* On to Tokyo, *short films released in May 1945 to explain to both Army and civilian audiences why some troops would be redeployed to the Pacific and to explain the point system for Army discharge. According to the Army history, Marshall "feared that once Germany was defeated an uninformed and unreasoning clamor to 'bring the boys back home' might play havoc with discipline and morale and greatly delay the defeat of Japan." The two highly effective films both featured Marshall and Stimson speaking directly to the troops, and the more informal* On to Tokyo *also had General Dwight D. Eisenhower, General Henry H. (Hap) Arnold, and General Joseph Stilwell answering typical GI questions about the fairness of different aspects of the point system (with Marshall candidly admitting, "Some individuals will get better breaks than others"). Capra directed the Technicolor* Two Down, *which he wrote with Gene Fowler, and codirected the black-and-white* On to Tokyo *with David Miller, as well as writing the script with Anthony Veiller.*

compromisingly realistic depiction of the costly battle for temporary possession of one Italian town in the winter of 1943–1944. *San Pietro*'s
honesty helped frighten away most of the brass from supporting Capra's
Special Coverage idea. Filmed without official authorization, but with the
approval of Capra (who proudly had it listed in his 1946 biographical
sketch as one of the films whose production he supervised during the war),
San Pietro ran into fierce opposition from the War Department, which did
not want to release what it considered an "antiwar" film. "If I ever make
a picture that's pro-war," replied Huston, "I hope someone will take me
out and shoot me." Capra helped Huston push the film through to completion, and it finally was released only after General Marshall saw it and
said, "This picture should be seen by every American soldier in training.
It will not discourage but rather will prepare them for the initial shock of
combat." Shorn of some of its grislier scenes by Capra at Marshall's request, *San Pietro* also was released to the public but not until shortly after
V-E Day.

The Army tried to compensate Capra for his frustrations by continuing
to promote him. After taking on the added title of assistant to the chief of
the APS for motion picture planning, he rose to his highest level in the
Army on May 11, 1944, when he was named assistant chief of the APS (a
post he shared with Colonel Charles S. Stodter), under the acting chief,
Lyman Munson, who took charge officially in July. Capra's name also had
been mentioned for the top job, but he loyally supported the choice of
Munson.

After London, Capra's only visit to a wartime combat zone came in July
1944, when he flew to Hawaii and spent a month organizing Special
Coverage operations in the Pacific for the final push against Japan.

"Frank hitched a ride on a plane," Chet Sticht recalled, "because he
just wanted to see what was going on."

"I didn't want to make the film," Capra said in a videotaped interview for
the United States Information Agency in 1975. "I had so many other things
to do."

The film was *The Negro Soldier.*

Initiated by Stimson's office as a way of motivating black soldiers to feel
they shared the same cause as their white counterparts—even though the
U.S. military remained segregated during World War II—*The Negro Soldier* finally was made mandatory viewing for GIs of all races. The surprising thing was that the film which emerged from the anxious Army
bureaucracy in February 1944 was so effective, for *The Negro Soldier*—as

mild as it was—played a significant role in the breaking down of the Army's racial prejudice and helped pave the way for the desegregation of the Army in 1948.

Capra encouraged a consensus approach to the production, both because it enabled him to spread the responsibility around in case of failure or backlash (there were some in the Army who feared the film would provoke race riots) and because he knew enough to recognize his own ignorance of the subject. "A lot of it was news to me," he admitted in the USIA interview.

His first choice to direct the film was his liberal colleague William Wyler, who commissioned an outline from Lillian Hellman and went on a research tour of black Army units with Marc Connelly, the author of *The Green Pastures,* and the man Capra called his "Negro consultant," Carlton Moss. A young playwright and radio writer, Moss had worked with Orson Welles and John Houseman on the promotion of the black *Macbeth* for the Federal Theater in Harlem, and Houseman had recommended him to the Army for *The Negro Soldier.*

Connelly's script "floored the professional race people in the War Department," Moss recalled. "He was a very pleasant, sensitive guy, but he made a *Green Pastures* out of it. It was tender but infantile: its tone was 'Look at these children with their guns.' It had nothing to do with the Army."

Wyler, meanwhile, left to make *The Memphis Belle.* Wyler's biographer, Axel Madsen, wrote that he did not want to make *The Negro Soldier* if it meant "saying exactly the opposite of what he had seen in Tuskegee and elsewhere in the South." Capra turned *The Negro Soldier* over to Stuart Heisler, a white man who had directed a 1940 Paramount feature in Georgia with an integrated cast, *The Biscuit Eater.* The script was left largely in the hands of Moss, who wrote it with advice from Ben Hecht and help in construction from Jo Swerling. Moss also played a major role on screen, as the preacher whose sermon is used as voice-over narration for the parts of the film dealing with the blacks' role in American history (focusing on military exploits and downplaying slavery) and in the modern Army (showing a young black soldier going through officer candidate school).

Moss was pragmatic about the limited goals of the project, telling the press in March 1944 that it was designed to "ignore what's wrong with the Army and tell what's right with my people." Since he and Heisler were not allowed to talk about Jim Crow in the Army, they deliberately set up shots to make that point visually. "You didn't *need* any dialogue, you didn't *need* any preachment," Moss explained in retrospect. "And you can't change a relationship by edict."

Once the project was launched, Capra kept a cautious arm's length until it was finished and approved for Army distribution.

"When the praise started coming in, he lapped it up," Moss recalled. "He's a guy who cannot afford *not* to take the credit. But I'll say this for him, we had all the money we wanted, and he did leave us absolutely alone. He was not unsympathetic to the subject, and when we'd run the dailies at night, he came in a couple of times and said, 'Umm-hmm.' I would pass him in the hall and say 'Hello' and he would say, 'How are you?' That was all.

"If Capra had been hostile, personally hostile in this area, the film would never have been made, he could have sabotaged it. If he had been of the racist tribe, he would have opposed it. I don't care what he said out of my hearing: here was a guy who was straight enough to keep his record clean."

Moss was named to HUAC as a Communist in 1951 by Hollywood agent (later producer) Meta Reis Rosenberg, who said he was a Party member in the early 1940s, an accusation which probably influenced Capra's comment in his book that he had to tone down the black rebelliousness Moss brought to the film. To the soft-spoken and diplomatic Moss, Capra's "ridiculous" comment caused "half a second of irritation," because he realized it had little to do with the reality of his virtually nonexistent working relationship with Capra. "He wrote the book at a time when that kind of thing was in the headlines—when Huey Newton and Eldridge Cleaver were making news by throwing their arms around. Not that I'm *not* a militant, but I wouldn't have had the job if I'd gone in there like a bull in a china shop; you never go into a battle without knowing what you can win."

After *The Negro Soldier* was screened by Litvak in October 1943 for Stimson, Marshall, Surles, and Osborn, it had to pass what the Army regarded as the final test, a screening for two hundred black journalists at the Pentagon. It was then, as historians Thomas Cripps and David Culbert put it in their study of the making of the film, that "Frank Capra, though he had little to do with the film, arrived in Washington to show 'his' production."

That triumphant screening, which Capra proudly describes in his book, actually was anticlimactic, according to Moss, who said, "They were all primed." Without telling Capra, Moss and Heisler had carefully plotted behind the scenes to mobilize black opinion makers and sympathetic liberal groups (including the Democratic Party) to create a climate of subtle pressure on the Army to release the film not only to the troops but to the public. The really decisive event, Moss said, was a screening in Harlem for black leaders who were skeptical of the Army's sincerity in making such a film: "If the community group would not accept it, forget it. They could have killed it." When the lights came on, that audience's only remaining concerns about the film were, "Now, who's going to see this? And are the white people going to see it?" From that point on, said Moss, the Army was "caught in a trap; the film could not be tampered with. And they were smart enough to see that everybody had got what he wanted."

Though it performed poorly at the box office when given a public release in April 1944 (a shortened version later was released, cut from forty-three to twenty minutes, and was more successful), *The Negro Soldier* was warmly received by blacks both in and outside the Army, and an Army survey of the white soldiers showed that 67 percent also had a highly favorable reaction to the film. And, as Cripps and Culbert wrote in 1979, "Only *The Negro Soldier,* of all wartime films depicting blacks, actually tried to weave the Negro into the fabric of American life; this characteristic made the Army's film a model for filmmakers wishing to break through ingrained industry stereotypes. . . . The existence of such a film indicated change within the Army—why not also in the civilian world?"

It was after the film was released that Capra had his first, and only, extended personal talk with Carlton Moss.

As Moss recalled, "It was in that time when everybody was planning his future and jockeying for position in Hollywood. The big thing these guys would ask me was, 'What are you going to do when the war is over?' By then I was kosher—it was after the glory. They all got interested in me, except me. Stu Heisler tried to get me to work with him after the war, but I knew there was no place for me in Hollywood; I could have had a career in the studios after the war, but it was clear that I would have had to make compromises I couldn't accept. So I formed an educational film company, and I'm still doing it today.

"One day near the end of the war, Capra called me in and talked to me, with the attitude that he was helping a young fellow. He said, 'Why don't you go to some of those rich colored guys and get some money and start a company for yourself?' That was the first time I knew he was thinking about me. With a kind of subdued passion I had never seen in him before, he said, 'There's *gotta* be some rich colored guys.'

"I said, 'Well, Colonel, there *are* some, but not enough to get the kind of money together to compete with the major studios.' He thought about that, and he acted crushed. Then he gave me some advice which he was passing on as if to a man who was drowning: he said, 'Why don't you leave the country?'

"I said, 'My father was born here. Let me get all the fruits I can get from this process, and after there aren't any more fruits for me to get, *then* maybe I can leave the country.' He looked disappointed.

"I think I had become identified in his mind with Rocky Washington [Capra's black friend from childhood]; in his sober moments he would talk to me about Rocky. And when he called me into his office that day, I suddenly *became* Rocky. He found himself wanting to express something— something romantic—it's in his films, too, he likes to fantasize about the ambitions and drives of the little guy. But if he had thought about it, he would have known damn well there probably was not enough money in the black community to make a short.

"I could sense that he was a minority person, but *he* didn't see that *I* belong here more than he does. I go back several generations; he's a newcomer."

As he prepared to leave the Army in the spring of 1945, Capra was putting the finishing touches to his long-delayed films about the German and Japanese people, two of his most fractious projects, dealing not only with the causes of the war but also with the problems that peace would bring.

From its origins as *Know Your Enemy: Germany*, *Here Is Germany* had the longest gestation period of any film made by Capra's unit, and by the time it was ready for screening, as Peterson put it, "There *was* no enemy Germany." It was released in October 1945 for American occupation troops.

The first version had been written by Bruno Frank and was directed at Twentieth Century–Fox in October 1942 by the German Jew Ernst Lubitsch, the master of sophisticated comedy who had made a controversial black comedy about Nazism, *To Be or Not to Be*, earlier that year. Lubitsch's *Know Your Enemy: Germany* was a dramatized account of the rise of German militarism through several generations, as personified by a symbolic German named Karl Schmidt. Only vestiges of that approach remained in the final version, a *Why We Fight*–style compilation on modern German history supervised by Gottfried Reinhardt, also a German Jew (son of the renowned stage director Max Reinhardt), who attributed the "endless" delays in making the film to "friction" within the War Department on the subject of postwar policy toward Germany.*

When he took over the project in 1943, Reinhardt recalled, "I asked

---

* *Others who worked on the film at various points included Litvak, Veiller, Peterson, Spigelgass, Huston, and William L. Shirer, who later wrote* The Rise and Fall of the Third Reich.

Capra, 'What's the official doctrine?' He said, 'Make up your own doctrine.' They had dumped this on him, and I think he couldn't have cared less. Frank was a very simple and straight-thinking person, a practical man with a very good sense of humor, patriotic, loyal, but politically naive—not reactionary, but on the whole conservative, and not an intellectual."

Reinhardt shaped the film as a warning against a postwar rebirth of German militarism. He wanted occupation troops to realize that "we must not make the same mistakes that we had made in World War I. I was afraid that the minute the war was over, it would become again a pro-German policy. I felt very passionate about it, so I sold my point of view, including a lot of concentration camp stuff. I was very proud of it."

Before it was released, the Capra unit rushed through production an even more emphatic anti-fraternization film for the occupation troops called *Your Job in Germany*, supervised by Ted Geisel, who wrote it with Anthony Veiller. Directed in part by Litvak, it was shipped to the troops on April 13, 1945, and was so up to date that it also included some of the first footage from the Nazi concentration camps, which still were in the process of being liberated by the Allied armies.

Capra was so busy with other projects that he "directed only the [narrator's] voice," Geisel recalled. "The nearest actors were at Fort Roach [the Hal Roach Studios in Culver City, used by the Army Air Forces for making training films], and I called them and said, 'Send over a couple of actors.' They sent me Sergeant John Beal and Lieutenant Ronald Reagan. I listened to Lieutenant Reagan and had the pleasure of saying, 'Don't call us, we'll call you.' Reagan didn't seem to have the understanding, that morning, of the vital issues" (Reagan later narrated *The Stilwell Road*)." Geisel hand-carried a print of *Your Job in Germany* to Europe to secure the approval of the Army commanders. Eventually they all passed it with the exception of General George S. Patton, whose admiration for the Nazis was so scandalous that Eisenhower would have to warn him that August to "get off your bloody ass and carry out the denazification program instead of mollycoddling the goddamn Nazis." Patton walked out on a screening of *Your Job in Germany* after giving it a one-word review, the same word he used for denazification: *"Bullshit."*

Though the BPR initially balked at allowing the film to be distributed to the American public, as a result of APS screenings for the Hollywood Writers' Mobilization and for sympathetic congressmen and journalists, *Your Job in Germany* did receive some play in American commercial theaters. Late in 1945, Warner Bros. redubbed the sound track and made a few other alterations in the film (which, like other government films, was in the public domain and not protected by copyright), releasing it as *Hitler Lives?*, credited to production supervisor Gordon Hollingshead and director Don Siegel. *Hitler Lives?* won the Academy Award as best documentary short.

Capra in later years recalled his shock at seeing the first Signal Corps photographs and motion pictures sent back in April 1945 from the newly liberated Nazi concentration camps (much of the American film of the camps was shot by George Stevens and his unit). Though the Allies had learned of the extermination of the Jews as early as August 1942 and the existence of the death camps was widely known by 1943, when Capra's film *The Nazis Strike* showed a concentration camp and stated that Hitler's plan was to "exterminate all those he considers 'inferior races,' " Capra told Bill Moyers in 1982 that he (like many others) did not believe those reports until he saw the photographic evidence at the end of the war, "a terrible, terrible shock."

For his televised interview with Moyers, Capra brought along some of the horrific photos of Nazi death camps he had saved in his files. "I was surprised when Frank Capra brought those still photos of the concentration camps with him to our interview," Moyers told the audience. "I hadn't expected it. He talked about them in a sad and incredulous voice." Though Capra's films helped defeat the Nazis, Moyers felt that Capra "was uncomfortable, enough so to bring the photos as an additional justification for having himself been a propagandist, even a propagandist on democracy's behalf."

Know Your Enemy—Japan is "very offensive" by postwar standards, acknowledged Pete Peterson, who worked on the film. It is a piece of unrestrained hysteria which purports to analyze the history and character of a people whose minds "we shall never completely understand," a people who follow "a system of regimentation so perfect it made Hitler's mouth water. . . . Defeating this nation is as necessary as shooting down a mad dog in your neighborhood."

One of Capra's pet projects, three years in production, it was "hampered from the beginning by the War Department's inability to decide what our policy toward Japan really was," according to historian William J. Blakefield. "The central question which caused the most difficulty was, 'Who in Japan is actually to blame for this war?' The Japanese people? The emperor? A small band of militarists?"

Although Capra later disclaimed personal acquaintance with Joris Ivens, the Dutch leftist documentary filmmaker, he hired Ivens in the spring of 1943 to supervise the film. Ivens recalled Capra telling him, "We know you very well, and your art of editing documentary film is very important to us, because we have many good editors but they are specialized in editing fiction films." Ivens spent about six months preparing a twenty-minute preliminary cut of *Japan* with his editor, Helen van Dongen, and screenwriter Carl Foreman. A month later, Capra told Ivens that the Army disapproved of his approach: "They can't accept your film and they said you have to stop the project and you should leave our unit." Ivens's political background also may have contributed to his ouster. But he remembered Capra "very generously" helping him find work as a consultant on William Wellman's 1945 feature *The Story of G.I. Joe*. "Capra felt very badly about it," Ivens said. "We had worked very well . . . [but] there was nothing he could do."

The problem was Ivens's insistence that the Japanese were like "everyone else" in their openness to democracy and his belief that the blame for the war should be laid not on the people but on Emperor Hirohito and the other militarists and politicians: "We had the idea of saying it was the same as Hitler's fascism on the other side of the world, and after the war the Emperor must be treated as a war criminal; why Hitler and not him?" The Army's disapproval of that approach proved to Ivens that "they had in their heads an idea of collaboration" with Hirohito "for their imperialist politics in the Indian Ocean."

Allen Rivkin, one of the writers who worked on the script after Ivens left, confirmed that "we couldn't call Hirohito a war criminal because we knew we had to deal with him later. For once the bureaucrats were right. When Ivens quit the picture [Ivens said he was fired], that's when we knew we couldn't deal with Hirohito, and it threw us into a tailspin. That's why it took so long."

The young journalist and future novelist Irving Wallace collaborated on several drafts of the *Japan* script before Capra and Geisel wrote the final version.* Wallace felt that he and his collaborators were "writing in a vacuum, without instruction," because the American high command "did not know how we should treat the Japanese, except to beat them in the field." But he was convinced that "the real problem was our boss, Frank Capra himself. . . . He was totally unsophisticated when it came to political thought. He knew only one thing, America had been good to him,

---

* *Wallace's collaborators included John Huston, who supervised the project for about two months in late 1944 and early 1945; Peterson; Foreman; and Geisel, who supervised the film's completion. Frances Goodrich and Albert Hackett also wrote a draft.*

America was beautiful. . . . For Capra it was not difficult. He came up with a simple foreign policy toward Japan. It added up to this: the only good Jap is a dead Jap. He did not say it in those words, but that was what his words added up to.

"You can believe me when I say that [Carl] Foreman and I fought this terribly, persistently, because it was all wrong. Foreman and I used to leave those meetings with Capra and say to each other, 'We can't allow Capra's attitude toward the enemy to be our government's policy in this picture for our troops, because while Capra doesn't understand it, the direction the film is taking is utterly racist.' How could we indict an entire people in our film?"

Wallace did not realize that the decision not to blame the war on the Japanese leadership but on the people had been passed along to Capra from higher echelons, and he was incorrect when he claimed that the final film manages to "separate the Japanese people from the Japanese military." Any modification that Wallace and Foreman managed to bring about could only have been one of degree rather than in the basic theme of the film, which proclaims: "This film tells the story of the Japs in Japan, to whom the words liberty and freedom are still without meaning."

Classified as "confidential" by the nervous Information and Education (I&E) division of Army Special Services in January 1945, the film underwent final revisions to eliminate what the Pentagon ironically felt was "too much sympathy for the Jap people." In what Blakefield called "a classic case of bad timing," it was released to the troops on August 9, three days after Hiroshima and the day the second atomic bomb was dropped on Nagasaki. The headquarters of General Douglas MacArthur cabled the Pentagon on August 28: "AFTER PREVIEW OF NEW FILM *KNOW YOUR ENEMY—JAPAN* RELEASE TO TROOPS BEING WITHHELD DUE TO CHANGE IN POLICY GOVERNING OCCUPATION OF JAPAN. ALSO RECOMMEND NO PRESS RELEASES OR SHOWING TO PUBLIC IN UNITED STATES." In MacArthur's attempt to persuade the Japanese to accept American-style democracy, "a film entitled *Know Your Enemy—Japan* was suddenly of very little value to anyone," Blakefield noted. The next day General Osborn ordered it withheld from release. It did not receive its first public screening until 1977.

MacArthur later ordered the shelving of a film the Capra unit put together for the Japanese occupation troops, the eighteen-minute *Our Job in Japan*, written by Foreman and the film's supervisor, Geisel. It called Japanese atrocities "so disgusting, so revolting, so obscene that [they] turned the stomach of the entire civilized world," but it also manifested a somewhat more conciliatory attitude, warning occupation troops against "pushing people around," and telling them to ensure "a fair break for everybody regardless of race or creed or color." *Our Job in Japan*, the last film completed by Capra's unit (in March 1946, long after Capra himself had left the service), was not released until 1982.

"When the matter comes to me in more formal fashion, I will express myself more formally," General Marshall wrote Capra on June 5, 1945, ten days before his discharge, "but in the meantime I wish you to know how much I value and how much I appreciate the work that you have done for the Army.

"Your *Why We Fight* series had a tremendous influence on morale and understanding and I think *Prelude to War* and *The Nazis Strike* will stand as motion picture classics of that character. . . .

"Altogether you have done a grand job and I want you to know that I am very grateful."

"I deeply appreciate the personal note you sent me," Capra replied on June 11. "It makes me very happy and very proud to know that you feel I've contributed my small two cents' worth to the greatest event in history.

"Providence has smiled on our country; for only Providence could have given America the magnificent leadership that is carrying us through. You, sir, epitomize that leadership, and I know how truly humble you must feel toward your great responsibility, and what pride you must feel in the success of our cause.

"As for me, I am eternally grateful for the opportunity of serving. Should any particular job come up in the future on which I could be of service, please know that I stand willing and eager to do it as a civilian, or to be recalled to active service until that particular job is done.

"Thank you, General Marshall, for your confidence and friendship. You have been an inspiration to me, and will remain so the rest of my life."

On June 14, Capra was summoned to Marshall's office. He was upset, fearing he was about to be given a new assignment.

Instead Marshall pinned on him the Distinguished Service Medal. The citation read: "From February 1942 to June 1945 Colonel Frank Capra, Army of the United States, rendered service of exceptional distinction, making a valuable contribution to the war effort. He was responsible for the production of a remarkable series of motion pictures at the personal direction of the Chief of Staff which graphically presented the causes leading up to the present war and the responsibility of the Axis powers for the tragic consequences. He portrayed in a classic manner the true character of the German and Japanese enemy. He prepared a series of films interpreting the character and customs of various of our Allies for the better understanding of the soldiers of our Army who were to serve in intimate contact with those Allies. At the further personal direction of the Chief of Staff he made a most important contribution through his production of the films *Two Down and One to Go!* and *On to Tokyo*, which provided for the soldier a clear understanding of the reasons and methods for the redeployment and demobilization plans which became effective on the defeat of Germany.

"The films produced by Colonel Capra under the direction of the Chief of Staff had an important influence on the morale of the Army. Colonel Capra also rendered an important service as Chief of the Army Motion Picture Unit and as Assistant Chief of the Army Pictorial Service."

Frank McCarthy later remembered: "General Marshall said, 'Get Capra in here—I want to give him this personally.' Capra is a very shy man, and when he received the award, he just smiled. When he left the room, we walked down the hall together and he said, 'Where is the men's room?'

"He was so emotionally moved that he went into the stall and threw up."

17. Liberty

"*I*t's frightening to go back to Hollywood after four years, wondering whether you've gone rusty or lost touch," Capra admitted to Tom Pryor of *The New York Times* in November 1945. "I keep telling myself how wonderful it would be just to sneak out somewhere and make a couple of quickie Westerns first—just to get the feel of things again."

The postwar security he craved could be found only under studio contract, but Capra found it necessary to pretend otherwise. In an article he wrote for the *Times* six months later, Capra insisted that he was "willing to gamble [his] hard-earned savings to gain independence" and that it was his craving for "individuality" which led to his "revolutionary" act of founding an independent production company, Liberty Films, Inc., in partnership with William Wyler, George Stevens, and Sam Briskin (its trademark the tolling Liberty Bell). The unheroic truth, though, was that after his creative and financial disappointment in his earlier attempt at independence with *Meet John Doe,* after his run for cover with *Arsenic and Old Lace,* and after years of following orders in the Army, Capra was afraid to take the risks of going independent again and did so only out of necessity, in a state of anxiety and self-doubt.

While weighing his future in the last months of his Army service, Capra was hoping to pick up where he had left off in Hollywood when Pearl Harbor interrupted his career. Just as he was doing then, he was looking for a safe haven as a studio contract director, preferably with a long-term deal. But when Sam Briskin tested the waters for Colonel Capra around Hollywood, the news was not good: unlike in 1941, studio offers were not forthcoming. Like it or not, going independent—with seed money from his and his partners' own pockets and with production financing for his first postwar film, *It's a Wonderful Life,* coming largely from Bank of America loans secured by the negative of the picture—was his only postwar option.

His public pose of determined optimism made a striking contrast to his private fears. Capra's 1946 analysis of the industry shortsightedly heralded the rise of independent companies as an antidote to studio "mass production" (most of the filmmakers he mentioned would soon be back in the studio folds) and welcomed the federal government's outlawing of block-booking, a reform he had long been advocating, as a boon to independents, since films now had to be "sold individually, standing on their own merits." But in retrospect Capra acknowledged that what he was trumpeting was the beginning of the end of the Hollywood which had enabled him to thrive before the war—a process that culminated in the 1948 consent decree the Justice Department forced the major studios to sign, cutting loose their theaters and depriving them of a guaranteed outlet for their productions. These changes, along with the simultaneous advent of television, effectively destroyed the studio system. Jimmy Stewart, who starred as George Bailey in *Wonderful Life,* said in 1988 that he had "often wondered" about Capra's postwar decline, and concluded that "Frank had this wonderful relationship with Harry Cohn, and I think the change in the studio system, the big studios going out of style, had a very profound effect on Frank."

Capra blamed his postwar problems on the industry's notoriously short memory—to many after the war, he recalled, he was "Frank who?"—and on the general lowering of production budgets and standards of quality during the wartime box-office boom, which, coupled with cost increases due to postwar inflation and labor militancy, threatened to make his "one man, one film" approach obsolete. There were elements of truth in those explanations, but they also were alibis for his personal failure to adapt to changing conditions and his inability to function independently.

Unlike Stevens, Wyler, and Stewart, Capra had experienced the war largely from a distance, but Paul Horgan felt that "Capra's war experience changed his whole vision of the cinema—during the war he dealt with historical material in a highly persuasive and percussive way, but at the expense of his concentration on fictional film later."

"Once he got into this government stuff, it gave him a new sense of values, and then he was dead," said screenwriter Ian McLellan Hunter, who worked with him after the war. "He was working with the people who were the heavies in his own pictures, and it turned him completely around. From that point on, in trying to develop scripts he developed nonsense."

"Something happened to him in that period," agreed Chet Sticht, who became secretary-treasurer of Liberty after returning from the Army. "I never knew exactly what it was that got into him, but he wasn't fighting like he used to. It was a strange thing—for some reason or other around about there he was inclined to give up things. Maybe he felt he'd been to the top and he was just coasting now. And then he got into remakes, which I was always arguing against. I think a guy shouldn't go and remake his old pictures."

"I *didn't* change," Capra insisted in 1984. "I was more sure of what I had been doing, more certain, more strongly forward than I was before the war." But the view of the movie industry he expressed to Tom Pryor in 1945 amounted to defeatism: "When you make a picture today you are bucking a system, and no independent producer is big enough to lick it. So, even if he has ideals and ideas, he has to compromise them if he wants to stay in business."

"I never saw any big change in Capra at all until he came back from the war," said Joe Walker, who photographed part of *Wonderful Life*. "He was more anxious. He wasn't the careful, happy director on *Wonderful Life* that he had been before the war."

The fact that "a large part" of the public "seem[ed] to have more or less forgotten" Capra and Stewart during the war (as *Variety* observed after *Wonderful Life* opened weakly) should have been only a temporary setback for Capra. Not only Stewart but also Capra's fellow directors who had spent the war in uniform—Ford, Huston, Wyler, Stevens—were, in time, able to regain their former prominence in the industry.

Hollywood's lack of enthusiasm for Capra on his return from service stemmed from an accumulation of factors unique to Capra: it was a reflection on his faltering box-office track record and his reputation for extravagance; a delayed backlash against his rebellious posture toward studio control before the war, both in his own career and on behalf of the Screen Directors Guild; and, perhaps, a resentment of his arrogance toward Hollywood during his Army years, such as his blast from London at Hollywood for "embarrassing" the troops with "flag-waving" war movies. Capra's assumption of moral superiority toward those who remained in the studios making entertainment movies while he was in uniform—even though he spent most of the war at Fort Fox—undoubtedly helped negate whatever rewards he expected his wartime service to bring him in Hollywood.

At an introductory Hollywood press conference on February 23, 1946, with his three Liberty partners, who, like him, were all ex-Army colonels, Capra complained, "Men in our position—and that goes for thousands of others all down the line, actors, directors, writers, technicians—need a helping hand from the industry and from the trade press. Unfortunately, we are not always getting it.''

It was in the fall of 1944, while still recovering from the shock of learning that no studios wanted him, that Capra had formed Liberty with Briskin, who had joined Lyman Munson's staff as a civilian aide after his heart attack and retirement from the Army. Capra remembered telling Briskin that he might quit Hollywood entirely and work in England. But Briskin told Capra that he had made his own decision about what to do after the war: rather than return to his old job at Columbia, he would start his own production company. He suggested that Capra do the same. Without waiting for the war to end, they announced their postwar company on January 29, 1945, and Liberty Films was incorporated on April 10, with Capra as president and major stockholder.

According to Capra, two weeks after the incorporation he asked Robert Riskin to become a partner, and *Variety* on May 1 said it was "presumed" Riskin would join Liberty, but Riskin's widow, Fay Wray, insisted that Capra made no such offer. In any case, Riskin, leaving the OWI with a successful record as a production executive, was no longer interested in being a junior partner to Capra. He was getting ready to make his own films, for release through RKO. His first postwar project as a writer-producer was an original story he had written with Joseph Krumgold, *The Magic City*, about a public opinion pollster whose discovery of a perfectly average American city drastically alters its character—a story with strong overtones of the work Riskin had done for Capra, particularly *Mr. Deeds*. Riskin's decision to go his separate way hurt Capra, who, though he would not admit it later, evidently wanted to direct *The Magic City*. "It goes without saying that I infinitely regret that precious collaboration," Capra wrote of Riskin in a 1946 article for the French magazine *Cinémonde*.

Magic Town, as Riskin's film was retitled, starred Jimmy Stewart and was filmed while *Wonderful Life* was in postproduction at the same studio. Capra claimed that he and Riskin "worked together on this script" (Riskin received sole screenplay credit) but that his former partner "wanted to make a picture without me, [to] prove himself." Capra also claimed that Riskin started directing the film himself but that when Riskin, "a lousy director, couldn't finish the picture," his brother Everett asked Capra to step in and save it. Capra said he declined ("Jesus, I wouldn't do that to him, that would *really* debase him"), but that as a favor he asked William Wellman to shoot "the last week or so."

"Wellman was the director right from the beginning," Wray said. "Bob

Riskin never even considered directing it." Stewart confirmed that Riskin did not direct any part of the film, and Wellman told John F. Mariani in 1975, "Frank's just being kind about it. I was in on that thing from the beginning, and I wish I never started it. It stunk! Frank and Bob had a big argument about the picture and Riskin asked me to do it. I told him this is the kind of picture only Capra could do. It's not my kind of film. In my book Capra's the greatest, and if you think *Magic Town* has anything good about it at all, there's something wrong with you."

With Riskin unavailable for Liberty Films, Capra went to Leo McCarey, the producer-director whose *Going My Way* had won the Oscar as best picture of 1944 and whose Rainbow Productions was making a sequel for RKO, *The Bells of St. Mary's*. McCarey was formally offered a Liberty partnership on May 7, 1945. "We were supposed to go together," McCarey recalled, "and we couldn't see eye to eye." On the same day McCarey said no to Capra and Briskin, the enfeebled United Artists decided to pass on a deal to distribute Liberty's films, a stark indication of how much Capra's status in Hollywood had eroded during his wartime absence from commercial production.

Capra desperately needed the partnership of another important film-maker to strengthen his bargaining power with distributors. Though he insisted on keeping a controlling financial interest, Capra was willing to offer his potential partner an equal voice in major company decisions such as story purchases and casting; creative autonomy during production, as long as the film remained within its budget; control of postproduction; and possessive credit (i.e., the director's name above the title). William Wyler, who also confessed to being "a little frightened of the future," found it a "very attractive idea," attractive enough to make him refuse another extended contract with Samuel Goldwyn. Wyler agreed on July 6 to join Liberty after he was discharged from the Army and fulfilled a remaining commitment for one film with Goldwyn.

That film was *The Best Years of Our Lives*, the classic drama of returning veterans painfully readjusting to life in postwar America. "I knew the chief characters of it intimately," Wyler said shortly after making it. "I lived with the fellows throughout the war years. Their reaction to civilian life was my very own." "Willy came back from the war a very nervous, uncertain man," recalled Tom Pryor, who interviewed him that September. "He doubted his own capacity to deal with the subject matter of *Best Years*—he was very humble, and he didn't want to make a picture that would not be worthy of the sacrifice so many men had made."

With Wyler aboard, Liberty was able to swing a deal on August 23 for the release of nine pictures by RKO. Meanwhile Capra and Briskin also were sounding out John Huston and George Stevens about joining them, but Huston declined because he felt he would not have enough clout in partnership with more experienced men, and Stevens, whose unit had been the first to film the liberated concentration camps, for a time was too disturbed by his wartime experiences to concentrate on his postwar career.

"We cut the barbed wire to go into Dachau, and that's beyond description," Stevens said in 1974, shortly before his death. "The only way you can talk about it is the photographs." The full horror hit Stevens when he realized that he was disgusted by the concentration camp inmates, that they roused in him feelings of "arrogance and brutality"; it was "a fierce thing to discover within yourself that which you despise the most." When asked what effect the experience had on his films, Stevens replied, "It has a most profound adjustment in your thinking. I don't suppose I was ever too hilarious again."

"He didn't *talk* anymore," Capra remembered.

Capra's first overture to Stevens had been made in the fall of 1944, and Stevens, who was still overseas, asked if he could defer his answer until he returned home. At the end of the war, Stevens told Harry Cohn he would return to Columbia, but he changed his mind, wanting to be free of studio control. After considering a partnership offer from McCarey, Stevens joined Liberty on January 1, 1946, shortly before Capra began shooting *It's a Wonderful Life*, the first Liberty film to go before the cameras.

The deal with RKO was modified to require three films from each producer-director, it was hoped at the rate of one per year from each man, though each was allowed until 1951 to deliver his quota. As Liberty publicity put it, "The time element in production will be relegated to a place of secondary importance, [and] quality of product both from an artistic and entertainment standpoint is to come first."

Most of Capra's initial Liberty projects had a determined focus on what he hoped was safely noncontroversial, escapist subject matter. Shortly before he began shooting *Wonderful Life*, he told Edwin Schallert of the *Los Angeles Times*, "People are numb after the catastrophic events of the past ten to fifteen years. I would not attempt to reach them mentally through a picture, only emotionally. Anything of a mental sort, anything apart from the purely human, will have to be incidental."

He planned at the end of the war to remake one of his more innocuous films of the 1930s, *Broadway Bill*, with Bing Crosby. But the remake had to be postponed because Capra could not obtain the rights to the original film from Columbia. Liberty had no stars or stories to offer in return. Capra also was piqued because Sidney Buchman, his first choice for a writer after Riskin, was still working exclusively for Cohn as a writer-producer; Capra's respect for Buchman's writing abilities evidently outweighed any concerns he might have had at that point about Buchman's political history.

Capra had "always wanted to make a Western," so in February 1945, within a week after he and Briskin announced their partnership, he wrote a brief outline called "Pioneer Woman," the story of Utah Carson, a shy cowboy (the part was written with Gary Cooper in mind) who leads a wagon train of two hundred mail-order brides to love-starved cowboys in California. Though Capra felt a "quickie" Western would be a relatively safe bet commercially, "Pioneer Woman" was no quickie project. It was conceived on such a sprawling scale that it proved to be dauntingly expensive, with or without Cooper, particularly because Capra wanted to shoot it in Technicolor. After an attempt to revive the project in 1949 at Paramount (which rejected it because the budget came to $2.76 million), Capra sold the story to MGM, which filmed it in 1951 as the black-and-white *Westward the Women*, directed by William Wellman and starring Robert Taylor.

Capra in the first days of Liberty looked to Broadway for a presold hit. He made an unsuccessful attempt in April 1945 to buy the film rights to Mary Chase's *Harvey*, a fantasy about the gentle tippler Elwood P. Dowd and his invisible companion, a six-foot rabbit named Harvey. Jimmy Stewart played Elwood in Universal's disappointing film version, directed by Henry Koster in 1950, which proved that the story was less suited to the screen than to the stage.

Shortly before Liberty moved into two adjoining seven-room bungalows at RKO (just down Gower Street from Columbia), Capra bought a comedy by Herbert Clyde Lewis and Frederick Stephani, "It Happened on Fifth Avenue," about a philosopher-bum who spends his winters at a millionaire's mansion in New York and summers at the millionaire's Florida estate. Even the title hinted of self-parody for Capra, and it was not long before he unloaded the property. Allied Artists released the 1947 film of the story, directed by Roy Del Ruth and starring Victor Moore.

He had another project in those first months of Liberty that was *not* escapist, *No Other Man*, a grim fable (to be filmed in Technicolor) about the aftermath of World War III, based on a 1940 novel by Alfred Noyes, the poet-in-residence at Throop when Capra was a college student. Capra bought the rights in October 1945, hiring Jo Swerling to write a screenplay that was not completed until the following August, when Capra's interest in socially conscious material had lessened considerably. A few second-unit background scenes were filmed in Italy during the summer of 1946 before Capra put the project aside.

After only a brief time in his new office considering stories for which he could muster little enthusiasm, he had begun to despair of the future of Liberty Films. Then he read a story by Philip Van Doren Stern, "The Greatest Gift."

When Mrs. Philip Van Doren Stern wrote Capra in 1978 to complain that he continually was dismissing "The Greatest Gift" in interviews by saying that *It's a Wonderful Life* was based on a "little Christmas card," Capra replied by suggesting that her husband's story meant as little to him as the unpublished story by the long-forgotten Lewis R. Foster on which he had based *Mr. Smith Goes to Washington*. He went right on referring to Stern's story as "a Christmas card," and though on an earlier occasion he had said that "the whole idea of this picture was right in that little Christmas card," he usually implied that it was the merest hint of a story and acted as if Stern were incidental to the film's creation.

Philip Van Doren Stern was a historian and novelist who was respected by scholars for biographies of Lincoln, Lee, and John Wilkes Booth, and a novel about the abolition movement, *The Drums of Morning*. While shaving on Lincoln's birthday, February 12, 1938, Stern thought of a story about an ordinary small-town American who contemplates suicide ("I wish I had never been born!") and is saved by his guardian angel, who grants his wish, making him see what a difference he has made to his family and townspeople. Early attempts to write it failed, but he often found himself telling the story to friends and was encouraged by their response. In the spring of 1943 he finally succeeded in getting it right, with the addition of the Christmas setting.

"The Greatest Gift" was rejected by every magazine to which he sent it, "But by this time I had become fond of the story that nobody wanted. I revised it again and had 200 twenty-four-page pamphlets printed at my own expense. I sent these out to my friends as Christmas cards, and one of them went to my Hollywood agent [Shirley Collier]. She wrote back, asking for permission to offer the story to the movies. I thought she was crazy."

RKO bought the film rights for $10,000 in 1943 at the urging of Cary Grant, and the story appeared in *Good Housekeeping* as "The Man Who Never Was" before being published in 1945 as a small book entitled *The Greatest Gift*. Dalton Trumbo, the first screenwriter hired to adapt it, recalled that the project was put on hold after its intended producer went on an alcoholic binge. Despite hiring Clifford Odets and Marc Connelly to rewrite Trumbo's draft, RKO was unable to come up with what it considered a satisfactory script. When Capra read the scripts, he agreed that none "had the spirit of the original."

He bought the material from RKO on September 1, 1945, for $50,000, and on the fourteenth hired Frances Goodrich and Albert Hackett to write a new adaptation. Before he was through, Capra would employ three more screenwriters. Michael Wilson, a young ex-Marine then little known in Hollywood, was signed to a writing contract with Liberty on January 2 and did what his widow, Zelma, has described as a "polish"; at the same time, Jo Swerling was working with Capra on scene revisions, continuing to do so into the film's production; and Dorothy Parker did a dialogue polish. The shooting script in Capra's files indicates that about a fourth of the scenes were rewritten by Swerling and Capra during the shooting, much more reworking than Capra had found necessary on the well-crafted Riskin scripts.

After a Screen Writers Guild arbitration, Capra was granted a screenplay credit (in third position) with the Hacketts, and Swerling was credited for "additional scenes." Though the guild gave no credit to Trumbo, Odets, Connelly, Wilson, or Parker, Wilson was acknowledged in the Academy *Bulletin* as "contributor to screenplay." *Wonderful Life* marked the first time since *Forbidden* in 1932 that Capra had received screen credit as a writer, and it also would be the last time the guild would grant him writing credit on one of his own features, despite his attempts on subsequent films.

Capra's insistence on screen credit for his writing contributions in the postwar era, while it had some basis in the case of *Wonderful Life*, was also one of the reasons for his drastic creative decline after that film. His egotistical need to deny the importance of the screenwriter to his films had already dealt a nearly fatal blow to his career by sabotaging his creative relationship with Robert Riskin, and from this point his need to be recognized as a writer himself would make it increasingly difficult for him to work with first-rate writers, finally throwing him back on his own limited resources and on the help of the fanatically anti-Communist Myles Connolly (who had made himself unavailable for *Wonderful Life* because of a falling-out with Capra after *Meet John Doe* over his lack of recognition on screen, a situation Capra later rectified).

Albert Hackett recalled telling his friend Riskin at the time of the *Wonderful Life* arbitration, "Capra is now fighting for getting his name on the credits to beat the writers, not so much for the picture he's doing now but for all those pictures Riskin did with him."

Capra's selective memory of the screenwriting process of *Wonderful Life* in later years may have stemmed not only from egotism but also from a need to purge the film retrospectively of questionable political influences. For in addition to Capra himself, six of the film's other eight screenwriters found their loyalty questioned during the Hollywood inquisition that began in 1947.

Capra's book fails to mention the contributions of Wilson and Parker, who were blacklisted (Parker, the celebrated wit and short story writer, was a prominent Hollywood radical, an early Screen Writers Guild militant, and a cofounder of the Hollywood Anti-Nazi League and the Motion Picture Artists Committee to Aid Republican Spain). And though Capra mentions Trumbo's script in his book, he does not acknowledge that he borrowed some ideas, and even a few lines of dialogue, from Trumbo, at the time one of the most successful screenwriters in Hollywood. Capra was not eager in retrospect to share credit with a man who was blacklisted after the October 1947 HUAC hearings as one of the Hollywood Ten and was sent to prison in 1950 for contempt of Congress.

Odets, on the other hand, admitted his former Communist Party membership to HUAC and named names in 1952, so it was possible for Capra to admit that he used some of Odets's work in the early part of the film. Hackett said, however, that it was he and his wife who decided to borrow Odets's powerful scene of the drunken druggist, Mr. Gower (H. B. Warner), slapping the young George Bailey for telling him that he is mixing poison with his medicine. Other elements derived from the Odets script include the scene of George as a boy saving his brother from drowning, the dance and moonlight walk in which George and Mary Hatch (Donna Reed) are surprised with news of his father's death, and the romantic rivalry over Mary between George and his friend Sam Wainwright (Frank Albertson), whom she rejects to marry George.

The Hacketts, whose work on *Wonderful Life* Capra disparaged in his book, were active in liberal politics and had taken outspoken stands on civil liberties issues. They were accused by the American Legion in 1952 of being Communist sympathizers; among the charges brought against them was their involvement in the Hollywood Writers' Mobilization at the time they wrote a draft of *Know Your Enemy—Japan* for Capra. When MGM, the studio to which they were under contract in 1952, asked them to write a letter disavowing any subversive associations and apologizing for any such involvements, the Hacketts wrote studio executive Louis K. Sidney,

"We are not Communists. We have never been Communists and never could be. We have never wavered in our devotion and loyalty to the United States." But they refused to write the apology and repudiation of their actions MGM asked for, because "We feel that if we wrote such a letter we would be violating every principle of democracy and freedom in which we believe. . . . We hope you understand why we must refuse your request. Why we must adhere to our principles. After all, we must live with ourselves for many years to come." As Hackett recalled, "We told them we wouldn't write a letter, and they said, 'We'll have to break your contract.' Then we got a lawyer and that was the end of it." They continued their screenwriting for MGM and later for other studios with only one interruption, to write their stage adaptation of *The Diary of Anne Frank*, which won the 1956 Pulitzer Prize (they also wrote George Stevens's 1959 film version).

The Hacketts never wanted to see *It's a Wonderful Life* because of their dislike of Capra, whom Goodrich called "that horrid man." They had clashed earlier over the political approach of *Japan*, but on *Wonderful Life* their dispute was over professional ethics. "He couldn't wait to get writing on it himself," Goodrich felt. And Hackett recalled, "We never had much to do with Capra, really. He'd just come out of the war and he was letting us go our way. We told him what we were going to do, and he said, 'That sounds fine.' We were trying to move this story along and work it out, and then somebody told us that [Capra] and Jo Swerling were working on it together, and that sort of took the guts out of it. Jo Swerling was a very close friend of ours, and when we heard that he was doing this we felt rather bad about it. We were getting near the end, and word came that Capra wanted to know how soon we'd be finished. So my wife said, 'We're finished right now.' We quickly wrote out the last scene and we never saw him again after that. He's a very arrogant son of a bitch."

Michael Wilson, thirty-one when he succeeded the Hacketts on *Wonderful Life*, before the war was an aspiring novelist and writer of Hopalong Cassidy film scripts, which, as he told HUAC in 1951, "are now corrupting our children on the television screens of the nation." He had been educated at Berkeley, where he had studied literature and American history, taking a particular interest in the sociology of American minority groups (born in Oklahoma, he himself was part Indian). Wilson served in the South Pacific as a communications analyst with the Marines in World War II, returning to Hollywood in late December 1945 with a fierce commitment to peaceful coexistence.

Capra claimed that before Wilson's HUAC appearance, he had not known anything about Wilson's politics. But, as Wilson told interviewer Joel Gardner in 1975, he joined the Communist Party in 1938 while at Berkeley, and he remained a member until the mid-1950s. After Wilson was subpoenaed by HUAC, the Marine Corps demanded he answer charges that he had attended Communist Party meetings since 1941 and had been a member since 1946 and an officeholder in 1946–1947. As he later would do before HUAC, he declined to answer such charges, telling the Corps, "While I have always remained faithful to my oath as a Marine officer, it is my firm conviction that such interrogatories violate my Constitutional rights and invade areas of private belief which, under our Constitution, are sacred and inviolable to interrogation."

Wilson's draft, or polish, of *Wonderful Life* has not surfaced, either in his papers or in Capra's, making it impossible to document the nature and extent of his contribution to the film, but it evidently served as the foundation for the revised final script of March 18, 1946, a copy of which exists in Wilson's papers and which subsequently was revised further by Swerling and Capra.

"Mike was not a great admirer of Capra," Zelma Wilson said in 1985. "He thought Capra was a very overestimated director. I don't think Mike felt that *It's a Wonderful Life* was a great movie; he thought it was pretty good, but he was a disenchanted Catholic, and he was not wild about pictures with angels. I remember him groaning about having to write dialogue with an angel, but he was a professional writer and he did his job."

Capra was pleased enough with Wilson's work to ask him to write a film adaptation of *The Friendly Persuasion*, Jessamyn West's 1945 book of short stories about a Quaker family in the Civil War era, which Liberty purchased on April 4, 1946. This was more provocative material: a vehicle for the pacifist convictions Wilson had brought back from the war. His adaptation, based primarily on a story called "The Battle of Finney's Ford," dramatized the conflict in a Quaker youth who goes into combat, feeling he has a higher duty to his country, but finds it impossible to kill and decides to become a stretcher bearer instead. In West's story, the Confederate raiders bypass Finney's Ford and the boy is able to go home without having to test his convictions, but Wilson's script, while emphasizing the pressure American society exerts on pacifist citizens, insisted that under the American system a man of principle can choose to remain loyal to his principles.

Capra, whose own wartime experiences led to occasional bursts of pacifist rhetoric after his return from service, planned *The Friendly Persuasion* as his next film for Liberty and RKO after *Wonderful Life*. But in the increasingly reactionary climate of 1946–47, the kind of socially conscious material which had won him his reputation in the thirties was making him increasingly anxious.

Capra said in 1984 that the kind of film he did not want to make after the war was *The Best Years of Our Lives*. "As a matter of fact," he said, "I didn't particularly like the story. Wyler would do a good job with anything, but it was maybe too downbeat for me. We didn't like the same stories at all." Al Keller claimed that Capra himself had wanted to make *Best Years*, but Capra denied it. There can be little doubt, however, that his retrospective statements on *Best Years* were colored by the reaction Wyler's film stirred in Hollywood and elsewhere.

Part of Capra's attitude simply may have been sour grapes, for Wyler's "downbeat" film far outperformed *Wonderful Life* at the box office and received more critical praise and awards. Capra's negativity toward *Best Years* probably also was influenced by historical revisionism and ideological hindsight: the militantly anti-Communist Motion Picture Alliance for the Preservation of American Ideals agreed with HUAC in 1947 that *Best Years* was among the Hollywood films that contained "sizeable doses of communist propaganda." "I wouldn't be allowed to make *The Best Years of Our Lives* in Hollywood today," Wyler commented at the time. "That is directly the result of the activities of the Un-American Activities Committee. They are making decent people afraid to express their opinions. They are creating fear in Hollywood. Fear will result in self-censorship. Self-censorship will paralyze the screen."

The Alliance, which worked closely with HUAC, was formed in 1944 as a backlash against the guild movements of the 1930s and in reaction to the allegations of rampant Communist influence in Hollywood. Its most prominent members included directors Sam Wood, Clarence Brown, and King Vidor; actors Adolphe Menjou, Gary Cooper, John Wayne, and Ward Bond; columnist Hedda Hopper; Walt Disney; and the antilabor leader Roy Brewer. While Capra was still in the Army, seemingly isolated from the fray, HUAC and the Alliance had been building up their dossiers on Hollywood leftists and liberals, preparing for the all-out attack launched by HUAC with its sensational Washington hearings in October 1947.

Despite his later protestations of naiveté, with his history of pro-guild activities, his sporadic public stands for liberal-leftist causes in the late thirties and early forties, and his image as the Hollywood champion of the "common man," Capra could not have avoided recognizing his vulnerability in the immediate postwar period. Moreover, his experience with John

Sanford in 1942, the delay of his own security clearance in World War II, and his brush with G-2 over his visit to the Soviet Embassy had taught him how the government dealt with those whose loyalty was under suspicion.

Several of the "friendly" witnesses at the HUAC hearings attacked films which they said promoted communism by being critical of the capitalistic system, and, by extension, of the American Way. Screenwriter Jack Moffitt, who was also the film critic for *Esquire* at that time, said that "the party line" in Hollywood manifested itself in "picture after picture in which the banker is presented as an unsympathetic man who hates to give a GI a loan" (in *Best Years*, banker Fredric March is criticized by the bank president for giving a GI loan to a veteran with little in the way of assets). Sam Wood told the committee that Communists in Hollywood "have nothing to sell. All they want to do is try to unsell America. . . . [I]f you go back in pictures you will find frequently the banker or the man in public life, the doctor, any one of them would be the heavy in the picture. I think it is particularly bad if that is constantly shown, every night you go to the pictures you see a dishonest banker, or senator, you begin to think that the whole system is wrong. That is the way they work on it."

Capra never was attacked by name in those hearings. In fact, it was remarkable how rarely his name was mentioned, since such criticism could have been construed as referring to his prewar films and since even *It's a Wonderful Life* came under suspicion in that atmosphere. But he could not ignore the warning signs, including one from abroad (sent him by his clipping service) which brought the talk out into the open.

"Frank Capra—Is He Un-American?" asked the British Communist paper the *Daily Worker* on April 5 in the headline over its favorable review of *Wonderful Life*. Calling it "one of those thought-stimulating films which Hollywood produces so rarely these days," John Ross wrote that "the hunt for dollars is again the target of Capra's attack. . . . The un-American Committee of the House of Representatives will probably denounce it as Bolshevik propaganda. This incredible body, now turning its attention to Hollywood, has received an assurance from Eric Johnston, president of the Motion Picture Association of America, that all 'subversives' will be driven out.

"Are they after Capra?"

Moffitt, whom Capra had wanted as one of his original *Why We Fight* writers, went out of his way to exonerate Capra before HUAC: "I do not mean that I think no picture should ever show a villainous banker. In fact, I would right now like to defend one picture that I think has been unjustly accused of communism. That picture is Frank Capra's *It's a Wonderful*

Life. The banker in that picture, played by Lionel Barrymore, was most certainly what we call a 'dog heavy' in the business. He was a snarling, unsympathetic character. But the hero and his father, played by James Stewart and Samuel S. Hinds, were businessmen, in the building and loan business, and they were shown as using money as a benevolent influence. . . . Mr. Capra's picture, though it had a banker as villain, could not properly be called a Communist picture. It showed that the power of money can be used oppressively and it can be used benevolently."

Such issues terrified Capra, whose later comments on *Best Years* may have been an attempt to rationalize away a fleeting desire to make a film about returning war veterans, a desire he may have abandoned when he realized what kind of trouble it might cause him. There is no doubt that Capra was beginning to feel the effect of the Motion Picture Alliance's anticommunism campaign by early 1946. When asked in 1984 what his first brush with the blacklist had been, Capra did not mention Sanford or the delay of his own security clearance in World War II. He said his first such experience occurred while he was casting *Wonderful Life* and was told to clear a certain actor with John Wayne, who was acting on behalf of "the government" and the Alliance. Capra did not identify the actor or say who had told him to call Wayne, but the cast of *Wonderful Life* included Ward Bond, one of the most aggressive Alliance members, who previously had appeared for Capra in *It Happened One Night, Broadway Bill,* and as the Red-hunting "G-man" in *You Can't Take It With You,* and whom Capra wanted so badly for Bert the Cop in *Wonderful Life* that he and John Ford rearranged their shooting schedules so Bond could appear both in that film and Ford's *My Darling Clementine*.

Capra insisted that he was irate at having to ask Wayne "who was O.K.," especially since Wayne ("that awful prick") had stayed in Hollywood "getting rich" and did not serve in the military during World War II, "and now he's presuming to tell people who they can hire." He said he called Wayne and gave him hell, because "I didn't care. I didn't give a shit who was a Communist or who wasn't."

There is no way to prove whether or not Capra was telling the truth about that phone call to John Wayne, but that he may have been perhaps can be inferred from a comment Wayne made about Capra many years later:

"I'd like to take that little dago son of a bitch and tear him into a million pieces and throw him into the ocean and watch him float back to Sicily where he belongs."

A list of actors and actresses Capra considered for *Wonderful Life* included Anne Revere, the Oscar winner in 1946 for best supporting actress in *National Velvet.* Revere was blacklisted in 1951 after taking the Fifth Amendment when HUAC accused her of having been a member of the Communist Party in 1944 and 1945; she later said she "had never held a Party card which they alleged to be mine," and that she would not name names "in order to protect my own career by destroying others'." She headed the list of five women considered for the role of Jimmy Stewart's mother in *Wonderful Life,* but the part went to Beulah Bondi, who was not on the original list but had played his mother in *Mr. Smith* and in two earlier films, *Of Human Hearts* and *Vivacious Lady.*

There is no evidence to indicate whether Capra was aware when he made *Wonderful Life* that there already were several references to him in the HUAC files, the earliest dating back to 1932 (the allegation about the Communist Party election petition) and 1938 (his support of the "Communist inspired" strike at the *Hollywood Citizen-News*); or that Army Intelligence had been maintaining a file on him since October 14, 1938, and that G-2 on June 7, 1940, noted that Capra was "listed as active in various projects advanced by 6.43a [code for another subject in its files]"; or that Capra's name had appeared (for what reason it is unknown) in a February 18, 1943, FBI report on "Communism in the Motion Picture Industry" and in a May 18, 1945, FBI report on another person.

Capra wrote in his book that 1947 was the year which "marked the beginning of an innuendo campaign [against him] that was to climax in a Kafkaesque nightmare of humiliation." But he also remembered 1946 as "the year the bottom fell out of the movie business" (it was for *him*, but not for Hollywood as a whole, since that year set a box-office record); his first inkling of the "innuendo campaign" may have come in 1946, perhaps when he was told to call John Wayne. And he may have sensed that more questions were being raised in December 1946, the month in which *Wonderful Life* was released. It was in that month that, according to Army Intelligence, "an informant of known reliability stated that Frank CAPRA of 215 N. Barrington Avenue, West Los Angeles 24, California, was carried as a contributor to the Joint Anti-Fascist Refugee Committee [an organization formed to aid refugees from the Spanish Civil War, with an active Hollywood section that came under attack from HUAC and the Hollywood Right]. The Los Angeles FBI has conducted no investigation on SUBJECT; however, in the course of other investigations persons of known reliability, who had known SUBJECT well, had stated that SUBJECT is a loyal American."

Even if he had not known until 1946 that his own politics were being scrutinized for dangerous signs of leftism, it is reasonable to assume that in such a volatile political climate Capra's acute sensitivity toward the loyalty issue would have influenced the political viewpoint of his first postwar film and made him try to shy away from anything that might be construed as politically risky. While promoting *Wonderful Life* in Beaumont, Texas, on March 4, 1947, Capra was asked about the growing allegations of rampant communism in Hollywood, and he replied, "Yes, there is communism in Hollywood, just like there is in Beaumont and Podunk, but ours is overemphasized because it's louder. Hollywood folks are as good Americans as those of any other town."

When asked in 1984 if he thought *Wonderful Life* contained autobiographical elements, Capra replied, "That's not such a profound statement, for Christ's sake, that it looks like the guy that made it. What the hell—who should it look like?"

Yet at the time he discovered the story, hardly anyone else would have recognized "The Greatest Gift" as a potential vehicle for Capra's screen "autobiography," for it was not the story of a wealthy and celebrated Hollywood movie director and recipient of the Distinguished Service Medal but the story of a common man named George Pratt who contemplates suicide because he is "sick of everything! . . . I'm stuck in this mudhole for life, doing the same dull work day after day. Other men are leading exciting lives, but I—well, I'm just a small-town bank clerk that even the Army doesn't want. I never did anything really useful or interesting, and it looks as if I never will."

The extent of Capra's identification with the character would have astonished those who knew him only through his successful public image and did not know that as he prepared his postwar comeback film he felt "a loneliness that was laced by the fear of failure." In lines he wrote for the film but did not use, Capra had George say after jumping into the river, "I was a 4-F. In my case it didn't stand for Four Freedoms, it meant Four Failures. Failure as a husband, father, business[man]—failure as a human being." The fundamental pessimism that counterbalanced the superficial optimism of his prewar films had been brought dangerously to the surface during the war years, triggering Capra's awareness of the fragility of his art and the hollowness of his personal beliefs. Like his surrogate on screen, George Bailey, he was undergoing a secret metaphysical crisis, wondering whether he "had put too much faith in the human race."

Capra and George Bailey share some profound biographical characteristics—their equation of lack of money with desperation and shame, their conflict between a yearning for financial comfort and a desire to serve the community, their thwarted technological ambitions, the fateful roles of their fathers' deaths in deciding their careers, the calming and conservative influences of their wives, their frustration over having to stay in their hometowns during World War II, their terror of anonymity, and, underlying everything, their doubting of their own worth and their temptation to suicide. As critic Stephen Handzo wrote, "One can find the wild oscillations of euphoria and despair of Capra's films in his own life. . . . Violent shifts of mood give his films the sense of life being lived." Never was that truth more evident than in *Wonderful Life*.

Not only did Capra discover in the story a host of autobiographical elements, he structured the film around plot elements that had worked for him in the past, for *Wonderful Life* caught him in a paradoxical mood: it was both a desperate attempt to recapture his old commercial and artistic standing in Hollywood and a resigned valedictory to filmmaking, a summing-up of his life and work. Capra was still only middle-aged—he turned forty-nine while he was shooting the film, and he was marking the twentieth anniversary of *The Strong Man*, his first feature as a director—but *Wonderful Life* shows that he sensed he was reaching the end of his creative powers and that the time had come to make a definitive artistic statement. And so it became, for after *Wonderful Life*, the rest of his film career was essentially redundant, his work that of a man opting out of active engagement with life and settling for a dispiriting on-the-job retirement.

Riskin's unwillingness to work with Capra after the war was a crucial turning point for the director. In his later attempt to undercut Riskin's importance to his career, Capra misleadingly cited *Wonderful Life* and *Mr. Smith* as examples of masterpieces he made without any help from Riskin. This, of course, ignores both films' ritualistic adherence to the Capra-Riskin formula and *Wonderful Life*'s striking echoes of such landmarks in their partnership as *American Madness* (the 1932 run on the Building and Loan, George's role as financial savior of the community), *Mr. Deeds* (the fickle nature of the people, the hero's nearly fatal selfishness and despondency, the miraculous appearance of a little man to show him the way), and *Meet John Doe* (suicide and Christmas).

Wonderful Life's basic plot and what was called during production the "unborn sequence"—the sequence of the angel showing George what his hometown would be like if his suicidal wish were answered and he had never been born—were taken from the original story. But Stern barely had sketched in George's past life, and the flashbacks which occupy most of the screen time became the most familiarly "Capraesque"—or "Riskinesque"—parts of the film, as the marginal George Pratt of the original story, "just a small-town bank clerk," evolved into George Bailey, the quasi-political community leader of Bedford Falls who heads the Bailey Building and Loan Association and who, despite his own limitations as a businessman, represents the only visible opposition to the economic tyranny of Lionel Barrymore's banker Potter. But there also were crucial differences between *Wonderful Life* and the Capra-Riskin films, ones which, in hindsight, point to the inevitability of the director's creative collapse.

When he explained in a 1968 public appearance why he did not want to film the first script RKO had commissioned for *The Greatest Gift*—the one by Dalton Trumbo—Capra gave a simple reason that spoke volumes: Trumbo's script "was about politics." Already by 1946, politics for Capra had become a dirty word.

Trumbo's George is a politician who rises from an idealistic state assemblyman to a cynical congressman contemptuous of the people he represents. He goes to the bridge to attempt suicide after losing a race for governor. The angel shows him Bedford Falls as it would have been not if he had never been born but as it would have been if he had gone into business instead of politics. Bedford Falls in Trumbo's nightmare sequence has changed from an idealized small town to a foul, polluted, overindustrialized modern city. Trumbo's script, though heavy-handed, is more politically sophisticated than Capra's film: there is no Potter to serve as George's nemesis, for George, in effect, serves as his own Potter—a ruthless modern businessman who carelessly spoils the town for his own profit. He bears little similarity to Barrymore's Scrooge-like Potter, a figure carefully distanced by Capra from the contemporary scene (he makes his first appearance riding in a horse-drawn barouche). Despite the charge that the portrayal of Potter made the film communistic, Potter's principal motivation in the film is not so much greed as an obsessive personal vendetta of this "warped, frustrated old man" against the Bailey family, the only people in town resourceful enough to keep him from taking complete control of the "discontented, lazy rabble." By moving from Edward Arnold's utterly credible Fascist in *Meet John Doe* to this melodramatic villain, a character with no equivalent in Stern's original story, Capra showed that he actually had *regressed* in political sophistication during the war.

The harsh, explicit social criticisms of Trumbo's script cut too close to the bone for Capra. The film shows the influence of Trumbo only in some aspects of George's darker side, particularly in the way it draws an analogy between George and Potter ("What are you but a warped, frustrated *young man?*" sneers Potter, who says that George "hates the Building and Loan almost as much as I do"), as well as in keeping some of Trumbo's whimsy with the angel, including dialogue for the scene in Nick's Bar in the unborn sequence and the penultimate line about an angel getting his wings every time a bell rings. Capra's film retreats from the Marxist implications of Trumbo's view of capitalism, carefully balancing its unfavorable (and unbelievable) portrait of an evil businessman (Potter) with a favorable portrait of a good businessman (George), as if to anticipate the defense of the film Moffitt would make to HUAC.

It's a Wonderful Life paints the Bailey-Potter conflict in the Manichaean rhetorical terms of the Populist Party in the 1890s, showing the extent to which Capra had become locked into an anachronistic, and by then reactionary, thought pattern. "Populist thought," Richard Hofstadter wrote in *The Age of Reform*, "showed an unusually strong tendency to account for relatively impersonal events in highly personal terms. . . . A villain was needed, marked with the unmistakable stigma of the villains of melodrama, and the more remote he was from the familiar scene, the more plausibly his villainies could be exaggerated." This weakness pervaded the film and helped account for the reservations of contemporary critics and audiences. In his review in *The Nation*, James Agee, who called it "one of the most efficient sentimental pieces since *A Christmas Carol*" (one of Capra's favorite books, and a pervasive influence on the film), nevertheless found it peculiar that "in representing a twentieth-century American town Frank Capra uses so little of the twentieth and idealizes so much that seems essentially nineteenth-century, or prior anyhow to the First World War, which really ended that century. Many small towns are, to be sure, 'backward' in that generally more likable way, but I have never seen one so Norman Rockwellish as all that."

And as critic James Wolcott observed in 1986, it is no accident that many of Capra's latter-day admirers tended to prefer his retreat from reality in the essentially reactionary *It's a Wonderful Life* to the passionately engaged social criticism of his 1930s classics *Mr. Deeds Goes to Town* and *Mr. Smith Goes to Washington:* "*It's a Wonderful Life* is the perfect film for the Reagan era, celebrating the old-fashioned values of home and hearth that everyone knows deep down have eroded. Its false affirmations . . . spring not from joy but from anxiety. . . . Like Reagan, Capra is a blue-sky optimist who filters out bad news. . . . But peel away the picturesque snows of Bedford Falls and you have a town as petty and stultifying as any that drove Sinclair Lewis to apoplexy."

Capra's postwar regression was manifested in his depiction of sexual politics in Bedford Falls. The fact that Donna Reed's Mary Bailey is a housewife and mother, unlike the Jean Arthur and Barbara Stanwyck single professional women in the Capra-Riskin films, reflects the prevailing mood of postwar America, in which women were being pressured to give their jobs back to returning servicemen and stay home raising children. Yet in *Wonderful Life*, Mary's yearning for marriage, home, and family is portrayed with considerable ambivalence by Capra, who emphasizes George's resistance and his agonized capitulation (in the deeply moving telephone scene with Mary, which Capra considered "one of the best scenes I've ever put on the screen"). George blames his wife and children for their role in keeping him in Bedford Falls and curbing his ambitions to be an architect and city planner; what finally drives him to attempt suicide is Mary's turning on him after his frightening outburst in the living room in which he smashes his models of a bridge and skyscraper. Capra's reaffirmation of family and small-town values at the end is accomplished, as critic Robin Wood put it, "with full acknowledgment of the suppressions on which it depends and consequently, of its precariousness."

Another limitation of *Wonderful Life*, built into the original story, was one of the elements which so excited Capra in the first place: its recourse to the supernatural. Clarence Oddbody, Angel Second Class (Henry Travers), is sent by heaven in answer to the prayers of George's family and friends in Bedford Falls and convinces him not to commit suicide by giving him "a chance to see what the world would be like without you. . . . Strange, isn't it? Each man's life touches so many other lives." This might have seemed an innocuous enough plot device except for Capra's decision to elevate George from "just a small-town bank clerk" to an important figure in the community, which made Clarence's intervention seem like a trivialization of the issues and too blatant a manipulation by the director.

Capra foreshadowed the supernatural elements of *Wonderful Life* in the potter's field sequence of his silent-film treatment "Heart Beats" (possibly the source of his lost 1920 feature *The Pulse of Life*), in which his selfish hero is shocked into recognizing his own deadness of spirit and rededicating his life to the service of mankind. The unborn sequence in *Wonderful Life* serves a similar function, but more ambiguously, for by 1946 part of Capra was trying to help his protagonist avoid responsibility, not face it. Unlike Trumbo, Capra follows Stern's lead by placing George in a world for which he had no responsibility at all because he had never been born, a world which has gone to hell simply because he wasn't there to stop it. Capra's unborn sequence is a powerful vision of despair—though labeled a "fantasy," the sequence was shot in the fashionable *film noir* style, and it much more closely resembles the reality of 1946 than the rest of the film—but politically it is Capra's ultimate cop-out, his way of washing his hands of the modern world and the clearest expression of how much his social optimism depended on Riskin (whose absence is felt in the unborn sequence just as strongly as George Bailey's) and how utterly distrustful Capra had become of the American public.

William S. Pechter noted that the supernatural resolution of *Wonderful Life* exposes the "fatal weakness" of Capra's work, his tendency to resolve impossible social dilemmas with "strangely perfunctory" happy endings that are imposed "*de force majeure.* . . . Yet, for those who can accept the realities of George Bailey's situation . . . and do not believe in angels . . . the film ends, in effect, with the hero's suicide. . . . Capra's desperation is his final honesty. It ruthlessly exposes his own affirmation as pretense. . . .

"Perhaps, having made *It's a Wonderful Life,* there was nothing more Capra had to say. His only fruitful alternative, having achieved a kind of perfection within his own terms, had to be to question the very nature of those terms themselves. Without a realization that the dilemma existed inherently in the terms in which he articulated it, he could, in effect, go no further. It remains only to note that he went no further."

Dead end though it was for Capra, *Wonderful Life* was a new beginning for Jimmy Stewart.

At their reunion on October 10, 1945, in the presence of Sam Briskin and Stewart's agent, Lew Wasserman of MCA (then a talent agency, before it bought Universal), Stewart impressed Capra as suffering from his own newfound insecurities. Shaken by his war experiences, Stewart in fact was thinking of quitting Hollywood and going back to Pennsylvania to run his father's hardware store. "As I tell story it evaporates into thin air," Capra wrote in his notes on that meeting. "Tell Stewart to forget it. Wasserman dying. Jimmy doesn't want to hear story."

But Stewart recalled, "Frank really saved my career. I don't know whether I would have made it after the war if it hadn't been for Frank. It wasn't just a case of picking up where you'd left off, because it's not that kind of a business. It was over four and a half years that I'd been completely away from anything that had to do with the movies. Then one day Frank Capra called me and he said he had an idea for a movie.

"He said, 'Now, you're in a small town and things aren't going very well. You begin to wish you'd never been born. And you decide to commit suicide by jumping off a bridge into the river, but an angel named Clarence comes down from heaven, and, uh, Clarence hasn't won his wings yet. He comes down to save you when you jump into the river, but Clarence can't swim, so you save *him*.'

"Then Frank stopped and he said, 'This story doesn't tell very well, does it?'

"I just said, 'Frank, if you want to do a movie about me committing suicide, with an angel with no wings named Clarence, I'm your boy.' "

Jean Arthur was Capra's first choice for Mary, even though she (like Stewart) was considerably older than the script indicated. But since making her final break from Harry Cohn in 1944, Arthur had returned to the stage. She was rehearsing the role of Billie Dawn in Garson Kanin's *Born Yesterday* (which she would leave during an out-of-town tryout in Boston) when Capra pursued her to New York to offer her the part. On November 16 she gave him her answer.

"I didn't think *It's a Wonderful Life* was such a great picture," Arthur explained in 1987. "I am awfully angry when he always says that's his favorite picture. I think Stewart did a great job, it was a great part, but I wouldn't have liked to have been that girl, I didn't think she had anything to do. It was colorless. You didn't have a chance to be anything."

Capra's thoughts went to his old flame, Ginger Rogers, but she also turned down the film because "the woman's role was such a bland character." He thought of Olivia de Havilland (again), Martha Scott, and Ann Dvorak. Then he saw Donna Reed in an MGM film. It probably was *They Were Expendable*, John Ford's saga of the early days of the war in the Philippines, released that December; Reed gave a strong and luminous performance as a Navy nurse. She was only twenty-four when she made *Wonderful Life*, but her fresh Iowa beauty made her an ideal match with Stewart.

The director surrounded Stewart and Reed with most of his favorite character actors, giving the film the feeling of a nostalgic reunion. "He had everybody in town in it," Stewart marveled, "all these great people— Lionel Barrymore and Tommy Mitchell and Ward Bond and Frank Faylen and Samuel Hinds and H. B. Warner and Henry Travers. It was like getting briefed again. Frank was in the middle of it, and he was the most excited of anybody."

Capra sensed that Stewart still had doubts about whether acting was an important enough profession for someone who had experienced what he had in the war, so the director asked the old pro, Lionel Barrymore, to give the star a pep talk. As Stewart remembered it, Barrymore told him, "Jimmy, don't ever forget that acting is the greatest profession ever invented. When you act you move millions of people, shape their lives, give them a sense of exaltation. No other profession has that power."

"I was terribly influenced by what he said," Stewart admitted.

Capra added a detail Stewart left out: when Stewart told Barrymore he didn't think acting was "decent," Barrymore asked him "if he thought it was more 'decent' to drop bombs on people than to bring rays of sunshine into their lives with his acting talent. Stewart told me that Lionel's barbs had knocked him flat on his ass, and that now acting was going to be his life's work."

"Everything seemed to click," Stewart remembered. "After a week or so of working I just knew that it was gonna be all right, because I fitted in, and I hadn't forgotten the things I'd learned before the war. It still meant a lot to me. I could have sworn that I'd never been away.

"It was Frank who really got me some confidence back in the business, and in acting. I knew from the way Frank took it that I could pick up where I had left off, that I still had what he liked from *Mr. Smith*, that I hadn't lost it. *This* was what had kept me awake nights."

Capra and Wyler both began shooting their first postwar films on April 15, 1946. Before turning the cameras on *The Best Years of Our Lives*, Wyler sent a telegram to Capra: "LAST ONE IN IS A ROTTEN EGG. WILLY." Capra wired back: "MY FIRST DAY WAS EASY BUT DO YOU KNOW THEY'RE USING SOUND TODAY? FRANK."

Though Capra did his best to conceal his anxiety from Stewart, the actor knew what a gamble Capra was taking, and he told the press, "There are two million dollars invested in this picture. I just can't let Frank Capra down." Actually, the film was budgeted at $2,362,427, and its production cost was about $3.18 million ($156,000 of which was Capra's salary). Including distribution charges to RKO, the total cost came to about $3.78 million, making it the most expensive film of Capra's career. "Frank was making a big picture and I had to sign all the checks," George Stevens recalled. "I said, 'Jesus Christ, I wish this Capra would stop spending so much money, I've got a sore arm.' "

"If movie producers look more worried than usual these days, it may be because Frank Capra is again at work," the AP's Bob Thomas wrote after visiting the set. "They might fear other directors will adopt his habits and cause filmmaking costs to soar."

On *Wonderful Life* Capra shot what was, for him, a relatively modest

350,000 feet of film, but he was four days over his eighty-four-day schedule when he wrapped principal photography on July 27. There were twenty-eight days of snow scenes, many filmed in the 90-degree-plus San Fernando Valley heat of June and July on the refurbished small-town set at the RKO ranch in Encino. "These big trucks would come in with the [artificial] snow," recalled Joseph Biroc, one of the film's three cinematographers, "and five minutes later it would be gone and they'd have to do it all over again." Since most of the film takes place at night, the company also had to work fifty-five slow and tiring nights, from dusk to dawn.

Hollywood labor unions and guilds, like American organized labor in general, had become much more militant since Capra had made his last feature, and despite his own prewar activism on behalf of the Screen Directors Guild, he did not like what had been happening while he had been making films for the Army. An eight-month strike in the studios called by the Conference of Studio Unions (CSU), which the rival IATSE and its Hollywood head Roy Brewer denounced as Communist-inspired, prompted violence against picketers by the studio police and fire departments outside Warner Bros. on October 5, 1945. Later that month, Dalton Trumbo, one of the most vocal supporters of the CSU, traded angry charges with Brewer, linking him with the imprisoned racketeers who formerly had run IATSE, Willie Bioff and George Browne. Brewer replied that his goal was to drive foreign, un-American (i.e., Communist) influences out of Hollywood. Capra, in the uncut manuscript of his book, also blamed the industry's postwar labor turmoil on Communist influences, claiming that the Hollywood Left had taken over the industry during World War II.

Though he continued to be active in the Directors Guild in the postwar years, Capra did not rejoin the board until May 1947, and he was less eager to be seen in the forefront on labor issues. Now that he was trying to make a go of it as an independent producer, Capra found the negotiations with union officials an unwelcome source of tension and a distraction from his creative tasks. Hollywood leftists served as a convenient scapegoat for labor slowdowns and cost increases that made it difficult for him to succeed after the war, but the run-ins he remembered most vividly on *Wonderful Life* were with the more conservative elements of Hollywood labor.

One of Capra's economy measures was to pay an additional five dollars to each extra who would bring his own car and park it on the set. "The Teamsters one night said no," recalled Chet Sticht, who had turned over his secretarial duties to Miriam Geiger and joined the SDG as the film's second assistant director. "They wanted their own people to drive the cars to the set, and Frank said, 'Thank you very much, we'll close down the picture.' One hour later they said, 'Sorry, we made a mistake.' " On another occasion, while Capra was preparing to film an elaborate night scene, the set went dark as IATSE called a sit-down strike. That dispute also was settled quickly, but it helped solidify Capra's disenchantment with postwar Hollywood.

On *Wonderful Life*, Capra also had the unpleasant experience of replacing his cinematographer, for the first (but not the last) time in his career. Having difficulty adapting to another cameraman after spending so much of his career working with the genial Joe Walker, Capra found the veteran Victor Milner (an Oscar winner for Cecil B. DeMille's 1934 *Cleopatra*) slow and pretentious; Sticht said Milner was so autocratic that "the electricians were about to drop a light on his head."

"Vic was a perfectionist," said Biroc, who started on the film as Milner's camera operator. "[Capra] was a perfectionist about the people and the dialogue, but not about lighting. He couldn't care less if it was a few feet this way or that way. Vic didn't like a lot of stuff that Capra was doing." On the third day, Milner made the mistake of asking Capra to leave the set until he was ready to shoot. Capra indignantly refused. Milner left the set, and the tension continued.

Capra turned to the one cameraman he knew he could trust. But he was afraid to make the request directly, so he asked Lu to call Joe Walker. Still under contract to Columbia, Walker "approached Harry Cohn cautiously, knowing he'd never forgiven Capra for leaving." He told Cohn, "This would mean a lot to me—let me do it for old times' sake," and Cohn replied glumly, "Guess there's nothing in it for me. No point in trying to make a deal; he won't come back." Cohn agreed to let Walker go, but only until he was needed back at Columbia by one of the female stars who specified in their contracts that Walker had to shoot their films.

"The first thing we did was to reshoot all of the big street scenes," recalled Walker, who rejoined Capra on May 20 during the shooting of the run on the bank, Liberty announcing that Milner's "illness" had caused his departure. Walker suggested to Capra that they train Biroc as his eventual replacement. After five weeks, Walker returned to Columbia to shoot *The Guilt of Janet Ames* for Rosalind Russell, and Biroc finished *Wonderful Life*. The screen credit went to Walker and Biroc, with Milner uncredited. Although working with three cameramen had been a trial for Capra, "it worked out very well," Walker felt, because the scenes each man shot were so different in feeling that "Biroc's stuff didn't have to match mine or Milner's."

But Capra was the one who had to make it all tie together, and despite his financial worries and cost overruns he did not cut corners.

"We had a night sequence with fireflies suspended on wires from fishpoles," Biroc recalled. "The film was processed the next morning, and when Capra saw it at three or four in the afternoon, he said, 'It's lousy.' So we started over. Capra and Bob Aldrich were the only directors I worked with who could do that, because they were *producer*-directors. Capra was really sharp. He knew what he wanted.

"And it's a funny thing—when that picture came out it was regarded as just a mediocre picture—and now it's a classic."

Recognizing that it meant the end of something more than just a movie, Capra on June 21 and 22 staged the most elegiac of all his endings, with Joe Walker (in his last work with the director) panning his camera lovingly across the Baileys' crowded living room, where, in Donna Reed's words, "as far as you could see the screen was filled with these wonderful character actors" singing "Auld Lang Syne" and "Hark, the Herald Angels Sing," and Ward Bond squeezing out the music on his accordion.

Although in later years on television *Wonderful Life* became regarded as the quintessential Christmas movie, it originally was to have been released nationwide on January 30, 1947, in the slack postholiday period. But RKO rushed it out for a December 21 opening at the Globe Theater in New York City (its Oscar-qualifying run in Los Angeles began on Christmas Eve) because Technicolor couldn't make enough prints of *Sinbad the Sailor*, which the studio had planned as its holiday film; and the general release of *Wonderful Life* was advanced to January 7. Despite belated promotional rescue efforts by Stewart and Capra, who went to New York together in mid-January and to Texas at the end of February, the box-office returns were disappointing; audiences embracing the astringent realism of *The Best Years of Our Lives* considered Capra's sentimental brand of filmmaking old-fashioned.

Bosley Crowther of *The New York Times* called the film a "quaint and engaging modern parable" but "a little too sticky for our taste." There were more favorable notices—*The Hollywood Reporter* declaring it "the greatest of all Capra pictures"; *Time* calling it "a pretty wonderful movie"; *Newsweek*, in a cover story, describing the film as "sentimental, but so expertly written, directed and acted that you want to believe it"—but the reviews that the defensive Capra took to heart were the ones from Crowther and those few critics who derided it, such as *The New Yorker*'s John McCarten, who complained that "Mr. Capra has seen to it that practically all the actors involved behave as cutely as pixies" and that the treatment of the story was "so mincing as to border on baby talk."

Wonderful Life received five Oscar nominations—including best picture, actor, and director—but no awards. The Academy gave the Oscars for best picture, director, and actor (Fredric March) to *The Best Years of Our Lives*, and Capra found little consolation in his Golden Globe for best director from the Hollywood Foreign Press Association, for Wyler also won the more prestigious New York critics' award.

With domestic rentals of about $3.3 million, *Wonderful Life* ranked twenty-seventh on *Variety*'s list of 1946–1947 releases. That was $480,000 less than the cost of making and distributing the film. To Capra's chagrin, *The Best Years of Our Lives* was an enormous commercial as well as critical success, with rentals of $11.3 million, a figure surpassed only by *Gone With the Wind* up to that time.

Wonderful Life barely was in release when Capra, in mid-January, 1947, first started talking about selling Liberty.

The immediate problem was cash flow. Each of the four partners was receiving $3,000 a week, paid from their own pockets, of which about 85 percent went to the IRS. With the evident failure of *Wonderful Life* and the inactivity of Stevens and Wyler, something had to be done quickly to minimize their losses. As of January 27, the partners agreed to cut their weekly paychecks to $1,000, with the remainder deferred until the fall. At the same time, to strengthen their corporate bargaining position, each of the three directors agreed to extend his contract by delivering a total of five, instead of three, pictures to Liberty. They also entered into discussions with veteran MGM director Victor Fleming (*The Wizard of Oz, Gone With the Wind*) to enter the partnership.

But the real problem was that Capra was fed up with independence. "It was the most gentlemanly way of going broke, and the fastest way, anybody ever thought of," he told Richard Schickel in 1971. "We didn't have enough capital, so we decided to sell Liberty Films, which was a very, very hopeless thing to do. My partners did not want to sell. But I got cold feet, and I'm the one who insisted that we sell. And I think that probably affected my picture-making forever afterward.

"Once you get cold feet, once your daring stops, then you worry a little bit. And when you worry about a decision, then you're not going to make the proper films anymore. That is, *I* couldn't. And I think that was the start. When I sold out for money, which is something that I had always been against anyhow, and security, I think my conscience told me that I had had it. Really. There wasn't any more of that paladin out there in front fighting for lost causes. . . .

"We shouldn't have sold it. We could have made it go. And it was a thing in my life I've regretted ever since."

Capra, however, did not have a hard time convincing Briskin and Wyler. Selling the company to a major studio seemed much more sensible to Briskin than the risks of running an independent operation. Wyler admitted, "I have no talent for business. I don't like it. What I want to do is direct pictures. But now I have to fuss with lawyers, make decisions about distribution, be a salesman and so on. I just don't know how."

George Stevens was the one who was hard to sell. "Dad believed so strongly in independence," George Stevens, Jr., recalled. "He thought it made good work possible. He wanted to stick it out until they could make Liberty work. Dad was living relatively modestly and was preparing to make a go of it. But Willy and Frank were in very different circumstances financially; they needed the income, and they couldn't wait another year or two for revenue to come in on their films."

The deal was negotiated for Liberty by Jules Stein, the head of MCA. Stein made approaches to MGM, Paramount, RKO, and Universal about hiring Capra, Wyler, and Stevens as contract directors and Briskin as a production executive in exchange for the purchase of their contracts, stock, and properties. Liberty demanded to be paid in the stock of the purchasing company, which would be taxed at the 25 percent capital gains rate rather than as personal income. MGM and Paramount were the most serious contenders, but the deal was slowed by Liberty's financial demands, by tax complications, and by Stevens's intransigence. Paramount had the inside track. Stein, it was reported in 1946, was its second-largest stockholder, and the Justice Department later alleged that after he acquired his stock, MCA "began to feed its clients to Paramount. This was done partly in order to enhance the value of the stock. . . . Paramount was made a captive market by MCA for its talent." It was one of the means by which MCA (dubbed "The Octopus" by a federal court judge) was rapidly taking control of the splintering Hollywood system; Stein's fee for the Liberty deal was taken in Paramount stock.

"The run of the indies to cover is imminent," *Variety* reported on February 12, describing Liberty as the "bellwether on the trail back" to the studios. Capra was only one of many independents who had been panicked by the sudden box-office drop in January 1947 following record ticket sales in 1946 (box-office receipts in 1947 fell 23 percent). Because of the economic squeeze, which caused layoffs all over Hollywood, independents found it much harder to obtain production financing from banks and loan-outs of stars from studios. "Against this bevy of fears and troubles," *Variety* observed, "is the security offered by a long-term contract with a studio—and the fact that a big and experienced organization will take over the worries of casting, space, advertising-publicity, selling, and the myriad of other things that enter in when a director, actor, or writer is his own boss."

Before selling out to Paramount, Liberty came close to consummating the deal with MGM.

Once again Capra put aside his more offbeat and ambitious projects, in this case *The Friendly Persuasion* and *No Other Man*, and took the safer route by filming a presold Broadway hit. On his trip to New York in January, Capra met with Howard Lindsay and Russel Crouse to discuss the purchase of the film rights to *State of the Union*, their Pulitzer Prize—winning play about a Republican businessman whose messy personal life echoes his political compromises in running for President of the United States. Capra had seen it on three successive nights in November 1945, shortly after its opening at New York's Hudson Theater, and had made preliminary inquiries about the rights then, but in the meantime the playwrights' agent and stage producer, Leland Hayward, had sold the rights to Paramount. Wyler, Stevens, and McCarey also were interested in directing the film, but Capra had the inside track with Lindsay and Crouse because of his financial success with the screen version of their stage production *Arsenic and Old Lace*.

RKO was the first studio to which Capra proposed *State of the Union*, but, especially after *Wonderful Life*, RKO was nervous over the projected budget of the political drama—$2.8 million. MGM became involved because Capra wanted to cast his romantic team from *It Happened One Night*, MGM's Clark Gable and Paramount's Claudette Colbert, as the ambivalent candidate Grant Matthews and his acerbic wife, Mary. But MGM refused to loan Gable. Capra then suggested that Metro buy Liberty and let him make *State of the Union* as his first film there, with either Gable or Spencer Tracy.

Balking at buying Capra and his company intact, MGM agreed on March 10 to a one-picture deal with Liberty and Paramount for *State of the Union*, starring Tracy and Colbert. MGM took a distribution fee, payment for production facilities, and $175,000 for Tracy's services, but it waived a share of the profits; Paramount sold Liberty the film rights and Colbert's services (her price was $200,000) in exchange for 18½ percent of the distributor's gross. For Capra the deal with MGM marked a triumph of sorts: after his two failed attempts to make a feature there, he finally had cracked the bastion of Hollywood's greatest studio.

But he knew only too well what price he was paying for giving up his liberty.

A tentative deal for selling Liberty was struck with Paramount on April 14. To settle Liberty's obligations to RKO, Paramount agreed to loan two stars to RKO and Liberty agreed to loan Stevens for a nostalgia piece set in his hometown of San Francisco, *I Remember Mama*. Liberty was granted 25 percent of the gross from the Stevens film, which it turned over to Paramount as part of its assets, along with its interests in *Wonderful Life* and *State of the Union*.

Stevens did not want any other part in the deal with Paramount, and he announced on April 16 that after making *I Remember Mama* he would consider a partnership with Leo McCarey. "It is with genuine regret that I have concluded to withdraw from a most pleasant association with Frank Capra and William Wyler," he told the trade press, "and I only arrived at this decision because of my sincere desire to retain my independent production status."

But McCarey, too, was having second thoughts about independence (he would sell his Rainbow Productions to Paramount a few months later), and Stevens soon returned to Liberty, still fighting the deal with Paramount. But he was met with a barrage of pressure from Paramount president Barney Balaban, Paramount board member Edwin L. Weisl, and Sam Briskin. Briskin "urged us to accept Paramount's offer," Wyler recalled. ". . . They assured us we would have the same independence as before, which didn't turn out to be true. We still had to have their approval of subject and budget. I guess there is no such thing as complete independence unless you put up your own money."

On April 29, George Stevens capitulated. The deal was closed on May 16, two days before Capra's fiftieth birthday.

Liberty, whose assets on March 31 were valued at $4,177,586, exchanged those assets for 135,000 shares of Paramount stock, valued at $23 each on the day of transfer, October 27, or $3,105,000; 4,000 of the Paramount shares (or $92,000) were surrendered by Liberty in partial payment for performance bonds (totaling $375,000 for each partner) to ensure that they would fulfill their contracts to Paramount. Frank and Lu Capra owned 32 percent of Liberty's stock at the time of the sale, Wyler and Stevens 25 percent each, and Briskin and his family 18 percent. So the Capras' pretax share from the sale amounted to $993,600, or, after the deduction for his performance bond, $964,160.

As Paramount contract directors, Capra agreed to make three films, Stevens four, and Wyler five, reflecting their degrees of prior activity for Liberty, which technically still existed as a Paramount subsidiary. Briskin became an assistant to the studio's production chief, Henry Ginsberg, with responsibility for supervising the films of his former partners. Each of the directors was to receive a $3,000-a-week salary up to a total of $156,000 per picture. They had no profit participation in their films.*

In an article entitled "The Price of Liberty," *Time* lamented, "Of all the independent movie companies in the Hollywood pool, Liberty Films, Inc., seemed most likely to become a big fish. . . . To Hollywood's independent companies, it was a shock to hear that one of the best had given up. The signatures with which the deal was settled seemed like the handwriting on the wall to the war-born independents."

Time's caption under the photo of the four smiling Liberty partners— taken at the press conference to announce their partnership only eighteen months earlier—was a fitting epitaph for Capra's dream of independence: *"Life was not wonderful."*

---

* It's a Wonderful Life *was lost forever to Capra in that transaction. Not only was the negative allowed to deteriorate (it later was restored by the American Film Institute), but the copyright was allowed to lapse, leaving the film in the public domain. Frustrated at not being able to control or profit from his suddenly popular film, Capra became involved in the early 1980s with the Hal Roach Studios in its controversial colorization of* Wonderful Life, *but after agreeing to pay half the cost in exchange for profit participation (and also giving preliminary approval to colorizing* Lady for a Day *and* Meet John Doe), *he changed his mind and launched a moral crusade against the process, declaring: "When you think of it in terms of money, sure, it's great, but when you think of it in terms of integrity, it stinks." Though Capra's flip-flop on the issue was reported by* The New York Times, *his subsequent public outcries left most people with the impression that his principles were as unbending as those of John Huston, who said after* The Maltese Falcon *was colorized, "It almost seems as though a conspiracy exists to degrade the national character, to drag it down to the lowest common denominator, to pass off falsehood as truth."*

18. "I have no cause"

"*A*nd so, here and now, I withdraw as a candidate for any office—not because I'm honest, but because I'm dishonest. I want to apologize to all the good, sincere people who put their faith in me. . . ."

Those words, which were written for the film, were spoken by Spencer Tracy at the end of *State of the Union*, Capra's elegy for his abandonment of socially conscious filmmaking. *State of the Union* was a pale reflection of Capra's greatness as a filmmaker, sapped as it was by the same fears and lack of moral commitment which fatally compromise his protagonist, the Republican presidential candidate Grant Matthews. "Unlike any of Capra's other films, *State of the Union* seems anxious to retreat into its subplot, one of romantic misalliance," William S. Pechter wrote in 1962. "And all the hoopla of its finale, as frenetic and noisy as anything Capra has put on the screen, cannot disguise the fact that the hero resigns from politics. . . . In one sense, this is Capra at his most realistic, but also at his least engaged. For the artist, withdrawal from the world—the world as he perceives it—is never achieved without some radical diminution of his art."

State of the Union originated with Helen Hayes, who told Howard Lindsay and Russel Crouse in June 1944 of her idea for a play about a presidential candidate who is carrying on an extramarital affair but rediscovers his love for his wife after being forced to campaign with her.

The playwrights made Grant, in Lindsay's words, "a man entirely divorced from politics and inexperienced in politics. . . . The example of [1940 Republican presidential candidate Wendell] Willkie was before us, and we decided to make him a businessman of sufficient importance to be well known and of sufficient depth of feeling to have strong opinions politically." Another important reason for using Willkie as a model no doubt was the fact (well known to political insiders) that he was having marital problems prior to the 1940 campaign. President Roosevelt commented privately that August, "Mrs. Willkie may not have been hired, but in effect she's been hired to return to Wendell, and smile and make this campaign with him."

Interrupted by their production of another play, Lindsay and Crouse did not meet with Hayes to discuss their outline until January 1945. As Lindsay recalled, she found the candidate's wife "too mousy a character" and suggested that she "keep throwing conversational arrows into her husband, deflating him whenever she thought he became pompous or self-important, which would give more edge and sharpness to her character. We thought that was a very good idea and adopted it."

But Hayes was not happy when she read their first two acts, so they bought her out. *State of the Union* played for 765 performances on Broadway, starring Ralph Bellamy and Ruth Hussey. Lindsay and Crouse agreed to sell the film rights to Capra in January 1947 with the stipulation that the film had to be released in time for the national conventions in the summer of 1948.

Capra checked into MGM on June 30, 1947, with principal photography scheduled to begin on September 29.

Claudette Colbert was his first choice for Mary Matthews, the candidate's wife, and though she would have helped supply the tartness the part still needed, their battles on *For the Love of Mike* and *It Happened One Night* made Capra wary of her. During her visit to his office on August 6, she demanded a change of cameraman. Capra wanted to use Joe Biroc, but Colbert said she was uncomfortable with anyone who had not photographed her before and insisted on George J. Folsey, a veteran under contract to MGM, with whom she had made several pictures at Paramount.

Capra had Colbert make tests with Biroc on August 28, but she was displeased with the results. Capra realized that her demands boded poorly for their relationship during the shooting—never in his career had he fired a cameraman on the demand of a star—and he offered the part to Maureen O'Hara, who rejected it on September 11. Capra urged Colbert to consider the effect replacing Biroc would have on the cameraman's career, but finally acquiesced, over the objections of Tracy, who felt Capra was allowing Colbert too much control.

On October 9, four days before she was to report for her first scene, Colbert insisted that she be allowed to go home every day at 5 P.M., an hour ahead of the typical industry quitting time. "By five in the afternoon I am tired and my face shows it," she told the press. "I cannot give good work after that hour and will not even consider trying." Capra asked MGM for Greer Garson or Katharine Hepburn as a replacement. Garson was unavailable, and Hepburn was offered the role on October 10. She had been hearing about the situation from Tracy; Colbert's departure, she recalled, was "not a complete surprise." Although Capra felt she was being altruistic in agreeing to step in at the eleventh hour, Hepburn insisted, "I wouldn't do anything just to help anybody out. I was interested in working with Capra." Hepburn felt "there was justice on both sides" of the Colbert-Capra dispute: "I think she didn't want to do the part. It wasn't all that thrilling a part. I didn't think that *State of the Union* was the greatest film ever made. It wasn't one of those remarkable films like *It Happened One Night*. I thought it was just O.K."

The other woman in *State of the Union* is Kay Thorndyke, Grant's mistress and a right-wing newspaper publisher who pushes him into running. In the play the newspapers have passed into Kay's ownership after a divorce, but Capra characteristically changed that to have her inherit them from her father, Lewis Stone—named Sam like Capra's father—who commits suicide after saying good-bye to Kay in the powerfully underplayed opening scene. Only twenty-two when she was cast as Kay, Angela Lansbury had received Oscar nominations for *Gaslight* and *The Picture of Dorian Gray* but had been foundering in roles ill suited for her unconventionally mature beauty and personality. Capra, she recalled, "saw that despite my youth I possessed the requisite 'authority' for the part. Which was more than I saw!"

Lansbury's offbeat casting resulted in one of the few genuinely bright spots in *State of the Union*. Her unsentimentalized, strangely sympathetic performance transcended the black-and-white writing of the character and showed that Capra had not completely lost his sensitivity in directing women, particularly those with a hard-boiled exterior. Still, the superficially outspoken but fundamentally submissive nature of Hepburn's character shows how much Capra's work was losing by his capitulation to postwar sexist ideology. In both *Wonderful Life* and *State of the Union*, the heroines are housewives and the "bad" women are career women, a striking reversal from his films with Barbara Stanwyck and Jean Arthur, and the beginning of the end for what had been one of the most refreshingly original aspects of his work.

At a Directors Guild of America seminar in 1981, with Joe Walker an honored guest, Capra made the astonishing statement that *State of the*

Union was his best film from a technical standpoint, contending, "It wasn't until then that I really felt I knew what I was doing as a director." Undoubtedly a defensive reaction to the creative decline that became starkly manifest with that film, Capra's statement baffled George Folsey, who could not believe Capra could consider it a better film than *Mr. Deeds Goes to Town* or *Mr. Smith Goes to Washington*.

Folsey's work with other directors usually had a sparkling visual texture, but *State of the Union* is drab by his standards, with its flat lighting and its static approach to staging and composition. The trouble started with the script by Anthony Veiller and Myles Connolly, which was much more rigid in its approach to adaptation than Capra's earlier film versions of plays, keeping many events offscreen and using such a minimal number of locations and secondary characters that the film looks cheap, despite its cost. The pacing is laborious, long-winded, and mechanically punctuated for laugh lines.

But that was not the whole story. After so many years of relying on the indispensable Joe Walker, Capra seemed to have developed an inability to think in visual terms. But for a preliminary discussion in which Capra said that he liked to use multiple cameras on occasion and that he liked to keep the blocking loose to allow the actors freedom, Folsey recalled, "I never had one single bit of conversation with Capra about the photography. I didn't have any problem with him, except for the fact that he would never talk about it.

"On the night of the second day of shooting, we looked at the first day's work. We all sat in the projection room, and Capra came in and sat alongside of the cutter [William Hornbeck]. Tracy rarely looked at rushes, but he was there because it was an important picture, and Capra was an important director, a big man.

"So we were all set. The stuff looked pretty good. But you never know whether somebody else is going to like it or not. The lights came on, and Capra sat there for a full minute and a half, two minutes. There was absolutely no movement, no sound at all, nothing. And everybody was sitting on pins and needles, wondering, What the hell has gone wrong?

"Finally Capra said, 'Well, let's go home,' and he got up and walked out.

"I went to [assistant director] Art Black and said, 'Art, he didn't say anything.' Art said, 'Well, if he didn't like it, he would have said so.' I said, 'It's a hell of a way to know.' Tracy was mad as hell. And he never came to look at rushes again. I don't blame him.

"At least have a conversation about it, it doesn't have to be favorable, but have an opinion, say *something*. There never was a moment of satisfaction from Capra on *State of the Union*."

Capra's creative catatonia was a function of his unwillingness to take a side on any political issue.

Though the play was at most a mild satire of political opportunism, its political viewpoint was clear enough, portraying Grant Matthews as a moderate Republican whose liberal tendencies are challenged by his dealings with reactionaries and special-interest groups from the "lunatic fringe" of American politics. He is allowed by his political bosses Kay Thorndyke and Jim Conover (Adolphe Menjou) to criticize organized labor, but not to criticize big business, and he renounces his candidacy at the end so that he can speak out as he pleases. Capra made the theme of Grant struggling to keep his integrity under pressure darker and more pessimistic; while Grant in the play at least passively resists making deals with people he despises, keeping alive some measure of self-respect, Capra's Grant Matthews makes deals and hates himself for it. The film not only added Grant's description of himself as "dishonest" and his apology to the American people but also amplified the impact of his self-abasement by having his remarks broadcast on national radio and television.

"The point the play makes is that every citizen of the United States should not leave politics alone but take a vital and responsible interest in it," the playwrights told *The New York Times* shortly before the film started shooting, adding that they would be "very much disappointed" if the film did not "make the point as emphatically as the play."

But in the film Grant's closing insistence that "I'm just getting *into* politics" seems hollow and tacked on, a feeble face-saving device both for Capra and for Grant after his declaration that "I have as much right to run for President as a gutter rat. . . . I lost faith in you. I lost faith in myself. . . . I forgot how quickly the Americans smell out the double-dealers and the crooks. . . . [T]hey didn't like me anymore. They were on to me. They knew I was a phony."

The defeatist tone of the ending reflects Capra's unusually close identification with the character. Though, as the film does not fail to mention, only a "native-born American" can become President, Capra otherwise could see himself in the self-made millionaire from the West whose picture appears on the cover of *Time*, the airplane builder with pretensions to be a political leader, the professional flag-waver who declares, "I like this country, Mr. Conover, it's been darn good to me," but idealistically insists, "The American Dream is not making money." Capra also could identify with the private Grant Matthews, the man torn apart by his divided ambitions and the conflicting demands of pressure groups, the man who sells out himself and the American people, the man who compromises his ideas to win election but becomes a lifeless puppet like John Doe, "a stooge mouthing words that aren't your own, thoughts that aren't your own," as Mary says to him in the film.

Though Capra was rebuffed by the Writers Guild in repeated attempts to win a writing credit on *State of the Union*, Veiller and Connolly expressed willingness to share their credit with him, and Veiller told the guild Capra had been actively involved in the writing. One of the scenes Capra surely had a large hand in writing was Grant's monologue to Mary as he lies on the floor of their bedroom on the first night they spend together in the campaign. It closely resembled the speech about being a "failure" that Capra wrote and discarded for George Bailey in *Wonderful Life*, and its personal echoes for the Capra of 1947 are unmistakable: "The world thinks I'm a very successful man—rich, influential, and happy. You know better, don't you, Mary? You know that I'm neither happy nor successful—not as a man, a husband, or a father."

Grant had spent the afternoon outside the White House, measuring himself against Washington, Jefferson, Lincoln, and other great men of history.

"They were happy men, Mary, do you know why? They had a cause. They had a cause they could die for—some of 'em did. I have no cause, Mary—beating your competitor is no cause to die for. Really isn't very much to live for. Always me first and everybody else second."

Even at the beginning of the film, Grant's political beliefs are much less clear, and his personality more cynical, than in the play. Capra puts into Grant's mouth a nonsensical jumble of contradictory political opinions, particularly on business and labor issues, on which he flip-flops from Republican to Democrat within single sentences, leaving the impression of a man who, like Capra himself, has dangerously little in the way of beliefs even before his supposed corruption and has developed a lifelong habit of speaking out of both sides of his mouth. His growing opportunism in the course of the campaign is only relative, robbing the story of much of its point.

Capra's fear of taking a stand was compounded by a problem that Lindsay and Crouse were able to circumvent by rewriting as topics of national interest changed: the fact that whatever political views were expressed in the film might be rendered obsolete—or controversial—by the time lag between the film's completion and release, despite the rush schedule he was obligated to follow.

Notes made by Capra on September 27, two days before he began principal photography, show the depth of his anxiety over the political climate in the country at that time and the fear he felt over the HUAC hearings that were about to take place in Washington. But those notes, which were bound into his script for *State of the Union* and evidently were intended for Grant Matthews to speak in the film, also show that he was initially in a defiant mood toward HUAC, before something happened to change his mind—quietly and clandestinely, as something happens to Grant in the Detroit hotel room when he is visited by the bitch-goddess of success, Kay Thorndyke.

HUAC, whose members now included a young Republican congressman from Southern California anxious to make his reputation as a Red hunter, Richard Nixon, had opened its frontal assault on Hollywood "Reds," taking testimony behind closed doors in Los Angeles that May from fourteen "friendly" witnesses, most of them from the Motion Picture Alliance; the witnesses included Adolphe Menjou, Robert Taylor, Leo McCarey, Jack L. Warner, and writers Howard Emmett Rogers, James Kevin McGuinness, and Rupert Hughes. And, as Ceplair and Englund wrote, "congressional investigators, working with FBI files, had compiled long lists of alleged Communists in the movie business. . . . During the hearings he held in Los Angeles in May 1947, [HUAC chairman J.] Parnell Thomas told the press that 'hundreds of very prominent film capital people have been named as Communists to us.' The providers were the Motion Picture Alliance for the Preservation of American Ideals." As a result, pink subpoenas were issued beginning on September 18 for forty-three Hollywood people to appear at public hearings that were held from October 20 to 30, while Capra was shooting *State of the Union*.

The liberals and leftists subpoenaed—labeled the "Hollywood Nineteen"—were actor Larry Parks; writers Alvah Bessie, Bertolt Brecht, Lester Cole, Richard Collins, Gordon Kahn, Howard Koch, Ring Lardner, Jr., John Howard Lawson, Albert Maltz, Samuel Ornitz, Waldo Salt, and Dalton Trumbo; writer-producer Adrian Scott; and directors Herbert Biberman, Edward Dmytryk, Lewis Milestone, Irving Pichel, and Robert Rossen. Parks, Collins, Kahn, Koch, Salt, Milestone, Pichel, and Rossen were not called to testify in those hearings; Brecht left the country after his testimony, and the remaining members of the original nineteen became known as the "Hollywood Ten" (or the "Unfriendly Ten") as a result of their testimony as "unfriendly" witnesses, which brought them jail sentences for contempt of Congress. One of the nineteen, Koch, was a Liberty contract writer, and two of the Hollywood Ten, Trumbo and Biberman, had contributed to the scripts of Capra films. Other writers who had been associated with Capra who were named as Communists at the hearings included John Sanford, Julius and Philip Epstein, Clifford Odets, and Irwin Shaw; Sidney Buchman was named by Roy Brewer as one who helped cause "chaos" and "anarchy" during the CSU strike; and Lionel Stander, who acted for Capra in *Mr. Deeds*, was named as a Communist. The "friendly" witnesses included Menjou, who then was acting for Capra in *State of the Union*, and Capra's current boss at MGM, Louis B. Mayer, who defended his studio's 1943 pro-Soviet film *Song of Russia* by comparing it to the Army's *"The Battle of Stalingrad"* (he meant Capra's *The Battle of Russia*). Capra was never criticized by name in the hearings, nor were films such as *Mr. Deeds* and *Mr. Smith*, and two witnesses took pains to defend Capra pictures from suspicion, Warner saying that his company's *Arsenic and Old Lace* had "no taint of communism" and Jack Moffitt exempting *It's a Wonderful Life* from the anticapitalist stigma. Other friendly witnesses included such prominent Hollywood figures as Gary Cooper, Robert Montgomery, Sam Wood, Leo McCarey, Walt Disney, and Ronald Reagan.

Capra, as he wrote in his book, was worried that he might get caught in the middle: he was afraid of the reaction *State of the Union* would stir up, "sure the House Un-American Activities Committee would not muff the opportunity to subpoena us all into a congressional spectacular called 'Film Reds on Parade.' " On October 25, he was quoted by the AP's Bob Thomas as saying of Hollywood, "I haven't seen the town so panicky since the banks closed in 1933."

Capra's September 27 notes in his script for *State of the Union* suggested that both communism and fascism were inimical to the American way of life, and that both extremes were bound to be rejected by free-spirited Americans. Capra nevertheless urged respect for those who exercised the right to an unfettered exchange of ideas, and invoked the names of Jefferson, Paine, Emerson, and Thoreau in extolling the American traditions of free speech and political dissent.

None of that brave talk made it into the film, only a comment by Grant to Mary on the "fear of the future, fear of the world, fear of communism, fear of going broke" that was tearing the country apart.

Some of the reasons Capra pulled his punches are suggested in his book. While filming another indictment of the flaws in the American political system, he could not help thinking of the ferocious backlash and the attacks on his patriotism he had provoked before the war with *Mr. Smith Goes to Washington:* "Courage made me a champion. . . . But the world was full of *ex*-champions. . . . What did they lose? The year 1947 showed me what they lost."

Capra's first instincts were to fight back, on-screen and off-, to defend the rights of those in Hollywood under attack from HUAC. But, like so many others in Hollywood, he quickly retreated in the face of the opposition and from what Michael Wilson called "the intimidation of a company town." The conservative novelist and screenwriter W. R. Burnett recalled in a 1982 interview, "A friend of mine, Frank Capra, tried to get me to sign petitions in their favor. I chased him out of the house. Why should I sign? If they want to be Communists and overthrow the government, let them take what they've got coming." Capra evidently abandoned that brief attempt at public protest and played no role in the futile protest against HUAC mounted by a special committee of the Screen Directors Guild, chaired by John Ford, in an attempt to counteract charges by director Sam Wood and others that, as Wood put it, "There is a constant effort [by alleged Communists] to get control of the guild."

Although it probably started earlier, Capra's book identified 1947 as the year when he first learned of an "innuendo campaign" questioning his own political sympathies. Before 1947 the information in government files about Capra's political views and associations apparently had not been taken seriously, as was indicated by the FBI's dismissal of a negative report on Capra in December 1946 with the notation that he was "a loyal American." But 1947 was the year in which Representative John Rankin (D-Mississippi), an influential member of HUAC, declared: "Everyone whose loyalty was questioned I would certainly get them out of the moving-picture industry."

Whether Capra's silence was purchased with the threat of a subpoena or some friendly advice by a member of the Alliance, or by another kind of deal with the witch-hunters, the evidence is clear that he became terrified enough in 1947 to begin surrendering his conscience. With Hollywood under siege both at the box office and from Washington, and while Capra watched more and more of his colleagues being driven out of the business, like most others still working in Hollywood he set about purging his work of any elements he could anticipate that anyone, anywhere, present or future, might find "un-American"—starting with the speech for

State of the Union. As Capra's friend and neighbor Gary Cooper told HUAC, "within these last few months" in Hollywood "it has become unpopular and a little risky to say too much. You notice the difference. People who were quite easy to express their thoughts before begin to clam up more than they used to."

Time commented in January 1948 that as a result of the HUAC investigation, Hollywood had become afraid to "take up problems that cut deep into contemporary life. . . . There was doubt that Frank Capra, already well into making *State of the Union*, . . . would have started this satire on U.S. politics under present circumstances." And *The New York Times* reported in February that *State of the Union* "has worried Capra a good deal, he says, for fear somebody of the alarmist ideology would accuse him of filming a subversive indictment of the democratic system. . . . 'I still expect criticism from various extremists,' Capra said, 'because it has become an indoor sport to attack pictures, but we'd all have to go out of business if we didn't make films about what's going on.' "

Capra's casting of Menjou in *State of the Union* was an ambivalent act, both a criticism of the far Right and protective coloration against it. Like the character he was playing, who boasts about running his own political spying operation, Menjou declared to a reporter on the set of *State of the Union,* "I've never missed an opportunity to conduct private investigations on my own." He told HUAC that "Edgar" Hoover, the FBI director, was "a very close personal friend of mine," and he unabashedly helped the Alliance and HUAC compile dossiers on suspected Hollywood "Reds."

"I am a witch-hunter if the witches are Communists," Menjou told HUAC on October 21, 1947. "I am a Red baiter. I make no bones about it whatsoever. I would like to see them all back in Russia. I think a taste of Russia would cure many of them." He added that "we are curing people every day. There has been an amazing change in Hollywood in the attitude of many people since this committee has started to function and also due to the activities of the Motion Picture Alliance."

In *State of the Union* Capra uneasily tries to make both amusing and sinister Conover's collecting dirt on Grant Matthews and Kay's eavesdropping on Conover as he talks about Grant in a phone call to one of his informants. Menjou's presence on the set was a constant and unnerving reminder to Capra of the events taking place in Washington. Though Capra tried to bar reporters from the set, Harold Heffernan of Hearst's *Los Angeles Examiner* recorded Menjou's "explosive assaults on producers, directors, writers, and actors who have reputedly become involved in subversive activities."

Capra was concerned about the press overhearing the arguments on the set between Menjou and Hepburn, a liberal Democrat and Henry Wallace supporter who gave back as good as she received from Menjou and other Red baiters. In May 1947, giving the keynote address at a Hollywood rally for Wallace, Hepburn had mockingly worn a bright scarlet dress as she attacked the witch-hunt, declaring: "J. Parnell Thomas is engaged in a personally conducted smear campaign of the motion picture industry. He is aided and abetted in his efforts by a group of super-patriots who call themselves the Motion Picture Alliance for the Preservation of American Ideals. For myself, I want no part of their ideals or those of Mr. Thomas.

"The artist, since the beginning of time, has always expressed the aspirations and dreams of his people. Silence the artist and you silence the most articulate voice the people have."

After her speech, McCarey, like Menjou a member of the Alliance, announced that he had decided not to cast Hepburn in his next picture because of her political views. She was said to have been put on the unofficial studio graylist by MGM until Capra asked to use her in *State of the Union*.

"One reason I gave the speech was that I felt, They really can't hurt me," Hepburn recalled. "I sort of came over on the *Mayflower*. And I didn't have to depend on movies for my living. But it was a mess for Hollywood at that time. It was hard for me to realize how violently people felt.

"Menjou passionately believed in what he believed. He was trying to cut my throat at the time we made *State of the Union* [he told HUAC that people attending her speech for Wallace were Communists]. But we were frightfully civilized on the set toward each other. I would pull his leg. I would just torture Menjou. Menjou was *ridiculous*."

Hepburn did not know anything about Capra's political problems at the time or even where he stood on the issues. She commented when told of his political problems, "I felt very sorry for people who were in a prominent position and depended on the motion picture business, who were desperate for a livelihood and for their family's livelihood.

"Capra seemed a sweet fellow, nice and easy, and I think truthful about how he felt. He certainly wasn't very left. I don't think he was a party man in any violent sense. He was a very fair man, I would say. He didn't like anyone to push him around or try to tell him what to do.

"Was he an immigrant? I didn't know. Well, I think *they* know more about what this country means than those of us who were born here and criticize it. Those of us who were born here, we take it for granted. Capra's complete originality, his own outlook, was that of a fellow from Sicily coming into this country.

"That was his politics: 'Pleased to be here.' "

Capra finished shooting *State of the Union* on December 7, seven days *ahead* of its seventy-five-day schedule. He accomplished that feat by not shooting an elaborate montage of Grant traveling the country making speeches, which was to have ended with his antilabor speech in Wichita, to which the film only alludes. The cut saved him $200,000, bringing in the film for about $2.6 million, but it made the film even vaguer politically.

The script said the speeches would take bold and progressive stands on specific contemporary issues, but the speeches were never written.

Capra feared the worst when the film was previewed before President Truman and 1,600 other guests at Loew's Capitol Theater in Washington on April 7, 1948. The screening followed a reception for Capra at the National Press Club and was sponsored by the White House Correspondents Association. It was MGM's idea, not Capra's; the Washington screening of *Mr. Smith* was too fresh in his mind.

"I'm all in one piece," the astonished Capra told a reporter after *State of the Union* was shown. "They didn't misunderstand. . . . As long as we can laugh our heads off at ourselves, we're all right . . . especially when the people in public office are doing the laughing, too."

The President, who was escorted into the theater by Capra and sat with him at the preview, was reported to have been delighted by the jibes at Republicans and by his own kid-glove treatment in the picture. The next morning the White House requested a print to run on the presidential yacht, and there was even a story in the press that *State of the Union* helped encourage Truman to run in 1948. Capra was so touched that in years to come he called Truman his favorite President. Harry Truman seemed like a real-life Frank Capra character to the director, though Capra could not bring himself to vote for Truman that November.*

* State of the Union, *like* Mr. Deeds, *also made a big impression on future President Ronald Reagan, who borrowed one of Tracy's lines in a decisive moment of the 1980 primary campaign. In the film, when the producer of his radio and TV show tries to cut him off in midspeech, Tracy snaps, "I'm paying for this broadcast," with exactly the tone of righteous indignation Reagan*

The Washington praise, in the end, was bittersweet for Capra. He came to recognize that the kudos for *State of the Union* from politicians who had been enraged by *Mr. Smith* were a sign of the new film's toothlessness.

State of the Union performed moderately well commercially—with rentals of $3.5 million, it ranked fourteenth on *Variety*'s 1948 list—but it stirred little excitement in the press.

Time blamed its timidity on the "corporate nausea" of Liberty and MGM over the prospect of filming the play as written: "The satirical carnage involved, and might antagonize, every major force in the nation's political life. Luckily, the movie was being made by a cinemagician who could turn bludgeons into lollipops."

The only member of the press who found *State of the Union* at all provocative was Lee Mortimer, the Hollywood columnist of Hearst's *New York Daily Mirror*, who accused Capra of "devilishly clever workmanship" in using the film "to peddle some peculiar 'advanced' political thinking. . . . This artful trickster hawks his propaganda to audiences through two wonderful and irresistible salespersons, Katharine Hepburn and Spencer Tracy. . . . This stuff slipped through the customers by one of the oldest dodges in the game, 'Sure, I'm against communism, but—' The big 'but' here seems to be a deep-seated dislike for most of the things America is and stands for. . . . The indictment against this country, its customs, manners, morals, economic and political systems, as put in the mouths of Tracy and Miss Hepburn, would not seem out of place in *Izvestia*."

Capra replied on April 26 with the most candid statement of his political views that he ever gave to the press.

"Your review of *State of the Union* knocked me into a tailspin," he wrote. "Not because you didn't like the picture—my professional abilities are public property, and I realize only too well my own shortcomings. I was astonished because of the subversive motives you imply in its making. You practically accuse me of being a traitor to our country.

"Naturally I realize that you are being zealous in your attempts to smoke out those who are with us and those who are against us. I have no quarrel with that. But if you come to the conclusion that I am a Communist manipulator or a Communist stooge, you are completely off your nut.

"Let me clear up a few things for you. I am a Catholic. My kids go to Catholic schools. I am a Republican. I even voted against FDR right along,

used in New Hampshire when his microphone was about to be cut off by a supporter of George Bush and he declared, "I'm paying for this microphone."

not because I didn't agree with all of his ideas, but because I thought he was getting too big for the country's good. I am passionately against dictatorship in any form. . . .

"I've served voluntarily in two wars. . . . I will volunteer against *any* American enemy. . . .

"I have two motives in making any picture; One, to entertain; two, to present a Christian doctrine. . . .

"I like this country, Mr. Mortimer, I like it just as it is, and I imagine so do you. So let's not play into the hands of the opposition by calling each other Communists."

The following day, Capra moved into his offices at Paramount. The three years he would spend there would be a struggle against the admission of defeat.

Thrashing in frustration under the fiscal conservatism of the Barney Balaban regime, supervised by his old partner Sam Briskin, and concentrating his creative energies on the kind of films he had described to Tom Pryor in 1945 as "pap," Capra saw one project after another fall through at Paramount, ostensibly for budget reasons. In those anxious days in the spring of 1948, Balaban decreed that no Paramount film should cost more than $2 million, yet in time Capra and other directors, including Wyler and Stevens, managed to fight their way around that rule. Wyler's first film at Paramount, *The Heiress* (1949) cost $2.6 million, and Stevens's first, *A Place in the Sun* (1951), cost $2,295,304; after being given only $1,921,000 to make *Riding High* (1950), Capra also managed to exceed Balaban's ceiling, spending $2,117,000 ($61,000 over budget) on *Here Comes the Groom* (1951). Nor was working at Paramount in that era a guarantee of artistic failure: though Capra made two of the worst films of his career there, Wyler's Paramount films also included *Detective Story* and *Roman Holiday* and Stevens made the classic *Shane.*

"They don't want experimental pictures from me," Capra complained to the press during the shooting of *Riding High.* "They want the surefire thing. Hollywood could and should go off the beaten track, but it is afraid. Every time things get a little tough, they don't want to take a chance."

Capra's disintegration as a filmmaker between 1948 and 1951, one of the most precipitous collapses in the career of any major American director, could not be blamed entirely on the studio's shortsightedness, nor on the problems imposed on the industry as a whole by the 1948 consent decree and the simultaneous rise of television, nor even on the climate of political fear that was spreading throughout Hollywood and the rest of the country in those years. All these things contributed to Capra's collapse, but he came closest to the truth when he admitted that it was his own lack of "courage" that finally drove him out of Hollywood.

The projects Capra initially presented to Paramount—*The Friendly Persuasion, No Other Man, The Flying Yorkshireman,* and *Pioneer Woman*— promptly were rejected. The shell-shocked Capra tried to find new properties that would seem more commercial.

Paramount had bought an original treatment called "A Woman of Distinction" by Hugo Butler and Ian McLellan Hunter, and "Capra glommed onto it," Hunter recalled. It was a romantic comedy about the female dean of a New England women's college who falls in love with a visiting British lecturer. Capra planned to start shooting in early 1949, with Katharine Hepburn or Jean Arthur and Cary Grant or Ray Milland. The studio balked at the cost of two expensive stars, and Capra offered to use an unknown man with Hepburn or Arthur (neither of whom ever was approached on the project), but Paramount still refused. Because of Capra's track record, the studio did not believe that he could make it for under $2 million.

Lu suggested it might be time to leave the movie business. It was a tempting idea. For the last several years he had been talking about moving to Red Mountain Ranch and spending the rest of his life as a gentleman farmer. In 1947 the Capras also built a summer retreat on Silver Lake in the High Sierras, near the town of June Lake, which he had first visited in 1920, followed by many hunting, fishing, and skiing vacations there. Their comfortable cabin, built to order from the pines that surrounded it, became Capra's preferred escape, his earthly "paradise."

But he was not yet ready to get away from it all. Although he knew he had little hope of recapturing his past greatness, he wanted to make another film, and after a few months of agonizing, he was willing to compromise his old standards by doing it the way Paramount wanted—on the cheap.

Capra suggested swapping "A Woman of Distinction" to Columbia for *Broadway Bill*. By using the racing footage filmed in 1934, he argued, it would be possible to make a musical version of *Broadway Bill* with Paramount star Bing Crosby (whose box-office appeal was slipping) for close to $2 million. Harry Cohn agreed to the deal in October 1948, when Paramount threw in Milland's services for "A Woman of Distinction" (which Columbia filmed in 1950, also starring Rosalind Russell, with Eddie Buzzell directing).

Though he chafed against Paramount's cost-cutting measures, Capra tried to go the studio one better. He argued that *Broadway Bill* (eventually retitled *Riding High*) could be remade even more cheaply if his salary ($156,000) and Crosby's ($150,000) were cut to the minimum in exchange for profit percentages. But that scheme—which eventually became common in Hollywood—was too cost-conscious even for Barney Balaban.

With Capra claiming Riskin declined an offer to rewrite *Broadway Bill*—though Fay Wray insisted Riskin's offer to work on it had been refused—Sam Briskin tried to dissuade Capra from rewriting Riskin's script without help, but Capra started work on his own. That lasted only briefly, as did his attempt to work with Richard Breen. Most of the rewriting was done by Melville Shavelson and Jack Rose, although Barney Dean and William Morrow did some last-minute polishing.

Capra could not resist trying to improve on the six screenwriters' work. Even more uncomfortable than he had been in 1934 with the central character, Dan Brooks, divorcing his wife and marrying her sister—particularly since the part was being played by Father O'Malley—Capra changed his considerably older version of Dan Brooks to a footloose bachelor on the run from a divorced Margaret Higgins (Frances Gifford), making Dan seem even more emotionally stunted. Although Capra asked the Writers Guild to let him share screenplay credit with Riskin, suggesting that Shavelson and Rose be given an adaptation credit, Riskin protested Capra's attempt to claim writing credit on the film, and the guild gave the sole screenplay credit to Riskin, with additional dialogue credit to Shavelson and Rose and story credit to Mark Hellinger.

Despite the pressure of adhering to his fifty-one-day shooting schedule from March to May 1949 and another clash with a cameraman—Ernest Laszlo, whom Crosby had urged on Capra to make himself look younger next to Coleen Gray's girlish Alice, was replaced in the third week of shooting with George Barnes, who had photographed *Meet John Doe*—Capra professed to find the shooting enjoyable because of Crosby and because the film was his first venture into pure escapism since *Arsenic and Old Lace*.

He took a Moviola to the Tanforan Race Track location near San Francisco to help in matching the footage he had shot there in 1934 with new reaction shots of Crosby and the rest of his cast, which included Clarence Muse and eight other actors from the original film. When *Riding High* was previewed on July 7 in Huntington Park, many in the audience reacted with laughter and outrage when they realized that Capra was recycling old footage. Retakes helped somewhat, but members of the public still complained after a second preview on August 3 in Pacific Palisades and after the film belatedly went into release in April 1950, accusing Capra of lowering his standards and trying to deceive them.

The reuse of old footage was the least of *Riding High*'s offenses, however. More astonishing, coming from Capra, were its funereal pacing, its garrulous and unfunny dialogue, the anxious inclusion of on-screen laugh reactions for every gag line, the five tiresome and distracting musical numbers, and, most distressingly, the lack of any genuine sympathy displayed by Capra toward his central character, a sure barometer of the director's now all but total self-contempt.

Unlike Grant Matthews in *State of the Union*—who, as his wife observes, at least *tries* to be honest—Crosby's Dan Brooks is a repellently amoral grifter who thoughtlessly exploits Alice's emotions to milk her for money (because Dan is not married in this version, the relationship carries little dramatic weight); smarmily patronizes his aging stablehand Clarence Muse (still named Whitey, or "Brother Whitey," though not physically abused by Dan as he was in the original); and callously pushes Broadway Bill to run despite his heart condition (Crosby displays little of the affection toward horses which Capra claimed was their reason for remaking *Broadway Bill*). Warner Baxter's Dan shared some of those flaws, but the original film kept a critical perspective on the character; Riskin and Capra gave the character more obsessiveness, more financial desperation, and less of the oily charm that the lackadaisical Crosby mechanically dispenses to con people. Miscasting was part of the problem, and so was Capra's new slapdash manner of shooting, but it was mostly Capra's overreliance on Crosby's image to gloss over his own cynicism toward the story, a sign of the director's own lack of creative and emotional engagement.

The commercial response to *Riding High* was only fair—it tied for twenty-eighth in the annual *Variety* tally, with rentals of $2.35 million—and, as Capra expected, the critics were as harsh as the preview audiences. Capra was most upset over Manny Farber's review in *The Nation*. He was outraged at Farber's mockery of his clumsy attempts to be racially englightened ("the movie drools democratic pride in Crosby's sugary relationship with his colored stableboy"), but what probably galled Capra most was that Farber put his finger squarely on some of the root causes of his creative decline: "*Riding High* (from riches to nags with Bing Crosby) catches some of the jumpy, messy, half-optimistic energy seen around race tracks, but leaves you feeling that you've been taken in like a carnival sucker. . . .

"As in all Capra films, the world is given to the underdog (the 100-to-1 entry, two-buck better, brat daughter—all win over the big, pompous, and rich), but the sleek, pampered technique, the grandiose talk, and eating habits of his down-and-out characters, and even the names (Imperial City, Pettigrew, Brooks) make for a plush, elegant movie that subtly eulogizes the world of powerful wealth. Capra's poverty boys are royalists in ratty boarding houses and leaky stables; when they eat at a hamburger stand, they treat the owner like a witless palace scullion. The gags always revolve around large sums of money, often rib a character for not being a liberal spender, delight in scenes that resemble a busy day at the Stock Exchange. Actually Capra only hates and attacks the humdrum plodder made humble by necessity; his smart-aleck jibes at artless, hard-working waiters or farmers invariably win sympathy where Capra intends you to snicker."

In the fall of 1949, Paramount bought a promising new script for Capra, *Roman Holiday*.

Elizabeth Taylor and Cary Grant were Capra's first choices for the romantic comedy about a runaway princess bored with her royal routine and an American newspaperman in Rome who shows her how to live. It was not entirely a retread of *It Happened One Night*, for Ian McLellan Hunter's contemporary screenplay had an energy and wit of its own, as well as a refreshing, nostalgically Capraesque irreverence toward people in high places. Capra apparently did not know that Hunter was fronting, in part, for Hollywood Ten member Dalton Trumbo, who had written the original story while blacklisted. "Can you imagine if Capra had known *Dalton* was involved?" Hunter laughed in 1984. "What would he have done? You have no idea what a pain in the ass it became for me [to front for Trumbo]. But Dalton, Ring Lardner, Hugo Butler, and Michael Wilson were my closest friends, and you couldn't turn down your friends when they were blacklisted."

When Hunter checked into Paramount on November 14 to begin re-writing, he found Capra "very uncertain in story discussions; I worked with him for fourteen weeks, and I can't remember him ever giving me an idea. He even had trouble visualizing scenes, which surprised me, because I remembered him as the director of God knows how many good films."

The writer did not know that Capra was already fretting about the possible political ramifications of *Roman Holiday*. Though her country was not identified in the script, Princess Anne was based on Great Britain's Princess Margeret, whose romantic flings, particularly on a trip to Italy, had raised many eyebrows in the press. In early October, Capra asked Paramount whether the British government might object to the film, and shortly thereafter the British Board of Censors warned Paramount that it might refuse the film an exhibition permit if it appeared to be based on Princess Margaret and her Italian escapades.

Capra pressed on, taking Paramount's advice to exercise caution, but after Hunter turned in his revised screenplay, the studio threw Capra a harsher blow, telling him on March 21, 1950, that the film would have to be made on a forty-day schedule, with no shooting in Italy and only stock footage for backgrounds, for about $1.6 million. "Paramount had some kind of phobia about making pictures that cost money," Hunter recalled, "and they said the film wouldn't make any money."

Capra kept *Roman Holiday* on his agenda until he decided to leave Paramount a year later. He passed it to William Wyler, who made it for Paramount in 1952–1953, with Audrey Hepburn and Gregory Peck. Hunter and John Dighton, who had done some rewriting for Wyler, shared screenplay credit, and Hunter won an Oscar for the story, although he, like Trumbo, had been blacklisted by then. Capra's stated excuse in his book for abandoning *Roman Holiday* was Paramount's cheapness. But he told the U.S. government in 1951 that he had dropped it because of the objection by the British.

"The kind of director I thought Capra was before I met him fights that kind of thing," Hunter commented. "He evaluates it and thinks it isn't antiroyalty, it's proroyalty because she's such a charming girl, so he says, 'To hell with you. If necessary we'll drop in a line about her visiting England.' That's what I missed in Capra. He had no fight left in him. I felt, 'Oh, shit, this guy's gone.'"

The next project Capra tried to get off the ground was an original story called "Red," dated March 29, 1950.

Despite its provocative title, "Red" had nothing to do with communism. It was a lurid melodrama about a fifty-year feud between two Kentucky families, with an ending that tried to introduce a note of Christian redemption for the brutalized protagonist, Red Gillis. But it is tempting to consider "Red" a projection of Capra's view of the political fratricide in Hollywood and of his attempts to find a way out, as the pacified Red does by leaving his hellish hometown at the end. After Paramount spurned "Red," Capra tried to sell it to MGM's Dore Schary, who found it repugnant.

Communism *was* the subject matter, in part, of two other stories Capra wanted to film.

The Trial—written not by Franz Kafka, but by Virginia Van Upp—was a bizarre, unintentionally comical religious allegory set in contemporary Palm Springs, revolving around the staging of the Passion Play as a tourist promotion at an Easter sunrise service. The characters in *The Trial* were drawn with heavy parallels to such biblical characters as the Prodigal Son, Salome, and the Centurion, and in the course of the incredibly convoluted plot, which also involves Communist-inspired violence in a strike at an Indio date ranch, the venality and lewdness of the modern world are exposed with a relish that would have made the Federico Fellini of *La Dolce Vita* drool with envy. Before sinking under the weight of its own hysteria—the conflicts are resolved with a miracle, a general religious rebirth, and the appearance of Jesus Christ Himself at the sunrise service—the script makes fumbling attempts at ideological complexity, arguing that American Christians scapegoat Communists for the world's problems rather than examining their own hypocrisy and materialism. Though it tries to have it both ways on the issue of domestic Communist influence, *The Trial* does make some critical observations about McCarthyism: the Salome character inflames the already overheated populace into a lynch mob with lies about the allegedly subversive ideas of the Prodigal Son, a cynical writer who experiences a religious rebirth. Paramount actually put this film on its production schedule on May 25, 1950, hiring Van Upp to rewrite her script for Capra, though it kept stalling the start of shooting.

That fall Capra proposed filming Giovanni Guareschi's critically acclaimed 1948 novel *The Little World of Don Camillo*, the story of a small-town Italian priest who becomes involved in postwar politics and a brotherly conflict with a local Communist. On Capra's behalf, Paramount made an offer to the Italian producer Giuseppe Amato, who controlled the film rights with Angelo Rizzoli, for an outright purchase or a coproduction, but they refused, insisting on producing it themselves with Capra directing. Capra's continued attempts to strike a better deal evaporated; he was offered a job directing the third film in the *Don Camillo* series in 1953, but he declined.

Paramount meanwhile rejected his offer to remake the backwoods melodrama *The Trail of the Lonesome Pine* (filmed three times previously, from the novel by John Fox, Jr.) as a low-budget location film with a semidocumentary feeling, telling him it wasn't interested in Frank Capra making programmers. Paramount also resisted his continuing attempts to make a Western, turning down both *Pioneer Woman* and his suggestion to remake the 1923 James Cruze epic *The Covered Wagon*. When it was reported that Bing Crosby might make a Western with Hopalong Cassidy, Capra even volunteered to direct that. After he gave up on *Pioneer Woman* in November 1950, selling his treatment to MGM for William Wellman to direct, Capra never tried again to make a Western.

By the spring of 1950, after almost a year of forced inactivity, he was beginning to despair of feature filmmaking altogether, telling the press that he was "gloomy about his future projects" and that he didn't know "where ideas are coming from that will seem worthwhile to him and safe to the studio." Watching *It Happened One Night* again only deepened his gloom: "I thought to myself, 'How fast the scenes come along, how full of entertainment it is! How much we gave them for their money in those days!'

"As I see it, we can solve this problem in one of two ways. We can set ourselves a budget of $500,000 on a picture, forcing ourselves to think up new ideas and new techniques in order to make one for so little. Or we increase—yes, I said increase—our production budget and give the public a whopping good show. Either way would be fine with me. . . . The television camera may have a great influence on us all. . . . [W]ho knows, you might make a picture in a week, or a day."

He was considering moving into television ("I'm completely sold on television," he had told *Variety* in 1948), though in his darkest moments he was on the verge of retiring to Fallbrook and limiting his filmmaking to noncontroversial, image-boosting educational films. In March 1950 he agreed to help Caltech make a film called *The Strange Case of the Cosmic Rays*, planned in part to celebrate Robert Millikan's work on the subject.

But he still had two pictures to go on his Paramount contract.

In his book he obscured the facts surrounding his departure from the studio. Making no mention of his months of effort in trying to make *The Trial* and *Don Camillo*, he telescoped events and wrote that after *Riding High* he went to production vice president Y. Frank Freeman and told him he preferred being suspended from his contract to having his projects constantly refused. Freeman, wrote Capra, suggested that he take over a Bing Crosby project the studio had in development, and Capra jumped at the chance even before learning the story line, Paramount agreeing to forgo the second film.

Stevens negotiated his release at the same time, agreeing to make one more Paramount film, *Shane.* "Paramount's policy has become one of standardization," he told the press, "and I don't think you can standardize good pictures." Studio executives were grumbling about the Liberty deal, which had not worked out to either side's satisfaction, and were looking for excuses to get out of it. Capra was the most frugal of the three former Liberty partners, but he was also the least productive and his films were the least successful; Paramount was as glad to get rid of Capra as he was glad to get rid of Paramount.

Capra failed to mention in his book that his contract was paid off in full even though he did not make the last film on his Liberty contract. But it was not paid entirely against the cost of his second Crosby film, which was released as *Here Comes the Groom;* for that Capra received his standard yearly salary of $156,000 plus $20,000 for Liberty expenses. After Capra left the studio, the irate Stevens discovered that Paramount had stuck Capra's $156,000 salary for the unmade film onto the budget of *Shane,* which was about to go into production, while trying to cut Stevens's own salary by stigmatizing him as a spendthrift. Stevens's departure after the release of *Shane* in 1953 left only Wyler working at the studio. Wyler departed in 1955 after making *The Desperate Hours;* he was the only one of the three former Liberty directors to work off his original Paramount contract in full.

Capra claimed that he told Paramount he didn't care what story he made for his last Hollywood film, but his contract was not settled until *after* he finished shooting *Here Comes the Groom.* He decided to leave Paramount only after the studio canceled his *next* production, *The Trial,* on February 28, 1951, the same day he did the final retakes for *Here Comes the Groom,* and his contract was settled on March 20.

Capra asked to make *Here Comes the Groom* when he heard that Paramount was developing an original story by Robert Riskin. Based on a treatment Riskin had written in 1947, "You Belong to Me," it was intended as a vehicle for Jimmy Stewart. After the failure of *Magic Town,* Riskin sold the story to Paramount, which planned to make it with Bob Hope, but producer Irving Asher and director Richard Haydn were preparing the film for Crosby when Capra took it over on August 18, 1950, with Asher staying on as associate producer.

In his search for scapegoats for the collapse of his career, Capra naturally was beginning to focus on writers, since he knew that so much of his past success was owed to them, especially to those who he felt had betrayed him by leaving his employ or by turning out to be ideologically suspect.

In the fall of 1948, while brooding over his enemies, he rashly decided to sell his magnificent collection of rare books. Once it had symbolized his own aspirations to be in the company of literary greatness. Now those aspirations seemed to mock him, and when Lu wondered why he was putting the books up for auction, he replied, "Because I hate 'em—that's why!"

He certainly did not need the money. Nor was the auction a sound business move. His collection was valued at $106,954, but the auction of 640 items by the Parke-Bernet Galleries in New York on April 26 and 27, 1949 (which included the printing of an elaborate catalogue entitled *The Distinguished Library of Frank Capra*), brought in only $66,948. If he had kept the books until his old age, they would have been worth many times that amount.

But it was not the money that mattered. Selling his books was a self-destructive act which, as much as anything, appeared to mark Capra's recognition that he was through as a creative artist.

It was during the shooting of *Here Comes the Groom*, on December 27, 1950, that Robert Riskin suffered a stroke and underwent surgery to remove a blood clot from his brain. Left partially paralyzed and confined to a wheelchair, he never worked again.

Riskin's 144-page original treatment was responsible for the film's basic flaw: the essential heartlessness of a story trying to pass itself off as a sentimental romance. Pete Garvey (the Crosby character) is a roving Boston newspaperman who returns from postwar Europe with two orphans as pawns in his attempt to win over working girl Emmadel Jones (Jane Wyman), a campaign of emotional blackmail that involves the systematic destruction of her relationship with her wealthy boyfriend. Pete's brash proletarian charm is supposed to keep the audience on his side (as in *It Happened One Night*, which the story superficially resembles), but Riskin on his own lacked the warmth necessary to keep the character from seeming anything more than a heel.

In his better days, Capra might have managed to infuse some genuine feeling into the plot, but the plot itself had seen better days, and all Capra was able to do was magnify its flaws. Going all out with the kind of vulgarity Riskin avoided, Capra and his writers (six of them, including Myles Connolly) tried to disguise the story's coldness by overloading it with goo in the style of Leo McCarey, and, like Pete, by exploiting the orphans in a relentless succession of mawkish scenes that make them grovel for the sympathy of both Emmadel and the audience. When Connolly warned Capra about Pete's emotional aloofness, Capra's solution was to throw in *another* orphan, a blind teenaged girl (Anna Maria Alberghetti) who auditions to come to America by singing the aria "Caro Nome" from Verdi's *Rigoletto,* one of five irrelevant musical numbers in the film, which also includes the Oscar-winning "In the Cool, Cool, Cool of the Evening" and the stupefying "Misto Cristofo Columbo," in which Louis Armstrong, Dorothy Lamour, Phil Harris, Cass Daley, and Frank Fontaine make cameo appearances.

Capra was uncomfortable with the mild elements of social criticism in Riskin's story and did his best to eliminate them or twist them out of shape. Like Jean Arthur in *You Can't Take It With You,* Emmadel is a secretary who becomes engaged to her boss; in the Riskin version her boss, Wilbur Stanley, is a notorious slumlord Pete exposes in his paper as part of his campaign to win back Emmadel. Capra made Wilbur (Franchot Tone) over into a fairly decent chap who treats her much more kindly than Crosby does. Capra also hewed to the conservative counsel of Connolly in stressing the virtues of domesticity by having Emmadel "housebreak" the roving Pete. *Here Comes the Groom* represents the culmination of the growing sexist trend in Capra's postwar work, mocking Emmadel's former occupation and having her succumb to Pete because of her emotional ambivalence toward the working world: "I'm gonna slow down. As a matter of fact, I'm gonna stand still! First egghead comes along can have me. I was born to be a mother, not a poised pencil."

Her weary capitulation to the defeat of "security" is accomplished with an unconvincing change of heart, in a scene Capra added to the script: "I used the walk down the wedding aisle that was straight out of *It Happened One Night,*" he recalled, "and I decided that if I was having to steal from my own pictures, it was time to take a long rest."

This remarkably sour comedy also includes a grotesque running "gag" about the FBI pursuing Pete for bringing the children into the country illegally. Though the threat initially is made in all seriousness by an INS official, the "FBI" man who shows up at the wedding actually is one of Pete's fellow reporters, there as Emmadel's final persuader; Pete also tries to win sympathy for his cause by playing on the orphans' hysterical fear of deportation. At the fade-out, Crosby croons, "Now, if a wedding is nigh—" and Wyman responds, "Bring your own FBI!" The intrusion of these unfunny elements into an attempt to make a light comedy showed how obsessive Capra had become about his own growing fears of governmental persecution ("This is still a democratic country," Crosby hopefully asserts at one point) and how impossible it was for him, that fall and winter of 1950–1951, to dismiss those fears with satire—how impossible, indeed, it had become for him even to make a comedy.

Here Comes the Groom, which opened on September 6, 1951, finished nineteenth on *Variety*'s annual list with rentals of $2.55 million. Capra did not make another feature film for more than seven years. During the shooting of *Here Comes the Groom,* he told Alexis Smith, whose playing of Wilbur's spinster cousin Winifred is one of its few delights, that he did not want to make any more movies because "It isn't fun anymore."

"I was shocked," she remembered. "I thought he was kidding at first, he seemed to be enjoying himself so much on the set, but he said, 'No, I'm serious. I don't mean it isn't fun here, I mean the pressures that come from the schedule and from money.' That drove him crazy. He said he wasn't used to the banks moving into a position of creative control. This was before the drastic changes in the industry became apparent, and he was probably ahead of a lot of people in realizing what was happening. But I remember being very disturbed by it, because I didn't think *Frank Capra* should just walk away from it."

19. "The Judas pain"

*T*here was more to Capra's malaise than his budget fights with Paramount.

He had been running for cover politically since learning of the "innuendo campaign" against him in late 1946 or early 1947. He cryptically admitted in his book that in 1947, "I began to act strangely, to look for 'villains.' " That year he lost his "courage" and his "soul stopped leaping upward." The intervening years, with HUAC, the Motion Picture Alliance, and other witch-hunting groups gradually assuming total control over Hollywood's thinking, were a time of dread for Capra.

His public line for years had been to trumpet the patriotism of most (but not all) of his Hollywood colleagues and to deplore any attempts to prove otherwise. But after the HUAC hearings in the fall of 1947, he tried to avoid direct answers when reporters asked him about the issue of communism in Hollywood, and privately he began to take the side of the witch-hunters in their drive to purge Hollywood of "subversive" influences.

A vivid example is a letter Capra wrote to his former Liberty Films partner William Wyler on June 16, 1950. Wyler had asked Capra to help him make cuts in the script by Ruth Goetz and Augustus Goetz for *Carrie*, based on Theodore Dreiser's novel *Sister Carrie*, about a girl who chooses an illicit liaison with a wealthy man over working in a sweatshop. *Carrie* was filmed in 1950 but was not released until 1952 because of Paramount's qualms over its political content, and then only after being expurgated by the studio to avoid controversy. As Wyler recalled, "The reason for the cuts, as it turned out, was the McCarthy era. *Carrie* showed an American in an unflattering light." Paramount production vice president Y. Frank Freeman called Wyler to his face "just a bleeding heart, a do-gooder, a peace-monger, in short a damn fool, but no Commie."

Capra, however, refused to help Wyler because (as he wrote in the letter) he considered the script and its portrayal of employer-worker relations tantamount to communistic propaganda against the United States, a Marxist slur on the capitalist system which, he reminded his fellow immigrant director, had amply rewarded both of them. Telling Wyler that Dreiser's characters were repellent caricatures who did not resemble most Americans he knew, Capra sternly lectured Wyler on the inadvisability of filming such a harsh criticism of his adopted country, despite his privilege to do so under the American system. Wyler replied with a scathing letter denouncing Capra, and the incident no doubt was one of the reasons that, as Philip Dunne remembered, "Willy didn't like him" until they were reconciled in later years.

The exchange of correspondence between Capra and Wyler was found among the papers Capra donated to Wesleyan University. Those papers (examined by the author in 1981 and 1984) also contained material from investigations conducted by self-appointed Hollywood Red-hunters. One such item, screenwriter Adele Buffington's 1953 seventeen-page whitelist of members of the Screen Writers Guild she considered suitable for government employment because of their anti-Communist beliefs, boasted about her role in helping to blacklist Michael Wilson, and described him as a Communist. The copy in Capra's files was one of the three copies sent by Buffington to the Motion Picture Alliance and to Alliance leaders Ward Bond and Cecil B. DeMille. Although Capra in 1984 professed ignorance of Bond's role in blacklisting, with the copy of Buffington's list in Capra's files was a cover letter sent from Buffington to Bond at the Alliance office in Beverly Hills.

DeMille, in addition to his work with the Alliance, helped run the Motion Picture Industry Council, an organization formed in 1949 by Roy Brewer and designed, as Ceplair and Englund wrote, "to bring the 'Communist problem' in Hollywood to the attention of the studio executives, publicize the efforts of the film industry to purge itself of 'subversives,' 'clear' repentant Communists, and heap vituperations on any HUAC witnesses who took the Fifth Amendment." DeMille also had an intelligence service of his own, The DeMille Foundation for Americanism, which compiled dossiers on the "leftist" affiliations of his fellow directors; the foundation supplied the dossiers to the California Senate's Committee on Un-American Activities, run by Senator Jack B. Tenney, and to HUAC.

The files Capra donated to Wesleyan also included a 1952 dossier on the political activities of fellow director Herbert Biberman, the blacklisted member of the Hollywood Ten who had helped Capra with the script of *Lost Horizon* and had been active with him in the Screen Directors Guild during the 1930s. A note on the Biberman dossier indicated that it was supplied to Capra by his attorney Mabel Walker Willebrandt, general counsel to the guild since 1938.

Willebrandt's initial reaction to the 1947 HUAC investigation, conveyed in confidential memoranda to John Ford and SDG executive secretary J. P. McGowan, had been scornful, but she suggested the guild try to stay out of the fray and not oppose the investigation, in order to avoid giving an impression of culpability. As the investigation took force, however, the woman who was known in the 1920s as "Prohibition Portia" turned her zeal to the cause of anticommunism. In 1950, she and Capra helped DeMille push through a change in the bylaws requiring a loyalty oath of all members of the SDG, and she also made it her business to help circulate information on alleged entertainment industry Communists and Communist sympathizers to such interested parties as Capra and J. Edgar Hoover.

The Biberman dossier was a motley grab bag, drawn from Los Angeles and New York newspapers, the West Coast Communist party newspaper *People's World,* the anti-Communist organ *Alert,* and from various informers, including those who had named Biberman to HUAC as a Communist. In addition to allegations about Biberman's affiliations with various leftist groups and individuals, the dossier included such other items as his unlisted telephone number, charges that he participated in a memorial gathering for Franklin D. Roosevelt and led a protest outside HUAC hearings, and a notice from the *Los Angeles Daily News* about his scheduled appearance with his wife, the blacklisted actress Gale Sondergaard, to read from his poetry at a Unitarian church.

Willebrandt used her official capacity with the SDG and her association with Capra to give credence to charges she made against people in the entertainment business. An example was a letter she wrote to Hoover on September 21, 1950 (with a copy to the files of the SDG), making scurrilous sexual and political accusations against a woman whom she said was the mistress of one of the leaders of the rival Radio and Television Directors Guild. Three days earlier, the RTDG had filed an unfair labor charge with the NLRB against the "employer-dominated" SDG. Willebrandt retaliated by charging before the NLRB that the RTDG was "Communist-dominated" and by smearing three of its past leaders. Her letter to Hoover (which enclosed her NLRB affidavit) alleged that a current leader helped his mistress spread Communist propaganda over the radio. Willebrandt mentioned Capra along with DeMille, McCarey, and David Butler in telling Hoover of the SDG's anti-Communist orientation, including its loyalty oath for members. The oath, however, was not made official until October 9, after she helped ramrod it through in one of the ugliest political fights in Hollywood history.

Capra, in his autobiography, extolled Mabel Walker Willebrandt's "wisdom," "courage," and "morality."

Capra was belatedly but centrally involved in the controversy over the SDG loyalty oath for members, the climax of three years of turmoil within the guild over the blacklist issue. His involvement left him tortured and ambivalent, and contributed to the destruction of his Hollywood career.

Ceplair and Englund wrote that the Directors Guild in the fall of 1947 "did not seem to disagree with [HUAC's] means or ends." But according to Gordon Kahn's 1948 book *Hollywood on Trial*, the guild in early October 1947 issued a public statement (concurred in by the Screen Writers Guild) vigorously expressing its opposition: "Official investigations into the political beliefs held by individuals are in violation of a sacred privilege guaranteed the citizen in this free Democracy. . . . [W]e hereby resolve to defend the reputation of the industry in which we work against attack by the House Committee on Un-American Activities, whose chosen weapon is the cowardly one of inference and whose apparent aim is to silence opposition to their extremist views, in the free medium of motion pictures."

Most of the efforts against HUAC by the SDG's liberal wing were conducted behind the scenes, however, and the guild's public opposition soon weakened and collapsed. Capra was a member of the SDG board at the time (he was elected to the board on May 20, 1946, and was reelected a year later), but after abandoning his own early impulse to speak out, he took no public stand on the hearings, once he realized how hot the issue was.

After the HUAC subpoenas were issued in September 1947 to directors Biberman, Dmytryk, Milestone, Pichel, and Rossen, and the rest of the Hollywood Nineteen, the SDG board appointed its special committee, with John Ford as chairman, to support the subpoenaed directors. Others on the committee were guild president George Stevens, vice president William Wyler, board members John Huston and George Sidney, and Merian C. Cooper. Wyler and Huston were also the leaders, with Philip Dunne, of the newly formed Committee for the First Amendment, a broad coalition of anti-HUAC Hollywood liberals who were trying to steer an uneasy middle course between defending the civil rights of the Nineteen and declaring their own opposition to communism, a strategy that proved disastrous. By trying to place distance between themselves and the Nineteen, they were playing into the hands of those who wanted a Hollywood blacklist. The liberal wing of the SDG made the same error.

On October 20, the day the hearings started, the SDG's special committee wired Speaker of the House Joseph W. Martin, Jr. (R-Massachusetts) and HUAC Chairman Thomas, calling on HUAC to ensure those under investigation their Constitutional rights. But the signers also felt it necessary to declare their own hostility to communism. The liberals in the guild were more concerned about their own careers than about the fate of the "unfriendly" witnesses, whom they were willing to use as scapegoats to demonstrate their own probity.

The right-wing director Sam Wood, a member of the Motion Picture Alliance, testified that day, "There is a constant effort to get control of the guild. In fact, there is an effort to get control of all unions and guilds in Hollywood. I think our most serious time was when George Stevens was president, he went in the service and . . . it was turned over to John Cromwell. Cromwell, with the assistance of three or four others, tried hard to steer us into the Red River, but we had a little too much weight for that." Asked to name the others, Wood replied, "Irving Pichel, Edward Dmytryk, Frank Tuttle, and—I am sorry, there is another name there. I forget."

At the SDG board meeting on October 21, Wyler and Ford expressed outrage over Wood's allegation about Communist influence in the guild, scorning it as patently false. It was proposed that another telegram be sent to Congress, denying the allegation, but Lesley Selander objected, making vague charges against some unnamed former board members. Ford rose eloquently to the defense of their Constitutional rights, reminding the board that Thomas Jefferson himself was once considered a radical. The board finally authorized another telegram, though it was much milder in tone than the one previously sent to Congress by the special committee, and at Ford's urging limited itself to contradicting Wood's allegation.

Huston went to Washington on October 26 with a planeload of stars and other members of the Committee for the First Amendment, including Philip Dunne, Humphrey Bogart and Lauren Bacall, Sterling Hayden, Gene Kelly, Danny Kaye, and Jane Wyatt, but their protest against HUAC was a fiasco, dissolving in recriminations within the group over whether or not they were there "supporting *rights*, not causes," as Dunne later put it.

"John Huston took to the hills shortly thereafter," recalled Abraham Polonsky, a writer-director who later was blacklisted after appearing before HUAC. "Finally there was one last meeting of the Committee for the First Amendment—Willy Wyler was still president, me, Phil Dunne, [screenwriter-composer] Millard Lampell, and a secretary. From our huge auditoriums it had shrunk to a little projection room on Sunset. Wyler said, 'Well, I guess it's no use. We oughta fold. But I can continue to say what I wanna say,' meaning he'd make his fight in his pictures. And Lampell pointed his finger at Wyler—he was always pointing his finger—and he said, 'You'll never make good pictures again.' "

Ten of the Nineteen were cited for contempt of Congress on November 24, 1947, and later that month, the blacklist began unofficially when three of the Hollywood Ten lost their jobs. Edward Dmytryk and Adrian Scott were fired by RKO and Ring Lardner, Jr., by Fox. Hollywood was faced with a decision about the future of the Ten and about the principle involved in hiring or firing them.

"The decisive collapse," wrote Ceplair and Englund, "was the producers' unexpected recourse to the blacklist. . . . [But] evidence exists to indicate that an important minority of powerful studio bosses—Mayer, Goldwyn, Schary [then with RKO], Cohn—were looking for a way to arrive at a different conclusion. If strong intra-industry support for the Ten had been forthcoming from some of the highly influential moderate and liberal screen artists who enjoyed social and professional access to high-level studio management, a number of key moguls might have hesitated."

Instead, at a meeting on November 24 and 25 at the Waldorf-Astoria Hotel in New York, the Association of Motion Picture Producers, the Motion Picture Association of America, and the Society of Independent Motion Picture Producers, reacting to mounting public hysteria in support of HUAC, decided to abandon the Ten and formulate a policy of self-regulation. Known as the "Waldorf Statement," it was released on November 25 and emblazoned on the front page of *Daily Variety* the next day under the headline "JOHNSTON GIVES INDUSTRY POLICY ON COMMIE JOBS":

". . . [W]e will not reemploy any of the 10 until such time as he is acquitted or has purged himself of contempt and declares under oath that he is not a Communist.

"On the broader issue of alleged subversive and disloyal elements in Hollywood, our members are likewise prepared to take positive action.

"We will not knowingly employ a Communist or a member of any party or group which advocates the overthrow of the government of the United States by force or by any illegal or unconstitutional methods.

"In pursuing this policy, we are not going to be swayed by hysteria or intimidation from any source. We are frank to recognize that such a policy involves danger and risks. There is the danger of hurting innocent people. There is the risk of creating an atmosphere of fear. Creative work at its best cannot be carried on in an atmosphere of fear. We will guard against this danger, this risk, this fear.

"To this end we will invite the Hollywood talent guilds to work with us to eliminate any subversives; to protect the innocent; and to safeguard free speech and a free screen wherever threatened. . . ."

On November 27, an unpublicized five-hour emergency meeting was called at MGM with representatives of SAG, the SWG, and the SDG by the West Coast committee set up by the producers to implement the Waldorf Statement (chairman Mayer, producer Walter Wanger, 20th Century–Fox's Joseph Schenck, Paramount's Henry Ginsberg, and Schary). The producers were represented at the meeting by Mayer, Wanger, RKO's N. Peter Rathvon, and Edward Cheyfitz (for the AMPP and the MPAA). Sheridan Gibney, George Seaton, and Harry Tugend represented the writers, Wyler and Ford the directors, and Ronald Reagan the actors.

While blaming the Red-baiting Motion Picture Alliance and other friendly witnesses for provoking the crisis, the producers also expressed resentment at both HUAC and the defiant Hollywood Ten for putting them in what they felt was an impossible position. They wanted the guilds to help them do the dirty work, arguing that ostracizing the few would protect the many. The guild representatives objected, John Ford expressing anger that the producers were trying to buck the issue to the guilds, and Reagan and Gibney making forceful arguments that such a blacklist would be contrary to guild bylaws as well as illegal under the laws of California, the Wagner Act, and the Taft-Hartley Labor-Management Relations Act of 1947.

Reagan, in his testimony as a friendly witness before HUAC that October, did not name names, and he defended the civil rights of alleged Communists. However, as was revealed after he became President of the United States, he was secretly cooperating with the blacklist by acting as an FBI informer (code name: T-10), one of at least eighteen informers in the film industry used by the FBI in that period, and he told the FBI that the Communist Party should be outlawed in the United States.

When skepticism was expressed at the November 27 meeting between the guild representatives and the producers that the blacklist could be limited to ten people, the producers took refuge in what would become their familiar legal fiction: that no Hollywood blacklist existed. The decision about whether to employ the Hollywood Ten (or anyone else), they claimed, would be purely voluntary for each company. That stance had been suggested by the producers' chief counsel, former Secretary of State James F. Byrnes, as a way of getting around the legal pitfalls involved. Yet the producers privately made it clear at the meeting that their position was a façade, that a blacklist henceforth was in effect against those whose actions, as the Waldorf Statement put it, "have been a disservice to their employers and have impaired their usefulness in the industry." Clearly not only the Hollywood Ten were in jeopardy of losing their jobs, but instead of acting to protect their endangered members, the three guilds surrendered.

At a heated general membership meeting of the SDG on December 2, Robert Rossen was booed when he urged that the guild protest the firing of Dmytryk, and the handful of other dissidents at the meeting (among them Biberman, Milestone, Pichel, Huston, Ralph Ceder, Bernard Vorhaus, and Vincent Sherman) also were booed and shouted down as DeMille, McCarey, Wood, George Marshall, and other conservatives pushed through a resolution declaring that the SDG would deny office to anyone who would not sign a non-Communist affidavit.

The guild action was largely symbolic, since section 9H of the Taft-Hartley Act already required that if a labor organization wanted to be protected by the National Labor Relations Board, each of its officers had to sign an affidavit "that he is not a member of the Communist Party or affiliated with such party, and that he does not believe in, and is not a member of or supports any organization that believes in or teaches, the overthrow of the United States Government by force or by any illegal or unconstitutional means."

The vacillating guild president, George Stevens, frankly expressed to the membership the acute discomfort he felt over being politically vulnerable, in the postwar era, for his comradeship with America's Soviet ally in World War II. His remarks made evident his understanding of the ironies (not to say the absurdity) of placing such retrospective blame. But Stevens, who in many ways typified Hollywood liberalism, in the end was willing to abandon the radicals to keep himself and his kind from sharing their stigma. His equivocation on the blacklisting of the Hollywood Ten at the guild's membership meeting and his support of the loyalty oath was a climactic moment in Hollywood liberals' surrender to HUAC.

After a motion for a secret ballot failed, the guild's loyalty oath for officers was passed by a show of hands, 119 to 9. The guild's only qualification was to state that it did not deny "the civil right of any person to be a member of the Communist Party." But it also stated "that a member of the Communist Party has an obligation to the Communist Party which transcends his other obligations and shall transcend his obligation to the Screen Directors Guild."

*   *   *

As a board member of the SDG, Capra was required to sign a non-Communist affidavit or resign his office. There may have been an element of indecision, or tacit protest, in his decision to sign his affidavit on April 6, 1948, but then to leave the board when his term expired that May. He was reelected to the board two years later, on May 16, 1950, six days before the name of the guild was changed to the Screen Directors Guild of America, Inc. With the cold war about to get hot in Korea, he showed no hesitation this time about signing his affidavit.

DeMille and his cohorts on the newly elected board brought pressure in the summer of 1950 to extend the loyalty oath to the entire membership, something no other Hollywood guild required at that time, although the Screen Producers Guild later would do so as well (the Motion Picture Alliance pushed unsuccessfully for an industrywide mandatory loyalty oath). DeMille's plan was opposed by the newly elected SDG president, Joseph L. Mankiewicz, though he had been nominated originally by DeMille at the May 28 meeting. The first sign of friction came when Mankiewicz objected to DeMille's attempt to nominate him as part of a slate of officers, including DeMille's cronies Albert S. Rogell, Vernon Keays, and Lesley Selander, who later helped lead the campaign for the loyalty oath as vice president, secretary, and treasurer; Mankiewicz was elected after his nomination was withdrawn and he was renominated as an individual by George Sidney. Then a Republican, Mankiewicz willingly signed the non-Communist oath required of guild officers under Taft-Hartley, but he defied DeMille by declaring that forcing the members to sign too would be an illegal infringement on their civil rights; under Taft-Hartley, a union could deem a member unemployable only for dues delinquency.

As an immigrant, Capra had always felt extraordinarily sensitive and vulnerable on the loyalty issue, and the resurgence of nativism in America at the onset of World War II—brought home by his sister Ann's classification as an "enemy alien"—made him more anxious than ever before to demonstrate his loyalty to the service of his adopted country. But in the climate of postwar hysteria, and with Red-baiting Sen. Joseph McCarthy (R-Wisconsin) now in full cry, Capra's wartime service and decorations did not put his loyalty beyond question. In those days, even deportation was not out of the question for naturalized citizens who were deemed not "American" enough.

On June 25, the Korean War began, leading to an all-out assault on suspected "Reds" in the United States. As he had done before when America entered the two world wars, Capra hastened to offer his services to the Army. Though he insisted in 1984 that he "stayed out" of making films about the Korean War "because I really didn't understand it, I didn't know what they were fighting about," an SDG press release described "Colonel Frank Capra" as among the guild members who were "eager and ready to go" to Korea. But while Ford made plans to shoot a combat documentary for the Navy, *This is Korea!*, Capra languished in Hollywood, wondering what could have gone wrong. "No word yet to Frank from the Signal Corps on his return to active duty," *The Hollywood Reporter* obligingly noted on August 17, the day before it was announced he would direct *You Belong to Me* for Paramount.

It was on August 18 that the DeMille faction took advantage of Mankiewicz's absence on a European vacation to push a resolution supporting a loyalty oath for members through the SDG board. DeMille first had raised the idea at an emergency meeting he called with Capra, Willebrandt, and DeMille's guild factotum, Al Rogell. DeMille, according to Rogell, said he had "heard from a very reliable source in Washington that Joe McCarthy, who was in the headlines almost every day, had threatened to come to Hollywood, and his aim was the Directors Guild." Though no such investigation ever materialized, Rogell, to "keep McCarthy and his group out of here," brought the proposal for a loyalty oath to a vote at an emergency board meeting, while Mankiewicz, who had not been informed of the impending vote on the proposed amendment to the bylaws, was sailing back to New York.

Capra initially sidestepped voting on the issue. He was one of six other board members not present at the meeting, though he was the only one who was in town. He claimed he was busy working at Paramount when the one-hour board meeting began at 5 P.M.

Willebrandt the day before had given the guild her opinion that barring Communists and like-minded people from membership would be legal, and urged that such a step be taken. After weighing the idea of asking only for an oath for new members, the board decided unanimously that a ballot would be mailed to the general membership on an oath for all members, along with its urging of a yes vote.

"SCREEN DIRECTORS' GUILD DEMANDS NON-COMMY OATH OF MEMBERS," *Daily Variety* headlined its report of the meeting.

Despite Capra's absence, his name, like that of Mankiewicz, was attached to a public statement issued by the board explaining its action: "We, as representatives of one of the world's greatest industries, must make our position known to America and to the world on behalf of this industry. We sincerely hope and know that all guilds, unions, and other motion picture organizations and affiliates will follow our move."

The proposed oath (subsequently announced in a trade advertisement) read: "I am not a member of the Communist Party or affiliated with such party, and I do not believe in, and I am not a member of nor do I support any organization that believes in or teaches, the overthrow of the United States Government by force or by any illegal or unconstitutional methods."

The fact that the ballots were numbered contributed to an atmosphere of fear in which only fourteen directors dared to check the "no" box under the text of the proposed loyalty oath. There were 547 "yes" votes; 57 ballots were not returned, the guild explaining that some of those represented directors who were working on location or were in Europe. The official tally was not announced until October 13.

No record exists today of how Capra and other individual members voted. The ballots themselves were destroyed at a general membership meeting on October 22. But other guild records indicate that Capra supported the oath after the ballots were mailed, before experiencing a temporary change of heart.

After landing in New York, Mankiewicz publicly questioned the timing of the board vote, the open ballot, and the lack of an open discussion. He subsequently used much stronger language to Capra and the other board members: "Russia is the only place I know where the populace is not entitled to a secret ballot." Under Taft-Hartley, he insisted, "we have not the right to deny a man the right to work because he won't sign an affidavit," warning that such a requirement would be a useful tool in blacklisting.

With the vote tally of the membership running so heavily in favor of the oath, its proponents did not feel they needed to wait for the balloting's completion to proclaim victory, although they were not yet ready to do so publicly. At an August 31 meeting of the Executive Committee, a sort of board-within-the-board, it was decided that the producers be informed that the oath was becoming part of the guild bylaws. Although Capra had not been present at that meeting, at the September 5 board meeting (chaired by Mankiewicz, who although president had no vote on the board), it was Capra who moved that the committee's recommendations be accepted, and the board unanimously agreed.*

The board then accepted the recommendation of George Marshall's Bylaws Committee that a blacklist be made available to the producers of guild members who did not sign the oath: on a motion by DeMille, sec-

---

* According to Mankiewicz, DeMille later proposed that in addition to taking a loyalty oath, "every director, at the conclusion of a film, file a report on all the actors he has used in that film, in terms of their Americanism, loyalty, and patriotic attitudes. These reports were to be kept in a dossier in the SDG files, and the producers were to have access to them, in order to know whether they were hiring good Americans."

onded by Capra, the board voted unanimously to send out a "not in good standing" list of those members along with a separate list of members in good standing. According to *Daily Variety*, the blacklist of directors who did not sign the oath was to be placed in the guild's quarterly report to studios and producers.

George Stevens, then a board member, later recalled that he and Capra, "a great friend of mine, fell totally apart on this [blacklisting]." Stevens remembered Capra telling him, "They've got the goods on some of these guys," and "he mentioned a director's name that happens to be the same last name as Paul Robeson's" (Mark Robson, a liberal member of the guild, was a Mankiewicz supporter).

With the membership vote completed, the loyalty oath bylaw and its blacklist provision were approved at the board meeting of October 9. But the blacklist provision caused a strenuous debate, sparked by Mankiewicz's warning that any widespread revolt against the oath could lead to civil war within the guild and by his own statement of opposition to the blacklist. When he used the word "blacklist," Mankiewicz recalled, "I looked right at Jack Ford when I said it, and Ford jumped a foot. He didn't want any part of a blacklist, which I'd hoped would be the case." (Mankiewicz's use of the word also drew protests from board members who approved of the measure.)

Ford told the board that not only Mankiewicz would be among those blacklisted by the guild for not signing the oath, but also Merian C. Cooper, his producing partner in Argosy Pictures and a member of the guild. A brigadier general in the U.S. Army, Cooper had been chief of staff in China for General Claire Chennault and later deputy chief of staff for all Air Force units under General Douglas MacArthur. Mankiewicz's biographer, Kenneth L. Geist, wrote: "According to Mankiewicz, Cooper told his friend and colleague John Ford that even if DeMille put a pistol to his head, he would not sign a loyalty oath that was not required by the government."

After winning Ford's moral support, Mankiewicz drew the line for the board: as *Daily Variety* reported two days later, he "made the flat statement that he would not sign the SDG's oath, even though, as an officer of the guild, he signed a government loyalty oath as required by the Taft-Hartley law."

DeMille, equally defiant, moved that the oath be mailed to the members without further delay, and Tay Garnett seconded the motion, which was passed unanimously. Then Lesley Selander, with Rogell seconding, moved that the blacklist provision be made part of the official bylaws.

Now Capra switched his position on the blacklist provision, perhaps influenced by Ford, whom he greatly respected, and also perhaps because he had now had time enough to think about what it really meant. Capra, Mark Robson, and Clarence Brown were recorded as objecting to the Selander-Rogell motion. When the vote was taken on the loyalty oath bylaw, Capra voted against it because of the blacklist provision; Robson, Brown, and Ford were also in opposition, according to *Daily Variety*, and a letter Capra later wrote to the board provides further confirmation that his was one of four dissenting votes. But they were in the minority, and the bylaw passed. (According to Geist, the board "eventually adopted a compromise measure of sending out only a list of members not in good standing. The reason for their lack of good standing was to be furnished to the producer upon inquiry.")

Mankiewicz, unwilling to let the matter rest, pressed for a general membership meeting to make it clear to directors that they were in danger of being blacklisted if they refused to sign the oath. Ford expressed strong opposition to calling such a meeting because he feared it would set the membership against the board. DeMille tried to placate Mankiewicz by claiming that the loyalty oath fight was not directed at him personally, but was necessitated by the Korean War.

Though he remained adamant to the board about calling a membership meeting, Mankiewicz backed off the next day in a telephone conversation with Ford. But the matter did not rest there.

"SDG SCHISM ON 'BLACKLIST' " read the banner headline in *Daily Variety* on October 11, over a detailed account of the "bitter debate" at the board meeting. The subhead proclaimed, "MANKIEWICZ WILL NOT SIGN OATH."

The trade paper called the proposal to send producers a list of guild members who would not sign the oath "tantamount to a blacklist" and predicted that it would cause "a serious schism" in the guild. The provision was "said to have come under such heavy fire from Mankiewicz that he won the support of board members Frank Capra, Mark Robson, Clarence Brown, and John Ford. . . . However, the proloyalty oath faction on the board spearheaded by DeMille and Rogell won out in the final vote on the bylaw and its 'blacklist' provision."

Panicking over being publicly identified as an opponent of blacklisting, Capra tried to backtrack from the tentative support he had shown for Mankiewicz's position. At a meeting called by the furious DeMille faction that night—which they kept secret from Mankiewicz partisans, some thinking that Mankiewicz had leaked the news to *Daily Variety* as a disruptive measure—Capra agreed to join a DeMille-sponsored committee to recall

Mankiewicz from his presidency and signed a petition to start guild machinery in motion for a recall vote by senior directors.*

Capra offered a justification for his actions in a seven-page letter to the board dated November 1, after the DeMille faction had been repudiated by the general membership. He distorted the stance he had taken by implying that he had been consistently opposed to the blacklist provision, even though he had actively supported it before the October 9 meeting. He insisted that his ultimate support for a loyalty oath and his participation in the recall move against Mankiewicz were motivated not by any desire to impose a blacklist on the SDG membership, but to avoid the public impression in a time of war that members of the guild were disloyal. While claiming (like DeMille) that he personally was not impugning the patriotism of Mankiewicz or his faction, he felt their actions had caused disunion and brought a damaging impression of disloyalty into the open.

Mankiewicz, for his part, felt that the subhead of the October 11 *Daily Variety* article about the SDG schism—"MANKIEWICZ WILL NOT SIGN OATH"—misrepresented his position and "could not only bring discredit upon the guild, but upon my own good name and character," because he had been willing to sign the oath as a guild officer under the requirement of the Taft-Hartley law, as the article stated.

"I think that during the day and night of Wednesday, October 11," Mankiewicz later told the guild membership, "I considered every possible result and ramification that might eventuate from that story in the trade paper, except that it should be assumed by anyone in [his] right mind that I could have given the story to the paper. It could never conceivably have occurred to me that men whom I have known and with whom I have worked for as long as twenty years and that many members of a guild to which I have given so much of my time and my energy would have simply assumed my guilt."

The source for the article, according to Geist, was the DeMille faction; Capra conceded in his letter to the board that Mankiewicz had not leaked the information, and expressed regret that he and the other recall com-

---

* Besides DeMille and Capra, the signers of the petition included board members Tay Garnett, Frank McDonald, Albert S. Rogell, William A. Seiter, Lesley Selander, Richard Wallace, and John S. Waters; and Gordon Douglas, Leo McCarey, George Marshall, Andrew Stone, Ed L. Walker, and Jules White. The committee to recall Mankiewicz, as subsequently constituted, included Capra, DeMille, Garnett, McDonald, Rogell, Seiter, Selander, Wallace, Waters; board members David Butler and Clarence Brown; Henry King, McCarey, Marshall, and Stone. The board members who did not participate in the recall movement were Claude Binyon, Frank Borzage, Merian C. Cooper, John Ford, Walter Lang, Mark Robson, George Sidney, and George Stevens.

mittee members had used it as an excuse for their drive to oust the guild president.

The recall ballot read in its entirety: "This is a ballot to recall Joe Mankiewicz. Sign here ☐ Yes."

DeMille and guild secretary Vernon Keays on October 12 worked surreptitiously to prepare recall ballots for directors they felt would not support Mankiewicz, hoping to achieve the 60 percent vote tally required (167 of the 278 senior directors) before Mankiewicz and his supporters could mount a defense. "Fifty-five names were scratched from the list," wrote Geist, "and in a movement reminiscent of the sequence from Capra's *Meet John Doe* (1941) in which the corrupt reactionary played by Edward Arnold sends out uniformed cyclists to stave off the ideological threat of Gary Cooper, motorcycle messengers were dispatched into the night to hand-deliver the ballots." Geist added: "Ironically, Capra was among the members of the recall committee." John Huston called it "a putsch in the night."

"Did you know, for Christ's sake, there's a fucking recall action on against you?" Mankiewicz's brother, Herman, shouted to him on the phone that night. "Johnny Farrow said some guy just drove up on a motorcycle to his house to get him to sign the petition."

While the results of the membership vote on the loyalty oath were announced with "pride" in the trade press on October 13, Huston, with some difficulty, was rounding up twenty-five Mankiewicz supporters to petition for a membership meeting. Ironically, Huston's petition contained a loyalty oath which all twenty-five petitioners took in order to be considered in good standing with the guild.*

That same day, Capra and his fellow members of the recall committee sent out a four-page telegram trying to have it both ways on the blacklisting issue by engaging in the familiar Hollywood fiction that there was no such thing as a blacklist, while still making it clear that the oath would enable producers to blacklist anyone who was refused membership or was drummed out of the guild for refusing to sign it.

Declaring that Mankiewicz's characterization of the new bylaw as a blacklist was "UNTRUE AND WAS CHALLENGED BY THE BOARD AS INCENDIARY," the recall committee insisted that "A MEMBER WHO CHOOSES NOT TO COMPLY WITH

---

* *The petitioners were Huston, H. C. Potter, Peter Ballbusch, Michael Gordon, Andrew Marton, George Seaton, Maxwell Shane, Mark Robson, Richard Brooks, John Sturges, Felix Feist, Robert Wise, Robert Parrish, Otto Lang, Richard Fleischer, Fred Zinnemann, Joseph Losey, William Wyler, Jean Negulesco, Nicholas Ray, Billy Wilder, Don Hartman, Charles Vidor, John Farrow, and Walter Reisch.*

THE BYLAW REQUIRING A NON-COMMUNIST OATH MAY STILL BE EMPLOYED, BUT HIS EMPLOYMENT BECOMES A MATTER OF INDIVIDUAL NEGOTIATION WITH HIS EMPLOYER."

Implying that Mankiewicz was responsible for the article in *Daily Variety*, the telegram concluded, "MR. MANKIEWICZ HAS, THEREFORE, PITTED HIMSELF AGAINST THE LEGAL GOVERNING BODY OF THE GUILD, ITS BOARD OF DIRECTORS. HE REPUDIATES THE DEMOCRATIC VOTE OF ITS MEMBERSHIP. HE STANDS WITH 14 AGAINST 547. THE ISSUE IS WHETHER MR. MANKIEWICZ IS TO RULE THE GUILD. . . .

"OURS IS A DEMOCRATIC ORGANIZATION. WE RESPECT MR. MANKIEWICZ' RIGHT AS A MEMBER TO VOTE 'NO' ON THE BYLAW. THEN HE, AS A MEMBER OF THE GUILD, WILL HAVE THE SAME RIGHT AS OTHER MEMBERS TO STAND WITH THE MINORITY OF 14. HOWEVER, NOW, WE MUST DISAVOW MR. MANKIEWICZ' RIGHT TO USE HIS OFFICE AS PRESIDENT IN SUCH A DICTATORIAL MANNER AS TO RENDER THE DEMOCRATIC PROCEDURE OF THE BOARD OF DIRECTORS IMPOSSIBLE. BY HIS ACTIONS HE HAS LEFT US NO ALTERNATIVE BUT TO RECOMMEND THAT HE BE RECALLED ACCORDING TO THE DEMOCRATIC METHOD PROVIDED IN THE BYLAWS, NAMELY BY YOUR VOTE."

On October 16, Capra picked up his copy of *Daily Variety* and read the headline "MANKIEWICZ RECALL TO FAIL." He learned that Mankiewicz had decided to win the battle but lose the war. The guild president had taken "much of the wind out of the recall petitioners' sails" by signing the member's loyalty oath. Capra read an advertisement in which thirty-eight directors urged the members of the guild not to vote on the recall until after a membership meeting could be held and another ad in which Mankiewicz himself declared: "My personal feelings remain unchanged. If anything, they have been strengthened. . . . As long as I am president of the Screen Directors Guild of America, I will continue to fight for the right of every member to an open discussion and a closed ballot. As an American, I will fight as long as I live to maintain that distinction which is so intrinsically and inherently American—the distinction between properly constituted governmental authority and the attempt of any individual or group of individuals to usurp that authority."

Capra also learned on October 16 that Huston's group had succeeded in forcing a membership meeting to discuss the Mankiewicz recall on October 22. But he now realized that he had misjudged Mankiewicz, both for believing him the source of the *Daily Variety* article and for believing him implacably opposed to signing the member's loyalty oath. On October 18, Capra drafted a telegram on behalf of the recall committee that would have called off the recall movement and praised Mankiewicz for his change of heart, while also defending the American rights of freedom of thought and action. But according to Capra's letter, DeMille, who wanted Mankiewicz to show signs of apology, blocked approval of the telegram, although he agreed to discuss it with Mankiewicz.

At an emotional board meeting that night called in an attempt to conciliate the warring parties, Mankiewicz produced a letter from *Daily Variety* editor Joe Schoenfeld stating that the guild president had not been the source of its article (an ally and confidant of Mankiewicz and his faction, Schoenfeld later became one of Capra's agents at William Morris). "Almost to a man," Mankiewicz told the membership four days later, "the board members admitted to me openly and privately that they had never known the true facts and that they were shocked at the falseness of [the] accusations."

The board unanimously voted in principle to support a revision of the bylaws to provide for a closed ballot in future voting by the membership. Capra moved that the board give Mankiewicz a unanimous vote of confidence, and it did so.

Fed up with the internecine warfare, Capra sent a telegram of resignation from the board on the following night in what *Daily Variety* called "open protest against the failure of the DeMille-Rogell-Marshall faction to go through with the plan to recall the recall movement. This had been discussed at the SDG board meeting the previous evening, when the board gave Mankiewicz a surprise unanimous vote of confidence.

"However, the following day [at an informal meeting with several board members present in DeMille's office at Paramount], DeMille demanded from Mankiewicz an act of contrition, which Mankiewicz flatly refused. DeMille then dropped the idea of recalling the recall, and Capra walked out on him and the board."

Because of his resignation from the board and from the recall committee, Capra was absent from the seven-hour general membership meeting attended by 298 guild members and others (holding 64 proxies) at the Beverly Hills Hotel on October 22, a tumultuous occasion at which Stevens, Wyler, Huston, and others systematically demolished the case of DeMille and the recall committee, whose actions Mankiewicz called "so foreign to everything I have ever known or learned or thought as an American."

DeMille read a list of alleged Communist front groups with which he said some of the petitioners had been affiliated and warned that the *Daily Worker* and *Pravda* would "gloat over the spectacle" taking place within the guild. "To accentuate the fact that we weren't born in this country," as Fred Zinnemann put it, DeMille mocked the accents of foreign-born directors in reading the names of the petitioners, referring to Billy Wilder, William Wyler, and Fred Zinnemann as "Vilder," "Vyler," and "Tzinnemann." The audience "booed him until he sat down," Mankiewicz remembered. ". . . When DeMille heard those boos, he knew the meeting had turned against him. He was beat."

Wyler, a native of France, rose to say, "I am sick and tired of having people question my loyalty to my country. The next time I hear somebody do it, I am going to kick hell out of him. I don't care how old he is or how big."

Stevens made a long and careful attack on the recall movement "and in fact defended the Constitution of the United States," Huston recalled. Stevens finished by criticizing the guild for being "interested in nothing besides the fight against communism" and by announcing both Capra's and his own resignations from the board.

Capra's absence from the meeting was regretted by his close friend William Wellman, who said that "a guy I am very proud of and very fond of has resigned because he can't stand it any longer." Rouben Mamoulian urged Stevens to remain on the board, and Harold Daniels, with a second by Boris Ingster, proposed that the membership ask *both* Stevens and Capra to remain on the board; the motion was passed unanimously.

The Russian-born Mamoulian, reminding the members that he and other founders of the guild had been accused of being "red, left, revolutionaries" in the 1930s, expressed anguish over DeMille's assault on foreign-born directors.

"It was the first time anybody had ever mentioned my accent," Mamoulian recalled in 1985. "That man sat there with his red face—it was a terrible moment, and it has haunted me all this time. DeMille said we should be governed by real Americans, that there were too many accents, and I said I was a better American than he was, because he was just born here and I *chose* the place. We saved the guild. They were going to start wearing marching shoes."

The coup de grâce to DeMille and his faction was delivered by John Ford, who, after sitting silently for most of the evening, rose to announce, "My name is John Ford. I am a director of Westerns. I am one of the founders of this guild . . . [and] I would like to state that I have been on Mr. Mankiewicz's side of the fight all through it. I have not read one item of print in the newspaper or trade papers. I have not read one telegram or one ballot or one recall notification. I have been sick and tired and ashamed of the whole goddamned thing. I don't care which side it is. If they intend to break up the guild, goddammit, they have pretty well done it tonight. . . .

"We organized this guild to protect ourselves against producers. . . . Now somebody wants to throw ourselves into a news service and an intelligence service and give out to producers what looks to me like a blacklist.

I don't think we should . . . put ourselves in a position of putting out derogatory information about a director, whether he is a Communist, beats his mother-in-law, or beats dogs.

"I don't agree with C. B. DeMille. I admire him. I don't *like* him, but I admire him. . . .

"Everybody has apologized. Everybody has said their say, and Joe has been vindicated. What we need is a motion to adjourn."

But Mankiewicz insisted on discussing the conduct of the recall committee, and Ford, to a huge round of applause, picked up on a suggestion made earlier by others and said: "I believe there is only one alternative, and that is for the board of directors to resign and elect a new board of directors. They are under enough fire tonight. It appears they haven't got the support of the men that elected them."

Before the remaining board members formally resigned and DeMille walked off the podium disdainfully, Ford and Mankiewicz jointly won passage of a motion that the guild be run in the interim by an executive committee consisting of its five past presidents—Capra, John Cromwell, George Marshall, George Stevens, and King Vidor. In addition, Mankiewicz was directed by the membership to name a committee to investigate the recall movement.

The following day Willebrandt (whose attempt to resign as guild counsel had been rejected at the meeting) told Mankiewicz that the bylaws made rule by an executive committee illegal, so on October 25 Mankiewicz assembled five remaining members of the junior board and the five ex-presidents at Lucey's Restaurant in Hollywood and had the remnant board elect a new board and new officers under Mankiewicz: Ford was named first vice president, Capra second vice president, Stevens secretary, and George Sidney treasurer. Capra was mollified by Mankiewicz's assurance that he would write a letter recommending that members sign the loyalty oath, which Capra thought would help quell the public questioning of guild members' patriotism.

But Mankiewicz's letter of October 26 (published the next day in *Daily Variety*), though calling on members to sign the oath "as a voluntary act," infuriated Capra all over again with its insistence that "the late and lamentable rift within our ranks had nothing whatsoever to do with the pro or con of a loyalty oath. . . . And yet there exists a wicked and widespread misconception to the contrary—both within our industry and without. A misconception that continues to vilify and smear both our persons and our guild. It is essential that you help to remove that misconception."

Mankiewicz's contradictory actions left the final impression that he felt the real issue was not the loyalty oath but the undemocratic way the guild had enacted it. But Capra thought Mankiewicz's letter was as deceitful as anti-American Soviet propaganda about the causes of the Korean War. He proceeded from the mistaken assumption that Mankiewicz was suggesting the guild controversy had arisen not from the loyalty oath but from a dispute over the use of guild funds by officers who had been part of the anti-Mankiewicz faction.

On October 31, Mankiewicz notified the new board that Capra had submitted his resignation from the board, in his letter postdated November 1. Capra reminded the board that Mankiewicz had been "in violent opposition to a loyalty oath for all guild members. . . . Mr. Mankiewicz' letter to the members is not to me a sincere attempt to heal the rift. It is vindication and sanctification for himself and his disciples, and consignment to hell for the opposition." But Capra's letter also expressed regret that he and others in the guild had acted badly.

Capra was replaced by Vidor as second vice president, the loyalty oath became a fact of life for members of the guild, the guild adopted rules preventing another such abuse as the Mankiewicz recall, and at the end of his term on May 27, 1951, Mankiewicz left office voluntarily and quit Hollywood for New York, George Sidney replacing him as president.

Still fuming because Mankiewicz (after consulting with Stevens, Sidney, and Vidor) had refused to read his seven-page resignation letter to the board in October, Capra decided to vindicate himself by seeking reelection to guild office. He had been mulling over the idea of sharing the letter with the general membership, and at the start of the campaign in February, someone leaked the letter to the press. That May, Capra was returned to the board, as first vice president.

The loyalty oath remained part of the guild bylaws until 1966, when the U.S. Supreme Court upheld a lower court's ruling that the guild could not deny membership to six directors who refused to sign it when the Screen Directors International Guild merged in 1965 with the Directors Guild of America (as the guild was renamed in 1960). During the entire history of the guild's loyalty oath, only one director was successfully barred from membership for refusing to sign it—Charlie Chaplin, before he became an exile from the United States in 1952.

Capra's obsessive concern with the October 11 *Daily Variety* article reporting the schism in the guild over blacklisting, though it gave him a convenient scapegoat for his own actions by allowing him to pretend that the article and not the oath itself was responsible for the public controversy, was based on a very real fear of the reaction such news could engender. It was one thing to object to a blacklist in private but another to be seen in public as taking such a stand—and yet another to attempt to distance himself from the controversy.

The controversy came at a particularly sensitive time for Capra, since he was waiting for word from the Army about service in the Korean War. It was reported in *Daily Variety* on August 28 that the federal government would require a loyalty oath from everyone involved in making government films on the "current global crisis." All filmmakers working in military or restricted secret installations would be investigated by the Army and the FBI, and "much more caution is being exercised as regards total loyalty to this country than was evident during World War II."

A week after the story of Capra protesting the SDG's blacklisting provision was broken by *Daily Variety* it was picked up (as DeMille had predicted) by the *Daily Worker*. The Communist Party newspaper, which in August had decried Capra's descent from his "notable progressive films in the 1930s" into "silly horse-racing stories," mentioned Capra's protest in an article on October 18 ("Screen Directors Guild Split on 'Loyalty Oath' ") derived entirely from the *Daily Variety* article. It stated: "The blacklist provision of the loyalty oath bylaw was especially attacked by Mankiewicz and he was backed up by board members Frank Capra, Mark Robson, Clarence Brown, and John Ford, the trade paper said." As a result, a citation was placed in Capra's HUAC file: "CAPRA, Frank. Supports revolt against loyalty oath in Screen Directors Guild. *Daily Worker*, October 18, 1950, page 11."

Ironically, since the *Daily Worker* was a week behind *Daily Variety* with the news, the HUAC files did not reflect the fact that Capra had tried to backtrack from his tentative support for Mankiewicz by joining the recall committee after *Daily Variety* wrote about the October 9 meeting. Nor did the *Worker* article or the HUAC files reflect the fact that what Capra opposed at the meeting was not the oath itself, only the blacklist provision of the bylaw, and that he otherwise was one of the oath's most vigorous supporters.*

---

* *The HUAC files on Capra also cited items from* People's World, *noting that in 1942 the paper had reported his promotion to lieutenant colonel by the U.S. Army and that he was planning to produce the* Know Your Ally *series; an article in the paper that year by Sergei Eisenstein mentioning Capra also was cited in the files. Army Intelligence was another reader of* People's World, *noting that in 1944 it "quoted* Hollywood Reporter . . . *as having stated that Russia had a plan for a series of programs to be given at the House of Cinema Workers in Moscow[,] which programs were to include productions by CAPRA."*

The out-of-date information from the *Daily Worker* was also placed in Capra's G-2 file on October 25, and it helped raise a red flag when G-2 searched the HUAC files and other "appropriate files" for "derogatory information" on Capra in July 1951. A G-2 report by Maj. A. J. Sutton on July 12 indicated that: "CAPRA was reported to have associated with left-wing groups, and to have been one of several motion picture directors who were plotting a line of attack on the Congressional Investigation of Communism in the motion picture industry. SUBJECT considered possibly subversive. Flagged in TAG [The Adjutant General of the Army] 21 November 1950. Also flagged in Sixth Army."

G-2 apparently had been tipped off even before the SDG board vote on the loyalty oath bylaw that something was amiss with Capra, for it requested that the FBI investigate him. The results were submitted to G-2 on October 9, the day the vote was taken. The FBI report itself is still classified, but it may have been the one which the FBI made on Capra "alleging Comm[unist] sympathies," as G-2 summarized it in November.

As a result of that report, G-2 opened an active case on Capra, which ended his attempt to return to service in the Signal Corps. In its November 21 memo entitled "Personnel Action on Officer—CAPRA," G-2 wrote the commanding general of the Sixth Army at the Presidio of San Francisco: "It is requested that the Chief, Operations Branch, Security and Training Division, Office of the Assistant Chief of Staff, G-2, Intelligence, be consulted before the following-described officer is appointed to the Officers' Reserve Corps, the National Guard of the United States, or called to active duty."

When asked for his comment, the deputy chief signal officer, Major General Kirke B. Lawton, who had known Capra while head of the Army Pictorial Service during part of World War II, tried to protect him by writing a memo for the record on November 16 stating that while "Colonel Frank Capra will not be called to active duty for the present . . . this decision was not based on the attached [FBI] report."

But no more was heard of Capra's offer to reenlist.

It took a while for Capra to realize that the Army had cut him loose, for as late as January 18, 1951, he was writing the Italian producer Giuseppe Amato that he could not make *The Little World of Don Camillo* that year because of his expected return to Army service.

On January 22, 1951, there was a vivid public demonstration of Capra's vulnerability when the State Department announced that it had filed a formal objection, on behalf of Columbia Pictures, to the U.S.S.R.'s use of

Mr. Deeds Goes to Town and *Mr. Smith Goes to Washington* as anti-American propaganda.

State said the Soviets were "twisting" the films to make them serve their purposes, and that the version of *Mr. Deeds* showing in the Soviet Union had been truncated to end with Deeds's commitment to a mental institution for giving his money to the poor. According to *Daily Variety*, the Soviets claimed that the films had been captured from the Nazis, who had "chopped up the pictures to provide the distorted versions."

The popularity of Capra's films in the U.S.S.R., in addition to being noted by HUAC and G-2, probably was among the derogatory information in State's file on Capra, some of which is still classified. State notified G-2 in 1951 that Capra had traveled to Moscow and Leningrad in 1937, and it apparently also told G-2 about Capra's clandestine meetings with Ambassador Litvinov in 1942. In 1954, during the U.S. Senate investigation of the *Why We Fight* series and those who made the films, Capra felt compelled to deny any personal involvement in the production of *The Battle of Russia*.

Paramount settled its contract with Capra on March 20, 1951, shortly after HUAC began its final purge of Hollywood "Reds."

Earlier that month, HUAC issued the first of 110 subpoenas for an intensified new round of hearings which began that month and continued into the fall. Capra, who suffered in that period from stomach troubles and a severe bout of depression, was so panicky that he told the press he wanted to leave town immediately, abandoning *Here Comes the Groom* in postproduction, but that the studio had persuaded him to stay until the editing was completed.

"I hoped he would go on making films," Dimitri Tiomkin recalled, "but one day he said to me in an outburst of resentment: 'Nobody can compel me to make motion pictures. I don't have to!' I thought he was merely discontented and would get over it." But in April Capra sold his "Brentwood bivouac" (as *The Hollywood Reporter* called it) to agent Abby Greshler for the fire-sale price of about $100,000, half of its original dollar value in the late 1930s ("If we had it today we'd be *billionaires*," Capra lamented to his son Tom in 1984), and began preparation to move his family permanently to Red Mountain Ranch.

HUAC investigators William Wheeler and Courtney E. Owens were looking into the controversy over the SDG loyalty oath. Committee chairman John S. Wood (D-Georgia) came to Hollywood to oversee the investigation and to take testimony from unidentified witnesses on May 10 behind closed doors at the Drake Hotel ("Not all of them were coopera-tive," he said). According to a May 15 article in *The Hollywood Reporter*, "The investigators here have questioned no less than six members of the guild, and it is expected that some of those talked to, and perhaps others, will be subpoenaed."

The next day, Capra checked off the Paramount lot. He told *Daily Variety* that he had "no plans whatever, and would take a holiday on his ranch. He indicated, however, that if a suitable property came along which he liked, he would undertake it."

He escaped being called to testify in HUAC's public hearings, but as the hearings progressed, his past tendency to hire screenwriters who later were accused of being Communists or Communist sympathizers be-came increasingly obvious. Writers who had worked on Capra films and were blacklisted in 1951–1952 included Sidney Buchman, John Sanford, Robert Lees, Fred Rinaldo, Lillian Hellman, Carl Foreman, Dorothy Parker, Jerome Chodorov, Hugo Butler, Michael Wilson, and Ian McLel-lan Hunter; Frances Goodrich and Albert Hackett found themselves tem-porarily under a political cloud after the American Legion accused them of being Communist sympathizers. Other writers who had contributed to Capra films included two of the Hollywood Ten, Herbert Biberman and Dalton Trumbo; Carlton Moss exiled himself from the film industry be-fore being named as a Communist before HUAC; several others, including Marc Connelly, were graylisted; and Clifford Odets, who like Connelly had contributed to *It's a Wonderful Life,* turned informer before HUAC, as did Leopold Atlas, one of the writers in Capra's World War II unit.

Though Capra may well have felt that he had no choice but to leave Hollywood, he preferred the public to think it was solely his decision, and Paramount did not contradict him. There was, in any event, a lingering ambiguity about his preemptive departure which perhaps could only have been resolved if he had stayed in Hollywood and events had played them-selves out to the end. Max Youngstein, who was Paramount's advertising and publicity director from 1949 until shortly before Capra's departure, later recalled that he "had my ear to the ground" and knew of Capra's political "graylisting," but that he felt Capra was still employable when the filmmaker left Paramount: "I think it was his personal choice, kind of a disgust with the industry." The liberal Youngstein, who described himself as having been "so violently opposed to HUAC," felt that the suspicions against Capra were "the most ridiculous" imaginable, because Capra was "the number-one representative in our business of the best of America's dreams."

Capra told the press at the time that he had asked to be released from his contract because of Paramount's cancellation of *The Trial* (a script which had some critical comments to make about the witch-hunt); in his book, however, Capra did not even mention *The Trial* but said he asked to be released from his contract because of his frustration over Paramount's fiscal conservatism in canceling a whole string of projects between 1947 and 1951, including *The Friendly Persuasion* and *Roman Holiday*.*

In the uncut manuscript of his book, Capra explained the cancellation of those two projects differently: he said *he* had canceled them when he discovered that their screenwriters, Michael Wilson and Ian McLellan Hunter, were alleged to be Communists.

Both films eventually were made by William Wyler, and the fact that Wyler made one of them, *Roman Holiday*, for Paramount in 1952–1953 indicates that it could well have been Capra's own decision, not the studio's, to drop the project in 1951. Less than a month after Capra settled his contract, *The New York Times* reported that Wyler was reading the script of *Roman Holiday* with "a view to making it his next production at the studio now that Capra has left Paramount."

But Capra introduced a note of ambiguity in his uncut manuscript by claiming his discovery that Wilson was under suspicion took place on September 20, 1951—which was six months *after* Paramount settled Capra's contract—and by stating that he learned even later that Hunter was under suspicion. The manuscript claims Capra's first revelation came when Lu called him in from the garden at Red Mountain Ranch to see Wilson defying HUAC on live TV. Capra describes his feelings of betrayal as he watched Wilson testifying, feelings he claims were intensified when he subsequently learned that Hunter, Hugo Butler, and four other (unnamed) persons who had worked for Liberty Films were accused of being Communists, causing him to cancel *The Friendly Persuasion* and *Roman Holiday* to avoid being further tainted. Yet he had settled his contract with Paramount on March 20.

That discrepancy contradicts Capra's assertion in the same manuscript about why he dropped the projects, and raises the possibility that he was simply scapegoating his two screenwriters, in retrospect, for his own political problems that drove him out of Hollywood. He said in 1984 that he regretted not having made *Roman Holiday* and *The Friendly Persuasion*,

---

* Capra's book misstates Paramount's loosely enforced $2 million budgetary ceiling as $1.5 million.

but he did not regret leaving Paramount: "I'd gotten sick of the whole goddamn thing. Paramount just sickened me."

Furthermore, Capra's asserted ignorance of the writers' political situations before the late date of September 20, 1951, is difficult to accept, since Hugo Butler had been named as a Communist before HUAC by screenwriter Richard Macaulay on October 23, 1947, nearly *four years* before Capra's supposed revelation; Hunter was named as a Communist before HUAC on September 19, 1951, by screenwriter Martin Berkeley, who also named Butler; and the charges against Wilson had been no secret in Hollywood before his HUAC appearance. Wilson received his pink subpoena from HUAC on June 13, 1951, and after being fired by Darryl F. Zanuck from Twentieth Century–Fox, he wrote a friend on September 5, "I have been 'laid off,' which is the studios' temporary euphemism for blacklisting me. There was a time when studios waited until a man was in contempt of Congress before blacklisting him; but today the mere announcement that I have a subpoena and that I oppose this committee's aims costs me my job. . . . [F]reedom of speech is costly these days."

Five days before his HUAC appearance, Wilson wrote his mother and father, who had expressed dismay over his stand, "Have Americans been sold on the Big Lie—that the principles on which our country was founded sound 'un-American'? . . . To save my 'career,' I am indeed given only one other alternative: if I were to repudiate all my past beliefs and associations, if I were to perjure myself by smearing patriotic Americans as conspirators and traitors, if I were to jump on the bandwagon of these venal politicians and beat the drum for a third World War—then like the scum Dmytryk,* I could continue to work in the motion picture industry.

"Surely, whatever your own beliefs, you cannot see this as an alternative for a decent human being—to turn Judas, to sell my birthright and worship the Almighty Dollar for the sake of expediency for the sake of my career, or for the sake of your shame as to what people will think. It is not my *career* that is really at stake at all—it is my survival as a free writer. . . . If I have any worth as a writer it is because I have been a worthy citizen."

He quoted the words of Thomas Jefferson: "It behooves every man who values liberty of conscience for himself, to resist invasions of it in

---

* *Edward Dmytryk, a member of the Hollywood Ten who had turned informer to resume his directing career.*

the case of others, or their case may, by change of circumstances, become his own. It behooves him, too, in his own case, to give no example of concession, betraying the common right of independent opinion, by answering questions of faith, which the laws have left between God and himself."

Wilson's work for Capra was touched upon in the writer's appearance before HUAC, although Capra's name was not mentioned. "I contributed to a picture called *It's a Wonderful Life*," Wilson told the committee, and he said, "I feel that this committee might take the credit, or part of it at least, for the fact that *The Friendly Persuasion* was not produced, in view of the fact that it dealt warmly, in my opinion, with a peace-loving people."

HUAC counsel Frank S. Tavenner, Jr., continued the pattern of the committee's public exoneration of Capra by replying, "Of course, this committee has no knowledge of the intimate details of your contract or your relationship with your employer."

When asked, "What knowledge have you of the activities of the Communist Party in the moving picture industry?" Wilson took the Fifth Amendment, "and in so doing I wish also to protect the rights of every American citizen to the privacy of belief and association. . . . I think subversion is being committed against the Bill of Rights here today."

The right-wing movement of which HUAC was a part was aimed at a wider target than the radical Left. It was aimed at the much larger group of those who had, from time to time, espoused progressive ideas. As Albert Maltz observed, "One is destroyed in order that a thousand will be rendered silent and impotent by fear."

What happened to Wilson's script after Capra and Paramount dropped it was a case in point. Wyler had it changed to make the Quaker youth become a killer. The Quakers in Wyler's 1956 Allied Artists film *Friendly Persuasion*, as Pauline Kael observed, "are there only to violate their convictions." Although Wilson while blacklisted had won an Oscar for Stevens's *A Place in the Sun*, the SWG in 1953 had amended its rules permitting production companies to deny screenplay credit to blacklisted writers. Wyler and Allied Artists decided to release *Friendly Persuasion* without any screenwriter credit at all, the only such instance in the history of Hollywood. A public controversy erupted after Wilson received a Writers Guild Award and an Oscar nomination (the Academy subsequently disqualified him), and he sued Wyler, Allied Artists, and the vestigial Liberty Films over the denial of credit.

The case, which was settled out of court, became a landmark in the ongoing battle to destroy the blacklist. After Wilson's death in 1978,

Wyler claimed that the denial of credit was "a decision I regretted but had no control over," and that the controversy "should in no way minimize or detract from my high esteem of Michael Wilson, both as writer and citizen." But a memo written by Wyler for his files on April 8, 1954, contradicts this, indicating he had talked to Y. Frank Freeman about buying the script from Paramount and had received assurance from Freeman that he could deny credit to Wilson. Zelma Wilson said in 1985, "Mike just blamed Wyler. He was very angry. Wyler could have given him credit." *

While trying to explain and justify his abandonment of *The Friendly Persuasion* and *Roman Holiday*, Capra in the uncut manuscript of his autobiography seemed to recognize some of the tragic irony of the situation when he took pains to praise the scripts highly and to make it clear that he did not consider the scripts communistic—only their authors.

"I don't give a fuck about Capra," Ian McLellan Hunter commented in 1984 when told of Capra's explanation, "but I'm sorry to hear this, because I like his films. There were a lot of professional Red-spotters out there, and one of them may have taken him aside and said, 'You're working with half the Commies in Hollywood.' *That* would have scared the shit out of him. He gravitated to blacklisted people; it probably was the Buchmans of the world who gave his pictures their faintly liberal tinge. And he spent the rest of his life trying to straighten himself out."

Though the Army didn't want him, Capra found another way to demonstrate his loyalty when, during his final days at Paramount, he was asked to become a civilian staff member of the Defense Department's top-secret think tank Project VISTA.

Named after its headquarters at Hotel Vista del Arroyo in Pasadena, Project VISTA had as its official mandate "a study of ground and air tactical warfare with especial reference to the defense of Western Europe in the immediate future," which was of "compelling interest . . . in view of the situation then current in Korea."

Of the 113 members of VISTA's scientific and technical staff, 39 were from the faculty at Caltech, and its chairman was the school's president,

---

* During his years of blacklisting, which ended in the early 1960s, Wilson collaborated with fellow blacklistees Biberman and Paul Jarrico on the independent prolabor film Salt of the Earth and also contributed to the scripts of David Lean's The Bridge on the River Kwai and Lawrence of Arabia. In 1985, the Academy awarded Wilson a posthumous Oscar for Kwai, along with Carl Foreman, who also had been blacklisted, but their awards were not included on the televised Oscar ceremony.

Dr. Lee A. DuBridge, who invited Capra to join VISTA that spring of 1951. Capra had become friendly with DuBridge through the Caltech Associates, an alumni group which, in addition to its primary purpose of raising money, regularly assembled on the campus for briefings on the latest scientific developments.

Though Capra wrote that the position he was offered by DuBridge had nothing to do with filmmaking, in fact he originally was VISTA's director of motion picture production, heading its documentary films (or MOVION) group, one of fifteen groups into which the project was subdivided. That job was later given to the veteran Hollywood cameraman Alfred L. Gilks when Capra was shifted to the eleven-man Psychological Warfare (or PSY-CHON) group, headed by Dr. Earnest C. Watson, dean of the faculty at Caltech and vice chairman of VISTA.

Other VISTA groups were studying advanced concepts of nuclear, chemical, biological, and radiological warfare. Though VISTA's civilian staff members were given access to military secrets, the Defense Department advisers were not allowed to show actual war plans to the civilian staff, and the final report of February 4, 1952 (partially declassified in 1980), admitted that "this quite legitimate precaution may lead to some artificiality and lack of realism in the overall framework of the VISTA report." Capra nevertheless expressed wonderment in his book at VISTA's proposals, which ranged from a harebrained scheme to project propaganda onto clouds above cities under siege ("Projection of symbols, such as the cross, might be effective with religious troops") to more sinister recommendations, including the vigorous development of chemical warfare ("demanded by the presumed capability of the Soviet Union in chemical warfare") and "the tactical employment of atomic weapons on such targets as troop concentrations, supply dumps, and transport facilities," delivered by a combat-ready Tactical Atomic Air Force "for early use in Europe."

Capra was fingerprinted in June as part of his application for an interim security clearance, which he expected would be processed without a hitch, given his distinguished Army record. He began attending VISTA briefings and preparing recommendations for anti-Communist propaganda films.

But when the preliminary investigation of Capra by G-2 found derogatory information in its files and those of HUAC, the State Department, and the FBI, G-2 decided on August 17 that "an interim letter of consent will not be issued." On September 10, G-2 asked the Los Angeles office of the FBI to conduct an investigation, which eventually extended to the point of agents visiting his childhood home on Albion Street. They told the current owner, Frank D. Munoz, that Capra was being considered for a job "making films for the Army."

On September 11, Capra was told by VISTA that there was a delay in his security clearance. Despite the evident absurdity of the situation, he realized he would have to move swiftly and decisively to save his reputation as a loyal American.

He addressed his first formal response, that same day, to G-2. Despite his experiences with clearance procedures for himself and others in World War II, he still was feeling his way through the procedures of the postwar Truman loyalty program (a program that investigated the lives of millions of Americans), and he did not, at this point, know of the existence of the Army-Navy-Air Force Personnel Security Board, which would decide his case.

He could not hide his feelings of outrage and betrayal as he recited his record of devotion to his adopted country as a filmmaker, a voluntary member of the U.S. Army in both World War I and World War II, a recipient of the Legion of Merit and the Distinguished Service Medal, a Catholic, and a vehement foe of communism. Far from questioning the right of the government to probe into its citizens' loyalty and beliefs, he supported its right to do so, regardless of the harm it might cause to the reputations of some innocent people in exonerating others.

"**F**rank Capra has been dropped from the [VISTA] Staff . . . ," Army Intelligence was notified by the Army's Los Angeles Ordnance District on September 20, "but the application for clearance has not been abandoned, because there is a strong possibility that his services can be used later if appropriate clearance is received."

Capra was not consoled by the fact that a dozen other members of the VISTA staff, and several others considered for staff positions, also were under investigation; G-2 felt that "there appear to be an inordinate number of questionable personalities connected with or in the process of becoming connected with" the project. Capra was one of the two personalities considered "especially worthy of mention . . . [i]n this connection"; the other was the prominent chemist Linus Pauling. Pauling was chairman of Caltech's division of chemistry and chemical engineering, but his opposition to nuclear weapons testing and advocacy of multilateral disarmament caused some in the cold war era to label him pro-Soviet; Pauling did not become a VISTA staff member, but went on to win the Nobel Prize in chemistry in 1954 and the Nobel Peace Prize in 1962. Disturbed by the sweeping aspersions being made against VISTA staff members, which he considered unfounded, Lee DuBridge assured Capra of his support, and Dean Watson indicated to Capra that VISTA was doing all it could to have his case brought to a conclusion.

Capra tried to show bravado, but as the weeks dragged on, and the months dragged on, and he continued to receive only vague and noncommittal responses to his increasingly agitated inquiries to the Army and Secretary of Defense Robert A. Lovett, he was beginning to believe that this "Kafkaesque nightmare" really was happening to him.

In early August Capra had submitted two papers to VISTA, one calling for the production of a documentary film by the Army Signal Corps under VISTA staff supervision, *A Photographic Report of VISTA Conclusions.* "The motion picture is your best salesman," declared Capra, who suggested "we secure a handful of Hollywood scriptwriters who are clearable security-wise, and perhaps a few top-notch directors for the actual staging. This latter may not be necessary if we could get some smart officers to take an interest in the staging. But the scriptwriters seem to be a must." (No such film was produced.)

His pièce de résistance—which he found embarrassing in retrospect— was a sixteen-page paper, "Regarding the Content of Psychological Warfare."

In it he called war "a stupid, disastrous, uncivil method of settling disputes. . . . That's why we never hit the first punch. But as free people, we have more to fight for, and we always hit the last punch." Capra saw the cold war, however, in apocalyptic terms, calling it "a death struggle . . . between the free world and the slave world. . . . THE COLD WAR IS A BATTLE FOR THE MINDS OF MEN." His emotional anti-Soviet rhetoric was motivated not only by his perception of a threat to the material and spiritual benefits of the American way of life—a perception shared by most Americans in 1951—but it also expressed a more subtle anxiety about what the cold war was doing to his mind and to the minds of his fellow countrymen. The paper became his elegy for the American Dream: "Our history has been one of obstacles met and conquered. Defeat is foreign to us. We still believe in hope. The happy ending is a national characteristic. That's why when the chips are down, we're so tough to lick. We don't believe in it.

"But today our thinking is all defensive. The Soviets are calling the shots. We are boxing according to their plan. That doesn't come natural to us. We could take a licking that way."

Capra defined the struggle between capitalism and communism in terms reminiscent of the *Why We Fight* series: "We are not fighting for more territory, or more oil, or to impose our will on others by force, but . . . we are fighting to keep our individual freedom—to keep from being taken over by sheer force . . . we either fight or become Soviet slaves like the Poles, the Hungarians, and the Czechs. . . . We will not start a war, but are only defending ourselves against a cynical inhuman philosophy that is out to destroy all that we hold dear. . . .

"No more morning paper—no more radio—television—or movies. No more labor unions, or churches, or Elks Clubs, or Ladies Aid Societies.

"No more meeting with friends—no more shooting our mouth off for or against anything we please. No more voting for those *we* think should run things.

"No more small business, no more corner grocery stores—no more gas stations—no more owning your own farm—or even your own home. . . .

"No more baseball games—or song hits. No more cosmetics, silk stockings, or idolizing of pretty women.

"No more working when and where you want to. No more going fishing when you feel like it.

"No more trial by jury or impartial judges. No more Congress or Supreme Courts, and what is worst of all, no more friend[s]—for we all will be distrusting each other for fear of informers. In fact, we would be existing in a living hell of fear—fear for our husbands, our wives, our children. Fear of being taken away at night by secret police and never being heard from again."

Yet Capra felt that such measures were justifiable against Communists foreign or domestic, for "All Communists in U.S. and Allied countries are traitors and are capable of treason and sabotage. All take orders from Moscow. They have chosen to renounce allegiance to their own peoples and countries. They are not Americans, Chinese, Russian, or French. They are Communists."

His recommendations included a ruthless psychological warfare offensive directed at "Enemy Satellite Peoples," including: "Give hints of new and mysterious weapons . . . that will make Russia barren and foodless without an American soldier setting foot on Soviet soil. . . .

"Hint at targets that would be bombed overnight in case of war: factories—mines—refineries—railroads. Make the local population fearful of working in these places.

"Finally, sabotage and assassination of Russian and national stooge overlords will be the beginning of the end of their slavery."

Most tellingly, he urged that American propaganda "Play up the prostitution of arts and sciences. How all composers, writers, artists, and scientists must conform to the 'party line' or be liquidated. Surely there must still be some vestiges of intellectual honesty left in Russian artists and scientists."

Capra's paper was not included in the final report of Project VISTA. But the report alluded indirectly, in a footnote, to the clearance problems faced by Capra and other staff members: "There is a tendency in certain quarters today to consider objectivity and the ability to get oneself inside the other fellow's skin, sense his feelings and think his thoughts, as subversive. This tendency must be checked or the services of some of our ablest men will be lost to the country."

Before leaving Hollywood, Capra had written a letter on April 2 to Y. Frank Freeman in Freeman's capacity as president of the Association of Motion Picture Producers, suggesting a series of radio broadcasts to promote the film industry, emphasizing Hollywood's love affair with the American Dream and, not incidentally, minimizing its flirtations with communism. Freeman forwarded the letter to the militantly anti-Communist Motion Picture Industry Council. Ronald Reagan was secretary of the MPIC in 1951, and its executive secretary was Art Arthur, a screenwriter who had worked with Capra's unit in World War II.

The MPIC lacked the funds to implement Capra's idea, but Art Arthur brokered him an invitation from the State Department to serve as an adviser in its intensified cold war propaganda campaign. Capra accepted on June 18, 1951, five days after being fingerprinted for his Project VISTA security clearance. But he managed to avoid a final commitment to State until his clearance problem arose in September. Then he hastened to become active in the Film Advisory Committee of its U.S. Advisory Committee on Information, hoping the protective coloration of the State Department would help settle the question of his loyalty.

One of Capra's proposals to VISTA had been a series of films called *Why We Arm*, a cold war equivalent of the *Why We Fight* series based on the ideas he outlined in his paper on psychological warfare. Dean Watson hoped to lobby for the film series with Secretary of Defense Lovett when he went to Washington in early September, but he could not obtain an appointment and instead reported to Capra that there was a delay with his security clearance. (In a confidential report on October 2, G-2 repeated its charge that "Subject is considered possibly subversive.") So Capra took the proposal to the State, with the assurance that he was just the man to counteract the work of Hollywood Communists. Dean Acheson's State

Department, which was somewhat more liberal than the Pentagon on loyalty issues, adding to the flak it was receiving from the Right, apparently
did not regard the denial of Capra's clearance as a fait accompli, for it
allowed him to attend meetings of the Film Advisory Committee in Washington on September 24 and November 30 while he continued to press
Defense for vindication.

Writing Assistant Secretary of State for Public Affairs Edward W.
Barrett on October 9, Capra expressed what seemed to be a somewhat
forced enthusiasm over returning to the propaganda field despite the tensions inherent in collaboration between the government and Hollywood,
and assured Barrett, who was in charge of U.S. information activities in
foreign countries, that although Hollywood had been tainted by communism, the industry was ready to do its part in the fight against it. The next
day he sent a dignified SOS to Robert Lovett, one of the pillars of the
American establishment. He told the defense secretary it wasn't his clearance that was at stake now, it was vindication of his character as a patriotic
American. He vowed to do whatever he could to rid himself of the heinous
accusation of disloyalty.

Lovett replied on October 30 that it was routine for "a final clearance"
to be granted "only upon completion of a satisfactory background investigation" and, if necessary, a review by the security board. "In your particular case, however, the [board] has no record of ever having received
that matter for review, and it would thus appear that the application for
clearance is still in the process of investigation. As you probably realize,
the investigative machinery, of necessity, operates quite slowly."

The language was becoming increasingly Kafkaesque.

Colonel Frederick D. Sharp of the Army General Staff wrote Capra on
October 17 that "this office will do what it can to try and expedite the
completion of your investigation, but it must be appreciated that such
investigations, which run into the thousands, are a time-consuming process."

It was nine days before Christmas 1951, and, in a grim echo of George
Bailey staring disconsolately into the snowy river in *It's a Wonderful Life*,
Frank Capra, racing back home from Pasadena to Red Mountain Ranch,
was thinking of killing himself by crashing his car into a bridge.

His violent death at age fifty-four would have occasioned mixed judgments in the press, which he had courted so shrewdly on his way to the top.
The obituaries would have been unusually ample for the death of a movie
director, but if he had died in 1951, he would have been described as a

failure, a has-been, a man who had squandered his talent for reasons not entirely explicable by the fact that he had sold his independent production company.

Few people knew that December that Capra was reeling from the "bitterest and most humiliating experience of my life": at VISTA head-quarters, he had just been shown a letter from the Army-Navy-Air Force Personnel Security Board denying him a security clearance and accusing him of disloyalty to his country. Years later he still could hardly believe it possible that after all he had done and been, he was being branded as "a lousy Communist spy. . . . Jesus, loyalty—if there was anybody loyal to this country it was me."

Capra's copy of the letter from the security board (dated December 14) arrived in Fallbrook by registered mail on December 19. Signed by Colonel Victor W. Phelps, MPC, Army member of the board, it notified Capra that "your case has reached the second step," that of screening and review by the board in private, without his presence. The third step was the right to appeal with a hearing by the Industrial Employment Review Board.

"This letter will formally notify you that the Army-Navy-Air Force Personnel Security Board, after careful consideration of the information available to it at this time, has tentatively concluded that it cannot grant consent to the request for your proposed access to certain classified matter at California Institute of Technology, VISTA Project."

This letter finally specified the charges against him:

"In 1938 you were a member of a Communist inspired picket line in a Hollywood Citizens Newstrike [the reference was to the strike at the *Hollywood Citizen-News*].

"In 1941 you were sponsor and national vice-chairman of the Russian War Relief, which was strongly Communist infiltrated.

"In 1941 you were active in the National Federation for Constitutional Liberties, cited by the Attorney General in 1942 as having the main function of defending Communist Party members.

"In 1943 you contributed to the Joint Anti-Fascist Refugee Committee, also cited by the Attorney General as being a Communist organization.

"You have for a number of years closely associated with motion picture writers and other individuals reported to be or to have been members of the Communist Party.

"In 1942 and 1944 you received considerable propaganda literature direct from Russia.

"You are reported to have been active in attempts to halt Congressional investigation of Communist influence in the motion picture industry."

Before the security board would make its ruling, Capra was given ten days to submit "such written material as you may wish to explain or refute the information set forth above."

Capra wept "tears of shame" in his wife's arms. Lu suggested he call Mabel Walker Willebrandt for advice.

"Hit hard," Capra remembered Willebrandt telling him. "Be wrathful. It's your world that's being destroyed, not theirs."

Capra holed up with Chet Sticht in the outlying bungalow he had converted into an office at Red Mountain Ranch. The office had a couch bed and a fireplace, and they stayed there around the clock from December 19 to 29, not pausing for Christmas, working furiously on a response. "I've never seen Capra more upset than he was at this time," Sticht recalled. "That was the biggest shock in his life. He had a tremendous reaction toward the government, that *any* government could act like that. He was absolutely horrified, and he was mad as hell. He couldn't understand it. He had a great love for this country, and knowing him as well as I do, I know there was nobody more patriotic than Capra was. But all of Hollywood was suspect. We dug up everything we could think of that would counteract the charges."

While they assembled the history of his professional, military, religious, charitable, and political activities into an approximately 350-page dossier he called his Security Board File—in 1984 Capra described the ostensibly self-exculpatory document as "this mea culpa book . . . a book about my life"—Capra anxiously sent out letters asking several old friends for testimonials on his character, wondering how much trust he still had left with anyone. Though he took a pugnacious tone with the security board, vowing to go public with his self-defense if necessary, in fact he dared not go public, for he did not trust the public to help him: as Potter had told the desperate George Bailey in *It's a Wonderful Life*, "Why don't you go to the riffraff you love so much and ask them to let you have your $8,000? You know why, because they'd run you out of town on a rail." Most of Capra's former Hollywood friends did not know what was happening to him.

Blaming his problems in obtaining help from his friends on the fact that it was the holiday season, Capra frantically wired the security board asking for more time, but the extension did not arrive until after he mailed his dossier on December 29. It included letters attesting to his character from

John Ford, Myles Connolly, Lyman Munson, Y. Frank Freeman, and Father John F. Connolly, S.J., dean of Loyola University in Los Angeles. He gave as character references such well-known Hollywood anti-Communists as Willebrandt, DeMille, McCarey, William Wellman, Clarence Brown, and Eddie Mannix. He said that Jimmy Doolittle and Jimmy Stewart were among his friends, and he also listed nine present or retired Army officers as references, including Frederick H. Osborn, Frank McCarthy, and General George C. Marshall (whom Joseph McCarthy recently had accused of being a Communist sympathizer).

Capra's first and most detailed plea for help was a December 19 letter to John Ford, his professional colleague of the longest duration and a man whose own loyalty was unquestioned because of his service with the OSS and the Navy, which recently had promoted him to rear admiral. Capra knew that Ford was both staunchly anti-Communist and one of the last people in Hollywood who still had the guts to speak his mind.

Vehemently declaring his innocence of Communist sympathies, Capra reminded Ford of his credentials as an American patriot and dedicated foe of communism, pointing particularly in that regard (as he had done in his September 11 letter to Army Intelligence) to his record with the Screen Directors Guild.

"AM SHOCKED AT LETTER," Ford replied in a telegram to Capra. "WHAT WERE WE FIGHTING FOR?"

"I was terribly shocked and worried last week when an Investigating Officer came to me concerning the security risks of my friend, Frank Capra," Ford reiterated in his letter to the security board on December 24.* "I suppose these things are necessary, considering the state of the world as it is today, but nevertheless, it causes one to think when a man of Capra's attainments as an Officer of the United States Army, a gentleman, and a loyal American Citizen has to be investigated."

Capra had sent Ford a copy of the letter from the security board and outlined the responses he intended to make to the charges. To the one about his support of the strike at the *Hollywood Citizen-News*, Capra claimed he merely had been observing the picketing, not participating in it, although photographs he claimed were arranged deceitfully by Biberman had made it appear otherwise for Communist propaganda purposes. He also claimed to have been unaware at the time, like other guild members, that Biberman and Frank Tuttle were Communists.

* The version of Ford's letter quoted here is the typewritten, hand-corrected draft in the collection of his papers at Indiana University's Lilly Library.

Capra did not have to mention to Ford that one of the pictures had shown the two of them with Biberman, supporting the strike on behalf of their guild, nor that Biberman had gone to jail in 1950 as one of the Hollywood Ten. He also did not mention to Ford that he had written a letter to the chairman of the Newspaper Guild's publicity committee during the strike declaring his and other SDG colleagues' support.

Ford attempted to explain their involvement in the strike to the security board: "I was with Capra at the time. We stopped by to see what the excitement was and I believe we were photographed. Capra has never been in a picket line as far as I know . . . and I am quite sure that nothing in the world would convince Capra to get in a picket line other than [to protest] something that is drastically opposed to the interests of his beloved United States of America."

"Oh, what a lot of shit," Philip Dunne commented in 1985 when told of Ford's explanation of Capra's presence on the picket line; Dunne was there representing the Writers Guild, and was a friend of Ford's, as well as the screenwriter of the director's *How Green Was My Valley*. Clearly recalling how he, Capra, and Ford (along with Biberman and SAG president Robert Montgomery) "spent about five minutes walking up and down the picket lines and had our pictures taken," Dunne said, "Ford has this completely wrong. Jack was not a rational man, he was an emotional man, and he liked to heighten the dramatic interest. This is an emotional letter."

Though Ford had been among the founders of the SDG in 1935 and Capra did not join until 1937, Ford also told the security board, "Frank Capra and I joined hands in our Guild some sixteen years ago when the 'Commies,' 'Fellow Travelers,' 'Bleeding Hearts' or whatever you want to call them, tried to infiltrate the Motion Picture Directors Guild [sic]. Together with 99% of our Guild members we waged a very successful fight and kept them out."

Ford's account of a battle over Communist infiltration of the guild was highly exaggerated. Although HUAC informer Martin Berkeley, who testified in 1951 that he helped raise money for the *Citizen-News* strike when he was a Party member, claimed that "one of the purposes of the Party" was "the formation of a Directors Guild" and Tuttle testified in 1951 that there were seven directors who had been Communist Party members (himself, Biberman, Dmytryk, Michael Gordon, Jules Dassin, Bernard Vorhaus, and John Berry), Tuttle added, "The work of the directors in the Screen Directors Guild was very ineffectual as far as any real Communist angle was concerned. About all they were able to do was to propagandize for liberal candidates and the candidature of our own people during guild elections to the board of directors. I think only Mr. Biberman, Mr. Dmytryk, and I were ever elected to the board. As you can see, there were so few directors who were Communists that the Communists were content to have elected as many liberals as possible."

Capra and Biberman in fact were not enemies but allies when they served together as officers of the guild. When Capra was elected to his second term as president in May 1939, a year after he and Ford and Biberman made their appearance together at the *Citizen-News*, Capra sent Biberman what the latter considered at the time an effusive telegram of thanks for his support. Biberman, who had resigned from the board to devote more time to his directing career, in return praised Capra's skillful and equitable direction of the guild.

Capra's letter to Ford flatly denied the charges that he had been active in the National Federation for Constitutional Liberties and a contributor to the Joint Anti-Fascist Refugee Committee. Both organizations were favorite targets of Red-hunters and drew support from the Hollywood Left.

The National Federation for Constitutional Liberties, an active opponent of HUAC and a defender of people accused of "subversive" activities, was prominently listed in the 448-page report, *Communist Front Organizations*, published by California's Tenney committee in 1948. The report called the group "one of the most important Communist-front organizations in the United States . . . set up to attract those who would not openly affiliate themselves with Communist groups if apprised of the facts." The allegation that Capra was active in the National Federation for Constitutional Liberties had been found by G-2 in "appropriate files."

The Joint Anti-Fascist Refugee Committee, established by veterans of the Spanish Civil War to aid Spanish refugees, was also labeled a "Communist front" by the Tenney committee, which said that its policy was "in concert with the foreign policy of the Soviet Union. . . . It should be unnecessary to add that the only refugees in whom this front has shown interest are Communist refugees." The allegation that Capra was a contributor to the Joint Anti-Fascist Refugee Committee had been made to the FBI in December 1946 by "an informant of known reliability."

Giving the security board a year-by-year list of his many charitable contributions since 1935, Capra urged the board to view his support of charitable causes, like his other activities, in the context of his life history and character. He explicitly denied that he was a Communist or a fellow traveler or a potential traitor. The board should not be misled by any event that might appear to suggest the opposite, he insisted; he had been innocent of any knowledge of communism when it was alleged that he had leftist associations, and while those on the left of center exaggerated his involvement in social causes, they probably did so to exploit his presidency of the Directors Guild or the Academy.

Capra did not deny having contributed to Russian War Relief, of which the Tenney committee had written, "It should be understood that the Russian War Relief is, in every respect, a satellite front of the Communist party and that it is not an organization similar to the American Red Cross." Russian War Relief in fact enjoyed broad support across the political spectrum in Hollywood, as elsewhere in the United States. Capra's name had appeared as one of the sponsors of an advertisement in *The New York Times* on October 10, 1941, among "These eminent Americans [who] ask your help on behalf of the Russian people," a list of 309 names which included Sidney Buchman, Pearl S. Buck, Charles Chaplin, Ronald Colman, John Garfield, Ira Gershwin, Ben Hecht, Lillian Hellman, John Huston, New York's Governor Herbert H. Lehman, Ernst Lubitsch, Archibald MacLeish, Rouben Mamoulian, Thomas Mann, Lewis Milestone, Dr. Robert A. Millikan, Gale Sondergaard, Frank Tuttle, Walter Wanger, and Orson Welles, as well as many other prominent figures from the worlds of the arts, education, politics, and religion, who were "moved not only by their humanitarianism but actuated by their common-sense Americanism." "While it is undoubtedly true that many well-intentioned loyal Americans were tricked into believing that the Russian War Relief was a bona fide American agency," the Tenney committee wrote, "the hard core of Communist influence and direction is evident." The fact that Capra's name appeared in the *Times* ad had been noted in his HUAC file.

Capra told Ford that it would be absurd to draw the conclusion from his support of Russian War Relief during World War II that he was pro-Communist, since it was a common cause at the time and he also gave money to relief organizations for the British, French, Greek, and other peoples during the war. He had no idea why he might have been listed as an officer of Russian War Relief. In fact, though the security board claimed Capra was "national vice-chairman" in 1941, *The New York Times* ad listed Dr. Henry Sloane Coffin of Union Theological Seminary as the vice chairman. Barely restraining his amazement at the naiveté of the security board's statement that Russian War Relief "was strongly Communist infiltrated," Capra dryly suggested to the board that such a statement was tautological, and reminded the board that the Soviet Union also was an American ally in 1941.

Capra admitted to the board that he was one of the sponsors of a Russian War Relief benefit at the Shrine Auditorium in Los Angeles on

October 9, 1942, but mocked the notion that it showed him to be un-American, since his fellow sponsors included Los Angeles Mayor Fletcher Bowron, Edward Arnold, Ronald Colman, Mary Pickford, and Robert Millikan. The benefit was a fervent tribute to the fighting spirit of the U.S.S.R., organized by the Russian-born Dimitri Tiomkin and featuring performances of Shostakovich's *War* Symphony, with Leopold Stokowski conducting, and of the composer's "Song for United Nations," sung by Nelson Eddy. Both the "Internationale" and "The Star-Spangled Banner" were performed, there were speeches by Madame Maxim Litvinov and by Marc Connelly on behalf of the Hollywood Writers' Mobilization, and the crowd "went wild with enthusiasm" (the *Los Angeles Times* reported) when the Soviet army heroine Lieutenant Liudmila Pavlichenko called for a second front against Hitler. At the time, it did not seem un-American to support an embattled ally.

Without mentioning his back-channel dealings with Ambassador Litvinov in 1942 for Russian war footage, an offense for which he had barely escaped being court-martialed, Capra ridiculed the security board's charge that "in 1942 and 1944 you received considerable propaganda literature direct from Russia," noting that all the film footage and documents he had received from the Soviets and other allies pertained to the war effort (the 1944 reference apparently was to his efforts to photograph the activities of the Lend-Lease supply line into the U.S.S.R., which also had been monitored by G-2), and he was anxious to downplay the significance of the laudatory material on *The Battle of Russia* and the other *Why We Fight* films that he had received near the end of the war from Soviet director Vsevolod Pudovkin, dismissing it as nonpolitical and dealing only with cinematic matters.

Capra's Security Board File included the texts of speeches, interviews, letters, and other public statements he had made since 1941, by which he meant to demonstrate his love for his adopted country. If he were a Communist, he conceded, all of this display of patriotism could have been an act, but he wondered whether it would not have been detected during his Army service by such men as Marshall, Stimson, and Churchill.

Dropping the sarcasm, Capra made a powerful, heartfelt plea for the security board not to make a false judgment about his loyalty and thereby ruin him and his family. Not content with reminding the board of its duty to be fair and correct before making any such judgment, he went further, subtly implying that the board's very function was a violation of democratic principles, and arguing that it played into the hands of Communists by creating division between citizens and their government.

Nevertheless, Capra found two of the charges difficult to refute.

He admitted to Ford that he was concerned about the accusation that he was "reported to have been active in attempts to halt Congressional investigation of Communist influence in the motion picture industry," an accusation that evidently stemmed largely (if not entirely) from G-2's misleading charge on July 12, 1951, that "CAPRA was reported to have associated with left-wing groups, and to have been one of several motion picture directors who were plotting a line of attack on the Congressional Investigation of Communism in the motion picture industry." But, ignoring the telegram he had drafted for the Academy in 1938 protesting the Dies committee (which Darryl Zanuck had talked the board out of sending), his years of proclaiming Hollywood's patriotic bona fides, his brief attempt to circulate a petition on behalf of colleagues under government attack as alleged subversives, and his recent stand (however belated and tentative) against the blacklist provision of the SDG loyalty oath, Capra simply and heatedly denied the accusation to Ford, dismissing it as unsubstantiated and unattributed.

"Reference is made to the fact that Frank Capra, or Col. Capra as I prefer to call him, objected to the Congressional Investigation of Hollywood Communists," Ford wrote in his letter on Capra's behalf. "If so I never heard him mention it. I don't believe he did. Frankly, I objected to it loudly and vociferously. I'll now go on record as saying I think it was a publicity stunt and the taxpayers would have saved a lot of money in railfares . . . if the investigation had started in Washington.

"Still . . . I reiterate, I've never heard Col. Capra mention it, even when Congressman Thomas, the Chairman of the Committee, went to jail [J. Parnell Thomas was convicted in 1948 of taking kickbacks and was incarcerated in a federal institution with two members of the Hollywood Ten].

"I shall close by saying that I think that Col. Capra, Distinguished Service Medal, etc., etc., etc., has always been a shining light and example for good Americans to follow here in Hollywood or elsewhere. In my humble way I think he is a truly great American."

The other charge that had Capra concerned was the one that he had "for a number of years closely associated with motion picture writers and other individuals reported to be or to have been members of the Communist Party." (No mention was made of the charge in HUAC's files that a man named Frank Capra signed the 1932 Communist Party election petition.)

Conceding to Ford that there was some substance to the charge that he had associated with writers who were Communists, Capra tried to minimize it by singling out Sidney Buchman as his only close writer associate whom he had had inklings was a Communist, and by inaccurately claiming that he had terminated his relationship with Buchman because of their disagreement over Buchman's opposition to Roosevelt's Lend-Lease plan in 1939 (though Roosevelt did not announce Lend-Lease until December 1940). (Ford told the security board, "To the best of my knowledge Capra's only close friend with communistic leanings was one Syd [*sic*] Buchman; which ended in a row over Buchman's politics and unfriendly attitude to the Administration.")

Capra failed to mention to Ford that he had had dealings with Buchman as late as 1942, when Buchman had recommended John Sanford as a writer for the *Why We Fight* series. Nor did Capra mention to Ford that Buchman—who had admitted his former Party membership to HUAC on September 25, 1951, after being named by Martin Berkeley six days earlier—was only one of many writers he had worked with who were accused of being Communists (or Communist sympathizers), which was the reason he had to hedge by not dismissing the charge out of hand.

In his "mea culpa" to the security board, Capra did not mention a disagreement over Lend-Lease (or, as he revised the story in the uncut manuscript of his autobiography, over the 1939 Nazi-Soviet pact). He stated instead that he had terminated his relationship with Buchman when he learned that Buchman was a Communist. Later he would admit that he knew Buchman was a Communist when Buchman wrote *Mr. Smith;* in that version, Capra claimed he didn't care, yet Buchman said that Capra was "terribly suspicious" of him because of his Party membership and that Capra "had the impression that I wanted to betray him."

Capra also offered up to the security board the names of two other writers who, like Buchman, had been accused before HUAC of having been Communists: Michael Wilson and Ian McLellan Hunter.

The naming of these three names by Capra evidently was not an isolated incident. While trying to maintain his moderately critical but not entirely adversarial above-board position toward the Hollywood witch-hunt, Capra, according to his own account of events, at some time in that period began to play a dangerous double game: he had begun to inform on his colleagues to the government. The evidence suggests he did so in the hope that he would avoid being subpoenaed and blacklisted himself.

In letters he wrote to the U.S. government during his security clearance crisis in 1951 and 1952, found among his papers at Wesleyan, Capra is on record attempting to demonstrate his bona fides as a loyal American by pointing out that both the Los Angeles office of the FBI and the State Department had been in contact with him on a regular basis for service as a political informant.

Although the FBI refused the author's Freedom of Information Act request and the Justice Department turned down a subsequent appeal for the FBI's files on Capra, Capra indicated in his September 11, 1951, letter to Army Intelligence that the Los Angeles FBI office frequently relied on him as a source of information about individuals and their political beliefs. And while serving on the State Department's committee on film propaganda, Capra was extensively involved in the political clearing of screenwriters for department projects, according to his letter of January 10, 1952, to the security board's Colonel Phelps.

How long Capra may have been informing before September 1951 cannot be determined from the available evidence, but it was as early as 1947, the year his "soul stopped leaping upward," that he admittedly "began to act strangely, to look for 'villains,' " around the time of the HUAC hearings that had such a profoundly terrifying effect on him and his work. If cooperating with the FBI, which worked closely with HUAC, kept him employable and kept him from the shame of being called to testify publicly before the committee, it may not have been enough to provide lasting protection. As Victor S. Navasky wrote in his book *Naming Names*, "In a rational world, getting off one list should mean getting off all lists," but the world of the witch-hunt was not a rational world, particularly when the heat was turned up on Hollywood by HUAC with its 1951 round of hearings.

Navasky's case histories show that those who sought clearance to avoid the Hollywood blacklist or graylist could find they had to keep proving their loyalty repeatedly, since clearance was the business not only of the various studios but also of the American Legion, the Motion Picture Alliance, the Motion Picture Industry Council, American Business Consultants (publisher of *Red Channels*), Aware Inc. (publisher of *Counterattack*), and the rest of what Navasky calls the "free-lance enforcer network." Those who cooperated with the FBI in private, thinking their informing was a confidential means of demonstrating their loyalty once and for all, often found that they were mistaken, that they had to keep doing so in different forums and with increasing openness. Nor was even public informing before HUAC an absolute guarantee that one's employability in Hollywood would not suffer as a result, as Larry Parks and others learned. And, as Capra learned, declaring himself an FBI informer seemed to have little effect on whether, with the other questions hanging over him, he was judged fit for a security clearance.* That may have contributed to his sense of bafflement and outrage, but a higher standard of loyalty clearly was required for access to U.S. military secrets than for being allowed to continue working in Hollywood. Capra temporarily dropped the informing line of defense after finding it didn't work when he tried it in his first letter to the government about his clearance problems, although he brought it up again in his January 10 letter while waiting anxiously for notification of the final decision, and he continued demonstrating his cooperation with the witch-hunt in the interim by naming names in his Security Board File, a ploy that proved more effective.

Although Sidney Buchman and Michael Wilson probably never knew that Capra had named their names to the security board, they made their feelings clear on the subject of informers. Explaining his decision not to name names, although he admitted his own former membership in the Communist Party, Buchman told HUAC that "it is repugnant to an American to inform upon his fellow citizens. . . . I realize my position may doom a career which has taken twenty years to build, but I have to take that risk." After his testimony in September 1951 and his blacklisting, Buchman's defiance of a second HUAC subpoena in 1952 resulted in his being found guilty of contempt of Congress on a House vote of 314 to 0; he was fined $150 and given a suspended one-year jail sentence, and did not work again in films under his own name until the 1960s. Despite his principled testimony before HUAC, taking the First rather than the Fifth Amendment in order to refute testimony that could have been injurious to others, the fact that Buchman was not sent to prison convinced many leftists that Harry Cohn had "bribed the Committee to get him off, [but] no evidence has been produced to substantiate this claim," Navasky reported. Buchman died in France in 1975.

Wilson, shortly before his death in 1978, told Navasky, "My attitude toward informers has remained from the start unforgiving. I'm not one who says, Let bygones be bygones. I don't defend my attitude in terms of principle. It's just a visceral reaction, that's all. I just don't like the fuckers. Socially I don't acknowledge their existence. I wouldn't say hello. I have good friends who don't do that—and that's their right. It is simply

---

* Nor was obtaining a security clearance a finite event. As David Caute wrote in The Great Fear: The Anti-Communist Purge Under Truman and Eisenhower, "Neither the loyalty nor the security program ensured that, once investigated and cleared, a man would stay cleared. For this there were two parallel reasons. First, every new promotion or transfer entailed a new check; secondly, as laws and executive orders succeeded one another, imposing increasingly stringent criteria, old cases had to be reconsidered in the light of new standards."

not my attitude." If Wilson had known that Capra informed on him, Zelma Wilson commented, "I think he would have been surprised. They were a perfect combination, these people and Frank Capra: they were very romantic and idealistic, and they genuinely believed peace was possible. When he rejected them out of his life, he was hanging himself."

Ian McLellan Hunter, who had successfully resumed his scriptwriting career after being blacklisted, died in 1991. When told in 1984 that Capra had named him to the security board, Hunter commented, "Capra didn't mean anything to us, because he couldn't say whether somebody was in the Communist Party. Martin Berkeley [who named 161 names to HUAC, also including Hunter's wife, the former Alice Goldberg] was something else, because he was a member of the bloody Party, and he could tell about people he knew in the Party. Capra's naming names didn't mean a thing. The town was full of people who were willing to say, 'I think . . .' "

But as for Capra himself, said Hunter, "The blacklist killed him—that panic. In effect, he was a victim of the blacklist. [But] he had the soul of an informer."

Capra's philosophy of life, such as it was, was Darwinian, learned in his early experiences on the streets. As he said when asked in an interview for this book if he had worried about being blacklisted for his activities with the Screen Directors Guild in the thirties, "Fuck, I didn't get worried about being blacklisted. How could they blacklist me? I'd blacklist *them*." But the romanticization of informers in the United States during the postwar Red Scare did not entirely remove the shame Capra evidently felt over his naming of names, for, unlike the "friendly" witnesses before HUAC, he kept his clandestine.

In choosing the names of Buchman, Wilson, and Hunter to offer up to the security board, Capra may have felt, like many of the others who named names in that era, that naming only people who already had been publicly accused by others of having been Communists (as those three men had been accused before HUAC), or naming a person who had admitted his past membership in the Communist Party (such as Buchman), somehow mitigated the fact that he was naming their names to the government. As Navasky wrote in *Naming Names*: "If there is one refrain that keeps asserting itself—almost like a chorus—in the reminiscences and explanations of those who played the informer, it is, 'I only named those who were already named.' The idea seemed to function as a sort of security blanket not merely for those who now profess shame but also for those who express ambivalence about what they did, as well as those who defend their acting as informer. . . .

"That naming as Communists people whom the committee already knew as Communists was not harmless or morally neutral seems to have been implicitly understood by many of those who testified. . . . Each naming went out like a burglar alarm to the free-lance enforcer network, reminding them that there was a subversive to be fired, harassed, or embarrassed, a career to be derailed; reminding his children and their friends that they had a pariah for a parent; reminding neighbors that they had best keep their distance."

By collaborating surreptitiously with the witch-hunters and not choosing a public forum such as a HUAC hearing for his naming of names, Capra was allowed to escape (for the time being) the public scrutiny and eventual opprobrium visited upon those who collaborated openly with the committee, such as the director Elia Kazan, who made his first appearance before HUAC on January 14, 1952, the same day Capra received his formal notification by mail that the security board, "after consideration of the information submitted by you and in your behalf," on January 5 had granted him a conditional clearance, "specifically limited to California Institute of Technology, Project VISTA. If you should be desired for employment on classified Army, Navy, or Air Force contracts by some other employer. . . . a new authorization must be requested." Lu cried and Frank broke out a bottle of champagne.

Capra sent emotional messages of thanks to Ford and Willebrandt, telling Willebrandt that the whole mess seemed like a case of mistaken identity. And then, sadly, he felt it necessary to write Secretary Lovett a craven letter of propitiation and support for the security board's inquisitional methods, which he now appeared to regard as patriotic.

"I was hurt by that," Capra acknowledged in 1977, in one of his rare public comments on his security board crisis. "I love America. After all it has done for me, I'd never turn on her. . . . But that blacklist thing was not America. America is above that sort of thing. This country is much bigger than that. I have no rancor."

Three days after writing his letter to Secretary Lovett in 1951, Capra left for India, at the request of the State Department, to represent the United States Information Agency and the American film industry at the International Film Festival of India. He remembered his outraged reaction when the USIA's Turner Shelton called him on January 10 and implored him to help counteract the influence of the Soviet and Chinese delegations at the festival. He initially declined, bitter over the irony of being asked to help the United States crusade against communism overseas while he still was waiting for the security board to attest to his loyalty, but Shelton assured him that he had been given a clean bill of health as far as State was concerned. On the twelfth Shelton called back and tipped him off that his clearance was coming through from the security board (it had been mailed on the eighth); when it arrived, Capra went to India as if as a quid pro quo, plunging with frenzied abandon back into the role of a flack for the American government, even though he felt he had been "practically commandeered" into it by Shelton.

"At meetings, in homes, in private interviews, and at lunches that we organized for certain groups of people, I kept hammering on the freedom of the artist," he wrote the State Department in his report on the trip. "Because of my reputation with these people as a maker of films, and as a champion of the common man in my films, I could see that my reasoning carried weight." But he warily asked U.S. government officials that all of his meetings be "screened," because "I met dozens of people every day, and I wanted to know who they were so that my words wouldn't be twisted around and used for Commie propaganda."

Though praising the craftsmanship of Soviet filmmakers, he spoke pugnaciously against the propagandistic aspects of their films, and vowed "to make the Indian government hate the Communists before I was through." He boasted he wasn't long at the festival before "The Stars and Stripes were going up, and the Hammer and Sickle was going down," but he still kept talking obsessively about communism and its threat to artistic freedom and urging his fellow filmmakers to resist state control, which he said forced the artist to become a publicity agent for a dominant political ideology.

Seemingly oblivious to the ironies involved and admittedly disoriented by the turn of events, Capra took pains to reassure the Indians that the investigation by what he called "the un-American committee" had had no detrimental effect on Hollywood's artistic freedom. He insisted that "any producer could make any picture he wished in America," including one opposing the American role in the Korean War, even if no one went to see it. The Indian press reported that while Capra felt "some of the Communistic-minded people might have tried to influence" films "with their ideas, indirectly or otherwise," he also felt the issue was of "little importance" and insisted that most people in Hollywood "lead normal lives."

"I know some of our films stink," Capra conceded, "but they stink less than the products of some other countries."

Capra disavowed any knowledge of a Hollywood blacklist, but "The left-wing press kept asking me about Communists in Hollywood, whether

I thought the un-American committee had a right to inquire into the political beliefs of artists, and so forth," he reported to the State Department. "I very carefully explained the un-American committee was not inquiring into the *political* beliefs of artists, but was inquiring into the *subversive* beliefs of artists."

Some of the Indian journalists recognized what was happening to Capra.

At a press conference in Bombay on January 25, Capra "answered a barrage of questions with the self-confidence of the successful American," wrote the local publication *The Current*, but "When someone asked him why his recent pictures . . . did not have the same purposeful, humanistic trend of the prewar films, Mr. Capra cryptically remarked, 'We've grown old.' . . . Then suddenly becoming serious, Capra explained that during the war, many of the directors who joined the services were cut off from pictures for five long years. When they came back, they were mellowed, older and wiser, but afraid to tackle anything unusual or bold."

Although Capra escaped going through what Navasky called the "degradation ceremonies" of HUAC's public hearings, that did not keep him from feeling much the same feelings of shame as those who did go through the public abasement, as his "mea culpa" dossier makes clear.

Indeed, the clandestine nature of Capra's informing deprived him of even that superficial, temporary sense of absolution conferred by HUAC upon public informers and condemned him to live a lie—as the informing itself had condemned him to a life with "no more friend[s]—for we all will be distrusting each other for fear of informers. . . . a living hell of fear." When he finally gave a sketchy account of his security board crisis twenty years later in his autobiography (a book whose very title raises the interlocking questions so crucial to Capra of identity, credit, and naming of names), he could not bring himself to tell his readers that he had been an FBI and State Department informer and that he had named the three writers to the security board. But Capra carefully preserved the evidence of his own guilt, and the fact that he ultimately released the Security Board File and letters relating to it for public scrutiny, when he donated them to Wesleyan University in 1980, suggests that, whether consciously or not, he finally felt some need to unburden himself of the shameful secret he had been carrying around for so many years.

It was no coincidence that Capra, voluntarily or not, stayed away from feature filmmaking for much of the time the blacklist remained in force. Nor was it a coincidence that after he made his Hollywood comeback with

A Hole in the Head (1959), he began to suffer the incapacitating headaches, later diagnosed as "cluster headaches," which would afflict him for almost eleven years. "I believe the headaches were an unexplained phenomenon that helped me quit directing gracefully," he said. They went away only after he completed his autobiography and went public for the first time with the partial story of his security board crisis. As Joe Walker's wife, Juanita, put it, "Maybe he had a lot to get out of his mind."

One night in 1960, while lying in bed unable to sleep because of the pain inside his head, Capra asked himself what had caused it, and then he answered his own question: "It's the Judas pain. You welshed, compromised, sold out."

*T*horeau wrote of his bean field that it "attached me to the earth, and so I got strength like Antaeus." Capra hoped Red Mountain Ranch would do the same for him, but his posh version of Walden Pond proved to be as frustrating as Hollywood.

"When Capra quit the picture business, he was going to be The Land Owner down here," said Chet Sticht, who followed him reluctantly to Fallbrook in 1951. "That lasted about two and a half years. Watching trees grow is not too exciting. Hell, you can't suddenly quit something you've been doing and come down here and vegetate."

Outwardly Capra did not appear to be vegetating as he threw himself into the ranching business with the energy he once had devoted to his films. He planted thousands of new avocado and citrus trees (eventually he had 16,000 trees on the ranch) and built quarters for the Okies and braceros he brought in to pick them. Because the olive oil market had dried up with the reopening of Italian and Greek exports after World War II, he tore out his remaining olive trees and started a poultry business with 4,000 hens. "He would go around in a jeep, wearing old clothes and looking like a wetback," Sticht recalled. "I think Frank never forgot he was born in Italy," said George F. Yackey, a Fallbrook friend. "He had his hand on that shovel pretty hot."

Capra tried to put his college education to practical use by devising "scientific" new methods of stimulating growth in his orchards. He kept a card file with a separate card for each tree on the ranch to monitor their development for grafting purposes, devised an experiment measuring the growth of avocados by water displacement, and dug a 100-foot-long compost heap, blowing air into horse manure with hoses to force bacterial development. He also built a small earth dam and a concrete reservoir, remodeled the old main house, and erected barbed-wire fences and gates.

And because Capra was "spooked by atomic bombs" during the Korean War (as Yackey put it), he built an underground bomb shelter with enough room to sleep twenty-five and kept it stocked with food and water, telling his ranch foreman, James Pruitt, "If anything happens, this is for the workers. I always feel like I owe these people something."

The first few months of almost frantic activity, which coincided with Capra's security clearance crisis, were undertaken in the hope that his new life as a rancher—a means of developing a more stable income than motion pictures, and a sentimental attempt to re-create his father's dream—would wipe out the frustrations of what he felt was a misspent life in the movie business, and in the hope that the hundred miles separating Fallbrook from Hollywood would keep him free of the political taint which had driven him back to the soil, feeling "dried-up inside."

Within a year of his first retirement to Red Mountain Ranch, however, Capra was back at work on film projects—but not for the studios, which he avoided, evidently for fear of having the loyalty issue reopened.

AT&T brought him back to make *The Sun,* a pilot film for a children's television series to boost its corporate image and to brighten the benighted postwar image of science. For the maker of the *Why We Fight* series, the four films he made in the Bell Telephone science series between 1952 and 1958 were no mere diversion but a return to propaganda, although of the more sophisticated Madison Avenue variety, which did not seem like propaganda at all.

Capra had just received his security clearance and was about to leave for India when he received the first call from Donald Jones, who had been assigned to recruit and supervise the creative staff of the series for the N. W. Ayer & Son advertising agency. "I had been going through everyone I could think of in show business who was interested in science," Jones recalled, "and Capra was the only one I ever considered seriously. Gene Milford [Capra's former editor, then an Ayer consultant] recommended him to me. He said, 'Frank's really bugged about science. Whenever you work with Capra, you learn something.' "

When Jones called, the project Capra had been developing for Caltech about cosmic rays was stalled for lack of funding, but Capra was in the process of supervising and helping to write (with Charles Newton) a Caltech recruiting film, begun in 1950 as *Choosing Your Future* but not released until 1954, as *Careers for Youth.* Intended to counteract the image of the typical Caltech student as an antisocial egghead, it showed "Technical Tommy" as a fun-loving, regular, all-American guy and pushed

Capra's concern for rounding out a scientific education with the humanities. Capra never paid full attention to the film, however, assigning the direction to Edward Bernds, and though it was an effective enough sales pitch, Capra was accurate in considering it an unimaginative piece of filmmaking. But he was able to use the script he had prepared at Caltech with Charles Stearns for *The Strange Case of the Cosmic Rays* as the springboard for one of his Bell science films.

Capra eventually came to see the series as a way to act out his pedagogical aspirations through the use of film, a chance to turn his filmmaking abilities to something more worthwhile and stimulating than *Here Comes the Groom*. But though Jones claimed that "Capra was interested right away," Capra, by his own account, initially had deep misgivings.

When asked in 1984 how he got the job, he said cryptically that he had been recommended "by some people like the FBI—they had their picking of people and knowledge of this and that. I didn't want to do it. I tried to get out of the Bell science series like crazy. I got a lot of money [for feature films], and I didn't want to deal with crappy little stuff for children, for schools."

But he undoubtedly realized that the AT&T job was a way of going back to work quietly and rehabilitating his own image. Although Jones claimed to know nothing about "some people like the FBI" recommending Capra for the job, he made some suggestive allusions to the political situation Capra had left behind in Hollywood. Capra bragged in *The Name Above the Title* that he was wooed from features by the flattery of the AT&T board and its chairman, Cleo F. Craig, but Jones said, "The AT&T people had to be told who Mr. Capra was. I had a little biography made up [by Jeanne Curtis Webber, later a researcher for Capra on the first film in the series] to present to the company so that they could decide, 'Do you want to talk to him?' It heavily stressed how Mr. Capra was a solid member of the motion picture community, a churchgoer, a family man, a man who did not have a lot of scandal attached to his name. He had an unhappy first marriage, but a lot of people do, and since then he's been a solid member of the community. There were not a lot of people in Hollywood about whom you could say that. I mean, they knew he was not going to turn out to be a member of the Unfriendly Ten. The fact that he had experience doing documentary films [with the Army], not strictly entertainment, certainly loomed in the decision also. [The biography mentioned Capra's recent trip to India to combat communism and his State Department advisory work as well, while pointedly characterizing him as apolitical.]

"Frankly, I never knew his politics until later, when we had a lot of late-night talks. He was bitterly disappointed in some of his colleagues who turned out to be Communists and who told him they weren't. This was at the height of the blacklist—a very unpleasant business. He was not bothered so much that they were Communist Party members: what bothered him was that they did not tell him the truth. Frank is the kind of person who is quite open; he doesn't tell little fibs like other people do."

Daily Variety columnist Sheilah Graham printed the surprising news in April 1952 that Capra was working on a television series about "rockets, atom bombs, 'n' things." But the official announcement was not made until that October. Commuting from the ranch and spending some of his nights in a room he kept at the Beverly Wilshire Hotel, Capra began work behind locked doors at 9100 Sunset Boulevard with Art Black, Chet Sticht, and editor Frank Keller (they also had a smaller office at Paramount). On the interoffice Teletype to Ayer in New York, Capra insisted that he be referred to as "Mr. X." Jones thought the secrecy was due to the "experimental" nature of Bell's first venture into television, but Capra appeared paranoid about his furtive return to Hollywood, as if he hoped to keep his enemies, real and imagined, as much in the dark as possible about what he was doing until it was a fait accompli.

The man who had pursued publicity almost obsessively before 1951 now ran from it as he ran from controversy. To his mingled relief and chagrin, the press virtually ignored him until the first program in the series, finally titled *Our Mr. Sun*, made its long-delayed debut on CBS on November 19, 1956. It was followed by *Hemo the Magnificent* (CBS, 1957, about the circulation of the blood), *The Strange Case of the Cosmic Rays* (NBC, 1957), and *The Unchained Goddess* (NBC, 1958, about the weather, produced by Capra but directed by Richard Carlson). As Capra reemerged into the public eye, the press began to ask the uncomfortable question, "Why doesn't Frank Capra make movies?"—to which he could only give such cryptic answers as "People just aren't laughing anymore. . . . It may be that nowadays there is so much fun poked at us by others that we do not like to make fun of ourselves. . . . The chill has replaced the chuckle. . . .

"Communism just isn't funny."

At the same time he was beginning work on the science series, Capra also agreed to make a film on communism for the State Department.

The Defense Department in May 1952 had revived his proposal for a *Why We Arm* series. It was passed from Defense to State, where it was retitled *Peace With Freedom*, and Capra was hired to develop a pilot script with Myles Connolly, who recently had cowritten (with John Lee Mahin)

Leo McCarey's rabid diatribe against the domestic Red Menace, *My Son John*. "Poor old Myles," Philip Dunne called him. "He was a fairly decent fellow, a poetic fellow who wrote little airy fantasies, but he was caught up in this strange mania. It went further than a neurosis. It was a psychosis." Capra was living under the constant dread of having to repeat the trauma of his security clearance—a measure of that dread was his insistence as late as 1984 that his clearance "*Never* came back," by which he apparently meant that it was always conditional—and he was reluctant in the extreme to become involved in another government project. But when the offer came it was one he could not refuse, lest he be accused again of disloyalty.

Connolly's script, completed in September 1952, was titled *YOU*. Though it mostly was an unsophisticated by-the-numbers fulmination against what Connolly referred to as "The Evil Empire" of communism (against which "*the free men of the world, their patience ended,*" had risen to the defense of South Korea), there were some more subtle and double-edged overtones to the script, particularly in its extended passages on the suppression of individual thought and artistic freedom in the Soviet Union. The parallels with the recent experiences of Capra and other American artists with the security board and HUAC were hard to overlook.

"And who are 'the socially dangerous'?" asked *YOU*. "*Anybody . . . anybody this People's Commissariat cares to describe as such.*" The script suggested showing the FBI's fingerprint files ("without identifying them") in a sequence depicting the means by which totalitarian governments, also including Hitler's and Mussolini's, try to reduce the individual to "Mr. Zero."

"YOU are *not* Mr. Zero," the script insists. ". . . YOU are *not* a particle in the proletariat. . . . YOU are *not* a sheep. YOU are not an insect. . . . YOU are *not* a mere number in a census, not a mere item in the ledger of the State."

The State Department discreetly shelved the project, but in 1953, through Cecil B. DeMille, it offered Capra a job supervising the productions of the government's foreign propaganda arm, the United States Information Agency, then a part of State. DeMille headed a Hollywood advisory committee to the USIA, and Capra served as a member of the committee, but Capra told DeMille that he was busy on the science films and that while he was available to make a film for the government (such as *YOU*), he was reluctant to assume another administrative role like the one he had in World War II, because of Washington's increasing tendency toward taking pervasive control of filmmakers.

Capra felt secure enough under the wing of AT&T that he could afford to reject the protective coloration of a full-time government job. But after he delivered *Our Mr. Sun* on April 10, 1954, he realized what an illusion that was.

Conflicts had arisen over the cost and content of the science films. Each of his four films wound up costing about $400,000, about three times as much as originally estimated, and AT&T lost "huge" amounts of money, recalled animator Shamus Culhane, who wrote that every time Don Jones asked AT&T for more money, "He might just as well have asked for a pound of bone marrow." "The science films were sort of finicky films to do," said Chet Sticht. "They were slow, and they had a lot of animation. You couldn't hurry them. But AT&T tried to operate it like a business, and sometimes you can't make films like a business. Capra couldn't make anything by the dozen."

Most of the overruns went for direct production costs, especially for animation; Capra received only $40,000 in salary for *Mr. Sun*, and about $55,000 for each of the three other films, plus modest amounts over the years for the sale of foreign rights. "His tax people were a little aghast that he would go to work on TV shows," Jones recalled. "He was being pushed by Abe Lastfogel [head of the William Morris Agency, which represented him] and others to go back into features." Despite his nominal income from AT&T, he was not hurting financially. He was making a considerable profit raising avocados and citrus at Red Mountain Ranch, which reached a peak annual net of about $400,000 by the early 1960s, in addition to the appreciation in the value of the land; he also continued to rake in money from stock dividends and splits and from his profit participations on his old films, on which he and his lawyers had the foresight to include a share of profits for television rights.

Jones felt that Capra "was given a great deal of autonomy" on the science films, but Capra did not see it that way, complaining bitterly about his feelings of being creatively as well as financially subservient to Ayer and AT&T. Each subject had to be approved by the ad agency, which also had the final cut on the films (a common practice for that era in the TV industry). Some of the eminent scientists who served as informal advisers to AT&T and had helped supervise the preparation of subject outlines before Capra became involved also tried to exert their influence during production. But Capra resisted his creative straitjacketing for the first two years before giving in and surrendering any pretense that it was "one man, one film."

The scientific advisers criticized Capra's approach for its excessive whimsy and its determinedly puerile level of addressing the audience. Strenuous objections were made to Capra's use of anthropomorphic cartoon characters representing forces of nature (Mr. Sun, Chloro Phyll, Hemo the Magnificent, Meteora the Goddess of Weather), and some critics also objected to the series' lowbrow approach. But the films were used for many years in schools, where they were warmly received; Capra's own grand-children knew him not as the maker of *Mr. Smith* but as the maker of *Mr. Sun.*

The criticism of the series was stinging to Capra, however, particularly at a time when his better films had fallen out of fashion, because in his flight from serious filmmaking into what he considered "crappy little stuff for children, for schools," he had deliberately set a limit on the intellectual ceiling of the programs, talking down to his audience in order to sidestep any possible ideological problems.

Before approving Capra's contract for the three films to follow *Mr. Sun,* Ayer in 1954 insisted on more control, demanding that he accept a for-mally constituted Scientific Advisory Board to monitor every phase of production. Using Capra's cost overruns as leverage, Ayer also demanded that he provide fully elaborated scripts for its approval. Seeing no alter-native to accepting these strictures, he agreed, but in a November 12, 1954, letter to his agent Bert Allenberg, he candidly expressed his self-disgust for doing so.

But cost overruns were not the only club the ad agency was holding over Capra's head. They also raised the question of his loyalty to his country.

Ayer wanted him to sign a clause requiring that he endeavor to avoid hiring anyone under a political cloud or alleged to be involved with any group the government considered un-American. Asked by the Morris Agency on June 29, 1954, if he had any objection to the blacklisting clause, Capra emphatically replied that he did not, other than not wanting to be responsible for members of the Scientific Advisory Board. But through his agents he resisted the inclusion of the clause in the contract, because Ayer also wanted the right to cut the films to remove blacklisted partici-pants. That not only would have further eroded Capra's creative control but also would have necessitated costly reshooting.

Capra's conflicted feelings about the blacklist and about McCarthyism were expressed in a letter he wrote, but did not send, to Lee DuBridge on July 22, shortly after the televised hearings in which Joseph McCarthy attacked what he claimed were communistic influences in the United States Army. Even though the Army-McCarthy hearings had ended in disgrace for the Wisconsin senator, Capra continued to identify with the witch-hunters. While admitting that McCarthy's tactics caused damage, he felt McCarthy's critics did not seem to understand that the damage he caused was an unavoidable result of combating the even more dangerous threat of communism.

While Capra was defending McCarthyism, Ayer also was demanding the right to fire him if he were guilty or even accused of a crime or any other (nebulously defined) breach of decorum. Insisting on legal protection he was willing to disregard for others in the industry whose loyalty was under a cloud, Capra objected to being put in jeopardy by the mere accusation of wrongdoing. He made noises about quitting, telling Allenberg in the November 12 letter that he had lost interest in the science series. But he didn't quit.

The contract Frank Capra Productions had entered into with Ayer on August 20, 1954, which was amended on November 17, was not among Capra's papers when the author read them. But the papers included a signed employment contract for the science series between Capra and Frank Capra Productions, dated November 15, 1954, that included a clause obligating him to avoid even the appearance of involvement with any group the government considered un-American.*

Capra's refuge from the morass of politics, he wrote in the unmailed 1954 letter to DuBridge, was God.

He had turned back to the Church during his security clearance crisis, "revalidating" his twenty-year marriage to Lu in a Catholic ceremony on April 19, 1952, before Father Alfio Mondini at the Mission San Antonio de Pala, an Indian mission near Fallbrook. The scripts of Capra's science films and many of his other film projects after 1952 reflected his born-again Catholicism, which frequently caused friction with more secular-minded colleagues. His growing involvement with the church led to his being invested into the Knights of Malta in 1972 (through the recommendation of John Ford) and becoming a lay minister of the church in 1978, allowing him to distribute Holy Communion. But late in life he acknowledged the uncertainty of his religious beliefs.

"The agnostic in me is not completely gone," he said in 1984. "If I have to go to church, I go to a Catholic church. I believe that, but not too strongly. I don't know if there *is* a God. But I do know that religion is

---

* *Capra's crediting his job on the science series to sponsorship "by some people like the FBI" may shed light on records in his heavily censored Army Intelligence file indicating that on November 20, 1954, he was the subject of another security review, which was concluded in his favor.*

responsible for an awful lot of deaths, war, and hate. So you get a little bit worried that religion probably is man-made. And yet deep down within you, there is the matter of your own soul. What is that? When you're dead, you weigh just the same as when you were alive. What have you lost? What is death? What is life? If you start anywhere, from any angle, you run into a stone wall."

Robert Riskin, who had been an invalid since his stroke in 1950, died on September 20, 1955, shortly after being honored with the Writers Guild's Laurel Award for lifetime achievement.

After Capra wrote in a 1977 *Los Angeles Times* article that Riskin was "one of my dearest friends," Fay Wray replied in an unpublished letter to the *Times* that during her husband's long illness, "many concerned friends visited Bob. Frank Capra was not one of them." Capra was one of the many people who left telephone messages when Riskin was taken ill, but Wray was too busy to return the calls. Capra's later explanation for his failure to visit Riskin was that he felt unwelcome.

Riskin himself had always seemed to rise above the rancor surrounding his relationship with Capra. When Jo Swerling, a frequent visitor, was pacing back and forth in front of Riskin's wheelchair, he suddenly turned to Riskin and said, "It is appalling that Frank has never been to see you. He should have been here. He should be here now." Riskin looked up sharply at him from his wheelchair and said: "You're talking about my best friend."

Life as a gentleman rancher began to turn sour on Capra, just as his life in Hollywood had turned sour on him. And, ironically, it was a political scandal in his country retreat that drove him back into the movie business.

The Capras made little concerted effort to socialize with their neighbors in Fallbrook, even though they sent Lulu and Tom to the local schools. "When Capra came here he joined the Rotary Club," Chet Sticht noted, "but that didn't work out, because you had to attend meetings." Still, "Frank was not some first-class prima donna," recalled a local druggist, Leighton Harrison; though he "was never the type for having big wingdings. . . . Here it was like he never met a stranger. He'd sit and talk half a day to a bum, if the bum would talk to him." Most social occasions at Red Mountain Ranch, however, despite his negative feelings toward Hollywood, revolved around Capra showing one of his own films, in a basement playroom decorated with his Oscars, to his small circle of family and cronies. "Capra would play over any picture you wanted," George

Yackey said. "I guess I saw *It's a Wonderful Life* ten times." And he showed his home movies, which were as amateurish as anyone else's; in October 1959 he made a short film of a local tribute he staged for Duke Snider, the Los Angeles Dodgers outfielder, who also had an avocado ranch in Fallbrook. It was no substitute for creative activity, but as Sticht put it, "It kept him off the streets."

Lu did not seem comfortable in Fallbrook. Her asthma was affected by the vegetation, and she "never was interested in farming, even when she was down here," said her brother, Jim, who took over the management of the ranch after Pop Warner died in November 1952. She dutifully became involved with Bett Sticht in a local children's charity, The Angels Society, which ran a thrift shop. When asked how she otherwise passed the time in Fallbrook, her brother thought for a moment and then said, "She sewed a lot, you know."

Capra's "scientific" methods at the ranch were backfiring. The card file he kept on his trees turned out to be of little practical value, but his overdevelopment of the land and his mass production of compost stimulated growth to the point that it contributed to a general decline in the area's avocado prices, eventually forcing him to lease his picking operations on a fifty-fifty split to the Eadington Farming Company. When prices rose again, at the same time Capra's trees came into their maturity, it "killed him" to have to share the profits with Eadington, Warner said.

Red Mountain Ranch was the largest ranch in Fallbrook, and some resented Capra's wealth and aloofness, particularly after he became involved in local politics and published an advertisement in the *Fallbrook Enterprise* in April 1954 trumpeting his "professional accomplishments and earning capacities," including ownership of "my own Producing Companies," as qualifications for public office over a less affluent political foe. He titled the ad "The Good Old American Way." When a neighbor called him to task for his materialism, Capra beat a hasty public retreat: "The *spiritual* values are the only *real* values. . . . I was trying to make light of material accomplishment."

The trouble began after Capra was appointed to the board of the Fallbrook Public Utility District (FPUD), effective December 17, 1953, the only public office he ever held, and became embroiled in a political dispute that bore a disturbing similarity to the plot of *Mr. Smith Goes to Washington*—with Capra playing the Claude Rains role.

"It wasn't much of an office," Capra insisted in 1985. "All you could control were the water rights."

But there was no more vital issue in Fallbrook than water rights. Capra himself wrote in 1954 that "water is the 'lifeblood' of Fallbrook."

Before 1946, land development was limited by the scarcity of water and the high cost of irrigation. Water pumped from wells and from the nearby Santa Margarita River was sufficient for growing olives but not for the full-scale production of citrus and avocados. In 1924 a movement was started to raise money to dam the river and use the water which flowed down into the Pacific Ocean through the large Rancho Santa Margarita. Despite repeated attempts to lobby Congress and federal government agencies, including a pitch to the Public Works Administration during the New Deal era, Fallbrook did not have enough clout and population to raise the money. The issue was further complicated during World War II when the Rancho Santa Margarita became the Camp Pendleton Marine Base.

In 1946 FPUD hired George Yackey as its chief water engineer and general manager to push for the dam and to find other ways of bringing water to their orchards, such as piping it in from the Colorado River. A tentative agreement was reached in 1949 between FPUD and Camp Pendleton to build a reservoir for joint use. But on January 25, 1951, the Navy and the U.S. Department of Justice sued FPUD to reclaim all rights to the water in the river for Camp Pendleton. Many of the district's property owners were named in the suit, including Capra, who along with his neighbors was accused of "unlawful interference" with "the rights of the United States of America" and of "complete disregard of the need of water in question for National Defense" by "combat forces of the United States Marine Corps now engaged in warfare in the Far East."

Capra was roused to action by what he felt to be an assault on both his property and his patriotism, but in the early stages of the fight he tried to keep his name out of the public debate because, as Yackey put it, "He was afraid it might tarnish him."

As part of a propaganda campaign that also included pro-FPUD articles in the *Los Angeles Times, Reader's Digest,* and *The Saturday Evening Post,* Capra agreed to make a 16mm color documentary film called *The Fallbrook Story* for the local Chamber of Commerce. But his name did not appear on the screen. "I don't think Frank wanted to have his name associated with the picture," Yackey explained. Released in 1952, *The Fallbrook Story* was shown in Washington and Southern California to raise support for FPUD against "the unjust federal officials who were prostituting the real government." Though copies still exist in Fallbrook, the film, which is like a crude parody of a Frank Capra film, was discreetly overlooked in Capra's autobiography. When asked about it in 1985, he responded, "Well . . . it wasn't *much* of a film. It was just to keep me busy. I wanted to see the country. It didn't have much to say."

Ostensibly funded by the Chamber of Commerce and by individuals in

Fallbrook, the film was made largely through silent financing from the conservative *Los Angeles Times,* which warned, "If private water rights can be taken, any kind of rights can be taken." The script was written by *Times* feature writer Ed Ainsworth and the photography was by Hollywood cameraman Lee Garmes, who had a ranch in Fallbrook. Don Porter narrated with *Why We Fight* solemnity, and the host was Cecil B. DeMille.

The Fallbrook Story used some familiarly "Capraesque" rhetoric about "the little fellows" fighting the system but only as a smokescreen for a defense of the big ranchers and their traditional way of doing business in Fallbrook: when the big ranchers "feuded over dividing up the water, as will happen in the arid West. . . . they did things in the American Way. They didn't try to take any water from the little fellows up and down the creeks, who used a tiny bit of irrigation water or pumped a well": no, the big ranchers made a "private agreement"* which "simply and properly divided up what was left after the smaller owners had used their share. And under that doctrine of sharing the water, Fallbrook prospered."

To Capra, the suit by the federal government was much more than a fight over water rights, more than a threat to drain his property dry and put him out of business as a rancher—it was a symbol of the threat to his stake in the American Dream from communism, McCarthyism, Americanism, and all the other "isms" that were ruining his life. The rhetoric of the film could just as well have been describing Hollywood under the blacklist: "Some vague fear suddenly had invaded Fallbrook this day early in 1951. It was intangible, but none the less deadly. The whole town was infected, although no one knew the real nature of the rumors or their source. . . . [One man] went home profoundly disturbed, feeling there was some unknown danger threatening everything he had worked for. . . .

"Which way of life is to prevail in the United States? Shall it be the evil one? Are Americans to be ruled, in fear, by the mailed fist of internal tyranny? Are non-elective [*sic*] usurpers of power in Washington to prevail over the American people? Is Liberty to die? Is freedom to become but a memory?"

The Fallbrook Story painted a picture of "a hamlet that has united in simple faith to fight greed, tyranny, and oppression." But as Capra would learn firsthand when he joined the board of FPUD, there were deep schisms within the community over the proposed dam and the rights to the water in the Santa Margarita River.

---

* *A stipulated judgment in the Superior Court of San Diego County in 1940 between the two major landowners at the time, Rancho Santa Margarita and N. R. Vail.*

Opponents of the dam charged that it was a scheme to benefit the big ranchers and the real estate interests by condemning the property of small landowners to provide water for the big ranches and raise their property values. The opposition was led by a group of small farmers owning several thousand acres condemned by FPUD for the dam in July 1951 and in January 1955; the small farmers called themselves the Willow Glen Water Users Protective Association, a name that inescapably summoned up images of the Willet Creek Dam which Jimmy Stewart tries to stop in *Mr. Smith.**

"As a matter of fact, it *wasn't* fair," Yackey admitted in 1985 of the Fallbrook condemnation. "But that land is all sitting there owned by FPUD and ready to go."†

Some of Capra's own land had been condemned by FPUD. In 1949 and 1950, the district used its right of eminent domain to buy sixty acres of his ranch at thirty dollars an acre as the site of its main regulatory reservoir, a move Sticht said made Capra "furious." Capra considered suing the district to force the closing of a well it maintained on his property, but he dropped the idea after the district did so voluntarily.

He switched to the other side as a result of the federal suit and the controversy over the Santa Margarita dam project, which demonstrated even more powerfully that everything could be taken away from a Fallbrook citizen who did not become directly involved in the politics of water rights.

So he shed his misgivings about politics and in 1953, at the urging of his local attorney, Franz R. Sachse, he accepted appointment to the board of FPUD. It was part of a power squeeze in which the two opponents of the dam on the five-man board, John H. Griffin and Alfred G. von Normann, who had been elected in 1952 to four-year terms, were "kicked off the board," as Yackey put it, persuaded to resign in favor of compromise candidates, Capra and B. M. McDonald, a rancher and nursery owner.

Because of Capra's public image as the champion of the "little guy," many in town were surprised when he became the most vocal supporter of the dam on the board and in ads he placed in the *Enterprise*. He naively expected that "everybody would agree with him," said Yackey. But within

* Ironically, the only reference to the FPUD controversy in any previous book on Capra was Charles Wolfe's statement in Frank Capra: A Guide to References and Resources (1987) that Capra was "in the style of a Jefferson Smith, leading his neighbors in a fight to protect local water rights to the Santa Marguerita [sic] River."

† The federal suit did not go to trial until 1958 and finally was settled out of court in 1968, with the river water being divided on a 60-40 basis between the Navy and the district. But as of 1992 the dam remained unbuilt and the land FPUD's property.

six months after his appointment to the board, Capra already had come under personal attack.

He was accused of stealing community water which leaked from the reservoir onto his land (people in Fallbrook called the reservoir "Big Leaky"), and, more seriously, he was accused of scheming to have FPUD annex 520 acres of his own land for the dam—the steep, rocky, undeveloped part adjacent to Rainbow Creek, a tributary of the Santa Margarita— even though that land was not in the district. Capra expressed outrage over the charges, but shortly before leaving the board, he acknowledged that his Rainbow Creek property "might be affected by such condemnation action." Even if that part of his land had not been affected, Capra, as the district's largest landowner, stood to benefit greatly from the building of the dam, because it would have improved his ranching business and raised the value of his real estate. His conflicts of interests made him increasingly uncomfortable during his tenure on FPUD.

This latest "whispering campaign" against Capra, as Yackey called it, reached a crescendo in the spring of 1954, when two other board seats were up for election and the performance of the current board was being debated. Capra denied in one of his *Enterprise* ads that he and the other board members were "selling you down the Santa Margarita River." But he felt he was "without too much right to talk, since I was only 'appointed' and not elected by the voters. . . . If the voters vote 'no confidence' in what the present board stands for, I for one will step out of the picture and let the other boys have a go at it."

He stayed on the board after more than two-thirds of the vote went to his side, but with the legal battle over the dam dragging on, he began to miss meetings with increasing frequency, telling the board that it was "due to pressure of work in Hollywood, and my conscience is bothering me." He had begun to miss meetings in July 1954, during the time that he was negotiating his contract with Ayer for the rest of the science series and was being subjected to another questioning of his loyalty.

Capra not only accepted the repugnant job of continuing the science series, he began to reconsider his aversion to feature filmmaking: in April 1956, he made a development deal with Columbia Pictures to remake his classic *Lady for a Day* (a fact he did not mention in his book, claiming he initiated the project in 1960). His willingness to put up with the humiliation of crawling before Ayer and back to Harry Cohn was motivated not simply by his sense of stagnation in Fallbrook, though that certainly was a factor, but also by events which literally were driving him out of town.

His disenchantment with ranching intensified after the discovery in

1955 that his avocado trees, like those of most ranchers in the area, were infected with a mysterious fungus (or "root rot") that was slowly destroying them and eventually forced him out of the ranching business altogether. The immediate cause of his return to Hollywood, however, was not the plague or his creative anomie but the growing Fallbrook water scandal and his panic-stricken flight from the FPUD board on June 6, 1955.

When Capra was not missing meetings, he was trying to duck the issues. On January 10, 1955, when the board reaffirmed its support for the condemnation of land for the dam project, and also took a stand in favor of a proposed amendment of state law to "allow districts to annex noncontiguous property," the vote was 4 to 0 on both issues, with only Capra abstaining. As the minutes of that meeting explained, "Director Capra stated that inasmuch as he was the owner of approximately 500 acres adjoining Rainbow Creek which might be affected by such condemnation action, he wished to abstain from voting, however he was not voting against it and was very much in favor of such action."

The controversy intensified four days later when FPUD filed another land condemnation suit against about three hundred of the small landowners. The Willow Glen Water Users Protective Association made its futile protest directly to Capra on March 20, giving him lists of questions which he and the other board members tried to answer in the *Enterprise* and at a meeting on March 28 that overflowed the small FPUD headquarters. Capra resigned from the board and left town a little over two months later, with almost a year remaining in his term of office, in a state of considerable haste and confusion.

"Within three weeks my family is moving away from Fallbrook," Capra wrote the board in his letter of resignation on June 6, "because we are tearing down the old [ranch] house and will build a new one. This will take at least six months." He said he would be spending most of his time in Hollywood, and weekending with his family in June Lake (they later moved into a rented house in Fallbrook until the new house at the ranch was ready for occupancy). "So you will readily see that . . . attending meetings in Fallbrook will be quite a problem for me. . . .

"Believe me when I say that my resignation has nothing to do with all the dirt and mud that is being thrown around by those interested in keeping Fallbrook from obtaining vital water storage. I know how wild and untrue are the snide insinuations that have been made about me, so I have to conclude that all the other charges fall into the same category.

"I am resigning only because I cannot properly serve the community."

Yackey thought that Capra did not want to face the public in an election, which he would have had to do in May 1956: "I don't think he would have taken a chance on running for a job and not getting elected. He was very easily hurt. I don't think he was being hurt so bad, but he was very proud. That's what drove him."

Something even worse was happening at the time: the "snide insinuations" were spreading beyond Fallbrook.

At the board meeting on April 11, 1955, "Director Capra brought out the fact that there were rumors about a [San Diego County] Grand Jury investigation of the District and officers, and suggested that if such were the case, he believed that the board should welcome such investigation and request that the Grand Jury proceed with it immediately."

The Grand Jury did conduct an investigation of FPUD, calling thirty-two witnesses, including Capra, who testified in San Diego on July 28. His testimony was never made public, but the fact that he had been summoned to testify was reported by the *San Diego Union* and the Associated Press. He refused to comment to reporters at the courthouse other than to reaffirm his support for the dam "regardless of what happens to the government suit against the district," and to deny the Big Leaky charge, claiming, "I've lost millions of gallons of water to the district because of the Red Mountain dam and a well the district has there."

An interim report of the Grand Jury on October 3, 1955, criticized the FPUD board and Yackey on nine counts of "irregularities in the operations," but the jury returned no indictments, "believing that the best interests of the County and the District would be served by corrective methods."

In the matter of Big Leaky, the Grand Jury found "no evidence of bad faith or culpability on the part of either the District or Mr. Frank Capra," but otherwise it was sharply critical. In its final report on February 6, 1956, it charged the board and Yackey with "autocratic and secretive methods" and noted that complaints had been received that "proceedings for purchases of land condemned for the proposed Fallbrook dam are being pressed with little or no regard for legitimate interests of the small property owners." While conceding (in its interim report) that the condemnations "have evidently been carried out in accordance with law," the Grand Jury stated its belief that "the District has not shown due and proper regard for the personal and moral rights, feelings, and natural apprehensions of the property owners involved." It urged that the "directors and the general manager concern themselves to a greater degree with the personal and property interests of all members of the District, including minority groups."

*　　*　　*

The Frank Capra who returned to Columbia to remake *Lady for a Day* in 1956 was a shell of the man who had made the original in 1933. Like most of the other projects he worked on in his later years, the remake foundered at Columbia because of "script problems," a euphemism for his increasingly incoherent sociopolitical ideas and for his inability to cope with the changing times in a meaningful way.

There had been proposals to remake *Lady for a Day* for several years before Capra became involved. When Hal Wallis asked to buy it as a vehicle for Oscar winner Shirley Booth at Paramount, Harry Cohn offered it to Capra instead, with the hope of luring Booth to Columbia. Capra was unsure about whether to keep the Damon Runyon story in period or to modernize it; he was uncomfortable with the raffishness of the gangster milieu and wanted Dave the Dude to settle down, marry his moll, and go straight; and he could not resist injecting cold war rhetoric into the story. Unable to persuade HUAC informer Abe Burrows or his old friend Garson Kanin to work on the script, and dissatisfied with Herb Baker's modern treatment set in Greenwich Village (which Columbia liked), Capra drafted a new opening involving Korean War orphans on an Oregon apple farm and retitled the story *Ride the Pink Cloud*. Cohn insisted that Capra hire another writer, but after reading Harry Tugend's modern version, Cohn dropped the project. Capra vainly tried to rekindle the studio's interest until 1960, when Columbia allowed him to shop it elsewhere and he made a deal with United Artists to remake it in period as *Pocketful of Miracles*, his last feature film.*

In his book Capra skipped the entire episode of the attempt to remake *Lady for a Day* at Columbia, pretending that he returned to the studio to film the biblical tale *Joseph and His Brethren*, from the cycle of novels by Thomas Mann. But it was not until September 17, 1957, after almost a year and a half on *Lady for a Day*, that Capra was shifted to *Joseph*, a troublesome property previously worked over by several writers, including HUAC informer Clifford Odets and blacklist ringleader John Lee Mahin. Whatever their political coloration, most of the important writers in Hollywood by now were leery of working with a tottering and insecure director who had made his envy and contempt for writers well known in the industry ("*Fuck the writers*," he was fond of saying), and Capra, despite his own inability

---

* *The final script was a patchwork credited to Hal Kanter and Harry Tugend, based on the screenplay by Robert Riskin. Jimmy Cannon and Myles Connolly were uncredited, as was Capra, who failed to convince the Writers Guild that he, rather than Riskin, should receive credit for adapting Runyon's story.*

as a scriptwriter, compounded the problem by remaining stubbornly determined to prove that he could do it all himself.

He turned in a partial screenplay for *Joseph* on January 7, 1958, but Columbia was unhappy with it and a week later cut off his development money. Studio executive Ben Kahane, in breaking the news to Capra's lawyer, Mabel Walker Willebrandt, expressed regret that the studio was unable to work with the man who had been so instrumental in its past. In his book, Capra attributed the collapse of the project to Harry Cohn's death, which did not occur until six weeks later.

It was increasingly apparent to everyone that Capra had lost his touch. His last two features had been failed attempts to recapture his past glories, and since then he had been in embittered exile, making children's films for TV. A lingering fondness still existed in Hollywood for Capra's light comedies of the 1930s—in 1956 Columbia remade *It Happened One Night* as a musical, *You Can't Run Away From It*, with Dick Powell directing Jack Lemmon and June Allyson—but the more overtly socially conscious Capra films were no longer in step with the times. Rather than admit that *Mr. Deeds*, *Mr. Smith*, and *Meet John Doe* were too passionate, too engaged, too disturbing to the status quo to be acceptable in the 1950s, the Hollywood and critical establishments simply ridiculed all of his work, good or bad, past and present, as "Capracorn." It was a designation he fought, then used as a rationalization for his failure to reestablish himself, and finally adopted as a badge of honor when his old films came back into fashion in the 1970s. But his problem went much deeper than being old-fashioned, and it was not unique to Capra.

"Security, regularity, order, and the life of no imagination were the command of the day," Norman Mailer wrote of the 1950s. "If one had any doubt of this, there was Joe McCarthy with his built-in treason detector, furnished by God, and the damage was done. In the totalitarian wind of those days, anyone who worked in Government formed the habit of being not too original, and many a mind atrophied from disuse and private shame."

So, too, in Hollywood.

Though Capra's government clearances and his rehabilitation through AT&T made it safe enough for him to go back to work in the studios by the late 1950s, he did so in a state of mind in which, as Dalton Trumbo wrote of Hollywood in his 1949 pamphlet *The Time of the Toad*, "unconventional ideas or unpopular thoughts are carefully concealed by self-censorship." Michael Wilson wrote during the blacklist era that Hollywood films were suffering from "a pervading anti-intellectual quality, an absence of *ideas*, a disdain for rational motive." He wondered, "Why do informers have to make themselves out as idiots?"

"**T**oday I may not have a thing at all. . . . We're drifting and the laughs are few," Frank Sinatra sings under the credits of *A Hole in the Head* (1959), Capra's first feature in the eight years since events of the blacklist era drove him out of town. This remarkably glum and cynical "comedy," which most critics over the years have dismissed as impersonal hackwork, had as many autobiographical overtones as *Mr. Deeds Goes to Town* or *It's a Wonderful Life.*

A Sincap (Sinatra and Capra) coproduction packaged by Abe Lastfogel for the William Morris Agency, *A Hole in the Head* was released by United Artists, as was Capra's subsequent feature, *Pocketful of Miracles.* UA's general vice president in that era was Capra's friend Max Youngstein, who had worked with Capra at Paramount and had kept in touch with him in the intervening years. Youngstein recalled that it was "a very tough job" to convince Capra to make another feature: "So much of it was based on [how] Frank just got turned off by the things that happened and people that wouldn't keep their word. It was hard to convince him I would let him have enough creativity without interfering. I convinced him both of those pictures could be turned into something that was modern but still was making the kinds of statements he wanted to make." Youngstein said he disregarded Capra's earlier political problems in helping him return to features: "If he came to me and wanted to make a picture and I liked it, I couldn't care if every guy in Congress called him—I know what he stood for." But, added Youngstein, it also was "a little tough to get people to accept him back. A lot of those people didn't know whether he still had it. They wouldn't take the trouble to sit down and see how vital he was and how his brain was still functioning."

A Hole in the Head was based on Arnold Schulman's Broadway play, which in turn was based on his 1955 live television drama *The Heart's a Forgotten Hotel.* Schulman's screenplay was rewritten, without credit, by the ubiquitous Myles Connolly, and the characters were transformed from Jews to Italians. Sinatra plays Tony Manetta, a small-time promoter who runs a shabby Miami Beach hotel, The Garden of Eden, but dreams secondhand dreams of opening another Disneyland in Florida. Tony is about to be evicted from his hotel ("A rumor like that spreads, I'm dead"), and is brutally rebuffed when he tries to hustle backing from an old friend, gangster Jerry Marks (Keenan Wynn). He dumps his irresponsible beatnik girlfriend Shirl (Carolyn Jones) to romance the genteel widow Mrs. Rogers

(Eleanor Parker) for her money, but finds he has no stomach for the deception, admitting, "I'm nothing but a bum." Just when it appears he will have to give up his son (Eddie Hodges) to his brother Mario (Edward G. Robinson) in exchange for the hotel rent, Tony falls in love with Mrs. Rogers, the irascible-but-lovable Mario has a change of heart, and they all romp on the sand together as the sun sets on Miami Beach.

Tony's self-contempt, his insecurity, his anguished search for the big score, his permanent stench of failure, and even his rootless existence in a hotel all came uncomfortably close to the bone for Capra, who was undergoing the same kind of humiliation in Hollywood. Capra's ambivalent but in the end gratuitously harsh portrayal of Shirl—she is punished for her considerable charm and sex appeal by having her try to talk Tony into abandoning his son—showed how estranged the director had become from his earlier empathy with independent women. The 1959 model Frank Capra, who, as Andrew Sarris put it, had "returned with the triumphant new look in conformity," was more comfortable with the safely domesticated Mrs. Rogers, so helpless without a man that she'll buy the most heartless line.

Fatally unsure of itself, *A Hole in the Head* in fact alternately deplores and celebrates conformity, and its forced happy ending carries none of Capra's old emotional charge. The ostensible message is the familiar one from *You Can't Take It With You*, that it's possible to be both happy and poor, but the real message is the futility of dreams. The viewer is left with a pervasive sense of self-betrayal, which Capra perhaps allowed to dominate the story because of his own overwhelming guilt over his sellout as an artist and his betrayal of his colleagues to the witch-hunters (Edward G. Robinson, the film's symbol of capitulation to the system, had been a prominent Hollywood liberal before he crawled before HUAC to escape the graylist). As Donald Willis observed of *A Hole in the Head*, "The most interesting scene is the nightmarish conclusion to the Jerry Marks episode [an episode original to the film], in which Marks admits that he was wise to Tony all along and that he let him go on only because he was an old friend. It's a real shocker because, when finally the ugliness in the movie surfaces, the movie turns out to be even uglier than it appeared to be."

Capra's first color feature also looks ugly, which is surprising coming from the distinguished cinematographer William Daniels but characteristic of a director who had no sense of how to use color dramatically or aesthetically. The most distressing element of the visual style of *A Hole in the Head* was that Capra always managed to put his camera in the wrong place for every shot, a function both of his unfamiliarity with the wide screen and of his inability to shoot his scenes with a clearly defined dramatic and moral point of view. Though his old skill with actors was the last to desert him—Sinatra's desperation is utterly credible, and his scenes alone with Eddie Hodges are done with an astringency that gives them genuinely touching moments amid the general bathos—Capra had no idea what his *attitude* should be toward the characters, and the result is an evasive camera that jumps all over the place within a scene, trying its damnedest to remain neutral, in compositions that are uniformly flat and lifeless.

To make *A Hole in the Head* Capra had to accept the conditions of the new, decentralized Hollywood, in which the stars called the shots and powerful agents like Lastfogel served as arbiters of creative disputes. It galled Capra mightily that Sinatra was the senior partner in the joint venture (Sinatra owning two-thirds of the picture to Capra's one-third, and receiving a salary of $200,000 to Capra's $100,000), and Capra's book unfairly blamed Sinatra for the lackadaisical style of the film, claiming that the star was unwilling to take the time to shoot it properly. Sinatra's preference for the first take was well known—Capra in a more complimentary mood compared him to Stanwyck—and if the director did not stand up to his star, it was mostly because Capra was anxious to bring in *A Hole in the Head* with the minimum of fuss and expense, proving that he could be as efficient as any TV director. Only rarely using multiple cameras or takes, he filmed it for $1,890,605 in just forty days between November 10, 1958, and January 9, 1959, eight days ahead of schedule, and he rushed through the editing so that Sincap could beat a tax deadline.

Capra's return to feature filmmaking received a mixed response from the critics. His old friend Philip K. Scheuer of the *Los Angeles Times* called the film a "pleasant diversion. . . . For eight years Hollywood has been unaccountably and, I am sure, needlessly deprived of the know-how of this director." But Scheuer also noted that Capra's stated intention of making *A Hole in the Head* "just for laughs" was "something of a departure for the director. . . . It was Capra's habit to mix messages with his comedy, you will recall, and there was a lengthy period in which their invariably liberal tone lost favor around the country."

Capra had "curiously neglected" his career since 1951, agreed Bosley Crowther of *The New York Times:* "That was too long for one of the finest and wittiest directors in Hollywood to have kept himself *hors de combat* while the movies were fighting for their lives. And it was particularly fearful and depressing because his major production in that time was a quartet of one-hour documentaries on scientific subjects for the television screen. . . . But now Mr. Capra is back with us—and not only back, but also in such form as to make one toy vaguely with the notion that maybe it is good for a director to rest a bit once in a while. . . . [*A Hole in the Head* is] a thoroughly fresh, aggressive, and sardonic comedy of the sort that sets one to thinking about the comedies of the good old days."

A strikingly different judgment was rendered by the young Peter Bogdanovich, writing in the Los Angeles magazine *Frontier*. Titled "Crusade Forgotten," Bogdanovich's review called the film "overlong, meandering, and mawkishly sentimental," and pointed to the change in the Capra protagonist from Gary Cooper and Jimmy Stewart to the cynical Sinatra as symptomatic of decline not only in Capra but in America as well. For Capra, he wrote, *A Hole in the Head* "could have been little more than a well-paying job to be done—not a point of view, not a crusade." Dismayed that "Mr. Capra seems not only to have forgotten his past, but to be in direct opposition to it" by catering to the middle-class complacency of the Eisenhower era, Bogdanovich declared, "If Mr. Capra has truly forgotten his values, ideals, and crusades of the '30s and '40s, there are still those of us today who have not."

In an interview with *Variety*'s Fred Hift before he made *A Hole in the Head*, Capra showed his awareness of the change in his artistic personality, and hinted broadly at the reason: "Comedy is really the highest of all the arts. To succeed with it, you have to first know the facts and the basis of life on which to comment in a human way. Comedy, after all, is based on what should be, not on what is. I think that, possibly, the East-West ideological conflict has tended to unbalance the base of what is and what should be. We've lost that certainty during the last ten to fifteen years, and unless you are quite sure of your base, unless it's steady, comedy is difficult to achieve."

A Hole in the Head was a box-office success when it was released on June 17—with rentals of $4 million it tied for eleventh with *Hercules* on *Variety*'s annual list—and it served its purpose by making Capra bankable for another project. But its success was ephemeral. Today it is remembered mostly for an Oscar-winning song by Sammy Cahn and James Van Heusen, "High Hopes," which was adapted for use by Sinatra as John F. Kennedy's campaign song in the Wisconsin and West Virginia presidential primaries of 1960. The song seldom was used in the campaign after West Virginia because of negative reaction to Kennedy's association with Sinatra, but that did not stop Capra (a Nixon man) from boasting that it helped win the nomination for the future President. In later years, "High Hopes" became a theme song for television tributes to Capra himself.

* * *

While trying to make his comeback in features, Capra also was reenlisting in the cold war.

Though in later years he tried to pass himself off as "a pacifist against all war, not just Vietnam, all kinds of war" and said that if he were to make another film for the government he would title it *Why We Should Not Fight*, Capra in 1957 tried to help the Air Force sell its proposal for a two-part Bell science show on intercontinental ballistic missiles (with the Air Force having control over the script), but Ayer passed on the idea, considering it too propagandistic. Although Capra said in 1984, "I think [the wars in] Korea and Vietnam were mistakes—they weren't fought to win, all those people died for no reason whatever, and a lot of people lost faith in the American government," he had tried to rejoin the Army as a propagandist in the Korean War, and in 1958–1959, at the invitation of John Ford, he served on a Hollywood committee advising the Navy and the Defense Department on two troop orientation films Ford directed in 1959, *Korea— Battleground for Liberty* and *Taiwan—Island of Freedom,* as well as on scripts about other Asian countries of growing interest to the military, including Vietnam and Cambodia. Capra was asked to direct one of those films, but he kept his involvement limited to his advisory role, for which he received a commendation from the Defense Department in 1961.

The last time Capra's security clearance was at issue was in 1960. He had been invited to participate in the secret National Strategy Seminar at the Army War College in Pennsylvania that June, along with such other worthies as Allen W. Dulles, Henry Cabot Lodge, General Omar N. Bradley, and William F. Buckley. The invitation brought about a three-month review of his case by Army Intelligence.

After reading Capra's response to the old charges of involvement with "questionable organizations," a G-2 adjudicator decided, "I believe him." Further investigation in the files of the FBI and HUAC revealed only one new charge against him since 1954, an allegation that he had supported the American Committee for Protection of the Foreign Born, a group the attorney general had listed as a Communist front; another G-2 officer dismissed that charge by commenting, "Subject has successfully answered all other allegations, and I believe he could clear this one up." The clearance was granted on February 24, 1960.

Though the blacklist began to crumble that same year, Capra had been so traumatized by his years in political limbo that living as if he had to keep proving his loyalty had become a reflexive gesture.

His eagerness to travel the film festival and symposium circuit whenever State and the USIA asked him was his most public way of demonstrating his allegiance to America over and over again. As he put it in 1962, "I'm proud to go wherever they ask this immigrant to go." Whether it was to New Delhi or Berlin, Belgrade or Teheran, Toronto or Brasilia, Prague or Moscow, Capra was the Willy Loman of Americanism, presenting himself as "the apostle of the individual" and a crusader for artistic freedom from political tyranny. In truth he was a professional Commiebasher who earnestly debriefed his government patrons on his impressions of Third World and Communist delegations, Iron Curtain countries, and his attempts to outtalk leftist filmmakers—although, as time passed, his encounters with fellow directors, political leaders, and private citizens on his trips abroad resulted in a certain mellowing of his knee-jerk antagonisms. When he met Nikita Khrushchev at a *Time* magazine reception in Moscow on November 7, 1963, he found that "the little bastard had a lot of schmaltz—he liked to laugh, he had a lot of jokes—everybody liked him."

Capra's government was grateful.

"Frank was a wonderful ambassador," George Stevens, Jr., former director of the USIA's motion picture service, recalled in 1986. "His work was widely known and he was respected, and he had that wonderful enthusiasm and personal magnetism. He represented his country very well. Frank made a very interesting life for himself by going abroad and attending meetings instead of curling up in a chair somewhere." The USIA recorded Capra's patriotic message in 1975, producing a four-part series of videotapes, *Frank Capra: The Man Above the Title*, which it translated into several languages and used around the world; one of the tapes was shown in the town square of Bisacquino shortly before his 1977 USIA-sponsored homecoming.

Capra's indefatigable service to his country brought him an invitation to the White House from President Kennedy, postmarked on November 21, 1963, for a luncheon with leaders of the film community to be held on December 10, an event regarded in Hollywood as a long-overdue official recognition of the growing cultural status of motion pictures. Capra received the invitation on the day of Kennedy's funeral. He was a guest of President Johnson, who invited him to a White House state dinner in 1964 and a luncheon in 1967, and of President Ford, who took him golfing with Barry Goldwater and celebrated Capra's seventy-eighth birthday on May 18, 1975, with Frank and Lu at a private dinner in the White House.

Yet Capra never saw his role as a U.S. government propagandist as "political." He shied away from taking stands that were at odds with the American mainstream, and his love for America was something he considered beyond partisanship, beyond question, a matter of the heart (he was fond in later years of quoting Pascal's dictum, "The heart has reasons that reason knows nothing of"). "If you're a real artist, forget the politics," he told the audience at the Directors Guild seminar on his work in 1981. "Forget all politics. Because if you politicize yourself, what you do is cut yourself in half." But when he made that argument during a 1976 panel discussion in Mexico City, the director Costa-Gavras, the maker of *Z* and *State of Siege*, reminded Capra that he had been the inspiration for every political filmmaker, since he was, after all, the maker of *Mr. Smith Goes to Washington*.

Between 1959 and his retirement in 1966, Capra managed to make only one more feature film, the leaden and preachy *Pocketful of Miracles* (1961), which was so shockingly inferior to *Lady for a Day* that it effectively ended his Hollywood career, and a visually undistinguished and simple-minded short called *Rendezvous in Space* (1964), shown at the New York World's Fair to promote NASA's upcoming space shuttle and Manned Orbiting Laboratory program. Most of his creative energy in those years was spent hustling and developing a desperately long and diffuse list of film or television projects which either did not come to fruition or were made by somebody else. "Nothing ever jelled," Chet Sticht recalled. "Again he went into one of those strange periods when he wasn't fighting. He went through a bad psychological period in which he was bitter about everything, and in some way he lost confidence in himself."

The Frank Capra who flogged his wares around Hollywood until his final retirement in 1966 was visibly insecure, off-puttingly defensive, and, underneath it all, terminally afraid of any project or collaborator whose political views might get him into trouble. That habitual sheepishness, that loss of self-definition, affected all of his dealings with people. The man who had once told the United States Army, "In any discussion of film, where *I* sit is the head of the table," now could not stand up to more strong-willed executives, writers, and stars in a changing industry that too often answered his messages with "Frank who?"—if it answered them at all. Hearing that question from secretaries and telephone operators who weren't old enough to remember *It Happened One Night* would drive him into an intolerable rage, for beyond the humiliation of it, the question echoed his own inner doubts and confusion.

"I have a feeling he was actually *glad* to withdraw into retirement," said Eugene Vale, a novelist and screenwriter who worked on several of Capra's late projects. "He was scared and determined not to go on. Capra always struggled with fear. That comes through in *The Name Above the Title*, when he keeps saying he's got to be the boss, got to be the master. There is a great deal of fear attached to that, because if he wanted to be the total boss, he had to take the blame, too."

The failure of Red Mountain Ranch, though it had helped drive Capra back to Hollywood, was also, in Sticht's view, one of the factors that helped undermine his confidence. By the early 1960s, the root rot was spreading uncontrollably in Fallbrook, and in January 1964, after receiving a report from a scientist at UC Riverside who had been using his land to study the fungus, Capra realized it was futile to continue ranching. "The one thing that saved Capra down here was his appreciation of the land, his affinity for the land," Sticht felt. "But it went sour after the fungus spread all over, and he went sour on Fallbrook. It would have been silly just to keep pouring money into it; the IRS takes a dim view of constant losses. Capra's an emotional guy. He'd put a lot of money into the ranch, a lot of effort into it—not money so much as effort; he'd put a lot of *himself* into it—and it was a blow to his ego. I think he looked on the place as his Shangri-La Retirement Heaven, and then it went bad."

The ranch was losing as much as $100,000 a year by the time Capra abandoned farming in 1971. But as its value as farming property plummeted, its value for real estate development rose steadily, along with the rest of Fallbrook. The Capras moved in January 1970 to the Palm Springs area and put the ranch up for sale that October.

According to Capra, they moved to the desert because of Lu's health, but Chet Sticht thought it also was because of his depression over the failure of the ranch and because he had always considered the desert his "lucky place": it was the place where he and Riskin had worked on their scripts. But the Capras' $450,000 white stone ranch house at 49280 Avenida Fernando, on the eighteenth fairway of the La Quinta Country Club—underneath a gargantuan American flag that had flown at the 1932 Los Angeles Olympics—was difficult to maintain, and they had trouble keeping servants. So they sold the house in 1980 and leased a cramped three-room bungalow at the La Quinta Hotel, where they could order meals from room service and have maids do their cleaning.

Because Capra initially overpriced it at $2.5 million, Red Mountain Ranch proved difficult to unload. To obtain a tax break, the Capras in 1972 donated fourteen acres of the ranch, including the house, to Caltech, for use as a conference retreat. And in 1977, they finally found developers who were able to buy the remaining acreage for an aggregate price of $2.05

million. Frank and Lu had incorporated the ranch in 1972 for the purpose of distributing shares on an annual basis to their children in order to avoid heavy inheritance taxes. They liquidated the corporation in 1973, and in 1974 Frank and Lu's assets went into a living family trust for Frank, Jr., a film producer; Lulu, a professor of literature and philosophy; and Tom, a television producer; and for their ten grandchildren. At the peak of their holdings, Frank and Lu were worth about $5 million, much of it in land and blue-chip stocks—though Capra continued to talk poor mouth to the press, telling *The Washington Post* in 1972, "I wasn't really wise financially—I'm the poorest director you ever saw."

"**P**ocketful of Miracles was a terrible mistake, and Capra should have known it from the inception," Eugene Vale said of Capra's last feature. "I was embarrassed when he showed it to me. Obviously he expected my comment to be 'Frank, you've done it again,' but I couldn't do that. The fact that he did a remake of *Lady for a Day* may have been a self-destructive act, punishing himself. He no longer had the guts to do something original and creative, so he sought the insurance of an established hit. But *Pocketful of Miracles* didn't fit the times; even its title had no meaning."

Filmed from April 20 through late June 1961, in Panavision and Technicolor, *Pocketful* cost about $2.9 million but brought in rentals of only $2.5 million after it opened nationwide on Christmas Day following a week's showcase run at two theaters in New York. Ticket sales were not helped by bizarre advertisements in the *Los Angeles Times* featuring a grinning photo of Richard Nixon: "When Richard Nixon Laughs, Everybody in Los Angeles Laughs! Lucky Him! He's just seen Frank Capra's newest picture—and the screen's biggest laugh-getter—*Pocketful of Miracles!*" Some of the reviews were nostalgic and indulgent—*The Hollywood Reporter* called it "a Christmas sockful of joy, funny, sentimental, romantic . . . frankly capricious"—but most read like obituaries.

"Mr. Capra and his energetic troupe manage to get a fair share of laughs from Mr. Runyon's oddball guys and dolls," wrote A. H. Weiler in *The New York Times*, "but their lampoon is dated and sometimes uneven and listless. . . . Repetition and a world faced by grimmer problems seem to have been excessively tough competition for this plot."

Elaine Rothschild of *Films in Review* felt that "this unbelievable and unfunny comedy proves only that director Frank Capra has learned nothing and forgotten nothing in the 28 years that intervened between the two pictures. *Pocketful of Miracles* is not merely out of whole cloth, but out of

638 F R A N K   C A P R A

date, and watching it is a painful experience." She referred to Capra as "a once talented director."

In one of the most candid passages of his book, Capra admitted that his last features failed for "deeply personal, deeply moral" reasons: "I had lost my courage. . . . [A]nd the people said, 'Capra—we've had it from you.' "

And yet Capra also tried to pass the blame to other people. During the shooting he took out his frustrations on the unhappily miscast Bette Davis, who hated the role of Apple Annie but did it for the money ($100,000) after Shirley Booth, Helen Hayes, Jean Arthur, and Katharine Hepburn turned it down. Privately Capra blamed Lastfogel, who packaged *Pocketful* and served as mediator between the director and the stars, for convincing him that he had to share creative control in order to remain bankable. Capra's public wrath in his book, however, was focused on his Dave the Dude and producing partner Glenn Ford, whom he castigated for running the show. But he avoided a confrontation with Ford during shooting, because the two were less than equal partners* and it was only Ford's casting that made the film a "go" project five years after Capra first tried to launch it: Frank Sinatra, originally cast in the role, backed out in a disagreement over the script, and Kirk Douglas, Dean Martin, and Jackie Gleason rejected the part outright. Max Youngstein, who described Ford as "the only guy we could find," felt that Ford's casting "threw everything out of kilter, including [Capra's] own enthusiasm, which was a very important part of what made Frank Capra click." Capra retaliated for his diminished stature in the industry by shifting the blame from its real causes to Glenn Ford. In the uncut manuscript, Capra was more honest, admitting that he had used Ford as a scapegoat.

The cluster headaches Capra first suffered on April 20, 1960, while representing the American film industry at the dedication of Brasilia, occurred on the day *Pocketful* was announced in the trade press; they were associated in his mind with guilt over how he had changed from a social critic into an establishment icon and with the trauma of going back to work in Hollywood. During the shooting they afflicted him with a vengeance, making it virtually impossible for him to function. He would lie in abject pain on the couch of his dressing room at Paramount and writhe for hours on the floor of his apartment at the Beverly Comstock Hotel, cursing and holding his head, scraping his face raw with a wet washcloth. Sodium

---

* Though each was to receive 37½ percent of the film's profits, Ford was paid $350,000 up front and Capra only $200,000, and because the film did not earn back its cost, Capra never received an additional $50,000 in deferred salary or the $100,000 he was to recoup in first position from his and Ford's profits.

phosphate injections gave only temporary relief, Demerol and sleeping pills were of little help; no neurologist could cure "the Judas pain."

The headaches continued intermittently for years, and in that "forgotten decade" of the 1960s, Capra later admitted, "I often thought of suicide. I came close to it a lot of times. I thought I would rid my wife of myself, but when I thought of my family, I couldn't do it."

There were many other scapegoats.

Capra's book identified a veritable cabal of sinister and immoral forces running rampant during his last years in Hollywood: "the hedonists, the homosexuals, the hemophili[a]c bleeding hearts, the God-haters." But the religiosity Capra insisted on shoehorning into all of his projects (even *A Hole in the Head*, in which Sinatra is made to mutter uncomfortably, "I wish I was religious") seemed jarringly out of place in the sleazy milieu of *Pocketful of Miracles*, whose very title suggested a link in Capra's mind between religion and commercial success. Such ostentatious piety helped account for the widespread perception that Capra was increasingly out of touch with reality.

He went down some labyrinthine ways in his later years in Hollywood, begging embarrassed studio executives to let him film the life of St. Paul, starring Frank Sinatra, and a host of other religious tales, including Eugene Vale's screenplay of Louis de Wohl's novel *The Joyful Beggar*, filmed by Michael Curtiz in 1961 as *Francis of Assisi*; *Dear and Glorious Physician*, the Taylor Caldwell novel about St. Luke, also adapted by Vale; John Fante's script *The Carpenter of God*, about St. Joseph, for television with Danny Thomas; a film based on the Sermon of the Mount; a story of a priest in Las Vegas; *Mother Cabrini*; *The Agony and the Ecstasy*, Irving Stone's novel about the conflicts between Michelangelo and Pope Julius II over the painting of the Sistine Chapel; a comedy about a monk, *Brother Bertram*, rejected by Sinatra and Elvis Presley but accepted by Sidney Poitier, who said he would commit to anything Frank Capra wanted him to do without reading the script; and *Joseph and His Brethren*, which he was still pitching as late as 1975.

Nor did Capra's catchall list of sinners and scapegoats explain why a powerful triumvirate of stars—Dean Martin, Sinatra, and Bing Crosby—lost interest in an abortive Columbia feature (1959–1960) about Jimmy Durante and his partners Eddie Clayton and Lou Jackson after Capra turned in his formless and bathetic treatment of Gene Fowler's book *Schnozzola* (Garson Kanin and the Hacketts, among others, had passed up his offers to write the script); why Colonel Tom Parker was not interested in having Elvis Presley appear in Capra's story "The Gentleman from

Tennessee" (1959), about a rock star being used as a political demagogue to seduce the youth of America, an intriguing but half-baked idea too obviously derived from the Kazan-Schulberg film *A Face in the Crowd**; or why Dame Rebecca West did not think Capra had the political sophistication to make a film (in 1962) of her book *The Meaning of Treason*, about the British World War II traitor Lord Haw-Haw; and it did not explain why Capra failed to make a comedy-adventure story called *Circus*, which he prepared in Spain for six months in 1963 as a vehicle for John Wayne after the original director, Nicholas Ray, had a heart attack.

Neither Wayne nor the producers liked the story line developed by Capra and Joe Sistrom, which gently lampooned his all-American image, and rather than lock horns with the Duke, Capra fled back to the United States, abandoning the project to Henry Hathaway, who filmed it as *Circus World*. "By that time," Capra recalled, "I hated the story, I hated circuses, I hated animals, I hated Wayne, I hated everything."

Lu was his mainstay, as always. She had suffered a heart attack while he was in Spain preparing *Circus*, and it was the beginning of her slow and agonizing decline from emphysema. Frantic with worry, Capra flew back five times to be with her, but with characteristic self-effacement she devoted her energies to bucking up his spirits, writing him cheerful, ego-boosting letters and minimizing the gravity of her own problems. In one letter, she told him how she wept with admiration while watching a scene from *Mr. Deeds Goes to Town* on television in her hospital room.

But the once-great director could take little solace from his old movies when he was no longer bankable, even on television. He could not bring himself to mention in his book that he had tried to jump on the bandwagon of Alfred Hitchcock's successful TV series with an anthology series of his own, *The Frank Capra Comedy Theater*, or that he had flogged a series idea about congressional page boys, *Reveille in Washington*, a toothless throwback to *Mr. Smith*. As time went on Capra was willing to try just about anything: in 1965 he expressed interest in directing an episode of the ghoulish sitcom *The Addams Family*, starring Carolyn Jones, and in 1976 he almost was lured out of retirement by Columbia to direct the pilot for a short-lived series based on *Mr. Deeds Goes to Town*.

Nothing more clearly demonstrated Capra's problems in the 1960s than his failed attempt to make a film of a play by one of America's brightest young writers, Gore Vidal.

---

* *"The Gentleman from Tennessee" later served, along with* Meet John Doe, *as the inspiration for an unpublished novel Capra wrote between 1966 and 1985 about an American fascist movement,* Cry Wilderness.

*   *   *

In *The Name Above the Title,* Vidal was portrayed as the "gay blade" who made Capra flee *The Best Man* in a fit of righteous timidity, although not, as one might have suspected, for political or homophobic reasons, but because of what Capra claimed was Vidal's desire to propagandize for atheism.

The Best Man, which opened on Broadway in March 1960, was set during that year's presidential campaign. In it two Democratic candidates threaten each other with blackmail: the liberal candidate (modeled on Kennedy and Adlai Stevenson) is smeared because of his philandering and a nervous breakdown, and the Red-baiting conservative (modeled on Nixon) is threatened with the exposure of an ancient homosexual indiscretion which his rival finally refuses to make public, even though it might win him the nomination. The idea of the play, Vidal wrote, was to take the Nixon figure, "a man of exemplary private life, yet monstrous public life, and contrast him to a man of 'immoral' private life and exemplary public life. . . . Then demonstrate how, in our confused age, morality means, simply, sex found out. To most Americans, cheating, character assassination, hypocrisy, self-seeking are taken quite for granted."

The Capra who made *Mr. Smith* might have made another great film out of *The Best Man,* but the Capra who made *A Hole in the Head* took on the property only to muddy it up, to sidestep the theme of McCarthyism, which tempted him but cut too close to the bone. He and Myles Connolly set about rewriting the play for United Artists to purge it of what Capra felt were un-American overtones in its criticisms of political hypocrisy.

Capra was on the floor of the Democratic convention in Los Angeles that July when Kennedy won the nomination, soaking up atmosphere for *The Best Man.* He was not immune to the Kennedy mystique, telling Lulu (a Harvard graduate student then and a Kennedy supporter) that Kennedy was sounder on communism than Stevenson and praising his precocious political skills. But Capra remained a Republican, and he warned her about the vicious tactics Communists, Communist sympathizers, and liberals would be using against his man Nixon during the campaign. His daughter also was opposed to nuclear weapons, but Capra thought that was a dangerous cause, playing into the hands of communism.

The Capra-Connolly script for *The Best Man* invents a new protagonist: the hero is no longer the man who refuses to blackmail his opponent because "one by one, these compromises, these small corruptions destroy character" but the dark horse of the title, who receives the nomination when the two leading candidates cancel each other out—*The Best Man* in their grotesquely sentimentalized version is the guileless young mixed-race governor of Hawaii, their muddled notion of a John Doe for the 1960s. After reading the script, UA's Max Youngstein wrote Capra on January 24, 1961, that he was "laying it on too thick to make the point. . . . [The Hawaiian governor] is far from being my concept of someone to root for. He is a *schnook* Boy Scout. . . . He spouts clichés at the rate of one a minute, and while many of those clichés have great truths behind them, no one can take that many, back-to-back, without vomiting."

Capra offered to quit the project shortly after that, but he hung on until November, waiting until after *Pocketful* finished shooting and Vidal turned in his own screenplay; Franklin Schaffner replaced him as director of *The Best Man.*

"It was sad, as he records," Gore Vidal said in 1984. "He was resentful, and quite rightly so, because he was maneuvered out. He was justifying himself in his book; nobody likes to be rejected. Presumably he had read the stage version, so he knew what was in it. He told United Artists he wanted to do the film, and I was brought up on Frank Capra, so at first I thought, 'Well, yeah, Frank Capra—interesting idea.'

"Then I saw that thing he made with Ann-Margret and Bette Davis, what was the name of it? *Pocketful of Miracles.* I realized that this was one of the all-time bad pictures, so I was already highly suspicious.

"I didn't work for him. We chatted for a week [August 9–16, 1961], and I came to the conclusion that he was absolutely the worst director in the world for this project. He wanted the [Hawaiian] candidate to dress up as Abraham Lincoln reciting the Gettysburg Address, and I thought, 'Oh, Jesus . . .' I said, 'Frank, this is a different era, different politics. I'm the author of *The Best Man,* and it's going to be done my way or not at all.' And it *was* done my way, eventually."

"**F**rank, cut out this talk of retiring," John Ford publicly admonished him at a tribute to Capra from Los Angeles civic leaders on May 12, 1962. "Fill your pockets full of miracles instead of avocados."

Capra did not retire for four more exasperating years. He finally gave up after spending two of those years arguing with Columbia over a project called *Marooned,* from a Martin Caidin novel about a mission to rescue an American astronaut orbiting helplessly in his disabled space capsule.

The frustrated scientist in Capra was stimulated by the idea of making a film about rocketry and space travel. In January 1964, at a time when all his feature projects had turned cold and he was talking with Don Jones about making more science films for another sponsor, he accepted a

$125,000 offer to make the *Rendezvous in Space* short for the Martin Marietta Corporation, a major NASA supplier. His research led him to *Marooned*, and after he struck a deal with Columbia on March 27, work on both projects progressed simultaneously.

Rendezvous in Space, which Capra made in rented quarters at Paramount, included a series of fatuous "man-on-the-street" interviews with Danny Thomas asking actors playing ordinary people their Capra-scripted opinions of space travel; documentary views of outer space; and fairly minimal animated sequences showing the development of rocketry, with comments by an anthropomorphic Moon and Mr. Space. In conjunction with a full-scale live model of a shuttle docking with a Manned Orbiting Laboratory, the film opened on September 10 at the New York World's Fair on a huge wall screen in the circular Hall of Science, where it would continue to play for eleven years, though according to a Martin Marietta spokesman it "became obsolete in about six months."

"Something less than a stirring flight of fancy," Bosley Crowther called the last Frank Capra film in *The New York Times*. Crowther found the space scenes "no more exciting or convincing than a cheap science-fiction film. For the most part, it is a juvenile depiction that affronts [the] intelligence." But he reserved his strongest objections for the interview sequence: "The suggestion that average citizens are as stupid and indifferent as this is not flattering to an audience that is sufficiently interested to stand patiently to view the film."

Capra checked into his old studio, Columbia, for the last time on June 15, 1964. For the next two years, as he raced back and forth between Hollywood and Fallbrook, where the root rot was spreading like prairie fire, and worried over Lu's deteriorating health, he shopped *Marooned* from star to star, fought with NASA to obtain its cooperation, stroked the Defense Department, and argued helplessly with Columbia about budget while hacking Walter Newman's brilliant but overlong screenplay into almost unrecognizable bits (eleven drafts) in a futile attempt to bring the budget down to the $3 million demanded by Columbia worldwide production chief Mike Frankovich. But in retrospect that unrealistic budget seemed to be an illusory issue designed to force Capra out, since *Marooned* cost $8 million when it finally reached the screen under John Sturges's direction in 1969, with Frankovich (having left his executive post) producing and Frank Capra, Jr., as associate producer.

Capra felt that Frankovich simply coveted *Marooned* for himself. Columbia's waning interest in Capra probably also stemmed from his inability to fight for Newman's script and for his own creative control, as well as his difficulty in attracting stars to the project. Although Kirk Douglas and Anthony Quinn were agreeable, it was turned down by, among others, Jack Lemmon, Sophia Loren, James Garner, Steve McQueen, and Frank Sinatra. The straw that broke Capra's back came on April 20, 1965, when Jimmy Stewart turned down the role eventually played by Gregory Peck (when asked in 1988 why he had done so, Stewart claimed not to remember being offered a role in the film).

The only directing Capra did on *Marooned* was to supervise the filming of a few preproduction background shots at Cape Kennedy from October 4 to 11, 1965, four months before he first began making noises about quitting and six months before he walked out of Columbia in disgust and hid out in June Lake, refusing to take the studio's phone calls. It was on May 24, 1966, that he instructed his agent, Joe Schoenfeld of William Morris, to tell Frankovich he was no longer interested in haggling over the budget of *Marooned*. His anger was partly assuaged when he agreed on July 18 to a $54,000 settlement plus 10 percent of the profits.

He told friends that Lu had convinced him to retire, but though his concern for her health was genuine, that was just another excuse. In later years, when he felt the pangs of creative sterility, he would use her emphysema as an alibi for why he was not working—saying shortly before her death in 1984, "If my wife's health improves, I'll go off to Colorado and open my own studio and make a picture for $200,000"—but nothing more was heard of that notion after she died, although when asked how he was passing the time by himself, he shouted, "Fuck *time!* I want to work! What do you think I'm dying for? I'm in great shape except that nobody wants me for a job. I want to direct—if people would let me alone to do my own picture."

In those rare instances when anyone approached him with a "go" project in his later years, Capra would go away. Perhaps he could not be criticized for rejecting such a motley bunch of offers as a 1972 documentary on *Frasier, the Sensuous Lion*, an elderly resident of Southern California's Lion Country Safari who was renowned for his sexual exploits; a 1975 television special starring Lucille Ball, who had played a bit part in *Broadway Bill*; *Mr. Krueger's Christmas* (1980), a sentimental, mildly religious half-hour TV drama with James Stewart and the Mormon Tabernacle Choir (Capra was uncomfortable because the Mormons were the producers); and *It's Still a Wonderful Life*, a later-abandoned TV sequel project with Stewart and Donna Reed playing their characters in later years, originally proposed by Reed to the author of this book and offered by Universal in 1982 to Capra, who responded, "That's the kind of goddamn thing a producer would suggest. They can go fuck themselves."

The most promising offer Capra spurned after his retirement came from

Francis Coppola, who summoned him to San Francisco in 1979 to ask him to be the executive producer of *Tucker,* a film Coppola was planning to direct about Preston Tucker, a maverick automaker who defied the Detroit establishment in the 1940s. Though he admired the *Godfather* films, Capra went into the meeting furious at Coppola for making the Vietnam War film *Apocalypse Now,* which he considered anti-American ("I never saw such a piece of junk in my life"). After he heard the story of Coppola's new project, Capra refused to be associated with it, because it accused Detroit of deliberately thwarting Tucker's attempts to build an innovative car—something Capra felt was an impossibility under the American system. The ten-minute meeting ended badly, but Capra's influence nevertheless was felt in the film Coppola finally made in 1987, *Tucker: The Man and His Dream,* as executive producer George Lucas insisted on making it less downbeat and more "Capraesque" by turning it into "an uplifting experience that showed some of the problems in corporate America."

A week after giving up on *Marooned,* feeling distraught but strangely exhilarated, Capra made the forty-mile drive down the mountain from June Lake to Bishop and bought research books, a typewriter table, and a chair so he could begin writing his autobiography.

Night Voices was the title he gave to the ninety-two-page manuscript he spewed out in six weeks at his cabin in June Lake. It was a raw, anguished confession of despair and self-hatred, a chronicle of the inner torment of a man who felt life was devoid of purpose and meaning and openly speculated about the temptation of suicide. The bilious but honest *Night Voices* was very different from the anxiously self-justifying document he submitted secretly to the security board in 1951 or the cleverly self-aggrandizing autobiography he finally presented to the world in 1971.

"It was a masochistic outpouring of all the humiliations he had suffered in those last years," said Eugene Vale, one of the people to whom Capra showed the manuscript. "There were things in it which were very gripping and involving, but the main thrust was getting even, saying, 'You bums, you despise me, you don't listen to me, don't return my phone calls.' Of course, everybody who would have read it would have said, 'Hey, I'm not going to return his phone calls if nobody else did.' And there was a lot of guilt, a deep-seated sense of guilt; he was punishing himself, dumping on himself. He was morose, he was finished, he was down. There comes a time when you rest on your laurels, and he couldn't.

"I was aghast, because I felt it was just possible that [someone] would print it. If it had been published, it would have destroyed the whole image of Capra.

"After reading the manuscript [on September 10], I called him and said, 'Frank, I'm getting into my car and driving up to see you.' It was a six-and-a-half-hour drive to June Lake, but I felt if I told him over the phone it would not work. When I saw him, I told him, 'Look, you have done marvelous films. People remember them. There are great pools of goodwill in the country, and in the rest of the world, toward you, so write your true autobiography—what you did accomplish. Emphasize the positive. You're entitled to it. You're a hero.'

"He listened."

Capra was taking a poll on whether to share his *cri de coeur* with the public. Lu voted yes, and so did Joe Schoenfeld. Another friend thought it a fascinating revelation of Hollywood. Garson Kanin told Abe Lastfogel that he found it both absorbing and appalling. Lastfogel, like Vale, was horrified by *Night Voices* and vehemently urged Capra to keep it private.

"To put it bluntly, it was hopeless," felt Paul Horgan, who was under the impression that the manuscript he read the following January was a "novel," not an autobiography. "It was amateurish beyond words. I struggled for several days with what to say about it, because I didn't want to encourage this. Capra had a great story gift, but it was a pictorial narrative sense; imaginative prose was not his *métier*. I urged him to write an autobiography, to write reality. I told him his life was a miniature history of Hollywood. He took it so nobly, so graciously, so generously."

When Horgan passed along that advice, Capra already had scrapped *Night Voices* and had started writing an autobiography which would itself be an audacious act of the imagination, re-creating his life into a myth, rescuing his films from oblivion, and turning a miserable down-and-outer into a born-again celebrity lionized by college students, television audiences, and world leaders.

The largely negative reaction Capra received to the reckless act of confession he tried to make in *Night Voices* made him understand that the world did not want him but his myth. In essence, the world wanted him to be somebody other than he really was, and he wanted the world's approbation so badly that he chose, to his ultimate unhappiness, to live the lie that the world wanted him to tell.

The outlines of the myth, the ritualistic invocations of Horatio Alger and the Star-Spangled Banner, had been clear ever since his first rush of celebrity in the 1930s, and by the time he attempted his Hollywood comeback, they had hardened into cement. While being honored on the television program *This Is Your Life* in 1959, shortly before the opening of *A*

Hole in the Head, Capra visibly squirmed as host Ralph Edwards extolled him as a "great humanitarian . . . an inspiration to young people every-where . . . the champion of the little man . . . a deeply religious man."

At the end of that first televised tribute to Capra, the USIA's Turner Shelton, who had called Capra in 1952 to recruit him for the trip to India and had been the first to tell him that he would receive his security clearance for Project VISTA, appeared to put the official seal of approval on Capra's patriotism. The close-ups of Capra's troubled face as he lis-tened to Shelton reflected his awareness of ironies unknown to the audi-ence, and they betrayed his bitter realization, in the midst of triumph, that his mythic role was choosing *him:* "Frank," said Shelton, "we of the United States Information Agency believe that your life is a perfect demonstration of the magic of America. And it is because of men like you, dedicated to your work and to your country, that America has been and always will be *free.*"

There was no such rhetoric in *Night Voices*.

In his first attempt at an autobiographical reconstruction of his shat-tered self-image, he envisioned the hellish events that would take place if he were to attempt another studio comeback—events quite similar to what actually had happened to him between 1956 and 1966. Capra's personal vision was sadly derivative: he explicitly compared his character's tour of contemporary Hollywood to Jimmy Stewart touring Pottersville in *Wonder-ful Life* and to Ebenezer Scrooge's nightmare visions in its literary ante-cedent *A Christmas Carol*; his fantasy of ill will, rejection, and disgrace also drew from the peasant phantasmagoria which was his father's stock-in-trade as a storyteller, but it resembled nothing so much as a Hollywood rewrite of *Faust*. Cast into the form of a drunken nocturnal dialogue with Lucifer about Capra's own damnation, interspersed with stomach-churning vignettes of Hollywood job-seeking, including a scene in which Capra sheepishly avoids Jimmy Stewart in a studio cafeteria, *Night Voices* was filled with such melodramatic, self-pitying contrivances—climaxed with Capra being tossed off a set he is visiting by studio goons—that it seemed unbelievably sordid even to its defensive author: Capra reflexively tacked on a happy ending, with Clarence, the angel from *Wonderful Life*, appear-ing to talk him out of suicide.

Night Voices made it clear that Capra's anguish on revisiting Hollywood stemmed not so much from the industry's obliviousness (most people in the story know very well who he is) and not from any general awareness of his being a political pariah but from his recognition that it was his own self-hatred that made people instinctively shun him. Capra accused himself of having lost his artistic judgment and daring, and hinted broadly at the events leading up to his fall from grace, though he could not quite bring himself to call the blacklist by its real name and had to put it into the form of a fable told by Lucifer (who speaks sometimes with the voice of Richard Burton and sometimes with the voice of blacklisted actor Lionel Stander) about how primitive man learned the soul-destroying art of political scapegoating.

On *This Is Your Life*, Ralph Edwards summed up Capra's story by saying, "The ten miles from the sidewalks of a crowded city to the golden hills of fame are long indeed. But your footsteps have covered them with honor and humility. Yours is a story truly American, Frank Capra— immigrant boy comes to the United States, makes his mark, and gratefully and unselfishly gives to his country the fruits of his accomplishments. . . ."

In *Night Voices*, Capra imagined his own death at a skid-row bar on Main Street in downtown Los Angeles, just ten blocks from the corner where he once peddled papers and seven blocks from his boyhood home on Castelar Street. He has drunk himself to death, though Lu, loyal to the end, insists it was a heart attack, brought on by his treatment in Hollywood.

At one of the innumerable tributes held for Capra after the publication of *The Name Above the Title*, toastmaster Hal Kanter introduced him as "a legend in his own book."

Even Capra had to laugh.

The most remarkable fact about *The Name Above the Title* was not that it was largely a work of fiction but that Capra succeeded so largely in passing off "autohagiography" (reviewer Elliott Stein's word) as fact. In part he succeeded because the Horatio Alger aspects of his story so compellingly evoked the American Dream at a time when faith in America was imperiled by the Vietnam War and the Nixon presidency that the book struck a chord even in people who should have known better but could not help *wanting* to believe it, like Lord Gainsford at the end of *Lost Horizon*. The book's punchy catchphrases about idealism were adopted as credos by young admirers who were unaware of the guilt-ridden ironies that underlay them: for Christmas 1981, Jane Fonda gave her producing partner Bruce Gilbert a plaque on which she had inscribed Capra's oft-quoted words, "Only the morally courageous are worthy of speaking to their fellow men for two hours in the dark."

One of the ways Capra made his fairy-tale account of his life seem believable was by mingling self-serving episodes with ones that gave the impression of ruthless candor toward his own failings but that actually served to paper over even more damning aspects of his life, the parts he found unspeakable, the parts the book was concocted to conceal. And though his bias against some of his nemeses was rawly apparent, it did not, as in the case of Harry Langdon, prevent Capra's version from being accepted by credulous film historians as fact, for if Capra was so harsh on himself, the subliminal logic went, his harshness toward others must be equally deserved. But the more subtly destructive portraits contained in *The Name Above the Title* were a more effective means of getting even than the all-out frontal assault of *Night Voices*, for Capra was able to make even Mack Sennett, Harry Cohn, and Robert Riskin seem relatively unimportant next to himself, not so much by attacking them, though barbs were embedded in his faint praise, but more by failing to do justice to their collaboration and support, as he failed even to mention many others who had given him handholds on his climb to the top.

When he was asked about errors in his book, Capra quipped that they were "intentional, of course," and when asked about omissions, he conceded, "It's not my *whole* life." The fiction began to unravel when Capra finally let go of his personal papers in 1980, an act that seemed to contain equal amounts of conscious self-aggrandizement and subconscious confession.

This was the book with the foreword by John Ford (written with help from his research assistant Katherine Clifton Bryant) attesting to its uniquely veracious approach to the history of Hollywood. This was the book which, despite the occasional skeptic (William Hughes in *The Nation* called it "something other than film history"), received mostly adulatory reviews upon publication in June 1971. "The most entertaining and honest memoir ever written by an American filmmaker," Peter Bogdanovich proclaimed it in *Esquire,* and Capra's old friend Tom Pryor went even farther in *Daily Variety:* "This is the finest, most entertaining book yet written about Hollywood, embracing the whole intricate, complex and generally stormy fusion of art and commerce. It has many dimensions, both personal and impersonal, with soaring *alleluia* and crushing *de profundis.*" Most gratifying to the author, no doubt, was Pryor's judgment that the "profoundly wise and soul-revealing" memoir "removes any suspicion of doubt" about the authorship of Capra's films with Robert Riskin, "for it demonstrates that he is indeed a first-rate literatus."

The Name Above the Title sold vigorously, was an alternate selection of the Book-of-the-Month Club (on Paul Horgan's recommendation), and led to a whole new career for its author as a television talk show pundit, pontificator in print, and lecturer on the college circuit. Tirelessly fashioning his image for posterity with the help of squads of media acolytes, Capra peddled a self-aggrandizing pseudopersonality which blended a veneer of down-to-earth humility and a message of rampant egoism, and whose essence Elliott Stein aptly described as "the dry rot of quack benignity." While traveling to about seventy-five colleges and universities, Capra was reinvigorated by the praise. "It was like the answer to all his troubles," observed Eugene Vale. "He couldn't make pictures anymore, but this way he could retire and still be the center of attention." Still, Capra could not help recognizing the incongruity of his mostly uncritical adulation by young, antiestablishment idealists, and he cryptically told an interviewer after a 1975 appearance at Sarah Lawrence, "I can't understand it, except in some way perhaps they've got some kind of hungers we don't know about. I feel this very strongly in the way they gather round me, ask me questions. I'm not a great performer. Maybe it's because it's what I stand for rather than what I am."

Although, to Capra's intense disappointment, the success of his autobiography did not lead to the publication of his thematically muddled and clumsily written novel *Cry Wilderness, The Name Above the Title* served its most crucial function by inspiring journalists, critics, and academics to reevaluate his film work, spurring revivals of his films in theaters and on television, bringing offers (which he rejected) to make new films, spawning endless remakes and imitations, and winning him some of the most prestigious awards from his industry and his country, including the American Film Institute's Life Achievement Award in 1982 and the National Medal of the Arts from President Reagan in 1986.

He came to represent something much larger than himself. John Ford called him "an inspiration to those who believe in the American Dream." "Maybe there really wasn't an America," said John Cassavetes, "maybe it was only Frank Capra." And during the depths of Watergate, William O. Douglas wrote that Frank Capra "set the homely virtues of small-town America against the greed of the marketplace, the corruption of politicians, and the dangers of fascism. He made a hero out of the most obscure person. Frank Capra entertained us; but he also brought tears to our eyes when we revisited with him the shrines of Jefferson and Lincoln and when he made us realize that in spite of all the overreaching and crime and immorality the heart of America was warm and her conscience bright."

The tributes to his work were heartfelt and richly deserved, yet in his bitterness Capra viewed all the adulation with some measure of irony and contempt. "Movies have great power, you know," he wrote a journalist friend, Rolfe Neill, in 1972. "Great power, my eye. Films can't hold a candle's wick to the power of the printed word. Intellectuals threw verbal stink bombs at my films at the time they were made. Thirty years later I write a book to tell the world how great—great! my films really were. And lo! Academia believes me."

But living with his myth was a burden for Capra, depriving him of much of the satisfaction of his newfound celebrity. The way he had fabricated the myth was one of his most closely held secrets.

He had made an earlier abortive attempt at an autobiography in 1961, writing an opening in the form of a film script, but dropped the idea because, he said, he was worried about how his family would react. Encouraged in 1966 by Horgan and Vale, by Random House chairman Bennett Cerf, and by Simon & Schuster editor-in-chief Robert Gottlieb, Capra began work December 5 on a sample section of his life story.

Those first seventy-six pages, a highly fanciful account of how he came to make *Fulta Fisher's Boarding House,* met a discouraging response. The publishers would not commit without reading a more substantial manuscript. Horgan's publisher, Robert Giroux of Farrar, Straus & Giroux, commented that Capra was writing a novel, not an autobiography, a criticism Capra scoffed at, thinking he should have the same dramatic license in telling his life story as he did in making a movie.

With a furious energy born of years of creative frustration and a determination to prove the scoffers wrong, Capra did not give up, even after Random House and Simon & Schuster rejected a longer sample several months later, but pressed ahead, writing largely from memory, aided by his wife's recall and by her voluminous scrapbooks. "The thing I've enjoyed about it," Lu said at the time, "has been that it was like living our whole life over again." Before he drafted each section, Lu and her sister-in-law, Marion Warner, prepared digests and chronologies and organized his personal papers in file cabinets in the basement playroom of his Fallbrook ranch house, where he did most of the writing. In a grudging concession to the factual approach, he did two days of research at the Academy of Motion Picture Arts and Sciences, the Directors Guild of America, and the Beverly Hills Public Library, where he read up on the Great Depression. Chet Sticht retyped the material as it emerged from Capra's typewriter. "Sometimes he'd get facts somewhat cockeyed," said Sticht, "so I'd correct them. I'd been there." None of Capra's helpers received an acknowledgment in the book, and three years after it was published and things were going well again, Capra decided he could make do with six-dollar-an-hour part-time secretaries and let Sticht go on six weeks' notice after thirty-nine years of loyal service.

In June 1968, the William Morris Agency sold Capra's work-in-progress to Macmillan for the modest advance of $3,000. As he contemplated his sprawling, far from completed draft, and faced the reality of turning it into a publishable book which could make or break his reputation, Capra recognized that he was in over his head. On September 12, shortly after signing the book contract, he went back to Eugene Vale—who had been giving him advice all along and had first urged him to paint himself in a heroic light—and (according to his diary) asked Vale to assist him in the remaining stages.

The final manuscript was delivered to the publisher more than two years later, on October 2, 1970. Capra cut huge chunks from his original 1667-page draft under the direction of his young editor and fan Jim Neyland, who also provided the misleading but suitably egoistic title; much of the material they cut came from the later sections of the manuscript, which became tediously diffuse as Capra tap-danced stubbornly around the rubble of his ruined career. But Neyland failed to prod Capra into writing more than a few close-mouthed pages about his family and his childhood, and he provided the final rationale for the whitewash of Capra's political personality by urging him to drop most of the material on the blacklist era, which the editor considered an unnecessary self-justification.

The news of its Book-of-the-Month Club Selection came while Frank and Lu were traveling through the Canal Zone in early March 1971 on the SS *Statendam*. After receiving the cablegram from Sticht, Capra went to the ship's bar with Lu and got roaring drunk, showing strangers the cablegram and boasting of his success. When he woke up the next morning, the cluster headaches were gone for good. Capra finally had managed to shed his troublesome identity as a filmmaker, exchanging it for the one he had so long coveted: an Author. As he said in 1984, "To me, making a picture is almost equal to writing a book."

Although his book does not acknowledge that he had any assistance, the surprisingly professional quality of much of its dialogue and expository prose, mixed with slapdash and amateurish passages more characteristic of Capra's style, clearly indicates a joint endeavor.

"I'm responsible for the book," Vale said in 1984. "You said that the book started a whole new life for Capra. Well, *I* started it for him. He got everything from me and through me. It is a very well-written book. When it became successful, he was as excited as a kid. There was a vast, vast difference from the morose, beaten man who had given up and retired.

"Now comes the typical Capra twist.

"He came to my house with the first copy of the book. In it was a beautiful inscription about how much he owes me, what I've done, and so forth. Later, someone stole it. I asked him for another copy, and he said, 'I can't remember what I wrote the last time. I just can't. Now all that is left is the smile of the Cheshire Cat.' And that's what he wrote in my book.

"That summed it all up, that summed up Capra in a nutshell, because he knew what he owed me and he wanted it forgotten. His attitude was, 'Ha, you fool, I'm laughing at you.' I gave this old man a new life and all I got was a grin.

"I liked him. I did not expect this. It so infuriated me I never talked to Frank Capra again."

The supreme irony, perhaps, was that the ending of Capra's autobiography, in which he tells of revisiting his boyhood home on Albion Street and borrows Thoreau's allusion in *Walden* to the Greek god Antaeus, who got his strength from his attachment to the earth, described an event which Capra later admitted never took place at all and which came from the imagination of John Ford.

Capra was searching for an upbeat ending when he sent Ford the manuscript. All of the endings he had tried seemed phony or clichéd. To his surprise, Ford took it upon himself to solve the problem: "I hope you will forgive my enthusiasm, but when I finished *The Name Above the Title*, with tears of gladness, I felt there was something missing in your last paragraph. Throughout the book there was a punch in every line. The story of a little Dago from Sicily who scrapped, fought, bit, chewed, without compromise, from the ghetto to become the world's greatest Director—I would like to see you end your book by going back to the ghetto—just random thoughts. . . ."

Ford suggested that Capra tell of revisiting the "decrepit and dilapidated" house "where we first lived as penniless peasants from Sicily" and saying a prayer while remembering how his mother, "God rest her lovely courageous soul, had fought to bring us up in this strange unfriendly land." Reminiscent of the scene in Ford's 1958 film of Edwin O'Connor's novel *The Last Hurrah* in which Mayor Frank Skeffington (Spencer Tracy) pays a visit to the Boston tenement in which he was born, Ford's ending for Capra's story (somewhat darkened when it was rewritten for *The Name Above the Title*) reflected a nostalgia for roots and beginnings that was characteristic of Ford but entirely uncharacteristic of the less sentimental Capra, who hated everything about the "house of pain" where he grew up and told the author of this book that he had not the slightest interest in revisiting the house on Albion Street.

*   *   *

The myth, in the end, brought little consolation.

After the euphoria of being a successful author faded, after the college tours stopped because of Lu's declining health, after his eyesight started failing and his dreams of completing another book collapsed, after he had said no to Hollywood for the last time, he was left with little to do but tend to Lu in her prolonged agony, which ended on July 1, 1984, and for the first time in fifty-two years left him alone with his doubts and anxieties.

"I want to get out of here, because I'm going nuts," he said that August, hiding out in June Lake. "When your wife is gone, the place really goes to hell. I've never in my life been so low. You just don't know what it's like. Sometimes I cry myself to sleep. I could die and nobody would know it.

"Since I can't do any work, I've gotta just stay here and vegetate. All that keeps me from going crazy is listening to music.

"Life is—everything is different. Life doesn't mean anything."

A year later, Capra suffered the first of a devastating series of strokes that eventually left him virtually helpless. He spent his declining years in a condominium at the Santa Rosa Cove, a security complex next to the La Quinta Hotel, in a becalmed, passive state, eating and sleeping and watching television in the company of his nurses and family. His grandchildren paid frequent visits, and a few old friends were allowed to see him.

Jimmy Stewart paid Capra a visit over New Year's 1988, and was shaken by what he found: "I hadn't seen him for a while, and when you know somebody over the years and you suddenly see him in bad health, it's a shock, a very miserable thing. The stroke really hit him hard. He's able to stand up and walk, sort of—he stood up and walked a little bit and then sat down again. He just says a few words. There isn't much reaction at all."

His former pastor at St. Francis of Assisi Church in La Quinta, Father Raymond Bluett, said of him that April, "He knows who you are, but he really doesn't know who he is anymore."

Frank Capra's heart finally gave out at 9:10 A.M. on September 3, 1991. He was ninety-four. Three days later he was buried next to Lu at the nearby Coachella Valley Cemetery.

More than half a century after Capra made his decision to forsake his scientific ambitions for motion pictures, I asked him if he thought he had made the right choice.

"Not particularly," he said.

"You think you would have been happier in science?"

"Yes."

"Why?"

"I would have done more."

"Where do you think you would have ended up?"

"With [Dr. Edwin] Hubble. As an astronomer. I could study the stars and the planets forever. I always wanted to know why, *why*."

"Then why didn't you do it? What changed your mind?"

"Pictures changed my mind. I was too far along in the movie business. But when I go to Caltech now and hear about things I'm not familiar with, like black holes, goddamn! I get mad. How the hell I ever refused that I don't know—what ever *made* me refuse it—"

"Did you think then that scientists were more respectable than movie people?"

"Even now. A movie director is not as important as an astronomer."

"An astronomer isn't as well known, perhaps."

"No, but they're known among themselves."

"So was it fame that was most important to you, then? Was that what made you make the decision?"

"Yes, it was. I wanted to be somebody."

"But you do have regrets."

"Yes. But it seems like motion pictures have a terrific hold on me. I don't know what it is. I guess it's the audience. The audience kept me in there. I had made something and had shown it to people, and they had liked it, applauded or something. That I think was what turned me to it, that was why I didn't quit. Although I certainly was sorely tempted."

Acknowledgments

When I began writing the American Film Institute's Life Achievement Award tribute to Frank Capra with producer George Stevens, Jr., in 1981, there were troubling questions lingering in my mind, aspects of Capra's story that didn't quite add up. Particularly baffling was the question of how this great director could have so utterly self-destructed after the late 1940s, in the most precipitous decline of any American filmmaker since D. W. Griffith. The explanation in *The Name Above the Title* was unconvincing: Capra's self-flagellation over selling his independent production company to Paramount Pictures hardly sufficed to account for his subsequent creative bankruptcy, his premature abandonment of his craft, and his long, embittered exile from Hollywood. I expected that in the course of researching the tribute I would find some answers to that question.

Still, I was unprepared for the impact of the revelations that awaited me. Working with Capra on his Life Achievement Award acceptance speech, meeting his colleagues, and beginning to dig into his collection of personal and working papers at Wesleyan University in Middletown, Connecticut, I realized how little I had really known Frank Capra from his public persona. To understand Capra fully, I had to reexamine everything I knew about his life—his entire life, not just his period of disintegration, which I came to see as the result of forces set into motion much earlier. I began work on this book in 1984, and it took more than seven years to assemble all of the pieces of the picture he had tried so long to keep hidden.

I once asked Capra why he thought there have been so few good biographies of movie directors, and he replied, "Because *they* didn't have wives who saved everything—I didn't know she was doing it." I express my gratitude here for the work of the late Lucille Capra (a former secretary) in organizing and maintaining his papers along with her husband's longtime personal secretary, Chester E. Sticht, and for Mrs. Capra's scrapbooks, which document the press coverage of her husband's career from the early 1930s through its end in the 1960s. Capra's papers, donated to Wesleyan in 1980 as The Frank Capra Archive, also include his manuscripts, dating back to 1915; his voluminous correspondence; his diaries; film production files; and the final shooting scripts, with the director's annotations, for most of his sound features and some of the silents, as well as some of his scripts for silent comedy shorts, scripts for the *Why We Fight* films, and scripts and treatments by Capra and other writers for many unmade projects. Though the papers did not contain all of the answers to the riddles of Capra's life, they made it possible for me to begin asking the right questions. I studied the papers extensively on a second visit to Wesleyan for ten weeks in the fall of 1984. I am grateful to David Rivel, who graciously assisted me during my second visit.

Although I made it clear to Frank Capra from the outset that this would be an unauthorized biography, he still was willing to grant me many hours of interviews, and I am grateful to him for that. We spoke frequently at his homes in La Quinta and June Lake, California, until he suffered a series of strokes in August 1985. Although he was not always candid, he often came forth with genuine self-revelation, usually when I presented him with hard facts dug up from documents or from my other interviews. Capra also enabled me to obtain his U.S. Army personnel records and his transcripts and other records from the Los Angeles Unified School District and from the California Institute of Technology, Pasadena, even though some of those documents contradict elements of the Capra myth.

I thank Frank Capra, Jr., for granting me a one-hour interview in 1987. Frank Capra's daughter, Lucille, and his son Tom did not respond to requests for interviews, although Tom and I had a pleasant lunch with his father at June Lake in 1984.

I had extraordinarily good fortune in tracking down and interviewing other people who had known Capra throughout his lifetime, including many from his distant past and many who had never been interviewed before about Capra. Of the 175 people I interviewed, Chester Sticht was my most inexhaustible source of factual information and close-range, insightful observations of Capra, his employer of thirty-nine years. My many visits in Fallbrook with Chet and his wife, Bett, were full of friendship and encouragement. Capra's niece Josephine Campisi, his nephew Joe Finochio (who worked with Capra as a sound recorder), and Joe's wife, Victoria Buchellato Finochio, helped me enormously in understanding Capra and the saga of their family, and Joe kindly let me use his invaluable oral histories of his uncles Ben and Tony Capra, Frank's older brothers (taped in 1965 and 1981). Other essential insights came from Capra's first cousin Josephine (Giuseppa) Rosato Bondi, born in 1892, who lived one block away from his family in Bisacquino and later moved to Los Angeles; Maria Lanza Oddo, his neighbor in Sicily and Los Angeles; his nephew Samuel W. Capra, who grew up in Lincoln Heights; and Antonino Troncale, his nephew in Sicily, who shared his family history and his painful memories of Capra's 1977 homecoming. Other members of Capra's family whom I interviewed included David Blangsted, Bernadette Capra, Tony Finochio, Everest Capra, Marguerite (Mrs. Tony) Capra, Remo Capra, Rose Troncale Capra, Sarah Capra Coughlin, Frank R. Hale, Jeanette (Mrs. Frank R.) Hale, and James Warner.

Many people from Capra's youth still were living in the Los Angeles area, and most had vivid and precise memories: others among them included his next-door neighbor on Castelar Street, Josephine Leone Campiglia; his boyhood pal Roscoe (Rocky) Washington; his grade school classmate Evelyn Weldon; eighteen people who attended Manual Arts High School during all or part of Capra's years there (1911–15), including Lt. Gen. James H. Doolittle and his wife, Josephine Daniels Doolittle, who helped me begin the process of locating other Manual alumni, such as Esther Gleason Schlinger, historian of Capra's class of Winter 1915, whose memories provided the key that unlocked the secret of his high school years; eighteen men with whom Capra attended Throop College of Technology, especially Earl Mendenhall, whose sharp recall helped me immensely in re-creating Capra's college days; and Capra's college sweetheart, Isabelle Daniels Griffis, who shared her memories over many pleasant visits and let me read Capra's love letters from 1920–21.

In addition to the Doolittles and Schlinger, people I interviewed from Capra's years at Manual Arts included his Winter 1915 classmates Evelyn Turner Loftin (who also sang and appeared in *Lost Horizon*), Millson (Mitt) Downs, Lynford E. Hess, Lillian Shattuck Draves, and Gwynn Wilson; and also Isabel Martin Campbell, Helen Jerome Eddy (who also acted in several Capra films), Percy Goodell, Ruth Hammond, Brig. Gen. Harold R. Harris, Virginia Titus Ives, Altha Mudgett Jackson, Frank D. Keeler, Bonnie Houston McLaren, and A. S. Menasco. The eight persons interviewed who remembered Capra from high school were the Doolittles, Downs, Hammond, Harris, Loftin, McLaren, and Schlinger; the two who said they knew him well were General Doolittle and Schlinger.

In addition to Mendenhall and General Harris, men I interviewed with whom Capra attended Throop included Olin L. Armstrong, Earle A. Burt, Philip S. Clarke, Robert W. Craig, Louis F. Essick, Robert W. Flory, Kenneth J. Harrison, James E. Hill, E. V. Hounsell, G. R. McDonald, Lloyd E. Morrison, Fred L. Poole, Charles F. Simpson, Charles W. Varney, Jr., Howard G. Vesper, and Lester O. Warner. Others who remembered Capra from Throop were Mrs. Griffis, Lois Keener Thome, and Chet Sticht, whose brother Robert was Capra's college roommate; I also interviewed Alfio M. Bissiri and Martin Wesseler, who attended Throop shortly after Capra left. Seven other Throop alumni corresponded with me: Ralston E. Bear, Frank R. Bridgeford, J. C. Burks, Paul N. Crosby, Clyde Keith, Gerald G. Spencer, and Prof. Ernest H. Swift; related correspondence was received from Mrs. Joseph A. Beattie, Mrs. C. A. Boggs, Donna Darnell, Mrs. Edward R. Hess, Mrs. Theron C. Hounsell, Mrs. Harvey W. House, Richard Pomeroy, Mrs. William C. Renshaw, Mrs. Alfred J. Stamm, and Mrs. William T. Taylor.

Interviews with Capra's collaborators in the film industry, particularly his longtime cameraman Joseph Walker; Walker's assistant Alfred S. Keller (who also helped me locate other Capra crew members); and sound mixer Edward L. Bernds (later a director himself) described a way of working considerably unlike the manner described by Capra to latter-day interviewers; those loyal members of his Columbia Pictures crew were hurt by his slighting of their contributions to his work in *The Name Above the Title*, and they did not hesitate to speak candidly of his flaws as well as his virtues. Bernds also supplied me with his diaries for 1935–39, which were a source of highly perceptive firsthand observations of Capra's personality and his working methods. Other Capra crew members I interviewed included Joseph Biroc, Eugene De Rue, Irving (Buster) Libott, George J. Folsey, Henry Freulich, Glenn Kershner, Gene Milford, Ted Tetzlaff, and John Warren.

Actors who appeared in Capra films and shared their insights with me included Jean Arthur, Ralph Bellamy, Priscilla Bonner, Viola Dana, Coleen Gray, Katharine Hepburn, Madeline Hurlock, Sam Jaffe, Donna Reed, Alexis Smith, Lionel Stander, Barbara Stanwyck, James Stewart, and Fay Wray.

Other professional colleagues of Capra who gave me the benefit of their perspective and experiences were Olive Carey, Fanya Graham Carter, Edward Dryhurst, Philip Dunne, Julius J. Epstein, Theodor S. Geisel, Albert Hackett, Henry Hathaway, Howard Hawks, Paul Horgan, Ian McLellan Hunter, John Huston, Donald Jones, Walter Lantz, Robert Lees, Dorothy McAdam, Brig. Gen. Frank McCarthy, Fred MacMurray, Colleen Moore Maginot, John Lee Mahin, Rouben Mamoulian, Samuel Marx, Carlton Moss, Charles Newton, Edgar A. Peterson II, Lee Plunkett, Gottfried Reinhardt, Allen Rivkin, Hal Roach, John Sanford, Leonard Spigelgass, George Stevens, George Stevens, Jr., Eugene Vale, Gore Vidal, Irving Wallace, John D. Weaver, and Max Youngstein. Rivkin, then with the Writers Guild of America, also helped me locate other screenwriters of Capra films.

Others who helped me understand various aspects of Capra's life and work included Vivian (Mrs. Olin L.) Armstrong, Father Raymond Bluett, Frank Bonfiglio, Jack Bonura, Katherine Clifton Bryant, Shirley Burt, C. C. Coleman, Jr., Shirley Collier, Gay Coleman Collins, Joe D'Amico, Teresa Scavo Guzzeta, Rudy Hartman, Frederick Horst, Bill Kircher, Harry Langdon (son of the comedian), Mabel (Mrs. Harry) Langdon (widow of the comedian), John Lanza, Louis Lanza, Sgt. William R. Loftin, Joanne Merlo Luchetta, Renee Messner, June Mohney, Connie Moreno, Frank D. Munoz, John Murio, Dorothy Nelson, Edward (Ted) Paramore III, Thomas M. Pryor, Murray Riskin, Augie Scavo, Philip K. Scheuer, Irene Mayer Selznick, Peter Swerling, Irene Thill, Juanita (Mrs. Joseph) Walker, Marion Bemis (Mrs. Gwynn) Wilson, Zelma (Mrs. Michael) Wilson, George F. Yackey, and Madge (Mrs. George F.) Yackey.

I remember my conversations with all these people as the most enjoyable experiences I had during the years I spent writing this book. I only regret that so many of them are no longer living and could not see the fruits of the endeavor in which they so generously assisted me.

Many individuals, archives, libraries, and institutions gave me extraordinary help in my research.

Geoffrey A. Bell, author of *The Golden Gate and the Silver Screen* (Fairleigh Dickinson University Press, 1984), the definitive history of filmmaking in the San Francisco Bay Area, guided me around San Francisco and Belmont and answered many questions by digging into the notes and source material he used for his own book. Kevin Brownlow, the premier scholar of silent-film history and author of the monumental *The Parade's Gone By . . .* (Alfred A. Knopf, 1967), passed along many research leads and helped me locate early Capra collaborators, as well as sharing his notes of interviews with Claudette Colbert, William Hornbeck, and Irvin Willat, and a tape of his interview with Stephen Goossón.

The scripts Robert Riskin wrote for Capra can also be found among the Riskin Papers in the Fay Wray Collection, Cinema-Television Library, University of Southern California, Los Angeles, and in the Library's general collection; also included in the Riskin Papers are clippings and other information on his life and work. Fay Wray's 1979 monograph *Biography of Robert Riskin as Screenwriter* is in the Margaret Herrick Library of the Academy of Motion Picture Arts and Sciences, Beverly Hills. She gave me copies of Riskin's 1949 correspondence on the writing credits for *Riding High.* I am grateful to her for helping me research her husband's career and his work with Capra. Some of the Riskin scripts at USC are semifinal drafts, but the rest of the working drafts of the scripts for the Capra-Riskin films may no longer exist: a request to see the story files of Columbia Pictures on the Capra titles turned up only synopses and other scanty material. Other collections I used at USC included the Hal Roach Papers, which provided production information on the *Our Gang* films written by Capra; the Warner Bros. Archives, which has scripts, contracts, and other information on the production of the Harry Langdon features for First National, and production records for *Meet John Doe* and *Arsenic and Old Lace;* the Metro-Goldwyn-Mayer collection, which includes script material on *State on the Union* and *Brotherly Love;* and the papers of Albert Lewin, Jack Oakie (including papers of Capra's attorney Loyd Wright), and Dimitri Tiomkin. Ned Comstock of the USC Cinema-Television Library kept me supplied with research leads; I am also grateful for the assistance of the Library's Bob Knutson and Leith Adams of the Warner Bros. Archives.

The Mack Sennett Papers at the Academy's Margaret Herrick Library include scripts, drafts, and/or synopses for all of the films Capra wrote for Sennett, as well as other material on their production. I am indebted to Sam Gill for guiding me through the collection and sharing his knowledge of Sennett. For the history of the Academy, and the 1933 Academy pay cut controversy, I made use of the Library's clipping files and the few official Academy documents which are available to scholars, such as its files of *The Academy of Motion Picture Arts and Sciences Bulletin,* 1930–33. Although I was not allowed direct access to the minutes of Academy board meetings, some information from the minutes was obtained for me by Academy librarian Linda Harris Mehr, who also provided data on Capra's membership and offices. I also consulted the papers of John Huston and George Stevens, and the Paramount Facts File, and I made frequent use of the Library's other resources. Anthony Slide of the Library let me pick his brain on Hollywood history, arranged my interview with Priscilla Bonner, and helped me locate Helen Jerome Eddy. Others who assisted me at the Academy included Howard Prouty, Patrick Stockstill, Carol Cullen, and Sue England. The Academy's Dan Woodruff showed me *Cavalcade of the Academy Awards.*

The files of the Directors Guild of America—including its minutes, transcripts of meetings, legal files, correspondence, documents, Capra's membership files, and the personal files of its first president, King Vidor—were opened to me by David Shepard, the dedicated film scholar who was then head of DGA Special

Projects. The DGA, however, subsequently refused me permission to quote from its files. David Shepard also helped me locate and screen some of the silent films on which Capra worked, and chose me to moderate the DGA's 1981 seminar "A Weekend with Frank Capra and His Films" in Indian Wells, California, giving me the opportunity to get to know Capra better and to become acquainted with Joseph Walker.

Hollywood biographer and veteran Associated Press correspondent Bob Thomas allowed me to use his research files for his biography *King Cohn: The Life and Times of Harry Cohn* (G. P. Putnam's Sons, 1967) in the Bob Thomas Papers at the University of California, Los Angeles. His files include notes of interviews he conducted in the 1960s with Capra and with various Capra collaborators, some of whom (such as Sidney Buchman and Sam Briskin) had died before I began my research; I have made use of that material throughout the chapters dealing with Capra's work at Columbia. At UCLA, with the assistance of archivists Audree Malkin and Birgitta Cooper, I also used the papers of Michael Wilson and William Wyler.

Bob Bookman, Ron Jacobi, John Byers, and Nick Nichols gave me access to story files of Columbia Pictures. The studio did not respond to repeated requests for other information about Capra, however, and since it would not officially disclose financial information about Capra's films to me, I obtained copies of Capra's profit participation statements, computer printouts of financial information, and other data (1935–85) and a copy of "Contract Abstract: Frank Capra" (1935) from a confidential source at the studio. Additional financial information on Capra and Columbia was found in The Capra Archive and in the Bob Thomas Papers.

At the State Historical Society of Wisconsin, Madison, I made use of the papers of Dalton Trumbo, Frances Goodrich and Albert Hackett, Howard Lindsay and Russel Crouse, Herbert Biberman and Gale Sondergaard, and Claude Binyon, and the legal and publicity files of the United Artists Corporation. I am grateful for the longtime support of the Historical Society's Barbara Kaiser; Sara Leuchter, Menzi Behrnd-Klodt, Sheila Ryan, and Maxine Fleckner also rendered valuable assistance.

The U.S. Army Staff Files and the Records of the Office of the Chief Signal Officer, U.S. Army, at the National Archives in Washington, D.C., contain script drafts, shot lists, correspondence, research documents, and other material pertaining to Capra's World War II films (the films are available for viewing at the National Archives, except for *Your Job in Germany*, which I found at the Library of Congress, where Patrick Sheehan facilitated screenings). Additional documentation on Capra and his World War II films was found in the papers of Franklin D. Roosevelt and Lowell Mellett at the Franklin D. Roosevelt Library, Hyde Park, New York, by librarian John Ferris; and in the papers of George C. Marshall and Frank McCarthy at the George C. Marshall Library, Lexington, Virginia, by assistant archivist-librarian Anita M. Weber. At the National Archives, I also examined the manifest of the SS *Germania*, on which Capra and his family emigrated to the U.S. from Palermo in 1903; the microfilmed 1910 U.S. Census, which gives data about the Capras' Lincoln Heights neighborhood of Los Angeles;

the declassified (at my request in 1987) World War II records of the U.S. Senate Special Committee Investigating the National Defense Program (known as the "Truman committee," after its chairman, Sen. Harry S Truman), in the Congressional Records Division; and the partially declassified (in 1980) final report of the Defense Department/Caltech Project VISTA (1952), in the Military Archives Division. Those who assisted me at the Archives included Linda Ebben, Edward Reese, Les Waffen, Wilbert Mahoney, and Teresa Wertan. William T. Murphy and William J. Blakefield also provided information on Capra's war films.

Capra's official U.S. Army personnel records from World War I and World War II were released to me by the Army at his request in 1985. I found background information relating to his period of World War I service in the Presidio Museum and Library, U.S. Army Presidio, San Francisco. Government records were released to me in 1986 through the Freedom of Information Act by the U.S. Army Intelligence and Security Command, Fort Meade, Maryland, which supplied 55 partially censored pages of its 226-page file on Capra; and by the U.S. Department of Justice Immigration and Naturalization Service, which supplied its records on Frank and Ben Capra (Tony Capra's naturalization papers and other documents were obtained from his widow, Marguerite Capra). The Federal Bureau of Investigation refused my request for its files on Capra, and the Justice Department turned down an appeal in 1986.

Gloria Hamilton of the Los Angeles Unified School District researched and copied Capra's grade school and high school transcripts and other records for me (Marguerite Capra supplied Tony's grade school records). Other material on Capra's high school years came from the archives of Manual Arts High School, to which I was given access by principal Karleen Marienthal and Cathy Silva; and from Manual alumnus Frank D. Keeler, who gave me his copies of school yearbooks and other publications from that period. Virginia Titus Ives, who at the time of my research was head of Manual's alumni association, helped in locating graduates. Capra's Throop College of Technology transcript was interpreted for me by Lyman Bonner, then registrar of the California Institute of Technology, Pasadena. Other documents pertaining to Capra and Throop were found in the archives of Caltech, the Caltech Library, and the private collections of Throop alumni Robert W. Flory and Charles W. Varney, Jr. Others who helped me at Caltech included alumni director Lee Weingarten, who enabled me to locate men who attended Throop with Capra; Jo Keeney, Sheila Fields, Paula Hurwitz, Rod Casper, Carol Bugé, and Charles Newton. Andrea Dobbe located a print of *Careers for Youth* and arranged for screening it and Capra's home movie of Albert Einstein. I thank Kathleen and William Scharf, caretakers of Caltech's Capra Ranch (formerly part of Capra's Red Mountain Ranch), for a tour and for other historical information.

Francesca Savoia expertly translated Italian material for me and shared her knowledge of that country's history and culture. I also am grateful to Jean-François Miller for his French and Italian translations.

Other individuals, archives, and organizations providing research material and assistance included C. L. (Les) Anderson of the San Francisco Boys and Girls

Club's Ernest Ingold Branch, former site of the Montague Studios; Cheryl Baumgart of Indiana University's Lilly Library, Bloomington; Jack Boyd of the Martin Marietta Corp.; David Bradley; Father Peter Brennan of St. Francis of Assisi Catholic Church, La Quinta, California; Margaret Burk; Calvary Cemetery, Los Angeles; Phyllis Chapman and Gertrude Gerke of the Sierra Madre Historical Society, California; Anita Clark, librarian of the *Omaha World-Herald;* Allison Cowgill of the Nevada State Library, Carson City; Dresser Dalhstead of Ralph Edwards Productions; Shirley Eder of the *Detroit Free Press;* John Flinn and Tory Hicks of Columbia Pictures; Forest Lawn Memorial Park, Glendale, California; Cindy Franco of the Records Office, University of California, Berkeley; Bert Gould of the Bay Area Archive; Judy Gracia of the Office of the Registrar of Vital Statistics, California State Department of Health Services, Sacramento; Hollywood Cemetery, Hollywood, California; David Hull of the Maritime Library, San Francisco; Larry Kleno; Paul Kozak and Patty Prendergast of the American Film Institute; Nellie Lide, researcher for the CBS News program *60 Minutes;* Joanne M. Lord, staff secretary of the San Diego County Grand Jury Commissioner; Patrick McGilligan; Ron Magliozzi of the Museum of Modern Art Film Study Center, New York; Ellen Mastroianni; Father Walter Mattiato of Mission San Antonio de Pala, Pala, California; Lee Mortenson of the Nevada Historical Society, Reno; Bernard F. Pasqualini of the Free Library of Philadelphia; Jan Reed, editor of the *Sierra Madre News* (California); Sharon Reeves, chief librarian of the *San Diego Union* and *Tribune;* Harry Rex; the Santa Maria Valley Historical Society, Santa Maria, California; Steve Seemayer and Pamela Wilson; Sandy Snider, associate curator, historical section, Los Angeles State and County Arboretum, Arcadia; Prof. Howard Suber of the Department of Theater, Film, and Television, UCLA; Delores Thill, city clerk of Sierra Madre, California; Kevin Thomas of the *Los Angeles Times;* Linda Valentino of the Los Angeles chapter of the American Civil Liberties Union; Ron Whelan, librarian of the John F. Kennedy Library, Boston; Bob White, editor of the *Fallbrook Enterprise* (California); and Barbara Williams of the Los Angeles Police Department.

Additional sources of public information were the Register of Births, Bisacquino, Sicily; the Nevada Department of State, Carson City; the Fallbrook Public Utility District (FPUD) (California); Indio Superior Court, Indio, California; the Los Angeles County Assessor and Registrar-Recorder; the Los Angeles County Superior Court; the County Clerk and the Clerk of the Second Judicial District Court, Washoe County, Reno, Nevada; the Riverside County Clerk, Health Department, and Recorder (California); the San Diego County Recorder; the San Francisco County Registrar-Recorder; the San Francisco Police Department; the Sierra Madre Police Department; the Westminster County Court, London.

I made use of the Los Angeles history collection of the downtown Los Angeles Public Library, including the Los Angeles City Directory, 1900/01 through 1932. Carolyn L. Garner and Elaine Zorbas of the Pasadena Public Library assisted me with the papers of the Pasadena Community Playhouse and the Pasadena Historical Landmarks Files. I also used public libraries in other cities in California, Nevada, and New York, and the libraries of the University of Southern California and the University of California campuses of Los Angeles, Riverside, and San Bernardino; Pasadena City College; the Louis B. Mayer Library of the American Film Institute, Los Angeles; the genealogical library of the Church of Jesus Christ of Latter-Day Saints, Los Angeles; and the John F. Kennedy Library.

To these friends, whose support during the writing of this book meant more to me than can be expressed here, I offer my heartfelt thanks: Donna Ayers, Glen Barrow, Ernest Callenbach, Charles Champlin, Kevin Cox, Patricia Edson, Paul Feehan, Barbara Frank, Herman Hong, Joan McDowd, Raphael O'Donoghue, Michael O'Shea, Michael Shovers, Julia Sweeney, Esme Takahashi, Annette Taylor, Elaine Thielstrom, David A. Walsh and R. Patricia Walsh, Janie Wilson, and a guy named Dan with the Santa Fe Railroad.

The O'Hara, McGahan, Van Dessel, and McBride clans literally made it possible for me to complete this book. I particularly thank Hetty O'Hara for her boundless tenacity and insights; Una McGahan, for her untiring dedication to this project; Noel O'Hara, for his sage comments as a fellow writer; my daughter Jessica McBride, Gwenn O'Hara Van Dessel, and Susan O'Hara, for acting as research assistants; Karl Van Dessel and Fiona O'Kirwan, for their help in a thousand daily ways; Susan, Gwenn, Tony Garrison, Stuart Bennett, Suzette and David McGahan, and Karl Van Dessel, Jr., for helping look after my son John, who showed patience and good cheer beyond his years; Lynn Garrison, an honorary member of the O'Hara clan, for his fierce loyalty and his historical erudition; Michael F. McBride, for his generosity in offering legal advice and his other support; Dr. Patrick E. McBride, for his advice on medical aspects of the book; and the following members of the McBride clan for their fidelity: Dennis, Genevieve, Kerin O'Brien, Kim Schappe, Kim Stanton, Mark, Melanie Aska, Shirley Porterfield, and Timothy.

I regret that my parents, Marian Dunne McBride and Raymond E. McBride, did not live to see the completion of this book. My mother was responsible for my first steps as a professional writer, and she never wavered in her enthusiasm for my choice of a career; my father, like her a newspaper reporter, guided me through the writing of my first book in the 1960s, and I was lucky to have his continuing advice and encouragement through much of this one.

I am most fortunate to have Maurice L. Muehle as my lawyer. Maury, whose interest in books rivals his interest in the law, is a shrewd and dedicated advocate of my book's integrity. I also am grateful to his thoughtful and cheerful assistants Teri LaMee, Diane Wolfberg, Lanla Gist, and Leslye Batton.

Every author should have an editor with the sensitivity, perceptivity, and skill of Bob Bender, and a publisher as devoted to the truth as Simon & Schuster. I also am pleased to work with such people as Bob's gracious assistant Johanna Li and a legal department that includes the astute Felice Einhorn and Leslie Jones. Before I came to Simon & Schuster, Jeff Smith went beyond the call of duty with his keen-eyed copyediting and his personal kindness. At Simon & Schuster, the manuscript benefited from the careful and thoughtful copyediting performed by film scholar Virginia Clark.

Even while my wife, Ruth O'Hara, was in the process of completing her own Ph.D. program, she devoted her formidable strength of character to all of the tasks involved in this book, both practical and conceptual. She was my live-in editor, and only she knows how much more. Until I married her, I never believed an author who wrote that he couldn't have written a book without his wife's support. Now I know what that means.

Joseph McBride
Los Angeles and Green Valley Lake, California
1984–1992

Notes on Sources

Frank Capra's autobiography, *The Name Above the Title*, was first published by Macmillan, 1971. Other books, monographs, and pamphlets on Capra and his work include *The Making of a Great Picture* (promotional book on *Lost Horizon*: Columbia Pictures, 1937); Carl I. Hovland, Arthur A. Lumsdaine, and Fred D. Sheffield, *Experiments on Mass Communications* (Vol. III of *Studies in Social Psychology in World War II*; a study of the effects on soldiers of the *Why We Fight* series and the *Army-Navy Screen Magazine:* Princeton University Press, 1949); *The Distinguished Library of Frank Capra* (Parke-Bernet Galleries, 1949); Richard Griffith, *Frank Capra* (British Film Institute, 1951); Hans Saaltink, *Frank Capra: Leven en Werken* [*Frank Capra: His Life and Work*] (Filmfront-Filmstudies, Netherlands, 1951); Bruce Henstell, ed., *Frank Capra: "One Man—One Film"* (transcript of an American Film Institute seminar: AFI, 1971); Donald Willis, *The Films of Frank Capra* (Scarecrow Press, 1974); Arthur B. Friedman, *Capra* (an interview conducted in the late 1950s for the Popular Arts Project of the Oral History Research Office of Columbia University; Microfilming Corporation of America, 1975); Richard Glatzer and John Raeburn, eds., *Frank Capra: The Man and His Films* (University of Michigan Press, 1975); Leland Poague, *The Cinema of Frank Capra* (A. S. Barnes, 1975); Thomas William Bohn, *An Historical and Descriptive Analysis of the "Why We Fight" Series* (Arno Press, 1977); Charles J. Maland, *American Visions: The Films of Chaplin, Ford, Capra, and Welles, 1936–1941* (Arno Press, 1977); Gregorio Napoli, *Il Ritorno di Frank Capra* [*The Return of Frank Capra*] (a pamphlet commissioned by the Banco di Sicilia on Capra's homecoming to Sicily: Ufficio Fondazione Mormino, Palermo, 1977); Victor Scherle and William Turner Levy, *The Films of Frank Capra* (Citadel Press, 1977); Dennis R. Bohnenkamp and Sam L. Grogg, eds., *Frank Capra Study Guide* (AFI, 1979); Allen Estrin, *Hollywood Professionals, Vol. 6: Capra, Cukor, Brown* (A. S. Barnes, 1980); Maland, *Frank Capra* (Twayne, 1980); Joseph McBride, ed., *Frank Capra* (Life Achievement Award program booklet, AFI, 1982); Raymond Carney, *American Vision: The Films of Frank Capra* (Cambridge University Press, 1986); Jeanine Basinger, *The "It's a Wonderful Life" Book* (Alfred A. Knopf, 1986); Charles Wolfe, *Frank Capra: A Guide to References and Resources* (G. K. Hall, 1987); Wolfe, ed., *Meet John Doe* (Rutgers University

Press, 1989); Lee Lourdeaux, *Italian and Irish Filmmakers in America: Ford, Capra, Coppola, and Scorsese* (Temple University Press, 1990); and Patricia King Hanson, executive editor, *Meet Frank Capra: A Catalog of His Work* (Stanford Theatre Foundation/National Center for Film and Video Preservation, 1990).

Scripts have been published for five Capra films: *Lady for a Day*, in Lorraine Noble, ed., *Four-Star Scripts* (Doubleday, Doran, 1936); *It Happened One Night*, in Noble, and in John Gassner and Dudley Nichols, eds., *Twenty Best Film Plays* (Crown, 1943); *Mr. Smith Goes to Washington*, in Gassner and Nichols, and in Jerry Wald and Richard Macaulay, eds., *The Best Picture, 1939–1940* (Dodd, Mead, 1940); *Meet John Doe*, in Sam Thomas, ed., *Best American Screenplays*, First Series, foreword by Capra (Crown, 1986), and in Wolfe, *Meet John Doe*; and *It's a Wonderful Life*, by St. Martin's Press, 1986 (shooting script), and in Basinger, *The "It's a Wonderful Life" Book* (transcription from the film).

Abbreviations used in the chapter notes below include: AMPAS, Academy of Motion Picture Arts and Sciences (Beverly Hills, California); AP, Associated Press; BTP, Bob Thomas Papers (UCLA); DGA, Directors Guild of America; *DV*, *Daily Variety* (Los Angeles); FCA, Frank Capra Archive (Wesleyan University, Middletown, Connecticut); FCI, Frank Capra interview by the author; FWC, Fay Wray Collection (USC); *HCN*, the *Hollywood Citizen-News*; *HR*, *The Hollywood Reporter*; HUAC, House Committee on Un-American Activities; *LAE*, the *Los Angeles Examiner*; LAHE, the *Los Angeles Herald-Examiner*; *LAT*, the *Los Angeles Times*; *NAT*, *The Name Above the Title* (original draft version cited as "*NAT* uncut"; *NYHT*, the *New York Herald Tribune*; *NYT*, *The New York Times*; *NYWT*, the *New York World-Telegram*; SDG, Screen Directors Guild (predecessor to the DGA); SWG, Screen Writers Guild (predecessor to the Writers Guild of America); UP, United Press; UPI, United Press International.

References to books and articles in the chapter notes are listed fully the first time only, except when the full reference appeared above or in the Acknowledgments; subsequent references include only the author's last name and the title.

1. "I felt nothing"   (pp. 9–27)

Capra's trip to Sicily was documented by the Italian newspapers *Giornale di Sicilia*, *La Stampa*, *Il Giorno*, *L'Ora*, *Il Messaggero*, *Lettera dall'Italia*, *Il Mattino*, *Gazzetta del Popolo*, and *Gazzetta del Sud*, and by the AP (April 15–May 27, 1977); by Radiotelevisione Italiana in its 1977 special *Mister Capra torna a casa*; and in Napoli, *Il Ritorno di Frank Capra*. Also consulted were Capra's diary and his contemporaneous notes and correspondence on the trip (FCA). Antonino Troncale's comments on Capra's homecoming are from his letters to the author of April 18 and June 18, 1985. Capra's "I felt nothing" remark is from a Toronto press conference reported in "Capra on His 'Roots,' " *Variety*, September 21, 1977, and his comment on Alex Haley's *Roots* is from FCI. Graham Greene's description of Capra is from his review of *You Can't Take It With You*, *The Spectator*, London, November 11, 1938.

The conditions which drove the Capras and others like them out of Sicily are analyzed in Robert F. Foerster, *The Italian Emigration of Our Times* (Harvard University Press, 1919), which served as the source for general data on emigration. Information on the history of Capra's family is from sources including Troncale's 1985 and December 9, 1987, letters to the author, and the author's interviews with Capra, other family members, and Maria Lanza Oddo; the oral histories of Ben and Tony Capra; the Los Angeles City Directory, 1900/01 through 1906; the U.S. Census of 1910; and various public records in the U.S. and Sicily. Francesco Capra's birth on May 18, 1897, was recorded in the Register of Births, Bisacquino, Sicily, No. 171, Part I, 1897. Capra discussed his birth with the author and in Walter Karp, "The Patriotism of Frank Capra," *Esquire*, February 1981. Documents on Antonino Troncale's attempt to emigrate to the U.S. are in FCA. Capra spoke of his father's horticultural talents in Geoffrey Hellman, "Thinker in Hollywood," *The New Yorker*, February 24, 1940.

Ben Capra's journey to America was documented in records of the U.S. Immigration and Naturalization Service. The primary source of information about the rest of the family's emigration on the SS *Germania* is the ship's "List or Manifest of Alien Passengers for the Commissioner of Immigration," May 24, 1903, U.S. Department of Justice, INS, in "Passenger and Crew Lists of Vessels Arriving at New York, 1897–1942," National Archives. Also consulted was the "Incoming Steamships" column, *NYT*, May 23 and 24, 1903. INS supplied Frank Capra's Certificate of Naturalization, U.S. Department of Labor, June 4, 1920, in the U.S. District Court, County of Los Angeles.

2. *"I hated America"*   (pp. 29–48)

Capra described his arrival in New York to the author, to Josephine Campisi, and in his acceptance speech for *The American Film Institute Salute to Frank Capra* (CBS-TV, 1982). Carey McWilliams's *Southern California: An Island on the Land* (Peregrine Smith, 1983; originally published as *Southern California Country: An Island on the Land*, Duell, Sloane & Pearce, 1946) is the best history of life in Los Angeles during that era. Also useful were McWilliams, *California: The Great Exception* (Current Books, 1949), and Kevin Starr, *Americans and the California Dream 1850–1915* (Oxford University Press, 1973).

The U.S. Census of 1910 gives the basic data on Lincoln Heights, the Capras, the Washingtons, and their other neighbors. The author's interviews with Capra's relatives and with others who grew up with him also provided valuable information for this chapter.

Capra's remarks about ghettos are from John McDonough, "Frank Capra: For the Veteran Director, It's a Wonderful Life," *Chicago Tribune*, April 16, 1978. His memories of having "a very nice mother" appeared in James Childs, "Capra Today," *Film Comment*, November/December 1972. Capra recalled his father's parties in a February 21, 1972, letter to *Philadelphia Daily News* editor Rolfe Neill, part of which was published as "Fun in a Sicily Madhouse" in the *Daily News*, March 31, 1972.

Documentation on Capra's grade school education includes his and his brother Tony's transcripts and a letter to Capra from his Griffin classmate Ralph H. Thompson, June 23, 1959, listing class members. Jean McDaniel's anecdote about Capra is from her letter to him of October 5, 1936. Capra's letter to President Gerald R. Ford, August 12, 1974, recalled his anger on learning in second grade that he could not become President. Capra's radio interview, *I'm an American!*, was for the U.S. Department of Justice series on NBC, March 23, 1941; the script by Dorothy Donnell and Capra, and their correspondence, are in FCA.

Tony Capra recalled peddling papers with Frank in his oral history and on *This Is Your Life: Frank Capra* (NBC-TV, 1959). Sources on Frank Capra's name changes include his birth certificate, his grade school diploma, his certificate of naturalization, his letter to Harry Stuart Winer, September 17, 1973, and his interviews with the author.

3. *"A terrible wop"* (pp. 49–67)

Primary sources for this chapter included the author's interviews with Capra and with eighteen other persons who attended Manual Arts High School during all or part of Capra's years there (1911–15). Documentation was supplied by Capra's high school transcript and by Manual Arts publications: *Manual Arts*, 1910–13; *Manual Arts Weekly*, 1913–16; *The Artisan* (yearbook), 1913–18; and *Fifty Years*, the Golden Jubilee Edition of *The Artisan*, 1959. An invaluable general reference source was former Manual teacher Florence Sprenger's *Spirit of the Toilers: An Intimate History of Manual Arts High School* (Taylor Publishing Co., 1977). Capra discussed Manual Arts in "Frank Capra to Confer S'50 Diplomas," *The Manual Arts Daily*, June 9, 1950. The enrollment situation was reported in contemporary newspaper articles found in the school's scrapbooks (1910–12).

Rob Wagner's publications include *Film Folk* (The Century Co., 1918), based on his articles in *The Saturday Evening Post*; his magazine *Rob Wagner's Script*; and Anthony Slide, ed., *The Best of Rob Wagner's Script* (Scarecrow Press, 1985). Wagner is discussed in Sprenger and in Gene Fowler, *Father Goose* (Covici-Friede, 1934). Wagner's questioning before a grand jury in the "Federal investigation of parlor Bolshevism" in Los Angeles was reported in "Chaplin May Testify," *Variety*, December 5, 1919. His advice to Capra about the film business is from his letter of January 1, 1918 (FCA). *Our Wonderful Schools* was covered in *Manual Arts Weekly* (April-June 1915). Wagner's comments on Capra appeared in "Our Cover Boy," *Rob Wagner's Script*, June 10, 1939.

Capra's involvement in the Adelphic Society was mentioned in *The Artisan*, Winter 1915, and in Sprenger, and was recalled by General Doolittle, Downs, and Loftin. Sources on Capra's involvement with Wagner's stage designing crew and with Maude Howell include Sprenger and various Manual Arts publications. Information on Capra's appearance in *The Crisis* is from articles in *Manual Arts Weekly* (1915).

Capra's interest in movies in 1917 was demonstrated in his Throop College of

Technology paper "A Treatise on Moving Pictures," December 1917 (FCA), and by Wagner's letter to Capra. Capra called *The Birth of a Nation* "the most important film ever made" in his foreword to D. W. Griffith's autobiography, *The Man Who Invented Hollywood*, ed. James Hart (Touchstone, 1972).

Salvatore Capra's ambition for Frank to become a lawyer was recalled by Maria Lanza Oddo, to whose father Salvatore confided it. Frank's plans to attend the University of California, Berkeley, were reported in "Many Famed Ones Leaving with Great Class," *Manual Arts Weekly*, January 26, 1915.

4. *"Cap"* (pp. 69–102)

Capra's transcript from Throop College of Technology (now the California Institute of Technology) provided basic documentation for this chapter. The date given by Capra in *NAT* for his entrance into college is proven incorrect by his high school and college transcripts. With the advice of Caltech registrar Lyman Bonner, the grading symbols used by Throop in 1915–18 (V, IV, III, II) were converted for this book to their equivalents in the lettering system (A, B, C, D), and his GPA, or grade-point average, was computed from the numerical equivalents of Capra's grades. *The Throop Tech*, September 1918, lists Capra as having received a "B.S. in Chemistry," but Bonner said the only authoritative source for a student's degree is his transcript, which lists Capra's degree as a General B.S. Bonner also said that an examination of the courses Capra took and the grades he received proves that he did not fulfill the requirement for a degree in Chemical Engineering, but only for a General B.S., which is described in the Throop *Catalogue*, January 1918 (the *Caltech Alumni Directory*, 1981, correctly lists Capra as having a General degree). Capra's B.S. thesis, *The Equivalent Conductance of Solutions of Picric Acid*, 1918, is in the Caltech Library.

College publications and documents consulted also included *The Throop Idea* (1913); *Throop Bulletins*, 1915–18; *Throop Annals of 1915*; the school magazine and yearbook, *The Throop Tech*, May 1916 through September 1918 (of which Capra was editor from October 1917 through April 1918); the Commencement Program, Class of War '18, September 15, 1918; *The Gnome Club Directory* (Caltech, 1981); and various issues of *The Caltech News*. Capra's college writings, in addition to his thesis and his articles in *The Tech*, include his papers (FCA): "Personal Efficiency," January 11, 1916; "The Butler's Failure" (short story), May 3, 1916, published as "The Butler's Adventure," *The Tech*, November 1916; and "A Treatise on Moving Pictures." His film treatment "Heart Beats," n.d. (c. 1919), also is in FCA.

Historical material on Pasadena and Los Angeles was provided by the Los Angeles City Directory, 1912 through 1918, and the Pasadena City Directory, 1915–16 through 1918–19; McWilliams, *Southern California: An Island on the Land*; and various issues of the *Pasadena Star-News*. Material on Sierra Madre and the Churchill Ranch includes: McWilliams; Edith Blumer Bowen, *Annals of Early Sierra Madre* (Sierra Madre Historical Society, 1950) and *Sierra Madre Vistas: A Pictorial History of Sierra Madre* (Sierra Madre Historical Society,

1976); Phyllis Chapman, "Marlborough Terrace" (unpublished); "Beautiful Sierra Madre," *Sierra Madre Vista*, March 17, 1888; and various issues of the *Sierra Madre News*.

Capra's 1929 self-portrait, written for Columbia Pictures, was quoted in Hellman, "Thinker in Hollywood," and was verified by Capra to the author. The University of California, Berkeley, Records Office said Capra never was a student there. The fact that Capra's family helped him through college was testified to by Josephine Campisi; Marguerite (Mrs. Tony) Capra; David Blangsted (Ann Capra's adopted son); Maria Lanza Oddo; and Roscoe (Rocky) Washington.

Information on Clinton Kelly Judy is from school publications and from his 1949 correspondence with Capra, as well as from other correspondence in FCA. Alfred Noyes's comments on Throop and Capra are from his autobiography, *Two Worlds for Memory* (Lippincott, 1958). Capra wrote about Noyes in an unsigned *Tech* article, "A Rare Treat," October 1917.

Capra wrote about his trip to the Eastman plant in "A Treatise on Moving Pictures." His essay "Manhattan Island" was published in *The Tech*, October 1916. Sources on the Pasadena Community Playhouse and Capra's involvement with it include the author's interviews with Capra, Chester Sticht, Isabelle Daniels Griffis, and Lois Keener Thome; Diane Alexander, *Playhouse* (Dorleac-MacLeish, 1984); papers of the Playhouse at the Pasadena City Library; and reviews of Playhouse productions, *Pasadena Star-News*, 1917–18 (none of the printed sources includes any references to Capra).

The account of the death of Salvatore Capra is drawn primarily from the recollections of Samuel W. Capra (the only eyewitness to the accident itself) and from Ben Capra's oral history; other details are from Capra's niece Sarah Capra Coughlin, who also was present at the ranch when it happened; Josephine Campisi, who was present later that day and heard Ann Capra's account; Frank Capra, who also was present later that day; and from Joe Finochio and David Blangsted. The event is documented in Certificate of Death: Salvator[e] Capra, Board of Health, State of California, filed November 20, 1916; and "Life Crushed Out By Gear While Alone," *Sierra Madre News*, November 24, 1916. Capra's account in *NAT* is mistaken not only about the date of the accident but also in other important details. The loan of the tuition money was discussed in Capra's 1934–35 correspondence with Edward C. Barrett (FCA), and by Caltech president Dr. Lee A. DuBridge on *This Is Your Life: Frank Capra* (NBC-TV, 1959).

Capra's existing U.S. Army records include incomplete data on his service during World War I; information about his enlistment in the spring of 1917 was supplied by Sticht and confirmed by Capra. Details of Capra's ROTC activities and military duties are in various articles in *The Tech*, 1917–18, and "Throop's Class Will Enter Service," *Pasadena Star-News*, September 16, 1918. Capra wrote about the war in the unsigned *Tech* editorials "Doing Our 'Bit,' " October 1917, quoted in this chapter, and "The Danger of Peace," January 1918 (he told the author that he wrote all of the unsigned editorials, such as these, during his tenure as editor); the unsigned poem about enlistment, "With Apologies to Shakespeare," appeared in *The Tech*, December 1917. Information on Capra's U.S. citizenship is from Capra, Sticht, and Capra's Certificate of Naturalization.

Sources on Isabelle Daniels Griffis and her relationship with Capra include the author's interviews with Mrs. Griffis; correspondence between Capra and Mrs. Griffis, 1920–80, especially Capra's letters of February 28, 1920; [August or September] 1920; and August 24, 1921. Capra's account of the July 4 weekend is from his article "Seniors' Blowout(s)," *The Tech*, September 1918, reprinted as "1918: Frank Capra and Friends Storm Yosemite Valley," *Caltech News*, December 1982; and from the author's interviews with Capra. The letters to Capra from Marion (Ellen) Andrews (Mrs. John P. Conrad), October 11, 1935, and Faith Van Horn Knox, February 12, 1935, are in FCA.

Warner Bros.' 1941 publicity biography of Capra, which states that he wrote for Mack Sennett while in college, is from the Capra biographical file at AMPAS; the Sennett Papers at AMPAS yielded no records of any work by Capra in that period, but the job also was mentioned in John McCallum, *Scooper: Authorized Story of Scoop Conlon's Motion Picture World* (Wood & Reber, 1960). The Class Prophecy, Retla Alter's "T.C.C. Engineers," *The Tech*, September 1918, was recalled by Capra in " 'Movies' Miss Their Chance, Capra Charges," *Pasadena Post*, February 28, 1936, and to the author.

5. *"I'm from Hollywood"*   (pp. 103–138)

Capra attempted in interviews with the author to perpetuate the myth from *NAT* of his almost total lack of film experience before *Fulta Fisher's Boarding House*, but when presented with contrary information, he elaborated on some of his activities. Richard Griffith's 1951 monograph *Frank Capra*, partially reprinted in Glatzer and Raeburn, *Frank Capra: The Man and His Films*, contains some information on that period, but the mythic version has been followed by most of the post-*NAT* writers on Capra, including Wolfe, whose *Frank Capra: A Guide to References and Resources* dismisses genuine evidence as fanciful. An exception is Nancy K. Hart's profile "Frank Capra" in Jon Tuska, ed., *Close-Up: The Hollywood Director* (Scarecrow Press, 1978).

The principal work on silent filmmaking in San Francisco is Bell's *The Golden Gate and the Silver Screen*, which unearthed a wealth of long-forgotten information. Other books consulted on the silent period for this and the next three chapters included *Motion Pictures 1912–1939* (Copyright Office, Library of Congress, 1951); Brownlow, *The Parade's Gone By . . .* ; Benjamin B. Hampton, *History of the American Film Industry* (Dover, 1971, originally published as *A History of the Movies*, Covici-Friede, 1931); Kenneth W. Munden, executive editor, *The American Film Institute Catalogue of Motion Pictures Produced in the United States: Feature Films 1921–1930* (R. W. Bowker, 1971); Brownlow and John Kobal, *Hollywood: The Pioneers* (Alfred A. Knopf, 1979); and Bruce T. Torrence, *Hollywood: The First Hundred Years* (New York Zoetrope, 1982). The San Francisco City Directory, 1921 through 1923, and telephone directories for this period (San Francisco Public Library) listed places where Capra lived and worked. Information on his sister-in-law Katie (Caterina Daniele Capra) is from Certificate of Death: Catharine L. Daniels, Department of Public Health, State of California, filed February 9, 1970.

Capra's 1920–21 letters to Isabelle Daniels Griffis give invaluable accounts of his activities in this period. The most informative printed source on Capra's vagabondage and early filmmaking experiences is Alva Johnston's profile "Capra Shoots as He Pleases," *The Saturday Evening Post*, May 14, 1938, drawn largely from an interview with Capra, which fills in important details on his 1918–21 period. Though Capra embarrassedly tried to debunk it in his sanitized *Time* cover story, "Columbia's Gem," August 8, 1938, Johnston's colorful piece (as Capra himself admitted to the author of this book) proved more accurate in many particulars than most later writing on Capra. Capra also gave clues to his activities in his article "My Crazy Hollywood!," *Sunday Pictorial*, London, June 15, 1938; and in information he provided for his entry in the *International Motion Picture Almanac*, 1930; a publicity biography in the pressbook for *Dirigible*, Columbia Pictures, 1931; "Fame's Paradox: The Story of Frank Capra," in the publicity booklet for *You Can't Take It With You*, Columbia, 1938; Warner Bros.' 1941 publicity biography and its pressbook for *Meet John Doe*, 1941; *Biographies* (pamphlet), Liberty Films, Hollywood, 1946 (George Stevens Papers); N. W. Ayer & Son, "Detailed Biographical Notes: Frank Capra" (1952) (FCA); "Biography Frank Capra" (1961) (FCA); the biography in the "Director's Choice" program brochure (AMPAS), November 2, 1968; and the transcript of "The American Film Institute Seminar with Frank Capra," May 23, 1978 (AFI).

The development of Capra's mythical accounts can be seen in various drafts for *NAT* in FCA, which also has his stories, treatments, and scripts for this period discussed in the text, as well as his 1917 Throop College of Technology paper "A Treatise on Moving Pictures" and fragments of his play *Don't Change Your Husbands*, n.d. (c. 1919).

Other articles with revealing information on this period and Capra's early film career include John D. Forlin, "Frank Capra," *New York Sunday Evening Tribune*, 1932 (FCA); Sidney Skolsky column, "Tintypes," February 27, 1934; Kirtley Baskette, "Hollywood's New Miracle Man," *Photoplay*, December 1934; John Stuart, "Fine Italian Hand," *Collier's*, August 17, 1935; Jim Tully, "Star Boss," *This Week*, November 14, 1937; Philip K. Scheuer, "Directors Last Long in Filmland," *LAT*, May 29, 1938; and Hellman, "Thinker in Hollywood."

Capra's World War I service is documented in his U.S. Army records; his December 19, 1946, affidavit for the INS; and various historical records in the Library of the Presidio; his surveying class papers are in FCA.

Information on Anita Baldwin, her children, her estate, and the U.S. Army Balloon School is from sources including Bowen, *Annals of Early Sierra Madre*; Porter Garnett, "Stately Homes of California, II: 'Anoakia,' " *Sunset*, 1914; C. F. Lummis, "The Building Up of an Ideal California Ranch," *Out West*, May/June 1914; Clarie Hosler Coombs, "Anoakia—Where No Harm Shall Befall," *Pasadena Daily News*, n.d. (c. 1915); and various articles in the *Sierra Madre News*, *Pasadena Star-News*, and *LAT*, 1915–79.

The 1919–20 film activities of Capra and his associates in Reno, Nevada, were covered in various articles in the *Nevada State Journal* (Reno) and the *Reno Evening Gazette*, August 28, 1919–April 25, 1920. See especially *State Journal:*

"Movie Star Heads Local Corporation," September 24; advertisement for the Tri-State Motion Picture Co., October 12 and 13; and *"Pulse of Life* New Reno Film," April 2; and *Gazette:* "Motion Picture Company Coming," August 28; "Plans for Motion Picture Studio Here Are Made," September 25; Tri-State advertisement[s], October 7 and 11; "Show Reno-Made Moving Picture," April 1; and a review of *The Pulse of Life* by The Playgoer, April 24. Further data are contained in Articles of Incorporation, Tri-State Motion Picture Co., Nevada Department of State, September 17, 1919; "Coast Picture News," *Variety*, January 24, 1920; Polk's Reno City, Washoe County, and Carson City Directory, 1920–21; Skolsky's column, February 27, 1934; and Liberty Films' *Biographies*. Records of the *Ann Austin Collins vs. Arthur Oscar Collins* divorce are from the Second Judicial District Court, Washoe County, Reno, decree filed December 6, 1919.

Screen Snapshots and the early history of CBC and Columbia Pictures are discussed in Hampton, *History of the American Film Industry*; Thomas, *King Cohn*; various articles in *Moving Picture World*, 1920; and in "How Col Bloomed on Hall Rooms," *DV*, October 21, 1940.

The *San Francisco Chronicle* extensively covered local filmmaking in this period. See especially, "Movie Concern to Open Studios in San Francisco" (the article that probably led Capra to Walter Montague), December 8, 1920; "Paul Gerson Does Much to Bring 'Movies,' " July 31, 1920; "Gerson Company to Begin Filming Picture Comedies," February 24, 1921; "Picture Studio Dedicated by Visiting Star," April 11, 1921; and "Belmont Chosen for Plum Center Studio," March 4, 1922. Also see "Movie Studio Is Opened—Permanent Home of Paul Gerson Pictures Corporation," San Francisco *Examiner*, April 11, 1921.

Waldon S. (Walt) Ball was remembered in Bert Gould, "Historical Note," *Journal of the SMPTE*, May 1969. Capra's small claims suit against Charles A. Warren, filed October 5, 1921, was listed in the October 7, 1921, issue of *Edwards Abstract from Records*, San Francisco, available at the San Francisco Public Library; the actual records of the suit no longer exist.

Documentation on the 1921 visit of the Italian battleship *Libia* was found in records of the Maritime Library of San Francisco, and in the coverage by the San Francisco *Chronicle, Examiner, Bulletin,* and *Call,* November 7–December 5, 1921. Giulio DeMoro's reminiscences of Capra's documentary appeared in his column "Nel Mondo dei Libri," *La Follia di New York*, July 1972. Capra recalled the film in his letter to DeMoro of October 27, 1972 (FCA).

Fulta Fisher's Boarding House was reviewed in *NYT*, April 3, 1922, and by Laurence Reid, *Motion Picture News*, April 15, 1922; *The Village Blacksmith* was reviewed in *NYT*, June 5, 1922. David F. Supple recalled Fireside Productions in his letter to Capra of June 18, 1959 (FCA).

Those who remembered Helen Howell included Capra, Josephine Campisi, Joe Finochio, Samuel W. Capra, and Isabelle Daniels Griffis. Further information was provided in "Film Actress, Director Wed," *Chronicle*, December 1, 1923, and Frank Russell Capra–Helen Edith Howell Marriage License, filed December 1, 1923, City and County of San Francisco. The career of William A. Howell was described in "Next Viola Dana Picture to Be Directed by Howell," *Moving Picture World*, January 10, 1920.

6. *The Gag Man*   (pp. 139–179)

The films Capra wrote at the Hal Roach Studios were identified through the studio's 1924 Payroll Ledger and Roach's "Date Book for 1924" in the Hal Roach Papers at USC, and through Capra's scripts in FCA. Additional information on those films came from the author's interview with Roach, the Roach Papers, the *Film Year Book 1925* (published by *The Film Daily*, New York and Hollywood), and from Leonard Maltin and Richard W. Bann, *Our Gang* (Crown, 1977). Capra's credits at the Mack Sennett Studios were assembled from the scripts in FCA and from the script, production, and publicity material in the Mack Sennett Papers at AMPAS, with additional production information on those films and the Harry Langdon features for First National from sources including Fowler, *Father Goose*; David Turconi, *Mack Sennett il "re delle comiche"* (Edizioni dell'Ateneo, Rome, 1961), and the French edition, *Mack Sennett* (Editions Seghers, Paris, 1966); William Schelly, *Harry Langdon* (Scarecrow Press, 1982); Joyce Rheuban, *Harry Langdon: The Comedian as Metteur-en-Scène* (Fairleigh Dickinson University Press, 1983); and Edward Dryhurst, *Gilt Off the Gingerbread* (Bachman & Turner, 1987). Scripts, contracts, and other information on the Langdon features for First National are in USC's Warner Bros. Archives.

Capra in interviews with the author claimed to remember none of the titles of any Roach or Sennett films he worked on, but he provided a few anecdotes about his employers and collaborators; he was more forthcoming on the Langdon features. His contemporaneous essay "The Gag Man," in Charles Reed Jones, *Breaking Into the Movies* (Unicorn Press, 1927), was reprinted in Richard Koszarski, *Hollywood Directors 1914–1940* (Oxford University Press, 1976); Capra recalled his firing by Sennett in his article "Anything for Laughs," *LAHE*, December 24, 1961. Also useful were Brownlow's notes of his interview with William Hornbeck, part of which appeared in *The Parade's Gone By . . .*

Other books consulted (in addition to those cited previously) included: *Film Year Book 1926* and *Film Year Book 1927* (*The Film Daily*); Mack Sennett, as told to Cameron Shipp, *King of Comedy* (Doubleday, 1954); Tay Garnett, with Fredda Dudley Balling, introduction by Capra, *Light Your Torches and Pull Up Your Tights* (Arlington House, 1974); Richard Schickel, *The Men Who Made the Movies* (Atheneum, 1975); Anthony Slide, *The Idols of Silence* (A. S. Barnes, 1976); Walter Kerr, *The Silent Clowns* (Alfred A. Knopf, 1979); Bryan B. Sterling and Frances N. Sterling, *Will Rogers in Hollywood* (Crown, 1984); Leonard Mosley, *Zanuck: The Rise and Fall of Hollywood's Last Tycoon* (Little, Brown, 1984); and the Los Angeles City Directory, 1925 through 1928. An influential source on Sennett and Langdon, with comments by Capra, is James Agee's essay "Comedy's Greatest Era," *Life*, September 5, 1949, reprinted in *Agee on Film*, Vol. 1 (McDowell Obolensky, 1958).

The rise of Capra and Langdon, and Langdon's decline, were covered thoroughly in the Hollywood trade press and other newspapers and magazines. The most important article was Katherine Albert's "What Happened to Harry Langdon," *Photoplay*, February 1932. Others which provided valuable information or background included Jean North, "It's No Joke to Be Funny" (Langdon interview), *Photoplay*, June 1925; Cal York, "Studio News and Gossip East and West," *Photoplay*, March 1926; Tom Waller, "*Long Pants* Promises to Be Harry Langdon's Greatest Film" and "Who's Who in *Long Pants*," *Moving Picture World*, January 22, 1927; "218 Critics Name 144 Best Films Shown in 1926, in Nation-Wide Poll," *Film Daily*, January 28, 1927; Grace Kingsley, "Frank Capra Leaves Langdon," *LAT*, February 23, 1927; "Langdon Will Direct and Title Own Pictures," *Variety*, March 2, 1927; "Inside Stuff on Pictures," *Variety*, March 9, 1927; Marquis Busby, "Comedy Styles Change" (Langdon interview), *LAT*, April 17, 1927; Norman Webb, "Story of the Box-Office," *Film Spectator*, August 6 and 20, September 3, October 1, 1927; Harry Langdon, "The Serious Side of Comedy Making," *Theatre*, December 1927; Leonard Hall, "Hey! Hey! Harry's Coming Back," *Photoplay*, June 1928; and Richard Leary, "Capra and Langdon," *Film Comment*, November 1972. *Photoplay* reviews quoted include: *Tramp, Tramp, Tramp*, August 1926; *The Strong Man*, November 1926; *His First Flame*, July 1927; and *Three's a Crowd*, October 1927; also quoted are the review of *The Marriage Circus* in *Moving Picture World*, April 11, 1925, and the review of *Long Pants* by Rush. (Alfred Rushford Grearson) in *Variety*, March 30, 1927.

Capra's job with FBO was listed in the Los Angeles City Directory, 1925. Two untitled scripts by Capra for the *Puppy Love* series are in FCA; information on the series is from "Puppy Love Through Pathé," *Variety*, June 18, 1924. Capra's comment on his hero "chasing ideas" is from Joseph McBride, "Frank Capra Sees Emerging Sense of Comedy & Idealism Among Student Filmmakers," *DV*, April 16, 1975, reprinted as "Capra Conks Creepy Pic Heroes," *Variety*, April 23, 1975.

Sources on Helen Howell include documents pertaining to the *Helen H. Capra vs. Frank R. Capra* divorce, Superior Court, Los Angeles County, California, 1928–1929; "Alienation of Love Charged in Balm Suit" (on the suit against Helen by Mrs. Elizabeth L. Coverdill), *LAT*, December 12, 1928; Capra to Loyd Wright, March 23, 1929 (Jack Oakie Papers, USC); and William Bartlett (Helen's son) to Capra, July 9, 1964 (FCA). Bartlett wrote Capra that his mother had died several years earlier, and Campisi told the author that Helen died about 1960. No further information on her death was found, nor could the author locate Bartlett or any other relatives of Helen except for Capra and members of his family.

7. *"Marrying the harlot"* (pp. 181–217)

For this and the seven subsequent chapters involving Capra's work for Columbia Pictures, the author relied greatly on his interviews with Capra; his personal secretary, Chester E. Sticht; his regular cinematographer, Joseph Walker; and his other crew members, actors, and colleagues at Columbia.

These interviews were supplemented with Thomas's interview notes for his

Harry Cohn biography *King Cohn* (BTP); "Harry Cohn Interview," notes prepared by Columbia for Muriel Babcock of *LAT*, March 26, 1928 (BTP); Slide's interview with Ralph Graves in *The Idols of Silence*; Brownlow's notes of his April 11, 1967, interview with Irvin Willat; the Willat oral history in Robert S. Birchard, *The Western in the 1920s* (American Film Institute, 1971); and Brownlow's notes of an interview with Colbert. The report in *Variety* that Willat had left *Submarine* because of a "nervous breakdown from overwork" was titled "Willatt's [*sic*] Forced Rest," July 11, 1928.

Material on the history of Columbia appears in Hampton, *History of the American Film Industry*; Rochelle Larkin, *Hail, Columbia* (Arlington House, 1975); Joseph Walker and Juanita Walker, foreword by Barbara Stanwyck, *The Light on Her Face* (ASC Press, 1986); and Edward Buscombe, "Notes on Columbia Pictures Corporation 1926–1941," *Screen*, August 1975. Other sources on the early sound era are Evan William Cameron, ed., *Sound and the Cinema: The Coming of Sound to American Film* (Redgrave, 1980), including an interview with Capra; *End of an Era*, an episode of the Kevin Brownlow–David Gill *Hollywood* series (Thames Television, 1980); Henstell, *Frank Capra: "One Man—One Film"*; and the 1981 DGA seminar "A Weekend with Frank Capra and His Films," in which Joseph Walker also participated.

Capra's scripts for *The Swim Princess*, *Smith's Burglar*, and *Smith's "Uncle Tom,"* along with production data and publicity material, are in the Mack Sennett Papers at AMPAS; the production file for *Brotherly Love* is in the Metro-Goldwyn-Mayer papers at USC; and scripts for several of Capra's features from this period, and for the unproduced *Hold Your Husband*, are in FCA. Additional biographical data on Joseph Walker are from Walker, "Summary—Partial List of Patents," n.d. (c. 1980); Marjorie Walker and Alfred S. Keller, "Joseph B. Walker, A.S.C.," 1981; and Keller's letter to the Board of Governors, AMPAS, October 12, 1981. Walker's work on the zoom lens was discussed in Joseph McBride, "Sawyer Award Kicks Up Controversy," *DV*, March 26, 1990.

Information on Lucille Warner Reyburn, Capra's second wife, came from the author's acquaintance with Mrs. Capra and his interviews with Capra and others including her brother, James Warner; her eldest son, Frank Capra, Jr.; Josephine Campisi; Chester and Bett Sticht; Jean Arthur; Barbara Stanwyck; C. C. Coleman, Jr.; Gay Coleman Collins; and Philip Dunne. Other sources included *The American Film Institute Salute to Frank Capra* (1982), in which Capra reminisced about their first meeting; the Records Office, UC Berkeley; the Oakland-Berkeley-Alameda Directory, 1923; the Santa Maria (California) City Directory, 1931–32; "Santa Maria Girl Weds Director," *Santa Maria Daily Times*, February 2, 1932; items in *St. Louis Post-Dispatch*, February 3, 1932, and *St. Louis Globe-Democrat*, February 4, 1932; "Frank Capra's Father-in-Law Dies at Age 72" (obituary of Myron Warner), *LAT*, November 29, 1952; Lucille Capra obituary, *DV*, July 3, 1984; Certificate of Death: Lucille Warner Capra, State of California, filed July 3, amended July 5, 1984; Last Will and Testament of Lucille R. Capra, November 25, 1974; and probate documents, estate of Lucille R. Capra, Riverside County, California, 1984–85.

Sources on Barbara Stanwyck include the author's interviews with Capra and Stanwyck; their articles about their working relationship, each titled "Guest Column," in the pressbook for *Meet John Doe*, 1941; Muriel Babcock, " 'Best Performances' Just Players Being Self," *LAT*, August 16, 1931; Glatzer's interview with Capra in Glatzer and Raeburn, *Frank Capra: The Man and His Films*; Ella Smith, *Starring Barbara Stanwyck* (Crown, 1982); Al DiOrio, *Barbara Stanwyck* (Coward-McCann, 1983); and Stanwyck's foreword to *The Light on Her Face*.

Other documentation pertaining to this period: "Fame's Paradox: The Story of Frank Capra"; Budd Schulberg, *Moving Pictures: Memories of a Hollywood Prince* (Stein & Day, 1981); Marguerite Tazelaar, "Failure to Be 'Yes Man' Started Swerling's Career in Hollywood," *NYHT*, April 29, 1934; "Lost and Found: The Films of Frank Capra," *The AFI News*, March 1975; and Neil Hurley, S.J., "An Interview with Frank Capra," *New Orleans Review*, Winter 1981.

Variety reviews quoted include: Sid. (Sidne Silverman), *The Matinee Idol*, April 25, 1928; *So This Is Love*, May 2, 1928; Mark. (Mark Vance), *That Certain Thing*, May 2, 1928; Land. (Robert J. Landry), *Submarine*, September 5, 1928, and *The Donovan Affair*, May 1, 1929; Rush. (Alfred Rushford Grearson), *The Younger Generation*, March 20, 1929; Sime. (Sime Silverman), *Flight*, September 18, 1929; other reviews quoted include: Mordaunt Hall, *Submarine*, August 31, 1928, and *The Donovan Affair*, April 29, 1929, *NYT*; and *Ladies of Leisure*, *Photoplay*, July 1930. *Flight* was discussed by Elliott Stein, "Capra Counts His Oscars," *Sight and Sound*, Summer 1972; and by Gerald Weales, "Frank Capra Against the Sandinistas," *The Nation*, February 16, 1980.

8. "The Man in the Street" (pp. 219–245)

Sources on the Great Depression include Richard Hofstadter, *The American Political Tradition* (Alfred A. Knopf, 1948); Arthur M. Schlesinger, Jr., *The Age of Roosevelt: The Crisis of the Old Order 1919–1933* (Houghton Mifflin, 1956); James MacGregor Burns, *Roosevelt: The Lion and the Fox* (Harcourt, Brace & World, 1956); William E. Leuchtenberg, *Franklin D. Roosevelt and the New Deal 1932–1940* (Harper & Row, 1963); Susan Estabrook Kennedy, *The Banking Crisis of 1933* (University of Kentucky Press, 1973); and Robert S. McElvaine, *The Great Depression: America, 1929–1941* (Times Books, 1984). Capra's contemporaneous observations appeared in Ruth Morris, "Capra Foresees Satirical Cycle; Many Subjects 'Ripe for Ridicule,' " *Variety*, February 2, 1932. He discussed his financial situation in Joseph S. Coyle, "The Smartest Thing I Ever Did Was . . . ," *Money*, July 1979.

Hollywood's economic problems in this era are documented in Hampton, *History of the American Film Industry*; Tino Balio, ed., *The American Film Industry* (University of Wisconsin Press, 1976); and Douglas Gomery, *The Hollywood Studio System* (St. Martin's Press, 1986). The industry's response to political issues raised by events of the Depression era is discussed in Larry Ceplair and Steven Englund, *The Inquisition in Hollywood: Politics in the Film Community 1930–1960* (University of California Press, 1979, and Anchor Press, 1983), and by Nancy Lynn Schwartz in her study of the formation of the Writers Guild and the blacklist era, *The Hollywood Writers' Wars* (completed by Sheila Schwartz; Alfred A. Knopf, 1982). Victor S. Navasky's *Naming Names* (Viking, 1980), though primarily about the blacklist era, also helped give a context for this chapter. The author's interviews with Philip Dunne provided valuable insights into Hollywood politics. All of these sources also were used for the subsequent chapters of the book.

Material on Capra and Columbia in this period, in addition to works cited earlier, includes Elmer G. Dyer, "Up in the Air with the Navy," *American Cinematographer*, October 1930; *Dirigible* publicity book, Columbia, 1931; Hal Hall, "An Interview with Frank Capra," *American Cinematographer*, February 1931; Joseph Walker, "Putting the Realism into *Dirigible*," *American Cinematographer*, August 1931; "Actress Hurt as Horse Gets Unruly," AP, October 5, 1931; Manny Farber, "Capra's Riding High," *The Nation*, June 10, 1950, reprinted in Farber's *Negative Space* (Praeger, 1971); Richard Koszarski, "Lost and Found," *Film Comment*, Spring 1971; and Richard T. Jameson, "Stanwyck & Capra," *Film Comment*, March/April 1981. Capra discussed Jean Harlow in Friedman, *Capra*. Reviews quoted include Mordaunt Hall, *Forbidden*, *NYT*, January 11, 1932, and "Bob Williams Marvelous in Last Picture" (*Platinum Blonde*), *Los Angeles Express*, November 5, 1931. A novelization of *Forbidden* by Arthur Housman, from the screen story by Capra, was published by Grosset & Dunlap, 1932.

The history of AMPAS was drawn in part from its own clipping files and from its official documents, including its files of *The Academy of Motion Picture Arts and Sciences Bulletin*, 1930–33, which contain basic data about membership, activities, labor contracts and codes, and conciliation and arbitration procedures; information obtained through Academy librarian Linda Harris Mehr from the Academy's minutes and additional records; and documents in FCA, including 1931 letters to Capra about his membership from AMPAS officers Fred Niblo and Lester Cowan. Books dealing with AMPAS history include Murray Ross, *Stars and Strikes: Unionization of Hollywood* (Columbia University Press, 1941); Louis B. Perry and Richard S. Perry, *A History of the Los Angeles Labor Movement* (University of California Press, 1963); Pierre Norman Sands, *A Historical Study of the Academy of Motion Picture Arts and Sciences (1927–1947)* (Arno Press, 1966); Ceplair and Englund, *The Inquisition in Hollywood*; Peter H. Brown, *The Real Oscar: The Story Behind the Academy Awards* (Arlington House, 1981); Schwartz, *The Hollywood Writers' Wars*; and Mason Wiley and Damien Bona, *Inside Oscar: The Unofficial History of the Academy Awards* (Ballantine, 1986). Capra's discussions of AMPAS and Hollywood labor issues in interviews with the author were useful, if somewhat evasive, as were his comments in David Robb, "Directors Guild Born Out of Fear 50 Years Ago," *DV*, October 29, 1985.

Robert Riskin's papers in the Fay Wray Collection at USC are the starting point for research on the life and work of Capra's most important screenwriter. Those interviewed on Riskin included his widow, Wray; his brother, Murray Riskin; Dunne; Thomas M. Pryor; Walker; Chester Sticht; and Keller. Wray wrote of him in her monograph *Biography of Robert Riskin as Screenwriter* and in her memoir *On the Other Hand: A Life Story* (St. Martin's Press, 1989). Riskin's account of his role in the formation of the Screen Writers Guild, "I Was Going Along Minding My Own Business," appeared in *HR*, May 7, 1936. The support of the SWG in 1938 by Capra and Riskin is acknowledged in three telegrams from Dudley Nichols to Capra, June 27 and 29, 1938 (FCA). Further information on the SWG is from Philip Dunne, *Take Two: A Life in Movies and Politics* (McGraw-Hill, 1980), and Todd McCarthy and Joseph McBride, "Bombshell Days in the Golden Age: John Lee Mahin Interviewed," *Film Comment*, March/April 1980, reprinted in Pat McGilligan, ed., *Backstory: Interviews with Screenwriters of Hollywood's Golden Age* (University of California Press, 1986).

Riskin's complaint that "so little is known" of the screenwriter's contribution is from an interview by Janet White, "Seeing Pictures," *Brooklyn Times and Union*, April 11, 1937. Other articles on Riskin which were useful for this and subsequent chapters include Dudley Early, "Mr. Capra and Mr. Riskin Go to Town," *Family Circle*, October 23, 1936; "Variations on a Theme," *New York American*, April 4, 1937; John T. McManus, "Sunny Spain for Mr. Riskin," *NYT*, April 11, 1937; G. Alexandrov and V. Nilsen, "How American Films Are Made," *Izvestia* (Moscow), May 16, 1937 (interview with Capra and Riskin, original and English translation by Robert S. Carr in FWC); Theodore Strauss, "Mr. Riskin Hits the Road," *NYT*, January 26, 1941; Jerry D. Lewis, "Top Story Man," *Collier's*, March 29, 1941; " 'He Looks Like a Mug,' Thought Riskin When He Met Capra, But They're Partners Now," *Washington Post*, May 25, 1941; David W. Rintels, "Someone's Been Sitting in His Chair," June 5, 1977, and " 'Someone Else's Guts'—The Rintels Rebuttal," *LAT*, June 26, 1977; Capra, " 'One Man, One Film'—The Capra Contention," *LAT*, June 26, 1977; and Sam Frank, "Robert Riskin" in Robert E. Morsberger, Stephen O. Lesser, and Randall Clark, eds., *Dictionary of Literary Biography, Vol. 26: American Screenwriters* (Gale Research Co., 1984). Sidney Buchman's comments on Capra and Riskin appeared in Bertrand Tavernier, "Sidney Buchman," *Positif*, June 1969.

Myles Connolly's novel *Mr. Blue* was published in 1928 by Macmillan. His work on the scripts of *Mr. Smith Goes to Washington* and *Meet John Doe* was acknowledged in "Screen Achievement Records Bulletin: Writers Cumulated Bulletin," AMPAS, 1939–1943, and was mentioned in his agent Bill Schiffrin's letter "Cross Fire on the Director-Writer Front," *LAT*, July 10, 1977, along with his contributions to *Lost Horizon, Mr. Deeds Goes to Town, State of the Union*, and *A Hole in the Head* (but not his work on *Here Comes the Groom* and *Pocketful of Miracles*).

Sources on Capra, Cohn, and Mussolini include the author's interviews with Eugene De Rue and Mahin; Thomas, *King Cohn*, and notes of his interview with Columbia's Harry Foster (on Capra's involvement with *Mussolini Speaks*) (BTP); "Director Capra to Visit Il Duce," *Atlanta American*, February 7, 1932; Andre Sennwald, *Mussolini Speaks* review, *NYT*, March 13, 1933; item on Ethiopia ban of Capra films, *New York Telegraph*, October 10, 1935; item on Mussolini film proposal in *Illustrated Daily News*, London, November 14, 1935; and Hellman, "Thinker in Hollywood."

Documents on Capra's February 29, 1932, revision of his Columbia contract are in FCA. Articles on Capra's European vacation, marriage to Lucille Reyburn, and honeymoon included: "Frank Capra Here for First Vacation in Several Years," *New York Mirror*, December 24, 1931; "Capra Back from Europe," *Brooklyn Standard Union*, January 23, 1932; Irene Thirer, "Frank Capra Bridegroom Today," *New York Daily News*, January 28, 1932; "F. R. Capra Weds Mrs. L. W. Reyburn," *Brooklyn Standard Union*, February 2, 1932; and "Picture Standards Lower This Year," *Montreal Gazette*, February 8, 1932. G. F. (Doc) Harris's letter to Capra, December 21, 1932, is in FCA. Benny Rubin recalled the Capras' honeymoon in Scherle and Levy, *The Films of Frank Capra*. Information on Dr. Robert Walter Brown is from the Santa Maria Historical Society; Boyd Stephens, *Who's Who in Santa Maria* (1931); and Vada F. Carlson, *This Is Our Valley* (Westernlore Press, 1959).

9. American Madness (pp. 247–288)

Sources on the Great Depression, Hollywood politics, the AMPAS, Columbia Pictures, and Robert Riskin used for the last chapter provided background for this chapter as well. I also am indebted, not only here but throughout this book, to Richard Hofstadter's *The American Political Tradition, The Age of Reform* (Alfred A. Knopf, 1955), and *The Paranoid Style in American Politics and Other Essays* (Alfred A. Knopf, 1965). Additional background for this period was supplied by Arthur M. Schlesinger, Jr., *The Age of Roosevelt: Vol. 2, The Coming of the New Deal* (Houghton Mifflin, 1959) and Kenneth S. Davis, *FDR: The New York Years 1928–1933* (Random House, 1985).

The official history of the Gianninis and the Bank of America is Marquis James and Bessie Rowland James, *Biography of a Bank: The Story of Bank of America N.T. & S.A.* (Harper, 1954). Riskin's decision to model the banker hero of *American Madness* (aka *Faith*) on A. H. Giannini was reported in Lewis, "Top Story Man"; Capra's claim that the model was A. P. Giannini was made in his 1973 interview with Glatzer in Glatzer and Raeburn, *Frank Capra: The Man and His Films*. His latter-day claims about coauthorship of the story are in *NAT*; the Glatzer interview; and Schickel, *The Men Who Made the Movies*. Those who discussed Hollywood politics and Capra's politics for this chapter included Capra, Edward Bernds (whose diaries for 1935–39 also were used), Dunne, Julius J. Epstein, Coleen Gray, Albert Hackett, Katharine Hepburn, John Huston, Samuel Marx, Pryor, Leonard Spigelgass, and Chester Sticht. Information on the founding of the Screen Directors Guild was provided by the author's interview with the last surviving SDG founder, Rouben Mamoulian, who died in 1987; the files of the SDG/DGA (1935–1985), including the guild's list of its founders, "The Original Twelve" (n.d.), Capra's application for membership (August 8, 1937), and "The Screen Directors Guild of America: Its Origin and Development" (1952); Mitch Tuchman's unpublished 1977 interview with King Vidor; and Robb, "Directors Guild Born Out of Fear 50 Years Ago."

Articles on AMPAS issues, including the 1933 pay cut controversy, and

Hollywood labor unrest, include: "The Talk of Hollywood," *Hollywood Herald,* January 7, 1933; "Academy Trying to Revive Producer Pact Dying in Guerrilla Warfare," *DV,* February 24, 1933; "Permanent Studio Pay Cuts Loom," *LAT,* March 5, 1933; "Studios to Shut Doors Unless Pay Cut Taken," *LAT,* March 8, 1933; "Film Academy Group Urges Code Changes," *LAE,* August 25, 1933; and Ralph Block, "Block Calls Academy Producers' 'Creature,' " *Motion Picture Herald,* June 8, 1935. See also Jack L. Warner, *My First Hundred Years in Hollywood* (Random House, 1964) and Mosley, *Zanuck: The Rise and Fall of Hollywood's Last Tycoon.* The Cagney arbitration is discussed in "Academy Insisting on WB-Cagney Mediation as Obligation to Industry," *Variety,* September 13, 1932; James Cagney, *Cagney by Cagney* (Doubleday, 1976); and Patrick McGilligan, *Cagney: The Actor as Auteur* (A. S. Barnes, 1982).

Capra's clearest public statement of his political views was in his letter to Lee Mortimer, April 26, 1948, published in part in Mortimer, "Capra Defends His *State of the Union,*" n.d. (1948), replying to Mortimer's column, "*State of the Union* is Mostly Anti," *New York Daily Mirror,* n.d. (1948) (copies of letter and columns in FCA). Capra's admiration for Franco was reported by Spigelgass and for Napoleon by Sidney Skolsky in his February 27, 1934, column. Sources on Capra's voting record include the author's interviews with Capra and Sticht; Capra's Security Board File, submitted to the Army-Navy-Air Force Personnel Security Board, December 29, 1951 (FCA); Capra's diary, November 7, 1972; "A Weekend with Frank Capra and His Films"; Capra to President Ford, August 12, 1974; and Frank and Lu Capra telegram to President-Elect Ronald and Nancy Reagan, November 5, 1980. Capra's reading of Karl Marx was reported in *NAT* uncut. Army Intelligence reports on Capra quoted in this chapter are 1st Lt. Philip J. Lombardi, "Agent Report," July 20, 1951; Yoshio G. Kanegai, "Agent Report," August 24, 1951; and "Summary of Information," G-2, October 10, 1951 (Army Intelligence file). MGM's dropping of *Soviet* for political reasons was reported in "Capra Returns to Col., *Soviet* Again Shelved," *Variety,* February 28, 1933. Capra's politics also were discussed in Raymond Durgnat, *The Crazy Mirror: Hollywood Comedy and the American Image* (Horizon Press, 1969); Elliott Stein's article on Capra in Richard Roud, ed., *Cinema: A Critical Dictionary* (Viking, 1980); Margaret Case Harriman, "Mr. and Mrs. Frank Capra," *The Ladies' Home Journal,* April 1941; McBride, "Frank Capra Sees Emerging Sense of Comedy & Idealism Among Student Filmmakers"; John F. Mariani, "Frank Capra," *Focus on Film,* No. 27, 1977; and Karp, "The Patriotism of Frank Capra." Capra's remark on the autobiographical nature of his films is from "Director's Choice," the transcript of a November 2, 1968, AMPAS seminar on *It's a Wonderful Life,* reprinted in Basinger, *The "It's a Wonderful Life" Book.*

The Capras' marriage was discussed in Schulberg, *Moving Pictures;* Capra, "Frank Capra Tells All," *NYT,* December 16, 1934; Stuart, "Fine Italian Hand"; "Columbia's Gem"; Carol Frink, "Frank Capra's Top Interest Is Children, Not Pictures," *Washington Times-Herald,* October 17, 1939; Harriman, "Mr. and Mrs. Capra"; G. A. Rolsnaag, "Noted Film Director Capra Charms DVC and Concord High School Movie Buffs," unidentified newspaper, October 17, 1972

(FCA); and Gloria Greer, "LQ Honors Favorite Son Frank Capra," *Rancho Mirage Chronicle* (California), March 18, 1982. Lucille Capra Bruch's comment on her mother was made in a radio interview with Faye Chessler, "Lulu Bruch Interview" (KWED, Seguin, Texas, 1972) (audio tape in FCA).

In addition to interviews previously cited, sources on Capra's relationship with his crew include Harrison Forman, "The Hollywood Star You Never See on the Screen," *Liberty*, April 10, 1937; "How Frank Capra Makes a Hit Picture," *Life*, September 19, 1938; and Henstell, *Frank Capra: "One Man—One Film."* The anecdote about Cohn's trick chair is from Dore Schary, *Heyday* (Little, Brown, 1979). Cohn's comment about Capra to Virginia Van Upp is from Thomas's interview notes (BTP), as is the Harry Foster story about the cutting of *Lady for a Day*. The June 6, 1935, Columbia-Capra Agreement is in FCA. Sidney Skolsky's description of Capra as "a big frog in a small puddle" is from his February 6, 1934, column. The joking use of ethnic names by Capra and Riskin was reported in Hellman, "Thinker in Hollywood."

Edward Bernds's comments on the making of *American Madness* are from an interview with the author and from Bernds's "Dear Frank Capra" letter, *Film Fan Monthly*, October 1971; Walker's comments are from interviews with the author and with Bob Thomas (BTP). An item in *Variety*, July 25, 1933, reported that the title *American Madness* was suggested by Harry Rapf. The *Milwaukee Sentinel* editorial on the film, n.d. (August 1932), was found in FWC; also quoted are reviews by William Boehnel, *NYWT*, August 5, 1932, and Abel. (Abel Green), *Variety*, August 9, 1932. *The Bitter Tea of General Yen* was based on the novel by Grace Zaring Stone (Bobbs-Merrill, 1930). Information on Radio City Music Hall and the opening of *Bitter Tea* is from coverage in *Variety*, December 20, 1932–January 24, 1933, and from Ronald Haver, *David O. Selznick's Hollywood* (Alfred A. Knopf, 1980). *Variety*'s review of the film by Shan. (Sam Shain), appeared on January 17, 1933. The fact that it was passed by the British Board of Censors was reported by Wolfe, *Frank Capra: A Guide to References and Resources;* see also "Talkie Insult to White Australia," *Truth*, Sydney, n.d. (c. February 1933) (FCA).

Sources on *Soviet* include Capra's comments from Glatzer's interview in Glatzer and Raeburn, *Frank Capra: The Man and His Films;* the author's interview with Marx, and Marx, *Mayer and Thalberg: The Make-Believe Saints* (Random House, 1975); Thomas's notes of his interview with Sam Briskin (BTP); various *Variety*, *HR*, and *LAT* articles, October 18, 1932–April 30, 1933; Sidney Skolsky column, March 2, 1935; and Johnston, "Capra Shoots as He Pleases." The story of Capra worrying over *Lady for a Day* is from Thomas's notes of an interview with Sidney Buchman (BTP); see also Thomas, *King Cohn.*

10. *"The catastrophe of Success"* (pp. 289–326)

The chapter title is from Tennessee Williams, "On a Streetcar Named Success," *NYT*, November 30, 1947.

Damon Runyon's story "Madame La Gimp" (source of *Lady for a Day*) was first published in *Cosmopolitan*, October 1929, and was reprinted in Runyon's *Guys and Dolls* (Frederick A. Stokes, 1931) and *The Bloodhounds of Broadway and Other Stories* (William Morrow, 1981). FCA has a copy of the agreement between Runyon and Columbia, September 19, 1932, for the sale of film rights. Runyon's September 8, 1933, telegram to Robert Riskin is in FWC; his public comments on *Lady for a Day* are from an untitled item in the *Dayton Journal* (Ohio), February 24, 1935 (FWC). The source of *It Happened One Night,* the story "Night Bus" by Samuel Hopkins Adams, was published in *Cosmopolitan,* August 1933, and was reprinted in William Kittredge and Steven M. Krauzer, eds., *Stories into Film* (Harper & Row, 1979). Eric Knight's story "The Flying Yorkshireman," which Capra purchased for filming, first appeared in *Story,* July 1937, and was reprinted in Knight, *The Flying Yorkshireman Novellas* (Harper, 1938).

Sources previously cited on Riskin were used again for this chapter. Additional articles pertinent to his working relationship with Capra and to the authorship issue include Sidney Skolsky column, February 6, 1934; W. R. Wilkerson, "Trade Views," *HR,* February 16, 1934; "Story's Thing, Says Cohn," *New York Telegraph,* March 19, 1934; Bland Johaneson, "All Films Are Miracles, Says Riskin," *New York Mirror,* May 24, 1934; Eileen Creelman, "Frank Capra, Director of Two of the Year's Biggest Hits, Talks of His Work," *New York Sun,* n.d. (September 1934) (FCA); Capra, "Frank Capra Tells All"; "Line of Attack All Important in Screen Work," *Columbus Dispatch* (Ohio), April 20, 1936; Riskin, "Has No Fixed Rules for Writing Scenarios," *Cincinnati Times-Star,* July 31, 1936; Rose Pelswick, "Famous Writer, Europe Bound, Bares Woes in Making Film," *New York Journal,* April 1, 1937; Riskin, "Meet the Creators of *John Doe,* Meet John Doe Himself," *Click,* March 1941. The origin of the story about Riskin and "The Capra Touch" was reported in Tom Stempel, *Framework: A History of Screenwriting in the American Film* (Continuum, 1988).

Capra's comments on his process of "constant collaboration" with Riskin were made to Sam Thomas's UCLA class on "The Literature of the Screen" and were quoted by Thomas in his *Best American Screenplays,* First Series. Capra's July 5 and October 6, 1977, letters to Charles Champlin of *LAT* regarding David W. Rintels's *LAT* articles on the Riskin-Capra controversy are in FCA. Capra's discussion of the scripts of *Broadway Bill* and *Riding High,* and his relationship with Riskin and other writers, is in his letter of July 25, 1949, to Alice Penneman of the SWG (FCA). Buchman's remarks on Riskin and Capra are from Thomas's interview notes (BTP) and from Tavernier, "Sidney Buchman." Capra's claim about letting actors run away with scripts is from Henstell, *Frank Capra: "One Man—One Film."* For background on the *auteur* theory, see François Truffaut, "Une certaine tendance du cinéma français," *Cahiers du Cinéma,* January 1954; André Bazin, "De la politique des auteurs," *Cahiers,* April 1957; Andrew Sarris, *The American Cinema: Directors and Directions, 1929–1968* (E. P. Dutton, 1968) and John Caughie, ed., *Theories of Authorship: A Reader* (British Film Institute, 1981).

John Ford listed *Lady for a Day* among his ten favorite films in a 1964 list for *Cinema* magazine, cited by Tag Gallagher in *John Ford: The Man and His Films* (University of California Press, 1986). Steven Handzo commented on the Capra-Riskin blend of sentiment and sarcasm in "Under Capracorn," *Film Comment,*

November 1972, reprinted in Glatzer and Raeburn, *Frank Capra: The Man and His Films.* The loss of the negative of *Lady for a Day* was discussed in Capra's diary for June 3, 1974, and in "Lost and Found: The Films of Frank Capra." The production cost is from Thomas, *King Cohn,* and the film rentals are listed in an audit of Columbia Pictures for Capra, c. 1940 (FCA).

Riskin told Philip K. Scheuer about the decision to make *It Happened One Night* in "Film Academy Awards Don't Prove a Thing, Says Riskin," *LAT,* March 10, 1935. Capra denied to the author that *It Happened One Night* was written for Robert Montgomery, but he said so in his 1934 interview with Creelman, and to Michael Mok in "Mr. Capra Comes to Town," *New York Post,* October 24, 1939; Riskin also said so in his 1936 article "Has No Fixed Rules for Writing Scenarios." Other sources on *It Happened One Night* include: Whitney Stine and Bette Davis, *Mother Goddam: The Story of the Career of Bette Davis* (Hawthorne, 1974); Larry Swindell, *Screwball: The Life of Carole Lombard* (William Morrow, 1975); Walker and Walker, *The Light on Her Face;* James Kotsilibas-Davis and Myrna Loy, *Myrna Loy: Being and Becoming* (Alfred A. Knopf, 1987); "Gable Goes Columbia," *The Ace in the Hole* (Columbia publication for exhibitors), November 22, 1933; William Boehnel review, *NYWT,* February 23, 1934; Sidney Skolsky columns, February 6, 1934, and March 2, 1935; coverage in *Variety,* February 27–March 27, 1934; and Robert Stebbins, "Mr. Capra Goes to Town," *New Theatre,* May 1936, reprinted in Glatzer and Raeburn, *Frank Capra: The Man and His Films.* See also Capra's comments on screen eroticism in his article "What Is Smut Worth?," *HR,* May 31, 1934.

Some of the quotes from Joseph Walker and Claudette Colbert are from Thomas's interview notes (BTP); Gable's comment to Colbert about Capra is from Thomas, *King Cohn;* also quoted are Colbert's remarks on *The American Film Institute Salute to Frank Capra* (1982). Capra discussed love scenes in Henstell, *Frank Capra: "One Man—One Film,"* and letting the audience "just look at your people" in the Glatzer interview in Glatzer and Raeburn, *Frank Capra: The Man and His Films.* Rentals for *It Happened One Night* and the comparison with *Lady for a Day* are from the audit of Columbia Pictures for Capra, c. 1940 (FCA).

Articles on the 1934 Academy Awards include "Best Bets for Academy Prize," *Variety,* March 13, 1934; AP item, March 17, 1934; Elizabeth Yeaman, "Scrupulous Honesty Marks Movie Awards," *Hollywood Citizen-News,* March 17, 1934; and Edwin Schallert column, *LAT,* March 19, 1934.

The birth of Frank Warner Capra (aka Frank Capra, Jr.) was reported on March 21, 1934, in "Boy Born to Frank Capras," *LAT,* and by the AP. The birth of John Capra was reported on April 25, 1935, in "Frank Capras Parents of Son," *LAT,* and by the AP. Frank and Lucille Capra's April 26, 1935, telegram to Albertina and Dimitri Tiomkin about John's birth is in FCA. Sources on John's medical history are listed in the notes for chapter 13.

Information on Paul H. (Scoop) Conlon is from Sticht; McCallum, *Scooper; Motion Picture Almanac,* 1935–36; and Conlon's obituary in *Variety,* February 8, 1961. Myles Connolly's remarks on Capra appeared in W. R. Wilkerson, "TradeViews," *HR,* March 2, 1934. Jim Tully's are from his article "Frank Capra," *Rob Wagner's Script,* March 3, 1934. Capra's 1982 comments on the

Oscar are in Robert Lindsey, "Oscars Make and Break Careers," *NYT*, March 28, 1982. The "impostor phenomenon" was described in Daniel Goleman, "Therapists Find Many Achievers Fear They Are Fakes," *NYT*, September 11, 1984.

Otis Ferguson's review of *Broadway Bill*, "It Happened Once More," appeared in *The New Republic* on December 19, 1934, and was reprinted in Glatzer and Raeburn, *Frank Capra: The Man and His Films;* Capra discussed the film in Larry Swindell, "Frank Capra: Canonized by Film Cultists," *Philadelphia Inquirer*, May 4, 1978. Capra's letter to Albert Lewin, January 18, 1935, is in Lewin's papers at USC. The new scenes written by Buchman are included as a four-page insert in Capra's working script (FCA); see also Thomas, *King Cohn;* Tavernier, "Sidney Buchman"; Capra to Penneman; and Thomas's notes of interviews with Buchman (BTP). Manny Farber's criticisms are from "Capra's Riding High."

Capra's 1934–35 illness was discussed with the author by Capra, Chester Sticht, Joe Finochio, and Josephine Campisi. It was reported in *HR*, November 12–December 17, 1934, and *DV*, November 13–December 14 (including the front-page report that he had been "seriously ill," in "Frank Capra Is Back in Cedars Hospital," December 3); "No Change in Frank Capra's State," *HCN*, December 10; "Capra Back to Studios," *Newark Call*, February 3, 1935; items in *Variety*, March 27 and April 10, 1935; an item in *DV*, April 4, 1935; Stuart, "Fine Italian Hand"; Boehnel, "Movie Fans to Gain by Capra's Return," *NYWT*, November 30, 1937; and Hellman, "Thinker in Hollywood." Capra told friends about his condition in various telegrams, December 10 and 24, 1934, and in a letter to Osman Wheatley, April 22, 1935 (FCA). He first rehearsed the "little man" story in Friedman, *Capra*. His comment to Philip K. Scheuer is from "Public Doesn't Want to Think, Says Capra," *LAT*, June 3, 1934. Myles Connolly's letter to Capra about St. Francis of Assisi, n.d. (mid-1930s), is in FCA.

Colbert's conversation with LeRoy Johnston prior to the 1935 Academy Awards was reported in Eleanor Barnes, "Colbert and Gable Win Movie Awards," the *Los Angeles Daily News*, February 28, 1935; Gable's remarks are from newsreel footage in *The American Film Institute Salute to Frank Capra* (1982); Cohn's acceptance speech was quoted by Sidney Skolsky in his March 2, 1935, column. Riskin's use of his Oscar as a doorstop was mentioned by Everett Riskin in Thomas's interview notes (BTP).

11. *"A sense of responsibility"* (pp. 327–350)

Previously listed sources on the formation of the SDG and on the history of AMPAS were used again for this chapter. Financial records of Columbia Pictures pertinent to this chapter include copies of Capra's profit participation statements; computer printouts of financial information on his films, and other data (1935–85); and "Contract Abstract: Frank Capra" (1935). Records from FCA include his June 6, 1935, contract with Columbia; budget breakdowns for *Mr. Deeds Goes to Town, You Can't Take It With You*, and *Mr. Smith Goes to Washington;* an audit of *You Can't Take It With You* for Capra, n.d. (c. 1940); the audit of Columbia Pictures for Capra (c. 1940); and Mabel Walker Willebrandt to William C. Miller of Price Waterhouse, June 3, 1960.

Capra mentioned his interest in directing Grace Moore in Creelman, "Frank Capra, Director of Two of the Year's Biggest Hits, Talks of His Work." Sources on his *Valley Forge* project include "*Valley Forge* for Col., Capra to Direct," *HR*, January 25, 1935; Betty Hynes, "Why Director Capra Is Termed a Genius," *Washington Herald*, October 13, 1938; Vernon Scott, UPI, November 27, 1971; and McBride, "Frank Capra Sees Emerging Sense of Comedy & Idealism Among Student Filmmakers"; and documents pertaining to Paul Horgan (1961–62) in FCA. Capra discussed his *Crime and Punishment* and *Anna Karenina* projects in *NAT* and "Frank Capra Projects," *Variety*, July 11, 1962. Edwin Schallert's column in *LAT*, November 12, 1938, reported on Capra's continuing desire to make a film of *Pagliacci*, which was discussed in Capra's telegram to Harry Cohn, July 9, 1935, and Cohn's telegram to Capra, July 10, 1935 (FCA). Information about Capra beginning work on *Lost Horizon* in 1935 is from "About the Author" in the Pocket Books edition (1939) of James Hilton's *Lost Horizon*, previously published by William Morrow, 1933; *The Making of a Great Picture*; Capra's telegram to Gene Lewis, June 4, 1935; "*Opera Hat* Replaces *Horizon* for Capra," *HR*, July 1, 1935; Capra, "Sacred Cows to the Slaughter," *Stage*, July 1936; and Early, "Mr. Capra and Mr. Riskin Go to Town."

Clarence Budington Kelland's story "Opera Hat," the basis for *Mr. Deeds Goes to Town*, was published as a serial in six installments in *The American Magazine*, April–September 1935 (which billed it as a "novel"). Descriptions of political aspects of *Mr. Deeds:* ("a genuine"), Leif Furhammar and Folke Isaksson, *Politics and Film* (Studio Vista, 1971); ("boosting"), George L. David, "*Mr. Deeds* Hinted as Cinema That Has Radical Strain," *Rochester Democrat Chronicle* (New York), October 18, 1936, quoting an unidentified writer in the English periodical *Cavalcade*; ("quasi-communistic"), Abel. (Abel Green) in his *Variety* review, April 22, 1936; ("a kind of Roosevelt"), Georges Sadoul, quoted in Willis, *The Films of Frank Capra*; and ("propaganda"), Durgnat, *The Crazy Mirror: Hollywood Comedy and the American Image*. The popularity of *Mr. Deeds* in the Soviet Union was reported in Johnston, "Capra Shoots as He Pleases"; see also the notes for chapter 19.

Capra discussed his finances in Coyle, "The Smartest Thing I Ever Did Was . . ." A UP dispatch of September 17, 1938, reported that Capra wrote in an SDG questionnaire that his income for the year was nearly $1 million; the figure was confirmed to the author by Sticht. Capra's claim that he "never asked for a penny" is from Thomas's interview notes (BTP). Sticht reported Capra's profit percentages on *Lady for a Day* and *It Happened One Night*. Profits earned by Capra for *Mr. Deeds, Lost Horizon, You Can't Take It With You*, and *Mr. Smith* are from records of Columbia Pictures. The June 6, 1935, Columbia-Capra Agreement is in FCA. Sources on Capra's settlement with Columbia (November 24, 1937) include Sticht and Charles E. Millikan to Louis E. Swarts, February 24, 1947 (FCA). A confidential source at Columbia reported that Capra was the only filmmaker of the 1930s to be earning continued profits from the studio as of 1985.

Information on Capra's Brentwood home is from Sticht and from coverage of Capra's land purchases in *LAE, LAT, HR*, and *Los Angeles Herald-Express*, February 1935–December 1938, and "Frank Capra's Estate Sold," *LAE*, September 16, 1951. The author viewed a 16mm color home movie, *Xmas '36—Brentwood*, which Capra made in 1936 of his house being constructed (FCA).

Capra's rare book collection is described in *The Distinguished Library of Frank Capra* and related documents (1935 and 1949) in FCA. See also Stuart, "Fine Italian Hand," and Early, "Mr. Capra and Mr. Riskin Go to Town."

The 1936 series of articles by Capra includes "A Sick Dog Tells Where It Hurts," *Esquire*, January; "Mr. Capra (Humanist) Shares a Bow," *NYT*, April 19; and "Sacred Cows to the Slaughter," *Stage*, July 1936.

Additional data on the formation of the SDG are from coverage in *DV* and *HR*, January 17–25, 1935, and from SDG documents, including "Articles of Incorporation of SDG, Inc.," January 18, 1936. Capra's boast about his anti-Communist stance in the guild is in his letter to John Ford, December 19, 1951 (FCA).

Capra's claim that AMPAS was down to only forty members was made to the author and in *NAT*; Sands's figure of 400 is from his *A Historical Study of the Academy of Motion Picture Arts and Sciences (1927–1947)*; see also Philip K. Scheuer, "Who Votes on Awards Given by Academy?," *LAT*, February 16, 1936, and Sidney Skolsky column, March 5, 1937.

Other coverage of 1936–37 AMPAS issues appeared in numerous articles in *LAT*, *HCN*, *LAE*, *Variety*, *DV*, *HR*, *Motion Picture Daily*, AP, and *The New York Morning Telegraph*. The text of Dudley Nichols's letter to AMPAS appeared in *HR*, March 9, 1936; Capra's reply was in "Acad. Mummifies Statuette, Capra Speaks O'er the Tomb," *DV*, March 10, 1936. The Jessel-Capra banter on Capra's second Oscar was quoted in "Rainer, Muni Gain Film Academy Awards," unidentified newspaper, March 5, 1937 (AMPAS).

Mr. Deeds was reported to be Riskin's favorite film in the 1941 article " 'He Looks Like a Mug,' Thought Riskin When He Met Capra, But They're Partners Now." President Reagan's quoting of *Mr. Deeds* is from his "Remarks at the Annual Meeting of the National Alliance of Business," October 5, 1981, Presidential Paper No. 881; the speech was featured on *60 Minutes* (CBS-TV, December 15, 1985), in a segment demonstrating Reagan's reliance on movie metaphors. Carole Lombard's turndowns of *Mr. Deeds* and Riskin were reported in Capra to Lombard, December 10, 1935 (FCA), and Swindell, *Screwball: The Life of Carole Lombard*. Background on Jean Arthur is from the author's interviews with Arthur and Capra; *NYT* articles by Judy Stone, "Jean Arthur: Still After Laughter," September 11, 1966; Guy Flatley, "From Mr. Deeds Goes to Town to Miss Arthur Goes to Vassar," May 14, 1972, and "When Jean Arthur Was the Gem of Columbia's Ocean," January 28, 1977; and John Springer et al., "Jean Arthur: Great Star as Great Lady," *Interview*, June 1972. George Stevens's comment on Arthur is from a 1974 interview by Patrick McGilligan and the author, parts of which appeared as "A Piece of the Rock: George Stevens," *Bright Lights*, no. 8, 1979. See also Hurley, "An Interview with Frank Capra," and Arthur Pierce and Douglas Swarthout, *Jean Arthur: A Bio-Bibliography* (Greenwood Press, 1990). The discussion of short men on the set of *Mr. Deeds* is from Edward Bernds's diary, January 24, 1936. Pauline Kael's criticism of Capra is from her collection *Deeper into Movies* (Little, Brown, 1973).

The *Izvestia* interview with Capra and Riskin is Alexandrov and Nilsen, "How American Films Are Made," with English translation by *Izvestia*'s Robert S. Carr (FWC). Bernds's comments on "The Capra method" are from his diaries, December 14 and 19, 1935, and January 8, 1936. Sources on Capra's growing reputation for extravagance include the author's interviews with Bernds, Alfred S. Keller, and Sticht; Ralph Wilk, item in *Film Daily*, February 19, 1936; budget breakdowns and other financial data for various Capra films; and Bernds's diaries (1935–39). Film rental figures for *Mr. Deeds* are from the audit of *You Can't Take It With You* and Columbia financial records. Walker's comment on Columbia accounting is from Thomas's interview notes (BTP).

The April 17, 1936, New York reviews of *Mr. Deeds* quoted include those by Frank S. Nugent, *NYT*; Bland Johaneson, *Daily Mirror*; and Kate Cameron, *Daily News*. See also the reviews by *The New York American*, n.d. (April 1936) (FWC); Robert Stebbins, "Mr. Capra Goes to Town," *New Theatre*, May 1936; and Paul Holt, *Daily Express* (London), September 1, 1936. Graham Greene's review in *The Spectator* (London), August 28, 1936, is reprinted in Glatzer and Raeburn, *Frank Capra: The Man and His Films*. Alistair Cooke's review was printed in Cooke, ed., *Garbo and the Night Watchmen* (Jonathan Cape, 1937; McGraw-Hill, 1971).

12. *"The doghouse"* (pp. 351–374)

Primary sources on *Lost Horizon* include the author's interviews with Capra and Sticht; with seven others who worked on the film: Bernds, Finochio, Sam Jaffe, Keller, Irving (Buster) Libott, Gene Milford, and Walker; and with Robert Gitt, who supervised the 1973–86 restoration of the film for the American Film Institute. Also used for this chapter were Tavernier's interview "Sidney Buchman"; Brownlow's interview with Stephen Goossón; Peter Bogdanovich's oral history *Leo McCarey* (AFI, Beverly Hills, 1968–69); and Bob Thomas's notes of his interviews with Capra, Buchman, McCarey, Frances Marion, Lewis Meltzer, Everett Riskin, and Lou Smith (BTP).

Principal documentation on the making of *Lost Horizon* and its aftermath also includes the novel by James Hilton (1933); Robert Riskin's final draft screenplay, March 23, 1936, with subsequent revisions (FCA); Bernds's diaries for 1936–38; Capra's 1936 article "Sacred Cows to the Slaughter"; the 1937 interview with Capra and Riskin by Alexandrov and Nilsen in *Izvestia*, "How American Films Are Made"; Columbia's *The Making of a Great Picture*, which includes a plot summary of the first public preview version; Dimitri Tiomkin and Prosper Buranelli, *Please Don't Hate Me* (Doubleday, 1959); Thomas, *King Cohn*; Walker and Walker, *The Light on Her Face*; Columbia financial records, also including "Summary of Income and Profits (1937–1946)" in a 1947 Columbia legal brief (BTP); and William H. Rosar, *"Lost Horizon:* An Account of the Composition of the Score," *Filmmusic Notebook*, vol. IV, 1978. Capra's contrasting later views of the film are from Schickel, *The Men Who Made the Movies*, and from Friedman, *Capra*. Franklin D. Roosevelt's remark about Shangri-La is from his press conference of April 21, 1942, in *Complete Presidential Press Conferences of Franklin D. Roosevelt*, vol. 19 (Da Capo, 1972).

Articles with information on *Lost Horizon*, and reviews, include W. R. Wilkerson, "TradeViews," *HR*, June 15, 1936; Eileen Creelman, "Picture Plays and Players," *New York Sun*, July 24, 1936; and April 22, 1937; "*Lost Horizon* Great: Triumph of Unlimited Appeal," *HR*, February 20, 1937; "Apologia for Gloria," *NYT*, February 28, 1937; Otis Ferguson, "Capra and Tibet," *National Board of Review Magazine*, March 1937; Frank S. Nugent, "Scanning *Lost Horizon*," *NYT*, March 7, 1937; Pelswick, "Famous Writer, Europe Bound, Bares Woes in Making Film"; "Bob Riskin Muses on *Lost Horizon* and Wisecracking to a B'way Chorine," *Variety*, April 7, 1937; McManus, "Sunny Spain for Mr. Riskin"; White, "Seeing Pictures"; Graham Greene's review in *The Spectator*, April 30, 1937, reprinted in Glatzer and Raeburn, *Frank Capra: The Man and His Films*; Sam Frank, "*Lost Horizon*—A Timeless Journey," *American Cinematographer*, April 1986; and Stephen Farber, "A *Lost Horizon* Film with Most Cuts Restored," *NYT*, September 3, 1986. The Santa Barbara preview of *Lost Horizon* was advertised (without the title) by the Granada Theatre in the *Santa Barbara Sunday Daily News-Morning Press*, November 22, 1936. Differing views on colorizing *Lost Horizon* were expressed by Frank Capra, Jr., in "Capra Jr. Says Father Wanted *Lost* in Color," *DV*, November 19, 1986, and by Capra Sr. in his appearance at the Palm Springs Desert Museum on January 9, 1985 (recorded by the author).

Sources on the split between Riskin and Capra include the author's interviews with Capra, Murray Riskin, and Fay Wray; Thomas's notes of interviews with Buchman and Everett Riskin (BTP); Cameron Shipp column, unidentified source, June 18, 1936 (FWC); McManus, "Sunny Spain for Mr. Riskin"; White, "Seeing Pictures"; Tavernier, "Sidney Buchman"; and Wray, *Biography of Robert Riskin as Screenwriter*. Myles Connolly's contribution to the script of *Lost Horizon* was cited in Shiffrin, "Cross Fire on the Director-Writer Front"; Herbert Biberman's contribution is mentioned in an undated (1936) letter to his mother (Biberman and Sondergaard Papers, State Historical Society of Wisconsin).

David O. Selznick's comments on the cutting of *Lost Horizon* are from his lecture "The Functions of the Producer and the Making of Feature Films," November 1, 1937, in *Memo from David O. Selznick*, selected and edited by Rudy Behlmer (Viking, 1972). Capra's dispute with Harry Cohn and his lawsuit against Columbia were covered in various articles in *Variety*, *DV*, *HR*, *Motion Picture Daily*, and other publications (March–November 1937); details of Capra's 1937 settlement with Columbia are from Sticht and from Millikan to Swarts (1947). Capra's 1935 discussions with Columbia about "supervising" films he would not direct were reported in "Columbia Will Spend Twelve Millions Here," unidentified source, July 3, 1935 (BTP). *If You Could Only Cook* was reviewed by M.B. in *NYT*, December 26, 1935. Capra's plans for an independent company were reported in Bosley Crowther, "Such Guys as Capra and Wellman," *NYT*, October 17, 1938.

Sidney Buchman's screenplay *Frédéric Chopin*, third draft, January 29, 1937, is in FCA. Other sources on the project (filmed in 1945 as *A Song to Remember*) include *NAT* uncut; Axel Madsen, *William Wyler: The Authorized Biography* (Crowell, 1973); and coverage in *HR* and *DV*, October 1936–December 1938, March 1 and 18, 1946. Buchman's September 25, 1951, testimony before the House Committee on Un-American Activities (HUAC) is in *Communist Infiltration of Hollywood Motion-Picture Industry* (U.S. Government Printing Office, 1951).

Capra's story about traveling through Nazi Germany with Riskin is from *NAT* uncut; his reactions to the U.S.S.R. are from *NAT* and the *Izvestia* interview. Elliott Stein's dispute with Capra about the Eisenstein meeting is in Stein, "Capra Counts His Oscars"; the first paperback edition of *NAT* was published by Bantam Books, 1972. For Sergei Eisenstein's political troubles, see Marie Seton's biography, *Sergei M. Eisenstein* (A. A. Wynn, 1952).

13. *"Columbia's Gem"* (pp. 375–400)

The activities of the SDG and its movement toward recognition received extensive press coverage, particularly in the Hollywood trade papers, from August 1937 to October 1938. In addition to sources cited earlier, documents read from the DGA files included membership rosters, July 1937 and September 17, 1937; correspondence and minutes of board meetings, 1937–39; "Policy and Program of the Screen Directors Guild, Inc.," June 13, 1938; Capra's statement on behalf of the SDG, July 21, 1938, published in part as SDG, "An Incorporated Report," *NYT*, August 7, 1938; and "The Producer–Screen Directors' Guild Basic Agreement of 1939," March 13, 1939, published in *DV* on May 6, 1939. Correspondence (1938) between Capra and Darryl F. Zanuck about SDG and AMPAS issues was found in FCA, as well as in *DV*: Zanuck's May 7 letter to Capra on the SDG negotiations was published in "SDG Stand False— Zanuck," May 9, and Capra's May 11 reply was published in "Capra in Answer to Zanuck Says Studios Suggested New Parley," May 12. Capra's letter to *NYT* on the SDG, "By Post from Mr. Capra," April 2, 1939, was reprinted in Glatzer and Raeburn, *Frank Capra: The Man and His Films*. See also Capra's article "Hollywood's Frankenstein," *Screen and Radio Weekly*, September 25, 1938.

Jack L. Warner's March 10, 1938, telegram to Capra about the Thalberg Award was found in FCA. Also filed there was 1938 correspondence on the abortive AMPAS response to the investigation of Hollywood by Rep. Martin Dies's HUAC: Donald Gledhill, executive secretary, AMPAS, to AMPAS board members, August 18 (which includes the text of Capra's proposed telegram protesting the statement of Dies committee investigator Edward F. Sullivan), and Gledhill to Capra, August 20. Donald Ogden Stewart's response to Sullivan is from "Anti-Nazi Leaguers Fight Red Aid Charge" and "Accused Film Writer Calls Communistic Charge Fiction," unidentified Los Angeles newspaper, August 16, 1938 (DGA). Capra's September 14, 1938, letter to AMPAS on the controversy over its producers branch, and Zanuck's September 15 letter to Capra, were published in W. S. Van Dyke II's September 19 advertisement in *DV*.

The HUAC citation on Capra's involvement in the 1938 strike at the *Hollywood Citizen-News* was noted in "Summary of Information," G-2, October 10, 1951, in Capra's Army Intelligence file; other information on the strike is from the author's interview with Dunne; SDG minutes, May 23 and June 6, 1938; Schwartz, *The Hollywood Writers' Wars;* and "Film Directors Give Aid," *Hollywood Citizen-News Striker,* June 1, 1938. Capra's May 26 letter to Frank Scully is in FCA.

Further material on the origins of the guilds, the 1938 HUAC investigation, and other political issues, in addition to Ceplair and Englund's *The Inquisition in Hollywood,* Dunne's *Take Two,* Navasky's *Naming Names,* and other references previously cited, includes William Gellermann, *Martin Dies* (John Day, 1944) and the HUAC hearings on *Communist Infiltration of Hollywood Motion-Picture Industry* (1947, 1951–1953), including Clifford Odets's testimony on May 19, 1952. Hollywood's response to the American Legion's "Americanization" campaign was reported on September 21, 1938, in "H. M. Warner Condemns All Isms," *Variety,* and "Zanuck Hits 'Pink Shirts'; Pledges Pix to Americanism," *DV. Ship Forever Sailing* (NBC Radio play directed by Capra, on the 1938 program *America Calling*) was covered in "Stars in Salute to U.S. Tonight at 'Rededication,' " *Los Angeles Herald-Express,* December 14, and "Re-Dedication!," *LAE,* December 15. The text of Capra's speech at the meeting of the Hollywood Anti-Nazi League is in FCA.

Biographical data on Mabel Walker Willebrandt are from the SDG document "Guild Counsel," 1949; Dorothy M. Brown's profile in Barbara Sicherman et al, eds., *Notable American Women: A Biographical Dictionary* (Harvard University Press, 1980); and Richard Gid Powers, *Secrecy and Power: The Life of J. Edgar Hoover* (The Free Press, 1987).

Magazine profiles of Capra published during this period include Johnston's "Capra Shoots as He Pleases"; the *Time* cover story, "Columbia's Gem"; and *Life*'s photo spread, "How Frank Capra Makes a Hit Picture."

Capra's earnings were discussed in September 17–24, 1938, press coverage of the SDG's NLRB hearings, including "As Salaries Go . . ." in the *Boston Transcript,* September 24, and were verified by Sticht. Sidney Skolsky's remark about Capra's wealth was made in his column of May 26, 1938. Capra commented on his 1938 income and his attitude toward wealth in Margo, "Capra Tells How Sex, Violence Get on Screen," *Chicago Daily News,* July 18, 1972. His esteem for *Walden* is mentioned in his letter to Jeanne Dittori, February 6, 1939 (FCA). Riskin's comments on the theme of *You Can't Take It With You* are from Virginia Wright, "Cinematters," *Los Angeles Evening News,* April 28, 1938.

Capra vs. Columbia Pictures Corp., a suit involving *A Song to Remember* (earlier prepared by Capra as *Frédéric Chopin*), was filed in Los Angeles County Superior Court, February 28, 1946; correspondence on the suit between Capra and Harry Cohn, and between Capra and his lawyer Louis E. Swarts, is in FCA; financial information on the film is from Columbia records.

Additional Columbia Pictures material from FCA on the shooting schedule, cost, and rentals of *You Can't Take It With You* was used for this chapter. The story about Capra losing Olivia de Havilland for the film is from Hellman, "Thinker in Hollywood." Manny Farber's description of Capra is from "Capra's Riding

High." Graham Greene's review in *The Spectator*, London, November 11, 1938, was reprinted in Glatzer and Raeburn, *Frank Capra: The Man and His Films*. Bernds's comments on Capra's shooting methods are from his diary. Capra's comments on James Stewart are from FCI and from Glatzer's interview in Glatzer and Raeburn, *Frank Capra: The Man and His Films*.

The burglary of the Capra home by Ralph Graham in 1938 was reported in "Fear Kidnapping of 3 Frank Capra Tots," *LAE*, July 11, and "U.S. Agents Probe Plot Against Three Capra Children," *Los Angeles Morning News*, July 12. Graham's comments are from "$2500 Received for Loot, Accused Says," *HCN*, March 25, 1939; "Film Raffles Gives Tip to Stars: Hide Gems," *New York Daily News*, March 26, 1939; and "Hollywood's Incredible 'Phantom Burglar,' " *New York Journal-American*, May 7, 1939.

Sources on the death of John Capra include Certificate of Death: John Capra, State of California Department of Public Health, August 23, 1938; and newspaper coverage, August–September 1938, including "Capra's Son Dies After Throat Operation," *DV*, August 24; "Capra's Film Triumph Saddened as Son Dies," *Los Angeles Evening News*, August 24; "Capra Boy's Death Cause Revealed," *LAE*, August 26; and "Inflamed Brain Blamed for Capra Death," *HCN*, August 26. Capra wrote about John in *NAT* and in "See My Psychiatrist," *Dodge Adventurer* and *Chrysler-Plymouth Spectator*, Summer 1980; his "lone wolf" description of John is from Bernds's diary, August 19, 1938. Saridda's and Lu's reactions to John's death are from *NAT* uncut.

14. *"My ancestors couldn't; I can"* (pp. 401–424)

The revised final draft of the screenplay *Mr. Smith Goes to Washington* by Sidney Buchman (and Myles Connolly, uncredited), April 1, 1939, with subsequent revisions, is in FCA; Connolly's work on the script is acknowledged in AMPAS's "Writers Cumulated Bulletin, 1935–1941" and is also mentioned in Schiffrin, "Cross Fire on the Director-Writer Front." A novelized version of the film by Charles Landery was published by Grosset & Dunlap in 1939. FCA does not have a copy of *The Gentleman from Montana*, the unpublished treatment (or "novel") by Lewis R. Foster credited as the source of *Mr. Smith*, and Columbia Pictures also said it has none; information on it came from the author's interview with Rouben Mamoulian, and from Gerald Gardner, *The Censorship Papers: Movie Censorship Letters from the Hays Office 1934 to 1968* (Dodd, Mead, 1987). Columbia's purchase of the film rights to Maxwell Anderson's play *Both Your Houses* (Samuel French, 1933) was reported in Sidney Skolsky's column, October 5, 1939. Capra's comments on Foster's story are from Henstell, *Frank Capra: "One Man—One Film"*; his letter to Mrs. Philip Van Doren Stern, February 12, 1979 (FCA); and from Eileen Creelman, "Picture Plays and Players," *New York Sun*, October 6, 1938.

Columbia records on *Mr. Smith* in FCA include "Revised Final Production Cost Report," 1939; "Selling Mr. Smith Singly" (press release), 1940; and a booklet of reviews and other press clippings distributed for publicity purposes; FCA also has a large file of additional press clippings. The 1940 audit of Columbia conducted for Capra contains a "Comparison—*Mr. Smith Goes to Washington* with *You Can't Take It With You*"; other financial information comes from Columbia sources previously cited. Capra's statement on the controversy engendered by the film, "Other Side of the Picture," appeared in the *Christian Science Monitor*, October 27, 1939, along with a comprehensive article by Richard L. Strout on the Washington reaction, "Now, 'Mr. Capra Goes to Washington' But the Senators Are Not Amused." See also articles on the reaction to the film in the *Washington Times-Herald*, *Washington Post*, *Washington Evening Star*, and *Washington Daily News*, and the *New York Sun* and *New York Telegraph*, October 18, 1939; *DV* review, October 4; William Edwards, *Chicago Tribune* Press Service, October 21; "Capra's *Mr. Smith* Goes to Washington and Solons, Seemingly, Can't Take It" and "Barkley's Blast," *Variety*, October 25; Frank S. Nugent, "Capra's Capitol Offense," *NYT*, October 29; William Boehnel, "Film Critic Replies to Senator Barkley," October 29; and Ralph Block, "Mr. Capra Misses the Train to Washington," *Rob Wagner's Script*, November 4, and Capra's letter in reply, November 18; James Hilton's *Sunday Graphic* column, London, November 19; and Graham Greene's review in *The Spectator*, London, January 5, 1940, reprinted in Glatzer and Raeburn, *Frank Capra: The Man and His Films*. Jim Preston's unhappiness with the film was reported by Merwin H. Browne, "Mr. Preston Goes to Hollywood, Comes Back Sadder But Wiser," *Buffalo Evening News*, November 11, 1939. Howard Hawks commented on Jean Arthur's drunk scene in Joseph McBride, *Hawks on Hawks* (University of California Press, 1982).

Buchman's HUAC testimony is from *Communist Infiltration of Hollywood Motion-Picture Industry*, September 25, 1951. Capra commented on Buchman's Communist Party membership in an interview with the author; *NAT* uncut; his Security Board File (1951); and his December 19, 1951, letter to John Ford. Buchman discussed the writing of *Mr. Smith* in Earl Wilson, "Scenarist Who Now Writes in Palm Springs Bungalow Recalls How $4 Columbia Room Really Got Him Started," *New York Post*, November 27, 1939; "Job of a Hollywood Writer Is No Cinch, Says Sid Buchman, Who Ought to Know," *New York Telegraph*, November 29, 1939; and in Tavernier, "Sidney Buchman." Hellman's comments on Capra's political viewpoint are from "Thinker in Hollywood."

Capra's contrast of Cooper and Stewart is from Pat McGilligan, "Frank Capra's Golden Age of Hollywood," *Boston Globe*, July 4, 1975. The description of Capra at FDR's press conference of October 11, 1938, is from John R. Covert, "Press Conference Thriller," *Philadelphia Bulletin*, October 12; Capra's comments are from ibid. and from W. A. S. Douglas, "Rolling Along," unidentified newspaper, October 18 (FCA); the transcript of the session is in *The Press Conferences of Franklin D. Roosevelt* (National Archives and Records Service, Franklin D. Roosevelt Library). Capra's criticism of Roosevelt's court-packing plan is from his letter to Mrs. E. Grey Diamond, July 12, 1979 (FCA). J. Edgar Hoover's letter to Capra, October 15, 1938, about Capra's October 13 visit to the FBI, is in FCA, as is the photo of Capra firing a Thompson submachine gun. The opening of Army Intelligence's file on Capra on October 14, 1938, is recorded in Yoshio G. Kanegai, "Agent Report," August 24, 1951 (Army Intelligence file).

Capra's 1966 disavowal of *Mr. Smith* is quoted in Judy Jack, "Capra: Rapport Through Comedy," *The Telescope*, Palomar College, San Marcos, California, n.d. (April 1966) (FCA). He discussed Senator Paine in James Childs, "Capra Today." Articles on the block-booking controversy include "Capra's *Mr. Smith* Goes to Washington and Solons, Seemingly, Can't Take It" and "Consent Decree," *Time*, November 11, 1940; Capra praised government action against block-booking in his article "Breaking Hollywood's 'Pattern of Sameness,' " *NYT*, May 5, 1946; Capra's amazed reaction to the Senate backlash is from "$10,000 for Film Plot!," *New York Telegraph*, October 27, 1939. Joseph P. Kennedy's supposed offer to buy the negative of *Mr. Smith* was discussed by Capra in Schickel, *The Men Who Made the Movies*, and in Shales, "Lights! Capra! Action!" FDR's reaction to *Mr. Smith* is from a letter by a sailor on the USS *Tuscaloosa*, Ed McAndrews, to William Arnold, n.d. (c. 1975) (FCA); the dates of FDR's December 3–16, 1940, cruise are from the ship's log in the Franklin D. Roosevelt Library.

Robert Riskin's departure to join Samuel Goldwyn was discussed in Katherine Smith, "The Case of Robert Riskin Will Set Precedent for Scenarist Publicity," *Washington Daily News*, September 26, 1938. The possibility of Capra also joining Goldwyn was reported in "Columbia's Gem"; item in unidentified Washington, D.C., newspaper, August 21, 1938 (FCA); "How Frank Capra Makes a Hit Picture"; and "Report Capra to Goldwyn as a Prod.," *Variety*, February 22, 1939. Capra's interest in directing *Gone With the Wind* is discussed in David O. Selznick to Dan O'Shea, September 21, 1938, in Behlmer, *Memo from David O. Selznick*.

Sources on the SDG negotiations include the minutes of SDG board meetings (1938–39), including Capra's proposed statement resigning as AMPAS president, and a statement on the history of the SDG negotiations written by Herbert Biberman, Frank Tuttle, John Cromwell, W. S. Van Dyke II, and Rouben Mamoulian (February 15, 1939); Joseph M. Schenck to Capra, February 17, 1939, and other correspondence in the DGA files; and "The Producer-Screen Directors' Guild Basic Agreement of 1939." *DV*, *LAT*, and *HCN* covered the 1938–39 negotiations. The SDG's awarding an honorary life membership to Capra was recalled by the guild's Adele Salem in a letter to Joseph C. Youngerman, October 31, 1951 (DGA), quoting the minutes of the May 19, 1941, meeting. Capra's role in the guild's achievement of a first cut for directors in 1964 was described in Robb, "Directors Guild Born Out of Fear 50 Years Ago." *Can We Forget?*, the 1939 CBS Radio program directed by Capra, was reviewed in *Variety* on January 25, 1939; the script by Mary McCall, Jr., is in FCA.

15. "We're *the front office*" (pp. 425–452)

The chapter title is from Margaret Case Harriman's April 1941 *Ladies' Home Journal* article, "Mr. and Mrs. Frank Capra."

Documents on the production and release of *Meet John Doe* and *Arsenic and Old Lace* are from FCA and from the Warner Bros. Archives at USC, which has contracts for both films. Capra's files contain legal documents on the establishment in 1939 of Frank Capra Prods., Inc. (FCP), and its dissolution in 1941; correspondence on *Doe* and *Arsenic*, including the so-called John Doe Letter from "EGF" to Riskin, n.d. (1941); Capra's February 20, 1943, letter to Col. Kirke B. Lawton detailing his earnings for the two films; Lloyd G. Rainey's accounting of FCP profits on *Doe*, December 31, 1943; an audit of *Arsenic* for Capra by Benjamin W. Solomon, August 28, 1948; and Willebrandt to Miller (1960). The Lindsay and Crouse Papers and the legal files of the United Artists Corp. at the State Historical Society of Wisconsin contain contracts and other material on the stage and film versions of *Arsenic*. The UA files also contain correspondence pertaining to Capra's discussions about becoming a partner in UA, including David O. Selznick to Alexander Korda, June 5, 1941, and Korda to Selznick, June 7, 1941; Mary Pickford's letter to Dennis O'Brien and other material are in Tino Balio, *United Artists: The Company Built by the Stars* (University of Wisconsin Press, 1976). Selznick's January 22, 1940, letter to Capra about "one-man jobs" is in Behlmer, *Memo from David O. Selznick*. Information on the terms of Capra's proposed contracts with Warner Bros. and with 20th Century–Fox is in a letter from Warners' Steve Trilling to Jack L. Warner, October 19, 1944 (Warner Bros. Archives).

FCA has the draft of July 27, 1940, with revisions through September 4, 1940, of the screenplay *Meet John Doe* by Robert Riskin (and Myles Connolly, uncredited); other script material is in FWC and in the Warner Bros. Archives. Riskin wrote about the film in "Meet the Creators of *John Doe*, Meet John Doe Himself," *Click*, March 1941. Connolly's contribution to the screenplay was acknowledged in AMPAS's "Writers Cumulated Bulletin, 1935–1941." Wolfe's book *Meet John Doe* contains material on the making of the film, as well as articles and reviews; Capra's April 8, 1941, letter to M. Gluck; and a version of the script. Sam Thomas's *Best American Screenplays*, First Series, contains another version of the script. FCA has the screenplay for *Arsenic* by Julius J. Epstein and Philip G. Epstein, October 16, 1941, with revisions through December 5, 1941. Also in FCA are the screenplays *The Flying Irishman* by Frances Goodrich and Albert Hackett, December 21, 1944, and *The Flying Yorkshireman* by Valentine Davies, July 21, 1947, and sales agreements pertaining to the film rights to Eric Knight's story "The Flying Yorkshireman."

Capra's official U.S. Army records were used in establishing the dates of his World War II commission and service; other documents relating to his commission are among the papers of the U.S. Senate Special Committee Investigating the National Defense Program (the "Truman committee"), 1943, at the National Archives; Liberty Films' "Biographical Sketch of Frank Capra," 1945, gives the date of his application for a commission erroneously. Sources on the Army's film production before and during the war include the following volumes in the official series *The United States Army in World War II* (Office of the Chief of Military History, Department of the Army): Dulany Terrett, *The Signal Corps: The Emergency*, 1956; George Raynor Thompson, Dixie R. Harris, Pauline M. Oakes, and Terrett, *The Signal Corps: The Test*, 1957; and Thompson and Harris, *The Signal*

Corps: The Outcome, 1966. Also consulted for this chapter was Forrest C. Pogue, *George C. Marshall: Ordeal and Hope, 1939–1942* (Viking, 1966). Capra's telegram to President Roosevelt, February 28, 1941, and the reply on the President's behalf by his secretary, M. H. McIntyre, March 4, 1941, are from the Franklin D. Roosevelt Library. The script by Dorothy Donnell, with material from Capra, for Capra's appearance on *I'm an American!* (U.S. Department of Justice, NBC Radio, March 23, 1941), and related correspondence between Capra and Donnell, are in FCA, as are his wartime correspondence with his wife, Lu, and his letter about his sister Ann's "enemy alien" classification, written to Selective Service Draft Board #242, Hollywood, August 3, 1942; Josephine Campisi and Chester Sticht discussed Ann's classification in interviews with the author. Riskin's letter to Capra from England, October 1, 1941, was published in *DV* and *HR*, October 9, 1941.

Sources on the history of Fallbrook, California, and Capra's Red Mountain Ranch are listed in the notes for chapter 20.

Information on the May 23, 1941, death of Capra's mother is from Certificate of Death: Serah [*sic:* Rosaria] Capra, Department of Public Health, State of California, filed May 26, 1941.

Numerous articles on Capra's proposed producing partnerships with Riskin, Goldwyn, Selznick, UA, and others, and the formation of FCP, appeared in *NYT*, *Variety*, *Motion Picture Herald*, *Time*, *HR*, *DV*, *Film Daily*, *Boxoffice*, and *Showmen's Trade Review*, 1939–41; see especially "Columbia's Gems," *Time*, July 24, 1939, and "Fold-Up of U.A. Dicker Admitted by Frank Capra," *HR*, August 15, 1941. Riskin's comment on "the sense of freedom" is from Strauss, "Mr. Riskin Hits the Road." Cohn's offer was reported in "Capra-Riskin May Yet Stay [at] Columbia," *Variety*, August 2, 1939; Thomas, *King Cohn*; and in Thomas's notes of an interview with Joseph Walker (BTP).

Capra's story about offering *The Flying Yorkshireman* to Chaplin is from *NAT* uncut; see also "Capra, Riskin After Chaplin for Fantasy," *Variety*, May 14, 1941. Capra's purchase of film rights to "Tomorrow Never Comes" and *The Jest of Hahalaba*: documents in FCA, 1941–42, and Virginia Wright column, *Los Angeles Daily News*, May 8, 1944. Capra's plans to film *Don Quixote*: "Capra Sets *Quixote* for Start on Jan. 1," *Variety*, August 21, 1940.

Articles on the making of *Meet John Doe* appeared in *NYT*, *New York Telegraph*, *PM*, *HR*, *DV*, *Motion Picture Daily*, *Time*, *Variety*, and *Boxoffice*, November 1939–April 1941; see especially Strauss, "Mr. Riskin Hits the Road," *NYT*; "Coop," *Time* (cover story on Gary Cooper and *Doe*), March 3, 1941; "Toomey Recalled in New Ending for *Doe*," *HR*, March 24, 1941; and John Chapman column, *Boxoffice*, April 26, 1941; also see "Capra, Riskin Sell *Doe* for $150,000," *DV*, n.d. (1945) (FCA), and "Lost and Found: The Films of Frank Capra." Eileen Creelman's review appeared in the *New York Sun*, March 13, 1941.

Capra commented on *Doe* in Henstell, *Frank Capra: "One Man—One Film"*; Schickel, *The Men Who Made the Movies*; and in an appearance with Jean Arthur at the University of California, Santa Cruz, June 9, 1975 (videotape in FCA). His remark that he never ceases to "thrill at an audience seeing a picture" is from Hellman, "Thinker in Hollywood," as are Hellman's comments on Red Mountain Ranch. François Truffaut's observation about Capra's tragicomedy is from his essay "Frank Capra, The Healer," in *The Films in My Life*, trans. by Leonard Mayhew (Simon & Schuster, 1978). Andrew Sarris's observation on *Doe* is from *The American Cinema*; Elliott Stein's is from Roud, ed., *Cinema: A Critical Dictionary*.

Capra's disavowal of interest in message films and his dismay over Hitler's fondness for *It Happened One Night* are from his interview with Allan Kellar, "Capra Set for Poison Film," *NYWT*, n.d. (1941) (FCA); Hitler's fondness for the film was reported in William L. Shirer, *Berlin Diary: The Journal of a Foreign Correspondent, 1934–1941* (Alfred A. Knopf, 1941). The idea for a comedy on gangsters fighting Hitler originated in the column "Every Word the Truth" by "Sparky" (R. Wesley Baxter) in *Refrigeration*, April 14, 1941; Capra's correspondence with Sparky, and related correspondence on *All Through the Night*, are in the Warner Bros. Archives.

Articles on *Arsenic and Old Lace* include Douglas W. Churchill, "Murder in Hollywood," *NYT*, November 9, 1941; "Nonchalant Cary Grant Plays Bouncing Booby," *Kalamazoo Gazette* (Michigan), November 16, 1941; "Capra Enroute Home for *Lace* Editing," *DV*, January 2, 1942; and "*Arsenic* WB Film Wow Now" (review), *HR*, September 1, 1944. Capra's abortive deal with Fox was reported in "Frank Capra Signs 3-Year Producing Deal with 20th-Fox," *Motion Picture Daily*, November 27, 1941, and "Capra Signs with 20th; May Do *Yorkshireman*," *DV*, November 27, 1941. Cary Grant's criticisms of *Arsenic* were quoted in his obituary on NBC-TV, November 30, 1986. Capra's complaint about the film's delayed release was conveyed to Warner Bros. by his attorney Martin Gang in a letter of January 19, 1944, to Roy J. Obringer (Warner Bros. Archives).

Capra's attendance at the May 1940 meeting in Hollywood with Signal Corps officers was reported in "U.S. Enlists Aid of Industry for National Defense," *Motion Picture Daily*, May 31, 1940. Other articles about his and Hollywood's recruitment for the war effort (1941) include "Signal Corps May Recruit from Hollywood Talent," *DV*, December 10; "Frank Capra Quits Films to Join the Signal Corps," *NYT*, December 13; "Wyler, Capra, Huston Headed for Signal Corps Service" and "Studio Employees Who Answered Call to Arms," *DV*, December 15; W. R. Wilkerson, "TradeViews," *HR*, December 15; and "Capra in Capital for Army Service," *HR*, December 31. Capra's project (or projects) *Combat Counter-Intelligence* and *Espionage* were discussed in "Capra's Service Picture," *Variety*, October 12, 1938, and "Frank Capra Short Film, *Espionage*, Gets U.S. Aid," *HR*, September 9, 1941; documents on the making of *Combat Counter-Intelligence* by Charles Vidor in 1942 are in the files of the Truman committee. The Capras' involvement in war relief efforts was reported in "Women of Industry Join Red Cross Drive," *HR*, July 1, 1940, and "Centralization of War Relief Work," *Boxoffice*, July 6, 1940. Background on Frederick H. Osborn is from Thomas Cripps and David Culbert, "*The Negro Soldier* (1944): Film Propaganda in Black and White," *The American Quarterly*, Winter 1979. John Ford's war service is discussed in Dan Ford, *Pappy: The Life of John Ford* (Prentice-Hall, 1979), and in Gallagher, *John Ford: The Man and His Films.* Sources on Robert Riskin's departure from Hollywood include Sidney Skolsky column, June 16, 1941; "Robert Riskin Joins British Information; Donates Services," *DV*, September 24, 1941; "Bob Riskin on His Way Back from London Stay," *HR*, December 15, 1941; and "Riskin Named Aide to Robt. Sherwood in OWI," *HR*, August 25, 1942.

16. *"That fellow Capra"*   (pp. 453–501)

Capra's official U.S. Army records, his Army Intelligence file, his Security Board File (1951), and his extensive World War II Teletype traffic, correspondence, and other files at FCA were among the essential sources for this chapter. Official documents on Capra and the films made under his supervision were found at the National Archives in the U.S. Army Staff Files; the Records of the Office of the Chief Signal Officer, U.S. Army; and the files of the Truman committee. Additional documentation came from the papers of U.S. Army Chief of Staff Gen. George C. Marshall and Brig. Gen. Frank McCarthy at the George C. Marshall Library; President Franklin D. Roosevelt and Lowell Mellett at the Franklin D. Roosevelt Library; John Huston and George Stevens at AMPAS; and William Wyler at UCLA. The papers of Robert Riskin in FWC supplied information on Riskin's activities with the Office of War Information (OWI).

Members of the Capra unit and other wartime associates interviewed by the author included Joseph Biroc, Dunne, Julius Epstein, Theodor S. Geisel, Albert Hackett, Paul Horgan, Huston, Robert Lees, Dorothy McAdam, McCarthy, Carlton Moss, Edgar A. Peterson II, Gottfried Reinhardt, Allen Rivkin, John Sanford, Spigelgass, Stevens, Chester Sticht, Irving Wallace, and John D. Weaver. Other interviews were conducted with William J. Blakefield, Edward (Ted) Paramore III, and Fay Wray. Also quoted were "George C. Marshall Interviews and Reminiscences for Forrest C. Pogue: Transcripts and Notes, 1956–1957," George C. Marshall Research Foundation, 1986.

The National Archives has scripts and shot lists for the *Why We Fight* films and other films made by the Capra unit; Capra's working scripts are in FCA. Sanford supplied copies of his correspondence with Capra, as well as his drafts of *The Battle of Russia*; the unproduced project *America's Friends: Russia*; and an untitled project on the U.S.S.R., as well as a copy of the Army Orientation Course Lecture #8, "The Battle of Russia," U.S. War Department, Bureau of Public Relations, 1941. Sanford's April 16, 1991, letter to the author explained why he did not admit to Capra that he was a Communist. Sanford wrote of his experiences with Capra in his memoir *A Very Good Land to Fall With: Scenes from the Life of an American Jew, Volume 3* (Black Sparrow Press, 1987), in which he also quoted from the letter Capra wrote him in May 1942. Synopses of the *Army-Navy Screen Magazine* are in the papers of Claude Binyon at the State Historical Society of Wisconsin. The 1944 screenplay *The Flying Irishman* by Frances Goodrich and Hackett is in FCA (the date of the RKO option is from a letter by Sidney L.

Lipstich of RKO to Donald A. Dewar, January 24, 1945); see also a note by Goodrich and Hackett on their copy of the script at the State Historical Society of Wisconsin.

The official U.S. Army histories by Terrett, *The Signal Corps: The Emergency*; Thompson et al., *The Signal Corps: The Test*; and Thompson and Harris, *The Signal Corps: The Outcome* provided basic reference points and background for the study of Capra's wartime work. Issues pertaining to Army filmmaking were discussed in testimony before the Truman committee on February 16 and April 3, 1943; see *Hearings Before a Special Committee Investigating the National Defense Program* (Part 17, U.S. Senate, 1943). Other official publications which were useful included the booklet *Information and Education Division* (U.S. Army, 1945); Maj. James E. Gibson, SC Reserve, "Producer: Signal Corps," *Signals*, March/April 1947; William J. Blakefield, *Documentary Film Classics Produced by the United States Government* (National AudioVisual Center, 1979, and 2nd ed., n.d.); *Media Resource Catalog* (National AudioVisual Center, 1986); and Mayfield S. Bray and William T. Murphy, *Audiovisual Records in the National Archives Relating to World War II* (National Archives, n.d.). See also "Army Orientation Films: Program Notes" for screenings of films produced by the Capra unit, September 21–22, 1943, under the auspices of AMPAS (provided by Peterson).

Sources on George C. Marshall include the first three volumes of Pogue's biography *George C. Marshall* (Viking): *Education of a General (1880–1939)* with Gordon Harrison, 1963; *Ordeal and Hope (1939–1942)*, 1966; and *Organizer of Victory (1943–1945)*, 1973. Books used for this chapter also included Adolf Hitler, trans. by Ralph Manheim, *Mein Kampf* (Houghton Mifflin, 1943, first published in 1925); Lowell Thomas and Edward Jablonski, *Doolittle: A Biography* (Doubleday, 1976); and Ladislas Farago, *The Last Days of Patton* (McGraw-Hill, 1981). See also Col. Beirne Lay, Jr., "Jimmy Stewart's Finest Performance," *Saturday Evening Post*, December 8 and 15, 1945.

The articles in *The Atlantic Monthly* which inspired the *Why We Fight* series were Stewart Alsop, "Wanted: A Faith to Fight For," May 1941, and Cleveland Amory, "What We Fight For," June 1941. Studies of the series include Hovland, Lumsdaine, and Sheffield, *Experiments on Mass Communication* (1949); Bohn, *An Historical and Descriptive Analysis of the "Why We Fight" Series* (1968, published in 1977); and William Thomas Murphy, "The Method of *Why We Fight*," *Journal of Popular Culture*, Summer 1972. See also Edward V. Johnson, Jr., *The Military Information Film: A Case Study of Internal Information in the Armed Services* (master's thesis, Boston University School of Public Communication, Division of Public Relations, 1967). Two superb histories of individual films produced by the Capra unit are Cripps and Culbert, "*The Negro Soldier* (1944): Film Propaganda in Black and White"; and Blakefield, "A War Within: The Making of *Know Your Enemy—Japan*," *Sight and Sound*, Spring 1983. Capra's most extensive interviews on his wartime films were George Bailey, "Why We (Should Not) Fight," *Take One*, September 1975; Prof. Oliver Franklin and Dr. Gene S. Weiss, *The Motion Picture in Persuasion*, in the USIA series of videotaped interviews *Frank Capra: The Man Above the Title* (1976); Karp, "The Patriotism of Frank Capra";

and Bill Moyers, on the PBS program *A Walk Through the Twentieth Century: WWII: The Propaganda Battle* (1984). See also "Capra Criticizes U.S. War Films," *LAT*, September 26, 1943; Arthur Bressan and Michael Moran, "Mr. Capra Goes to College," *Interview*, May 6, 1972; Mariani, "Frank Capra"; Bob Grace, "The Topic of Capra-corn," *Houston Chronicle*, April 4, 1982; and Robert Lindsey, "Frank Capra's Films Lead Fresh Lives," *NYT*, May 19, 1985. Richard Griffith, a member of Capra's unit, wrote of the experience in his monograph *Frank Capra*; see also Schickel, *The Men Who Made the Movies*; Scherle and Levy, *The Films of Frank Capra*; and Maland, *Frank Capra*. Capra's establishment of Liberty Films, Inc., is dealt with in the company's publicity booklets *The Story of Liberty Films, Inc.*, and *Biographies* (1946), found among the papers of George Stevens (AMPAS).

Additional books dealing with filmmaking during the war by Capra and others include: Agee, *Agee on Film*; Jay Leyda, *Films Beget Films* (Hill and Wang, 1964); Joris Ivens, *The Camera and I* (International Publishers, 1969); Mel Gussow, *Don't Say Yes Until I Finish Talking* (Doubleday, 1971); Richard Dyer MacCann, *The People's Films* (Hastings House, 1973); Madsen, *William Wyler: The Authorized Biography*; John Leverence, *Irving Wallace: A Writer's Profile* (The Popular Press, 1974); Edward Dmytryk, *It's a Hell of a Life But Not a Bad Living* (Times Books, 1978); Ford, *Pappy: The Life of John Ford*; Dunne, *Take Two*; John Huston, *An Open Book* (Alfred A. Knopf, 1980); Carlos Böker, *Joris Ivens: Film-Maker Facing Reality* (UMI Research Press, 1981); Mosley, *Zanuck: The Rise and Fall of Hollywood's Last Tycoon*; and Gallagher, *John Ford: The Man and His Films*.

Capra's wartime contacts with the Soviets are described in his Army Intelligence file; *NAT* and *NAT* uncut; and in Mariani's interview, "Frank Capra." Sources on Hollywood politics and Red-baiting before, during, and after the war used for this and subsequent chapters include Bruce Cook, *Dalton Trumbo* (Charles Scribner's Sons, 1977); Ceplair and Englund, *The Inquisition in Hollywood*; Dunne, *Take Two*; Navasky, *Naming Names*; and Schwartz, *The Hollywood Writers' Wars*. Also read were the HUAC *Hearings Regarding the Communist Infiltration of the Motion Picture Industry*, 1947, and the HUAC hearings on *Communist Infiltration of Hollywood Motion-Picture Industry*, 1951–53; Fourth Report of the Senate Fact-Finding Committee on Un-American Activities 1948: *Communist Front Organizations* (Senate of California, 1948); *Red Channels: The Report of Communist Influence in Radio and Television* (American Business Consultants, 1950); and *Guide to Subversive Organizations and Publications* (U.S. House of Representatives, U.S. Government Printing Office, May 14, 1951).

Additional articles used for this chapter include Wilkerson, "TradeViews," *HR*, December 15, 1941, and February 23 and 26, 1942; "Hollywood Faces Labor Shortage"; "Government Films Further Roosevelt's Aims, Says Holman," *The Washington Post*, February 9, 1943; "Federal War Film Held 4th Term Bid," *NYT*, February 9, 1943; "Mellett, War Dept. Clash Over *Prelude to War* Film," *HR*, February 11, 1943; John M. Fisher, "Congress Sees 4th Term Film," *Washington Times-Herald*, February 17, 1943; Dorothy Norman, "A World to Live In: The Strange Case of Carlton Moss," *New York Post*, n.d. (1944); V. I. Pudovkin,

"The Global Film," *Cinema Chronicle*, June 1945, reprinted in English translation by Jay Leyda, *Hollywood Quarterly*, June 1947; Philip Dunne, "The Documentary and Hollywood," *Hollywood Quarterly*, no. 1, 1945–46; Cedric Larson, "The Domestic Motion Picture Work of the Office of War Information," *Hollywood Quarterly*, Fall 1947; and Gordon Hitchens, "Joris Ivens Interviewed," *Film Culture*, Spring 1972.

17. *Liberty*   (pp. 503–534)

Documents on Liberty Films, Inc., were found in FCA; in the papers of William Wyler at UCLA; and in the papers of George Stevens at AMPAS, which contained most of the financial information cited in this chapter, including documents on Liberty stock ownership and on the sale of the company to Paramount Pictures on September 29, 1947. Jules Stein's ownership of Paramount stock at the time he served as agent for the Liberty deal is reported in Dan E. Moldea, *Dark Victory: Ronald Reagan, MCA, and the Mob* (Viking, 1986); Capra's October 1, 1947, agreement with Stein for payment in Paramount stock is in FCA. Capra's salary for *It's a Wonderful Life* was reported by Willebrandt to Miller (1960). Also useful were the Liberty publicity booklets *The Story of Liberty Films, Inc.*, and *Biographies*. Capra discussed his postwar plans with Thomas M. Pryor in "Mr. Capra Comes to Town," *NYT*, November 18, 1945, and with Edwin Schallert in "Emotional Appeal Capra's Film Goal," *LAT*, March 3, 1946. He wrote of his dreams of independent production in "Breaking Hollywood's 'Pattern of Sameness,' " *NYT*, May 5, 1946, and in "Il faut savoir faire un film avant de le commencer," *Cinémonde*, June 25, 1946, reprinted in *Positif*, December 1971. He recalled Hollywood's postwar "Frank who?" reaction in "Dialogue on Film: Frank Capra," *American Film*, October 1978, and discussed his decision to sell Liberty in Schickel, *The Men Who Made the Movies*. Stevens recalled his wartime experiences and his Liberty partnership in his 1974 interview with the author and Patrick McGilligan, parts of which were published as "A Piece of the Rock: George Stevens"; he also spoke about the concentration camps in the documentary film *George Stevens: A Filmmaker's Journey*. Wyler was interviewed about Liberty and Paramount by Madsen in *William Wyler: The Authorized Biography;* also see Wyler's interviews with Pryor, "Back to Work," *NYT*, September 16, 1945, and Irene Thirer, "Reality of *Best Years* Scares Wyler for Future," *New York Post*, November 11, 1946. Leo McCarey's explanation of his decision not to join Liberty is from Bogdanovich's oral history.

Sources of production information on *Wonderful Life* include documents in FCA and the Stevens Papers; Walker and Walker, *The Light on Her Face*; Mark Rowland's 1983 interview with Frances Goodrich and Albert Hackett in McGilligan, *Backstory*; and Basinger, *The "It's a Wonderful Life" Book*, which contains the original story by Philip Van Doren Stern, "The Greatest Gift" (1943); Stern's article "*It's a Wonderful Life* Started as the By-Product of a Shave," *NYHT*, December 15, 1946; a scene and dialogue transcription of the film (March 4, 1947); and the transcript of Capra's 1968 AMPAS seminar on the film. Mrs. Stern's 1978–79 correspondence with Capra is in FCA. The shooting script

(March 20, 1946) was published by St. Martin's Press, 1986; Capra's annotated working copy, with inserted changes through May 24, 1946, is in FCA. Stern's story first was printed privately by its author on December 20, 1943; it was published as "The Man Who Never Was" in *Good Housekeeping*, January 1945, and in book form, with revisions, as *The Greatest Gift* (David McKay, 1945). Biographical information on Stern is from Herbert Mitgang, "Philip Van Doren Stern Dies; A Specialist on Civil War Era," *NYT*, August 1, 1984. Trumbo's screenplay *The Greatest Gift* (1944) is among his papers at the State Historical Society of Wisconsin, with a note on his involvement in the project. Michael Wilson's contribution to the script was acknowledged in the "Writers Cumulated Bulletin 1946–1950" (AMPAS); his January 2, 1946, employment contract with Liberty is in the Wyler Papers; his January 22, 1946, draft is mentioned in a note by Capra in the director's working copy of the script (FCA); and Wilson mentioned his work on the film in his HUAC testimony on September 20, 1951. Sources on Dorothy Parker's work on the script include "Rambling Reporter," *HR*, March 1, 1946; the minutes of the April 28, 1946, Liberty board meeting (FCA); and Sticht.

Wilson's outline and drafts for the Capra project *The Friendly Persuasion* (1946–47) are in FCA and the Wilson Papers; the Wyler Papers include Wilson's drafts and the subsequent drafts rewritten by Jessamyn West and Robert Wyler for the 1956 Allied Artists film *Friendly Persuasion*, directed by William Wyler. The Wilson and Wyler Papers also contain documents pertaining to the denial of screen credit to Wilson, and to Wilson's lawsuit, *Michael Wilson vs. Liberty Films, Inc., Allied Artists, Paramount, William Wyler, Robert Wyler, and Jessamyn West et al.*, October 26, 1956. West's stories on which the script was based were collected as *The Friendly Persuasion* (Harcourt, Brace, 1945); she wrote about Wilson and the film in her journal *To See the Dream* (Harcourt, Brace, 1957).

Documents on the purchase and preproduction of *State of the Union* include the program booklet for the press preview (1948), and also "Dates Concerning Claudette Colbert" and statements by Capra and Art Black on Colbert, October 15, 1947 (FCA). FCA has Jo Swerling's scripts of *No Other Man*, 1946 and 1952, and Capra's outline "Pioneer Woman," February 2, 1945 (filmed in 1951 by William Wellman as *Westward the Women*), as well as correspondence and other documents on these projects. Wellman discussed Capra's involvement in *Magic Town* (1947) in Mariani, "Frank Capra."

Postwar Hollywood labor unrest and the growing Red scare are discussed in sources including *NAT* uncut; the HUAC *Hearings Regarding the Communist Infiltration of the Motion Picture Industry*, 1947, including the October 21 testimony of Jack Moffitt; and the HUAC hearings on *Communist Infiltration of Hollywood Motion-Picture Industry*, 1951–53; Robert Sklar, *Movie-Made America: A Social History of American Movies* (Random House, 1975); Cook, *Dalton Trumbo*; Ceplair and Englund, *The Inquisition in Hollywood*; Navasky, *Naming Names*; Schwartz, *The Hollywood Writers' Wars*; and Anne Edwards, *Early Reagan* (William Morrow, 1987). Capra's Army Intelligence file provided data on the investigations of his political involvements. His comment about 1946 being the year "the bottom fell out" of the film industry is from McDonough, "Frank Capra:

For the Veteran Director, It's a Wonderful Life." His 1947 remarks about communism in Hollywood are from Hugh Baker, "Jimmy Stewart in Real Life Same as on Screen, Fans Agree After Movie Star Visits in Beaumont," *Port Arthur News* (Texas), March 5, 1947. John Ross's article "Frank Capra—Is He Un-American?" appeared in *The Daily Worker* (Great Britain), April 5, 1946; a similar analysis appeared in Stig Almquist, "Är livet underbart?" ("Is Life Wonderful?"), with a letter by Georg E. Eriksson, *AT* (Sweden), August 17, 1947. The papers of Goodrich and Hackett at the State Historical Society of Wisconsin contain material on their political problems, including dossiers prepared on them by the American Legion (c. 1952) and their letter to Louis K. Sidney of MGM, July 21, 1952. Michael Wilson discussed his Communist Party membership in 1975 interviews with Joel Gardner for *I Am the Sum of My Actions*, UCLA Oral History Program, 1982. Material on Wilson's HUAC appearance and his investigation by the U.S. Marine Corps (also 1951), including his letter of August 22, 1951, to the Commandant of the Marine Corps, are in his papers. John Wayne's comment on Capra was made to David Shepard, who reported it to the author.

The formation of Liberty Films and its sale to Paramount were covered in *HR*, *Variety, Boxoffice Digest, DV, NYT,* and *Time,* 1945–47; see especially Hedda Hopper column with a letter from Capra quoted, n.d. (c. 1945) (FCA); "Helping Hand Requested for Returned Veterans," *Boxoffice,* February 23, 1946; "All's Not Gold Away from Fold," *Variety,* February 12, 1947; "Stevens Mulls Rainbow Offer," *DV,* April 16, 1947; and "The Price of Liberty," *Time,* May 26, 1947; articles on the subsequent departure of the Liberty partners from Paramount include "Budgets-Stories Snags Cue Exit of Capra, Stevens," *Variety,* April 4, 1951; Thomas F. Brady, "Hollywood Agenda," *NYT,* April 8, 1951; and "Wyler Prefers Sticking with Major Co. to Avoid Coin Worries, Biz Snarls," *Variety,* April 15, 1953.

Before Capra became involved with *It's a Wonderful Life,* an advertisement announcing the film as *The Greatest Gift* (with Cary Grant) appeared in *DV,* October 16, 1944; the production and release of *Wonderful Life* were covered in *HR, NYT, DV, NYHT,* AP, *Boxoffice Digest, HCN, This Week, Variety, NYWT,* and other sources, September 1945–March 1947; see especially Bob Thomas, AP, July 9, 1946, and "Capra-Stewart Due to Plug Lagging Life," *Variety,* January 15, 1947; also see Glatzer's interview with Capra in Glatzer and Raeburn, *Frank Capra: The Man and His Films,* and Swindell, "Frank Capra: Canonized by Film Cultists." James Stewart reminisced about the making of the film in *The American Film Institute Salute to Frank Capra* (1982). Ginger Rogers explained her rejection of the lead female role in *Ginger: My Story* (HarperCollins, 1991). Reviews of the film include Jack D. Grant, "*Wonderful Life* Splendid Start for Liberty Films," *HR,* December 19, 1946; John McCarten, "Angel of Whimsey," *The New Yorker,* December 21, 1946; "New Pictures," *Time,* December 23, 1946; Bosley Crowther, "The Screen in Review," *NYT,* December 23, 1946; James Agee, "Films," *The Nation,* December 28, 1946, reprinted in *Agee on Film,* and February 15, 1947; and "Capra's Christmas Carol," *Newsweek,* December 30, 1946. William S. Pechter commented on the film in his essay "American Madness" in *Kulchur,* Winter 1962, reprinted in his collection *Twenty-Four Times a Second:*

Films and Filmmakers (Harper & Row, 1971); Handzo in "Under Capracorn"; Robin Wood in "Ideology, Genre, *Auteur*," *Film Comment*, January/February 1977; and James Wolcott in "Less than Wonderful," *Vanity Fair*, December 1986.

The fate of the negative of *Wonderful Life* was reported in "Lost and Found: The Films of Frank Capra." Articles discussing the colorization controversy as it involved Capra and *Wonderful Life* include Lindsey, "Frank Capra's Films Lead Fresh Lives"; and Leslie Bennetts, "Colorizing Film Classics: A Boon or a Bane?," *NYT*, August 5, 1986. John Huston's remarks on the issue were transcribed by the author at Huston's DGA press conference of November 13, 1986.

Capra's plans to make *State of the Union* were reported by *HR, NYT, Variety*, and *DV*, December 1946–June 1947. His plans to make various other projects mentioned in this chapter were reported in the same publications and in *LAT*, 1945–48.

18. *"I have no cause"* (pp. 535–559)

The screenplay of *State of the Union*, by Anthony Veiller and Myles Connolly, September 16, 1947, with changes through November 28, 1947, is in FCA, along with Capra's September 27 notes on the American tradition of dissent; correspondence and production information; and promotional booklets. The papers of playwrights Howard Lindsay and Russel Crouse at the State Historical Society of Wisconsin include their original draft of *State of the Union, I'd Rather Be Left*, and their accounts of its genesis, among other documents pertaining to a plagiarism suit, *Millstein vs. Hayward et al.*, 1948, including Lindsay's deposition, n.d., which is quoted in the chapter. The play was published by Random House in 1946. Franklin D. Roosevelt's August 1940 remark on Mr. and Mrs. Wendell Willkie was quoted in "Tapes Offer a Rare Glimpse of the Private F.D.R.," *NYT*, March 2, 1988.

The HUAC *Hearings Regarding the Communist Infiltration of the Motion Picture Industry*, 1947, included the public testimony of the Hollywood Ten and the "friendly" witnesses that October. Notes on the futile protest against HUAC by a special committee of the SDG are in the section for chapter 19. Events of this period were documented by Ceplair and Englund, *The Inquisition in Hollywood*; Navasky, *Naming Names*; and Schwartz, *The Hollywood Writers' Wars*. Capra's Army Intelligence file was used again for this chapter. His letter about his political views to Lee Mortimer of the *New York Daily Mirror*, April 26, 1948 (FCA), was published in part in Mortimer, "Capra Defends His *State of Union*," replying to Mortimer, *"State of the Union* Is Mostly Anti." W. R. Burnett's story about Capra is from an interview with Ken Mate and Pat McGilligan, "Burnett," *Film Comment*, February 1983.

Wyler's papers include the various scripts for *Roman Holiday* by Ian McLellan Hunter and others (1949–53); Hunter's September 1949 script is also in FCA, along with related correspondence. The Writers Guild of America's decision to credit Dalton Trumbo with the story of *Roman Holiday* was reported in David Robb, "Trumbo Receives *Holiday* Credit," *DV*, October 22, 1991.

Scripts, financial information, correspondence, and other material on Capra's Paramount films *Riding High* (1949–50, including Capra's 1949 letter to Alice Penneman of SWG on the writing credits) and *Here Comes the Groom* (1947–51, including Robert Riskin's treatment, "You Belong to Me") are in FCA. Riskin's July 13, 1949, letter to Penneman on the *Riding High* credits was provided by Fay Wray. FCA has material on Capra's unproduced Paramount projects and his Caltech project *The Strange Case of the Cosmic Rays* (the basis for his 1957 TV film of that title). George Stevens's papers at AMPAS include a June 12, 1951, draft of a letter to Paramount's Y. Frank Freeman summarizing his complaints against the studio, including the charging of Capra's severance pay to the budget of *Shane*.

State of the Union and related political issues were discussed in Lindsay and Crouse letter to *NYT*, September 2, 1947; Bob Thomas, AP, October 25, 1947; Harold Heffernan, "Menjou Sees New Film Red Exposé," *LAE*, November 15, 1947; "Paradise Lost?," *Time*, January 19, 1948; Thomas F. Brady, "Hollywood Thrift," *NYT*, February 15, 1948; Lew Sheaffer, "Mr. Capra Goes to Washington and Returns All in One Piece," *Brooklyn Eagle*, April 18, 1948; Frank Coniff, "Thomas Film Probe Distorted by Leftists," *New York Journal*, April 19, 1948; "*State of the Union*" (review), *Time*, May 3, 1948; and Charles Aldredge, "Film That Changed History," *Variety*, January 5, 1949. William S. Pechter's comments on *State of the Union* are from his essay "American Madness." Ronald Reagan's borrowing of a line from the film was discussed on *60 Minutes* (1985).

The making of *Riding High* and *Here Comes the Groom* were covered in *HR*, *DV*, *NYT*, *NYHT*, and *Film Daily*, 1949–50; see also Pryor, "Robert Riskin Looks into the Crystal Ball," *NYT*, October 5, 1947; Farber, "Capra's Riding High" (review); and David Platt, "Hollywood's Part in Cold War," *Daily Worker* (New York), August 16, 1950. Capra's March 20, 1951, agreement with the vestigial Liberty Films (i.e., Paramount) for the termination of his services is in FCA. His unhappiness at Paramount, his unmade projects there, and the events surrounding his departure from the studio (see also chapter 19) were reported in articles including Brady, "Hollywood Recants," *NYT*, April 10, 1949; Ezra Goodman, "Hollywood Is Looking for the Sure Thing," *NYHT*, April 17, 1949; Otis L. Guernsey, Jr., "Capra Wants to Woo the Moviegoer Back," *NYHT*, April 16, 1950; Tex McCrary and Jinx Falkenburg, "New York Closeup," *NYHT*, May 30, 1950; Brady, "Studio Calls Off Religious Picture," *NYT*, February 28, 1951; "Capra, Par Call It Quits," *DV*, March 21, 1951; "Red Probers May Shift Hearings to L.A. to Prove They're Not 'Ogres,' " *DV*, May 8, 1951; "Probe Chairman Wood Deplores Job Reprisals Against Confessed Reds," *DV*, May 11, 1951; "Directors Guild Anti-Loyalty Oath Fracas Before Red Probe," *HR*, May 15, 1951; "Frank Capra Checks Off Par Lot Upon Canning *Groom*," *DV*, May 17, 1951; "Capra Exits Par" and "Probers to H'wood?," *Variety*, May 23, 1951; item on Capra's retirement, *DV*, March 14, 1952; Bob Thomas, AP, April 12, 1952; and item on sale of Brentwood home, *HR*, May 1, 1952; see also Swindell, "Frank Capra: Canonized by Film Cultists."

Information on Capra's sale of his rare books is from *NAT*; *The Distinguished Library of Frank Capra* (1949); and correspondence in FCA. Capra's interest in

TV production was reported in "Director Theorizes on Movies at the End of Two Decades," *Baltimore Sun*, June 5, 1932; "Capra Sees Pix-In-Your-Home Setup on a Television Fee Basis," *Variety*, April 14, 1948; and "Tele-Type," *DV*, May 10, 1950.

19. *"The Judas pain"* (pp. 561–610)

Capra's remarks on his headaches and "the Judas pain" are from Barbara Zuanich, "Columbia Pictures' Rise to Golden Year," *LAHE*, May 4, 1975.

The principal sources for this chapter include Capra's Army Intelligence file and material in FCA on his political troubles: his Security Board File, December 29, 1951, which he submitted to the Army-Navy-Air Force Personnel Security Board (ANAFPSB) in response to the denial of his security clearance for the Defense Department's Project VISTA at Caltech; a related file of letters, telegrams, and manuscripts grouped under the heading "VISTA 1951–1952"; and *NAT* uncut, which contains part of the Security Board File and other material about his departure from Hollywood and the denial of his clearance, including his contemplation of suicide (the account of these events in the published version of the autobiography is brief and evasive).

The quotes from John Ford's letter to ANAFPSB on Capra's behalf, n.d. (December 24, 1951), and from his telegram to Capra, n.d. (December 1951), are from Ford's draft copies in the collection of his papers at Indiana University's Lilly Library. The formerly top-secret *Final Report Project Vista: A Study of Ground and Air Tactical Warfare with Especial Reference to the Defense of Western Europe* (California Institute of Technology, February 4, 1952), declassified (with deletions) in 1980, was obtained from the National Archives. The advertisement Capra signed for Russian War Relief, "Russia's 'Scorched Earth' Calls to America's Green Fields," appeared in *NYT*, October 10, 1941; information on the benefit he sponsored at the Shrine Auditorium is from Isabel Morse Jones, "Shostakovich Concert Musical Event of Year," *LAT*, October 10, 1942.

Other important facets of this chapter emerged from correspondence and other documents in FCA on Capra's involvement with the Motion Picture Industry Council; his membership on the Film Advisory Committee of the U.S. Advisory Committee on Information, U.S. State Department; and his involvement in the political clearing of screenwriters for State Department projects (according to Capra's letter to Col. Victor W. Phelps, MPC, Army Member, ANAFPSB, January 10, 1952). The possibility of Capra's return to active duty in the U.S. Army was discussed in his Army Intelligence file: Maj. Gen. K. B. Lawton, "Colonel Frank Capra, 0900209," November 16, 1950, and Col. Egon R. Tausch, "Personnel Action on Officer—CAPRA," November 21, 1950; and Capra's interest in making government propaganda films was mentioned in "Rambling Reporter," *HR*, August 17, 1950, and an SDG press release, J. P. McGowan to *Film Daily*, "Directors and Assistants in the Reserve Force," n.d. (1951) (DGA). Capra's plans for the series of *Why We Arm* or *Peace With Freedom* films are discussed in his 1952 correspondence with Col. Tom B. Blocker and Dr. Earnest C. Watson, and outlined by Capra in his sixty-page submission to the State Department,

"Exploration of Themes and Research on *Peace With Freedom* Films," August 1, 1952 (FCA).

The HUAC *Hearings Regarding the Communist Infiltration of the Motion Picture Industry*, 1947, and the HUAC hearings on *Communist Infiltration of Hollywood Motion-Picture Industry*, 1951–53; and the Tenney committee report on *Communist Front Organizations*, 1948, were used again for this chapter.

Information from the DGA files on the guild's reaction to the 1947 HUAC hearings and to the institution of the blacklist includes telegrams and the minutes of SDG board and membership meetings. The SDG's public statement of October 1947 is from Gordon Kahn, *Hollywood on Trial* (Boni and Gaer, 1948). The Waldorf Statement was printed in "Johnston Gives Industry Policy on Commie Jobs," *DV*, November 26, 1947. The SDG's loyalty oath for officers was quoted in *DV*, December 4, 1947, and the guild printed the oath for members in a *DV* advertisement on October 13, 1950.

Ronald Reagan's FBI informing was revealed in 1985 by the *San Jose Mercury News* (California), based on documents obtained through the Freedom of Information Act: see "Unmasking Informant T-10," *Time*, September 9, 1985. Also see Moldea, *Dark Victory*, and Edwards, *Early Reagan*.

Political events of this period were documented in Ceplair and Englund, *The Inquisition in Hollywood*; Navasky, *Naming Names*; and Schwartz, *The Hollywood Writers' Wars*, although those books have little on the SDG. For a general history of the postwar Red Scare, see David Caute's *The Great Fear: The Anti-Communist Purge Under Truman and Eisenhower* (Simon & Schuster, 1978).

The reporting by *DV* of the 1950 movement to recall SDG President Joseph L. Mankiewicz was relatively thorough (see below), but Capra's role was only partially covered in the press. The chapter on the recall movement in Kenneth L. Geist's biography of Mankiewicz, *Pictures Will Talk: The Life and Films of Joseph L. Mankiewicz* (Charles Scribner's Sons, 1978), provided valuable material, including interviews with participants and a partial transcript of the October 22, 1950, membership meeting, and Mankiewicz made further comments in Elia Kazan's *Elia Kazan: A Life* (Alfred A. Knopf, 1988) and in Robb, "Directors Guild Born Out of Fear 50 Years Ago." Documents found in the DGA files revealed other aspects of the story of the attempted recall and the positions taken by Capra. Among those documents were minutes of board and committee meetings; the files of guild counsel Mabel Walker Willebrandt (including her September 21, 1950, letter to J. Edgar Hoover); and other documents and correspondence, including Capra's non-Communist affidavit as a guild board member, April 6, 1948; the October 11, 1950, recall petition signed by Capra et al.; and Capra's November 1, 1950, letter to the board, with a cover letter to Mankiewicz (parts of Capra's letter to the board were quoted in "Capra SDG Resignation Letter to Be Election Campaign Issue," *HR*, February 16, 1951). The October 13, 1950, telegram sent by Capra and the other members of the recall committee to the membership was published as "Text of Recall Telegram," *DV*, October 16; and Mankiewicz's October 26 letter to the guild membership by *DV* on October 27 in "Mankiewicz Asks Unity on SDG Oath." Related documents were found in FCA, including Capra's draft of his October

19 telegram of resignation from the board; the handwritten draft of his November 1 letter; and his notes on the reverse of the guild's November 25 "Unity Committee Report." George Stevens's comment on his falling-out with Capra is from Geist, *Pictures Will Talk*. The 1984 documentary film *George Stevens: A Filmmaker's Journey* contains interviews with Mankiewicz, John Huston, and Fred Zinnemann on the Mankiewicz recall movement.

Additional material found in FCA relating to Capra's political viewpoint in this period included his letter to Lee Mortimer of the *New York Daily Mirror*, April 26, 1948, published in part in Mortimer, "Capra Defends His *State of Union*," replying to Mortimer, "*State of the Union* Is Mostly Anti"; Capra's letter to William Wyler, June 16, 1950, and Wyler's reply; screenwriter Adele Buffington's seventeen-page, "LIST OF *ESTABLISHED ACTIVE ANTI-COMMUNIST MEMBERS* of the SCREEN WRITERS GUILD for PERMANENT JOBS OR PICTURE-ASSIGNMENTS with the *Motion Picture Division of the Office of International Information* (or any other Government Department or Agency employing writers)" (September 30, 1953), with related correspondence between Buffington and Ward Bond of the Motion Picture Alliance; and the dossier on Herbert Biberman sent to Capra by Willebrandt in 1952. Capra discussed his security clearance crisis with the author and in Richard K. Shull, "Weighty Words from an Old Warrior," *Indianapolis News*, April 20, 1977, and Catherine Chapin, "At 83, a Younger Capra Still Shines Through," KNT News Service, n.d. (1980) (FCA).

Capra's Army Intelligence file also includes the following documents, inter alia, from 1950: "Report of Agency Check" (FBI), October 9; and "Re: Screen Directors Guild Split on 'Loyalty Oath,' " October 18; and from 1951: Maj. A. J. Sutton, "Report of National Agency Check" (G-2), July 12; 1st Lt. Philip J. Lombardi, "Agent Report," July 20; Yoshio G. Kanegai, "Agent Report," August 24; "CAPRA, Frank, Director of Motion Picture Production, CIT, Project VISTA," September 12; Los Angeles Ordnance District, "Clearance Status for Project VISTA Staff Members," September 20; Sixth Army, "Project VISTA," September 21; "Report of National Agency Check," October 2; and "Summary of Information," G-2, October 10.

Among the documents in Capra's VISTA file are his 1951 papers "Regarding the Content of Psychological Warfare," August 9, and "A Photographic Report of VISTA Conclusions," August 10; correspondence (1951) including Capra's September 11 letter to U.S. Army Intelligence (in which he indicated that the Los Angeles FBI office frequently relied on him as a source of information about individuals and their political beliefs); Phelps to Capra, December 14 (detailing the charges against him); Capra to John Ford, December 19; and Lt. Col. John F. Cox, MPC, Army Alternate Member, ANAFPSB, to Capra, January 8, 1952 (notifying Capra of his security clearance).

Documents and printed material previously cited on Michael Wilson were used again for this chapter, as well as additional material from his collection at UCLA, including his letters to "Jules," September 5, 1951; to his parents, September 15, 1951; and to Carey McWilliams, May 27, 1952; and his *Hollywood Review* articles "Hollywood and Korea," January 1953, and "Hollywood on the

Brink of Peace," June 7, 1956. The quotation from Thomas Jefferson cited by Wilson is from a letter to Dr. Benjamin Rush, April 21, 1803, in *Writings* (Library of America edition, Viking, 1984). Correspondence and other documents concerning Wilson's denial of screen credit for *Friendly Persuasion* are in his and William Wyler's papers. See especially Wyler's "(Note for File)," April 8, 1954, and his deposition in Wilson's credit suit, March 1957; and a letter from Jack M. Sattinger, counsel and assistant secretary of Allied Artists Pictures Corp., to company president Steve Broidy, March 9, 1956, quoting the SWG clause which allowed Allied Artists to refuse credit to Wilson. The *Friendly Persuasion* credit issue was covered in *NYT, DV, LAT, Variety,* and *The Nation,* 1956–1959; see also William Wyler, "Credit Where Credit Is Due" (letter), *LAT,* April 16, 1978. Pauline Kael's comment on the film is from *Kiss Kiss Bang Bang* (Little, Brown, 1968).

Articles in *DV* on the SDG loyalty oath and the Mankiewicz recall in 1950 include "Screen Directors' Guild Demands Non-Commy Oath of Members," August 21; "SDG Schism on 'Blacklist,' " October 11; "Mankiewicz Recall to Fail," "Important Notice to All Members of the Screen Directors Guild" (advertisement), and untitled advertisement by Mankiewicz, October 16; "Directors Vote Full Peace," October 19; " 'Recall the Recall' Move Reported in SDG Board Rapprochement," October 20; and "Mankiewicz Wins; SDG Bd. Out," October 24; see also "Reds Ruled Off Gov't Films," August 28; "Communist Charge Enters Directors Guilds' Scuffle," September 20; "U.S. Supreme Bench Upholds Upheaval of DGA Loyalty Oath," December 6, 1966; and Robb, "Directors Guild Born Out of Fear 50 Years Ago." Articles from other sources include D.P., "Screen Directors Guild Split on 'Loyalty Oath,' " *The Daily Worker* (New York), October 18, 1950; "Directors Guild Anti-Loyalty Oath Fracas Before Red Probe"; and Michael Cieply, "The Night They Dumped DeMille," *LAT,* June 4, 1987.

Press commentary on the popularity of *Mr. Deeds Goes to Town* and *Mr. Smith Goes to Washington* in the U.S.S.R. includes Johnston, "Capra Shoots as He Pleases"; "Moscow Goes to Town with *Mr. Deeds* But Without Any Payoff," *Variety,* December 20, 1950; "Chinese Reds Seize All U.S. Films; Yanks Fear Propaganda Distortions," *DV,* January 2, 1951; "State Dept. Demands Soviet Cease Showing Stolen, Distorted U.S. Pix," *DV,* January 23, 1951; "Soviet Rebuffs U.S. on Return of 5 Films," *NYT,* September 22, 1952; and Handzo, "Under Capracorn." Capra's remark to Dimitri Tiomkin is from Tiomkin and Buranelli, *Please Don't Hate Me.*

Capra's comments in his role as a U.S. government spokesman in India are from his "Confidential Informal Report on International Film Festival in India" to Assistant Secretary of State for Public Affairs Howland H. Sargeant, 1952 (FCA), and from Patanjali, "No More Risks for Capra? Fighter Gives Up Fighting," *The Bharat Jyoti* (Bombay), February 3, 1952; " 'Show the Real India in Your Films,' Say Festival Delegates," *The Current* (Bombay), January 30, 1952; "Russian Contribution to Film Art: Mr. Frank Capra's Praise," *Times of India,* February 19, 1952; and "Box Office Only Criterion for U.S. Films," *Statesman,* February 19,

1952. Related material in FCA included Capra's "International Film Festival of India—DIARY," 1952, and his letters to his wife, Lu.

20. A Reputation   (pp. 611–655)

Drafts, correspondence, and other material pertaining to Capra's autobiography, *The Name Above the Title* (1966–71), including John Ford's draft of the ending (Ford to Capra, January 4, 1971), are in FCA, as well as Capra's unpublished autobiographical work *Night Voices* (June–July 1966). Reviews of *NAT* include Thomas M. Pryor, "Capra's Candid Autobiog Colorful Hollywood Saga," *DV*, May 7, 1971; Stein, "Capra Counts His Oscars"; Peter Bogdanovich, "Hollywood," *Esquire*, October 1972; and William Hughes, "Rites of the Bitch-Goddess," *The Nation*, November 27, 1972; see also Stein, "Frank Capra," in Roud, ed., *Cinema: A Critical Dictionary*. Capra commented on *NAT*'s errors in Nancy K. Hart's profile "Frank Capra" in Tuska, *Close-Up: The Hollywood Director*, and on his reception by college audiences in Mariani, "Frank Capra." His February 21, 1972, letter to Rolfe Neill was published in part as "Fun in a Sicily Madhouse." Lu Capra's comment on the writing of *NAT* is from Kimmis Hendrick, "The Capras Retire to a Joint Literary Effort," *The Christian Science Monitor*, March 9, 1970. Ford's characterization of Capra as "an inspiration to those who believe in the American Dream" is from his foreword to *NAT*; John Cassavetes's comment on Capra is from Glatzer and Raeburn, *Frank Capra: The Man and His Films*; and William O. Douglas's is from Scherle and Levy, *The Films of Frank Capra*.

FCA also has the manuscript of Capra's unpublished novel, *Cry Wilderness* (1966–85), loosely based on his film outline "The Gentleman from Tennessee" (April 22, 1959). Scripts, contracts, financial data, correspondence, and other documentation on *The Fallbrook Story*, *Careers for Youth*, his TV science films, *A Hole in the Head*, *Pocketful of Miracles*, *Rendezvous in Space*, and the many unproduced projects he worked on during this period are in FCA, as is his home movie *Duke Snider Day—Fallbrook* (1959). *NAT* uncut and Capra's diaries for 1963–80 provided further information on his projects and other activities.

Capra's ownership of Red Mountain Ranch, Inc. (RMR), in Fallbrook and his involvement with the Fallbrook Public Utility District (FPUD) are documented in FCA, and also in the minutes of FPUD, 1952–55; the records of the San Diego County Grand Jury; and various printed sources. Other important sources were the author's interviews in Fallbrook with Chester and Bett Sticht; James Warner, Capra's brother-in-law and ranch manager; and George F. Yackey, chief water engineer and general manager of FPUD in that period.

Historical material includes Harold R. Marquis, *Fallbrook, 1869–1977* (Fallbrook Historical Society, 2nd ed., 1977); "History of Red Mountain Ranch (1887–1951)" and other documents on the ranch (Caltech); William S. Ralston, "A Compilation of Historical Data on Water Development in the Fallbrook Area," July 15, 1974 (FCA); Carol Olten, "Fallbrook Adds a Salute to Film Honors for Capra," *San Diego Union*, March 4, 1982; and Laura Kaufman, "Capra Played Big Role in Fallbrook's History," "The History of Red Mountain Ranch," and

"Remaking a Garden Paradise," *Escondido Times-Advocate* (California), May 12, 1985. Capra's admission that he felt "dried-up inside" was made to Ann St. John, "On the Town," *HCN*, October 16, 1952.

Documents on the Camp Pendleton water suit and the controversy over the planned Santa Margarita Dam include *United States of America vs. Fallbrook Public Utility District et al.* (various corporations and fifty-three individuals including Capra), U.S. District Court, Southern District of California, Southern Division, January 25, 1951, and summons to Lucille Capra, August 29, 1951; "Interim Report Number Two: Investigation of Fallbrook Public Utility District by the 1955 San Diego County Grand Jury," October 3, 1955; "San Diego County Grand Jury Final Report 1955," February 6, 1956; "Final Report," 1956 San Diego County Grand Jury, 1957; and *United States of America vs. Fallbrook Public Utility District et al.* (including Frank and Lucille Capra), U.S. District Court, Southern District of California, 1958. Capra's resignation letter to the FPUD board, June 6, 1955, is in FCA. Related articles include Stanley High, "Washington Tyranny: Another Case Study," *Reader's Digest,* December 1951, and Ed Ainsworth and Cameron Shipp, "The Government's Big Grab," *Saturday Evening Post,* January 3, 1952. Coverage in the *Fallbrook Enterprise* included Capra's advertisement "The Good Old American Way," April 23, 1954; Capra's letter to V. D. O'Hearn (April 28, 1954), published as an ad on April 30, 1954; "To the People of Fallbrook," from board of FPUD, answering questions from the Willow Glen Water Users Protective Association, April 1, 1955; and "Capra's Loss Bemoaned," June 17, 1955. Coverage of the Grand Jury investigation in the *San Diego Union* (July 1955) included "Jury Hears Capra in Fallbrook Probe," July 29; see also "Frank Capra Summoned," *LAT,* July 27.

Books used for this chapter include Edwin O'Connor's novel *The Last Hurrah* (Little, Brown, 1956); Gore Vidal's play *The Best Man* (Little, Brown, 1960); Dalton Trumbo, *The Time of the Toad: A Study of Inquisition in America and Two Related Pamphlets* (Perennial Library, 1972); and Shamus Culhane, *Talking Animals and Other People* (St. Martin's Press, 1986). The April 30, 1952, HUAC testimony of Edward G. Robinson is in *Communist Infiltration of Hollywood Motion-Picture Industry.* Norman Mailer's comment on McCarthyism is from his essay "Superman Comes to the Supermarket," *Esquire,* November 1960, reprinted in *The Presidential Papers* (G. P. Putnam's Sons, 1963). Capra's unsent July 22, 1954, letter about Sen. Joseph McCarthy to Dr. Lee A. DuBridge is from FCA. Michael Wilson's observation on the blacklist era is from his article "Hollywood and Korea," and his comment on informers is from undated notes on HUAC witnesses in his papers at UCLA.

Capra's involvement in various U.S. government propaganda efforts is documented in FCA, through such material as his diaries; Capra, "Exploration of Themes and Research on *Peace With Freedom* Films"; the film script *YOU* by Myles Connolly, September 15, 1952; Capra's letter to Maj. Gen. B. A. Schriever, USAF, Commander, Air Force Ballistic Missile Division, October 24, 1957, on the proposed film about ICBMs; correspondence and Department of Defense scripts for the "People to People" series of orientation films, including *Korea—*

Battleground for Liberty and *Taiwan—Island of Freedom* (1958–59), with an August 22, 1961, "Outstanding Contribution Award" to Capra; Capra to U.S. State Department, "Report of the United States Delegation to the XIIIth Karlovy Vary International Film Festival," 1962; and Capra to U.S. State Department, "Report of Frank Capra" (on his visit to the U.S.S.R.), December 10, 1963. His comment about going "wherever they ask this immigrant to go" is from Army Archerd's column, *DV*, May 14, 1962; his view of himself as "the apostle of the individual" is from Charles Champlin, "Apostle of the Individual," *LAT*, May 7, 1971. Capra's May 7, 1953, letter to Cecil B. DeMille turning down an administrative position with the USIA is in FCA; Capra's advisory role was reported in "Chief of U.S. Propaganda Pictures Cites Hollywood Aid to Program," *DV*, January 17, 1954. Correspondence and other documents on Capra's participation in the 1960 National Strategy Seminar, U.S. Army War College, Carlisle, Pennsylvania, are in FCA; his Army Intelligence file contains documents on his clearance for the seminar (which also indicate that Capra's files had last been evaluated on November 20, 1954). Capra expressed pacifist sentiments and opposition to the Vietnam War in such interviews as Tom Zito, "Capra Looks at Film Industry That Passed Him By," *Philadelphia Inquirer*, January 17, 1971; Bressan and Moran, "Mr. Capra Goes to College" (1972); and George Bailey, "Why We (Should Not) Fight" (1975). Capra's disparagement of Francis Coppola's *Apocalypse Now* is from McDonough, "For Frank Capra, It's a Wonderful Life," and of Coppola's *Tucker* project from his diary of May 2, 1979; George Lucas's comments on *Tucker: The Man and His Dream* are from Robert Lindsey, "Francis Ford Coppola: Promises to Keep," *NYT*, July 24, 1988. Costa-Gavras's remark to Capra about political films is quoted in Capra to Ernesto G. Laura, June 11, 1977 (FCA).

Information on Capra's relationships with various U.S. presidents is from sources including Capra's diaries; his May 9, 1960, letter to his daughter, Lulu, about John F. Kennedy and Richard Nixon, in reply to her letter of May 4, 1960, and his July 18, 1960, letter to Lulu about Kennedy (FCA); a newspaper item citing Capra on "High Hopes" and the 1960 election, unidentified source, n.d. (1960) (FCA); Edward R. Murrow, Director, USIA, to President Kennedy, September 21, 1963 (John F. Kennedy Library); President Kennedy to Capra, November 21, 1963 (FCA); Helen Thomas, "Dinner with Johnson," UPI, April 14, 1964; and Capra to President Gerald R. Ford, August 12, 1974 (FCA).

The biographical notes "Frank Capra" and "Detailed Biographical Notes—Frank Capra," n.d. (1952), prepared for N. W. Ayer & Son, Inc., by Jeanne Curtis Webber, are in FCA; Webber wrote of Capra's science films in "Science Enlists the Capra Genius," *The Sign*, June 1957. Other articles on the series include Sheilah Graham column, *DV*, April 22, 1952; "AT&T Sets Costliest TV Show," *DV*, October 16, 1952; and William E. Haesche, Jr., "Our New Science TV Series Performs a Public Service," *Bell Telephone Magazine*, Spring 1957.

The question "Why doesn't Frank Capra make movies?" was asked by Herb Stein, "On the Hollywood Scene," *New York Morning Telegraph*, August 10, 1955. Capra's answers are quoted in Philip K. Scheuer, "Capra Once Again Shoots for Laughs," *LAT*, November 25, 1958; Murray Schumach, "Hollywood

Maverick," *NYT*, May 28, 1961; and John C. Waugh, "Capra Renews Hope for Comedy Genre," unidentified source, n.d. (1950s) (FCA). He also tried to explain his malaise in Fred Hift, "Capra of *Deeds & Smith* Sagas Sees Hollywood Now Over-Intellectual," *Variety*, July 16, 1958.

Capra's return to Columbia Pictures in 1956 to work on the remake of *Lady for a Day* and on *Joseph and His Brethren* is documented in the files of his lawyer Mabel Walker Willebrandt (FCA); and the story files of Columbia Pictures. See also Thomas, *King Cohn*, and Pryor, "Capra Return to Film Business," *NYT*, April 7, 1956.

A Hole in the Head was reviewed in 1959 by Scheuer, "*Hole in Head* Pleasant Diversion," *LAT*, June 18; Bosley Crowther, "Capra's *A Hole in the Head*," July 16, and "Return of a Native," *NYT*, July 26; and Peter Bogdanovich, "Crusade Forgotten," *Frontier*, October. See also Andrew Sarris, "The American Cinema," *Film Culture*, Spring 1963. Reviews of *Pocketful of Miracles* in 1961 include *HR*, November 1; Elaine Rothschild, *Films in Review*, December; A. H. Weiler, "Capra's *Pocketful of Miracles* Opens at Two Theatres Here," *NYT*, December 19; and "Acting Their Age," *Time*, December 29. See also Pechter's essay "American Madness" (1962). John Ford's plea to Capra to "cut out this talk of retiring" is from "Capra Feted at Dinner," *LAHE*, May 14, 1962. Bosley Crowther's review of *Rendezvous in Space*, "A Disappointing Science Film," appeared in *NYT*, September 10, 1964.

Capra's financial net worth of approximately $5 million originally estimated for the author by Chester Sticht, was confirmed by documents in FCA. See especially "Account Statement," Bank of America Trust Department, Palm Springs, California, to Frank and Lucille Capra, n.d. (November 9, 1981), listing the total market value of their assets (common stocks, government bonds, municipal bonds, real estate, invested cash, and miscellaneous) at $4,507,070, with an annual income of $266,227. Frank and Lu Capra's signing of the agreements establishing the Capra Family Trust took place on November 25, 1974, according to his diary of that date. Capra's remark about being "the poorest director you ever saw" is from Shales, "Lights! Capra! Action!" Sticht's dismissal on December 1, 1974, was noted in Capra's diaries for October 18, 1974, and February 11, 1975.

Fay Wray's July 14, 1977, letter to Irv Letofsky of *LAT* about Capra's relationship with Robert Riskin was found in FCA, as was correspondence between Capra and *LAT*'s Charles Champlin pertaining to David W. Rintels's 1977 attacks on Capra in *LAT*, "Someone's Been Sitting in His Chair" and " 'Someone Else's Guts'—The Rintels Rebuttal"; and Capra's article " 'One Man, One Film'—The Capra Contention."

Lu Capra's letters to her husband from the hospital, March 30, 1963, and n.d. (1963), are in FCA. Her death on July 1, 1984, at Eisenhower Medical Center in Rancho Mirage, California, was recorded in Certificate of Death: Lucille Warner Capra. Capra's 1985 strokes were reported in *LAHE*, *DV*, and *LAT*, August 12–22, 1985. His death on September 3, 1991, was recorded in Certificate of Death: Frank Capra, County of Riverside, Riverside, California, registered September 5, 1991.

Filmography

Code: DIST: Distributor; P: Producer; D: Director; AD: Assistant Director; S: Screenwriter; T: Titles; CAM: Cinematographer (in black and white unless otherwise indicated); WITH: Principal Cast Members; R: Release Date; L: Length (where known); FC, Frank Capra.

Miscellaneous Silent Film Work

1915 *Our Wonderful Schools.* DIST-P: Los Angeles Board of Education (produced with the help of D. W. Griffith's Reliance-Majestic Co.). D-S: Rob Wagner. CAM: Hugh McClung. FC may have taken part in the making of this documentary on the Los Angeles school system, partly filmed at Manual Arts High School in the spring of 1915. R: June 11, 1915.

1915–1918 While a student at Throop College of Technology in Pasadena, FC "earned a few dollars by selling 'gags' and situations for screen comedies to Mack Sennett," according to his 1941 Warner Bros. publicity biography; he also may have worked as a film editor for Sennett in this period, and he assisted newsreel cameraman Roy Wiggins in photographing the Mount Wilson Observatory.

1919 *The Outcasts of Poker Flat.* DIST: Universal. P: P. A. Powers. D: Jack Ford. S: H. Tipton Steck, from the stories "The Outcasts of Poker Flat" and "The Luck of Roaring Camp" by Bret Harte. CAM: John W. Brown. WITH: Harry Carey, Cullen Landis, Gloria Hope, J. Farrell MacDonald, and FC uncredited as an extra loading a steamboat. R: July 6, 1919. L: 6 reels.

1919 FC reportedly was an extra in various films made in Hollywood, including another Harry Carey–Jack Ford Western at Universal.

1919 FC worked as a laborer with the Christie Film Company in Hollywood.

1920 *The Pulse of Life.* DIST: None. P: Tri-State Motion Picture Co. (Reno, Nevada). WITH: Peggy Lawson, W. Montgomery, Denison Standing, Frank Russell [Capra?], Sylvia Goddisart. R: April 25, 1920. L: 6 reels. Individual production credits on this and the following film are unknown, but Tri-State's president was W. M. Plank, Ida May Heitmann was vice president, and FC was secretary-treasurer. It is likely that FC wrote the scripts for these films, but Plank probably directed them.

1920 *The Scar of Love.* DIST: None. P: Tri-State Motion Picture Co. (Reno, Nevada). WITH: Peggy Lawson. R: None. L: 5 reels. For other credits, see above. The only known reference to this possibly apocryphal film was an item in *Variety* on January 13, 1920, stating that filming on it and *The Pulse of Life* had been completed.

1920 *Screen Snapshots.* DIST: States' rights. P: Jack Cohn, Louis Lewyn, for CBC. L: 1 reel. FC was Lewyn's assistant and editor on the first few issues of this series of shorts about life behind the scenes in the motion picture industry; he probably also did some of the directing.

1921–24 FC worked as an assistant to Waldon S. (Walt) Ball at the Ball Laboratory in San Francisco, where he helped process feature film dailies (including the dailies for the 1923 location filming of Erich von Stroheim's *Greed*) and newsreel footage, and also shot and edited film on assignment from various Ball customers.

1921 Scenic documentary on San Francisco (title unknown). P: Charles A. Warren et al. T: FC. R: Unknown. FC sued Warren in October 1921 to collect his fifty-dollar salary.

1921 Documentary (title unknown) on the November 6–7 visit to San Francisco of the Italian warship *Libia.* P: The Italian Virtus Club of San Francisco. D: FC. T: FC, Giulio DeMoro. WITH: Admiral Ernesto Burzagli, officers and men of the *Libia,* Dorothy Valerga [Dorothy Revier], and citizens of San Francisco. R: December 3, 1921.

1921 *Life's Greatest Question.* DIST: CBC. P: George H. Davis, for Quality Film Prods./The Paul Gerson Pictures Corp. D-S: Harry J. Revier. CAM: Del Claussen. WITH: Roy Stewart, Louise Lovely, Dorothy Valerga [Dorothy Revier], Harry Van Meter, Eugene Burr. FC probably was AD on this film. R: December 10, 1921. L: 5 reels.

1921–22 *Fulta Fisher's Boarding House.* DIST: Pathé. P: G. F. Harris, David F. Supple, for Fireside Productions (San Francisco). D: FC. S: FC, Walter Montague, from the poem "The Ballad of Fisher's Boarding-House" by Rudyard Kipling. CAM: Roy Wiggins. WITH: Mildred Owens, Ethan Allen, Olaf Skavlan, Gerald Griffin, Oreste Seragnoli. R: April 2, 1922. L: 1 reel.

1921–22 *The Village Blacksmith.* DIST: Unknown. P: G. F. Harris, David F. Supple, for Fireside Productions. D: FC. S: FC (and Walter Montague?), from the poem by Henry Wadsworth Longfellow. R: June 1922 (?). L: 1 reel.

1921–22 *The Looking Glass.* DIST: None. P-D-S credits as above. From a story by F. B. Lowe. R: None. L: 1 reel.

1921–22 *The Barefoot Boy.* DIST: None. P-D-S credits as above. From the poem by John Greenleaf Whittier. Partially shot in the two-strip Prizma Color process. R: None. L: 1 reel.

1921–22 *"Curfew Must Not Ring Tonight."* DIST: None. FC's possible involvement unknown on this Fireside production from the poem by Rose Hartwick Thorpe. R: None. L: 1 reel.

1922 *The Broadway Madonna.* DIST: FBO. P: Quality Film Prods./R-C Pictures Corp./The Paul Gerson Pictures Corp. D-S: Harry J. Revier. CAM: Del Claussen. WITH: Dorothy Revier, Jack Connolly, Harry Van Meter, Eugene Burr, Juanita Hansen. FC probably was AD on this film. R: October 29, 1922. L: 6 reels. (Working title: *Mothers of Men.*)

1922–23 *Pop Tuttle the Fire Chief; Pop Tuttle's Grass Widow; Pop Tuttle's Long Shot; Pop Tuttle, Deteckative; Pop Tuttle's Polecat Plot; Pop Tuttle's Lost Control; Pop Tuttle's Lost Nerve; Pop Tuttle's Russian Rumor.* DIST: FBO. P: William A. Howell, Paul Gerson. D: Robert Eddy. S: A. H. Giebler. CAM: Roy Vaughan. WITH: Dan Mason, Wilna Hervey, Helen Howell, Oliver J. Eckhardt. R: August 1922 through May 1923. L: 2 reels each. FC worked as a prop man, AD, editor, and gag man on these installments of the Plum Center comedy series, filmed in Belmont and San Francisco.

1924 *Waterfront Wolves.* DIST: Renown Pictures. P: Paul Gerson, for The Paul Gerson Pictures Corp. D-S: Tom Gibson. AD: FC. CAM: George Crocker. WITH: Ora Carew, Jay Morley, Helen Howell, Hal Stephens, Dick La Reno. R: January 15, 1924. L: 5 reels.

1924 *Three Days to Live.* DIST: Renown Pictures. P: Paul Gerson, for The Paul Gerson Pictures Corp. D-S: Tom Gibson. AD: FC. WITH: Ora Carew, Jay Morley, Dick La Reno, Hal Stephens, Helen Howell. R: April 22, 1924. L: 5 reels.

1924 *Paying the Limit.* DIST: States' rights. P: Paul Gerson, for The Paul Gerson Pictures Corp. D-S: Tom Gibson. AD: FC. CAM: George Crocker. WITH: Ora Carew, Helen Howell, Eddie O'Brien, Arthur Wellington, Jay Morley. R: August 1924. L: 5 reels.

1924 FC worked as an AD for FBO (Film Booking Offices of America, Inc.) at its Hollywood studio in the spring of 1924. Titles of the films on which he worked are unknown. In June 1924 he worked on the scripts of two short comedies (titles unknown) in the Hollywood Photoplay Company's *Puppy Love* series, starring Gordon White.

Our Gang *Comedies*

Two-reelers for the Hal Roach Studios (produced by Roach and distributed by Pathé), listed in order of release:

1924 *Cradle Robbers.* D: Robert F. McGowan. S: Hal Roach (and FC, uncredited). T: H. M. Walker. CAM: Blake Wagner. WITH: Mickey Daniels, Mary Kornman, Joe Cobb, Allen (Farina) Hoskins, Ernie (Sunshine Sammy) Morrison. R: June 1, 1924.

1924 *Jubilo, Jr.* D: Robert F. McGowan. S: Hal Roach (and FC, uncredited), based on the title character of the serial *Jubilo* by Ben Ames Williams and the 1919 feature film adaptation starring Will Rogers. T: H. M. Walker. CAM: Art Lloyd, Robert Doran. WITH: Will Rogers, Mickey Daniels, Mary Kornman, Joe Cobb, Charles Parrott [Charlie Chase]. R: June 29, 1924.

1924 *It's a Bear.* D: Robert F. McGowan (and Mark Goldain, uncredited). s: Hal Roach (and Goldain, FC, uncredited). T: H. M. Walker. cam: Bob Walters. with: Mickey Daniels, Mary Kornman, Joe Cobb, Allen (Farina) Hoskins, Ernie (Sunshine Sammy) Morrison. r: July 27, 1924.

1924 *High Society.* d: Robert F. McGowan. s: Hal Roach (and FC, uncredited). T: H. M. Walker. with: Mickey Daniels, Mary Kornman, Jackie Condon, Andy Samuels, Allen (Farina) Hoskins. r: August 24, 1924.

1924 *Every Man for Himself.* d: Robert F. McGowan. s: Hal Roach (and FC, uncredited). T: H. M. Walker. cam: Art Lloyd. with: Mickey Daniels, Mary Kornman, Allen (Farina) Hoskins, Joe Cobb, Andy Samuels. r: October 19, 1924.

Mack Sennett Comedies

Two-reelers (unless otherwise indicated) for the Mack Sennett Studios (produced by Sennett and distributed by Pathé), listed in order of release:

1924 *Little Robinson Corkscrew.* d: Ralph Ceder. No s credit (FC, uncredited). T: J. A. Waldron. cam: George Crocker, George Unholz. with: Ralph Graves, Alice Day, Andy Clyde, Vernon Dent, Billy Bevan. r: September 21, 1924.

1924 *Riders of the Purple Cows.* d: Ralph Ceder. No s credit (FC, uncredited). T: J. A. Waldron. cam: George Crocker, George Unholz. with: Ralph Graves, Alice Day, Andy Clyde, Vernon Dent, Tiny Ward. r: October 19, 1924.

1924 *The Reel Virginian.* d: Ed Kennedy, Reggie Morris. s: Arthur Ripley, FC. T: J. A. Waldron. cam: George Crocker, Bob Ladd. with: Ben Turpin, Alice Day, Christian J. Frank, Sam Allen, Fred Ko Vert. r: October 26, 1924.

1924 *All Night Long.* d: Harry Edwards. s: Vernon Smith, Hal Conklin (and FC, uncredited). T: J. A. Waldron. cam: William Williams, Lee Davis. with: Harry Langdon, Natalie Kingston, Fanny Kelly, Vernon Dent. r: November 9, 1924. (Working title: *Over Here.* Preview title: *War Is Swell.* Remade as *The Leather Necker,* Columbia, 1935, starring Langdon.)

1925 *A Wild Goose Chaser.* d: Lloyd Bacon. s: FC (based on his play *Don't Change Your Husbands*). T: Felix Adler, A. H. Giebler. cam: George Crocker, Sam Moran. with: Ben Turpin, Madeline Hurlock, Trilby Clark, Jack Cooper, Eugenia Gilbert. r: January 18, 1925.

1925 *Boobs in the Wood.* d: Harry Edwards. s: Arthur Ripley (and FC, uncredited). T: J. A. Waldron. cam: William Williams, Lee Davis. with: Harry Langdon, Natalie Kingston, Vernon Dent, Marie Astaire. r: February 1, 1925.

1925 *Plain Clothes.* d: Harry Edwards. s: Arthur Ripley, FC. T: Felix Adler, A. H. Giebler. cam: William Williams, Earl Stafford. with: Harry Langdon, Claire Cushman, Jean Hathaway, Vernon Dent, William McCall. r: March 29, 1925.

1925 *Breaking the Ice.* d: Al Santell. s: FC, Jefferson Moffitt. T: Felix Adler, A. H. Giebler. cam: George Crocker, Sam Moran. with: Ralph Graves, Marvin Lobach, Alice Day. r: April 5, 1925.

1925 *The Marriage Circus.* d: Reggie Morris, Ed Kennedy. s: FC, Vernon Smith. T: Felix Adler, A. H. Giebler. CAM: George Spear, Lee Davis. WITH: Ben Turpin, Louise Carver, Madeline Hurlock, Sunshine Hart, William C. Lawrence, Christian J. Frank. R: April 12, 1925. (Working title: *Three Men*. Preview title: *Monsieur Don't Care*.)

1925 *Super Hooper-Dyne Lizzies*. D: Del Lord. S: Jefferson Moffitt, FC. T: Felix Adler, A. H. Giebler. CAM: George Spear, George Unholz. WITH: Billy Bevan, Andy Clyde, Lillian Knight, John J. Richardson. R: May 14, 1925. (Preview title: *Bedtime Stories*. Reissued in 1978 as *Super Power Automobiles*.)

1925 *Good Morning, Nurse!* D: Lloyd Bacon. S: Jefferson Moffit, FC. T: Felix Adler, A. H. Giebler. CAM: William Williams, Lee Davis. WITH: Ralph Graves, Olive Borden, Marvin Lobach, William McCall, Eva Thatcher. R: May 21, 1925. (Working title: *Pills and Spills*.)

1925 *Sneezing Beezers!* D: Del Lord. S: Jefferson Moffitt, FC. T: Felix Adler, A. H. Giebler. CAM: George Spear, George Unholz. WITH: Andy Clyde, Billy Bevan, Madeline Hurlock, John J. Richardson, Kewpie Morgan. R: July 19, 1925. (Preview title: *King Jazzbo*.)

1925 *Cupid's Boots*. D: Ed Kennedy. S: FC. T: J. A. Waldron. CAM: George Crocker, Bob Ladd. WITH: Ralph Graves, Christian J. Frank, Thelma Hill, Yorke Sherwood, Evelyn Sherman. R: July 25, 1925.

1925 *The Iron Nag*. D: Del Lord. S: FC, Jefferson Moffitt. T: Felix Adler, A. H. Giebler. CAM: George Spear, George Unholz. WITH: Andy Clyde, Ruth Taylor, Sunshine Hart, Billy Bevan, John J. Richardson. R: August 9, 1925.

1925 *Lucky Stars*. D: Harry Edwards. S: Arthur Ripley, FC. T: A. H. Giebler. CAM: George Crocker. WITH: Harry Langdon, Vernon Dent, Natalie Kingston. R: August 16, 1925. (Working title: *The Medicine Man*.)

1925 *Cold Turkey*. D: Eddie Cline. S: FC, Jefferson Moffitt. T: Felix Adler, A. H. Giebler. CAM: Vernon Walker, Bob Ladd. WITH: Alice Day, Sunshine Hart, Raymond McKee, Pat Harmon, Sam Lufkin. R: August 30, 1925.

1925 *Love and Kisses*. D: Eddie Cline. S: FC, Jefferson Moffitt. T: Felix Adler, A. H. Giebler. CAM: Vernon Walker, Bob Ladd. WITH: Alice Day, Raymond McKee, Sunshine Hart, Jack Cooper, Barbara Tennant. R: September 27, 1925.

1925 *There He Goes*. D: Harry Edwards. S: Arthur Ripley, FC. WITH: Harry Langdon, Peggy Montgomery, Frank Whitson, Vernon Dent. R: November 19, 1925. L: 3 reels.

1926 *Saturday Afternoon*. D: Harry Edwards. S: Arthur Ripley, FC. T: A. H. Giebler. CAM: William Williams. WITH: Harry Langdon, Vernon Dent, Alice Ward, Ruth Hiatt, Peggy Montgomery. R: January 31, 1926. L: 3 reels.

1927 (produced in 1925) *Soldier Man*. D: Harry Edwards (and FC, uncredited). S: Arthur Ripley, FC. T: A. H. Giebler. CAM: William Williams, Ernie Crockett. WITH: Harry Langdon, Natalie Kingston. R: November 27, 1927. (Working title: *Soldier Boy*.)

1927 (produced in 1925) *Fiddlesticks*. D: Harry Edwards. S: Arthur Ripley, FC. T: Tay Garnett. CAM: William Williams. WITH: Harry Langdon, Vernon Dent. R: November 27, 1927.

1928 *The Swim Princess*. D: Alf Goulding. S: James J. Tynan, FC (and

Nick Barrows, uncredited). T: Paul Perez. CAM: Ray Rennahan, Lewis Jennings (part Technicolor). WITH: Daphne Pollard, Carole Lombard, James Hallett, Irving Bacon, Andy Clyde. R: February 26, 1928.

1928   *Smith's Burglar.* D: Phil Whitman. S: Nick Barrows, FC (and Vernon Smith, Earle Rodney, uncredited). T: Paul Perez, Maurice Stephens. CAM: John W. Boyle, Frank Heisler. WITH: Raymond McKee, Ruth Hiatt, Mary Ann Jackson, Sunshine Hart, Otto Fries. R: December 9, 1928.

1929 (produced in 1927)   *Smith's "Uncle Tom."* D: Phil Whitman. S: Jefferson Moffitt, Earle Rodney, FC, Vernon Smith, Harry McCoy, Walter Lantz. T: Maurice Stephens. CAM: John Boyle, Lee Davis, Vernon Walker. WITH: Raymond McKee, Ruth Hiatt, Mary Ann Jackson, Irene Allen, Paralee Coleman. R: 1929.

Harry Langdon Features

1926   *Tramp, Tramp, Tramp.* DIST: First National. P: The Harry Langdon Corp. D: Harry Edwards. STORY: FC, Arthur Ripley, Tim Whelan, Hal Conklin, J. Frank Holliday, Gerald Duffy, Murray Roth. T: George Marion, Jr. CAM: Elgin Lessley. WITH: Harry Langdon, Joan Crawford, Edward Davis, Alec B. Francis, Tom Murray. R: March 17, 1926. L: 6 reels. (Working title: *Mr. Nobody.*)

1926   *Ella Cinders.* DIST: First National. P-D: Alfred E. Green. S: Frank Griffin, Mervyn LeRoy, from the comic strip *Cinderella in the Movies* by William Counselman and Charles Plumb. T: George Marion, Jr. CAM: Arthur Martinelli. WITH: Colleen Moore, Lloyd Hughes, Vera Lewis, Doris Baker, Harry Langdon. According to Moore, FC assisted Langdon in the filming of his cameo appearance. R: June 6, 1926. L: 7 reels.

1926   *The Strong Man.* DIST: First National. P: The Harry Langdon Corp. D: FC. STORY: Arthur Ripley. ADAPTATION: Tim Whelan, Tay Garnett, James Langdon, Hal Conklin (and Robert Eddy, Clarence Hennecke, uncredited). T: Reed Heustis. CAM: Elgin Lessley, Glenn Kershner. WITH: Harry Langdon, Priscilla Bonner, Arthur Thalasso, Gertrude Astor, William V. Mong. R: September 5, 1926. L: 7 reels. (Working title: *The Yes Man.*)

1927   *Long Pants.* DIST: First National. P: The Harry Langdon Corp. D: FC. STORY: Arthur Ripley (and FC, uncredited). ADAPTATION: Robert Eddy. COMEDY CONSTRUCTION: Clarence Hennecke. CAM: Elgin Lessley, Glenn Kershner. WITH: Harry Langdon, Priscilla Bonner, Alma Bennett, Betty Francisco, Alan Roscoe. R: March 26, 1927. L: 7 reels (original version, including a reel in Technicolor, which was cut before the national release).

1927 (produced in 1925)   *His First Flame.* DIST: Pathé. P: The Mack Sennett Studios. D: Harry Edwards. STORY: Arthur Ripley, FC. T: A. H. Giebler. CAM: William Williams. WITH: Harry Langdon, Natalie Kingston, Ruth Hiatt, Vernon Dent, Bud Jamieson. R: May 3, 1927. L: 6 reels.

1927   *Three's a Crowd.* DIST: First National. P: The Harry Langdon Corp. D: Harry Langdon. STORY: Arthur Ripley (and FC, uncredited). ADAPTATION: James Langdon, Robert Eddy. CAM: Elgin Lessley, Frank Evans. WITH: Harry Langdon, Gladys McConnell, Cornelius Keefe, Henry Barrows, Frances Raymond. R: August 28, 1927. L: 6 reels. (Working title: *Gratitude.*)

Feature for First National

1927   *For the Love of Mike.* DIST: First National. P: Robert Kane. D: FC. S: Leland Hayward, J. Clarkson Miller, from the story "Hell's Kitchen" by John Moroso. CAM: Ernest Haller. WITH: Ben Lyon, George Sidney, Ford Sterling, Claudette Colbert, Hugh Cameron. R: August 22, 1927. L: 7 reels. (No print exists.)

Features for Columbia Pictures (Silent)

1928   *That Certain Thing.* P: Harry Cohn. D: FC. S: Elmer Harris. T: Al Boasberg. CAM: Joseph Walker. WITH: Viola Dana, Ralph Graves, Burr McIntosh, Aggie Herring, Carl Gerard. R: January 1, 1928. L: 7 reels.

1928   *So This Is Love.* P: Harry Cohn. D: FC. S: Elmer Harris, Rex Taylor, from a story by Norman Springer. CAM: Ray June. WITH: Shirley Mason, William (Buster) Collier, Jr., Johnnie Walker, Ernie Adams, Carl Gerard. R: February 2, 1928. L: 6 reels.

1928   *The Matinee Idol.* P: Harry Cohn. D: FC. S: Elmer Harris, Peter Milne, from the story "Come Back to Aaron" by Robert Lord and Ernest S. Pagano. CAM: Phillip Tannura. WITH: Bessie Love, Johnnie Walker, Lionel Belmore, Ernest Hilliard, Sidney D'Albrook. R: March 14, 1928. L: 6 reels. (No print exists. Remade by Columbia in 1936 as *The Music Goes 'Round.*)

1928   *The Way of the Strong.* P: Harry Cohn. D: FC. S: William Counselman, Peter Milne. CAM: Ben Reynolds. WITH: Mitchell Lewis, Alice Day, Margaret Livingston, Theodore von Eltz, William Norton Bailey. R: June 19, 1928. L: 6 reels.

1928   *Say It With Sables.* P-D: FC. S: Dorothy Howell, from a story by FC and Peter Milne. CAM: Joseph Walker. WITH: Helene Chadwick, Francis X. Bushman, Margaret Livingston, Arthur Rankin, June Nash. R: July 13, 1928. L: 7 reels. (Only the trailer for this film exists.)

1928   *The Power of the Press.* P: Jack Cohn. D: FC. S: Frederick A. Thompson, Sonya Levien, from a story by Thompson. CAM: Chet Lyons, Ted Tetzlaff (and Joseph Walker, uncredited). WITH: Douglas Fairbanks, Jr., Jobyna Ralston, Mildred Harris, Philo McCullough, Wheeler Oakman. R: October 31, 1928. L: 7 reels. (Existing prints incomplete.)

Features for Columbia Pictures (Sound)

1928   *Submarine.* P: Irvin Willat, Harry Cohn. D: FC (FC replaced Willat and reshot all of his footage). S: Winifred Dunn, Dorothy Howell, from a story by Norman Springer. CAM: Joseph Walker. WITH: Jack Holt, Ralph Graves, Dorothy Revier, Clarence Burton, Arthur Rankin. R: August 28, 1928. L: 93 mins. (Working titles: *Into the Depths, Out of the Depths.* Released with music and sound effects.)

1929   *The Younger Generation.* P-D: FC. S: Sonya Levien, Howard J. Green, from the play *It Is to Laugh* by Fannie Hurst. CAM: Ted Tetzlaff, Ben Reynolds. WITH: Jean Hersholt, Ricardo Cortez, Lina Basquette, Rosa Rosanova,

Rex Lease. R: March 4, 1929. L: 75 mins. (Released with music and four talking sequences.)

1929   *The Donovan Affair*. P-D: FC. S: Howard J. Green, Dorothy Howell, from the play by Owen Davis. CAM: Ted Tetzlaff. WITH: Jack Holt, Dorothy Revier, William (Buster) Collier, Jr., Agnes Ayres, John Roche. R: April 11, 1929. L: 83 mins. (Also released in a silent version for theaters not equipped for sound.)

1929   *Flight*. P-D: FC. S: Howard J. Green, FC, from a story by Ralph Graves. CAM: Joseph Walker, Joseph Novak, Elmer Dyer. WITH: Jack Holt, Ralph Graves, Lila Lee, Alan Roscoe, Harold Goodwin. R: September 13, 1929. L: 110 mins.

1930   *Ladies of Leisure*. P-D: FC. S: Jo Swerling, from the play *Ladies of the Evening* by Milton Herbert Gropper. CAM: Joseph Walker. WITH: Barbara Stanwyck, Ralph Graves, Lowell Sherman, Marie Prevost, Nance O'Neill. R: April 2, 1930. L: 98 mins. (Also released in a silent version for theaters not equipped for sound.)

1930   *Rain or Shine*. P-D: FC. S: Dorothy Howell, Jo Swerling, from the play by James Gleason and Maurice Marks. CAM: Joseph Walker. WITH: Joe Cook, Louise Fazenda, Joan Peers, William (Buster) Collier, Jr., Dave Chasen. R: July 26, 1930. L: 87 mins.

1931   *Dirigible*. P-D: FC. S: Jo Swerling, Dorothy Howell, from a story by Lt. Comdr. Frank Wead, USN (and James Warner Bellah, uncredited). CAM: Joseph Walker, Elmer Dyer. WITH: Jack Holt, Ralph Graves, Fay Wray, Hobart Bosworth, Clarence Muse. R: April 3, 1931. L: 102 mins.

1931   *The Miracle Woman*. P-D: FC. S: Jo Swerling, Dorothy Howell, from the play *Bless You, Sister* by John Meehan and Robert Riskin. CAM: Joseph Walker. WITH: Barbara Stanwyck, David Manners, Sam Hardy, Beryl Mercer, Russell Hopton. R: July 20, 1931. L: 91 mins.

1931   *Platinum Blonde*. P-D: FC. S: Robert Riskin, Jo Swerling, Dorothy Howell, from a story by Harry E. Chandler and Douglas W. Churchill. CAM: Joseph Walker. WITH: Robert Williams, Loretta Young, Jean Harlow, Louise Closser Hale, Halliwell Hobbes. R: October 30, 1931. L: 82 mins. (Working titles: *The Blonde Lady, Gallagher*. Preview title: *The Gilded Cage*.)

1932   *Forbidden*. P-D: FC. S: Jo Swerling, from a story by FC. CAM: Joseph Walker. WITH: Barbara Stanwyck, Adolphe Menjou, Ralph Bellamy, Dorothy Peterson, Thomas Jefferson. R: January 9, 1932. L: 87 mins.

1932   *American Madness*. P-D: FC (FC replaced Allan Dwan and Roy William Neill as director, reshooting all of their footage). S: Robert Riskin. CAM: Joseph Walker. WITH: Walter Huston, Pat O'Brien, Kay Johnson, Constance Cummings, Gavin Gordon. R: August 14, 1932. L: 75 mins. (Preview title: *Faith*.)

1933   *The Bitter Tea of General Yen*. P: Walter Wanger, FC. D: FC. S: Edward Paramore, from the novel by Grace Zaring Stone. CAM: Joseph Walker. WITH: Barbara Stanwyck, Nils Asther, Gavin Gordon, Toshia Mori, Walter Connolly. R: January 11, 1933. L: 88 mins.

1933   *Lady for a Day*. P-D: FC. S: Robert Riskin, from the short story "Madame La Gimp" by Damon Runyon. CAM: Joseph Walker. WITH: May Robson,

Warren William, Guy Kibbee, Ned Sparks, Walter Connolly. R: September 7, 1933. L: 95 mins. (Working titles: *Madame La Gimp, Apple Mary, Apple Annie, Lovable Rogues*. Preview title: *Beggars' Holiday*. Remade by FC in 1961 as *Pocketful of Miracles*.)

1934 *It Happened One Night*. P-D: FC. S: Robert Riskin, from the story "Night Bus" by Samuel Hopkins Adams. CAM: Joseph Walker. WITH: Clark Gable, Claudette Colbert, Walter Connolly, Jameson Thomas, Roscoe Karns. R: February 23, 1934. L: 105 mins. (Working title: *Night Bus*. Academy Awards for best picture, director, writer, actor, actress. Remade by Columbia in 1956 as a musical, *You Can't Run Away From It*.)

1934 *Broadway Bill*. P-D: FC. S: Robert Riskin (and Sidney Buchman, uncredited), from the story "On the Nose" by Mark Hellinger. CAM: Joseph Walker. WITH: Warner Baxter, Myrna Loy, Walter Connolly, Helen Vinson, Clarence Muse. R: November 29, 1934. L: 90 mins. (Remade by FC in 1950 as *Riding High*.)

1936 *Mr. Deeds Goes to Town*. P-D: FC. S: Robert Riskin (and Myles Connolly, uncredited), from the story "Opera Hat" by Clarence Budington Kelland. CAM: Joseph Walker. WITH: Gary Cooper, Jean Arthur, George Bancroft, Lionel Stander, Douglass Dumbrille. R: April 12, 1936. L: 115 mins. (Working titles: *Opera Hat, Cinderella Man, A Gentleman Goes to Town*. Academy Award for best director. Adapted as an ABC-TV series in 1969–70.)

1937 *Lost Horizon*. P-D: FC. S: Robert Riskin (and Sidney Buchman, Myles Connolly, Herbert J. Biberman, uncredited), from the novel by James Hilton. CAM: Joseph Walker. WITH: Ronald Colman, Jane Wyatt, John Howard, Thomas Mitchell, Sam Jaffe. R: March 2, 1937. L: 132 mins. (original road-show version). (Academy Awards to art director Stephen Goossón and editors Gene Havlick and Gene Milford. Remade as a musical by Columbia in 1973.)

1938 *You Can't Take It With You*. P-D: FC. S: Robert Riskin, from the play by George S. Kaufman and Moss Hart. CAM: Joseph Walker. WITH: Jean Arthur, Lionel Barrymore, James Stewart, Edward Arnold, Ann Miller. R: September 2, 1938. L: 127 mins. (Academy Awards for best picture and director.)

1939 *Mr. Smith Goes to Washington*. P-D: FC. S: Sidney Buchman (and Myles Connolly, uncredited), from the story *The Gentleman from Montana* by Lewis R. Foster. CAM: Joseph Walker. WITH: James Stewart, Jean Arthur, Claude Rains, Edward Arnold, Thomas Mitchell. R: October 19, 1939. L: 128 mins. (Working titles: *The Gentleman from Montana, Mr. Deeds Goes to Washington*. Academy Award to Foster. Adapted as an ABC-TV series in 1962–63. Remade in 1977 as *Billy Jack Goes to Washington*.)

Warner Bros. Releases

1940 *Cavalcade of the Academy Awards*. P: Academy of Motion Picture Arts and Sciences. SUPERVISOR: FC. D: Ira Genet. S: Owen Crump. CAM: Charles Rosher (part color). COMMENTARY: Carey Wilson. WITH: FC, Walter Wanger, Bob Hope, Sinclair Lewis, Hattie McDaniel. R: April 4, 1940. L: 30 mins.

1941 *Meet John Doe.* P: FC, Robert Riskin, for Frank Capra Prods. D: FC. S: Riskin (and Myles Connolly, uncredited), from the treatment "The Life and Death of John Doe" by Richard Connell and Robert Presnell, based on Connell's short story "A Reputation." CAM: George Barnes. WITH: Gary Cooper, Barbara Stanwyck, Edward Arnold, Walter Brennan, James Gleason. R: March 12, 1941. L: 125 mins. (Working titles: *The Life and Death of John Doe, The Life of John Doe.*)

1944 (produced in 1941–42) *Arsenic and Old Lace.* P-D: FC. S: Julius J. Epstein, Philip G. Epstein, from the play by Joseph Kesselring (and Howard Lindsay and Russel Crouse, uncredited). CAM: Sol Polito. WITH: Cary Grant, Priscilla Lane, Raymond Massey, Josephine Hull, Jean Adair. R: September 1, 1944 (released to military audiences in 1943). L: 118 mins.

United States Army Films

Produced (unless otherwise indicated) for the 834th Signal Service Photographic Detachment, Special Services Division, U.S. Army, of which FC was commanding officer from June 1942 through August 1943, before the unit was transferred into the Signal Corps' Army Pictorial Service (he continued to supervise projects begun earlier). No individual credits were listed on screen; see chapter 16 for names of individuals who contributed to the films and other production information. During the latter years of the war, FC worked under the War Department Bureau of Public Relations and on joint projects with the British Ministry of Information; he was commanding officer of the Signal Corps' Special Coverage Section, Western Division, APS, supervising combat photography; and he served as assistant to the chief for Motion Picture Planning and as assistant chief of the APS.

1942 *Why We Fight: Prelude to War.* THEATRICAL RELEASE: May 13, 1943. L: 53 mins. (Joint winner of Academy Award for best documentary.)

1943 *Why We Fight: The Nazis Strike.* L: 42 mins.

1943 *Why We Fight: Divide and Conquer.* L: 58 mins.

1943 *Why We Fight: The Battle of Britain.* L: 54 mins.

1943 *Substitution and Conversion.* L: 6 reels.

1943 *Know Your Ally Britain.* L: 45 mins.

1943 *Why We Fight: The Battle of Russia.* THEATRICAL RELEASE: November 12, 1943. L: 83 mins.

1943 *Fast Company* (Working title: *OCS.* Unreleased.)

1943–45 *Army-Navy Screen Magazine* (50 issues; first 11 issues titled *The War*). L: 25 mins. (The *Seeds of Destiny* segment, after being distributed separately in 1946, won the Academy Award as best documentary short.)

1944 *The Negro Soldier.* THEATRICAL RELEASE: April 21, 1944. L: 43 mins. (alternate version: 20 mins.).

1944 *Tunisian Victory* (U.S. Army Bureau of Public Relations/British Ministry of Information). THEATRICAL RELEASE: March 16, 1944. L: 76 mins.

1944 *Why We Fight: The Battle of China.* L: 67 mins.

1944–45   *Staff Film Reports* (46 issues; classified). L: c. 25 mins. Re-edited for troop viewing as *Combat Film Bulletins* (34 issues). L: 20 mins.

1945   *Why We Fight: War Comes to America.* L: 67 mins.

1945   *Your Job in Germany.* L: 15 mins.

1945   *Two Down and One to Go!* THEATRICAL RELEASE: May 10, 1945. L: 9 mins. (Technicolor).

1945   *On to Tokyo.* L: 15 mins.

1945   *The Stilwell Road* (U.S. Army/British and Indian Film Units). L: 51 mins.

1945   *Know Your Enemy—Japan.* L: 63 mins. (Withdrawn after a brief release to the troops in August 1945, it did not receive its first public screening until 1977, as part of the PBS series *Films of Persuasion.*)

1945   *Here Is Germany.* L: 52 mins. (The original version, *Know Your Enemy: Germany,* made in 1942, was not released; *Here Is Germany* was reissued by Warner Bros. in revised form as *Hitler Lives?,* 1945, which won the Academy Award for best documentary short.)

1946 (not released until 1982)   *Our Job in Japan.* L: 18 mins.

Features for Liberty Films

1946   *It's a Wonderful Life.* DIST: RKO. P: FC, for Liberty Films (his partnership with George Stevens, William Wyler, and Sam Briskin). D: FC. S: Frances Goodrich, Albert Hackett, FC, Jo Swerling (and Dalton Trumbo, Clifford Odets, Marc Connelly, Michael Wilson, Dorothy Parker, uncredited), from the short story "The Greatest Gift" by Philip Van Doren Stern. CAM: Joseph Walker, Joseph Biroc (and Victor Milner, uncredited). WITH: James Stewart, Donna Reed, Lionel Barrymore, Thomas Mitchell, Henry Travers. R: December 21, 1946. L: 129 mins. (Working title: *The Greatest Gift.* Remade for television in 1977 as *It Happened One Christmas.*)

1948   *State of the Union.* DIST: MGM. P: FC, for Liberty Films. D: FC. S: Anthony Veiller, Myles Connolly, from the play by Howard Lindsay and Russel Crouse. CAM: George J. Folsey. WITH: Spencer Tracy, Katharine Hepburn, Van Johnson, Angela Lansbury, Adolphe Menjou. R: April 22, 1948. L: 124 mins.

Feature for MGM

1950   *Westward the Women.* DIST: MGM. P: Dore Schary. D: William A. Wellman. S: Charles Schnee, from a story ("Pioneer Woman") by FC. CAM: William Mellor. WITH: Robert Taylor, Denise Darcel, Hope Emerson, John McIntire, Julie Bishop. R: January 11, 1950. L: 116 mins.

Features for Paramount Pictures

1950   *Riding High.* P-D: FC. S: Robert Riskin, Melville Shavelson, Jack Rose (and Barney Dean, William Morrow, uncredited), from the screenplay

Broadway Bill by Riskin (and Sidney Buchman, uncredited) and the story "On the Nose" by Mark Hellinger. CAM: George Barnes, Ernest Laszlo. WITH: Bing Crosby, Coleen Gray, Clarence Muse, Charles Bickford, William Demarest. R: April 8, 1950. L: 112 mins. (Working title: *Broadway Bill*. A remake of FC's 1934 film *Broadway Bill*, including footage from the earlier picture.)

1951   *Here Comes the Groom.* P-D: FC. S: Virginia Van Upp, Liam O'Brien, Myles Connolly (and Arthur Sheekman, Charles Hoffman, Barney Dean, uncredited), from a story by Robert Riskin and O'Brien, based on Riskin's treatment "You Belong to Me." CAM: George Barnes. WITH: Bing Crosby, Jane Wyman, Alexis Smith, Franchot Tone, James Barton. R: September 6, 1951. L: 113 mins. (Working title: *You Belong to Me.* Academy Award for best song to Johnny Mercer and Hoagy Carmichael for "In the Cool, Cool, Cool of the Evening." FC introduced an NBC-TV adaptation of the film directed by Norman Morgan in 1956.)

Educational Documentaries

1951   *The Screen Director.* DIST: RKO. P: Grant Leenhouts, Gordon Hollingshead, for the Academy of Motion Picture Arts and Sciences' series of shorts *The Movies and You.* D: Richard Bare. WITH: FC, John Ford, Elia Kazan, William Wyler, Joseph L. Mankiewicz. R: March 13, 1951.

1952   *The Fallbrook Story.* P: Charles Peters, for the (uncredited) Fallbrook (California) Chamber of Commerce, the Fallbrook Public Utility District, and the *Los Angeles Times.* D: FC (uncredited). S: Ed Ainsworth. CAM: Lee Garmes (uncredited; color). HOST: Cecil B. DeMille. NARRATOR: Don Porter. WITH: Floyd Ahrend, Diane Kettering, Mary M. Melsheimer, George F. Yackey, California Lt. Gov. Goodwin J. Knight. R: 1952. L: 32 mins.

1954 (produced in 1950–54)   *Careers for Youth.* P: California Institute of Technology. P-S: FC, Charles Newton (uncredited). D: Edward Bernds (uncredited). CAM: Uncredited (color). WITH: Dr. Lee A. DuBridge, students and faculty of Caltech. R: January 25, 1954. L: 28 mins. (Working titles: *Life in an Institute of Technology, Choosing Your Future.*)

1956   *Our Mr. Sun.* DIST: Bell Telephone/CBS-TV. P: FC, for Frank Capra Prods., and Donald Jones, for N. W. Ayer & Son, Inc. D: FC. S: FC (and Aldous Huxley, Willy Ley, uncredited). CAM: Harold Wellman (color). ANIMATION: UPA. WITH: Frank Baxter, Eddie Albert, and the voices of Lionel Barrymore, Marvin Miller, and Sterling Holloway. FIRST TELECAST: November 19, 1956. L: 59 mins. (Working titles: *The Sun, Horizons Unlimited.*)

1957   *Hemo the Magnificent.* DIST: Bell Telephone/CBS-TV. P: FC, for Frank Capra Prods., and Donald Jones, for N. W. Ayer & Son, Inc. D-S: FC. CAM: Harold Wellman (color). ANIMATION: Shamus Culhane Prods. WITH: Frank Baxter, Richard Carlson, and the voice of Sterling Holloway. FIRST TELECAST: March 20, 1957. L: 59 mins.

1957   *The Strange Case of the Cosmic Rays.* DIST: Bell Telephone/NBC-TV. P: FC, for Frank Capra Prods., and Donald Jones, for N. W. Ayer & Son, Inc. D: FC. S: FC, Jonathan Latimer (and Charles Stearns, uncredited). CAM: Harold Wellman, Ellis Carter, Edison Hoge (color). ANIMATION: Shamus Culhane Prods.

WITH: Frank Baxter, Richard Carlson, Bil and Cora Baird's Marionettes. FIRST TELECAST: October 25, 1957. L: 59 mins.

1958   *The Unchained Goddess.* DIST: Bell Telephone/NBC-TV. P: FC, for Frank Capra Prods., and Donald Jones, for N. W. Ayer & Son, Inc. D: Richard Carlson. S: FC, Jonathan Latimer. CAM: Harold Wellman (color). ANIMATION: Shamus Culhane Prods. WITH: Frank Baxter, Richard Carlson. FIRST TELECAST: February 12, 1958. L: 59 mins. (Working title: *Meteora: The Unchained Goddess.*)

1959   *Korea—Battleground for Liberty.* DIST: Office of Armed Forces Information and Education, U.S. Department of Defense, in the series of People-to-People Orientation Films, produced in cooperation with the U.S. Navy. P: Rear Adm. John Ford, USNR, and Capt. George O'Brien, USNR. D: Ford. S: Lt. Comdr. Eric Strutt, USN. CAM: Photographed in 16mm Eastmancolor by U.S. Air Force cameramen. WITH: O'Brien, Kim-chi Mi, Choi My Ryonk. L: 30 mins. (Working title: *Korea—Land of the Morning Calm.*) FC served on a Hollywood committee in 1958–59, along with Ford, O'Brien, Capt. John Lee Mahin, USAF (Ret.), Maj. George Sidney, USAFR, and Capt. A. J. Bolton, USNR (Ret.), as a consultant on the production of this and the following film.

1959   *Taiwan—Island of Freedom.* DIST: Same as for preceding film. P: Ford, O'Brien, and Comdr. Mark Armistead, USNR. D: Ford. S: Strutt, W. T. Blume, Mahin. CAM: Photographed in 16mm Eastmancolor by U.S. Air Force cameramen. WITH: Lt. Comdr. Glenn Ford, USN (narrator). FC was a consultant, as above. (Working title: *Taiwan—The Island Fortress.*)

Features for United Artists

1959   *A Hole in the Head.* DIST: United Artists. P: FC, for Sincap Prods. (Frank Sinatra, Frank Capra). D: FC. S: Arnold Schulman (and Myles Connolly, uncredited), from Schulman's play. CAM: William H. Daniels (Panavision, DeLuxe Color). WITH: Frank Sinatra, Edward G. Robinson, Eddie Hodges, Thelma Ritter, Eleanor Parker. R: June 17, 1959. L: 120 mins. (Working titles: *All My Tomorrows, The Garden of Eden.* Academy Award for best song to Sammy Cahn and James Van Heusen for "High Hopes." An earlier version of the play, *The Heart's a Forgotten Hotel,* was produced on NBC-TV in 1955, directed by Arthur Penn.)

1961   *Pocketful of Miracles.* DIST: United Artists. P: FC, for Franton Prods. (Glenn Ford, Frank Capra). D: FC. S: Hal Kanter, Harry Tugend (and Jimmy Cannon, Myles Connolly, uncredited), from Robert Riskin's screenplay *Lady for a Day,* based on the short story "Madame La Gimp" by Damon Runyon. CAM: Robert Bronner (Panavision, Technicolor). WITH: Glenn Ford, Bette Davis, Hope Lange, Ann-Margret, Peter Falk. R: December 18, 1961. L: 136 mins. (Working titles: *Lady for a Day, Ride the Pink Cloud.* A remake of FC's 1933 film *Lady for a Day.*)

Short for the New York World's Fair

1964   *Rendezvous in Space.* Shown at the Hall of Science, New York World's Fair, through 1975. P: FC, for the Martin Marietta Corp. D: FC. S: FC,

Jonathan Latimer. CAM: Uncredited (color). WITH: Danny Thomas, Tom Fadden, Benny Rubin, Charles Lane, Andy Clyde. R: September 10, 1964. L: 18 mins. (Working title: *Reaching for the Stars*.)

Documentary Feature

1984 *George Stevens: A Filmmaker's Journey*. DIST: New Liberty Prods. P-D-S: George Stevens, Jr. WITH: FC, Katharine Hepburn, Elizabeth Taylor, Joel McCrea, Warren Beatty. L: 111 mins.

Television Specials Featuring Frank Capra

1959 *This Is Your Life: Frank Capra*. DIST: NBC-TV. P: Ralph Edwards. D: Richard Gottlieb. WITH: Edwards, Lucille Capra, Tony Capra, Edward G. Robinson, The Ukelele Club of Manual Arts High School. FIRST TELECAST: June 10, 1959. L: 30 mins.

1975 *The Men Who Made the Movies: Frank Capra*. D: PBS. P: Richard Schickel, for WNET (New York), Eastman Kodak. D-S: Schickel. CAM: Erik Daarstad, John A. Morrill, Tony Foresta. NARRATOR: Cliff Robertson. L: 88 mins.

1976 *Frank Capra: The Man Above the Title*. DIST: United States Information Agency. P: Larry Ott. Four-part series of videotaped interviews with FC: *The Motion Picture as Entertainment* (interview by Richard Schickel and Dr. John Kuiper), 42 mins.; *The Motion Picture in Persuasion* (interview by Prof. Oliver Franklin and Dr. Gene S. Weiss), 33 mins.; *The Motion Picture and Social Change* (interview by Dr. Robert W. Wagner and Jean DeBruge), 33 mins.; and *The Motion Picture and Science* (interview by Dr. Randall M. Whaley and Theodore Manekin), 32 mins.

1977 *Dialogue on Film: A Seminar Series with Master Filmmakers: Frank Capra*. DIST-P: The American Film Institute. Recorded April 5, 1977. WITH: Students of the AFI's Center for Advanced Film Studies. L: 60 mins.

1977 *Mister Capra torna a casa* [*Mr. Capra Goes Home*] DIST-P: Radiotelevisione Italiana (Italy). A documentary of FC's visit to Italy and his return to his hometown of Bisacquino, Sicily, in April 1977. L: 60 mins.

1981 *High Hopes: The Capra Years*. DIST: NBC-TV. P: Carl Pingitore, Frank Capra, Jr., for Columbia Pictures TV. D: Vincent Sherman. S: Richard Schickel. CAM: Al Francis, Chuck Wheeler, Travers Hill. WITH: Carl Reiner, Lucille Ball, Burt Reynolds, James Stewart. FIRST TELECAST: December 24, 1981. L: 60 mins.

1982 *The American Film Institute Salute to Frank Capra*. DIST: CBS-TV. P: George Stevens, Jr., for the American Film Institute. D: Marty Pasetta. S: Stevens, Joseph McBride. WITH: James Stewart, Claudette Colbert, Bette Davis, Joseph Walker, William Hornbeck. FIRST TELECAST: April 4, 1982. L: 90 mins.

1984 *A Walk Through the Twentieth Century: WWII: The Propaganda Battle*. DIST: PBS. P: David Grubin, for CEL/BDM, WNET (New York), and KQED (San Francisco). D: Grubin. S: Ronald Blumer, Bill Moyers, Bernard A. Weisberger. CAM: Grubin, Robert Leacock, Bodo Kessler. A documentary on U.S. and German propaganda films of World War II, featuring interviews with FC and German director Fritz Hippler. HOST-INTERVIEWER: Moyers. FIRST TELECAST: May 9, 1984. L: 60 mins.

1986   *Arriva Frank Capra [Here Comes Frank Capra]*. DIST: Radiotelevisione Italiana-RAI UNO (Italy). P: Dino Di Dionisio. D: Gianfranco Mingozzi. CAM: Safai Tehrani. Part of a TV series entitled *Stories of Cinema and Migrants*. WITH: Donna Reed, Lionel Stander, Hope Lange, Coleen Gray. L: 80 mins.

INDEX